Roy Rogers

Roy Rogers

*A Biography, Radio History, Television Career
Chronicle, Discography, Filmography, Comicography,
Merchandising and Advertising History, Collectibles
Description, Bibliography and Index*

by ROBERT W. PHILLIPS

McFarland & Company, Inc., Publishers
Jefferson, North Carolina, and London

**Frontispiece: Rogers in a publicity still
from his Mutual Radio days, ca. 1944–1945**

British Library Cataloguing-in-Publication data are available

Library of Congress Cataloguing-in-Publication Data

Phillips, Robert W., 1944–
   Roy Rogers : a biography, radio history, television career
chronicle, discography, filmography, comicography, merchandising
and advertising history, collectibles description, bibliography
and index / by Robert W. Phillips.
    p. cm.
   Filmography: p.
   ISBN 0-89950-937-1 (lib. bdg. : 50# alk. paper) ∞
   1. Rogers, Roy, 1911– . 2. Rogers, Dale Evans. I. Title.
PN2287.R73P55 1995
791.43'028'092 – dc20   94-31152
                                       CIP

Manufactured in the United States of America

McFarland & Company, Inc., Publishers
 Box 611, Jefferson, North Carolina 28640

This book is dedicated to
my loving wife since 1967,
Cece Phillips, who was practically raised
on U.S. Highway 80, in the back of the
family automobile, running back and forth
to California, as so many Americans did in
the 1940s and 50s, searching for a better
life in a land of promise

CONTENTS

ACKNOWLEDGMENTS

This work would not have been possible had it not been for several longtime collectors who virtually opened up their files, computer-stored information, and collections to me in an effort to contribute to a project they deemed not only worthwhile, but long overdue.

Raymond White, a history professor at Ball State University in Muncie, Indiana, has been particularly helpful. We shared our individual Roy Rogers bibliographies, each with about 500 different items, and then combined them. We also exchanged photocopies of information and computer lists for months. In addition, I am very grateful to the many fans, collectors, and past manufacturers and retailers of Roy Rogers merchandise, as well as artists, personal acquaintances of Roy Rogers and Dale Evans Rogers, and even those in the legal profession who provided various amounts of information and guidance. I sincerely hope that I do not leave anyone out, as many people's efforts went a long way in helping to produce a one-of-a-kind and first-of-its-kind book.

There are several individuals who made a very generous contribution, supplying hundreds of pages of information, photos, and facts obtained from their personal contacts with Roy Rogers, but for personal reasons, they prefer to remain anonymous. These persons know the contributions they made and how grateful I am.

I have extensive correspondence from individuals and companies that was full of information important to this work. Prints of personal photographs and permissions to use these are especially appreciated. I wish to thank the following individuals: D. J. Aarensen (Roy Rogers Restaurants, Franchise Consultant, New York), A and S Book Co. (Larry), Steve Ackerman (Baker and Hostetler, McCutchen Black, Counsellors at Law), Gene Andrewski, Glen Arvin, Phil Van Auken, Sam Austill, Robert Autry (Hardee's Food Systems), Thomas A. Basl, Baylor Children's Hospital, Gene Bear (television show host), Big Apple Comics (Arnie), Bill Black (Roy Rogers Western Classics, AC Comics), Mervin Bendewald (owner, Whiskey Dust/Big Sky Furniture), Ted Berkowitz, Earl Blair (Captain Bijou), David M. Bower (library assistant, the Museum of Radio and Television), Dan Brewer (Western artist), Bob Brown (artist, Roy Rogers material), Pat Browne (Bowling Green State University), Ray Centola, Larry Cisewski (Arrowcatch Productions), Jerry Carbone, Luis Carlo, Wanda Click, Ed Colbert (Hollywood celebrity photographer), Sidney E. Conner, Walter C. Cooper, Ben and Cecil Cunningham, Larry Curcio (Avalon Comics), Bill Curtis, Barbara Dacus-Wadlington, (Catering, Grand Kempinski Hotel, Dallas), Ed Davis (*Yippy Yi Yea* magazine), James Davis, Carol Derkits, Jason Dow, Hank Decato, Suzanne Edgar, Stan Edwards, Johnny Efird, Betty Eubank (Roy Rogers Enterprises), Dale H. Fellows (Morgan Litho), Jeff Ford (head of acquisitions, Carlton Television), Ft. Knox Security Products, Funny Business, Ken Galente (Silver Screen Photo), the Gallaghers, Donna Gehres (Gene Autry Western Heritage Museum), Tom Gill (Western Co. artist), Fred Goodwin (liner notes, Columbia Records), Don Gordley (Roy Rogers Hometown Exhibit, Portsmouth, Ohio), Danielle Gordon (Kraft General Foods), Frances Graham (editor, Antiques and Collecting Hobbies), Henry Greenbaum (Jay-Bee Magazines), J. L. Gutierrez, Randy Hadden, Rodgers Hambleton, Barrie Hanfling, Steve Hazlewood,

Jim Henley's Universe, Patrick Henrys (producer, Roy Rogers documentary, Ireland), Marilyn Hering, Dee Dee Hill (the Collection Agency), Allan Hodell, Ronnie Holub, Hope Cottage (Intake Department), LaRue Horsley, Nancy Horsley (executive secretary, Roy Rogers–Dale Evans Collectors Assn.), Helen Houser (assistant editor, Long Publications), Mary C. Janacky (manager, Licensing and Rights Administration, Western Publishing Co.), Jo Ann Janzen, William Jacobson (editor, Song of the West), Barry L. Jones, Charley Jones, Mike Johnson, Colin Jellicoe (Roy Rogers artist, England), Paul Kennedy, Norman Kietzer (editor, Westerns and Serials), Bob King (editor, Classic Images), Gerry Kramer, Anna Labbate, Steven C. Laird (Russell, Turner, Laird, Barkholtz & Jones, Attorneys at Law), Jack Lambert (owner, J. J. Hat Center, N.Y.), J. Layburn, Cheryl Laymon (president, Little Oak Enterprises), Henry Lee, Rhonda K. Lemons (Empire Publishing), Philip Levine (Philip M. Levine and Sons), Jennifer Lockman, Tony Lorio, Margo Lundell (editorial director, Western Publishing Co.), Joseph Macrie, Boyd Magers (Video West), Katherine M. McClinton, Kimbell McCurry (Industrial Screenprint), Diane McInerney, Elizabeth McCready (editorial department, Dell Publishing Co.), Norman Michaels, Mid-Town Video (staff), Jack Miller (Boot-sters Co.), Stephen C. Moody, Colin Momber, Len Morris (producer, Galen Films), Ben Moskowitz, Harry Moss, Karen Moy (editorial assistant, King Features), Museum of the Performing Arts, Lincoln Center (library reference staff), the National Cowboy Hall of Fame and Museum (staff), Jim Newton (Texas radio personality), New York Public Library (staff), Jerry Ohlinger's Movie Materials Store (Jerry and all the gang), J. F. Patrickus (J.P.'s Custom Handmade Boots), George E. Pitman, Dale Peiffer, Paula Phillips (Film Favorites), L. Gene Phillips, Kevin G. Pipes (Smoky Mountain Knife Works), Neil Pond, Pat and JoLain Probst, Ronnie Pugh (librarian, Country Music Foundation Library), Republic Pictures (Rights and Permissions), Re-Runs Books, Carol Rickard, Pat Roberts, Greg Robertson, Scott Robertson, Robert Rogavin (Four Color Comics), Roger's Comics, Roy Rogers, Jr., Gerald Saunders, Julie Semrau (editor, *Yippy Yi Yea* magazine), Randall W. Scott (Michigan State University Libraries), Second Childhood (staff), Jerry Sienco (video/ still collector), William G. Sizemore (grand executive director, Scottish Rite of Freemasonry), Dale Slye (Roy's cousin), Alan Smith, Bill Smith, Katherine Smith (record producer, deceased), Fred Sopher, Strand Books (staff), Kathy Streten (editor, Toybox magazine), John Spencer, Melvin Steinmetz, Elvin R. Sweeten (director, Gene Autry Oklahoma Museum), Dr. J. Stromer (professor, Queensborough Community College), Tom St. Aubwyn, Suncoast Video (staff), James N. Treadway, Hank Tuchman, Phil Van Auken (professor, Baylor University), Variety Clubs Children's Charity of North Texas, Joe D. Wallace, Frances K. Williams (personal secretary to Roy Rogers; general manager, Roy Rogers–Dale Evans Museum), Jeanette Williams (Lake Hughes, California), Stephen M. Williams (editor, Victor Valley Daily Press), Walter Williams (supplied hundreds of records), Stan Wilmanski (Roy Rogers Restaurants, franchise consultant), Jim and Judy Wilson (Double R Bar News). A very special thanks to Clovia A. James, Eugene R. Lehr, and Tracie C. Maupin, bibliographers, Reference and Bibliography Section, Copyright Office, Library of Congress, Washington, D.C., who came up with all the answers on copyrights, and to the staffs of the bureaus of vital statistics, county recorders, county clerk's offices, registrars, and departments of health in various states, and most especially to Pat Johnson, Jessica, and Valerie in Los Angeles County, California, and the Memphis, Tennessee, and Louisville, Kentucky, staffs, for many hours of work.

Finally, I wish to thank my grandfather, Joe Biggers (1887–1960), without whose influence I might never have written this book. My grandfather was as big a Roy Rogers fan as I was as a child in the 1950s. He introduced me to Roy's films and his comics, and he took me to see him in person at the Fort Worth Fat Stock and Exposition Show at the Will Rogers Coliseum. The memories are as clear as if the events took place yesterday. The "King of the Cowboys" never had any two bigger fans than this old gentleman and I.

INTRODUCTION

The study of Roy Rogers and any of the media in which he appeared is the study of an era, the pastimes of a people, the heroes of a country, then-current photography, Hollywood, art, and "Madison Avenue." One must grasp the era in order to understand how an individual could become rich and famous and gain entry into our history books as a legendary figure. I was not old enough in the 1940s to recall much of what that decade was all about, but I recall the 1950s very well. Dwight D. Eisenhower was president from 1953 on; the world had only been out of a major war for a few short years and the United States was engaged in another war in Korea. Television had not been around very long, and the amount of money a family had left over after meeting necessities determined the pecking order of who got televisions into their homes first. As the grandson of a woman who was crippled and took in boarders to supplement the income of her husband, who was also crippled and made fifty dollars a week as a carpenter during the better weeks, I recall we were about the last ones in town to get a television and then it was a present.

Gathering around a radio in one room to listen to action, suspense, and drama shows was a nightly affair and a part of everyone's lives until television came along. The "cowboy shows," as we called them at the time, were an important part of radio. Men and boys tended to like them more than women and girls, but all enjoyed them to some extent or didn't think any more about them than putting on a pot of beans for supper or going out into the garden to gather the onions and peppers for the meal. "The Roy Rogers Show" (Mutual network; 1944–1955) was one of these, and there wasn't a more popular show to be heard. He came on Thursday nights and was sponsored by General Foods.

When television came into our home, it took a long time for some programs to catch on. At first, we watched in the daytime, and the personalities we had listened to on the radio were the ones we were most likely to tune in on the tube. As soon as we learned that "The Roy Rogers Show" was on every Sunday evening, 5:30–6:00 P.M. (CST), we never missed a single episode. When a family went to the grocery store back then, the cereal aisle was never overlooked, even when there was no money for the cereal. These were the days before "pop tarts" and microwave meals, and schools stressed the importance of eating cereal. Roy Rogers' picture or likeness was in every cereal aisle, in every grocery store in the country, on the front of Post Cereal boxes (and the backs). Inside those boxes were premiums such as Roy Rogers trading cards or photos. On the backs of the boxes were advertisements that stated that by sending in a quarter with the box-top, you could expect in 4–6 weeks to receive a Roy Rogers sheriff's badge or set of photos. When Christmas time rolled around, the Roy Rogers industry had every base covered. There were toys of every variety for boys and girls; there were clothes and even bedspreads and lamps. Toys were sold in the well-known stores like Sears and Roebuck and Montgomery Ward and cost in the neighborhood of $5. That was a lot of money in the 1950s. Any Roy Rogers item was a class item that bore Roy's own seal of approval as an assurance to parents that it was a wholesome and quality item that was fairly priced.

Roy Rogers was as familiar a name in the schools as he was in homes because he sponsored a safety bike riding program in which all schools and youngsters could participate. Roy Rogers was not merely a cowboy hero to children, however. I recall that movie theaters were full of adults as well. I happen to know that my grandfather, who grew up in the days when the cowboy heroes were William S. Hart, Tom Mix, and Buck Jones, was crazy about Roy Rogers. If I did not beat him to the drugstore to get the new Roy Rogers comic each month, it would already be in our house. The comic books were as important a part of American life as the Sunday newspaper color comic sections. Dell Comics had an advantage over most of the rest. They were a perfect place for Roy. Just as he was the most colorful and classy of the "silver screen cowboys," Dell was the most colorful and classy company in the comic business. They used a heavily coated, extra slick cover as opposed to the flat pulp covers of many comics, and they used photo covers and photography that really stood out in the newsstands full of Western comics with illustrated (or "line-drawn") covers.

The 1950s was an era of real heroes when guys like Mickey Mantle and Audie Murphy were constantly in the news. It was hard for any parent to argue against any hero that was everywhere you went, telling kids to eat all the food on their plates, go to Sunday School, mind your parents, be kind to animals, ride your bicycle safely, and study hard. When the rodeo came to cities such as Fort Worth, Texas, many people went not to watch the bull-dogging or bronc busting but to see in person Roy Rogers, "King of the Cowboys," ride Trigger out into that big arena and put the horse through all his famous tricks. It might be hard to conceive of all this today, for we do not have cowboys like this anymore, and we do not have heroes like Roy Rogers anymore either.

All of these heroes rode into a final glistening sunset in the era this book addresses. We might, as adults now, realize that there were some huge money-minded corporations behind the making of icons like Roy. There were corporate giants in advertising—the Madison Avenue folks, the big publishing houses, Hollywood, network television, etc., and they had a lot to do with it all, but the story does not stop there and is not that simple. Although these organizations helped to create the image they desired

to sell, it would not have all come together if there had not been some mighty tall men to fill the saddles and if the powers-that-were did not have a person who could protect and maintain that image and thus protect the investment of all concerned.

There were, throughout these decades, dozens of "whisper" magazines, or "gossip" or "scandal" magazines as they were known then, that contained juicy bits of information on every actor that ever walked around the corner of Hollywood and Vine streets. Well, almost every actor. Roy Rogers was in many magazines throughout the heyday of his career, issue after issue, month after month. But today, when you go out and start rummaging through all the old stacks of magazines from the 1940s and 1950s found in used book stores and flea markets across the country, you can save your time looking through the gossip ones. The magazines in which you will find plenty of articles on Roy, his wife, and his kids, usually all together, are ones like *Look, Life, Saturday Evening Post, McCall's, Good Housekeeping, Better Homes and Gardens, Liberty, Screen Stars, Film Land, Modern Screen,* etc. The kind of man Roy Rogers has been, and the kind of character he has portrayed, are suited to these better titles. He provided the Hollywood gossip columnists with little to talk about. They did, however, occasionally follow him and his family to church, and there they got their stories and photographs. He was in all the "class" magazines, in stories aimed at the families of America.

Roy spent his lifetime, on and off the screen, living up to this image. It made him a legend. He was one of the "singing cowboy" matinee idols of the 1950s, acting in the "B" westerns of this strange era when the cowboy was seldom seen being vile and violent, a drifter hell-bent on revenge, killing everyone in gory fashion. Instead, he was seen shooting the gun out of the villain's hand, wounding him, or just chasing him out of town in order to get down to the serious business of singing a song to his horse, winning the heart of a decent young lady in distress, and trying to teach a code that was very similar to that of the Boy Scouts of America. Roy was a cowboy who completely represented the genre of Western film: he stood a little taller, looked a little more trim and neat (almost like a Marine Corps lieutenant of the Western set), sat a little taller in the saddle, rode a more magnificent-looking horse, and outfitted himself in attire that was somewhat more colorful and extravagant. At the same time he possessed a much more beautiful singing voice and had more yodeling ability than his competition. Roy Rogers was a little "un-realistic" say the Western purists, but one should keep in mind that the setting in which Roy rode was not so much the real Old West, but rather a semimythical present day setting out West. And his attire for a Western entertainer cowboy definitely has its roots in a real part of the Old West, that of the "Wild West Shows" that men like Buffalo Bill Cody owned and performed in. Rogers' films had a touch of class, like the "Wild West" shows. They were part Western musical events and part action films with solid story lines.

The saturation of America with Rogers memorabilia was carried out through radio, phonograph records, movies, comic strips and comic books, novels, toys, food products, television, clothing, etc. So the study of Roy Rogers, the man, Roy Rogers, the character, and the Roy Rogers comic book is a study of Americana and American popular culture in an exciting time—a story of how far one man can go in the entertainment world with enough charisma and determination. The collectible comics, like the collectible toys, are relics of a bygone era when real heroes existed and became legends serving as role models for the nation's youth.

There is a real story that begs to be told in the lives of Roy Rogers and his wife, Dale Evans. Only half of it has been told, and much of that is clouded with old publicity-generated tales and scenarios and by the routine omission of facts, an omission dictated for the most part by a Hollywood publicity department that was always suggesting, advising, and insisting on what should and should not be told. Over the past sixty years, there have been many biographical and autobiographical works on the Rogers' lives in the form of books, magazine articles, and recorded interviews, all of which have read largely the same, offering little if anything new of substance and forming a chain of rehashed publicity stories.

There have been a few critical evaluations, founded in ignorance and aimed at destroying their image in a contemptible manner. Until now, there has been little attempt at producing a scholarly and objective study. Roy and Dale have lived extraordinary lives in their climb from obscurity to stardom and have become legends as the result of publicity from their film studios and their personal publicity departments and because of the exemplary lives they have lived.

They have been caught up in a celebrity world most of their lives, and books that have told their story have only told part of it. For a researcher who has dissected and analyzed what has appeared in print during those sixty years, there were many gaps to be bridged, holes to be filled, and questions to be answered. I have been a lifelong fan of Roy and Dale, and my research will continue long after the publishing of this work until I am satisfied that every possible question has been answered.

The first two chapters of this book trace the lives and paper trails of two individuals who started out in life as an Ohio farm boy named Leonard Sly and a Texas farm girl named Lucille Smith and wound up, many failures and successes later, as "America's Favorite Western Couple." The publicity is examined and documents are studied that both support and contradict the publicity. It was inevitable that controversy would develop as the result of this exhaustive research. There are those who will not accept that the real people behind the part mythical image are as important to our traditional American values as the image itself. Underneath the symbols of the "King of the Cowboys" and the "Queen of the West" are two very real, and sometimes very ordinary, persons who developed, protected, and dedicated their lives to maintaining the image of these very important symbols. Two of the hardest-working people ever to set foot in Hollywood, they rose to stardom and became American symbols despite a mixture of conventional and unconventional fashions.

In addition to formally introducing the pioneering study of Roy Rogers Comics and Roy in the commercial art form, I have attempted in this work to locate and consolidate into one comprehensive reference source all information pertaining to the phenomenal life and career of Roy Rogers. Although some of this information culled from a thousand sources may seem trivial to some, such detail can be of significance to the future researcher, opening up new avenues to pursue. The author's forty-year Roy Rogers collection, especially those hundreds of items in the print media, which represent a generous amount of pure publicity but also an excellent source for factual detail, has made all of this possible. For the most part, it enables the researcher to find the answers in one text. In any instance, surely few, where this fails to be the case, the source of information is shown, along with a detailed and expansive bibliography that will enable the reader to pursue a topic in greater detail.

Biographical information on the subjects of this work has appeared in numerous books and hundreds of magazine articles over the past sixty years. Conflicting statements in these sources, as well as in countless published and recorded interviews with the subjects, are examined and annotated. Any entries made for the first time are fully supported by documentation or notes from my research that brought about a finding. Hundreds of pages of legal documents, hundreds of magazine articles, numerous published works, and published, recorded and filmed interviews have been used for reference and are shown in the bibliography.

Chapter 1

LEONARD FRANK SLY AND LUCILLE WOOD SMITH

Chapters 1 and 2 are presented in a chronological format so as to organize logically the hundreds of fragments of information about Roy Rogers (born Leonard Frank Sly) and Dale Evans (born Lucille Wood Smith) that have appeared in public documents, books, and magazine and newspaper articles, as well as in publicity materials and on items of merchandise. Data were also gathered from acquaintances of Roy and Dale, family members, fans and collectors, and other researchers.

1883
Andrew Earlin Sly was born at Portsmouth, Ohio.

Circa 1905
Andrew E. Sly, approximately 22, of Portsmouth, Ohio, and Mattie Womack, approximately 22–24, of Carter County, eastern Kentucky, were wed.[1]*

1906
Mary Elizabeth Sly was the first child born to Andrew and Mattie Sly; she was born in Portsmouth on April 14. The family was living on the river bank on Front Street.[2]

1910
Another girl, Cleda May, was born to the Slys on January 16.[3] The family's address was 112 E. Front Street. Andrew and Mattie Sly moved from Portsmouth to Cincinnati later that year.

1911
On November 5, Leonard Frank Sly was born to Andrew and Mattie Sly of 412 E. 2nd Street, in Cincinnati, Ohio, in the two-room, red brick tenement building close to his dad's workplace at the U.S. Shoe Co.[4] Dr. J. H. Caldwell, of Newport, Kentucky, just across the Ohio River from the Sly home, handled the delivery. Leonard looked very much like his father and had Choctaw Indian eyes.[5] He

was proud of Indian heritage all his life.[6] His mother was a petite (under five foot), brown-eyed woman. She had suffered infantile paralysis, but had been able to overcome most of the effects of the disease.[7] She was working in a laundry when she met Leonard's father. Andy, as he was known, worked as a skilled shoemaker in the lasting department of the shoe factory.[8] Another address for the Slys in Cincinnati was 1910 Ohio Avenue.[9] By the time of Leonard's birth, his father's employment background included working on the wharves, and being a carnival laborer, an acrobat, and an entertainer on a showboat.[10]

1912
Leonard's dad and his blind uncle Will built a 12 by 50 feet houseboat that friends called "Andy's Ark."[11] On July 12 they traveled back up the Ohio river to Portsmouth, where the Slys would live for the next eight years.[12] The sail, which was made from a dozen of Mattie's sheets, was torn to threads by a storm the first day. The water was so rough they had to hitch onto a boat pushing barges up the river. Andy worked his way up the irregular coastline while performing odd jobs, setting out nets for the fishing boats. They docked on the river bank east of Portsmouth's Chillicothe Street.

*

*Notes to the entire book begin on page 343.

On October 30, a baby girl was born to Walter Hillman and Bettie Sue Wood Smith, at the home of Bettie Sue's parents on Fort Clark Road in Uvalde, Texas.[13] They resided in Italy, Texas, about 35 miles southwest of Dallas, on property owned by the maternal grandparents. The presiding doctor in Uvalde filed the birth record with the county clerk of Uvalde County, showing the infant to be named Lucille Wood Smith.[14] Years later she was given an affidavit sworn by her mother that stated her name to be Frances Octavia Smith and gave her birthdate as October 31.[15] Many years later and far from her birthplace, she would marry Leonard and become Mrs. Roy Rogers. In a 1971 book that she authored, she recalls dreaming as a child that she would one day marry cowboy star Tom Mix.

1913
On March 26, Portsmouth suffered massive flooding for thirteen days that partially submerged buildings and endangered the lives of the city's inhabitants. Andy maneuvered his houseboat through what had once been the streets of Portsmouth, rescuing people from the swirling waters. The Scioto River Bridge was washed away by the devastating force. At one point, the water rose at the incredible rate of two feet an hour.

1914
On December 14, in Roswell, New Mexico, another baby was born, who was destined to become the second wife of Leonard Sly. She was Grace Arline Wilkins, and her parents were Prentice D. and Lucy Cross Wilkins.[16] On December 31, Robert Patrick Brady was born in Toledo, Ohio; he would become one of Leonard's best friends. He would also be a sidekick to Roy Rogers on radio, in film, and on television, as well as appearing in Roy Rogers and Dale Evans separate comic book episodes.

1915
On June 14, Leonard's baby sister Kathleen was born. The family's address was 1216 Front Street.[17]

1916
As the family increased in size and the older girls approached school age, it became necessary for the Slys to move away from the river's bank and beach at 1223 Mill Street, a

couple of blocks away.[18] The houseboat continued to be the Sly home.

1917–1918
Leonard began school at Union Street.[19] His ambition was to become a doctor.[20] Andy Sly made the purchase of a secondhand Maxwell touring car.

1919
For the first seven years of his life, the houseboat was home to Leonard and his folks. Then Andy Sly purchased several acres from earnings saved while working at the Selby Shoe Co. The family moved again, this time eleven miles up the Scioto River to a farm near Duck Run, Ohio, population fourteen.[21] Leonard was going on eight years old at this time. He helped his dad and uncle build the six-room clapboard farm house in this hilly brush country. There was no indoor plumbing and no electricity. Light on this small farm came from coal-oil lamps. Andy tried to eke out a living from the soil, but he was a city-boy who knew little about farming, and a kick from a mule nearly ended his life.[22] Needing more money for the family, he returned to factory work in Portsmouth. Mattie and the kids held down the farm. Leonard learned firsthand every kind of hard work that went with a farm. Being a doctor, or perhaps a dentist, was the only sort of career that ever crossed Leonard's mind, however. He learned to ride really well on a black mare named Babe, a gift that his dad surprised him with, and he won a race at the Scioto County Fair. The Slys were a close family. When Andy was home and mealtime was over, there was always time for music.[23] Leonard's introduction to the movie cowboys was at the Portsmouth Theater, and his favorite cowboy was Hoot Gibson. He occasionally rode Babe to the theater and also saw his dad on these trips to town in case Andy hadn't made it home for the weekend. Leonard rode a horse not only to school and to movies, but also to prayer meetings and square dances.

1920
Meanwhile, the Smith family, including Frances and her younger brother Hillman, moved from Texas to Osceola, Arkansas, a town that sits on the banks of the Mississippi River.

Leonard Sly's first grade class at Union St. School, c. 1918; Leonard is in the front row (far left).

1922

Sometime near this date Leonard hurt his shoulder by falling out of a cherry tree, an injury that would give him problems for the rest of his life. Leonard's first dramatic role was playing Santa Claus in a grammar school play.[24]

1923

For his twelfth birthday, Leonard got his first rifle, a .22 Winchester carbine, but he wasn't permitted to shoot it unattended for another year.[25] Being the oldest kid around, he was called upon to babysit the younger children of neighboring families, one of which lived in the community of Otway, several miles up Duck Run Road. At Otway, Leonard began calling square dances, so well, in fact, that he was a favorite of everyone for miles around Duck Run.[26] When playing for the dances, he used his mom and dad's guitar. They taught him to play at an early age, and he and the girls picked up on yodeling as well, something he would do in fine style the rest of his life.[27] He knew a lot of cowboy songs, and everyone enjoyed hearing him sing. Leonard's teacher, Guy

Bumgarner, had a great influence on his character. It was Bumgarner who organized a 4-H club and encouraged Leonard to join the organization. At the age of twelve, Leonard raised a black Poland China piglet (named Martha Washington) to a champion sow for the 4-H contest held at Scioto County Fair. Leonard had another pig named Evangeline, but Martha Washington was the one who won him $5 and a week-long trip to the 4-H Club Congress in Columbus, Ohio. It was in Columbus that he got his first taste of city life, riding for the first time in an elevator in the Neil House Hotel. Another of his teachers had a much less positive impact, and Leonard suffered a lashing with a whip-like cane. Unable to stand the beating, he threw a rock at the abusive teacher.

Circa 1924

Leonard's sister Mary married a man named Johnson and moved to California.

1926

Leonard enrolled at McDermott High School, about four miles down a few winding roads. He was good at sports and learned to play the clarinet during his first two high school years.

1927

There are numerous photographs of Leonard, identified as school year 1926-1927, that show him in either the seventh or eighth grade, but never specify which. It would seem likely that he lost anywhere from one to several grades because there is a photograph of his first school year, 1916-1917, at five to six years of age. In the later photographs, he appears considerably older than any of his classmates.

*

April 1: In Arkansas, Frances Smith was fourteen and a half years of age and according to public records filed in the state of Tennessee, she married Thomas F. Fox.[28] These records state that they "went to live in the state of Arkansas," which implies that the union took place in Tennessee, or at least outside the state of Arkansas. There are several published accounts of this marriage. In version (a) she eloped with several other couples, got married to "a youthful sweetheart" in a mass wedding in Blytheville, eighteen miles north of their Osceola home, and called her mother from the home of the groom's mother in Tennessee.[29] In version (b) she and her boyfriend lied about their ages to obtain a license, drove to Blytheville, and got married in the home of a minister. They then drove to her new mother-in-law's home in Tennessee, where she called her mother and announced she was "Mrs. Frances Fox."[30] In version (c) she met her first steady, a "boy from a neighboring town," who was in his late teens. He applied for a marriage license in the area "Gretna Green," lying about his age and hers. They drove to his town, married in the home of a minister, and went to his mother's home in Tennessee, where Frances phoned her mother.[31] In version (d) she ran away and married her "high school boyfriend."[32] Apparently no application or marriage license was ever filed.[33] In versions (a) and (b), Frances moved with her folks to Memphis in late 1927, when she was 15. She had been deserted by her husband twice. On November 28, a son was born to her at Baptist Hospital in Memphis and she named him Thomas Frederick Fox, Jr.[34]

1928

Leonard was still playing shindigs wherever he could.[35] He was still considered one of the best square dance callers in those parts.[36] He met a man who owned a thoroughbred horse farm and was able to improve his horsemanship. Most of his horseback riding was done bareback, as no one could afford fancy saddles and saddles had no place on a farm. He bought a second-hand guitar for twenty dollars at a Cincinnati pawn shop.[37] Leonard's close friends during this time were Lowell Crabtree, a square dance caller, and the boys of the Clell Hiles family.[38]

Leonard left McDermott High in his sophomore year when the family moved to Cincinnati, where seventeen-year-old Leonard labored beside his father in the shoe factory. He worked days and attended school at night. His parents turned the farm over to his married sister Cleda. Leonard, his mother, and his sister Kathleen moved into the small duplex Andy occupied in the city, and he and his dad worked at the U.S. Shoe Factory.[39] Mary wrote often from California, talking of the beauty of the countryside and her letters made the Sly family want to see her and California, as well. That year Kathleen married a man named O'Dell, who came from McDermott.

*

May 1: According to Tennessee documents, Fox, an Arkansas resident, brought Frances to Memphis "ostentatiously on a visit" and deserted her.[40] She lived with her folks and provided her own and her son's support after this date. In version (a) early in this year (Tommy was a few months old), Frances and her husband moved back to Blytheville. It was here that he left the final time. On Easter, Frances returned to Memphis with Tommy to visit her folks. All versions indicate that her husband wrote to say he wanted a divorce. In version (b), Frances' husband pleaded for divorce in May-June.[41] In version (c), she received a good-bye note from husband. Her folks suggested they adopt Tommy, but she insisted on keeping him and supporting him herself.

1929

Leonard and his folks returned from Cincinnati when possible to visit family and friends at Duck Run. As much as he wanted to be in the city, Leonard missed the open spaces and hunting found in the country. Leonard and his dad hated the grueling shoe factory work, but they were fortunate to have it because that year the country entered into the Depression.

*

Circa April: Frances Fox enrolled in business school. She was a stenographer at an insurance firm and made her radio debut as Frances Fox. According to Tennessee documents signed by Frances, she filed for divorce on May 4, 1929. On September 24, Frances' divorce from Thomas F. Fox was granted by Judge H. W. Laughlin. Her mother and an aunt, Ruth Massey, provided the court with testimony on Frances' behalf, for grounds of desertion. She was awarded custody of Tom.[42]

1930

The month was June. Leonard had long wanted to go to California.[43] His job had no future, and the time was right for making the move. It was the first time in a while that the household had been excited. Leonard and his father had nearly two hundred dollars saved between the two of them. The 1923 Dodge was packed with their belongings, as well as with Leonard, his parents, an aunt, and the family dog.[44] They pointed the car west. It was an adventure for a boy who had never been far from home, but it became even more so, as the trip was not without incident. After several days on the road, the old vehicle's bearings just played out in Magdelina, New Mexico. No sooner did they get it going again, than it broke down in Arizona. The Slys picked up another automobile along the way to use for parts, and towed it along to make the trip. At least part of the way, they also pulled a small trailer. Leonard would manage to hold on to some of these old cars throughout his lifetime.[45] This is the same year that John Steinbeck wrote the novel *The Grapes of Wrath*, and the photo of the Slys making this trek out West looks as though it came right out of the book. Upon arriving in this "promised land," Leonard and his dad drove gravel trucks that Mary's husband owned, hauling to road construction crews.[46] Leonard even managed to do some boxing at 50 cents a round. They stayed with Mary and her husband a while

and then returned to Ohio after four months.[47] But almost immediately, Leonard was on his way back to California with Mary's father-in-law.[48] Jobs were scarce all over, including California. On one of the two trips, they were hitchhiking into town after the car had broken down, when a cowboy picked them up. He was the first real cowboy Leonard had met.[49] This is also the year that Leonard acquired his first motorcycle.[50]

*

On November 29, Frances Smith Fox, age 18, and August Wayne Johns of Mississippi, age 22, applied for a marriage license.[51] They were joined in matrimony on the 30th, by Robert G. Lee, probably a justice of the peace.[52] Chasing the rainbow of a show business career, as she has put it, Frances moved to Chicago with her son Tommy.[53]

1931

On this trip to California, Leonard found work at the Fox Hill Golf Course. In the spring he worked driving more dump trucks (Model Ts), while helping to build a stretch of highway from Newhall to Castaic. His folks sold their Ohio property to some neighbors, the Hiles family, and moved to California.[54] Leonard and Andy worked for the same company, driving trucks, until the company went bankrupt, and then both were out of work again. Andy managed to rent a house close to Mary's, probably at 4044 DePew Avenue in Lawndale.[55] Leonard, his dad, and a cousin Russ Scott found work picking peaches in Tulare.[56] Judging from some published accounts, Leonard picked peaches for the Del Monte Packing Co. in the San Joaquin Valley.[57] Leonard had his twenty-dollar guitar with him, and at night, after a hard day in the fields, he and his dad would get their instruments and entertain the other workers. After the summer, they returned to Lawndale. They had day labor for a while, but nothing permanent. Then Leonard, or "Len" as he was called, became a professional entertainer of sorts. The last thing that Andy wanted was to work in a shoe factory again, but he thought he had little choice. There was an opening for such work in Los Angeles, so he decided to go there. Len turned to the one thing he knew something about and wanted desperately and that was to try to make a living playing music. Len and his cousin

The Slye Brothers, c. 1930–1931. Leonard is holding the banjo.

Russ Scott played the Arrow Theater on L.A.'s Main Street for two dollars pay.[58] Then he and another cousin, Stanley Sly, got together and billed themselves as the Slye Brothers.[59] Although Western music was popular at the time, the money was low for performers. Roy and Stanley would work a place for a week and then strap their guitars on the handlebars of a motorcycle they had acquired. During the day they looked for labor jobs. They played everywhere they could get someone to stand still (or dance) and listen to them—beach parties, lodges, square dances, and socials of all kinds. They did not have a prearranged payment method worked out with the "house." They played first and then "passed the hat." An agent spotted them after they'd played a square dance and arranged for them to be booked into theaters. The places in which they found themselves performing left a lot to be desired. Soon the agent didn't even show up. After a while, Stanley decided to give up, but Len was more determined. He joined Uncle Tom Murray's Hollywood Hillbillies, where he played for free for the experience. In the summer of 1931, there was an amateur radio show in Inglewood called "Midnight Frolic" that was broadcast every Saturday night from midnight to 6 A.M.[60] Len was urged to audition for the show by his sister, who brought the opportunity to his attention. He played guitar, mandolin, banjo, and sang, but suffered a case of stage fright and was a long way from winning this on-the-air contest. The next day, the manager of a Western group, the Rocky Mountaineers, called and offered him a job as singer/guitarist.[61] The pay was nothing, but they had a weekly radio spot broadcast from Long Beach over radio station KGER, and they could advertise to people who needed a band. Len accepted the offer. He sang lead until an ad was placed in a local paper for a singer.[62] He stayed in the Long Beach area for six months.

1932

While performing in Long Beach, Len met a young woman by the name of Lucile Ascolese of 4025 Robison Avenue in Lawndale.[63] Lucile and her girlfriend Opal spent their lunch hour at the Long Beach radio station, watching the Rocky Mountaineers perform. Lucile was attractive, dark-haired,

and brown-eyed. Len was soon singing just to her. After a few weeks, he worked his way into the audience to get acquainted. He learned later that Lucile had told her mother that the singer was the man she would marry. Lucile was the only daughter of Joe Ascolese and Vinchinea Mele Ascolese, a respectable Italian-American couple residing in Wilmington, a coastal town near Long Beach. She was a native Californian, was fairly ambitious, and at eighteen years of age was attending high school and the Chicago College of Beauty in Long Beach. At the time, Len was so broke he never considered the idea of dating, so whatever romance there was had to take place in the radio station when he serenaded her. Since he was in the band making music, she had to be content dancing with others. The Depression was still going strong, and girls didn't expect expensive dates. Sometimes after the shows, Len would go with Lucile to meet her parents. The young couple enjoyed being together, going to the beach, to movies, or just driving around in his 1929 Ford Tudor Sedan that he had purchased for about $150 and was paying for on time payments.[64]

Canadian-born, former Santa Monica lifeguard Bob Nolan joined the Rocky Mountaineers for a while but then departed. During the time he was with the group, he and Len sang lead duets together.[65] After Nolan left, Len ran an ad in *Variety* magazine for a lead singer.[66] Missouri-born Vern Spencer answered the ad and joined the group. One member of the group was married and had a small cottage, and this is where they all lived when they weren't performing.[67] Life was cramped in the small house, as they struggled to make a living with their music. Before long, the Rocky Mountaineers disbanded. Len, Vern, and Bill "Slumber" Nichols joined Bennie Nawahi's International Cowboys, which consisted of them, a Mexican, and a Hawaiian.[68] They were still two years away from anything that smelled of the big time.

A palomino colt is foaled in Santa Cietro, California, near the Mexican border, south of San Diego, and is named "Golden Cloud" by his owner Roy Cloud. He will soon race at Caliente Race Track, and eventually become Roy Rogers' "Trigger."[69]

*

According to published accounts, Frances was experiencing health problems in Chicago, mostly due to malnutrition. She was working for an insurance company, still looking for entertainment work, and worrying about her son Tommy. She decided to go back to Texas, where her folks had moved.[70] Upon her arrival, she spent two weeks in the hospital recovering from malnutrition and anemia. According to court documents, her husband was abusive to her and Tommy.[71]

1933

In June of this year, the International Cowboys band played Warner Bros. Theater in L.A., singing "Tumbling Tumbleweeds" right through an earthquake. It wasn't long, however, before this group was also history. Len then put together another group consisting of himself, Vern ("Tim"), "Slumber," "Cactus Mack," and "Cyclone" (a fiddler). They called themselves the O-Bar-O Cowboys after an old brand.[72] Lucile had finished high school and beauty college by this point in time. Len's folks met her and decided they liked her.[73] In May, Len proposed to Lucile via a radio broadcast and the song "Hadie Brown" which ends with the line "Won't you be my wife?" Len, 21, and Lucile, 19, were married on Wednesday, May 8, by Justice of the Peace Kenneth E. Morrison in Santa Ana, with William A. ("Slumber") Nichols and his mother, Laura M., in attendance.[74] Lucile's mother gave the wedding band. There was no honeymoon.

After the short wedding ceremony, the band's agent called, and they had to hit the road.[75] The O-Bar-O Cowboys might have lasted a little longer had they not been talked into this ill-fated performance tour. It marked the first of what would be a lifetime of tours for Len. He was interested in making money, getting publicity for the band, just surviving. Len and the O-Bar-O Cowboys departed on a six-week "barnstorming" tour of the Southwest in the Pontiac belonging to fiddle player "Cyclone."[76] They played from the California border across into Texas in such towns as Yuma, Miami, Safford, Willcox, and Lubbock. They were on the road almost two months.[77] The contract wasn't too good and barely supplied them with enough money to cover meals and gasoline. It was a hundred and twelve degrees in Yuma, Arizona, and after playing two shows, they left as broke as they arrived. In Phoenix, the promoter told the city they would be coming at a date far later than they actually arrived. As a result, they had to lay over in Phoenix for almost a week and by the time they were to perform, they were so weak from hunger, they could barely play. They didn't set any box-office records. Miami, Arizona, was a mining town. When the band arrived, the mines were shut down, so everything was shut down. Worse still, they were less than impressed to learn that no one there had ever heard of them.[78] The first thing they did when they hit a town was to go parading down the streets using a megaphone and announcing they had arrived to play. The last thing Len did in this town was to give up his wristwatch to pay the motel bill. Safford, Arizona, was more successful; they netted four dollars each. Then came Wilcox, the hometown of "Cactus Mack." The band members were so excited by all the hoopla that greeted them because of a hometown boy coming back to perform that they went all out, buying a lot of floor wax and having circulars printed up for a square dance. The crowd was large, and "Cactus" was so moved that he decided to stay home. It was the most attention he had gotten in a long time, and he couldn't bring himself to leave it for the hunger of the road again. "Cyclone" decided to give up as well and head back to sunny California. It was with great difficulty that he was persuaded to remain with the band to go on to Roswell, New Mexico. Without him, they would not have been able to go on because he was their transportation. It was June when they arrived in Roswell, and after having blown six tires (hot Arizona asphalt and thin rubber don't mix), they were still ahead of schedule.[79] They stayed in a tourist court in Roswell, talking the manager into a little credit. Money was so scarce, they hunted rabbits and shot hawks in order to put a little food in their stomachs.[80] On the air, they offered to trade a yodeling song for a lemon pie. Grace Arline Wilkins, an eighteen-year-old ash-blonde, about 5'9", ventured to the radio station with her mother and her brother to offer a lemon pie in exchange for a performance of the "Swiss Yodel." Len and Arline became better acquainted when he returned the pie plates the next day.[81]

The members of the band had been assured by the booking agent that folks of the Southwest would appreciate the fine Western music their band made. As was the practice at the time, they would perform on radio a few minutes for free in order to let the audience know where they would be playing in the evenings, and they hoped to pick up a little cash in these performances. It was pretty hard work because they usually had to do the radio slots early in the morning, after playing somewhere the night before.

No one was getting rich out on the road, and the O-Bar-O Cowboys soon went the way of other groups, disbanding after they wrapped up the tour in Lubbock, Texas.[82]

According to numerous magazine articles, Len spent a year's time on the Sutherland Ranch being a real cowboy, learning all about tending cattle, branding, roping, etc. after the O-Bar-O Cowboys disbanded. This supposedly was in New Mexico when Len was on the way back to California.[83] When he left the ranch, he had just about enough money clinking in his jeans to get a cup of coffee.

After Len returned to L.A., he and Lucile got their first house, a "$30.00 a month furnished duplex apartment on 88th Place."[84] She had been living with her parents. Items received from wedding showers helped them set up housekeeping, and Tim Spencer taught her how to cook. Len did minor radio stints, one after another, and his employment instability apparently affected his life in general. Then, along with Tim Spencer, he joined "Jack and His Texas Outlaws" and performed on Radio KFWB, another no pay situation.[85] At night, Len played cafes with another musician, Curly Hoag, for a dollar a night. Len wanted his old trio to stay together and still believed they could make it in the music business, but Tim Spencer went to work in a Safeway grocery store sacking groceries and Bob Nolan went to Bel-Air Country Club and began caddying. They liked the regular paychecks and meals, but Len talked to them and managed to convince them to make another stab at performing together, just the three of them.[86] (Bill "Slumber" Nichols took off for Texas, and "Cyclone" went home to Kansas.) In December 1933, Len, Spencer, and Nolan got together again and joined Jack and His Texas Outlaws, creating a unique, three-part harmony yodeling that gained such popularity that the radio station offered them their own show.[87] They found a sponsor, changed the band's name to "The Pioneer Trio," and received the fantastic sum of $35 a week pay. Len managed to rent a rooming house at 1453 Tamarind Avenue in Hollywood,[88] a mere two blocks away from radio station KFWB, where they performed on an early morning program.[89] (The WB in KFWB stands for Warner Brothers.) An article featuring their band appeared in Bernie Milligan's column, "The Best Bets of the Day," in the *L.A. Herald-Examiner* because of their rendition of the song "The Last Roundup." Play and practice is all the group did. They all stayed together in the small house, and they practiced as much as 8–10 hours a day, which was common for musical groups at this time.

Lucile couldn't adjust to life with a musician husband, however. She worked days as a beauty operator, and he kept late night hours performing. She wouldn't let him sleep late.[90] Lucile was pregnant and became very irritable when he attempted to practice, mocking him and creating disturbances to run interference. Len felt his ability was being greatly impaired by her behavior.[91] Lucile was jealous to the point that she couldn't stand for him to dedicate a song to female listeners as he emceed their radio show, and she was reading his mail. According to Len, she falsely accused him of infidelity in front of his friends.[92]

*

In the fall of 1933 or 1934, Frances landed a radio job in Louisville, Kentucky, at station WHAS. She performed as "Marion Lee" for a while. For a better-sounding stage name, Joe Eaton, program director, suggested "Dale Evans." At some point between arriving and leaving Louisville, she met and began dating pianist/arranger Robert Dale Butts.[93] Tommy became ill and was sent to her folks' farm in Irene, Texas.[94] By this point, her husband had deserted her at least once.[95]

1934

In California, a radio announcer's slip or intentional introduction of the band as the "Sons of the Pioneers" brought about a name change. He explained that they were too young to be pioneers of anything, and they liked the catchy sound of the new tag.[96] Len and the band played as the Gold Star Rangers in a morning slot on the radio and as the Sons of the Pioneers in the evenings.[97] Soon they received invitations to appear on bigger radio shows with well-known performers such as Jo Stafford. In March of 1934, they began expanding their group by adding a virtuoso fiddler and bass singer by the name of Hugh Farr from Llano, Texas, making themselves a combo. Farr was known for his ability to play both country and jazz. Len's pay was increased to $40 a week, with paydays every Wednesday.[98] The rent was nine dollars a person per week, for cramped quarters.[99] This situation eventually had to take its toll on the marriage, and Len and Lucile began having more marital problems. According to Lucile, Len took her to her mother's house in Wilmington in June, went after a pack of cigarettes, and, instead of returning, sent her a special delivery letter stating he was disgusted with married life and was washing his hands of her.[100] Soon after this episode, however, they were reconciled. About July 12, after another argument, Lucile threatened to commit suicide and gave Len a scare.

A big break soon came about for Len and the band when the group signed with Decca Records. They had their first recording session on August 4.[101]

In the meantime, Lucile went to work for a Mrs. Ward, in Wilmington, for $15 a week, the state minimum requirement for such work.[102] On August 18 or 19 (Lucile's version) or August 9 (Len's version), they split for good. According to a magazine article, they came to a mutual agreement and would remain friends, but divorce proceedings were begun. Apparently Lucile is the one who left, as she had possession of the car and wouldn't give it up, despite Len's demands. According to court documents, Len, on August 25, 1934, told her he had gotten an attorney and was filing for divorce. Lucile got an attorney and filed for separate maintenance on August 29, on grounds of mental

cruelty, mentioning a woman "of bad repute in Arizona," name calling, and a flying "glass tray." She wanted Len's Model A Ford Tudor Sedan, $50 a month alimony, and attorney's fees. Len answered her complaint on September 5 and on that day filed a cross-complaint, complaining of mental cruelty because of her accusations and her attitude and behavior regarding his occupation.[103] He also charged that she and her mother had arranged an abortion after he had proudly bragged to everyone of being an expectant father.[104] According to the *Modern Screen* article, November 1955, their biggest problem was his hours spent with the band in a schedule contrasting with hers and general incompatibility. Lucile was not happy being an entertainer's wife.[105] On September 13, the court recommended that Len pay Lucile's attorney fees, court costs, and $8 a month for alimony, at least until the divorce became final. Len got the automobile. In papers filed September 27, Lucile made it plain that she didn't want a divorce but separate maintenance and alimony instead. Len moved just around the corner into a Hollywood boarding house at 5841 Carlton Way, where he occupied one room.[106] The rent was $7 a week and included two meals.[107]

During this period Arline was living in L.A. and attending business college. Len and she had corresponded since their first meeting.[108]

The band was still playing as the staff band at KFWB.[109] They were performing nearly every night and beginning to see some real money for their work. On December 15, "Tumbling Tumbleweeds" hit #13 on the charts. In late 1934, the Sons of the Pioneers recorded several hundred selections for Standard Radio to make records to be sold to radio stations all over the country in syndicated fashion. (These recordings took place until mid-1935.)

During this period Len acquired an automobile that he was reportedly told had previously been owned by Clark Gable.[110]

1935

The divorce trial for Len and Lucile was set for February 25, but apparently one or both of them did not show up. It was reset for, and held on, April 10 and 11. They both appeared with counsel, and the divorce was granted to Len on May 28, but under California law, they had to wait one year for it to become final.

Len and the Sons of the Pioneers appeared with Will Rogers in a Salvation Army benefit in San Bernardino, California, the last show before his death in a plane crash in Alaska.[111] In July, Len received his first fan letter.[112] Len and the band appeared on film together, making their debut in *Radio Scout*, which was probably a short, and then *The Old Homestead*, a Liberty picture.[113] Their next appearance was in a Republic film starring Gene Autry that was titled *Tumbling Tumbleweeds*, after their hit recording. Gene Autry was Hollywood's number one silver screen cowboy at the time. The band worked in another show called *The Open Spaces*. During mid–1935, the band, which remained on KFWB, added Hugh's brother Karl, a singer/guitarist. The next film exposure for the group came in the form of a short subject film *Slightly Static* and then *Way Up Thar*, an educational short. The final film for them this year was *Gallant Defender*, a Charles Starrett vehicle. The Sons of the Pioneers obtained a contract to play background music for Columbia's Charles Starrett films.

*

On December 25. Frances and August Johns separated.

1936

On June 8, in open court, Len received his divorce. He got the automobile but had to pay court costs. Lucile got the real estate they had acquired.[114] On June 10, Len, Arline, and the Sons of the Pioneers were on their way to Texas, where Len and the band performed at the Texas Centennial and appeared in the Autry film *The Big Show*. But first they made a brief stop in Roswell, New Mexico, where Len and Arline entered the Chaves County clerk's office to apply for a marriage license. On June 11, Len, 24, and Arline, 21, were married by the Reverend D. B. Titus. Arline's parents, Mr. and Mrs. P. D. Wilkins, Jr., were witnesses to the event. The license was recorded in the clerk's office on June 12.[115]

The Texas Centennial was held at the Dallas fairgrounds, a little southeast of the downtown area. Len and Arline and the group spent six to eight weeks in Texas. Dale Evans also was appearing there, but remarkably, their paths did not cross.[116]

Back in California, Len tried out in a screen test for Universal Studios as a solo cowboy, when sagebrusher Buck Jones moved to Columbia studios, leaving an empty cowboy slot. A young white-hatted Bob Baker beat Len to the draw, so to speak. Baker achieved a small degree of success, and Len kept his singing job. Probably Len's first appearance on sheet music or a songbook is *The Sons of the Pioneers Song Folio #1*, published by Cross and Winge of San Francisco. Songbooks were an item continuously connected with his career (see Chapter 12). The Sons of the Pioneers performed on Peter Potter's "KNX Hollywood Barn Dance."[117]

At the end of December, Len had a dangerous bout with pneumonia.

*

On May 13, Frances Johns appeared in court to file for divorce from August on the grounds of cruelty.[118] August Johns appeared on May 16 and made waiver. On May 29, Judge Humphries granted the divorce.[119] At this time her pay at WHAS was $30 a week.

Keeping the name "Dale Evans," Frances auditioned with Jimmie Jeffries on Dallas' WFAA Radio "Early Bird" program and landed another job. Tommy stayed at the farm, and Dale visited him on weekends. Robert Dale Butts moved from Louisville to Dallas, where he went to work for WFAA Radio as an arranger and pianist.

1937

According to an oft repeated story, Len was in a hat store in Glendale when he heard about a screen test at Republic studios for "singing cowboys" from a hopeful who entered the store.[120] Len was in the store getting his only hat cleaned and blocked. He headed to the studio but had to sneak through the gate in a group of workers returning from lunch.[121] He met producer Sol C. Siegel, who knew him as one of the Sons of the Pioneers and agreed to an audition. Len sang "Hadie Brown" because of the yodeling part. He also sang "Tumbling Tumbleweeds" and one other song. This is at least the second time that Len used this song to bring about a change in his life. The screen test with director Joe Kane was successful, but Len was reminded of another contract still in force. At Columbia, he explained his opportunity and was released, provided he found a replacement for his part in the group. Len went to Sunset Beach where Pat Brady, a singer, comedian, and bass player, was appearing at Sam's Place, an after-hours hangout for musicians. Pat accepted the offer and became a singer with the Sons of the Pioneers.

On October 13, Len signed a contract with Republic Studios. Immediately, the studio officials decided that his name was not right for a cowboy and gave him a new name, Dick Weston.[122] Republic star Gene Autry was threatening to walk out if he didn't get a new contract, and Republic used singing cowboy Dick Weston as leverage against him.[123] *The Old Wyoming Trail* with Charles Starrett was released November 8, with Len singing with the Sons of the Pioneers, his last film credit as Len Slye. Len had a bit part as Dick Weston in the Three Mesquiteers film *Wild Horse Rodeo. Variety* magazine reviewed his performance in this film, which was released December 6. Len was about to be making $75 a week.[124] On October 19, Len and the group recorded at ARC Records; it was their first recording together in quite a while.[125]

*

On September 13, Robert Dale Butts and Frances Octavia Johns filed an application for marriage in Dallas, Texas. On September 20, the Rev. A. Paul Dougherty united them in marriage at the Greenville Avenue Christian Church.[126]

SOURCE MATERIAL

Books

Davis, Elise Miller. *The Answer Is God.* New York: McGraw-Hill, 1955.

Morris, Georgia, and Mark Pollard. *Roy Rogers: King of the Cowboys.* San Francisco, CA.: Collins Publishers, 1994.

Raskey, Frank. *Roy Rogers: King of the Cowboys.* New York: Julian Messner Co., 1955.

Rogers, Dale Evans. *The Angel Spreads Her Wings.* Westwood, NJ: Fleming H. Revell Co., 1956.

_____. *Angel Unaware.* Old Tappan, NJ: Fleming H. Revell Co., 1953.

_____. *Dale—My Personal Picture Album.* Old Tappan, NJ: Fleming H. Revell Co., 1971.

_____. *My Spiritual Diary.* Westwood, NJ: Fleming H. Revell Co., 1955.

_____. *To My Son—Faith at Our House.* Westwood, NJ: Fleming H. Revell Co., 1957.

_____. *Woman at the Well.* Old Tappan, NJ: Fleming H. Revell Co., 1970.

_____, with Jane and Michael Stern. *Happy Trails: Our Life Story.* New York: Simon and Schuster, 1994.

Roper, William L. *Roy Rogers: King of the Cowboys.* Minneapolis, MN: T.S. Denison & Co., 1971.

Rothel, David. *The Roy Rogers Book.* Madison, NC: Empire Publishing, Inc., 1987.

_____. *The Singing Cowboys.* San Diego: A.S. Barnes & Co., Inc., 1978.

Rovin, Jeff. *Country Music Babylon.* New York: St. Martin's Press, 1993.

Stowers, Carlton, with Roy and Dale. *Happy Trails.* Waco, TX: Word Books, 1979.

Sword, Elmer. *Roy Rogers Hometown Photo Album.* Portsmouth, OH: Portsmouth Area Recognition Society, 1982.

Witney, William. *Trigger Remembered.* Toney, AL: Earl Blair Enterprises, 1989.

Published Interviews

Michael Bane, 1992.

Joan Winmill Brown, 1980.

Tom Carroll, Jerry Osborne, 1991.

Mark Goodman, 1975.

Jackson Griffith, 1991.

Lydia Dixon Harden, 1991.

Bill Kelly, 1981.

Bart McDowell, 1972.

John F. Maloney, 1979.

Bill Miller, 1992.

Neil Pond, 1992.

David Rothel, 1977, 1987.

Bob Thomas, 1975.

Recorded Interviews (with Roy Rogers)

Jim Wilson, WIOI, Portsmourth, 1992.

Cincinnati radio, 1992.

Filmed Interviews

"AM-Philadelphia" (TV), 1975, 1981.
Len Morris, Galen Films, 1992.

"The Republic Pictures Story," AMC-TV, 1991.

Articles by Roy and Dale have appeared in such publications as: *American Classic Screen, American Magazine, Christian Reader, Jack and Jill, Screen Guide,* and *Modern Screen,* 1940s–1980s.

Chapter 2

THE "KING OF THE COWBOYS" AND THE "QUEEN OF THE WEST"

1938

Enter Trigger, formerly "Golden Cloud," who appeared in *Adventures of Robin Hood* with Errol Flynn, a film in which he was ridden by Olivia De Havilland. He was a six-year-old palomino.[1] The studio folks were not satisfied with Len's new name of "Dick Weston." After they searched for a name with more flair, they finally agreed upon "Roy Rogers." Len was a great admirer of Will Rogers, so the surname suited him fine. He was a little reluctant about the "Roy" part, however, because of a "LeRoy" he knew as a kid. But he had to agree that "Roy" wasn't "LeRoy" and did sound good with "Rogers." Republic staff men Bill Saal and Moe and Sol Siegel took part in the decision, along with boss Herbert Yates. Sol Siegel seems to have been the man who came up with both names, but Yates approved. Republic's publicity crew conjured up the image they wanted to project for "Roy Rogers" and started the myth that Roy Rogers was born and raised on a ranch in Cody, Wyoming. The residents of Cody, however, had never heard of any Rogers family with a son named Roy who went to Hollywood and became a movie star. They searched records, not just in Cody, but in all of Wyoming.[2]

Republic wasn't overly impressed by their research, and very little about these discoveries was ever leaked to the press. It was several years before American magazines stopped using the Wyoming story, and it persisted even longer overseas. This myth continued until 1949.[3]

On August 22, vaudeville actor Roy Rogers filed suit against Leonard Slye and Republic Productions for $150,000 damages and an injunction against the use of his name for the new cowboy star.[4] An out-of-court settlement was reached on November 17 by a dismissal with prejudice filed by the attorney for the plaintiff. Republic and Roy were able to retain the name and Republic retained the "picture rights."[5]

Len's first feature film as "Roy Rogers" (which was going to be titled *Washington Cowboy* when it was slated for Autry) was titled *Under Western Stars* and was filmed in Lone Pine early in 1938. It was shot in nine days. The palomino mentioned above was used in Roy's first films but was renamed "Trigger." Trigger became a film character right away, played by both the real Trigger and any number of horses that doubled for him.

With Gene Autry away from the studio for about six months, Roy Rogers got star status at Republic. In April, Roy was in Dallas for the premier of *Under Western Stars* at the Capitol Theater. He and the Sons of the Pioneers went on stage and sang prior to the film itself, a common practice with premiere showings in those days. Roy got the group signed for seven years with Republic to provide his supporting music. The *Dallas Morning News* provided "Roy Rogers" in his first film review. The film became the first "B" Western to show at the Criterion Theater on Broadway in New York, and it was voted "Best Western of the Year." Roy made his first trip to New York City, a city that became very important to his career and popularity. He participated in the Victory Parade that lasted for ten hours. The rule prohibiting horses was set aside for Roy Rogers to enable him to ride Trigger between the governor's and mayor's cars.[6]

Variety reviewed Roy Rogers, and he was also reviewed by Bosley Crowther in the *New York Times*. He was an immediate hit with the public and was already receiving 28,000 pieces of fan mail weekly. Arline was helping answer the mail by sending back signed photos of her husband. Len "Roy Rogers" Slye tried to solicit help from Yates, but there was no interest from Republic. He finally rented a truck and dumped a load of fan mail on the lawn of Yates' office to make his point. Roy's personal appearances were earning him $150 an evening.[7] He would drive throughout the night, make several appearances, and then be back on the road. When he wasn't on location filming, or on tour promoting a film, or in the recording studio, he was lining up appearances or doing one-night stands to help defray the cost of the mail staff. He eventually hired four women to answer the mail and send out autographed photos (made at his own expense).

Len had a solo hit recording as Roy Rogers: in July, "Hi Yo Silver" hit #13 on the charts. Probably the first sheet music to be issued with Roy alone on the cover was "Dust," by Santly Bros.–Joy, Inc., from his first feature film.

The "B" Westerns Roy appeared in took from eight days to two weeks to shoot. A fancy silver-laden saddle, the first of several he would own in the future, was evident in the first film. It is believed to have been made by Edward H. Bohlin, maker of the "World's Finest" saddlery.[8] Roy was offered a standard trial contract with Republic.[9] When Yates attempted to use pressure on Roy by hinting at putting another cowboy on the horse, he was informed that Roy owned the horse.

"Seein' Stars" by Feg Murray (a syndicated cartoon panel) included Roy and Trigger and was probably the first drawn likeness of Roy printed in the papers, aside from possible Republic Productions work associated with the films.[10]

*

Dale Evans, now a singer on WFAA Radio, Dallas, was on the cover of *Rural Radio* in August. Throughout her career, she would be seen with many different hair colors, from blonde to red to brown.[11]

1939

Roy Rogers was now living in a five-room wooden house, and his film wages were $100 a week. The studio put eye drops in Roy's eyes to keep him from squinting, but found that the public liked him with the squint. In June, *Real Screen Fun*, a "girlie" magazine, published a photo of Roy and other actors in a still from his film *Shine On Harvest Moon*.[12] (This was one of the very first magazines to carry a picture of Roy, and it is probably the only time his photo appeared in this type of publication.)

That year Roy appeared at the Garden Theater in his hometown of Portsmouth.[13] During this visit he saw old friends such as his former teacher Guy Bumgarner and his wife Nell.[14]

Roy hired horse trainer Jimmy Griffin to train Trigger.[15] He performed with Trigger at the New York World's Fair in Flushing Meadows, Queens, an event which marked the beginning of his "national splash" in personal appearances. "Roy Rogers Day" was proclaimed in New York City.

*

Seeking opportunities for their careers, the Butts moved to Chicago. He found work at NBC as an arranger, and Dale landed a job as a singer with Jay Mills' Orchestra and played the Edgewater Beach Hotel. Dale obtained a job with the Anson Weeks Orchestra, touring the Midwest and West Coast. She and Roy would soon cross paths. She had to drive hundreds of miles from engagement to engagement, doing "one-nighters." This arrangement lasted for a year.[16]

1940

In March, Roy hired a personal manager, W. Arthur (Art) Rush, who would be with the cowboy for approximately the next fifty years and play a very important role in his success.[17] Working under Rush, E. James (Jim) Osborne handled Roy's financial affairs.

Roy acquired another palomino that

Roy in an early publicity still, ca. 1938.

year, "Little Trigger," who would be around for many years. "Little Trigger" often portrayed the character "Trigger" on the road, along with other doubles, while the "old man," as he was known, stayed in California.

Yates was notorious for not being generous with pay raises. When Roy approached him with a request for a raise and an idea about product endorsement, he was refused the raise but given a contract clause that released him to pursue additional commercial avenues. This was an important event because it led to the birth of a merchandizing empire that would last for a couple of decades.[18] On a trip to New York City, Art Rush and Roy let it be known to manufacturers that he was willing to lend his character name and image to their products. Products tied to other Hollywood cowboys, especially toys, were already popular and meant a lot of additional cash for the cowboy stars. The manufacturers responded enthusiastically to this request from Roy and Art Rush.[19]

According to published accounts, there was a real fight between Roy and three rowdies who were trying to spoil a serenade requested by the owners of a restaurant. One guy was knocked out, and he and one of his friends took the door off the hinges and ended up on the sidewalk. Fortunately, Roy was able to walk away from these adversaries.

At this time Roy and Arline were considering adopting a child. While in Dallas, Roy had lunch at a variety club with two acquaintances, Bob O'Donald and Bill Underwood, local theater owners showing his pictures, who were on the board of directors of Hope Cottage, an orphanage in Dallas. They assisted him in the adoption of an infant girl.

Roy's salary was increased to $150 per week during 1940.[20] According to popularity polls, Rogers had become the "Number 2 Singing Cowboy," second only to Autry.[21] Roy was seen in photos plugging Wheaties cereal, and magazine advertisements began appearing with Roy promoting such items as electric ranges and dog food. Art Rush put together a transcribed, syndicated radio show for Roy called "Manhattan Cowboy," and Roy made an appearance on Louella Parsons' radio show.

*

Dale Evans and her husband were living in Chicago, and his parents were living with them. Her son Tom was in junior high school. Dale was performing at the Balinese Room in the Blackstone Hotel and at supper clubs in the Sherman and Drake Hotels and also appeared over WWBM Radio and sang at the famous Chez Paree Club. In addition, she was singing on CBS and NBC radio shows. She was working her own show, "That Gal from Texas," over CBS Radio when she answered a call from Hollywood for a screen test.

1941

By now, Roy's tours had taken him over 100,000 miles. There were only four states in which he had not appeared: Maine, Vermont, and North and South Dakota.

Roy and Arline adopted an infant girl after they and Arline's mother traveled to Texas to visit Hope Cottage.[22] They had to wait until the baby was four months old before taking her home, and during this time, a representative of the orphanage traveled to California and spent a couple of weeks living with the Rogers to determine that they were fit parents to adopt.[23] Having met the requirements, they picked their new daughter up at the orphanage. Her name was Cheryl Darlene, and she was born in 1940.[24]

Magazine articles stated that Roy Rogers lived on a California ranch and swam a lot. He was reported to be five feet eleven inches tall, to have blonde hair, blue eyes, and to weigh one hundred and sixty-five pounds. He was making eight films a year and touring heavily. He appeared with the Cactus Cowboys, consisting of Joe Caliente, fiddle; Jake Watts, guitar; "Windy" Bill McKay, doghouse bass; and Bobby Gregory, accordion. Roy had begun entertaining at orphanages during his personal appearance tours, something that he continued throughout his career.

That fall Roy and Arline bought a home with six acres at 4704 Whiteoak Avenue in Encino, in the San Fernando Valley, close to the chicken farm he had purchased for his parents. The home, which once belonged to actor Don Ameche, had a huge Spanish-style house with a swimming pool, tennis court, guest house, citrus orchard, and corral.

*

In California, after several disappointing tryouts, including a screen test at Paramount, Dale Evans landed a one-year contract with 20th Century–Fox through her agent Joe Rivkin. When she revealed that she had a teenage son, however, Rivkin ordered her to pass him off as her brother.[25] Dale Evans, along wth her son Tom, returned to L.A. to live. Her mother (who had flown to Chicago) accompanied them for a visit. After Dale had worked things out at NBC, Robert Dale and his folks made the move also, and they all rented a house in West L.A.

1942

A magazine addressed the so-called "feud" that was rumored between Gene Autry and Roy Rogers, a rumor both said was nonsense.[26] The studios would often create this kind of story to boost the popularity of their stars. Magazines had Roy trailing behind Autry and William (Hopalong Cassidy) Boyd as the number-one cowboy. Roy's management team worked hard on his first big publicity build-up and image change, which resulted in the birth of many more "trademark" characteristics for this cowboy and his horse. He had become a superb rider and marksman and sang in a distinctive Western-flavored voice; America was enthralled with this image. When Autry joined the Army Air Corps, the publicity department took full advantage of this opportunity to build Roy's new image and Trigger got as much attention as Roy.

Len "Roy Rogers" Slye was now 30 years of age and had a wife and child. Their family was about to be expanded, for that summer Arline learned she was pregnant. With World War II underway, there was speculation that Roy would be drafted, even though he had a family.

With Gene Autry gone, Roy quickly moved up to "Number 1 Singing Cowboy." Now that his career was solidly established, Len and Arline filed a petition in Los Angeles County Court on August 22 requesting that they be allowed to change their names to Roy Rogers and Grace Arline Rogers in order to simplify their lives. Their request was granted on October 6.[27]

Under the direction of Joe Kane, Roy's films had departed from the historically set "Old West" days of Billy the Kid, Buffalo Bill Cody, and Wild Bill Hickok. He was now a good samaritan cowboy in a modern day West.[28] There was a succession of actresses playing Roy's leading ladies, including pretty Linda Hayes. The title "King of the Cowboys" was created for Roy by Yates. Film magazines of the day covered every step that the cowboy made, whether on tour, at a filming location, or at home. Roy also enhanced his image by appearing at the World's Championship Rodeos around the country.[29]

Roy made a sweeping tour of army bases in Texas for the 8th Service Command. In another patriotic effort typical of his high energy in performances, he made 136 appearances in 20 days to sell war bonds in cities all over Texas, where he was sponsored by the state, the Interstate Theater Circuit, the Theater Owners of Texas, and Republic Productions. He performed for bond sales activities, stage canteens, base hospitals, and underprivileged children. Roy and Trigger were photographed in front of the Alamo, in San Antonio, Texas, at Sheppard Field in Wichita Falls, Texas, and with Governor Stevenson of Texas. Trigger impressed everyone with his rumba dance routine.

That summer Roy was photographed on Trigger (actually "Little Trigger") on the lawn across from the Capitol building in Washington, D.C. This was a rare occasion when for unknown reasons he was wearing a black hat.

Roy made his debut at the 17th annual Madison Square Garden Rodeo, October 7–25, outfitted in all white attire with red boots.[30] After 19 days, he set a new attendance record. Two hundred cowboys and cowgirls competed here.[31] Roy and Arline took in the sights of the city, and it was reported that Roy liked New York and New York liked him.[32] Trigger celebrated a birthday in the city with a party thrown in his honor, complete with cake. The city's famous Stage Door Canteen hosted a performance by Roy, Trigger, and the Sons of the Pioneers. Trigger really impressed the press with a publicity gimmick that would be used repeatedly. He stepped into the Dixie Hotel and at the registration desk, signed in with an "X." As part of the stunt, the horse went upstairs to Roy's room and then dined in the restaurant.

Roy's spurs were becoming famous. Fred Allen recorded over the radio for posterity the sound of these spurs, and Roy presented Mayor La Guardia of New York City with a pair of silver spurs.

One of Roy's attention-getters at personal appearances was to go out in the center of a main street in the city or town, usually in front of the theater at which he was appearing, and ride Trigger, making him rear and do other tricks. Roy entertained at

Roy and "Trigger" during Texas Tour, 1942. (Probably Little Trigger.)

Merchant Seaman's base, Sheepshead Bay, Brooklyn, and he and Trigger entertained at the New York Infirmary for Women and Children and at St. John's Home in Brooklyn.

*

When Joe Rivkin entered the military, Dale was referred to Art Rush for an agent. Dale had a 43-week stint with Edgar Bergen on the Chase and Sanborn radio show. She was entertaining troops in U.S.O. shows at military camps all over the West and South-west. She performed about six hundred shows for U.S.O. and the Hollywood Victory Committee, and her husband, Robert Dale, often went along as her piano player.

Dale and her family attended Hollywood First Baptist Church. She and R. Dale

Arline, Cheryl, and Roy at home, ca. 1942.

(as she always referred to him) lived in a Spanish-style, eight-room house in Westwood, at 10470 Kinnard Avenue.[33] After she had a dispute with Art Rush because his time was taken up by top client Roy Rogers, she hired Daniel M. Winkler as her new agent.

1943

Roy toured Canada this year. In January he was invited to the White House for President Franklin D. Roosevelt's 61st birthday. He presented Mrs. Roosevelt with a pair of spurs.

On April 16, Arline entered the hospital. On April 18, something Roy and Arline hadn't thought was possible a year earlier happened. A baby girl was born to them at Hollywood Presbyterian Hospital, and they named her Linda Lou. Roy even wrote a song in her honor.[34]

One magazine reported that the only time Roy drank was when he had a Scotch prior to an interview. Roy and Arline only attended parties on occasion and preferred to do their socializing at home with barbe-cues. (Ironically, the exact same thing was reported in magazines covering the home life of Robert Dale and Dale Evans.[35])

Roy and Trigger were featured on the cover of *Life* in the rearing pose that had already become a trademark.[36] By now, Trigger was beginning to share marquees with his rider.

Horses were not the only animals that interested Roy Rogers. He had collected a small zoo and aviary. He eventually owned almost twenty dogs, a situation that had his neighbors up in arms. Roy was particularly interested in homing pigeons, and all 95 of his pigeons were registered for army duty. One bird in particular, "Lone Ranger," had won first place in three races and was once clocked at 50 miles per hour. Another great winner would be "Blue Chicken, No. 316."[37] Some of the races covered 700 miles. "Lone Ranger" even appeared in one of Roy's films.[38] Described as a "racing pigeon addict," Roy belonged to the North Hollywood Studio City Pigeon Racing Club.[39]

A *Life* article stated that Roy's closest competitor was Hopalong Cassidy. Roy was voted number one Western star in polls conducted by various film magazines, i.e., *Box Office, Showman's Trade Reviews,* and *Motion Picture Herald*, and would remain in that position until the polls ended in 1954. In December another record, *Think of Me,* hit the charts at #18. Decca Records was selling 6,000 Roy Rogers records per week.

Roy's draft status was 3-A at this point. Although he didn't go into the active military, he did do much for the war effort at home, as he worked to sell war bonds and reportedly sold more than any other Hollywood star. Before the end of the war, he received a citation from the U.S. Treasury Department for having sold over a million dollars worth of bonds. Roy found it really easy to draw large crowds of youngsters and their parents because a cowboy on a golden palomino was a tough act to beat. He became extremely popular with the servicemen and gave a lot of his time and energy to entertaining them. Roy's shows for underprivileged children got a lot of notice, as well as his rounds of camps and base hospitals. A big morale booster, he was quickly becoming a hero to young and old alike. The studio was taking no chances, however. Just in case he might be drafted, a young cowboy actor by the name of Monte Hale had been added to Republic's roster and groomed as a possible replacement.

Republic was launching one of its biggest publicity campaigns, and it was for Roy. Whitman Publishing Co. was producing Roy Rogers books now. Whitman was the world's largest publisher of children's books and was owned by Western Printing Co., which would play one of the biggest roles in Roy's success. As part of the publicity campaign, ads for Roy's films were appearing in national magazines. The film *King of the Cowboys* was about to be released, and a song book, *Roy Rogers' Own Songs*, was published by American Music. In one of the many events that furthered the publicity campaign, Roy took part in the Sheriff's Rodeo at the coliseum in Los Angeles with Betty Hutton, Allen "Rocky" Lane, another popular Republic cowboy star, and new actress Dale Evans. In June the publicity campaign placed 192 billboards across the country carrying 24-sheet movie posters at a cost of $500,000.[40] The billboards showed Roy and Roy on Trigger and announced that he was the "King of the Cowboys" and that Trigger was the "Smartest Horse in the Movies" (see Chapter 7). That year Roy was voted "Number 1 Money Making Western Star."[41]

While Roy was on a tour of army camps, he stayed in San Antonio's Gunter Hotel, where Trigger received star treatment. He was quartered in the lobby and got heavy media attention. The hotel had a special box stall built to accommodate him for three days. The Double R Bar brand that was about to become a trademark name was designed for him by leather craftsman Bob Brown. Although it appears that it was never registered as a real trademark, it would figure importantly when Roy began marketing his own brand of products.

As she had the previous year, Arline accompanied Roy on his tour with Trigger, which lasted between ten and sixteen weeks. His rodeo circuit logged 50,000 miles this year.[42] Seventy-five hundred U.S. theaters were showing his pictures, including 126 in Chicago. Roy performed a week of stage shows at Chicago's Oriental Theater, a record money week for the house. His golden palomino and expensive and unique attire, which included a $150 saddle, put him ahead of the competition. Trigger knew over sixty tricks and was learning more. A lot of money was used for trainers such as Glenn Randall, who taught the "Trigger" horses and others used by Roy for the many tricks and routines that were part of Roy's shows.

Roy was backed at Madison Square Garden this year by the "Ranch Girls" during his October performances; one number called "Home on the Range" used the largest herd of Texas Longhorns in existence.[43] This year the purse was nearly $100,000 (for competition events), five times greater than that of any other 1943 rodeo. Roy had his photo taken with cowgirls, Garden executives, and even Gene Autry, who was in uniform. The New York visit had him working every day for bond drives, China relief, servicemen's canteens, orphanages, and hospitals. It was reported that "Not since the death of Valentino had a motion picture star garnered so much publicity space as was freely given to Roy Rogers."[44]

*

Thanks to Winkler and Rush, Dale Evans signed a contract at Republic Studios, as her path and Roy's came closer together. Her first film was *Swing Your Partner* with Lulu Belle and Scotty. She also appeared in the film *Hoosier Holiday*. Still a year away from making a film with Roy, Dale appeared in nine more films, one of which was *Here Comes Elmer*. Her option was renewed at the end of the year.

Dale met Roy Rogers while she was appearing at Edwards Air Force Base near Lancaster, California, with the Sons of the Pioneers, with whom she had made some recordings back in Chicago in 1940. In December, Dale Evans appeared in her first Western, *War of the Wildcats* (Republic), starring John Wayne. (The film was also known as *In Old Oklahoma*.)

1944

The birth of a phrase that would become almost as well known in American vernacular as baseball and apple pie was taking place, and again, it was a Yates idea. He cast Dale Evans as Roy Rogers' leading lady in *The Cowboy and the Senorita*. "Roy and Dale" would be burned into American hearts and imaginations forever. As a result of this move, Dale became a part of Roy's road shows and was soon with Roy on NBC Radio. Inasmuch as a great majority of their income was produced from personal performances, it appears likely that Dale was on Roy's payroll now when she was not before the cameras making films.

In April, Roy was introduced in a new medium, *Roy Rogers Comics*, Four Color #38, and it was reported that the first million copies of this issue sold out in twenty-four hours.[45]

A cowboy star's customized attire becomes his personal trademark. A magazine writer referred to Roy's attire as a "rainbow rig."[46] His shirts were now elaborately designed with everything that denoted cowboys and the romantic West, from horseshoes to stars, cactus to yellow roses. His hats were also custom designed. Many different Triggers were now being seen in films, personal appearances (even close-ups, contrary to accounts in later years), advertising, books, merchandise, and comic books, but they were accepted as one horse by the public, out of unawareness, loyalty, or blind devotion to the film cowboy.[47] The character horse Trigger, was gaining legendary status.

This year the Rogers moved into a colonial home in Van Nuys, in an exclusive section of the Valley, a quiet place on the outskirts of "Tinsel-Town."[48] He was closer to the studios and wanted a place with neighbors. Arline's parents had moved from their Roswell home at 701 East Second Street to a home nearby, and her mother visited often.

The Roy Rogers World Championship Rodeo was being formed for touring. It made its debut during the summer at the Los Angeles Coliseum.[49] Roy would make $150,000 a year from rodeo appearances.[50] He was touring twice a year, with the trips lasting weeks at a time. Roy rode Trigger on the Paul Revere ride stretching from Boston to Concord, Massachusetts, for a bond drive. He made a nearly three-week appearance at the Madison Square Garden Rodeo in the fall. While in New York, he attended the opening game of the World Series at Yankee Stadium, where he met Babe Ruth, Jack Dempsey, and even former president Herbert Hoover. He also attended a showing of the play *Oklahoma* on Broadway with Art Rush and met Frank Sinatra.

In November, Roy went on the air with a program sponsored by Goodyear Tire and Rubber Co. Rush was completing a large-scale merchandising program for toys and attire. The Rohr Co., which was formed to manage Roy's business ventures, is believed to have been a co-partnership between Roy and Jim Osborne (financial whiz), Philo Harvey (attorney), and Arthur Rush (personal management). Roy's income was on the verge of making another leap, and his popularity was spreading. His film *Song of Nevada* was playing at two elite theaters, Grauman's Chinese Theater and Cathay Circle, houses that did not normally host Western films.

*

Dale Evans appeared in Republic's *Casanova in Burlesque* with Joe E. Brown and *Hitchhike to Happiness*. Dale's husband was arranging her songs and scoring Republic's films, eventually even Roy's. Her son Tom had graduated from high school and would enter the University of Southern

Dale had her sights on roles other than cowgirls. Publicity still from mid–1940s.

California. Due to the strain their careers were placing on their relationship, Dale and R. Dale were not getting along well.

1945

Dale Evans' reputation was enhanced that year when she received the "Queen of the West" title in an Erskine Johnson award as the top-ranking Western movie heroine. Roy took five of the top ten Western films and was among the top ten male singers (in all categories). Dale Evans' thirteenth film,

Song of Arizona, was about to be released, and she complained about always getting fourth billing, which thwarted her desire for more fame and for different kinds of roles. She threatened to leave Republic and was quoted as saying: "A heroine in a Western is always second string. The cowboy and his horse always come first." In Roy's films, the billing was Roy, his costar Trigger, his sidekick, and then his leading lady.

Fans who heard that Dale was upset about getting fourth billing poured letters into magazines, saying that they wanted her to stay in Roy's Westerns. Roy and Dale were made "King and Queen" of the Heldorado Days celebration at Las Vegas, Nevada.

Roy appeared at Col. Jim Eskew's Texas Rodeo at the Arena in Philadelpia, September 23–30. Based upon available information, Roy had either purchased the Eskew Rodeo, entered into a business relationship with Col. Jim Eskew, or had hired Eskew to run his rodeo, which began the previous year, under the management of the Rohr Co. The Roy Rogers Rodeo made its second appearance in Los Angeles and featured two pretty cowgirls, Frances Langford and Virginia Mayo.[51] Many stars turned out, and the crowd swelled to 80,000. Then the rodeo toured a circuit taking in Los Angeles, Houston, St. Louis, Chicago, Indianapolis, Cleveland, Detroit, Philadelphia, Boston, and New York, with many smaller cities included. Roy held special matinee shows for underprivileged children. In October, Roy made his final appearance for a while at the Madison Square Garden Rodeo because he now had his own rodeo. The show grossed over a million dollars by the final performance.[52]

Republic studios announced that Roy would kiss the leading lady in his next film to test the reaction. Boys wanted no part of that "mushy stuff" taking place with their hero. But according to some reports, other fans thought the romance might keep Dale in the pictures. Director Witney returned to Republic upon discharge from the Marines, to create a new direction for Rogers' films.[53]

In the meantime, Roy's draft board sent him a letter stating he was now classified 1-A. This meant he was close to being drafted, but his classification was soon changed to a 3-A because of a change in the deferment age.

*

Dale was now having marital problems. She says in her book *Dale—My Personal Picture Album*, "As I rose in my career, my marriage declined."[54] She described the situation as "a typical Hollywood tragedy." She and R. Dale separated on September 22, and she and Tommy moved to North Hollywood. Frances Octavia Butts filed for divorce from Robert Dale Butts on the grounds of mental cruelty in Los Angeles on October 10, 1945.[55] On November 12, they signed a mutual property settlement agreement drawn up by their attorneys. They split everything down the middle amicably, including the bank accounts, savings bonds, life insurance, house, furniture, and cars, with Robert Dale paying off the mortgage on the house. He got the 1941 Plymouth, and she got the 1941 Chevy. On November 13, the judgment was entered in the court.[56]

As a friend of the family and Roy's leading lady, Dale was spending time with the Rogers family, and photographers captured numerous shots of them all at various events and functions.

1946

It was reported that Roy liked shark fishing in the Pacific and had landed a 243-pound hammerhead, taking first prize in a competition. Roy also liked to relax by riding his motorcycle or bowling. His nonprofessional activities also included participation in the Mason Lodge, where he was a member of the Scottish and York rites and also a Shriner.[57] Roy joined the lodge because he was impressed by its work with children's hospitals.

By this time, there were 700 Roy Rogers fan clubs in the U.S., and it was reported that he was receiving 90,000 letters a month.[58] Fans even yanked hair from Trigger's mane and tail for souvenirs. Roy and Dale were frequently visited on film sets for interviews and photo sessions. Roy was a favorite for Feg Murray's syndicated comic panel, "Seein' Stars," and the Sunday editions were produced in color. It was evident that he had captured imaginations around the world and his popularity wasn't limited to the U.S. because *Ciné Revue*, an oversized French pulp publication, came out featuring Roy on the front in what was one of the largest covers of Roy ever to be published.

Roy in publicity photo from mid–1940s.

Fans were fascinated by Roy's apparel. The numbers were seldom consistent, but it was reported that Roy had fifty cowboy outfits (many duplicated) and thirty pairs of boots with the "thunderbird" design.[59] He went through a lot of Stetsons as well.

That year Roy's "Weekly Roundup" radio show debuted over NBC, sponsored by Miles Laboratories. Roy and Dale went on location to Bill and Alice Licken's 6,000 acre Flying L Ranch in Dougherty, Oklahoma, outside of "Hereford Heaven," where they

were filming *Home in Oklahoma*. After finishing their filming, Roy and Dale went off to
Nevada, where they stayed at the Last Frontier Hotel while appearing in the Heldorado
Rodeo and filming *Heldorado* on Vegas'
Freemont Street. Some filming was also done
at nearby Boulder Dam. Dale suffered a fall
from horseback during the filming and went
over the horse's head onto a pile of rocks.
While they were on location, Roy bought a
600-acre ranch outside Vegas so the gang, including the Sons of the Pioneers, could relax. Expenditures like this were not a problem because Roy's annual take was reported
to be $250,000.[60] Trigger's value was now
placed at $20,000.[61]

On Sunday, October 27, Arline checked
into the hospital. On Monday, October 28,
1946, Roy and Dale were appearing in his
rodeo in Chicago when he was informed that
he had a new son. Roy Rogers, Jr., nicknamed "Dusty," was born at 8:37 A.M. at
Madison Hospital in Los Angeles.[62] He was
delivered by cesarean section. Newspapers
of the day announced that "Dusty" was the
"Prince of Cowboys." Roy hurried home to
see the baby and visit with Arline. Several
days later, he and the girls were eating at the
Wilkins' home when he received a call from
the hospital.[63] Roy and Mrs. Wilkins rushed
to Arline's side. Only six days after child-
birth, Arline died of an embolism on Sunday, November 3, at 9:25 A.M.[64] The couple
had celebrated their tenth anniversary that
June. Arline's death was the first of the
tragedies that would haunt Roy's life and
career. Arline's funeral was held November
6 at Forest Lawn Cemetery in Glendale.[65]

Despite his loss, Roy had to continue to
meet the demands of his professional life.
That fall he performed at WLS Radio's National Barn Dance at the Illinois State Fair in
Springfield. Apparently, Dale didn't make
this show, perhaps because of the horseback
accident. Here Roy was backed on stage by
the Prairie Ramblers (Western singer Louise
Massey's group). At this event, Roy gave
away cowboy suits. Giving toys to the kids
on such occasions was also a common practice.

*

On November 18, Dale's divorce became
final. Tom enlisted in the armed forces. His
enlistment papers showed that Dale Evans,
Hollywood actress, was his mother.[66] Republic, upon hearing from the military, requested that they not leak this information
to the press.

1947

That spring Roy purchased a new retreat at
Lake Hughes, seventy miles north of
Hollywood. By settling into Sky Haven
Ranch, he became the community's first full-
time citizen. Child-care for his children was
an ongoing responsibility. It was reported
that Roy's in-laws wanted him to give up the
children, but he refused.[67] He had a stand-in
named Whitey Christensen, and his mother
Marian looked after Roy's children at Lake
Hughes. Mrs. Virginia Peck was employed
at the Rogers place as a nanny and remained
there for nine years before going to work for
Roy's neighbor Rex Allen.

After filming *Apache Rose*, Roy underwent a permanent, major image change. He
put away the rounded crown hat for a fully
customized, streamlined version (see Chapter 8). His outfits were much more elaborate,
and many emphasized long suede leather
fringe, with a myriad of contrasting colors
and patterns for a more "trademark" appearance. This attire was used for personal
appearances and photo sessions, lending
itself well to the color pictures that were
becoming more frequent. Much of his attire
for the new color films and personal appearances was now being designed by Ben
the Rodeo Tailor of Philadelphia.[68] He had
a new plastic show saddle and tack for personal appearances, a red, white, and blue
one with the thunderbird design and a blue
plastic lariat.[69]

Roy reportedly received over 900,000
fan letters this year. He had five girls employed to answer fan mail, and his record
sales amounted to 25,000 per month by this
point. Gene Autry left Republic's corral for
good, going over to Columbia Pictures, and
Yates didn't want to take any chances. To be
sure that Roy stayed in the number one position, budgets were increased and color pictures utilized.

Dale was still not happy with her roles
and allowed her contract to lapse after filming *Bells of San Angelo*. She went back to
radio and appeared on the "Jimmy Durante

Show" and the "Garry Moore Show." Republic offered a different type of role if she would agree to return to the studio. As a result, she appeared in *The Trespasser* with Bill Bakewell.

It was reported that Roy and Dale had become close friends and shared a lot of conversation and problems. Roy had been married twice, had been widowed, and was now a single parent to three children, one an infant. Dale had had several past marriages, as well as ups and downs in her career, so she and Roy enjoyed spending much time together and soon had a strong relationship.

Gene Autry initiated the practice of portraying himself on screen. Going a step further, Roy was now patterning his life as closely as possible in every aspect to that of his film character. The leading lady in his films would become his leading lady at home. When he finished singing about life on the Double R Bar Ranch of movie sets, he would go home to life on his own Double R Bar Ranch. It took away almost all traces of fantasy that would have been attached to his films and radio shows and may have added to their appeal for all ages. Many of the nation's adults didn't go along to his films simply to chaperone the kids, and they didn't read his comics merely because their children couldn't read yet. Adults enjoyed Roy Rogers too. He represented wholesomeness and quality in everyday American life.

Louella Parsons, a Hollywood gossip columnist, wrote an article that may have been designed to quell any talk of Roy and Dale's relationship blossoming a little too soon.[70] Parsons had insinuated on her radio show that there was a romantic involvement between Roy and Dale. In the article, she made no apology for her earlier comments, as apparently she meant no harm, but she allowed Roy to state his position in his own words. He said that he was not getting married anytime soon to anyone, but the relationship between Roy and Dale continued to be explored in magazines. One story stated that she had been an understanding companion, confidante, and friend to Roy and his kids. It was fairly obvious to all observers just where the relationship was headed. Dale wrote a song called "Don't Ever Fall in Love with a Cowboy," but she appeared to be doing just that.

Roy and Dale enjoyed fishing together, and they went to Big Bear Lake, a California resort.[71] Dale later stated in her book *Dale — My Personal Picture Album* (1971) that she and Roy were together most of their waking hours, and their attraction for one another naturally grew.

In September, Cheryl, the first Rogers child of school age, began first grade at Lake Hughes School.[72] The school was a large one-room house up "the school road" (a dirt road) from the Trading Post, which consisted of the post office and a filling station.[73] There were thirty-nine children enrolled, and 1947 was the first year that two teachers were employed.

Cheryl had received movie offers because of her "doll-like beauty similar to Shirley Temple," but Roy preferred that she debut in his films.

Dale appeared in the film *Slippy McGee* with Don Barry. Although their current film work kept Roy and her separated at the studio and usually on the road, they crossed paths in Atlantic City, New Jersey. She was there on tour, singing with the Sons of the Pioneers, and Roy drove down from New York, where he was debuting his Roy Rogers Thrill Circus at the Polo Grounds of the Palisadium and taking care of business with Art Rush.

Roy and Dale had dinner dates, and he talked to her about returning to his films and shows, but to no avail. The fans of "Roy and Dale" were screaming for the two to go back together in pictures. The executvies at Republic had failed to realize what these fans wanted. They kept getting letters demanding that Dale get back in the saddle.

Everything was becoming "Roy and Dale," and everywhere they went, the cameras were even far behind. Roy and Dale were even writing songs together.

Louella Parsons, who admitted that she liked Roy, reported on October 19 that Roy and Dale would be wed in January 1948. And she dropped a bombshell that Dale would eventually appreciate. Highlighting Dale's career, Louella told fans that Dale had a twenty-year-old son.

When Roy and Dale were at the Chicago Stadium for a rodeo performance, matters moved forward. They were sitting astride Trigger and Pal in the chutes, waiting to do their act, when the "King" proposed to the woman who was destined soon to become the "Queen," in more ways than one. In November, Roy and Dale returned to California and announced their engagement to the world. On Tuesday, December 30, Roy or a representative phoned the county clerk's office in Murray County, Oklahoma, and provided the information for the application for a marriage license.[74]

The big day finally arrived on Wednesday, December 31. In Oklahoma, at the Flying L Ranch belonging to their friends Bill and Alice Lickens, Roy and Dale were married in a private ceremony to which friends and family were invited, almost fifty guests in all. Bill Lickens gave Dale away, and Art Rush was the best man. Oklahoma governor Roy Turner attended, as did Dale's son Tom (who was enrolled at the University of Southern California), his fiancée Barbara, and her sister. Dale's mother, father, and aunts drove up from Texas, despite miserable blizzardlike weather conditions. The Flying L Quartet entertained. The Reverend W. H. "Bill" Alexander, an Oklahoma City minister of the First Christian Church, performed the ceremony. According to Roy, the minister was two hours late because he rode a horse to the ranch for the sake of authenticity.[75]

1948

Bad weather had Roy and Dale snowbound and forced them to spend two weeks of their honeymoon on the Oklahoma ranch. When they were finally able to travel, they drove through Texas, where they stopped to visit Dale's parents.

Now that they were married, Dale had a change of heart and found Herbert Yates to tell him she was ready to get back in the saddle. The years were now full for the couple, with winters and springs spent filming and doing radio shows. The newlyweds often drove up to 150 miles to reach a filming location. Summers included vacation time and family outings. Recordings and photography were a constant part of their lives, along with personal appearance tours, weeklong engagements, and rodeos that took place in the fall. Interviews were seemingly endless, and merchandising was a continuing enterprise.

Roy and Dale's first home, on Vine Street in Hollywood Hills, was formerly owned by actor Noah Beery. Overlooking Hollywood, it sat on two acres of land and had six bedrooms and six baths. The Lake Hughes home served as an ideal location for their wedding party, where they hosted 600 guests, including Roy's sisters and parents, who all lived in California at this time.

In a letter to her dad, Dale described Roy as "the most giving person I'd ever met." She said he was a devoted family man, a man who was forever talking about his wife and two daughters, and that his devotion to them was not for publicity. She said he was "totally un-affected, very down-to-earth, and not the least bit phony."

At some point soon after their marriage, Dale made a commitment to the Christian faith, and shortly thereafter Roy followed. Articles stated that Roy's commitment took place after a stormy evening and cocktail party at their home, an event celebrating the completion of another film for Roy. The evening of the following day, Sunday, found Roy in church. The pastor at the time was Jack McArthur. On Palm Sunday, Roy and his daughter Cheryl were baptized. Their faith and religious commitments would see Roy and Dale through tough times in the future.

One difficulty Dale faced at first was getting along with her stepchildren. With a new mother in the home, there was some natural resentment from the girls that had to be overcome. Dale gave up smoking after one of the girls remarked that their real mother hadn't smoked. Cheryl was attending Cheramaya Public School, and Linda was beginning kindergarten. It was reported that the kids were calling their new stepmother by her given name.[76]

Dale passed up an opportunity to appear in the London stage production of *Annie Get Your Gun* in order to spend more time with the children during this crucial period. Around March, a possible contract dispute with Republic was mentioned in a magazine.[77] Dale remained in a strong position because she was the only female Western star to be included in the Western division of *Motion Picture*'s poll of "Top Money-Making Stars"; she was in ninth place.

Roy and Dale married in heavily publicized Oklahoma wedding.

Dale Evans' comics were born this year. They began with photo covers and then fluctuated between those and line art covers. The stories and artwork were fairly unbelievable and portrayed her as a self-sufficient Hollywood cowgirl heroine, without a cowboy hero. The comic was not really suited for her, as she was presented to readers as a cowgirl Supergirl. It did, however, give her other media vehicles besides films. The photo covers show her, among other settings, in her rodeo appearances with Roy, although, because of contractual reasons, he was not shown. In fact, in the photos, his initials were removed from the tapaderos on her stirrups. She and her horse Pal were riding in their pulp adventure pages for DC Comics.

Dale's son Tom married Barbara Miller at the Fountain Avenue Baptist Church in Hollywood. Tom was majoring in music, while Barbara attended UCLA, where she was specializing in music and physical education. They both had teaching careers in mind. Cheryl and Linda were junior bridesmaids; two hundred people attended the reception.

Roy Rogers merchandise was becoming a veritable bonanza, producing millions with "tie-in" items. The market for such items was increased by the magazine covers and articles that appeared frequently, featuring all aspects of the Roy Rogers family. Roy and Dale were being called Hollywood's most colorful couple. Roy's interest in animals was one of the topics mentioned in the press. He was raising palomino ponies and had twenty-eight brood mares.[78] He also had eleven hound dogs, a German shepherd named "Bullet," who was destined to be a star, and a white German shepherd, Spur, who appeared with Roy on numerous comic book covers.

Roy still toured with his rodeo each fall, and his elaborate show attire was changing again, with new styles designed by "Nudie" Cohen, a custom tailor in California who specialized in glitzy stage costumes. Trigger was the image of fashion for horses in film, with diamond-shaped silver ornaments on his tack and "RR" initials on the tapaderos. Eighty million tickets had been sold in the past year for Roy's films, and two thousand theaters in England featured his pictures as well. In the fall, Roy's rodeo played Crosley Field, Cincinnati, and Cleveland Children's Hospital, where Trigger pushed a child in a wheelchair.

Another way that Roy contributed to the welfare of young people was through his work with 4-H clubs; he attended meetings and conventions whenever possible. Roy was also working as an advocate for safety among school children in cooperation with the National Safety Council. He helped organize an annual competition that would eventually have thousands of schools participating. The first year saw an enrollment of 1500 schools. Roy and Dale presented the awards in person for many years. One of the awards was a golden statuette of Trigger mounted on a walnut base.

"The Roy Rogers Show," transcribed, was on the radio Sundays at 6 P.M. on the Mutual Network, with Quaker Oats (Mother's Oats) as its sponsor (see Chapter 4). Roy and Dale were joined by Foy Willing and the Riders of the Purple Sage. Numerous Roy Rogers premiums were offered, and contests were run by Quaker. Dale wrote a song entitled "Happy Trails" that would eventually become the closing theme for their first radio show and then their television series. She was signing her "Dale Evans Roundup" columns in the *Dale Evans Comics* with "Happy Trails."

1949

That April, Roy and Trigger put their prints in the sidewalk at Graumann's Chinese Theater in Hollywood, while Dale, the Riders of the Purple Sage, and Hoot Gibson watched.

Roy and Dale vacationed that summer in New York, one of their favorite places. On this occasion, the couple saw the Broadway play *South Pacific*. That fall they drove to Connecticut for a look at New England's brilliant array of autumn colors.

The fall also took Roy, Dale, and Gabby Hayes to the Annual Fat Stock Show (rodeo) in Houston, Texas, where they were guests at oilman Glenn McCarthy's Shamrock Hotel.[79] The show played to over a half million people in its two-week run. Trick shooting and trick riding acts were featured, and Foy Willing and the Riders of the Purple Sage also appeared. Dale was honored with "Dale Evans Day" in Houston, and she received a proclamation naming her "Texas' Favorite Daughter." In November, Dale learned she was pregnant, but she managed to appear in six more of Roy's films before bowing out again.

Roy's dogs remained a strong interest. He now had twenty-four dogs, including a hound "Slim," who was winning field trials. That fall Roy and Dale attended the annual Coon Dog Hunting Trials at Corona, California, a two-day event in which they entered six of their coon dogs.

Roy and Dale celebrated their second

anniversary in San Francisco. They heard a little Chinese girl named Robin sing, and Dale made note of this name for a child they would soon be having. Dale was back working with Roy in his films because fans had persisted in plying the studio to have her reclaim her place in the saddle beside the "King of the Cowboys." The first film was *Susanna Pass.*

On December 31, Roy was featured in a newspaper comic strip syndicated by King Features Syndicate and drawn by artists John Ushler and Peter Alvarado. Dale eventually appeared in these adventures, although the two were usually kept apart in the comic book stories. Another event that occurred late that year was the organization of the Roy Rogers Riders Club, a special fan club. It was reported that 1,700,000 youngsters joined within ninety days of its formation.

1950

Every Saturday, 5,000 U.S. theaters were filling for four showings with fans eager to see Roy clean up the West. Forty daily newspapers were also carrying the Roy Rogers comic strip at this time. Roy was enjoying hit records with RCA Victor. When *Life* magazine conducted a poll among children, asking, "What person would you most like to resemble?" Roy, the only cowboy listed, made the list among sports heroes, generals, and presidents.[80]

Newspaper advertisements carried Roy's photo in the Quaker Oats contests. Five-foot-tall likeness displays were seen in grocery stores. Premiums continued to expand as Roy proved to be one of the best cereal salesmen ever. The department stores across the country were full of Roy Rogers toys and books. Only the manufacturers of quality toys were used to make Roy Rogers products, however. Many toys were made by the Marx Co. The Sears Roebuck catalogs were full of Roy Rogers items. Quaker Cereals was running newspaper ads for a contest to name Trigger's son.[81] The first prize was a week spent with Roy. According to figures reported in *Look* magazine, there were now three thousand Roy Rogers Riders Clubs and over three thousand stores with "Roy Rogers Corrals," where the RR brand products were sold.

Dale contracted German measles and

was forced to spend more time at home to safeguard her pregnancy. The baby was due in late summer. Dale was in danger of having a miscarriage, and it was learned that she had Rh-negative blood and Roy had Rh-positive. Special preventive care was taken as a result. On Saturday, August 26, at Presbyterian Hospital, Olmsted Memorial, Robin Elizabeth Rogers was born. She was Roy and Dale's first child together and the fourth child for the Rogers household. To the heartbreak of her parents, it was learned that Robin had heart problems and was afflicted by Down's Syndrome.

Dale's sorrow over her baby's problems may have been a factor in her participation in the Billy Graham Crusades in Houston, New York, San Diego, and Washington that year.

On November 1, Roy and Dale left for a personal appearance tour that took in twenty-eight cities. Their schedule was so hectic that between Toledo, Ohio, and Huntington, West Virginia, there was not even time to stop in Roy's hometown of Portsmouth, Ohio. What time Roy and Dale had off from touring, filming, etc., they spent with the children, concentrating on family activities such as picnics, horseback rides, barbecues, hikes, and swimming.

Roy celebrated his twelfth year at Republic, and the studio surprised him with a cake with twelve candles. There was excitement on location of *Twilight in the Sierras*, Roy's seventy-third feature film for Republic, when Roy, his six guns loaded with blanks, cornered a mountain lion, when the animal ventured out and acted up.

The Roy Rogers Riders Club of Klamath Falls, Oregon, baked the world's largest cake to celebrate Roy's birthday. Covering a Ping-Pong table, it measured three feet high and weighed a full ton. Three thousand kids helped eat it.

That year Roy did an unusual tour of 26 one-night stands in small towns; it was supposedly the first tour to omit the larger cities. He was, of course, accompanied by Trigger, who wore specially made rubber shoes when performing on stages. Twenty of the towns he visited proclaimed a "Roy Rogers Day." Roy planned to repeat this type of tour yearly. There was one show that he made and Trigger did not. Trigger's caravan, guided by trainer Glenn Randall, became stranded in

"America's Favorite Western Couple" in publicity photo, ca. 1949–1950.

an Iowa snowstorm and had to be dug out by a volunteer crew of fans.

1951

Robin was eight months old in April when the family moved to Encino in the San Fernando Valley, where they bought a sprawl-ing place with a pool. The address was 5330 Amestoy Avenue. It was a ten-room, Spanish stucco, ranch-style house on five acres (or nine, depending on the source). A tree in the middle of their new patio was a city monument because of its age. Roy had a large vegetable garden, a fruit orchard, and a large variety of animals as usual. Cheryl had her own pony, who was named "Tony." Roy named the place the "Double R Bar Ranch."

Roy and his father built a two-room house onto the main structure to accommodate Robin and her full-time nurse, "Cau-Cau" (Claudia). Robin required a nurse because she was a very fragile baby. That June, *Movie Stars Parade* had a one-page photo of Roy and Dale feeding Robin, who was nicknamed "Stormy," according to the title and caption. "Stormy Takes a Bow" mentions that Dale was resuming her film career after being off work while she was pregnant. To complicate matters, Robin developed polio in August.

The schedule for the Rogers family was a busy one. On an average work day, Roy and Dale got up at 4:30 A.M. and returned home at about 8:30 P.M. Roy's parents had moved from their chicken ranch to a smaller place in Van Nuys, and Roy's father took the children to school. Depending on their ages and homework, bedtime ranged from 7:30 P.M. to 8:30 P.M. This was the girls' first year at camp. Cheryl went to a religious conference camp at Forest Home, while Linda spent a week at the PTA's Camp Radford.

Robin was baptized at St. Nicholas Episcopal Church. Roy, Dale, Cheryl, and Linda were confirmed there and joined this church.

After he filmed Republic's *South of Caliente*, Roy's second seven-year contract with the studio ended. His career was at a strong point, since he had just tied for third place with actor Stewart Granger in the poll for Most Popular Male Star conducted by *Country Gentleman* magazine. He began filming *Son of a Paleface* with Bob Hope for Paramount. Because of the clause in the contract with Republic that resulted from an incident that occurred about 1940, Roy had the merchandise right to his likeness, voice, and name. Republic owned the rights to the films, however. Roy wanted to produce a television series, but Republic didn't want this competition because it wanted to edit his films to fifty-four minutes and package them for television. This dispute created a legal problem that could only be solved in court.[82] Roy's radio show would cancel if he couldn't carry the sponsor, General Foods, to television.[83] Unable to make any money from Republic's marketing of his films to television, Roy refused to renew his contract with the studio. On July 10, Roy and General Foods signed a contract for sponsorship of his television show.

On October 18, the Roy Rogers vs. Republic Productions trial began.[84] It was held on the second floor of the Los Angeles Federal Building. Roy usually had to appear in full Western costume because he had to run back and forth between the *Son of Paleface* set and the courthouse. The trial lasted four and a half weeks, with Roy emerging victorious, having won the first round. He began working on his television series, but Republic appealed the decision. Television was here to stay and scaring the pants off the studios.

In May the first issue of *Roy Rogers' Trigger Comics* appeared on the market. Pal and Trigger looked too much alike for black and white television shows, so Roy bought Buttermilk, a buckskin gelding, for Dale.[85]

In the fall of 1951, probably during an appearance at the Houston rodeo, a Texas oil and cattle man, John B. Ferguson of Wharton, offered to buy Trigger for $200,000. The oilman wanted the famous horse for his son, as well as for breeding purposes.[86] He was immediately turned down, but rumor held for a time that the cowboy was indeed about to sell the "Smartest Horse in the Movies." Kids all over the country reacted by sending Roy money, in case he needed to raise money by selling Trigger. Roy responded by printing tons of "Certificates of Honorary Shareholder" of Trigger and mailing them on request.

Roy was working frantically to get as many television episodes produced as was possible while Republic was under a temporary injunction not to show his films on television. The premiere episode of "The Roy Rogers Show" on NBC, Sunday, December 30, at 5:30 P.M., was "Jail Break" (see Chapter 11). The theme song of the television show was "Happy Trails." Roy and Dale were shown singing it together at the end of the 30-minute show as the credits rolled.

1952

On August 12, in Los Angeles, actress Mabel Smeyne (aka Mabel Smaney) filed a law suit against Roy Rogers Enterprises, Roy Rogers, and thirteen others, seeking $186,000, plus court costs and general relief. She alleged that Roy and others recklessly failed to control Trigger, allowing him to kick her. She claimed permanent internal and external injuries to the head, chest, and breast. Trigger had kicked her on August 13, 1951, during the filming of *Son of Paleface*,[87] according to the petition. Roy's attorneys demanded a jury trial, and it was set for October 21, 1953.

A couple of days before Robin's second birthday, she developed mumps, as did the rest of the children. Tragedy plagued the Rogers family again. After also acquiring encephalitis, Robin Elizabeth died of respiratory failure on August 24, just two days before her birthday.[88] She was buried at Forest Lawn Mausoleum on her second birthday. Dale found the loss of Robin so stressful that her hair turned completely white by that fall. She soon began to write a book about Robin titled *Angel Unaware*.

That August the film *Son of Paleface*, Roy's first film since leaving Republic's corral, starred him and Trigger, along with Bob Hope and Jane Russell, in a Paramount comedy filmed in color. Roy and Trigger were guests of Jane Russell and Bob Hope at a luncheon at the studio commissary.

In September, Roy and Dale boarded a train to New York City, via Dallas. They preferred to travel by train whenever possible, although Trigger traveled in a specially built tractor-trailer-van costing $25,000. While in Texas, they visited Dale's folks and drove to Hope Cottage in Dallas to begin the process of adopting another little girl. During this trip, Dale also filmed *Symphony of Life*, a short religious color film. The Santa Fe Chief took them from Dallas to Chicago. They performed at the rodeo there, and there was a big parade down State Street. Roy and Dale performed at the Harvest Moon Festival at Chicago Stadium. While they were staying in Chicago's Blackstone Hotel, a logo was devised for the Roy Rogers merchandise, and the Roy Rogers "Plus Brand" was born. It appears that this brand was never registered as a trademark, however.

Roy and Dale continued by train to New York, where they appeared at the Madison Square Garden Rodeo after an absence of six years. They did forty-three performances in less than thirty days. The attendance of 700,000 broke all-time records for Madison Square Garden. Against the advice and wishes of officials, Roy and Dale insisted on singing a religious song. They were told it would destroy their careers. The lights were dimmed as they sang "Peace in the Valley" to the distinct approval and pleasure of the audience.

Roy continued to have a widespread appeal to young people. One radio-television columnist stated: "As far as the youngsters are concerned, it's better that they thrill to a 100 percent perfect cowboy than to follow the adventures of some slimy gangster." Roy had recently been voted the favorite star of Britain's boys under fifteen, and 27 percent of these boys said they would rather be Roy than anyone else. He came in number two, second to James Mason, on the girls' poll. These findings were the result of an official government inquiry in England.[89]

After leaving New York, Roy and Dale did several one-night stands as they worked their way home. In Ohio they performed at Cincinnati Gardens. While visiting Ohio, they learned of an orphan boy with a history of health problems, mostly from abuse. Roy and Dale decided that this child, who was in an orphanage across the river in Covington, Kentucky, would be a good brother for Dusty. When they were making the decision to adopt Sandy, Roy told Dale: "Mama, anybody can adopt a strong healthy kid who has everything going for him, but what happens to a little guy like this? Let's take him."[90]

After leaving this area, Roy and Dale made a quick swing through Dallas to Hope Cottage and were home in time for Dusty's birthday on October 28. And what a birthday present, as Dusty had a brother Sandy (Harry John David Hardy), but there was a bonus. Roy and Dale also brought home another child they were in the process of adopting, a little Choctaw Indian girl, Mary Little Doe, whom the family nicknamed "Dodie."

Sandy was five years old, only a few months younger than Dusty. Roy took the two boys on a hunting and fishing trip to Marysville, California. Sandy was still suffering nightmares from abuse, and there were physical problems as well. He had spent a lot of his infancy in a back brace and was almost two before he could walk. He suffered rickets and still had coordination problems.

Roy, an expert marksman, gun safety advocate, and hunting and trap-shooting enthusiast, taught Dusty how to shoot and care for a gun. Dale owned a new .38 revolver that Roy had given her, and target practice was a favored activity at the Rogers shooting range behind the house.

Boating and fishing were also activities Roy and Dale liked to share with the children. They took Cheryl on fishing trips to Catalina Island on a boat belonging to a friend, Spade Cooley, a Western bandleader. Part of the family's recreational time was spent on their fishing boat moored at Paradise Cove, near Malibu. Roy and Dale owned a thirty-five-foot house trailer that they used at the beach for the girls' sleeping quarters during summer outings. Roy, Dusty, and Sandy camped under the stars in sleeping bags. Roy also took along his sixteen-foot speedboat, the *Yellow Jacket*.

Roy's radio show was moved to a Thursday time slot, and Pat Brady joined the radio cast. Among other items, Roy Rogers Pop-Out Trading Cards were offered as premiums from General Foods.

That year Roy received the award for the Best Western Show on television. His popularity remained strong. There were now 2,000 Roy Rogers–Dale Evans fan clubs in operation in the U.S., and Roy employed twenty-three people to handle fan mail. Roy was reportedly receiving a million fan letters per year. The fan club in London contained 50,000 members and was the largest fan club for any individual in the world. The Roy Rogers Riders Clubs were sponsoring a roping contest. Bill Alexander (the minister who married Roy and Dale) and Dale wrote "Cowboy's Prayer," which was used to open meetings of Roy Rogers Riders Clubs, numbering 5 million members.

Trigger's popularity also remained high. He was credited with knowing fifty-two tricks, and his show-stealing antics made a lot of press. Trigger was sometimes called the "Barrymore of horses." The original Trigger,

born in 1932, was now twenty years old. He was reported to weigh 1100 pounds and to stand "Terry Moore high" (Moore was a very popular movie actress at the time). There were reportedly Trigger fan clubs, and Trigger received thousands of fan letters from all over the world. The letters were answered on paper autographed with a hoof print.

In addition to his horse, Roy's attire and accessories continued to play an important part in his image. One of the stories that continued to circulate year after year was that Roy didn't own any clothes that were not Western, and he was quoted as saying that he wouldn't even know how to walk in a regular pair of shoes.[91] Roy's saddle and accessories were made of hand-tooled leather inlaid with silver, gold, and rubies and were insured for $50,000. The artist who did the Western sketches for Roy's saddle was the famed Tillman Goodan, who was also instrumental in artwork seen in the *Western Roundup* series of comic books that featured Roy.

1953

That winter a judge made the adoption of Dodie official, and in the spring Sandy's adoption became legal. Sandy was taken to the Children's Hospital in L.A. for evaluation, where it was discovered that he had a learning disability. That summer the children traveled with Roy and Dale during their school vacation and became part of the show. Roy purchased an old PT boat and turned it into a recreational fishing boat named "The Flamba." He kept it at Wilmington Harbor, and the family spent as many weekends as possible at the beach.

The Rogers household staff had grown to compensate for the five children. The ranch was beginning to look like the United Nations. Between the family and staff, there were American whites, American blacks, an Native American, a Swede, and a Filipino; other nations would eventually be represented. The majority of the staff lived at the ranch, with females outnumbering males ten to four. With the purchase of 130 acres in Chatsworth, the ranch was large enough to hold all the people and even to be used for filming. The new ranch featured a low-level mansion and was also named the "Double R Bar."

Family photo just prior to Marion's arrival, ca. 1953.

The press continued to be fascinated by the Rogers family, and a couple of the children debuted in television episodes that year. Ever the model parents, a family photo reveals the book *Mothers of America* in the household. Dusty and Sandy were dressed in matching attire, except for their ties, and the girls' outfits sported Dale's initials. Many of their outfits were as elaborate as those of their parents. The Little Golden Records on the market were sold in colorful sleeves illustrated with Roy, Dale, Pat, Trigger, and Bullet. Roy and Dale received the Golden Apple awards from the Hollywood Women's Press Club for being "the most cooperative stars" of the year.

Ralph Edwards' "This Is Your Life" television show featured Roy and his family, the Sons of the Pioneers, Bill Alexander, and Roy's sisters, Mary Johnson, Cleda (Mrs. Al) Willoughby, and Kathleen (Mrs. Ted) Cox. The show also mentioned Roy's menagerie, which now included 10 cows, 25 sheep, numerous ducks, chickens, geese, a fox, a raccoon, and a bobcat, not to mention his ever-growing canine population. Ralph Edwards stated that he had received more requests for the life of Roy Rogers than for that of any other person. As a momento of the occasion, the program's sponsor, Prell shampoo, had Ray and Dale's picture painted by David Miller, noted Southwest artist.

All of this publicity helped to sell a great deal of merchandise. The American Thermos Bottle Co. produced a Roy Rogers–Dale Evans thermos and lunch box. There would be several different sets of these made over the years.

Religion remained an important part of Roy and Dale's life. They belonged to the Hollywood Christian Group, which sponsored retreats at Forest Home Christian Conference Center in the mountains near San Bernardino. Dale accepted the position of vice-president of the group. While on a trip to New York and Detroit, Art Rush spoke with evangelist Billy Graham about Roy and Dale becoming part of his crusade in London. Later that year Billy Graham visited with them at their home to plan a United Kingdom tour with his crusade that would follow the completion of their first overseas performance.

Roy stated in interviews that after his court battle with Republic, all the studios were afraid of him and blacklisted him because he had stood up for his rights. Republic's appeal was still pending, but appeal time was on Roy's side. His television series was entering its third season and had won awards. Even if Republic won the appeal, the damage to Roy would be minimal.

In July, Dell Publishing produced a new comic series with a high-gloss cover that featured "The Queen of the West." Dale Evans Enterprises was formed and filed copyrights for her likeness and name on comics and other items.

On October 20, Roy's attorneys filed an affidavit for continuance of the Smeyne personal injury trial because of his busy schedule, and it was granted. The trial was eventually reset for January 27, 1954.

That year Roy had a chance meeting with his first wife, Lucile, and her mother. During their brief conversation, she reported that she was happily married.

1954

After the court initially postponed the Smeyne trial until January 28, both parties' lawyers agreed to yet another trial date of October 25, 1954.

"Rearing on Trigger" had long been Roy's trademark pose, used in every medium, but this month it was issued in the largest format ever. The Sunday edition, February 7, 1954, of the *Philadelphia Inquirer* in its Colorama section boasted a classic color photo of Roy and Trigger on a 12¾" by 16¼" cover page.

During this winter, Roy and Dale began their overseas tour via Idlewild Airport in New York and toured Glasgow, Edinburgh, Birmingham, Liverpool, Belfast, and Dublin. Then they went on to London to work with Billy Graham for the last eight days of his crusade. Overly enthusiastic fans pulled the fringe from Roy and Dale's clothing, and their car was nearly toppled. By the time they reached Liverpool, both were sick with pneumonia due to Great Britain's cold, wet winters. In Liverpool, they were both in bed with pneumonia, but had to perform or face a law suit. While entertaining at Dunforth Orphanage in Edinburgh, they met thirteen-year-old Marion Fleming, destined to become their foster child. At the end of the stars' performance, the children entertained, and Marion sang "Won't You Buy My Pretty

Flowers?" (Marion had a brother and two sisters at the orphanage.) English law prohibited adoptions by those not living in England, but Roy and Dale were granted the right to be Marion's foster parents. After a visit to the Chatsworth ranch and many extensions of the visit, Marion managed with the help of a Chief Constable Merriles to become a permanent member of the Rogers household. Marion was nicknamed "Mimi," making her an official member of the nicknamed Rogers clan.[92]

The Rogers household staff underwent some changes during this period. After nearly nine years at the Rogers home, Virginia Peck left to care for the children of neighbor Rex Allen, another Western film star. She was replaced by Pearl White and then Ruth Minor.

Dales's book *Angel Unaware* was now number three on the list of popular nonfiction. Royalties from the sales went to the National Association for Retarded Children.

Roy still found time for hunting, fishing, and especially trapshooting, which he did at the Aqua Sierra Gun Club. He bought the "finest gun" he ever had owned from friend Clark Gable.[93]

Roy and Dale were back at Madison Square Garden for the 29th Annual World's Championship Rodeo, September 30–October 11, with Pat Brady, Nellybelle, Trigger, and the Sons of the Pioneers. Roy had been voted into the Garden's Hall of Fame for setting an all-time, one-day, box-office record.

On October 26, after another day's postponement by the court, the Smeyne trial began in Los Angeles Superior Court.[94] On October 27, Louis ("Slim") Gaut, Paul Holman, and John Kenny testified for the plaintiff. Roy spoke for himself and Trigger. On October 28, Leo Adelstein and Fred Summers testified for Smeyne, while Edwin McNeil and H. J. Strathearn took the stand for Roy and Trigger. Then the jury and other participants went to Paramount studios to watch *Son of Paleface*. On October 29, the jury was out only thirty-nine minutes and rendered a verdict in favor of Roy and Trigger. Whether the horse was actually "Little Trigger" or one of the other doubles was irrelevant. Trigger was the horse at issue. Smeyne had to prove the accident happened and that Roy was negligent, but she was unable to do so (see Chapter 10 and Appen-

dix). Roy and his Triggers surely won the hearts of the twelve members of the jury, as they had done for the previous fourteen years.[95] In the end, Mabel Smeyne was ordered to pay Roy $148.25 in court costs. She did not give up, however. On November 12, her attorneys filed a motion for a new trial on five counts, one being that a member of the jury mentioned to Roy after the filming that Trigger was a beautiful horse. In a hearing on December 10, the motion was denied. Smeyne's attorneys were finished, but she was not. On December 27, she filed papers to act as her own attorney.

Roy made an appearance on "Cavalcade of America," ABC-TV, in what was the beginning of years many such appearances that would last into the 1990s. Roy, Dale, Cheryl, Linda, and Dodie went to Hawaii on United Airlines and did a stage show in Honolulu. On New Year's Eve, Roy and Dale celebrated their seventh wedding anniversary.

1955

On January 6, Mabel Smeyne appealed the lower court judge's denial for a new trial to the state appellate court.

A tabloid magazine published an article that Manuel Shaw wrote about Roy and Dale in which he accused them of all sorts of atrocities for the sake of publicity and even claimed that they had adopted their children for that reason. Naturally, they were both very upset by this attack.[96]

Roy received a parchment scroll as an award for distinguished achievement from Equestrian Trails, Inc., for making the horse popular with millions of American youngsters. At this point, Roy's name was second only to Walt Disney's in the number of character-related items produced. Frontiers, Inc., was formed to control these interests. It is believed that this was the first incorporating and that Roy Rogers Enterprises and possibly Roy Rogers' Frontiers (which may have been formed later) were smaller companies for dividing up control of copyrights, etc. Trigger shared the spotlight in Roy's comics as issue 92, *Roy Rogers and Trigger*, arrived on the stands. The radio shows ended this year, with Dodge as the final sponsor. General Foods continued sponsoring the television series with Post

Cereals and Jell-O. By the end of his association with Post, Roy's picture or likeness would have appeared on 2½ billion boxes of cereal and in a multitude of magazine ads. On May 7, 1955, *Billboard* magazine filled entire pages (two on Roy, two on Gene) to let the television stations of the country know that there were now Roy Rogers and Gene Autry films available for purchase. The films had been edited to 53 minutes and 20 seconds and released to MCA TV Film Syndication for sale to the stations. Sixty-seven of Roy's films were in the package.

"The Bible Tells Me So," written by Dale, was published by Famous Music Corp., New York, that year, and the sheet music was released by Paramount–Roy Rogers Music Co.

On May 27, Roy's attorneys filed for dismissal of Mabel Smeyne's appeal because she had not followed the rules an attorney must follow for appealing a case. The motion was granted by the lower court, and on June 15, the appellate court agreed and dismissed the appeal.

That summer someone tried to dig up some dirt to hurt Roy's public image. Information was apparently given the media regarding Roy's first wife, Lucile. Roy probably contacted *Modern Screen* because in November the magazine carried the story "The Truth About My First Wife" by Roy, an article that was interesting more for what it didn't say than what it said.[97]

1956

Early that fall, In Ai Lee arrived from Korea. She was renamed Deborah Lee and known affectionately as Debbie. Dr. Bob Pierce with World Vision assisted in finding this member of the family. Debbie was age three, about five months younger than Dodie.

Roy and Dale participated in Easter sunrise services at Walter Reed Hospital in Washington, D.C. They visited with President and Mrs. Eisenhower and attended the National Presbyterian Church. Later they received a letter from the Eisenhowers stating how much they had enjoyed their visit.

Attendance records were broken at the Ohio State Fair when Roy, Dale, the children, and Pat Brady performed. They

stopped on the way to the fair to visit Duck Run and Roy's old homeplace. Roy and Dale were making special guest appearances on television variety shows, singing, taking part in comedy skits, doing interviews, etc. They also played the Iowa State Fair, and they appeared at the Houston Fat Stock Show and Rodeo February 22–March 4.

The "Roy Rogers Pledge to Parents" was used like a personal Good Housekeeping Seal to guarantee the quality of the Rogers line of merchandise. The Roy/Dale lunch box sets had sold more than 3½ million units.

In the early years, Roy insisted on doing most of his own stunt work. Even later, after the studio heads were adamant about their star being too valuable to jeopardize with stunt work, he still performed most of his mounts, many fight scenes, and a number of the tricks with Trigger. Roy had been doubled in stunts by his fishing buddy Spade Cooley and famed stunt men Yakima Cunutt, David Sharpe, and particularly Joe Yrigoyen.

Roy went on his first African safari this year, and there would be several future ones.

1957

The "Roy Rogers Show" was popular on NBC Sunday evenings; it was sponsored by Post Cereals, Maxwell House Coffee, and Baker's Instant Chocolate Mix. One hundred eighty-six newspapers now carried the syndicated comic strip. Scioto County's favorite son was shown holding a 4-H alumni recognition award presented to him in Portsmouth. Each comic book issue was selling at the rate of 2 million copies. On January 6, Roy and Dale appeared on the "Ed Sullivan Show," sharing the spotlight with emerging rock and roll superstar Elvis Presley. Conservative America saw Elvis only from the waist up, but they got to see all of Roy and Dale, head to toe.

The original Trigger had earned his retirement, having served faithfully in films, photos, personal appearances, and television series. He was twenty-five years old.

1958

Roy bought NBC's interest in the television episodes of the "Roy Rogers Show" and put them back on television in the form of reruns on various channels across the country on Saturday mornings. He sold the shows to the

Nestle Co. for six years for 1.5 million, and they went into syndication through 1960.[98]

Dusty and Sandy were by now attending a military school and returning home on weekends. Cheryl was attending Kemper Hall, a girl's school in Kenosha, Wisconsin, where she was enrolled for one year.[99] While Roy, Dale, and Dodie were visiting her, Roy was presented with a new war bonnet by Ed LaPlante, a Chippewa Indian, and Morris Wheelock, an Oneida Indian.

Roy's career was winding down somewhat, so he was at last able to spend more time with his family. But changes were taking place at home too. Roy's mother died at the age of 76, and his father suffered a stroke. The rigors of show business, constant travel, and stunt work, combined with stress over family tragedies, began to take their toll on Roy's health. While on a deer hunt with friends in Utah, he suddenly had trouble breathing and his arms starting hurting. The symptoms continued when he got back home, and he found he had developed angina pectoris. On doctor's orders, he had to slow down and work to rebuild his health.[100]

In April the last monthly issue of *Roy Rogers and Trigger Comics*, #124, appeared. The comic then was issued bimonthly. Dale made an appearance in a "Matinee Theatre" episode, "Anxious Night," on NBC. Roy appeared in a "Bold Journey" episode, "I Follow the Western Star," on ABC. The Hollywood Walk of Fame was dedicated, with three stars in the walk for Roy and three for Dale. Roy was having some of his shirts with the "private" double-eagle design made by Rodeo Ben in Philadelphia; the cost of each was about $150.[101]

Roy and Trigger received the Richard Craven Award from the American Humane Society, an award presented annually for outstanding feats performed by animals before a live audience in theater, rodeo, or other entertainment. (Television and film feats were not eligible.) This award marked Roy's 25th anniversary in show business.

The children were growing up. After finishing high school, Cheryl married William Rose at St. Michael's Episcopal Church, with Linda as Maid of Honor. A month later, Marion married Dan Eaton at the Rogers ranch. Dusty and Sandy were now enrolled in a different military school,

one in Woodland Hills, California, where they were able to be home evenings, instead of only weekends, as was the case at their other school.

1959

On the 50th wedding anniversary of Roy's parents, Roy and Dale repeated their wedding vows at St. Nicholas Episcopal Church in Encino.

In August, Roy visited Portsmouth, Ohio. Friends, family, and fans packed every inch of the downtown area to watch him participate in the "Roy Rogers Day" festivities. The mayor presented him with a key to the city at the "Roy Rogers Esplanade."[102] James W. Secrest, a second cousin of Roy's on his mother's side, introduced the resolution to build the shrine. Roy, with his sons Dusty and Sandy at his side, cut the ribbon dedicating the new McDermott Post Office. The first letter to have the new postmark was from Roy to Dale, and a copy was framed and displayed in the facility. The athletic field was named in Roy's honor, and he unveiled a commemorative stone marker. At the Scioto County Fair, he was honored once again, as he returned to the scene of his early 4-H Club triumphs.[103] Roy showed a gun collection totaling 98 pieces that included cap and ball pistols, a Texas Ranger Colt (with a handle that was a horse's head with ruby eyes), antique dueling pistols, and an old Springfield rifle.

Roy's game room was full of heads from exotic wild animals he had killed in big game hunts such as the one in Nairobi, South Africa, where it was claimed that he was one of the most outstanding hunters ever to visit the country. In the 1950s, he hunted bear in the High Sierra mountains of California. In the game room, there was also a table made from rhinoceros hide and a stool with the legs and feet of a zebra. The African trip led Roy to invest $4300 in taxidermy. An adjoining area of the ranch house contained trophies that he won displaying skills in skeet shooting, pigeon racing, boat racing, and rodeo competition. Roy challenged the new "adult cowboys" to contests in all-around competition in horsemanship, roping, pistol and shotgun skill, as well as box-office draw, because disdainful remarks had been made about the "singing cowboy" image. He was stressing perhaps that it was "tougher" being a good role model for children than being the kind of antihero that was becoming popular.[104]

Roy was reputed to be a millionaire, with real estate holdings in the San Fernando Valley, plus part ownership in 24,000 acres of Arizona land and interest in a Texas boat business, a golf course, a gun club, an auto agency, and more. He and Dale were still performing in the state fair circuit yearly. *Queen of the West, Dale Evans Comics*, #22, was the last issue of Dale's comic.

Three children of the Rogers family were married, Tom, Cheryl, and Marion, and they were living in their own homes.[105] The other five, Sandy, Dusty, Linda, Dodie, and Debbie, were shown on an album cover with Roy and Dale. Roy was endorsing Eastman Kodak cameras and film, and ads appeared in magazines showing all the family members who were still at home.

Roy made a cameo appearance, along with other Western stars, in Bob Hope's film *Alias Jesse James*.

1960

According to a comic book story supposedly written by Roy, Trigger sired a colt whose mother was Buttermilk.[106] One must be very careful in accepting anything as fact that was used in a comic book. This story turned Buttermilk into a mare. Roy had earlier stated, "So I bought her a buckskin gelding with a beautiful black mane and tail, whom she named Buttermilk." Numerous other sources relate that the horse was a gelding. Needless to say, comic book space had to be filled, but these types of stories were written as if they were true accounts.

Dusty graduated from Ridgewood military school and enrolled at Chatsworth High School (Roy had recently dedicated the new building). Roy had been teaching Dusty to rope. Debbie and Dodie also learned to ride.

Although Roy and Dale no longer had the exposure to fuel heavy product sales (the television series had ended, Roy's feature films were history, and his comics were all but gone), Roy was involved in other business enterprises. He owned a car dealership on Ventura Boulevard (as well as Western clothing stores). He had approached Hartland Plastics with an idea of manufacturing

plastic figures of the televison cowboy heroes, and they had produced Roy and Trigger and Dale and Buttermilk as part of the series. The 1960s saw the end of the trail of the commercial tie-in bonanza with merchandise, at least to any significant degree. A few product endorsements would remain, but the majority had ended. In the future, however, these toys and other items would surface as collectibles, bringing high prices. Roy sold the television series rerun rights to CBS-TV, ending the syndicated viewings. The sponsors were Nestle's and Ideal Toys. The shows would be seen into 1964. In newspaper ads, Roy was seen plugging Nestle's Strawberry Flavored Quik. Roy stated in a story that Trigger knew about fifty tricks but stated in another article a few pages away that the figure was closer to seventy-five, so the Trigger legend continued.

Roy went to Alaska to visit the spot where Will Rogers and Wiley Post were killed in a plane crash.

1961

Linda was now attending Kemper Hall Girls School, but she eloped with Gary Johnson to Vegas before graduation.

Roy's King Features Syndicated comic strip, running since 1949, ended this year. The weekly circulation peaked at 63 million.[107]

That year a tragic occurrence produced the first scandal ever to be connectd with Roy. Roy, Dale, Spade Cooley, and his wife Ella Mae had enjoyed fishing excursions together, and some of their trips had even been covered by film magazines. Spade backed Roy on his RCA Victor recordings. They resemble each other a lot, especially at a distance, and it has been reported that Spade doubled some for Roy in films. Spade even owned a beautiful palomino horse. Happy times were history for him, however. Spade murdered his wife after she told him during an argument that she was having an affair with Roy. Published accounts related that Spade even apologized to Roy just before he died in 1969 for having believed the story. Spade was sentenced to the Vacaville, California, prison. After doing a special performance right before he was due to be paroled, he died of a heart attack backstage.[108] According to another source, Ella Mae had bragged about the affair to another friend, stating that Roy came to see her on Saturdays when Spade was away at rehearsal.[109]

1962

The Rogers clan that remained at home learned to drive in the famous jeep, Nellybelle. Wedding bells were not far away for the rest of the girls.

Roy still enjoyed skeet and double-trap-shooting and used a mesquite wood-handled shotgun. There was another African safari this year. Roy had twenty-nine mounted heads in his den from game that he shot in Kenya and Tanganyika. He also took up a new activity, learning to fly.

On June 6, Guinn "Big Boy" Williams, sidekick to Roy in a couple of 1940s films, died. Roy mourned the passing of another friend, Hoot Gibson.

Roy and Dale continued to do well financially, with merchandise bringing in 30 million dollars a year.[110] Seventeen states wanted Roy to build a Disneyland-type "Roy Rogers Frontier Town" in their area. Dale's book *Angel Unaware* had sold over 700,000 copies. In *TV Guide*, writer Davidson said that Roy and Dale's Chatsworth ranch was worth $200,000.

Dale was doing all the cooking at home these days for Roy and the four kids, with frequent outdoor barbecues. Family activities also included prayer meetings on Monday nights, and they attended the Chatsworth Community Church.

1963

Roy and Dale gave up the ranch at Chatsworth and moved to the green hills of Hidden Valley, where they lived among the horse-raising set.[111] *March of Comics*, #250, another Roy and Dale issue, was the last Roy Rogers comic with original stories to be produced until the Hardee's giveaway comic in 1991. (The Hardee's comic was, in fact, never given away, but sold instead by mail order.) Gordon Jones, Roy's sidekick in several films, died. The deaths of so many colleagues must have been one more reason that Roy and Dale were glad to participate in the Billy Graham Crusade that summer in Los Angeles.

1964

Sandy and his girlfriend Sharyn were becoming serious. He and Dusty worked for a real estate promoter digging ditches. Sandy had become almost as much of a collector as Roy, collecting Civil War items.

Roy's dad spent his final years in a convalescent home, where Roy visited every day he was not on the road. Arline's parents were still close to the Rogers family. Marion and her husband had a new baby boy, David Andrew Eaton. Mrs. Miner was still with the Rogers and was known affectionately as "Granny."

Roy and Dale decided to rest and skip their summer tour for what may have been the first time. The family, with the exception of Roy and the two oldest girls, went to Hawaii in July, staying at the Moana Hotel. Roy did not join them because he was experiencing problems with his vertebrae from all of the years of horseback riding and speedboat racing and was preparing for surgery. When Dale and the kids came back from Hawaii, he underwent surgery at UCLA Medical Center. He then developed a staph infection in the hip area, where the doctors removed part of the bone, and he had to wear a body cast. He became critically ill and was dangerously close to death. On Thursday, August 17, Roy was transferred to the Bel-Air Convalescent Home, between Oceanside and Sacramento.

That same day Debbie and some friends were returning from a mission to help children in Tijuana, Mexico, when the left front tire blew out on the school bus. Debbie, age 12, and a friend of the family were both killed in the accident. Art Rush broke the news to Roy after Dale made sure that televisions and radios were removed from his room. The heartbreaking news put him back in intensive care. The funeral was held at Forest Lawn, where daughter Robin lay.

Roy soon recovered enough to return home, but Dale developed diabetes that year. To express her grief and faith in God's will, with the loss of her daughter, she wrote *Dearest Debbie* and donated all royalties to World Vision. A magazine article appeared about Debbie and Robin, with photos of Roy, Dale, Dodie, and Debbie, entitled: "Our Two Angels Will Never Be Lonely Now."

Before long there was more tragedy in the Rogers family when Marion's husband died in an auto accident.

In the mid–1960s, Cheryl became acquainted with her natural family through Dale's efforts. She spent three to four weeks in Oklahoma with them; the family included several sisters and brothers, as well as a grandfather.

Roy bought land in the desert near Victorville, California, as plans for the museum began to materialize. Roy had earlier visited both Will Rogers museums in preparation for this venture.

The "Roy Rogers Show" on television became history this year.

1965

In January, Sandy graduated from high school and decided to enlist in the army. Because he was 17, Roy and Dale had to sign for him to do so. In February the paperwork was signed at Fort MacArthur in San Pedro. Sandy wanted to go to Vietnam. He left Sharyn behind and took off for basic training at Fort Leonard Wood, Missouri. Then it was on to Fort Knox, Kentucky, for advanced training. Dale visited him there for his graduation. He was transferred to Fort Polk, Louisiana, where he got orders for Germany, his request for Vietnam having been denied. The army didn't believe he was qualified for battle, but he continued to urge them to reconsider his request. After he succeeded in getting into the Tank Corps, he and Sharyn planned their marriage.

Roy had leased the Apple Valley Inn, was operating it, and planning his museum. He, Dale, and their remaining children moved to this little town, just over the hill from Victorville in the Mojave desert country. It was just Roy, Dale, Dusty, and Dodie, a big change for the Rogers. In the spring, Dusty graduated from Victor Valley High School. Dale was on the lecture circuit.

The fall found Sandy in Germany. On October 31, Dale's birthday, they learned of Sandy's death in Frankfurt, Germany, from an accident stemming from a drinking incident with his buddies. They found it difficult to carry on with their shows because of the ugly gossip regarding the circumstances surrounding his death, but their faith and strength pulled them through. The military funeral for Pfc. John David Rogers was held at Forest Lawn, November 4, adding sadly to the Rogers population there.

That year Roy also bid a final farewell to another loved and trusted member of the family, Trigger, dead at age thirty-three. Roy told no one for over a year. Unable to face burying his close friend, he had him mounted. He would later be displayed in the museum. Dale and Dusty protested the idea, arguing for a funeral and a final resting place with a monument in a pet cemetery. The Smithsonian Institute had asked Roy for Trigger, but he turned them down. At least until 1989, Roy was still signing autographs "Roy Rogers and Trigger."

Dusty performed in the Youth for Christ film *To Forgive a Thief*. It premiered in Portland, and Roy attended.

1966

Too much time apart and too little communication forced an estrangement between Roy and Dusty. Dusty struck out on his own for Ohio and found employment in a supermarket.[112]

Roy added his support to the campaign of California's Republican governor Ronald Reagan. As antiwar sentiment swept the country in the form of massive demonstrations against the government, Roy and Dale, always the patriots, made arrangements to visit U.S. troops in Vietnam. The purpose of the trip was twofold. They boosted the morale of the troops with their performances, and they got to talk with some soldiers who knew Sandy. The tour included Wayne West and the Travelons, a group that played at Roy Rogers' Apple Valley Inn and included a cousin of Roy's, Dick Slye. The show was organized by the USO Shows and the Hollywood Overseas Committee. Roy and Dale stayed in Saigon at the Meyer Kord Hotel and were welcomed by General Westmoreland. They got to hear firsthand what a fine soldier Sandy was and how many friends he had. Longtime entertainer Martha Raye was part of the show. They performed 34 shows in 17 days and received citations "For Service to Morale of Armed Forces in SE Asia."

Dale received the "Texan of the Year" award from the Texas Press Association in ceremonies at San Antonio, and Roy and Dale spoke at the convention.

1967

The Roy Rogers Museum was built. It incorporated a former bowling alley located close to the Inn and now looked like a fort. Trigger was placed on display at the museum.

Roy's first showbiz sidekick, Smiley Burnette, died on February 16. A few months earlier Herbert J. Yates, head of Republic Productions and Roy's longtime boss, had died.

Dusty learned the construction trade and was employed by Yoder Construction, where he met the boss' daughter. Wedding bells were heard once more, as Dusty and Linda Yoder made their vows to each other on November 18. The family made the trip east, and Dodie was the bridesmaid. The news of Dusty's wedding made the press wires, and it was announced to the world that the "Prince of the Cowboys" was wed.

Because of concerns about his health, Roy quit smoking, an activity he enjoyed but would not indulge in before children, fearing the effect it might have on them.[113]

Dale sang "Ave Maria" at President Nixon's Christmas party. She was named "California Mother of the Year" and attended ceremonies in New York City.

1968

Roy's Uncle Will died, only three months away from his 90th birthday. In the late sixties, Roy visited an ailing Gabby Hayes, his longtime sidekick. It had been reported that there might have been an estrangement between them for a while.

1969

On February 9, Gabby Hayes, Roy's sidekick on stage and off, died. Roy often related that Gabby was like a father, brother, and buddy all rolled into one. For years, Roy had mourned the passing of family and friends and had to do so again when Roy Barcroft died. Barcroft had kept Hollywood good guys hopping, mostly in pursuit of him as a bad guy. Another friend died, John English, who directed several of Roy's films.

Roy lent his name to a huge and fast-growing chain of restaurants owned by Marriott Corporation, and Roy Rogers Restaurants came about. Roy and Dusty made personal appearances at restaurant openings. The two also returned to Portsmouth, where they rode on a 4-H float in the Sesquicentennial Parade with Roy's former teacher Guy Bumgarner.

In the fall Dodie married Air Force Staff Sgt. Tom Faro. On December 28, Marion was again married, this time to Bill Swift. Roy and Dale became grandparents again when Shawna was born to Linda and Dusty.

1970

Roy Rogers' career in show business had by now spanned four decades. He was the most celebrated Hollywood cowboy in history, and he continued to have hit records with Capitol. His story of triumph and tragedy was known the world over, and when the word "cowboy" was mentioned, Roy's image came to mind. It seemed as if everyone he had performed with through the years and others who were so much a part of the family, were all dying. Ex-employee and friend Virginia Peck died of a massive heart attack.

Dale was named "Texas Woman of the Year" by her home state.

1971

Tom Fox, Dale's son, was the minister of music and his wife Barbara was the organist at Calvary Baptist Church in Los Gatos, California. He taught orchestra, glee club and choir.

Dale and Roy served as grand marshals in the Tournament of Roses Parade in Pasadena. Along with the Sons of the Pioneers, they performed at the New York State Fair in Syracuse. Roy made an appearance in Toronto, Canada, and Dale traveled to Rome and then to the Holy Land.

Dale's book *Dale—My Personal Picture Album* was published by Revell.

Raymond Hatton, Roy's second sidekick and partner in several films, died on October 21. On February 27, Pat Brady died of a heart attack in a Colorado sanitorium. He had checked in the day before for treatment of alcoholism.[114]

1972

Roy and Dale were beginning to give a lot of interviews, and this would continue into the 1990s. Possibly because crystal balls didn't predict a renewed interest in silver screen cowboys, Roy Rogers Enterprises failed to renew copyright registrations on many of the comics, television shows, books, etc., that came up for renewal in the 1970s, so many of these items are now in the public domain. The first issue of *Roy Rogers Comics* (Four Color #38) was in this group.[115]

Cheryl, Dale, Roy, October 30, 1973, at the Village Theater in Hollywood.

1973

Roy, Dale, and some of the children performed at the Seattle World's Fair. They closed the show with the hymn "How Great Thou Art." ABC-New York, televising the event, threatened to cancel if they refused to omit the word "Christ" from the last verse. They did refuse, and ABC canceled. On other occasions, the networks tried to edit out the last two minutes of their shows, wherein they would close with a hymn. Not being able to accomplish this successfully, the networks resorted to cancellation.

Roy and Dale appeared at the Kansas State Fair with the Sons of the Pioneers on September 22 and 23.

1974

Roy spent a lot of time in the recording studios; he was now recording for 20th Century Records and continuing to have hits.

In June, Tim Spencer died; he was one of the original Sons of the Pioneers and a close friend to Roy and Dale.

1975

Roy and Dale had by this time performed at more than 6,000 benefits. They now had fifteen grandchildren, and their first great-grandchild, Elizabeth, was Dodie's daughter. Dodie's natural mother had become a friend of the Rogerses and visited them on occasion. She had remarried and Dodie had five half brothers.[116]

Roy and Dale were now performing at six or seven state fairs a year.[117] Roy received the 1st Annual Thomas Great American Award. He attended the grand opening of three Roy Rogers Family Restaurants in Long Island, New York. There would soon be 240 of these restaurants. The attendance at the museum was running up to 100,000 per year. *Esquire* published an interview-article on Roy, which was greatly upsetting to the family.

1976

On February 18, Andy Devine, another of Roy's comic sidekicks, died.

Roy and Dale's income was reportedly

now one million dollars per year.[118] They received yet another honor when they were inducted into the Cowboy Hall of Fame in Oklahoma City, and Roy's purple and yellow boots were placed in the Kennedy Center's bicentennial exhibit of 200 years of memorabilia in Washington, D.C. America's "King of the Cowboys" was back on the Hollywood range after all these years. *Mackintosh & T.J.* was filmed in Texas and there was a reception thrown for Roy and country singer Waylon Jennings at the Palomino Club in L.A. for the debut of Roy's new film. Jennings sang the songs in the film.

Construction was completed on the new museum, which was named the Roy Rogers–Dale Evans Museum. It was located in Victorville, just off Interstate 15, and replaced the one in Apple Valley. It cost $500,000 according to one source.[119] Roy and Dale personally supervised the moving of artifacts and memorabilia from one museum to the other. The Trigger statue, actually in the image of Little Trigger or another of the doubles with the white stockings, is out front and is two stories tall. The lobby contains oil portraits of Roy and Dale. All the artifacts and memorabilia that tell the story of this couple are enclosed in glass cases on 32,625 square feet of floor space. Trigger is insured for one hundred thousand dollars. Trigger, Jr., will be displayed here, as well as Buttermilk, and Bullet.[120] The old truck that hauled the Slye family to California is there. In an outdoorlike setting stand the animals that were such a great part of Roy and Dale's lives. His $50,000 silver- and gem-inlaid saddle is here, along with the wardrobes of fancy attire that he and Dale have worn over the years. For the millions of Roy and Dale fans and the curious, this place is open seven days a week. Their house is in Apple Valley, seven miles from the museum. It is a two-story, Spanish-style home overlooking a golf course.

Dale was writing one book after another, mostly of a religious nature, but telling about show business life and the effect it had on family life. She made a speaking engagement tour to publicize these books. It was like "old home week," as she appeared on a WFAA Radio talk show in Dallas and on NBC Radio in Ft. Worth.

1977

Roy and Dale appeared as grand marshals in the Tournament of Roses Parade in Pasadena, California, on New Year's Day.[121] Roy was now racing horses and eventually owned 40. In a claimer race, he lost racehorse "Triggaro" (a black horse). He had another racehorse he raced at Hollywood Park that was named "Run Trigger Run."[122] In addition to racing horses, Roy spent part of his leisure time astride his forty-horsepower Honda 550 cc. motorcycle.

Dusty, his wife, and his new son Dustin Roy moved to Apple Valley, and he continued work as a construction supervisor and did some television shows and some disc jockey work, as well as singing.

Lloyd Perryman, longtime Sons of the Pioneers member, died May 31.

1978

Dusty built a new home for his parents, who were alone for the first time in their marriage now that Dodie had married and moved away. Roy underwent triple bypass heart surgery this year. A painting of Roy and Dale by Everett Kinstler, a well-known Western comic book artist, was unveiled at a ceremony at the Cowboy Hall of Fame.

1979

Roy and Dale made a trip to London. They were now grandparents of sixteen and great-grandparents of four. There would be no more grandchildren, but many more great-grandchildren. *Happy Trails: The Story of Roy Rogers and Dale Evans*, an autobiography with writer Carlton Stowers, was published by Word Publishing, Waco, Texas. Roy was still performing at benefits, and he and Dale visited Nashville, where they performed at the Opry House in a benefit for country singer Hank Snow. Reports said Roy had some descendants of Trigger on the ranch (see Chapter 10 and Appendix).

1980

Bob Nolan, one of the original Sons of the Pioneers and a memorable character in Roy's films, died June 16. The original Sons of the Pioneers, including Roy, who was Len Slye when he belonged to the group, were elected to the Country Music Hall of Fame in Nashville that year.

Roy's career experienced an upswing as

baby-boomers looked nostalgically at the legendary cowboy. Collectors and collector associations began to surface, and Roy's films were rerun on television (mostly cable channels) and were made available on video tape. The image of Roy still epitomized the honest, clean-living American cowboy. Western clothes had become chic, and Western music was reaching new audiences, with resounding applause, as America looked for her heroes. Roy's real heyday was over, but he made many appearances and gave interviews. He was often quoted as saying, "I think I'm the only cowboy who started his career making Westerns, and finished with the same horse."[123] Dale did the "Kings in Conflict" tour, talking on radio and television stations about Christianity and giving interviews. In April, Roy and Dale made the cover of the *Saturday Evening Post* in an issue devoted to religion.

Roy's endorsement of products began to increase again, fueled by the nostalgia craze. Many new products were forthcoming. Eventually, there were even extravagant and expensive items for gun enthusiasts and hard-core collectors. Most of the items were being sold in the gift shop at the Roy Rogers–Dale Evans Museum or by mail order. Scores of items began to appear in the flea markets and city stores as well that were "Roy Rogers" items, but were not connected with his companies. Roy was again being asked back to the studio to record.

1981

Roy was making a lot of appearances at the grand openings of his restaurants; there were now 325 of them. With his film career behind him, he had less desire for the fancy, custom-made boots and he bought his size 8B's off the shelf.[124]

1982

The great-grandchildren numbered six by now. Roy stated that if he were twenty years younger, he would adopt another family. He and Dale had spent their careers giving to charities and were still doing so.

Dusty formed a new Country and Western band named the High Riders, and his relationship with his father had been mended. "Roy Rogers Homecoming Day" took place in Portsmouth, Ohio, on Labor Day, September 6. Dale was unable to at-

tend, but Roy enjoyed the occasion. He went to Duck Run, his old residence, and met with childhood friends, sisters Cleda Willoughby and Mary Moreland, and other relatives. Roy met with the press and put his prints in a cement block on the Roy Rogers Esplanade, as Art Rush and radio personality Zeke Mullins assisted. "Scioto County's Favorite Son," as he was named, met with his cousin Ethel Slye. The crowd attending the parade was estimated at 10,000. This was Roy's first visit here since 1969. He was attired in a turquoise satin shirt lined with leather and sequined fringe, a white Stetson, and red neckerchief. The mayor read the proclamation making this date "Roy Rogers Day." Roy yodeled for an enthusiastic audience. Walt Yarbrough of the National Powerboat Association interviewed Roy on the Ohio river bank. A luncheon was given in his honor at the American Legion Hall, where he received the Spirit of Freedom plaque from the SOF Foundation and was named Honorary Sheriff of Scioto County by Sheriff John Knauff. Then he was presented with a watercolor painting of the Duck Run homeplace by artist George Little. Roy was also given a painting *Range War* by Marlboro artist Robert Young and a letter from President Ronald Reagan for his "Volunteerism" for having performed over 6,400 benefit shows, more than any other Hollywood star. Art Rush called Roy "America's Greatest Hero," and Gene Autry sent a mailgram. On May 9, country singer Barbara Mandrell's song, *I Was Country When Country Wasn't Cool*, mentioning Roy, debuted on the charts, where it stayed for thirteen weeks, gaining the number 1 position.

1983

By this time, Roy Rogers had had over one thousand product endorsements. The Roy Rogers–Dale Evans Collector's Association was founded by Elmer B. Sword in Portsmouth on December 7. The Roy Rogers Hometown Exhibit was put together through the efforts of Sword and others and forms part of the Portsmouth Area Community Exhibits. It opened officially September 2, 1984. The collectors held their first annual convention at the Ramada Inn near Shawnee State College. Three weeks later Roy made an unannounced visit and was shown the exhibit. While he was making personal appearances on behalf of his restaurants, he paid a visit to the mounted patrols of Boston, New York City, and Philadelphia, giving each patrol a horse as a good will gesture. He suggested that each horse be named "Trigger."

1984

Roy visited his hometown, the exhibit, and relatives in September. In the week of November 5, near Roy's birthday, Futura Productions from Hollywood filmed the Portsmouth exhibit for their television show "Fan Fare." Dale joined Roy in Portsmouth for the premier of the Roy Rogers–Dale Evans Convention. Dale had received awards from the American Legion, American Bible Society, National Film Society, and the National Committee for Child Abuse, among many other organizations.

1985

An old shoulder injury from childhood was flaring up again, and Roy had to give up bowling. He joked to audiences that his horse was getting higher off the ground all the time and his bowling ball was getting heavier. Roy was still in good shape, however, because he won a celebrity trapshoot, outshooting Jerry Mathers ("Leave It to Beaver") and Robert Stack ("The Untouchables"). He used the twenty-five-year-old rifle that he bought from Clark Gable. Roy was raising colts on a sixty-seven-acre ranch near the museum, where he owned seventeen horses. He got closer than he had in thirty-five years to matching Trigger's beautiful color. He named this horse "Triggario."[125]

1986

Roy was part of Thousand Trails, Inc., which opened forty-five RV parks. Happy Trails Resorts, which Roy was also part of, opened its first facility in Arizona, at Surprise, twenty-five miles west of Phoenix. This facility has a Roy and Dale Gallery filled with costumes, movie posters, children's games, and other memorabilia. Roy and Dale attended the opening ceremonies.

Dale was appearing on the religious PTL (Praise the Lord) shows, and they both attended Billy Graham events. *Angel Unaware* was in its 28th printing, and Dale was finishing her 22d book, *The Home Stretch*, a book about aging gracefully. She made two public appearances each month for her books, which were being reviewed by the Christian Book Association in Washington, D.C.

Roy received the Pioneer Award from the Academy of Country Music. He was also named Honorary American Indian of the year by the American Indian Exposition, which he attended. He and Dale taped "wrap-around" shows in Knoxville, Tennessee for Happy Trails Theater, and his old films were shown on television, accompanied by nostalgic chit-chat.[126] After a trip to Maryland to visit his sister Mary, Roy flew to Columbus, rented a car, and drove to Portsmouth unannounced to visit his sister Cleda and his old friend, Ethel Duncan, with whom he attended school.

The fourth annual Golden Boot Awards show was held Friday, August 15, at the new Warner Center at the Marriott Hotel in Woodland Hills, California. The prime rib dinner cost $75 and the proceeds went to the Motion Picture and Television Country House and Hospital.

Dawn Licensing Agency worked out the details with Art Rush to become the exclusive agent for new lines of Roy and Dale merchandise. Howard Haftel was the company president, and seven companies were licensed initially to produce and sell fifteen products.[127]

The opening of the Smithsonian Institute Show featured photos of Roy and Trigger. On May 22, Roy and Dale and Gene Autry received U.S.O. Distinguished American Awards during ceremonies in Anaheim. Roy's sister Cleda said it was still hard for Roy to believe he had achieved such fame. She stated that he was "overwhelmed."[128]

1987

There were now 90,000 members in the Thousand Trails Resorts, and RV parks had been organized all over the country. Roy, as spokesman, attended the first year anniversary celebration in January. Six to seven hundred members attended. In June, Roy's sisters Mary and Cleda attended the Roy Rogers Festival in Portsmouth. Dale was also there and was presented with a plaque by the Scioto County commissioner at the awards show.

In the fall, the fifth annual Golden Boot Awards were presented in ceremonies held at the Los Angeles Equestrian Center.

1988

Roy was a member of the National Committee to Draft televangelist Pat Robertson for president. The television commercial was airing in seven states. Roy was elected into the Country Music Hall of Fame and now had two spots, the first as a member of the Sons of the Pioneers. Dale was still traveling thousands of miles a week on the speaking circuits. She and Roy were supporting churches and missionaries, and Dale appeared in Avon Park, Florida, at the Noon Rotary Club Benefit to raise money for Polio Plus. Her book *Only One Star* was issued by Word Publishing.

Americomics (AC) was selling numerous memorabilia items such as buttons, reproductions of movie posters, lobby cards, etc.

1989

On New Years Day, Roy's longtime manager Art Rush died, and in March, Roy's sister, Mary Moreland, died. As Roy was all but retired, Dusty took over the manager/agent chores. There were a number of older women who cared for the museum and looked after Roy's interests, screening people for interviews. New exhibits at the museum were being added: newspaper and magazine articles covering Roy's career, including Hollywood gossip columnist Hedda Hopper's column 1938–1958.

In late March, Roy and Dale participated in the openings for the Oscar Awards Show.

The 200-plus films and television episodes with guns firing around him had taken a toll on Roy's hearing for some time, and he finally decided to be fitted with hearing aids. He also suffered another bout with pneumonia (he had been stricken in 1976). "Happy Trails Theater" was history after several years on television. It had allowed Americans to see many (twenty-six per season) of the Rogers "oaters" they might have not seen otherwise.

1990

On April 13, Hardee's acquired all 784 Roy Rogers Restaurants from Marriott Corp. for $365 million. Now they would be Hardee's–Roy Rogers Fried Chicken.

On October 7, Roy and Dusty were in Lone Pine, California, for the Sierra Festival dedicating the site of Roy's first Republic feature film, *Under Western Stars*. It was a two-day event cosponsored by the California Arts Council and the Inyo Council for the Arts. Roy sang a song he had recently written, "Alive and Kickin'," for the crowds there.

Roy underwent heart bypass surgery again on October 21 at St. Mary Desert Valley Hospital, a four-hour procedure to correct an aneurysm in his aorta, and he developed a serious case of pneumonia. His condition weakened, and his sister Cleda visited California to help him during his six- to eight-week convalescence. Still as tough as ever, he recovered, but his doctor prescribed an inhaler to help him attain more lung power. Roy received over nineteen thousand "get well" letters. The *National Inquirer* had printed a request from Dale for letters to cheer him up.

There was a Roy Rogers Award presented at the Shotgun News Trade and Gun Shows. Roy attended this organization's SGN IX–West Convention at the Bally's Grand Hotel in Reno, Nevada, on November 16.

Roy, Dale and Dusty were in Nashville for the Country Music Association awards, and on October 8 and 9, Roy and Dusty attended the 50th annual BMI Awards. On October 10, they attended the ASCAP awards.

Randy Travis—Happy Trails, a special film presentation of a Montana cattle drive with Roy, Randy, and others was shown on Nashville Network cable television, October 17.

On October 19, the 1st Roy Rogers–Dale Evans Celebrity Golf Tournament was held at Spring Valley Lake Country Club in Victorville. Roy's team came in second. He participated in the 4th annual Charlton Heston Celebrity Shoot in Orange County, California.

In August, Roy recorded his tracks for a new LP for RCA. The other singers' tracks, such as those of Randy Travis, Emmylou Harris, etc., would be recorded separately and then all would be mixed by studio technology. Thirty-eight artists showed up, however, to sing with Roy on his signature song, *Happy Trails*.

New Year's Eve was Roy and Dale's 43d wedding anniversary.

1991

The requests for personal appearances and interviews never ceased. Roy was quoted in interviews as saying: "But a lot of 'em [people making requests] forget that I made these pictures a long time ago [Laughs]. They don't know how old you are; I guess they think you're still the same age as they see you on the screen." And, after all these years, Roy admitted to being tired of the road and personal appearances. There were plenty of family members to keep life interesting, however. There were now sixteen grandchildren and twenty-two great-grandchildren with another on the way.

In June, Roy developed pneumonia again and spent a week in the hospital. As Roy Rogers described the museum in a letter: "To my way of thinking [it] is the most beautiful scene in the world. The morning sun slides over the mountains, and the tumbleweeds roll lazily over the high desert country of California. I think this is about as close to the Great Reward as I ever expect to get in this life."[129] And Roy talked about his guns: "When I was riding the Hollywood range with that single-action six-shooter strapped on, I felt somehow connected to the past. Sometimes with the gun in my hand standing under the western sun, I felt like I was closer to some of the great events that shaped our country, in a way I had never experienced before."[130]

Roy told Associated Press reporter Joe Edwards in a telephone interview that he still rode his motorcycle, and, in fact, rode it to and from the museum each day. He said he watched his favorite daytime television show at home, "The Guiding Light" (noon, pst). Roy stated in interviews that he was happy, didn't need anything, didn't want anything, had trusts set up for all the kids, and just liked to take it easy.[131]

April 8–11, Roy, Dale, and Dusty entertained returning troops from the Gulf War at Thousand Trails Resort, Sahara Hotel, Las Vegas. May 17–19, Roy and Dale attended the Western Music Festival at the Gene Autry Museum in L.A., where tributes

were made to Roy and Gene. Fifty-six people attended Roy's 80th birthday party (and Dale's 79th) in November. The *Tribute* LP had already hit over 300,000 in sales, and the new record out with Clint Black, *Hold on Partner*, had climbed to #36 in L.A.

1992

There were more "Roy Rogers covers" adding to the many that had already appeared over the years. Roy was invited as a guest to Music of the West, "A Tribute to the Singing Cowboys," a three-day celebration at the Gene Autry Western Heritage Museum in L.A., May 15–17. Roy, Dale, and the Sons of the Pioneers were among the honorees.

Although Roy was at the museum every morning shaking hands with his fans, he gently refused to sign any autographs, saying that if he did so, he would have to stay there all day. He liked to take an afternoon nap between watching television shows, which included "Matlock" and "Evening Shade."

In April, the Hardee's folks were in trouble with their plans to convert all the Roy Rogers Restaurants they had bought in January 1990 to Hardee's facilities.[132] After many customers became upset with the change, they had to spend $4 million to convert them back to Roy's name.

Everyone remained concerned about Roy's health because he had suffered several problems. But to everyone's surprise, Dale had a heart attack and required a quadruple bypass. She recovered well, however. Then another surgery was necessary because of complications from the first. Roy himself apparently drove Dale to the hospital. He had been planning to surprise many fans by attending the Roy Rogers Festival in Portsmouth, but with Dale recuperating in the hospital, he decided to stay at home. On May 29, he landed in the hospital with Dale because he suffered chest pains, possibly related to the stress created by Dale's illness. She had been transferred from High Desert Hospital to Loma Linda Community Hospital, where she and Roy had rooms next to each other.

Awards and honors continued to come to Roy. He received the *Music City News* "Living Legend Award" June 8 and was on the related television broadcast, via satellite, from the museum. A documentary film *Roy Rogers, King of the Cowboys* was produced by Kees Ryninks of England and directed by Roy Rogers fan Thys Ockersen of Holland. Highway 18, in Apple Valley, California, was officially named "Happy Trails Highway" in a resolution passed in July by the state assembly. A made-for-television movie on Roy titled *Roy Rogers, King of the Cowboys* was produced by Galen Films for American Movie Classics and Republic Pictures. It was shown over AMC-TV during the entire first week of December, beginning the 3d. Roy's life story was told in his own words through much film footage, a lot of it taken by Roy over the years with his 8mm camera. Thys Ockersen's documentary showed for two weeks, December 30 to January 12, at New York's Film Forum Theater. The lobby hosted a great photo tribute to the star. The second feature was Roy's 1949 classic, *The Golden Stallion.*

1993–1994

A Broadway musical about the careers of Roy and Dale from their meeting through the 1950s, was produced in 1993, titled *Roy, Dale and Me* (as told by Trigger). It debuted at Branson, Missouri, then went to London, and then came back to Broadway. The Bower-Cohen Co., Los Angeles, worked with the New York production group, which was responsible for the notable plays *Cats* and *Les Misérables.*

Negotiations were underway with Nickelodeon and another company to produce a Roy Rogers cartoon series. Republic backed out of this project. Initially, fifty-five episodes were planned, with Fred Wolf doing the animation. Ten thousand sets of the AMC-TV documentary, packaged along with uncut versions of four of Roy's films, had been sold as of March 1993.

Dale returned to taping her "Date with Dale" religious programs for the Turner Broadcasting Network, and Roy and Dale continued to appear at fundraiser dinners. One was a $300 per plate event on February 12 at the Beverly Hilton Hotel for Uni-Health. Another was February 19 at the Grand Kempinski Hotel in Dallas for the Variety Clubs Children's Charities of North Texas, where the dinner cost $100 per plate.

In an interview in *TV Guide*, Roy was asked what he watched on television. He responded "Guiding Light," sports, the Nashville Network, "Dr. Quinn, Medicine Woman," and "Rush Limbaugh." Roy paid tribute to Limbaugh: "He's taught me so much about politics that I can't help but think that our government would benefit by paying some attention to him." Roy is further quoted as saying that Limbaugh makes you think. Roy and Dale were still participating in Billy Graham events, including one on April 29 in Los Angeles, where they were joined by Gene Autry and Clayton ("The Lone Ranger") Moore.

Roy and Dale continued to be honored at banquets across the country, and made live appearances at such places as Branson, Missouri, the new fast-growing country music capital, and at the annual Western Music festival in Tucson, Arizona, as well as on television, especially Dale's "A Date with Dale" show, broadcast over TBN (Trinity Broadcast Network) cable channel. They were honored by the Salvation Army, an event hosted by evangelist Billy Graham.

A new book came out, entitled *Roy Rogers, King of the Cowboys*, essentially a coffee table book by Georgia Morris and Mark Pollard, based upon the AMC documentary shown in 1992.

Groundbreaking has taken place for a 25 million dollar "Rogersdale, USA" tourist attraction, to be built on thirty-five acres in Victorville, consisting of an entertaining and shopping complex.

Roy and Dale twice became great-grandparents again in 1994. Roy and Dale have recorded tracks for a new gospel record. They lost a grandson (Cheryl's son) in an accident, summer, 1994. An "official" biography on the couple was in the works by Jane and Michael Stern.

Chapter 3

MUSICOGRAPHY

*I would like to gratefully acknowledge the past discographies of the Sons of the Pioneers and Roy Rogers that were produced by Ken Griffis, David Rothel, Walt Cooper, and Jerry Osborne. This discography results from that information and information from my own collections and research. (An asterisk [*] indicates that song was not issued originally; ** indicates that the song was issued much later on an LP.)*

1934

Decca Records. DATE: August 4 and or 8 (sources disagree). Unless otherwise specified, recordings took place in Los Angeles. MUSICIANS: Vocal, Leonard Slye, Bob Nolan, Tim Spencer; guitar, Leonard Slye; fiddle, Hugh Farr. This was the first recording session of Leonard Slye with the Sons of the Pioneers. MASTERS: DLA 10, "Way Out There" (Bob Nolan), #5013; DLA 11, "Tumbling Tumbleweeds" (Bob Nolan), #5047; DLA-12, "Moonlight on the Prairie" (Nolan/ Spencer), #5047; DLA-13, "Ridin' Home" (Bob Nolan), #5013.

Standard Transcriptions

DATES: Unknown. Several hundred songs including the following: "Swiss Yodel," "When Roundup Time Is Over," "Hear Dem Bells," "Giddyap Napoleon," "Ain't We Crazy," "Sidewalk Waltz," "Bells of Baltimore," "White Mule of Mine," "Sweet Betsy from Pike," "She Came Rollin' Down the Mountain," "Grandfather's Clock," "Little Brown Jug." Standard radio recordings include the following: "Put On Your Old Gray Bonnet," "Dear Old Girl," "Gospel Train," "Dese Bones Gwine to Rise Again," "Lone Star Trail," "Little Red Barn," "Hills of Old Kentucky," "Little Annie Roonie," "Jim Crack Corn," "Rufus Rastus Johnson Brown," "Jordan Am a Hard Road to Travel," "Threw It Out the Window," "Cowboy's Night Herd Song," "Railroad Boomer," "Nancy Till," "Black Sheep Blues," "Cider Schottische," "When You and I Were Young Maggie," "When the Bees Are in the Hive," "Dear Old Western Skies," "Hadie Brown," "At the End of the Lane," "Gentle Nettie Moore," "When the Work's All Done," "Prairie Whing Ding," "Leaning on the Everlasting Arm," "Down the Lane to Happiness," "Sweet Genevieve." (Len is either singing or playing the guitar on these.)

1935

Unless otherwise specified, the recording company is Decca Records. DATE: March 7 and or 8. MASTERS: DLA 122, "I Follow the Stream" (Bob Nolan), #5083; DLA 123, "There's a Round-Up in the Sky" (Bob Nolan), #5083; DLA 124, "I Still Do"* (Bob Nolan); DLA 125, "The Roving Cowboy" (Bob Nolan), #5218.

DATE: March 13. MASTERS: DLA 138, "When Our Old Age Pension Check Comes to Our Door" (M. Stone), #5082; DLA 139, "Will You Love Me When Our Hair Has Turned to Silver?" (T. Spencer), #5082; DLA 140, "When I Leave This World Behind" (B. Nolan), #5218; DLA 141, "Popeyed"* (Unknown).

DATE: October 9. MASTERS: DLA 241, "Over the Santa Fe Trail" (T. Spencer), #5232; DLA 242, "Song of the Pioneers" (T. Spencer), #5168; DLA 243, "The New Frontier"* (Unknown); DLA 244, "Echoes from the Hills" (Nolan), #5168.

The Sons of the Pioneers in a pure hillbilly pose.

DATE: October 16. MASTERS: DLA 245, "Kilocycle Stomp" (H. and K. Farr), #5178; DLA 246, "Cajon Stomp" (H. Farr), #5178; DLA 247, "Kelly Waltz"* (Unknown); DLA 248, "Westward Ho" (T. Spencer), #5275.

1936
DATE: May 4 and or 8. MASTERS: DLA 358, "Hills of Old Wyomin'" (Robin/Rainger), #5222; DLA 359, "A Melody from the Sky" (Alter/Mitchell), #5222; DLA 360, "We'll Rest at the End of the Trail" (Rose/Fulton), #5248; DLA 361, "Texas Star" (DeRose/Breen/Barrett), #5232.

DATE: June 18. MASTERS: DLA 382, "Blue Bonnet Girl" (G. Spencer), #5243; DLA 383, "Ride, Ranger, Ride" (T. Spencer), #5243.

DATE: June. PLACE: Dallas, Texas. MASTERS: #61926, "Way Out There" (B. Nolan), #5358; #61927, "Tumbling Tumbleweeds" (B. Nolan), #5358, #46027, #29814. (Note: Issued in three different Decca series as singles; not released until February 1937.)

DATE: July 3. MASTERS: DLA 411, "Empty Saddles" (Hill/Brennan), #5247, #46160; DLA 412, "Blue Prairie" (Spencer/Nolan),

#5248; DLA 413, "I'm an Old Cowhand" (J. Mercer), #5247; DLA 414, "One More Ride" (B. Nolan), #5275.

1937
COMPANY: American Record Co. (ARC) issued records under the following labels: Banner, Melotone, Oriole, Perfect, Romeo, Conquerer (CQ), Harmony (HR), Columbia (CO), Okeh/Vocalion (O/V), and Coral (CL). (In February 1938, ARC became Columbia. Songs were issued simultaneously on different labels with the Okeh and Vocalion bearing the same record number.) Columbia would occasionally issue simultaneously in two different series.

DATE: October 19 and or 21. MUSICIANS: Vocal, Leonard Slye, Bob Nolan, Lloyd Perryman; guitar, Lloyd Perryman, Karl Farr; violin, Hugh Farr. MASTERS: LA 1482, "My Saddle Pals and I" (Slye), #ARC 8-03-56, CQ 8941, HR 1935, O/V 03236; LA 1483, "I Love You Nelly" (Unknown), ARC 8-02-62, CQ 8941, O/V 03913; LA 1484, "I Wonder If She Waits for Me Tonight" (B. Nolan), #CQ 8949, O/V 04136; LA 1485, "When the Roses Bloom Again" (Edwards-Cobb), #ARC 8-02-

Karl Farr, Bob Nolan, Tim Spencer, Hugh Farr and Len Slye in the mid–1930s.

62, CQ 8949, CO 20226, 37627, Q/V 3916; LA 1486, "Heavenly Airplane" (B. Nolan), #O/V 05725; LA 1487, "Billy the Kid" (A. Jenkins), #HR 1033, O/V 04136; LA 1488, "Power in the Blood" (L. Jones), #ARC 8-04-60, CO 20334, 37757, O/V 03399; LA 1489, "Let's Pretend" (B. Nolan), #ARC 8-03-56, O/V 03236.

COMPANY: ARC. DATE: October 26. MASTERS: LA 1490, "Love Song of the Waterfall"* (Unknown); LA 1491, "Song of the Bandit"* (Nolan); LA 1492, "Down Along the Sleepy Rio Grande" (Slye), #ARC 8-01-51, HR 1033, O/V 03880; LA 1493, "Just a Wearying for You" (Bond/Stanton), #ARC 8-01-52, HR 1070, O/V 03881; LA 1494, "Smilin' Thru" (A. Penn), #ARC 8-01-52, HR 1070, O/V 03881; LA 1495, "Kelly Waltz" (Unknown), HR 1035, O/V 04264; LA 1496, "Open Range Ahead" (B. Nolan), #ARC 8-01-51, CO 20500, O/V 03880; LA 1997, "Cajon Stomp" (Farr), O/V 04264; LA 1498, "Blue Juanita"* (Unknown); LA 1499, "Send Him Home to Me" (B. Nolan), O/V 04328; LA 1500, "At the Rainbow's End" (B. Nolan), O/V 04329.

DATE: October 28. A & R: Art Satherly.

MUSICIANS: (Records carry name "Roy Rogers," but he did one final session with the Sons of the Pioneers as Leonard Slye, same personnel, on December 14.) Vocal, Roy Rogers; lead guitar, Karl Farr; violin, Hugh Farr; bass, Bob Nolan; rhythm guitar, Roy Rogers. MASTERS: LA 1500(?), "Cowboy Night Herd Song"** (Rogers); LA 1501, "That Pioneer Mother of Mine" (T. Spencer), #ARC 8-04-51; LA 1502, "When the Black Sheep Gets the Blues" (Unknown), #ARC 8-04-51; LA 1503, "Hadie Brown"** (McWilliams/J. Rodgers/Rogers).

DATE: December 14. MUSICIANS: Vocal, Leonard Slye, Bob Nolan; guitar, Lloyd Perryman, Karl Farr; violin, Hugh Farr; bass, Pat Brady. MASTERS: LA 1539, "Hear Dem Bells" (Unknown), #O/V 04187; LA 1540, "One More River to Cross" (Unknown), #CO 20500, O/V 05725; LA 1541, "You Must Come In at the Door" (T. Spencer), #O/V 04187; LA 1542, "Lead Me Gently Home, Father" (W. Thompson), #CO 20334, 37757, O/V 03399; LA 1543, "The Devil's Great Grandson" (B. Nolan), #CO 20499; LA 1544, "Dwelling in Beulah Land" (Unknown), CQ 9447, O/V 05428;

LA 1545, "When the Golden Train Comes Down" (Nolan), #CQ 9448, O/V 05347; LA 1546, "The Hangin' Blues"* (Unknown); LA 1547, "Hold That Critter Down" (Nolan), #CO 20499; LA 1548, "Leaning on the Everlasting Arm" (Unknown), #CQ 9447, O/V 05428; LA 1549, "What You Gonna Say to Peter?" (Unknown), #CQ 9448, O/V 03347; LA 1550, "At the Rainbow's End" (Nolan), #O/V 04328; LA 1551, "The Touch of God's Hand"* (Nolan); LA 1552, "Lord, You Made the Cowboy Happy"* (Nolan).

1938
COMPANY: ARC. DATE: March 4 and or 30. A & R: Art Satherly. MUSICIANS: Vocal, Roy Rogers (other session personnel unknown). The four songs were used in Roy's first feature film, *Under Western Stars*. MASTERS: LA 1616, "That Pioneer Mother of Mine" (T. Spencer), # O/V 04051, CQ 9007; LA 1617, "Dust" (Marvin/Autry), #O/V 04050; LA 1618, "When a Cowboy Sings a Song" (Tinturin/Lawrence), #O/V 04050; LA 1619, "Listen to the Rhythm of the Range" (Marvin/Autry), #O/V 04051, CQ 9007.

COMPANY: ARC. DATE: June. PLACE: New York City. MUSICIANS: Same. MASTERS: 23091, "Hi-Yo Silver!" (Unknown), #O/V 04190, CQ 9060; 23092, "A Lonely Ranger Am I" (DeLeath/Erickson), #O/V 04263; 23093, "Old Pioneer" (T. Spencer), #O/V 04263; 23094, "Ridin', Ropin'" (Rogers), #O/V 04190, CQ 9060.

COMPANY: ARC. DATE: September 1. The last three songs will be used in Roy's second feature film, *Billy the Kid Returns*. A & R: Art Satherly. MUSICIANS: Vocal, Roy Rogers; guitar, Karl Farr; bass, Pat Brady; violin, Hugh Farr; rhythm guitar, Lloyd Perryman; steel guitar and accordion, unknown. MASTERS: LA 1706, "I've Sold My Saddle for an Old Guitar" (Allan), #O/V 05310, CQ 9431; LA 1707, "When Mother Nature Sings Her Lullaby" #O/V 04389, CQ 9059; LA 1708, "Colorado Sunset" (Conrad/Gilbert), #O/V 04453; LA 1709, "There's a Ranch in the Rockies" (Unknown), #O/V 04453; LA 1710, "The Sun Is Setting on the Prairie" (Cherkose/Colombo), #O/V 04389, CQ 9059; LA 1711, "When I Camped Under the Stars" (T. Spencer), #O/V 04544, CO 38907;

LA 1712, "Born to the Saddle" (Cherkose), #O/V 04544.

1939
COMPANY: ARC. DATE: April 11 and or 17. A & R: Art Satherly. MUSICIANS: Vocal, Roy Rogers; steel guitar, Frankie Marvin (possibly); other musicians, unknown. MASTERS: LA 1858, "Somebody's Smile" (King), #O/V 04840; LA 1859; "I've Learned a Lot About Women" (J. Marvin), #O/V 05094, CQ 9430; LA 1860, "The Man in the Moon Is a Cowhand" (Rogers), #O/V 05028; LA 1861, "She's All Wet Now" (Rogers), #O/V 05094, CQ 9430; LA 1862, "I Hope I'm Not Dreaming Again" (Rogers/Rose), #O/V 05310, CQ 9431; LA 1863, "The Mail Must Go Through" (Samuels), #O/V 04840.

COMPANY: ARC. DATE: April 18. MUSICIANS: Same. MASTERS: LA 1871, "Headin' for Texas and Home" (Unknown), #O/V 04923, CQ 9692; LA 1872, "Rusty Spurs" (W. Wood/R. Wood) #O/V 05028, CQ 9333; LA 1873, "Let Me Build a Cabin" (Cherkose/Natteford/Kraushaar), #O/V 04961, CQ 9334; LA 1874, "Here on the Range" (T. Spencer), #O/V 04961, CQ 9334; LA (n/a), "Ridin' Down the Trail" (Unknown), #O/V 04923, CQ 9692.

COMPANY: ARC. DATE: June. PLACE: New York City. MASTERS: Unknown.

1940
Unless otherwise specified, the company is Decca Records. DATE: August 4 and or 29. A & R: Dave Kapp. MUSICIANS: Vocal, Roy Rogers; Spade Cooley's Orchestra, the Buckle-Busters. MASTERS: DLA 2102, "Chapel in the Valley" (Unknown), #5895; DLA 2103, "You Waited Too Long" (Whitley/Rose/Autry), #5876; DLA 2104, "Nobody's Fault but My Own" (Unknown), #5876; DLA 2105, "No Matter What Happens My Darling" (Unknown), #5895.

DATE: September 3. MUSICIANS: Same with the addition of Jimmy Wakely's Trio. MASTERS: DLA 2110, "Silent Night, Holy Night" (Mohr/Gruber), #5883; DLA 2111, "O Come All Ye Faithful" (J. Reading), #5883; DLA 2112, "Wondering Why" (Rogers/Lange/Porter), #5916; DLA 2113, "Life Won't Be the Same" (Porter/Lange),

Pat Brady, who took Len's place in 1937.

#5916; DLA 2114, "Round That Couple and Swing When You Meet" (Unknown), #3733 CL 64016; DLA 2115, "Chase the Rabbit, Chase the Squirrel" (Unknown), #3733, CL 64016; DLA 2116, "Bird in a Cage and Three Rail Pen" (Unknown), #3734, CL 64017; DLA 2117, "Round That Couple and Swing When You Meet" (Unknown), #3734, CL 64017; DLA 2118, "Boy Around the Boy, Girl Around the Girl" (Unknown), #3735, CL 64018; DLA 2119, "Lady 'Round the Lady, and Gent Solo" (Unknown) #3735, CL

Roy's singing was featured in his life story in the comics. *It Really Happened Comics*, No. 8.

64018. (The last six songs are square dance tunes with Roy doing the calls.)

DATE: September 10. MASTERS: Unknown.

DATE: November 4. MASTERS: Unknown.

DATE: November 29. MUSICIANS: Vocal, Roy Rogers; Spade Cooley's Orchestra, the Buckle-Busters. MASTERS: DLA 2247, "New Worried Mind" (Daffan/Davis), #5906; DLA 2248, "Time Changes Everything" (T. Duncan), #5908; DLA 2249 "Yesterday" (Harrison/Wilhite), #5908; DLA 2250, "Melody of the Plains" (Berlau/Sive), #5906.

1941

DATE: August 25. MASTERS: DLA 2685, "Don't Be Blue, Little Pal, Don't Be Blue" (Kanter/Jurgens), #5986; DLA 2686, "You Were Right and I Was Wrong" (J. Crockett, Jr.), #6074; DLA 2687, "I'm Trusting in You" (Rose), #5986; DLA 2688, "I'll Be Honest with You" (Rose/Autry), #6016.

DATE: September 4. MUSICIANS: Same. MASTERS: DLA 2726, "Down by the Old Alamo" (Porter/Lange), #5987; DLA 2727, "I Know I Shouldn't Worry, but I Do" (Foree/Reilly/Conners), #6060; DLA 2728,

Roy in a singing and guitar playing pose for *Under Western Stars*, publicity photo, 1938.

"A Gay Ranchero" (Espinosa/Tuvim/ Luban), #5987; DLA 2729, "Blue Bonnet Lane" (C. Walker), #6016.

DATE: September 12. MUSICIANS: Same. MASTERS: DLA 2756, "It's Just the Same" (J. Crockett, Jr.) #6074; DLA 2757, "Don't Waste Your Love on Me" (Unknown), #6037; DLA 2758, "I've Sold My Saddle for an Old Guitar" (Allan), #6092; DLA 2759, "A Man and His Song (Unknown), #6037. (Between the years of 1940 and 1942, Roy recorded 34 songs for Decca Records.)

1942
DATE: March 4 and or 20. MASTERS: DLA 2955, "You're the Answer to My Prayer" (Unknown), #6041; DLA 2956, "Little Old Church on the Hilltop" (Beacon), #6060; DLA 2957, "She Gave Her Heart to a Soldier Boy" (Sanders/Bryan), #6041; DLA 2958, "Think of Me" (Loring/Cross/Rogers), #6052.

1943–44
Roy didn't do any recording for the usual record releases in 1943 and 1944, probably because of the war and the shellac shortage.

1943–47
COMPANY: Republic Pictures. Many recordings were made that would be used for soundtracks for Roy's movies. In addition to writing a lot of original songs, his group would record their own version of "Your Hit Parade" radio show songs. Songs include the following: "My Saddle Pals and I," "Silver Stars," "Purple Sage," "Eyes of Blue," "The Everlasting Hills of Oklahoma," "Rainbow Over Texas," "My Adobe Hacienda," "Cowboy Country," "I'm an Old Cowhand"; a medley composed of "Springtime in the Rockies," "Tumbling Tumbleweeds," "Highways Are Happy Ways," "Mexicali Rose," "Git Along Little Dogies," "Don't Fence Me In," "Utah Trail," "It's an Old Custom," "The Cowboy Jubilee," "Ride 'Em Cowboy," "Lights of the Old Santa Fe," "Ride Ranger Ride," "The Lonesome Cowboy Blues," "Red River Valley," "On the Old Spanish Trail."

1945
Unless otherwise specified, the record company is RCA Victor. DATE: August 4 and or

10. MUSICIANS: Vocal, Roy Rogers, Sons of the Pioneers; conductor, Perry Botkin; piano, Frank Leithner; bass, Joseph "Country" Washburne; drums, John Cyr; accordion, Earl Hatch; viola, Leon Fleitman; trumpet, Robert Kimic; clarinet, Jack Mayhew; saxophone, Morton Friedman; violin, Sam Freed, Mischa Russell, Gerald Joyce; cello, Cy Bernard. MASTERS: D5-AB-1113, "Along the Navajo Trail" (Markes/Charles/ Delange), #20-1730-A, #20-3075; D5-AB-1114, "Don't Blame It All on Me" (Barrett/ Wilkins), #20-1730-B; D5-AB-1115, "You Can't Break My Heart" (Cooley/S. Rogers), #20-1782-A; D5-AB-1116, "You Should Know" (Barrett/Wilkins), #20-1782-B.

1946
DATE: January 6 and or 10. MUSICIANS: Vocal, Roy Rogers, Sons of the Pioneers; guitars, Karl Farr, Charles R. Roberts; bass, George "Deuce Spriggins" Braunsdorf; violin, Mischa Russell, Alexander Murray, Harry B. Bluestone, accordion, Fred Tony Travers; clarinet/saxophone, Barnet Sorkin. MASTERS: D6-VB-2004, "Rock Me to Sleep in My Saddle" (Marion), #20-1815-A; D6-VB-2005, "I Wish I Had Never Met Sunshine" (Evans/Haldeman/Autry), #20-1815-B, #21-0113; D6-VB-2006, "A Little White Cross on the Hill" (F. Rose), #20-1872; D6-VB-2007, "I Can't Go On This Way" (F. Rose), #20-1872-B.

DATE: September 4. MUSICIANS: Vocal, Roy Rogers and Country Washburne Orchestra. MASTERS: "I'm Restless" (F. Rose), #20-2236-B; "I Never Had a Chance" (F. Rose), #20-2124-B; "No Children Allowed" (D. Parker), #20-1994, 21-0113-B, 48-0116-B, 48-0028-B; "My Heart Went That-a-Way" (D. Evans/R. Rogers), #20-1994, 21-0114, 48-0028; "My Chickashay Gal" (S. Cooley/ S. Rogers), #20-2124-A.

1947
DATE: February 24. MUSICIANS: Same. MASTERS: "Do Ya or Don'tcha" (S. Cooley/ S. Rogers), #20-2437-A; "Dangerous Ground" (S. Nelson/M. Leeds/E. Nelson), #20-2236-A.

DATE: March 3. MUSICIANS: Vocal, Roy Rogers; conductor, Country Washburne; guitar, Jimmy O. Wyble; fiddle, Billy Hill, Nicholas Pisani, Carl Hunt; accordion,

Arthur A. Wensel; steel guitar, Noel Boggs; drums, John Mountjoy; bass, Stanley Puls. MASTERS: D7-VB-484, "I've Got a Feelin'" (M. Leeds/F. Wise/S. Nelson/E. Nelson), #20-2320-B; D7-VB-485, "Saddle Serenade" (Markes/Stone) #20-2437-B; D7-VB-486, "Make Believe Cowboy" (C. Lucas), #20-2604-B.

DATE: May 7 and or 18. MUSICIANS: Vocal, Roy Rogers; orchestra conductor, Spade Cooley; guitar, Earl E. Colbert; steel guitar, Noel Boggs; bass, Stanley Puls; fiddle, Billy Hill, Harry Simovitz, Spade Cooley; piano, John Haynes; accordion, Larry DePaul; drums, John Mountjoy. MASTERS: D7-VB-547, "On the Old Spanish Trail" (Kennedy/Smith), #20-2320-A, 20-3074. (At this session, a few square dance tunes with Roy doing the calls may have also been recorded.) "Skip to My Lou," #21-0127; "Rickett's Reel," #21-0127; "Old Joe Clark," #21-0128; "Sycamore Reel," #21-0128; "Oh Dem Golden Slippers," #21-0129; "Lucky Leather Breeches," #21-0129.

DATE: October 8 and or 23. PLACE: Chicago. MUSICIANS: Vocal, Roy Rogers; conductor, Dave Boehme; guitar, Karl Farr; steel guitar, Jesse Colvard; bass fiddle, Pat Brady; accordion, August Klein; fiddles Chuck Hurter, George Kayser, Dave Boehme; piano, Franklin Wolfe; drums, Thomas C. Summers, Jr. MASTERS: D7-VB-1094, "San Fernando Valley" (G. Jenkins), #20-3075; D7-VB-1095, "Roll On Texas Moon" (J. Elliott), #20-3073; D7-VB-1096, "Don't Fence Me In" (C. Porter), #20-3073; D7-VB-1097, "Home in Oklahoma" (J. Elliott), #20-3076.

DATE: October 24. PLACE: Chicago. MUSICIANS: Same. MASTERS: D7-VB-1098, "Yellow Rose of Texas" (P.D.), #20-3074; D7-VB-1099, "A Gay Ranchero" (Tuvim/Luban/Espinosa), #20-3076; D7-VB-1100, "Hawaiian Cowboy" (R. Allen), #20-2804; D7-VB-1101, "Hasta La Vista" (J. Jackson), #20-3050.

DATE: December 1. MUSICIANS: Vocal, Roy Rogers, Lloyd Perryman, Ken Carson, Bob Nolan, Tim Spencer; guitar, Karl Farr; fiddle, Hugh Farr; bass, Pat Brady, George "Shug" Fisher. MASTERS: D7-VB-2133, "Blue Shadows on the Trail" (Lange/Daniel), #20-

2780; D7-VB-2134, "Pecos Bill" (Lange/Daniel), #20/2780; D7-VB-2135, "That Palomino Pal o' Mine" (Kenwood/Kingsley), #21-0077-A; D7-VB-2138, "Home on the Range" (Higley/Kelley), #21-0077.

DATE: December 3. MUSICIANS: Vocal, Roy Rogers; conductor, Billy Hill; steel guitar, Earl "Joaquin" Murphey; bass, Alan Barker; accordion, Milton DeLugg; fiddle, Billy Hill, Carl Hunt, Max Fidler; piano, Richard Anderson; drums, Jackie Mills. MASTERS: D7-VB-2150, "I Met a Miss in Texas" (Cunliffe/Fulton), #21-0030-A; D7-VB-2151, "That Miss from Mississippi" (Unknown), #20-3313; D7-VB2152, "I'm A-Rollin'" (Unknown), #20-3313; D7-VB-2153, "I'm Gonna Gallop, Gallop, Gallop to Gallup, New Mexico" (Sheridan/Franklin), #20-2917; D7-VB-2154, "The Kid with the Rip in His Pants" (J. Owens), #20-3154-B; D7-VB-2155, "Dusty" (D. Evans/R. Rogers), #20-3154-A.

DATE: December 4. MUSICIANS: Vocal, Roy Rogers; conductor, Billy Hill; bass, Alan Barker; fiddles, Billy Hill, Carl Hunt, Max Fidler; accordion, Milton DeLugg; piano, Richard Anderson; guitars, John Weis, Cameron Hill; steel guitar, Earl "Joaquin" Murphey; drums, Jackie Mills. MASTERS: D7-VB-2156, "With a Sweep of My Sombrero" (L. Penny), #21-0030; D7-VB-2157, "Old Fashioned Cowboy" (Howard/Erwin), #20-2917-B; D7-VB-2158, "Betsy" (Shand/Kapp/Eaton), #20-3059-A.

DATE: December 9. MUSICIANS: Vocal, Roy Rogers, Bob Nolan, Lloyd Perryman, Ken Carson, Tim Spencer, Karl Farr, Hugh Farr; bandleader, Hugh Far; bass, Pat Brady, George Fisher, Alan Barker; guitar, Hugh Farr, Norman Malkin, Cameron Hill; steel guitar, Earl "Joaquin" Murphey; fiddle, Hugh Farr, Billy Hunt, Carl Hunt, Max Fidler, Mort Herbert; accordion, Stanley Ellison, Milton DeLugg; drums, Jackie Mills; piano, John Haynes, Richard Anderson. MASTER: "Pecos Bill" (Daniel/Lange; story by Erdman Penner), #(W) Y-375.

DATE: December 11. MUSICIANS: Vocal, Roy Rogers, George "Gabby" Hayes, the Lore of the West Singers; Country Washburne Orchestra. MASTER: "Lore of the West," Pt. 1-4 (Washburne/Carling), #(W)Y-394. (Apparently Roy was too busy to hit the recording studio, or the head of the merchandising department didn't want anything to interfere with the sales of the *Lore of the West* record set. Only one song was recorded.)

1948
DATE: Unknown. MUSICIANS: Vocal, Roy Rogers; Frank Worth Orchestra. MASTER: "Roy Rogers' Rodeo" (J. Richards), #(W)Y-413.

1949
DATE: August 24. MUSICIANS: Vocal, Roy Rogers, Dale Evans, Foy Willing and the Riders of the Purple Sage; conductor, Frank Worth, steel guitar, Joaquin Murphey; fiddle, B. Gill, K. Sirinsky, Harry Simovitz; cello, C. Bernard; guitar, R. Idriss; viola, L. Kievman. MASTERS: D9-VB-720, "May the Good Lord Take a Likin' to Ya" (P. Tinturin), #20-0373; possible recordings at this session—"Christmas Night on the Plains" (C. Walker), #21-0125, 48-0128; "Wonderful Christmas Night" (Porter/Mitchell, #21-0125, 48-0128.

DATE: September 3 and or 20. MUSICIANS: Vocal, Roy Rogers; conductor, Billy Hill; guitar, Jimmy Widener; bass, A. Caldwell; drums, Pee Wee Adams; organ, F. Haynes; fiddle, Billy Hill, A. Soldi. MASTERS: D9-VB-743, "Little Hula Honey" (Leeds/Hayes), #2100148, 48-0152; "Mommy, Can I Take My Doll to Heaven?" (C. Coben), #21-0148, 48-0152; "Next to the X in Texas" (Altman/Britton/Micketla), #21-0173-B, 48-0207-B.

DATE: December 1 and or 14. MUSICIANS: Vocal, Roy Rogers, Lloyd Perryman, Ken Curtis, Tommy Doss; conductor, Robert Bain; bass, L. Edelman; guitar, J. W. Marshall; organ, K. Pandit. MASTERS: D9-VB-789, "Stampede" (D. Rice/F. Willing), #21-154-A, 48-0161-A; D9-VB-799, "Church Music" (B. Russell), #21-154-A, 48-0161-A.

DATE: Unknown. MUSICIANS: Vocal, Roy Rogers, Dale Evans, unidentified vocalists and orchestra. MASTERS: "The Old Rugged Cross" (G. Bennard), #(W)P-286; "In the Garden" (C. A. Miles), #(W)P286; "What a Friend We Have in Jesus" (Scriven/Fischer), #(W)P-286; "I Love to Tell the Story" (Hankey/Fischer), #(W)P-286; "Since Jesus Came into My Heart" (McDaniel/Gabriel), #(W)P-286; "He Is So Precious to Me" (C. H. Gabriel), #(W)P-286; "Where He Leads Me" (Blandy/Norris), #(W)P-286; "Love Lifted Me" (Rowe/Smith), #(W)P-286.

DATE: Unknown. MUSICIANS: Vocal, Roy Rogers, the Roy Rogers Riders; Frank Worth Orchestra. MASTERS: "Me and My Teddy Bear" (Winters/Coots), #21-0331, 47-0227; "Buffalo Billy" (Redmond/Cavanaugh/Weldon), #21-0331, 47-0227; "Frosty the Snowman" (Nelson/Rollins), #21-0374; "Gabby the Gobbler" (C. Coben), #21-0374-B.

1950
DATE: July 8. MUSICIANS: Vocal, Roy Rogers, Dale Evans. MASTERS: EO-VB-3720, "Smiles Are Made out of the Sunshine" (R. Gilbert), #21-0373; EO-VB-3721, "Easter Parade" (I. Berlin), #21-0423-B; "Yellow Bonnets and Polka Dot Shoes" (Carpenter/Stewart), #21-0399-A, 48-0399-A; "No Bed of Roses" (D. Evans/R. Rogers), #21-0399-B, 48-0399-B.

DATE: July 21. MUSICIANS: Vocal, Roy Rogers and quartet; conductor, Jack Hayes; steel guitar, Noel Boggs; guitar, Jimmy Wyble; bass, G. F. Boujie; fiddle, Billy Hill; organ, D. Bacal; drums, Muddy Berry. MASTERS: EO-VB-3730, "Peter Cottontail" (Nelson/Rollins), #21-0423-A, 21-0173-A; EO-VB-3731, "Ride Son Ride" (D. Liebert), #21-0414-A; EO-VB-3732, "The Story of Bucky and Dan" (Howard/Erwin), #21-0414-B; EO-VB-3733, "Cowboy Heaven" (F. Marvin), #21-0458, 48-0458.

1951
DATE: April 4 and or 27. MUSICIANS: Vocal, Roy Rogers; conductor, Frank Worth; guitar, Jimmy Bryant; bass, P. Tonniges; piano, D. Ferris; viola, L. Kievman; cello, R. Kramer; trombone, A. Lincoln; fiddle, B. Gill, K. Sirinsky, H. Sims; trumpet, G. Werth; steel guitar, Speedy West. MASTERS: EL-VB-623, "Buckeye Cowboy" (R. Rogers/D. Evans), #21-0479-B; EL-VB-624, "Don't Ever Leave Me"** (Kay/Worth); EL-VB-625, "I Wish I Wuz" (S. Kuller/L. Murray), #21-0479-A; "Piney Jane" (C. Walker), #21-0458-A, 48-0458-A.

Popular Western Swing bandleader Spade Cooley backed Roy on RCA Victor recordings.

DATE: June 29. MUSICIANS: Vocal, Roy Rogers; conductor, Frank Worth; steel guitar, Speedy West; bass, P. Tonniges; drums, L. Singer; guitar, Jimmy Bryant; fiddle, B. Gill, D. Holguin, H. Sims; piano, D. Ferris. MASTERS: EL-VB-658, "Horseshoe Moon" (G. Walker), #20-4424, 47-4424; EL-VB-659, Unknown recording; EL-VB-660, "Home Sweet Oklahoma" (T. Glazer), #20-4424, 47-4424.

DATE: Unknown. MUSICIANS: Vocal, Roy Rogers and the Roy Rogers Riders; Frank Worth Orchestra. MASTERS: "Good Luck, Good Health, God Bless You" (Adams/Le-Royal), #21-0496-B; "The Lamp of Faith"

(S. Fenne), #21-0496-A; "Katy (The Hop-
pingest Kangaroo)" (C. Coben), #21-0438-A,
47-0263; "Yogy the Dogie" (Kennedy/
Alstone), #21-0438-A, 47-0263.

DATE: July. MUSICIANS: Vocal, Roy Rogers
and the Roy Rogers Riders; unidentified
musicians. MASTERS: EL-VB-672, "The
Three Little Dwarfs" (S. Hamblen), #20-
4301, 47-4301; "The Kiwi Bird" (Whitcup/
Gierlach), #20-4664, 47-4237; "The Little
White Duck" (Barrows/Zaritzky), #20-4664,
47-4664; "Punky Punkin'" (Unknown),
#20-4237, 47-4237; EL-VB-685, "Daddy's
Little Cowboy" (T. Spencer/Rowe/G.
Spencer), #20, 4301, 47-4301.

DATE: Unknown. MUSICIANS: Vocal, Roy
Rogers; Frank Worth Orchestra. MASTERS:
EL-VB3828, "The Masked Marauder — Part
One" (Richards/Worth), #20-0297, 47-0297;
EL-VB3829, "The Masked Marauder — Con-
clusion" (Richards/Worth), #20-0297, 47-
0297; "The Television Ambush — Part One,"
"The Television Ambush — Conclusion,"
(Richards/Worth), #45-5328.

1952
DATE: Unknown. MUSICIANS: Vocal, Roy
Rogers. MASTERS: E2-VB-5215, "Egbert, the
Easter Egg" (Corday/Carr), #20-4526, 45-
5336, 47-4526.

DATE: March 4 and or 5. MUSICIANS: Vocal,
Roy Rogers; backup vocalists, R. Linn,
W. Reeve, G. Mershon, B. Dole; conductor,
Henry Rene; steel guitar, Noel Boggs; bass,
A. Lambert; drums, Muddy Berry; piano,
S. Wrightsman; fiddle, Billy Hill; guitar, Ed-
die Kirk; electric guitar, Jimmy Bryant;
organ, Paul Sells. MASTERS: E2-VB-5284,
"There's a Cloud in My Valley of Sunshine"
(Hope/ Moraine), #20-4634, 47-4634; E2-VB-
5285, "A Four Legged Friend" (J. Brooks),
#20-4634, 47-4634; E2-VB-5286, "Peace in
the Valley" (T. A. Dorsey), #20-4732,
47-4732; E2-VB-5287, "Precious Memories"
(Martin/ Jones), #20-4732, 47-4732.

DATE: April 4 and or 21. MUSICIANS: Vocal,
Roy Rogers, Dale Evans, The Whipporwills;
backup vocalist, Georgia Brown (Juanita

**Right: The advertising for Roy's musical
Westerns even showed the songs that were performed.**

Here's America's favorite entertainer in a musical adventure you
won't want to miss!

ROY ROGERS
King of the Cowboys
and
TRIGGER Smartest
Horse in the
Movies
in

DALE EVANS
George Cleveland
Harry Shannon
Grant Withers
BOB NOLAN
and the
**SONS OF THE
PIONEERS**

Songs
"Take It Easy"
"Lucky Me, Unlucky You"
"Song of the Rover"
"Down In The Old
Town Hall"
"Western Wonderland"

A REPUBLIC PICTURE

Vastine); conductor, Jack Hayes; mandolin, Doug Dalton; bass, Dusty Rhodes; accordion, Paul Sells; guitar, Roy Lanham, Gene Monbeck; drums, S. Weiss; fiddle, Harry Bluestone, Mischa Russell, Billy Hill. MASTERS: E2-VB-5313, "California Rose" (Livingston/R. Evans), #20-4709, 47-4709; "You've Got a Rope Around My Heart" (Unknown), #20-4950, 47-4950; E2-VB-5314, "Hazy Mountains" (D. Evans), #20-4950, 47-4950; "Happy Trails" (D. Evans), #20-4709, #47-4709.

RCA Victor unissued recordings. Information is not confirmed on these recordings. "Bambo the Black Sheep," "Floppy the Bashful Puppy," "Dream of You," "Pine Trees in Heaven," "Smiles," "When You Dream." The following songs were issued in Canada on Quality Records (information also not confirmed): "The Bible Tells Me So," "Lonesome Valley."

Mid–1950s
Roy and Dale backed by the Mitch Miller Orchestra recorded Little Golden Records for children. See Chapter 12.

Unless otherwise specified, the record company is Capitol Records.

1970
DATE: October 5. RELEASED: "The Country Side of Roy Rogers," CAP ST 594. (LP)

1971
DATE: May 15. RELEASED: "A Man from Duck Run," CAP ST 785. (LP)

1972
DATE: June 15. RELEASED: "Take a Little Love and Pass It On," CAP ST 11020. (LP)

Early mid–1970s
RELEASED: "Christmas Is Always," CAP ST 2818. (LP) Roy stopped recording for Capitol Records because the company often asked him to learn new material at the last minute when he arrived for a recording session at the studio.

1980
COMPANY: MCA Records. RELEASED: "Ride, Concrete Cowboy, Ride." This was the theme song to the film *Smoky and the Bandit 2*,

sung by Roy and the Sons of the Pioneers. It was released as a single and made the charts.

1980s
Several of the companies for whom Roy worked in the past transferred the masters into LP concepts and released albums made up of many of the old favorites. A record company in Germany that specializes in releasing old American recordings released *The King of the Cowboys* (Bear Family Records, BFX 15124) (LP), featuring Roy with the Sons of the Pioneers. Most of the selections are secular. MCA Records, which owned all the old Decca masters, released "Empty Saddles" (MCA 1563) (LP), also mostly secular selections.

1986
Roy and Dale had recorded over 400 songs at this point. MCA released old material on cassette and titled it "Melody of the Plains." Songs included: "Time Changes Everything," "Melody of the Plains," "Nobody's Fault but My Own," "I'm Trusting in You," "Wondering Why," "I'll Be Honest with You Dear," "Blue Bonnet Lane," "Chapel in the Valley." "Lore of the West" is rereleased, cassette only, RCA CAK-1074.

1990
COMPANY: RCA Records. DATE: Unknown. Stan Moress approached RCA head man, Joe Galante, with the idea of Roy recording again. Roy wasn't excited at the prospect but agreed. He had only recently gone into the studio to record "Happy Trails" with Randy Travis. He sang duets with all the stars involved in the *Tribute* album, via the sound engineers. The "Happy Trails" song with Randy Travis, was released on Travis' LP, *Heroes and Friends*. The *Tribute* LP by Roy was released in September/October, 1991. It was issued on CD, and there were a number of special limited edition vinyl picture discs made available.

Extended Play (EP) and Long Play (LP) Discography

EPs

Hymns of Faith (two-record set), RCA Victor EPS 3158, 1954.

Pecos Bill, Bluebird EYA-5.

Roy Rogers Roundup, RCA Victor EPA-253, WP-253. "My Chickashay Gal," "A Little White Cross on the Hill, "I Wish I Had Never Met Sunshine," "No Children Allowed," "My Heart Went That-a-Way," "Dusty."

Roy Rogers Souvenir Album (two-record set), RCA Victor EPB-3041, 1952. Exists in 78 RPM record set as well; Musical Smart Set. Contains songs from eight of Roy's movies. Released by Republic Pictures Corp. See LP's for song listing.

Sweet Hour of Prayer, RCA Victor EPA-2-1439, 1957.

LPs

The Best of Roy Rogers, RCA Camden ACL1-0953. "My Chickashay Gal," "Don't Fence Me In," "I Wish I Had Never Met Sunshine," "Blue Shadows on the Trail," "My Heart Went That-a-Way," "A Gay Ranchero," "The Yellow Rose of Texas," "That Palomino Pal o' Mine," "Along the Navajo Trail," "On the Old Spanish Trail," "Roll On Texas Moon," "Rock Me to Sleep in My Saddle."

The Best of Roy Rogers, Curb Records D4-77392 (Cass), D2-77392 (CD). "Lovenworth," "Money Can't Buy Love," "Happy Anniversary," "These Are the Good Old Days," "Candy Kisses," "Tennessee Waltz," "Send Me the Pillow That You Dream On," "He'll Have to Go," "You and Me Against the World," "In Another Lifetime," "Lay Some Happiness on Me," "Talkin' About Love."

The Bible Tells Me So, Capitol ST-1745, 1962. "The Bible Tells Me So," "Whispering Hope," "Just a Closer Walk with Thee," "In the Sweet By and By," "Peace in the Valley," "Pass Me Not," "It Is No Secret," "Amazing Grace," "Take My Hand, Precious Lord," "The Love of God," "I'd Rather Have Jesus," "How Great Thou Art."

Christmas Is Always, Capitol ST-2818, 1967. "It's the Most Wonderful Time of the Year," "Happy Birthday, Gentle Savior," "Christmas Is Always," "I'll Be Home for Christmas," "Star of Hope," "A Christmas Prayer,"

"Merry Christmas, My Darling," "December Time," "Let There Be Peace on Earth," "What Child Is This," "Sweet Little Jesus Boy," "What Color Is Love?" "Sleigh Ride/ Jingle Bells."

Classic Country Western, Radiola Records 4 MR-2, 1984.

The Country Side of Roy Rogers, Capitol ST-594, October 5, 1970 (released again by Stetson Records as HAT-3116). "Money Can't Buy Love," "I Washed My Face in the Morning Dew," "The Blizzard," "Down Home," "Okie from Muskogee," "The Fightin' Side of Me," "Green Green Grass of Home," "The Night Guard," "Vision at the Peace Table," "You and Me Against the World."

The Days of the Yodeling Cowboy, vol. 2, Cowgirlboy Records (Unknown #).

Decca/Coral, John Edwards Memorial Foundation, AFM 721 (contains songs from the 1930s). "Way Out There," "Tumbling Tumbleweeds" (1934), "Kilocycle Stomp" (1935), "A Melody from the Sky, "Bluebonnet Girl" (1936).

Empty Saddles, MCA Records MCA 1563, 1983. "I'm an Old Cowhand," "Tumbling Tumbleweeds," "A Melody from the Sky," "One More Ride," "Over the Santa Fe Trail," "Westward Ho," "Cajon Stomp," "Empty Saddles," "When I Leave This World Behind," "Blue Prairie," "Roving Cowboy," "Blue Bonnet Girl," "Kilocycle Stomp," "Echoes from the Hills."

The Good Life, Word Records WSA 8761, 1977. ("Old Time Religion"/"Cowboy Camp Meeting"/"Everytime I Feel the Spirit"/ "Ezekiel Saw De Wheel"/"Do Lord"), "Love of the Children," "God's Gonna Do It," "Lord Have Mercy on My Soul," "I Found It in Jesus," "Home Where I Belong," "He Walks with the Wild and the Lonely," "Jesus Walk Past Me," "Through It All," "Happy Trails."

Happy Trails to You, 20th Century–Fox, 467, 1975 (released again by Nostalgia Merchant Records). "Cowboy Heaven," "A Very Fine Lady," "Hoppy, Gene and Me," "Tennessee Stud," "Happy Trails," "Don't Cry Baby," "On the Old Spanish Trail/Along the Navajo Trail/Blue Shadows on the Trail," "Cold, Cold Heart," "Good News, Bad News," "Don't Ever Wear It for Him."

(Roy recorded a dozen songs for 20th Century–Fox in 1974.)

Hoppy, Gene and Me, Nostalgia Merchant (Unknown #), 1974. (Originally released on 20th Century Records, titled "Happy Trails to You." Songs are same as LP above.)

Hymns of Faith, RCA Victor LPM-3168, 1954, 10-inch LP. "The Old Rugged Cross," "In the Garden," "What a Friend We Have in Jesus," "I Love to Tell the Story," "Since Jesus Came into My Heart," "He Is So Precious to Me," "Where He leads Me," "Love Lifted Me."

In the Sweet By and By, Word Records, WST-8589, 1973. "In the Sweet By and By," "Jesus in the Morning," "If I Can Help Somebody," "I'll Fly Away," "Peace in the Valley," "On the Wings of a Dove," "The Cowboy's Prayer," "Softly and Tenderly," "This Little Light of Mine," "Whispering Hope," "Star of Hope."

Jesus Loves Me, RCA Victor, Bluebird LBY-1022, 1959; RCA Camden, CAL 1022, 1960. "Read the Bible and Pray," "Jesus Loves Me," "Do What the Good Book Says," "I'll Be a Sunbeam," "The Circuit Ridin' Preacher," "Did You Stop to Pray?," "Watch What You Do," "Wonderful Guest," "The Lord Is Counting on You," "The Bible Tells Me So," "A Cowboy Sunday Prayer," "I'll Pray for You Until We Meet Again."

Legendary Songs of the Old West, Columbia Records P4 15542, 1981. Columbia Special Products, four-record set, including forty songs, eight of which are 1930s ARC recordings by Roy Rogers and the Sons of the Pioneers. "Song of the Bandit," "Hold That Critter Down," "Open Range Ahead," "Billie the Kid," "Cowboy Night Herd Songs," "I Sold My Saddle for an Old Guitar," "Hadie Brown," "When the Black Sheep Gets the Blues."

Lore of the West, RCA Camden CAL-1074, 1966.

Mackintosh & T. J., RCA (Penland Productions), APL 1520. "All Around Cowboys," "Back in the Saddle Again," "Ride Me Down

Easy," "Gardenia Waltz," "Bob Wills Is Still the King," "Shopping," "(Stay All Night) Stay a Little Longer," "Crazy Arms," "All Around Cowboy."

A Man from Duck Run, Capitol Records ST-785, c. 1971. "Lovenworth," "If I Ever Get That Close Again," "I Never Picked Cotton," "Everything Changes," "Happy Anniversary," "Come Sundown," "You Brought Me Love," "Take Your Time," "Happiness," "Spotted Dog Named Sam."

Many Happy Trails, Teletex C-7702, 1984, two-record set, Roy, Dale, Dusty. "Skyball Paint," "Silver on the Sage," "Lookin' Through the Eyes of a Fool," "Bread Upon the Water/Count Your Blessings," "Christmas on the Plains/Silent Night/O Little Town of Bethlehem," "Texas Plains," "Pretend," "Happy Anniversary," "Happiness," "May the Road Rise Up," "Didn't You," "Hoppy, Gene and Me," "Great Day/When the Roll Is Called Up Yonder/When the Saints Go Marching In," "This Is My Country/This Land Is Your Land/God Bless America," "Make Someone Happy/You're Nobody Till Somebody Loves You," "Though Autumn's Coming On," "Country Lady," "You and Me Against the World," "King of the Cowboys," "Happy Trails."

Melody of the Plains, MCA Records MCAC-20361, 1986.

Okeh Western Swing, Columbia Records EG-37324. (Various Artists)

The Original Pioneer Trio Sings Songs of the Hills and Plains, AFM (Unknown #).

Pardners, Walt Disney Productions (nine songs by Roy, all previous recordings), unknown date.

Pecos Bill, RCA Camden CAL-1054, 1964.

Peter Cottontail and His Friends, RCA Camden CAL-1097, 1968.

Peter Cottontail, Golden Records 81, 1962.

Roll On Texas Moon, Bear Family Records BDP-15203 (Picture Disc), 1986. (These are 1948 RCA Victor recordings.) "The Yellow Rose of Texas" (D7-VB-1098-1), "Don't Fence Me In" (D7-VB-1099-1), "A Gay Ranchero" (D7-VB-1095-1), "Roll On Texas Moon" (D7-VB-1095-1), "I Met a Miss in

Texas" (D7-VB-2151-1), "On the Old Spanish Trail" (D7-VB-0547-2), "May the Good Lord Take a Likin' to Ya" (D7-VB-0720-1), "San Fernando Valley" (D7-VB-0720-1), "I'm A-Rollin'" (D7-VB-2152-1), "Little Hula Honey" (D9-VB-0743-1), "California Rose" (E2-VB-6313-2), "Home in Oklahoma" (D7-VB-1097-1), "Rock Me to Sleep in My Saddle" (D6-VB-2004-1), "Old Fashioned Cowboy" (D7-VB-2157-2), "There's a Cloud in the Valley of Sunshine" (E2-VB-5284-1), "Along the Navajo Trail" (D5-AB-1113-1).

Roy Rogers, Columbia Records, Columbia Historic Edition FC-38907, 1984. These were originally ARC recordings, released through Columbia; they are mostly secular songs and some previous issued mixed with unissued material from the 1930s. "Ridin', Ropin'," "That Pioneer Mother of Mine," "She's All Wet Now," "A Lonely Ranger Am I," "The Mail Must Go Through," "Headin' for Texas and Home," "Old Pioneers," "When I Camped Under the Stars," "Dust," "My Little Lady (Hadie Brown)."

Roy Rogers: Country Music Hall of Fame, MCA 10548. "I'm an Old Cowhand," "Moonlight on the Prairie," "You Waited Too Long," "Chapel in the Valley," "Melody of the Plains," "New Worried Mind," "Yesterday," "Time Changes Everything," "Don't Be Blue, Little Pal, Don't Be Blue," "I'm Trusting in You," "A Gay Ranchero," "Blue Bonnet Lane," "Don't Waste Your Love on Me," "A Man and His Song," "She Gave Her Heart to a Soldier Boy," "I Sold My Saddle for an Old Guitar."

Roy Rogers and Dale Evans Song Wagon, Golden Records GRC-6, c. 1950s. Reissued as *16 Great Songs of the Old West*. "Song Wagon," "I Ride an Old Paint," "Whoopee-Ti-Yi-Yo," "Home on the Range," "Colorado Trail," "The Railroad Corral," "Tumbling Tumbleweeds," "Cool Water," "The Streets of Laredo," "The Night Herding Song," "Red River Valley," "Doney Gal," "Goodbye, Old Paint," "Bury Me Out on the Lone Prairie," "The Cowman's Prayer."

Roy Rogers and the Sons of the Pioneers— The Republic Years, Varese Sarabande Records STV-81212, 1984. Sarabande Records issued a very important LP produced

from the original Republic Pictures 78 RPM acetate masters recorded in the 1940s and 1950s. Most of these selections are from the soundtracks of Roy's Republic feature films. "My Saddle Pals and I," "Silver Stars, Purple Sage, Eyes of Blue," "The Everlasting Hills of Oklahoma," "Rainbow Over Texas," "My Adobe Hacienda," "Cowboy Country," "I'm an Old Cowhand," "Springtime in the Rockies/Tumbling Tumbleweeds/Highways Are Happy Ways," "Mexicali Rose," "Git Along Little Dogies," "Don't Fence Me In," "Utah Trail," "The Cowboy Jubilee," "Ride 'Em Cowboy," "Lights of Old Santa Fe," "It's an Old Fashioned Custom," "Ride, Ranger, Ride," "The Lonesome Cowboy Blues," "Red River Valley," "On the Old Spanish Trail."

Roy Rogers, King of the Cowboys, Bear Family Records BFX-15124, 1983. "Hawaiian Cowboy" (D7-VB-1100-1), Hasta La Vista (D7-VB-1101-1), "(There'll Never Be Another) Pecos Bill" (D7-VB-2104), "I'm Gonna Gallop, Gallop, Gallop to Gallup, New Mexico" (D7-VB-2153-1), "Stampede" (D9-VB-789-1), "With a Sweep of My Sombrero" (D7-VB-2156), "Saddle Serenade" (D7-VB-485-1), "Make Believe Cowboy" (D7-VB-486-2), "Horseshoe Moon" (D7-VB-658-1), "Church Music" (D7-VB-799), "The Story of Bucky and Dan" (EO-VB-3732-1), "Cowboy Heaven" (EO-VB-3733-1), "Ride, Son, Ride" (EO-VB-3731-1), "Don't Ever Leave Me" (E1-VB-624-1), "Buck-Eye Cowboy" (E1-VB-623-1), "A Four-Legged Friend" (E2-VB-5258-1).

The Roy Rogers Show, Radiola Records MR-1032, May 8, 1945, 1974.

Roy Rogers Souvenir Album RCA Victor LPM-3041, 10-inch, 1952. "Don't Fence Me In," "The Yellow Rose of Texas," "San Fernando Valley," "A Gay Ranchero," "Home in Oklahoma," "Along the Navajo Trail," "On the Old Spanish Trail," "Roll On, Texas Moon."

Roy Rogers Souvenir Album, RCA Victor and Musical Smart Set (two 78-RPM records), 1940s. "Don't Fence Me In," "On the Old Spanish Trail," "Home in Oklahoma," "Along the Navajo Trail," "San Fernando Valley," "A Gay Ranchero," "Roll On Texas Moon," "Yellow Rose of Texas."

Roy Rogers, Tribute, RCA 3024 1R (LP), 2R (CD), 4R (Cass), 1991. "That's How the West Was Swung" (Roy, Kentucky Headhunters), "Here's Hopin'" (Roy, Randy Travis), "Hold On Partner" (Roy, Clint Black), "Tumbling Tumbleweeds" (Roy, K. T. Oslin, Restless Heart), "Little Joe the Wrangler" (Roy, EmmyLou Harris), "When Payday Rolls Around" (Roy, Ricky Van Shelton), "Final Frontier" (Roy, Kathy Mattea), "Don't Fence Me In" (Roy, Lori Morgan, Oakridge Boys), "Rodeo Road" (Roy, Willie Nelson), "Alive and Kickin'" (Roy only), "King of the Cowboys" (Dusty), "Happy Trails" (Roy, Dale, Dusty and Friends).

Skip to My Lou and Other Square Dances, RCA Victor P-259. "Skip to My Lou," "Rickett's Reel," "Old Joe Clark," "Sycamore Reel," "Oh Dem Golden Slippers," "Lucky Leather Breeches."

Songs of the Hills and Plains, AFM Records AFM 731. "Cowboy's Night Herd Song," "Railroad Boomer," "Nancy Till," "Black Sheep Blues," "Cider Schottische," "When You and I Were Young, Maggie," "When the Bees Are in the Hive," "Dear Old Western Skies," "Hadie Brown," "At the End of the Lane," "Gentle Nettie Moore," "When the Work's All Done," "Prairie Whing Ding," "Leaning on the Everlasting Arm," "Down the Lane to Happiness," "Sweet Genevieve."

Sons of the Pioneers, Columbia Records, Columbia Historic Edition FC-37439, a mixture of the religious and secular material and the issued and unissued. "Song of the Bandit," "At the Rainbow's End," "Hold That Critter Down," "When the Golden Train Comes Down," "Cajon Stomp," "You Must Come In at the Door," "The Devil's Great Grandson," "Cowboy Night Herd Song," "Send Him Home to Me," "The Touch of God's Hand."

Sons of the Pioneers—Country Music Hall of Fame, MCA 10090. "Way Out There," "Tumbling Tumbleweeds" (1934), "There's a Round-Up in the Sky," "When Our Old Age Pension Check Comes to Our Door," "Echoes from the Hills" (1935), "Hills of Old Wyomin'," "Ride, Ranger, Ride," "One More Ride," (1936).

Sons of the Pioneers—Days of the Yodeling Cowboys, Vol. 2, Cowgirlboy Records LP 5002. "Old MacDonald," "Peekaboo," "Oh Susannah," "Mandy Lee," "Kingdom Coming," "Get On the Golden Train," "Strawberry Roan," "Cabin in the Lane," "Abdul Abulbul Ameer," "A Sandman Lullaby," "A Summer Rain," "Dear Eveline," "Bluebonnets," "The Glendy Burke," "Pop Eye's Spiritual," "West of the Rio Grande."

Sons of the Pioneers—In the Beginning, Vol. 1, Cowgirlboy Records LP 5013. "I Wish I Had Stayed in the Wagon Yard," "Some Folks," "Billy the Kid," "Dixie," "Swanee River," "Big Rock Candy Mountain," "Little Old Sod Shanty," "Beautiful Nell," "Dolly Day," "Beulah Land," "Darling Nellie Grey," "Chicken," "Old Rover," "Keep a-Inchin' Along," "Climb Up Chillun," "Falling Leaf."

Sons of the Pioneers—In the Beginning, Vol. 2, Cowgirlboy Records LP 5014. "Bugler's Blues," "Old Cherry Orchard," "Crawdaddy Song," "Old Black Mountain Trail," "My Old Kentucky Home," "Get Away Old Man," "Eighth of January," "Power in the Blood," "Coming Thru the Rye," "Memories of the Range," "Birmingham Jail," "New River Train," "I Want to Follow a Swallow Back Home to Colorado," "Lane County Bachelor," "Open Up Dem Pearly Gates," "Cowboy's Dance Song."

Sons of the Pioneers, Standard Radio Transcriptions, Pt. 1, Outlaw Records CSR 5. "Swiss Yodel," "When Round-up Is Over," "Hear Dem Bells," "Giddyap Napoleon," "Ain't We Crazy," "Side Walk Waltz," "Bells of Baltimore," "White Mule of Mine," "Sweet Betsy from Pike," "She Came Rollin' Down the Mountain," "Grandfather's Clock," "Little Brown Jug."

Sons of the Pioneers, Standard Radio Transcriptions, Pt. 2, Outlaw Records CSR 6, CSR 6C. "Put On Your Old Gray Bonnet," "Dear Old Girl," "Gospel Train," "Dese Bones Gwine to Rise Again," "Lone Star Trail," "Little Red Barn," "Hills of Old Kentucky," "Little Annie Roonies," "Jim Crack Corn," "Rufus Rastus Johnson Brown," "Jordan Am a Hard Road to Travel," "Threw It Out the Window."

Sweet Hour of Prayer, RCA Victor LPM-1439, 1957 (released again by Stetson Records HAT-3088). "What a Friend We Have in

Jesus," "In the Garden," "The Light of the World Is Jesus," "The Old Rugged Cross," "Near to the Heart of God," "Sweet Hour of Prayer," "I Love to Tell the Story," "Where He Leads Me," "He Is So Precious to Me," "Since Jesus Came into My Heart," "Love Lifted Me."

Take a Little Love and Pass It On, Capitol ST-11020, 1972. "Candy Kisses," "I'll Try a Little Sadness On for Size," "Lay Some Happiness on Me," "Tennessee Waltz," "Leavin' the Leavin' Up to You," "Talkin' About Love," "These Are the Good Old Days," "He'll Have to Go," "Pass It On," "Send Me the Pillow You Dream On."

Way Out West, Country Music Foundation Records, includes songs from 1934 through 1936 sessions. "Way Out There" (1934), "There's a Round-Up in the Sky," "Roving Cowboy," "Over the Santa Fe Trail," "Echoes from the Hills" (1935), "A Melody from the Sky," "Blue Bonnet Girl" (1936).

The West, Golden Records (unknown #) by Roy and Dale.

Children's Records

78s/45s

Gabby the Gobbler, RCA Victor, 45 rpm: 48-0374; 78 rpm: 21-0374, 1955. ***If You Ever Come to Texas/Dusty Skies***, Beltone Records, 78 rpm: E-0263 (Matrix B7 19½), sung by Dale. ***Roy Rogers' Cowboy Songs***, RCA Victor, AV3240/324 EP (6 songs), 45 rpm. ***Friends and Neighbors/The Little Shoemaker***, Roy and Dale, 1950, Disney Records.

Lore of the West, RCA Victor #Y-388, "Little Nipper Series" (two 78 RPM records, stories, picture set?), 1940s.

(*See* Chapter 12 for Little Golden Records.)

LPs by Dale Evans

Country Dale, Word Records (unknown #). ***Dale Evans Sings***, Allegro 4116, 1940s Elite high-fidelity 10-inch. ***Faith, Hope and Charity***, Word Records (WST 8566). ***Getting to

Know the Lord, Capitol Records (unknown #). ***Heart of the Country***, Word Records (unknown #). ***It's Real***, Capitol ST-2772, 1967. ***Reflections of Life***, Manna (unknown #). ***Totally Free***, Word Records (Unknown #).

Others

Heroes and Friends, Warner Bros. 26310, Randy Travis LP. Roy sings "Happy Trails" with Randy. ***The Singing Cowboy***, Warner Bros. 3671, 1982. Includes song "Last of the Silver Screen Cowboys" by Rex Allen, Jr., Rex Allen, Sr., and Roy. ***Smokey and the Bandit 2***, soundtrack from film, MCA Records 1980. Roy Rogers and the Sons of the Pioneers do one song, "Ride Concrete Cowboy, Ride." Also appeared on soundtrack to *Rustler's Rhapsody* in 1984. ***Television's Greatest Hits***, TeeVee Toons TVT 1100. This contains a version of "Happy Trails" by Roy.

Audio Cassettes

No attempt is made to show cassettes that have duplicate LPs. ***The Best of Roy Rogers***, Curb D4-77392. ***The Cowboy Album*** (cassette only), Kid Rhino R4-70403. ***Happy Trails***, by Roy. ***Lore of the West***, RCA Records CAK-1074, 1986. ***Many Happy Trails***, Teletex, 2-cassette set, C7702. ***Roy Rogers Columbia Historic Edition***, CBS, Inc. FCT 38907. ***Roy Rogers Country Music Hall of Fame Series***, MCA, MCAC 10548. ***Roy Rogers Melody of the Plains***, MCA, MCAC 20361. ***Sons of the Pioneers Columbia Historic Edition***, CBS, Inc. FCT 37439 (featuring Roy Rogers). ***Sons of the Pioneers Cool Water***, RCA and BMG 8406-4R. ***Sons of the Pioneers Empty Saddles***, MCA, MCAC 1563. ***Sons of the Pioneers Standard Radio Transcript 1934–35***, vol. 2, Outlaw CSR 6 C. ***Sons of the Pioneers Tumbleweed Trails***, MCA 730. ***Sons of the Pioneers Tumbling Tumbleweeds***, MCA, MCAAC 20359 (featuring Roy Rogers). ***Sons of the Pioneers Tumbling Tumbleweeds, the RCA Years***, vol. 1, RCA and BMG 9744-4R. ***Tribute***, RCA 3024-4R.

Chapter 4

RADIO HISTORY

Information available on syndicated radio shows is sketchy at best. I wish to thank the many collectors and dealers of old-time radio shows who were able to offer the episode titles shown. I have chosen to add some information appearing in book form for the first time that I believe will give the reader some insight into the programs. For Len Slye/Sons of the Pioneers radio history, see Chapter 1.

1943
TITLE: "Tommy Riggs and Betty Lou Show." Broadcast at NBC, Roy and Trigger guest star.

1944
TITLE: "The Roy Rogers Show." TYPE: Transcribed. TIME/PLACE: 8:30 P.M., Tuesdays, Mutual Network. SPONSOR: Goodyear Tire and Rubber Co. DEBUT: November 21, 1944. CAST: Roy Rogers, the Sons of the Pioneers, the Farr Brothers, Pat Friday, Perry Botkin Orchestra, and special guest stars. ANNOUNCER: Vern Smith. THEME SONGS/MUSIC: "Smiles Are Made Out of Sunshine," "It's Roundup Time on the Double RR Bar." CLOSING: Roy, "Goodbye, good luck, and may the good Lord take a likin' to ya'." END OF SERIES: 1945

1945
Sample episodes of "The Roy Rogers Show": January 23—"Sara Berner." January 30—"Tom Barnes, Texas Ranger." May 8 VE Day—"Pecos Bill"; Guest, Porter Hall.

1946
TITLE: "Weekly Roundup." TIME/PLACE: Saturday P.M., NBC. SPONSOR: Miles Laboratories. CAST: Roy Rogers, Dale Evans, Gabby Hayes, Sons of the Pioneers. September 8: "All Star Western Theater."

1947
May 3: "All Star Western Theater."

1948
The public relations department of the radio stations and Mutual network airing the Roy Rogers Show would have "conference calls," in which announcements would be made pertaining to sponsor's ads, contests, and revisions. Some of this information is courtesy of Professor Ray White, Ball State University, Muncie, Indiana. This information was originally obtained from the manuscript division of the Library of Congress. TITLE: "The Roy Rogers Show." TIME/PLACE: 6:00 P.M., Sundays, Mutual Network. SPONSOR: Quaker Oats. CAST: Roy Rogers, Dale Evans, Foy Willing and the Riders of the Purple Sage. Sample episodes—March 30: "Case of the Mysterious Puppet." August 29: "Plot Against the Bank." September 6: "Mystery of the Circle E Ranch."

1949
Conference call of September 15 discussed the sponsor's offer of a spoon and fork salad server set. Episode, September 19: "Horse Thieves of Paradise Valley." Conference call, September 23, discussed sponsors offer of a four purpose pitcher-mug for 35 cents and one trademark. (This is the mug that has been confused with the Roy Rogers mug in various collectibles books. This one is the "Toby" mug.) Episode, September 26: "Ghost Town Men." Conference call of September 26 discussed a Roy Rogers' contest:

Here's the sensational Roy Rogers Movie offer made by Quaker Oats. It's a giant

Roy with Sons of the Pioneers, performing over KTRH Radio. (Informal publicity photo.)

opportunity, your chance to be in a real wild-west movie with Roy Rogers and get paid for the privilege. One Thousand Dollars in Cash and get all expenses paid for the trip to Hollywood with your Mom or Dad. Besides there are 15,500 other chances to win in this Quaker Oats Contest. Quaker Oats is awarding 500 pairs of Roy Rogers Cowboy Boots as second prizes. 500 Roy Rogers Watches as Third prizes. 1,500 fourth prizes of Roy Rogers Cameras. 1,000 Roy Rogers Binoculars as fifth prizes. 1,000 Roy Rogers Record Albums. 1,000 Roy Rogers Coloring Sets. And 10,000 additional prizes, big 4-color posters of Roy Rogers and Trigger. What is more, everybody who enters gets a beautiful color postcard of Roy Rogers, Trigger, Gabby Hayes and Dale Evans!

All you do: Write a second line to rhyme with this line: 'Quaker Oats is good to eat' or 'Mother's Oats is good to eat.' You know Quaker and Mother's Oats are the same!

By early 1950 this radio show was being broadcast over 561 Mutual Radio Stations.

1950

Conference call of January 25 discussed the sponsor's offer of seven packages of Vaughan's Flower Seeds for 15 cents and one trademark. The callers also discussed another sponsor offer of a Roy Rogers Badge that used the following promotion:

> Here's your chance to get a 14 carat, gold plated Roy Rogers Deputy Sheriff's Badge, just like the one Roy wears in his Western pictures. There are three secret features in this special Roy Rogers Badge—one, a hidden signal whistle for signaling your pals in the dark; two, a built in mirror for flashing signals in the daytime, and three, a secret code compartment—hidden slot for hiding code messages.

Conference call of March 16 discussed the sponsor's offer of a Roy Rogers Cup:

> Quaker oats is offering you a Roy Rogers Souvenir cup that has a wonderful likeness of Roy and his autograph, molded into a Lustrox cup. It has a spout that makes it

Newspaper Quaker Oats Roy Rogers Premium advertisement.

a handy milk pitcher or it can be used as a drinking cup. It holds half a pint. Just send one trademark from Quaker or Mother's Oats and $.35 to Roy Rogers, Box Q, Chicago 77, Illinois.

Conference call of April 12 discussed the sponsor's offer of Vaughan's Flower Seeds. Conference call of May 27 announced: "This is the last broadcast of the current contract. 'The Roy Rogers Show' leaves the air after this broadcast for a five week hiatus in July. We have received a renewal order from Quaker Oats." Company memorandum of July 18 discussed the sponsor's offer of twenty-seven different miniature bird trading cards. Conference call of September 6 discussed the opening of another Roy Rogers contest:

In 25 words or less, complete this sentence: "I like Quaker Oats, the giant of the cereals, because..." or "I like Mother's Oats, the giant of the cereals, because..." Then send it with your name and address and one Blue Star from a package of Quaker Oats or Mother's Oats to Roy Rogers, Box Q, Chicago 77, Illinois.

First prize—Trigger Boy, a palomino horse, or $2500 in cash. Roy Rogers Rainj-Coats and Helmets to the next 500

boy winners; Dale Evans Dolls to the next 500 girl winners; Rubber Cowboy Boots to the next 500 boy winners; Dale Evans Cowgirl Suits to the next 500 girl winners; Roy Rogers Sweaters to the next 500 winners; Roy Rogers Square Dance Record Albums to the next 500 winners; Roy Rogers Golden Colored Spurs to the next 1,000 winners; Roy Rogers Cowboy Band Harmonicas to the next 2,000 winners; and Roy Rogers Bantam Flashlights to the next 10,000 winners.

1951

Conference call of January 17 discussed sponsor's offer of Vaughan's Flower Seeds beginning January 21. Conference call of January 22 discussed the sponsor's offer of Gene Autry items:

Here's your chance to get five, all-new, pocket size Gene Autry Comic Books. Five different, western adventures of Gene Autry and his famous horse, Champion. Every 32-page, action-packed story is complete, new, never before published, and is not on sale anywhere. The supply of these books is limited so hurry and get yours. See details on the package or simply send ten cents in coin and a boxtop from Quaker Puffed Wheat or Puffed Rice with your name and address to Gene Autry, Box L, Chicago 77, Illinois.

Another offer used the following promotional:

> Here's something terrific! Your chance to get a Roy Rogers Branding Iron Ring! A gleaming gold-colored ring that you can do amazing things with! It has your own initial made into a real western brand for branding your schoolbooks, baseball, pocketbook, cap, and other belongings! It has a secret inked cap. Take it off and there is your very own initial made into a real western brand! Every brand is different for every initial! And that's not all that makes this Roy Rogers Branding Iron Ring so exciting to own and wear! You also get on it a miniature of Roy Rogers own western brand—the famous Double R Bar Brand that Roy uses on his own ranch! You also get a lucky horseshoe design on this ring! You also get an embossed picture of Roy Rogers himself—and his famous horse, Trigger. You can adjust this handsome gold-colored ring to fit any finger whether you're a boy or a girl. All you do is send only 15 cents in coin with your name and address and one Blue Star from a package of Quaker or Mother's oats. Print the initial you want us to put on your ring and send with 15 cents and one Quaker or Mother's oats Blue Star to Rogers, Box Q, Chicago 77, Illinois.

February 1: "Rustlers in Paradise." Conference call of May 2 made the following announcement:

> Attention: All stations carrying "Roy Rogers" Sundays at 6 to 6:30 P.M. NYT, for Quaker Oats Company. In accordance with our conference call of Friday, April 13, the last "Roy Rogers" broadcast will definitely take place on Sunday, May 13, 1951.... The Quaker Oats Company, thru their agency, Sherman and Marquette, has given us an order for the following program: Sundays, 6–6:30 P.M. NYT, "Challenge of the Yukon," starting Sunday, June 10, 1951. (This program will broadcast on a sustaining basis on Sundays, May 20, 27, and June 3, 1951.)

New General Foods show. TITLE: "The Roy Rogers Show." TIME/ PLACE: Friday p.m., NBC. SPONSOR: General Foods (Post's Cereals). CAST: Roy Rogers, Dale Evans, Pat Brady, the Whippoorwills, Milton Charles Orchestra. ANNOUNCER: Art Ballinger. Art Rush Production. THEME SONGS/MUSIC: "It's

Roundup Time on the Double RR Bar." COMMERCIALS: Roy. CLOSING: Roy and Dale sing theme song. Sample episodes—October 12: "Ed Bailey's Bad Luck." October 19: "Night Riders." October 26: "Old Prospecting Friend." November 2: "Doug Manson Gang." November 9: "Counterfeiters." November 23: "Lawman's Badge." December 7: "Eight Convicts." December 14: "The Bride." December 21: "Christmas Show." December 28: "Outlaws," aka "Manson and Morris."

1952
January 4: "Back from the Past." January 11: "Cattle Swindle." January 18: "The Owlhoot Trail." January 25: "Wake of the Storm." February 1: "Rustlers in Paradise Valley." February 8: "The Jinxed Ranch." February 15: "The Gold Fields." February 19: "Professor Manson and Wife." February 22: "The Hideaway." February 29: "Smugglers." March 7: "John Kennedy, Escaped Outlaw" (director, Tom Hague; script, Ray Wilson; music, Milton Charles; cast, Rye Billsbury, Herb Butterfield, Dorothy Faye Southward, Bill Green, Don Harvey, Howard McNeer; closing theme, "Happy Trails"; song, "There's a Horseshoe Moon in the Sky"). March 14: "Lee Bulow and Gang." March 21: "Herb Selby Trapped." March 28: "Gold in the Desert." April 4: "Sid Kenyon's Frogs." April 11: "Rene Egan Case," aka "Evidence for Egan Case." April 18: "Paradise Valley Sweepstakes" (possible air date). August 25: "Paradise Sweepstakes." September 4: "George Allison." September 11: "Fish That Told a Story." September 18: "Red Danger and Black Death," aka "Red Danger, Black Gold." September 25: "Rip Roaring Rodeo Yarn." October 2: "Pat Gets Roy into a Fix." October 9: "Fred's Ranch." October 16: "Indiana." October 23: "Lee Fox and Len Dean." October 30: "The Howling Mine." November 6: "Range War." November 13: "Rancher's Son," aka "Richest Rancher." November 20: "Greatest Horse in the West." The commercial advertised Pop-out Trading Cards premiums (in cereal boxes). November 27: "Feuding Fathers." December 4: "Last Stagecoach." December 11: "Boiling Treasurer." December 18: "Dale Plans a Surprise." December 25: "Night Before Christmas."

1953
January 1: "Prison Break." January 8: "The

Key." January 15: "Albert Larrimore Sutton." January 22: "Valley Wide Rodeo." January 29: "Jeff Kaufman's Dude Ranch." February 5: "Jane Farmer." February 12: "The Blizzard." February 19: "Jewel Robbery" (sources show two different shows for this date). February 19: "Centennial Celebration." February 26: "Checkered Neckerchief." March 5: "Chocera, Apache Chief." March 12: "Charles Ryder, Rancher."

March 19: "Black Gold in Paradise Valley." March 26: "Dog Story." Unknown Air Dates: "Blackmail Over Adoption," "Missing Atomic Scientist," "$50,000 Jewel Fraud," "Bergen and McCarthy."

1954

Dodge Motors Division of Chrysler Corp. becomes sponsor. Series ends in 1955.

Sample Program
"The Roy Rogers Show"
May 8, 1945 (V-E Day Broadcast)
Mutual System, Tuesday Evening
Sponsor: Goodyear Tire and Rubber Company

ANNOUNCER: "Friends, tonight as usual, Goodyear brings you Roy Rogers, but because of the great news we've all been hearing, we want you to know that we will interrupt this program instantly for any late news flashes. Meanwhile, you'll hear Bob Nolan and the Sons of the Pioneers, Pat Friday, the Farr Brothers, Perry Botkin's Orchestra. Goodyear's guest tonight, motion picture villain, Porter Hall. And now, for the greatest name in rubber, Goodyear invites you to meet America's greatest Western star, Roy Rogers."

(Applause)

Roy sings "I've Got a Locket in My Pocket," backed by Botkin's Orchestra (popular rendition).

(Applause)

ROY: Howdy folks, and welcome from me and the gang and Goodyear to tonight's get-together. We've rounded up a few new, and some of the old songs for the occasion. And one of the West's most [stammer] legendary stories. But right now, it's time for you to meet our guest for this evening, one of the swellest actors who ever foreclosed a mortgage on poor little Nell, Mr. Porter Hall. Hiya, Porter.

(Audience boos)

PORTER: Roy, Roy, Roy. That's a nice welcome after you *asked* me to come over to your get-together.

ROY: Well, shucks, don't mind the folks, Porter, they've seen you as the villain in so many pictures, they just can't keep from booin' at you.

PORTER: Well, I'm so misunderstood, Roy, [by] anyone who's ever seen me in pictures. I'm a "no-good-unprincipled-critter." Now honest, Roy, you know I'm not that way at all ... much [laugh].

ROY: Porter, I'm surprised at you. Why, I think I'd much rather play your part than my own. The heavy in the picture ... he ... well, he always gets his own way, and you get most of the close-ups. You know, where you sneer and twirl your mustache, and make everyone in the audience hiss at you.

PORTER: That's the real trouble, Roy. I never know if they're hissing at the character, or the real actor playing the part.

"Premiums" offered by Roy's sponsors kept youngsters tuned into every exciting episode of his radio and TV shows. (Ad, Roy Rogers Comics No. 66, Phillips Archives.)

ROY: Well, when Porter Hall is playing the part [stammer] as, as the villain, it isn't the actor they're hissing, you can believe me. But just to give you a break Porter, we've got a sketch [stammer] for you to play in tonight, about one of the West's most amazing characters. And just to prove that you're the star and the hero, I'm not even going to play in it. How's that?

PORTER: Well, that's what I call really being a hero. Giving a whole story to a screen badman [laugh]. But what're you gonna do, Roy?

ROY: Well, first of all, Porter, I'm going to keep an eye on you, and make sure you don't forget yourself and steal the ranch. Then, I'm just gonna sort of keep the get-together moving, like right now, when I call on the Sons of the Pioneers to dedicate a song to you.

MUSIC: Sons of the Pioneers sing "Ragtime Cowboy Joe," changing the lyric after the first verse to "Ragtime Porter Hall."

(Applause)

ANNOUNCER: Today, when congratulations are being offered all over the world to the millions who worked and fought for victory in Europe, Goodyear would also like to propose a toast, a toast of its own and to its own. A toast to the 24,783 of its men and women in the Armed Forces. It's "Well Done" to those in Europe. It's "Good Luck" to those in the Pacific. And here's a toast too, to the 100,000 Goodyear employees at home [for] the war work they've contributed and are continuing to contribute to final victory. To them, "Good Work," and let's keep punching hard until the Japs get theirs.

(Pause)

ROY: It's the Farr Brothers' furious fiddle and galloping guitar, and "Cajon Stomp."

MUSIC: Instrumental.

PAT FRIDAY: Roy, gee, Roy. I'm sorry I'm late. I miss much?

ROY: Well, hello there, Pat Friday. You missed a couple of good songs, but you're in plenty of time for the story Porter Hall and I are going to tell tonight.

PAT: Porter Hall? Do I know him? [To Porter], Are you my Uncle Every?

PORTER: That's right. Every Friday [laugh]. I am now fabulously wealthy, and I intend to buy you the finest ranch in the West.

PAT: Oh, but I already have a ranch.

PORTER: Oh, but I didn't know. But ... oh ... uh ... you deserve a much bigger one. Now, uh, if you'll just give me the deed to your present property.

PAT: Here you are, Sir.

PORTER: Uh-huh, heh, heh, heh, heh [three unintelligible words]. Now I have you in my power.

ROY: Doggone you, Porter Hall. Unhand that girl and give her back that deed.

PAT: Aw shucks, Roy, that isn't the deed to my ranch. It's just a song I'm going to sing tonight.

PORTER: Curses! Foiled again!

ROY: Not exactly, Porter, because if Pat'll forgive you and sing the song right now, you'll get the treat of your life. Folks, Miss Pat Friday, singing "Close as Pages in a Book."

(Song)

(Applause)

Sons of the Pioneers sing one line: "See them tumbling down..."

ROY: You know, you hear a lot about a cowman's pony, but there's another little animal I guess the West would've never been made without him. You find 'em packin' loads twice their own weight, where grubby prospectors worked [stammer] worked, tirelessly in the desert sand. You find 'em high up in the mountains where a less sure-footed animal will plunge his rider 5,000 feet down a sheer drop. Oh, maybe their voices aren't as musical as a cowhand's song, as he sings and quiets his herd, but ... I've yet to see a true Westerner who didn't cuss them ... and love them. The gentle sure-footed, little braying burro.

Sons of the Pioneers sing "Wanderers of the Wasteland."

(Applause)

ANNOUNCER: Now it's Roy Rogers, King of the Cowboys, and a new Western ballad, "Don't Blame It All on Me."

(Song)

(Applause)

ANNOUNCER: Say, Roy, you've got both Pat and me bustin' with curiosity about the yarn you and Porter Hall are going to tell. What's so different about it?

ROY: Well kids, tonight's story is about the greatest cowboy who ever rode a bronc, shot a six-gun, or roped a steer. As a matter of fact, he's the man who's taught the broncos to buck, invented the six-shooter, and considered the lariat his unimportant invention.

PAT: Oh no. Wait a minute, Roy.

PORTER: Now you wait a minute, Miss. Don't accuse Roy here of exaggerating. Roy, anybody knows the six-gun was invented by Samuel Colt.

ROY: That, Sir, is just a rumor. The six-gun was definitely invented by Pecos Bill.

PAT: Pecos Bill? Never heard of him.

PORTER: Female tenderfoots! Bah!

ANNOUNCER: But who was Pecos Bill, Roy? He sounds as fantastic as this Hall character here.

ROY: He's much more so, Vern. Pecos Bill is the most fantastic character the imaginations of thousands of cowboys ever dreamed up. And if you'll all just make yourselves comfortable, Porter Hall and I will tell you plenty about him.

(Musical introduction)

ROY: Now I'm not sayin' that Pecos Bill is dead, even today. To be honest, I don't know if Bill was ever born. They say he was born in Texas, and he was quite a baby ... weighed seventy-three pounds [chuckle] and stood more than four feet tall. He got lost out on the prairie one day and didn't have anyone to play with, so Bill wound up livin' and playin' with the coyotes. Well, just about Bill's ninth birthday, a cowboy who'd wandered off the trail came upon Bill, just as the big kid was havin' mornin' exercise ... [fades out and into dramatization]

Story of Pecos Bill

(Applause)

(Music)

ANNOUNCER: It's the whole Goodyear gang, led by Roy Rogers, the King of the Cowboys, singing "Skies Are Bluer."

(Song)

ROY: Well, it looks as if our time for tonight is like the water in a stream in the middle of the summer. It's all run out. But we've got more time again next week, and we'd like you all to be back sittin' with us at [stammer] at our "Goodyear Get-Together." We have some songs and music, and a little chatter, Western-style, and a rip-roarin' story about the old days that should please everybody. So, 'til next Tuesday, this is Roy Rogers, thanking Porter Hall for appearing with us tonight and sayin' for the whole Goodyear gang; "Goodbye, good luck, and may the good Lord take a likin' to ya."

Roy sings one line of theme song, "Don't Forget Smiles Are Made out of the Sunshine."

ANNOUNCER: Now this is Vern Smith, saying good-night for Goodyear, the greatest name in rubber. If you like the songs and stories of the West, don't miss tuning in next Tuesday, same station you're tuned to now. Same time of day on your clock, when Goodyear will bring you another get-together, with Bob Nolan and the Sons of the Pioneers, Pat Friday, the Farr Brothers, Harry Botkin and his orchestra, and starring the King of the Cowboys, Roy Rogers.

Theme music by orchestra: "Don't Forget Smiles Are Made out of the Sunshine" (fades out).

ANNOUNCER: The Roy Rogers program was transcribed.

(Theme music backup)

(Applause)

(ANOTHER) ANNOUNCER: This is V-E Day. Don't forget to buy another bond. A war half won is a job half done. This is the Mutual Broadcasting System.

Chapter 5

FILMOGRAPHY

A long eight years saw Len Slye go from singing gigs to radio shows to a recording contract with a major label, but all the fame and fortune wouldn't be realized until he became Roy Rogers. Republic Studio introduced the rootin'-tootin', two-gun hero, and the rest is box-office history. For a while, he and Gene Autry ran neck and neck, but all that changed in 1943, when Roy Rogers became number one for the duration.

A number of the films listed below are in the public domain. The Copyright Office in Washington, D.C., confirms the status, and several of these (the films) are so noted. They were originally registered with a one letter and three digit registration number. For the first time in a Roy Rogers filmography numbers are used which correspond with those found on stills and publicity photos for that film, a factor that potentially will be of great assistance in identifying such photographs.

Non-Starring Roles as Len Slye

Radio Scout, with El Brendel. *The Old Homestead*, with Mary Carlisle (Liberty) 1935. *Way Up Thar*, (educational short), produced by Mack Sennett, introduced Joan Davis. *Slightly Static*, (MGM) (short subject), September 7, 1935. *Gallant Defender*, with Charles Starrett (Columbia), November 30, 1935 (60 min.). *Song of the Saddle*, with Dick Foran (Warner Bros.), February 1, 1936 (58 min.). *The Mysterious Avenger*, with Charles Starrett (Columbia), January 17, 1936 (60 min.). *The Big Show*, with Gene Autry (Republic), November 16, 1936 (59 min.), filmed at the Texas Centennial. *The Old Corral*, with Gene Autry (Republic), December 21, 1936 (56 min.). *The Old Wyoming Trail*, with Charles Starrett (Columbia), November 8, 1937 (56 min.).

Non-Starring Roles as Dick Weston

Wild Horse Rodeo, with Three Mesquiteers (Republic), December 6, 1937 (55 min.). *The Old Barn Dance*, with Gene Autry (Republic), January 29, 1938 (60 min.).

Non-Starring Roles as Roy Rogers

Jeepers Creepers, with Weaver Bros. (Republic), 1939 (69 min.). *Dark Command*, with Claire Trevor, John Wayne (Republic), April 5, 1940 (91 min.). *Rodeo Dough*, with Sally Payne (MGM), November 9, 1940 (10 min.), Sepiatone. *Arkansas Judge*, with Weaver Bros. (Republic), January 28, 1941 (71 min.). *Brazil* (Republic), 1944 (91 min.), Rogers sings "Hands Across the Border." *Lake Placid Serenade* (Republic), 1944 (85 min.), Rogers sings "Winter Wonderland" (guest). *Hollywood Canteen* (Warner Bros.), 1944 (123 min.), Rogers sings "Don't Fence Me In." *Out California Way*, with Monte Hale (Republic), December 5, 1946 (67 min.), Trucolor. *Hit Parade of 1947*, with Eddie Albert (Republic), Trigger, Bob Nolan, and the Sons of the Pioneers. *Melody Time* (Walt Disney Productions, released through RKO Radio Pictures), 1948 (75 min.), Roy Rogers, Bob Nolan and the Sons of the Pioneers perform "Blue Shadows on the Trail" and "Pecos Bill."

Starring Roles

Under Western Stars (Republic), April 20, 1938 (65 min.), #704, filmed at Lone Pine, California.

Producer, Sol C. Siegel; director, Joseph Kane; screenplay, Dorrell and Stuart McGowan and Betty Burbridge; camera, Jack Marta; songs, Jack Lawrence, Johnny Marvin, Eddie Cherkose, Peter Tinturin, Charles Rosoff. CAST: Roy Rogers, Trigger, Smiley Burnette, Carol Hughes, Maple City Four, Guy Usher, Tom Chatterton, Kenneth Harian, Alden Chase, Brandon Beach, Earl Dwire, Jean Fowler, Dora Clemant, Dick Elliott, Burr Caruth, Charles Whitaker, Jack Rockwell, Frankie Marvin. SYNOPSIS: Roy is elected to Congress by running on a free-water ticket. He goes to Washington to fight for public ownership of the utilities. Our cowboy congressman wins his battle by showing films of his fellow ranchers facing dust bowl conditions. SONGS: "Dust," "Send My Mail to the County Jail," "When a Cowboy Sings a Song," "Back to the Backwoods," "Rogers for Congressman," "Pioneer Mother of Mine," "Rhythm of the Range."

Billy the Kid Returns (Republic), September 4, 1938 (58 min.). Filmed at Iversons' Ranch while Gene Autry was still on strike at Republic. Producer, Charles E. Ford; director, Joseph Kane; screenplay, Jack Natteford; camera, Ernest Miller; songs, Eddie Cherkose, Smiley Burnette, Alberto Colombo, Vern (Tim) Miller. CAST: Roy Rogers, Trigger, Smiley Burnette, Mary Hart (Lynne Roberts), Fred Kohler Sr., Morgan Wallace, Wade Boteler, Edwin Stanley, Horace Murphy, Joseph Crehan, Robert Emmett Keane, Al Taylor, George Letz (Montgomery), Chris-Pin Martin, Jim Corey, Lloyd Ingraham, Bob McKenzie, Oscar Gahan, Jack Kirk, Art Dillard, Fred Burns, Betty Roadman, Rudy Sooter, Betty Jane Haney, Patsy Lee Parsons, Ray Nichols, Ralph Dunn. SYNOPSIS: Billy the Kid temporarily abandons his greed and his lust for killing, at least to get through this episode. When Billy is killed outside the store (after the range wars), Roy comes upon the scene, and looks amazingly like Billy. No one believes that he is not the dead outlaw until Pat Garrett arrives and informs the law that Roy is a good guy. Roy is deputized and put undercover as Billy to catch the bad guys who are still terrorizing the nesters. SONGS: "Born to the Saddle," "Sing a Little Song About Anything," "Dixie Sales Song," "When the Sun Is Setting on the Prairie," "When I Camped Under the Stars."

Come On Rangers (Republic), November 25, 1938 (57 min.). Producer, Charles E. Ford; director, Joseph Kane; screenplay, Gerald Geraghty and Jack Natteford; camera, Al Wilson; musical director, Cy Feuer; editor, Edward Mann. CAST: Roy Rogers, Trigger, Mary Hart, Raymond Hatton, J. Farrell MacDonald, Purnell Pratt, Harry Woods, Bruce McFarlane, Lane Chandler, Lee Powell, Chester Gunnels, Frank McCarroll, Chick Hannon, Jack Kirk, Al Taylor, Horace B. Carpenter, Bob Wilke, Al Ferguson, Allan Caban, Ben Corbett, Burr Caruth. SYNOPSIS: Action-packed tale of the early days of Texas, with Roy, a former Ranger, being asked to call together other members of the Rangers and assist the cavalry. Outlaws are running rampant throughout Texas and practicing their own form of law and justice. SONGS: "Tenting Tonight," "I've Learned a Lot About Women," "A Western Love Song," "Song of the West."

Shine On Harvest Moon (Republic), December 30, 1938 (55 min.). Filmed at Vasquez Rocks. Director, Joseph Kane; screenplay, Jack Natteford; camera, William Nobles; editor, Lester Orlebeck. CAST: Roy Rogers, Trigger, Mary Hart (Lynne Roberts), Lulu Belle & Scotty, Stanley Andrews, William Farnum, Frank Jacquet, Chester Gunnels, Matty Roubert, Pat Henning, Jack Rockwell, Joe Whitehead, David Sharpe. SYNOPSIS: Fellow ranchers who were friends turn against each other when one of them develops the habit of rustling. Mary Hart is the bad rancher's daugther. Roy is the good rancher's son. Lulu Belle & Scotty sing and provide laughs. SONGS: "Shine On Harvest Moon," "The Man in the Moon Is a Cowhand," "I'm Dyin' to Find a Beau" (Lulu Belle), "Let Me Build a Cabin," "You're Really in the God House" (Lulu Belle), "Down the Trail."

Rough Rider's Round-Up (Republic), March 13, 1939 (58 min.). Filmed at Iversons' Ranch. Director, Joseph Kane; screenplay, Jack Natteford; camera, Jack Marta; editor, Lester Orlebeck; musical director,

Still from *Under Western Stars*. The Alabama Hills in background.

Cy Feuer. CAST: Roy Rogers, Trigger, Mary Hart (Lynne Roberts), Raymond Hatton, Eddie Acuff, William Pawley, Dorothy Sebastian, George Meeker, Jack Rockwell, Guy Usher, George Chesebro, Glen Strange, Duncan Renaldo, Jack Kirk, Hank Bell, Dorothy Christy, Fred Kelsey, Eddy Waller, John Merton, George Letz (Montgomery), Al Haskell, Frank Ellis, Augie Gomez, Frank McCarrol, Dan White. SYNOPSIS: This adventure is set after the Spanish-American War when Roy as a Rough Rider joins forces with other former soldiers and the Border Patrol to stop robberies of the gold shipments. SONGS: "When Johnny Comes Marching Home," "Ridin' Down the Trail," "Here on the Range."

Frontier Pony Express (Republic), April 12, 1939 (58 min.). Filmed at Iversons' Ranch. Producer and director, Joseph Kane; screenplay, Norman Hall; camera, William Nobles; editor, Gene Milford; musical director, Cy Feuer. CAST: Roy Rogers, Trigger, Mary Hart (Lynne Roberts), Raymond Hatton, Edward Keane, Monte Blue, Donald Dill-away, Noble Johnson, William Royle, Ethel Wales, George Letz (Montgomery), Charles King, Bud Osborne, Fred Burns, Jack Kirk, Bob McKenzie, Ernie Adams, Hank Bell, Jack O'Shea. SYNOPSIS: Roy is a rider for the Pony Express on the California route. He gets involved with a Confederate politician and a Confederate spy. And of course, the Yankees are contenders for California as much as the Confederates. But the Confederate politician is a crook and a traitor and really wants California's allegiance for his own selfish gain. SONGS: "My Old Kentucky Home," "Rusty Spurs."

Southward Ho! (Republic), May 19, 1939 (57 min.). Filmed at Andy Jauregui Ranch. Producer and director, Joseph Kane; screenplay, Gerald Geraghty; original story, John Rathmell and Jack Natteford; camera, Jack Marta; editor, Lester Orlebeck; musical director, Cy Feuer. CAST: Roy Rogers, Trigger, Mary Hart (Lynne Roberts), George Hayes, Victor Jory, Robert Barrat, Ralph Morgan, C. Henry Gordon, Robert Armstrong, Max Terhune, Janet Beecher, George

Letz (Montgomery), Guy Wilkerson, Charles Stevens, Hal Taliaferro, Lane Chandler, Ethan Laidlaw, Edmund Cobb, Billy Benedict, Tex Cooper, Leon Ames, Ferris Taylor, Kathleen Lockhart. SYNOPSIS: Ex-Confederate soldiers Roy and Gabby head for Texas so that Gabby can claim his inheritance, half interest in a ranch. The other half is owned by a "not-so-nice" ex-Union colonel that they had problems with during the Civil War. The federal government places the colonel in charge of the area, which is under martial law. The colonel finds that the cavalry captain and his troops are actually the outlaws that have been ravaging the countryside and terrorizing the people. The citizens all band together to catch the bad guys. SONGS: "Old Virginny," "I Hope I'm Not Dreaming Again," "Walk the Other Way."

In Old Caliente (Republic), June 19, 1939 (57 min.). Director, Joseph Kane; screenplay, Norman Houston and Gerald Geraghty; camera, William Nobles; editor, Edward Mann. CAST: Roy Rogers, Trigger, George Hayes, Mary Hart (Lynne Roberts), Jack LaRue, Katherine DeMille, Frank Puglia, Harry Woods, Paul Marion, Ethel Wales, Merrill McCormack. SYNOPSIS: During the settling of old California, nesters are being accused of a robbery. Roy is working for the other side but realizes that the nesters are innocent and that his boss is trying to frame the guileless homesteaders. SONGS: "Ride On Vaquero," "Sundown on the Rangeland," "We're Not Coming Out Tonight."

Wall Street Cowboy (Republic), August 6, 1939 (66 min.). Filmed at Red Rock Canyon. Producer and director, Joseph Kane; screenplay, Gerald Geraghty and Norman Hall; original story, Doris Schroeder; camera, Jack Marta; editor, Lester Orlebeck; musical director, Cy Feuer. CAST: Roy Rogers, Trigger, George Hayes, Raymond Hatton, Ann Baldwin, Pierre Watkin, Louisiana Lou, Craig Reynolds, Ivan Miller, Reginald Barlow, Adrian Morris, Jack Roper, Jack Ingram, Fred Burns, Paul Fix, George Chesebro, Ted Mapes. SYNOPSIS: It's the eastern Wall Street crooked dudes versus the honest Western cowboy. Roy can't make the payment on his ranch, which just happens to be quite rich in metal that the Wall Street crowd

needs. They're trying to force foreclosure to pick it up for a song. SONGS: "Me and the Rainbow Hills," "Ridin' Down the Rainbow Trail," "Ride 'Em Cowboy," "That's My Louisiana."

Arizona Kid (Republic), September 29, 1939 (61 min.), #921. Filmed at Iversons' Ranch. Author: Republic Productions, Inc. Reg. Republic Pictures Corp. reg. # LP 9159, following publication September 29, 1939, no renewal found. Producer and director, Joseph Kane; screenplay, Luci Ward and Gerald Geraghty; original story, Luci Ward; camera, William Nobles; editor, Lester Orlebeck; musical director, Cy Feuer. CAST: Roy Rogers, Trigger, George Hayes, Stuart Hamblen, Sally March, David Kerwin, Earl Dwire, Dorothy Sebastian, Peter Fargo, Fred Burns, Ed Cassidy, Jack Ingram, Ted Mapes, Frank McCarroll. SYNOPSIS: Roy is a Confederate captain torn between Missouri's pledge to the North and the marauding band of outlaws that is plaguing the Missouri border, under the guise of supporting the South. SONGS: "Home Sweet Home to Me," "Swing Low Sweet Chariot," "Lazy Old Moon."

Saga of Death Valley (Republic), November 17, 1939 (58 min.), #922. Filmed at Lone Pine. Producer and director, Joseph Kane; screenplay, Karen DeWolf; camera, Jack Marta; editor, Lester Orlebeck. CAST: Roy Rogers, Trigger, George Hayes, Donald Barry, Doris Day (not the Day of *Pillow Talk* fame) Frank M. Thomas, Jack Ingram, Hal Taliaferro, Lew Kelly, Fern Emmett, Tommy Baker, Buzz Buckley, Horace Murphy, Lane Chandler, Fred Burns, Jimmy Wakely, Johnny Bond, Dick Rinehart, Peter Frago, Ed Brady, Bob Thomas, Matty Roubert, Pascale Perry, Cactus Mack, Art Dillard, Horace B. Carpenter, Hooper Atchley, Frankie Marvin, Jess Cavan. SYNOPSIS: A gang of outlaws tries to make an easy buck by cutting off the water supply to the ranchers and making them pay for reinstatement. Don Barry is Roy's brother, unbeknown to both of them. The truth is revealed just as Barry meets an untimely demise. SONGS: "Shadows on the Prairie Tonight," "Ride, Ride, Ride," "I've Sold My Saddle for an Old Guitar."

Days of Jesse James (Republic), December 20, 1939 (63 min.), #923. Filmed at Iversons' Ranch. Producer and director, Joseph Kane; screenplay, Earle Snell; original story, Jack Natteford; camera, Reggie Lanning; musical director, Cy Feuer. CAST: Roy Rogers, Trigger, George Hayes, Pauline Moore, Hugh Sothern, Chief Thundercloud, Julian Rivero, Trevor Bardette, Gaylord Pendleton, Wade Boteler, Anna Demetria, Estelita Zarco. SYNOPSIS: A bank is robbed, and what better candidates than the James Boys for the evil deed? But it doesn't take Roy long to figure out that the villainous bank officials are the real culprits. SONGS: "I'm a Son of a Cowboy," "Saddle Your Dreams," "Echo Mountain."

Young Buffalo Bill (Republic), April 12, 1940 (69 min.), #924. Filmed at Iversons' Movie Ranch. Producer and director, Joseph Kane; screenplay, Harrison Jacobs, Robert Yost, Gerald Geraghty; original story, Norman Houston; camera, William Nobles; editor, Tony Martinelli; musical director, Cy Feuer. CAST: Roy Rogers, Trigger, George Hayes, Pauline Moore, Hugh Sothern, Chief Thunder Cloud, Trevor Bardette, Julian Rivero, Gaylord Pendleton, Wade Boteler, Anna Demetrio, Estelita Zarco, Hank Bell, William Kellogg, Iron Eyes Cody, Jack O'Shea, George Chesebro. SYNOPSIS: There are fights over mining land in New Mexico, and the Indians are harassing the Spanish folks who own a ranch. The cavalry comes to the rescue. SONGS: "Rollin' Down the Santa Fe," "Blow, Breeze, Blow."

Carson City Kid (Republic), July 1, 1940 (57 min.), #926. Director, Joseph Kane; screenplay, Robert Yost and Gerald Geraghty; original story, Joseph Kane; camera, William Nobles; editor, Helen Turner; songs, Peter Tinturin. CAST: Roy Rogers, Trigger, George Hayes, Bob Steele, Pauline Moore, Noah Beery, Jr., Francis MacDonald, Hal Taliaferro, Arthur Loft, George Rosener, Chester Gan, Hank Bell, Ted Mapes, Jack Ingram, Jack Kirk, Jack Rockwell, Tom Smith, Art Dillard, Hal Price, Yakima Canutt, Kit Guard, Curley Dresden, Oscar Gahan, Chick Hannon, Al Taylor. SYNOPSIS: Roy is a good-guy-

gunslinger, and he's a gunnin' for that varmint Bob Steele, who killed his brother. SONGS: "Gold Digger Song," "Are You the One?" "Sonora Moon," "Never Depart from My Darling."

Ranger and the Lady (Republic), July 30, 1940 (59 min.), #927. Producer and director, Joseph Kane; screenplay, Stuart Anthony and Gerald Geraghty; original story, Bernard McConville; camera, Reggie Lanning; editor, Lester Orlebeck; songs, Peter Tinturin; musical director, Cy Feuer. CAST: Roy Rogers, Trigger, George Hayes, Jacqueline Wells (Julie Bishop), Harry Woods, Henry Brandon, Noble Johnson, Si Jenks, Ted Mapes, Yakima Canutt, Chuck Baldra, Herman Hack, Chick Hannon, Art Dillard. SYNOPSIS: Sam Houston is off gallivanting around Washington, D.C., trying to attain statehood for Texas, and his assistant is trying to impose illegal taxes on anyone who travels the Santa Fe Trail. It's Roy Rogers, Texas Ranger, to the rescue, when a wagon train is charged those nasty taxes. SONGS: "As Long as We Are Dancing," "Nothing Compares to My Sweet Conchita."

Colorado (Republic), September 15, 1940 (57 min.), #928. Filmed at Red Rock Canyon. Producer and director, Joseph Kane; screenplay, Louis Stevens and Harrison Jacobs; camera, Jack Marta; editor, Edward Mann; songs, Peter Tinturin; musical director, Cy Feuer. CAST: Roy Rogers, Trigger, George Hayes, Pauline Moore, Milburn Stone, Maude Edburne, Hal Taliaferro, Vester Pegg, Fred Burns, Lloyd Ingraham, Jay Novello, Chuck Baldra, Tex Palmer, Joseph Crehan, Edward Cassidy, George Rosenor, Robert Fiske. SYNOPSIS: Roy and his brother fought on different sides during the Civil War; now Roy is sent to bring in the traitorous sibling. SONG: "Dreaming of You."

Young Bill Hickok (Republic), October 21, 1940 (59 min.), #1022. Filmed at Vasquez Rocks. Producer and director, Joseph Kane; screenplay, Norton S. Parker and Olive Cooper; camera, William Nobles; editor, Lester Orlebeck; musical director, Cy Feuer.

CAST: Roy Rogers, Trigger, George Hayes, Jacqueline Wells, John Miljan, Sally Payne, Archie Twitchell, Monte Blue, Hal Taliaferro, Ethel Wales, Jack Ingram, Monte Montague, Iron Eyes Cody, Fred Burns, Frank Ellis, Slim Whitaker, Jack Kirk, Hank Bell, Henry Wills, Dick Elliott, William Desmond, John Elliott, Jack Rockwell, Bill Wolfe, Tom Smith. SYNOPSIS: There's a foreign agent trying to take the Western territory with the help of a guerrilla band left over from the Civil War. Roy, as Bill Hickok, must put an end to the agent's vile deeds. SONGS: "Every Hour I Spend with You," "When the Shadows Fall Across the Rockies," "Rollin' Up and Down the Prairie," "Tamales," "We Are Going to Have a Cowboy Wedding."

Border Legion, aka *West of the Badlands* (Republic), December 5, 1940 (58 min.), #1021. Filmed at Iversons' Ranch. Producer and director, Joseph Kane; screenplay, Olive Cooper and Louis Stevens (based on a novel by Zane Grey); camera, Jack Marta; editor, Edward Mann; musical director, Cy Feuer. CAST: Roy Rogers, Trigger, George Hayes, Carol Hughes, Joseph Sawyer, Maude Edburne, Jay Novello, Hal Taliaferro, Dick Wessell, Paul Porcasi, Robert Emmett Keane, Ted Mapes, Fred Burns, Post Parks, Art Dillard, Chick Hannon, Charles Baldra. SYNOPSIS: Roy is a New York doctor who is forced to leave his home state because of a mix-up. He rapidly adjusts to the wild West and uses his fists, songs and guns to eliminate the bad guys who are doing disgusting things to his new Idaho neighbors. SONGS: "With My Guitar," "Yippy Ti Yi Yo," "Git Along Little Dogie."

Robin Hood of the Pecos (Republic), January 14, 1941 (59 min.), #1023. Filmed at Vasquez Rocks. Producer and director, Joseph Kane; screenplay, Olive Cooper; original story, Hal Long; camera, Jack Marta; editor, Charles Craft; songs, Peter Tinturin, Eddie Cherkose; musical director, Cy Feuer. CAST: Roy Rogers, Trigger, George Hayes, Marjorie Reynolds, Sally Payne, Cy Kendall, Leigh Whipper, Eddie Acuff, Robert Strange, William Haade, Jay Novello, Roscoe Ates, Jim Corey, Chick Hannon.

SYNOPSIS: Those rotten carpetbaggers have descended on Texas. Roy and Gabby have to keep them from plundering the townsfolk and the lovely land around the Pecos. SONG: "It's a Sad, Sad Story."

In Old Cheyenne (Republic), March 28, 1941 (58 min.), #925. Producer and director, Joseph Kane; screenplay, Olive Cooper; original story, John Krafft; camera, William Nobles; editor, Charles Craft; musical director, Cy Feuer. CAST: Roy Rogers, Trigger, George Hayes, Joan Woodbury, Sally Payne, J. Farrell MacDonald, George Rosenor, Hal Taliaferro, William Haade, Jack Kirk, Bob Woodward, Jim Corey, Cactus Mack, George Lloyd, Billy Benedict, Jack O'Shea, Edward Piel, Sr., Merrill McCormack, Ted Mapes, Fred Burns, Ben Corbett, Nick Thompson. SYNOPSIS: Roy is a newspaper reporter sent to Cheyenne to cover the story of Arapaho Brown because he's misbehaving something awful. But as luck would have it, the law is after the wrong man, and it takes Roy's shooting, fighting, and singing to prove poor Arapaho innocent and bring in the real bad buy. SONG: "Bonita."

Sheriff of Tombstone (Republic), May 7, 1941 (56 min.), #1025. Filmed at Vasquez Rocks. Producer and director, Joseph Kane; screenplay, Olive Cooper; original story by James Webb; camera, William Nobles; editor, Tony Martinelli; songs, Jules Styne, Sol Meyer, Peter Tinturin, Bob Nolan. CAST: Roy Rogers, Trigger, George Hayes, Elyse Knox, Harry Woods, Hal Taliaferro, Jay Novello, Roy Barcroft, Jack Rockwell, Addison Richards, Sally Payne, Zeffie Tilbury, Jack Ingram, George Rosenor, Jack Kirk, Frank Ellis, Art Dillard, Herman Hack, Vester Pegg, Al Haskell, Ray Jones, Jess Cavan. SYNOPSIS: Roy and Gabby ride into Tombstone, and Roy is immediately mistaken for a gun-wielding outlaw that the crooked mayor sent for to help him intimidate the town. Roy assumes this identity to get the goods on the bad mayor. Then the real gunsel comes to town, and Roy has to do some quick thinking and fast shooting to put the bad guys out of business. SONGS: "Ridin' on a Rocky Road," "Sky Bald Paint," "You Should Have Seen Pete," "Don't Gamble with Romance."

Nevada City (Republic), June 20, 1941 (58 min.), #1026. Filmed at Walker Ranch. Director, Joseph Kane; screenplay, James Webb; camera, William Nobles; editor, Lester Orlebeck; musical director, Cy Feuer. CAST: Roy Rogers, Trigger, George Hayes, Sally Payne, Fred Kohler, Jr., George Cleveland, Billy Lee, Joseph Crehan, Pierre Watkin, Jack Ingram, Art Mix, Syd Saylor, Hank Bell, Yakima Canutt, Rex Lease, Henry Wills, Bob Woodward, Jack Kirk, Fred Burns. SYNOPSIS: There's a feud going on between the stage line and the railroad, and some nasty ne'er-do-wells are performing sabotage on both parties and blaming it on the feuders. Amidst the gun battles, Roy and Gabby end the feud and bring in the bad guys. SONGS: "Whenever Stars Drift Over the Prairie," Mark Benton's "Iron Horse Is Dying."

Bad Man of Deadwood (Republic), September 5, 1941 (61 min.), #1024. Filmed at Iversons' Ranch. Producer and director, Joseph Kane; screenplay, James R. Webb; camera, William Nobles; editor, Charles Craft; musical director, Cy Feuer. CAST: Roy Rogers, Trigger, George Hayes, Carol Adams, Sally Payne, Henry Brandon, Herbert Rawlinson, Hal Taliaferro, Jay Novello, Horace Murphy, Monte Blue, Ralf Harolde, Jack Kirk, Yakima Canutt, Curley Dresden, Fred Burns, Lynton Brent, Lloyd Ingraham, George Lloyd, Robert Frazer, Archie Twitchell, Karl Hackett, Harry Harvey, Eddie Acuff, Tom London, Jack Rockwell, Ernie Adams, Jack O'Shea, George Morrell, Wally West, Bob Woodward, Pascale Perry, Horace B. Carpenter, Harrison Greene. SYNOPSIS: Falsely accused of foul misdeeds, Roy has to leave the town to unscrupulous businessmen who are trying to gain a monopoly of all the town's businesses. Gabby provides a job and a cover for Roy with his medicine show until the two of them can go back to town and run the bad guys out. SONGS: "Call of the Dusty Trail," "Joe O'Grady," "Home on the Rangeland."

Jesse James at Bay (Republic), October 17, 1941 (56 min.), #1121. Filmed at Iversons' Ranch. Producer and director, Joseph Kane; screenplay, James R. Webb; original story, Harrison Jacobs; camera, William Nobles; editor, Tony Martinelli. CAST: Roy Rogers, Trigger, George Hayes, Gale Storm, Sally Payne, Pierre Watkin, Hal Taliaferro, Roy Barcroft, Jack Kirk, Billy Benedict, Jack O'Shea, Rex Lease, Edward Piel, Sr., Jack Rockwell, Kit Guard, Curley Dresden, Hank Bell, Bill Wolfe, Ivan Miller, Lloyd Ingraham, Karl Hackett, Budd Buster, Fred Burns, Ray Jones, Fern Emmett, Bob Woodward, Chuck Morrison. SYNOPSIS: Those railroad rowdies are cheating honest people out of their land, and Roy is robbing railroads to give money to the ragged ranchers. SONGS: "Just for You," "The Old Chisolm Trail."

Red River Valley (Republic), December 12, 1941 (62 min.), #1122. Filmed at Iversons' Ranch. Director, Joseph Kane; screenplay, Malcolm Stuart Boylan; camera, Jack Marta; editor, William Thompson; musical director, Cy Feuer. CAST: Roy Rogers, Trigger, George Hayes, Sally Payne, Trevor Bardette, Bob Nolan, Gale Storm, Robert Homans, Hal Taliaferro, Lynton Brent, Pat Brady, Edward Piel, Sr., Dick Wessell, Jack Rockwell, Ted Mapes, Sons of the Pioneers. SYNOPSIS: The desert has no water, and Roy helps the ranchers raise a considerable sum to build a reservoir, which the government will subsidize. But the funds are swindled by the bad guys, who are pretending to be good guys. Roy, with his usual tenacity, saves the day, returns the money, and finds time for a song or two. SONGS: "Red River Valley," "Sunset on the Trail," "Lily of Hillbilly Valley," "When Payday Rolls Around," "Chant of the Wanderer," "Springtime on the Range Today."

Man from Cheyenne (Republic), January 16, 1942 (60 min.), #1123. Filmed at Red Rock Canyon. Producer and director, Joseph Kane; screenplay, Winston Miller; camera, Reggie Lanning; editor, William Thompson. CAST: Roy Rogers, Trigger, George Hayes, Sally Payne, Gale Storm, Lynne Carver, William Haade, Bob Nolan, James Seay, Pat Brady, Jack Ingram, Jack Kirk, Fred Burns, Jack Rockwell, Sons of the Pioneers, Al Taylor, Chick Hannon, Art Dillard, Frank Brownlee. SYNOPSIS: Two ladies get a kiss from government agent,

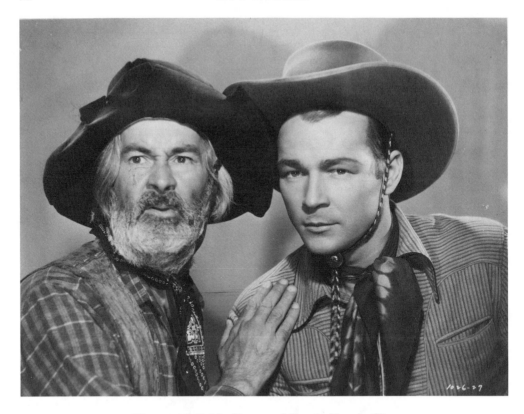

Close-up of Gabby Hayes and Roy in *Nevada City*.

Roy, and he discovers that one of them is actually a cattle rustler. SONGS: "Home Again in Ol' Wyoming," "When a Cowboy Start's a Courtin'," "My Old Pal," "Pal of Mine," "Happy Rovin' Cowboy."

South of Santa Fe (Republic), February 17, 1942 (56 min.), #1124. Filmed at Andy Jauregui Ranch. Producer and director, Joseph Kane; screenplay, James Webb; camera, Harry Neumann; editor, William Thompson; music director, Cy Feuer. CAST: Roy Rogers, Trigger, George Hayes, Linda Hayes, Paul Fix, Bobby Beers, Bob Nolan, Pat Brady, Arthur Loft, Charles Miller, Sam Flint, Jack Kirk, Jack Ingram, Hank Bell, Carleton Young, Lynton Brent, Robert Strange, Henry Wills, Jack O'Shea, Merrill McCormick. SYNOPSIS: A different mode for Roy. Airplanes, cars, machine guns, and mobsters dominate the scene, set in New Mexico. The plot involves gold mines and kidnapping. SONGS: "Song of Vaquero," "South of Santa Fe," "Yodel Your Troubles Away," "Trail Dreamin'," "We're Headin' for the Home Corral," "Open Range Ahead," "Down the Trail."

Sunset on the Desert (Republic), April 1, 1942 (54 min.), #1125. Filmed at Vasquez Rocks. Producer and director, Joseph Kane; screenplay, Gerald Geraghty; camera, Reggie Lanning; editor, Lester Orlebeck; musical director, Cy Feuer. CAST: Roy Rogers, Trigger, George Hayes, Lynne Carver, Frank M. Thomas, Bob Nolan, Beryl Wallace, Glenn Strange, Douglas Fowley, Fred Burns, Roy Barcroft, Henry Wills, Forrest Taylor, Bob Woodward, Edward Cassidy, Pat Brady, Cactus Mack, Sons of the Pioneers. SYNOPSIS: Roy has a double, and of course the double is a bad guy. When Roy is mistaken for the outlaw, he joins the gang to put the outlaws out of business, but then the real bad guy rides in and makes life tough for Roy. SONGS: "It's a Lie," "Remember Me," "Faithful Pal of Mine."

Romance on the Range (Republic), May 18, 1942 (63 min.), #1126. Producer and director,

Joseph Kane; screenplay, J. Benton Cheney; camera, William Nobles; editor, Lester Orlebeck; songs, Tim Spencer, Glenn Spencer, Sam Allen, Bob Nolan. Cast: Roy Rogers, Trigger, George Hayes, Sally Payne, Linda Hayes, Bob Nolan and the Sons of the Pioneers, Edward Pawley, Hal Taliaferro, Harry Woods, Glenn Strange, Roy Barcroft, Jack Kirk, Pat Brady, Jack O'Shea, Dick Wessell, Dick Alexander. Synopsis: The bad guys are rustling fur pelts, and Roy has to find a way to stop them. Songs: "Oh Wonderful World," "When Romance Rides the Range," "Rocky Mountain Lullaby," "Coyote Serenade," "Sing as You Work."

Sons of the Pioneers (Republic), July 2, 1942 (61 min.), #1127. Filmed at Iversons' Ranch. Producer and director, Joseph Kane; screenplay, M. Coates Webster, Mauri Grashin, Robert T. Shannon; camera, Bud Thackery; editor, Edward Schroeder; songs, Bob Nolan, Tim Spencer; musical director, Cy Feuer. Cast: Roy Rogers, Trigger, George Hayes, Marie Wrixon, Sons of the Pioneers, Forrest Taylor, Hal Taliaferro, Minerva Urecal, Bradley Page, Jack O'Shea, Frank Ellis, Tom London, Bob Woodward, Fern Emmett, Chester Conklin, Ken Cooper, Karl Hackett, Fred Burns. Synopsis: Sheriff Gabby is in danger of losing his job unless he can halt the rotten crooks who are burning barns and killing cows. He goes for Roy, who happens to be busy watching bugs. Roy agrees to put aside his interest in insects long enough to put the night crawlers in jail. Songs: "Things Are Never What They Seem," "Trail Herdin' Cowboy," "The West Is in My Soul," "He's Gone up the Trail," "Come and Get It."

Sunset Serenade (Republic), September 14, 1942 (58 min.), #1128. Director, Joseph Kane; screenplay, Earl Felton; original story, Robert Yost; camera, Bud Thackery; editor, Arthur Roberts; songs, Tim Spencer and Bob Nolan. Cast: Roy Rogers, Trigger, George Hayes, Helen Parrish, Onslow Stevens, Joan Woodbury, Frank M. Thomas, Bob Nolan and the Sons of the Pioneers, Roy Barcroft, Jack Kirk, Dick Wessell, Rex Lease, Jack Ingram, Fred Burns, Budd Buster, Jack Rockwell. Synopsis: A young lady from the East will be cheated out of her ranch unless Roy can stop the unsavory villain. Songs: "Song of San Joaquin," "I'm a Cowboy Rockefeller," "Mavoureen O'Shea," "He's a No Good Son of a Gun," "Sandman Lullaby," "I'm Headin' for the Home Corral," "For a Cowboy Has to Sing."

Heart of the Golden West (Republic), November 16, 1942 (56 min.), #1129. Producer and director, Joseph Kane; screenplay, Earl Felton; camera, Jack Marta; editor, Richard Van Enger. Cast: Roy Rogers, Trigger, Smiley Burnette, George Hayes, Ruth Terry, Bob Nolan and the Sons of the Pioneers, Walter Catlett, Paul Harvey, Edmund McDonald, Leigh Whipper, Hal Taliaferro, Cactus Mack, Hank Bell, Fred Burns, Carl Mathews, Horace B. Carpenter, Frank McCarroll, Art Dillard, Hall Johnson Choir. Synopsis: Time for the cattle to go to market, and the bad guy truckers are dealing dirty to keep all the business for themselves and away from the steamboat line. But Roy gets the goods on them and sends the cattle to market on the steamboats. Songs: "The River Robin," "Who's Gonna Help Me Sing," "Night Falls on the Prairie," "Cowboys and Indians," "River Chant," "Carry Me Back to Old Virginny," "Under Stars Over Texas."

Ridin' Down the Canyon (Republic), December 20, 1942 (55 min.), #1221. Producer, Harry Grey; director, Joseph Kane; screenplay, Albert DeMond; original story, Robert Williams and Norman Houston; camera, Jack Marta; editor, Edward Mann; songs, Tim Spencer and Bob Nolan. Cast: Roy Rogers, Trigger, George Hayes, Bob Nolan and the Sons of the Pioneers, Dee "Buzzy" Henry, Linda Hayes, Addison Richards, Lorna Gray (Adrian Booth), Olin Howlin, James Seay, Hal Taliaferro, Forrest Taylor, Roy Barcroft, Art Mix, Art Dillard. Synopsis: It's roundup time. The government needs horses for the war effort, but dishonest thugs decide it's easier to rustle than to roundup. Roy investigates, returns the horses to the rightful owners, and sings a few songs to boot. Songs: "Sagebrush Symphony," "Curley Jo," "Blue Prairie," "In a Little Spanish Town," "My Little Buckaroo," "Who Am I?" "When the Desert Sun Goes Down (Ridin' Down the Canyon)."

Idaho (Republic), March 10, 1943 (70 min.), #1222. Director, Joseph Kane; screenplay, Roy Chanslor and Olive Cooper; camera, Reggie Lanning; editor, Arthur Roberts; musical director, Morton Scott. CAST: Roy Rogers, Trigger, Smiley Burnette, Bob Nolan and the Sons of the Pioneers, Virginia Grey, Harry J. Shannon, Ona Munson, Dick Purcell, the Robert Mitchell Boy Choir, Onslow Stevens, Arthur Hohl, Hal Taliaferro, Rex Lease, Tom London, Jack Ingram, James Bush. SYNOPSIS: The town's judge is on an all-out crusade to do away with the immoral gamblers and drinkers and provide a safe, "clean" place to raise children. Roy is a state ranger and rides in to rescue the judge, the kids, and the town, not to mention the judge's pretty daughter. SONGS: "Idaho," "Whoopee Ti Yo," "Home on the Range," "Holy, Holy, Holy," "Lone Buckaroo," "Don Juan, Stop."

King of the Cowboys (Republic), April 9, 1943 (67 min.), #1204. Author: Republic Productions, Inc., Reg. Republic Pictures Corp. # LP 12006, following publication date, April 1, 1943, no renewal found. Director, Joseph Kane; screenplay, Olive Cooper and J. Benton Cheney; original story by Hal Long; camera, Reggie Lanning; editor, Harry Keller. CAST: Roy Rogers, Trigger, Smiley Burnette, Peggy Moran, Bob Nolan and the Sons of the Pioneers, Gerald Mohr, Dorthea Kent, Lloyd Corrigan, James Bush, Russell Hicks, Irving Bacon, Stuart Hamblen, Emmet Vogan, Eddie Dean, Forrest Taylor, Dick Wessell, Jack Kirk, Edward Earle, Yakima Canutt, Charles King, Jack O'Shea. SYNOPSIS: This is the movie that promoted Roy's new title. He's a combination rodeo performer and undercover agent, investigating the strange, exploding government warehouses. He and his buddies catch the saboteurs, ride and rope, and sing a song or two. SONGS: "A Gay Ranchero," "Ride Ranger Ride," "Ride 'Em Cowboy," "Red River Valley," "Roll Along Prairie Moon," "I'm a Old Cowhand," "They Cut Down the Old Pine Tree," "Biscuit Blues."

Song of Texas (Republic), June 14, 1943 (69 min.), #1223. Filmed at Lone Pine. Producer, Harry Grey; director, Joseph Kane; screenplay, Winston Miller; camera, Reggie Lanning; editor, Tony Martinelli. CAST: Roy Rogers, Trigger, Sheila Ryan, Barton MacLane, Harry Shannon, Pat Brady, Arline Judge, Bob Nolan and the Sons of the Pioneers, William Haade, Hal Taliaferro, Yakima Canutt, Tom London, Forrest Taylor, Eve March, Alex Nehera Dancers. SYNOPSIS: One of Roy's hired hands tells his daughter back East that he owns the ranch. Roy allows the young lady to believe it, but because of the deception, half the ranch gets sold to a crook who's out to get the other half. Roy has to win a wagon race to keep from losing all the ranch. SONGS: "Blue Bonnet Girl," "I Love the Prairie Country," "On the Rhythm Range," "Chapanecas," "Mexicali Rose," "Moonlight and Roses," "Rainbow Over the Range," "Cielito Lindo," "Far Away," "Whoopee Ti Yi Yo."

Silver Spurs (Republic), August 12, 1943 (65 min.), #1224. Filmed at Iversons' Ranch. Producer, Harry Grey; director, Joseph Kane; screenplay, John K. Butler and J. Benton Cheney; camera, Reggie Lanning; editor, Tony Martinelli; musical director, Morton Scott. CAST: Roy Rogers, Trigger, Smiley Burnette, John Carradine, Phyllis Brooks, Jerome Cowan, Joyce Compton, Bob Nolan and the Sons of the Pioneers, Hal Taliaferro, Jack Kirk, Kermit Maynard, Dick Wessell, Forrest Taylor, Byron Foulger, Charles Wilson, Pat Brady, Jack O'Shea, Slim Whitaker, Arthur Loft, Eddy Waller, Tom London, Bud Osborne, Fred Burns, Henry Wills. SYNOPSIS: Roy is the foreman on a ranch. The ranch is rich in oil, and there's always a less than honest critter about who wants the ranch, the oil, everything. The crook supplies a bride and alcohol, trying to coerce the rancher into his nefarious schemes. Roy saves the ranch and the oil for his boss. SONGS: "Jubilation Jamboree," "Tumbling Tumbleweeds," "When It's Springtime in the Rockies," "Highways Are Happy Ways," "When You Look for a Silver Lining (Back in Your Own Back Yard)."

Man from Music Mountain aka *Texas Legionnaires* (Republic), October 30, 1943, (71 min.) #1226. Producer, Harry Grey; director, Joseph Kane; screenplay, Bradford Ropes and J. Benton Cheney; camera, William

Cowboy King Appears At Brooklyn Strand

Roy Rogers and Ruth Terry make a romantic twosome for "Man From Music Mountain," at Brooklyn Strand.

By DOROTHY MASTERS

★ ★ ½★

Brooklyn Strand scoops Madison Square Garden in billing King of the Cowboys a week before the Rodeo brings him to town.

Peanuts, popcorn and sawdust don't go with the theatre deal, but Roy Rogers is on screen with some convincing arguments for his newly-acquired sovereignty.

"Man From Music Mountain" does all right by the man, by its music and by the mountains, too, what with Roy slated for impressive heroism and both singing and scenery every bit worthy of God's Country.

It's the godless who don't fare so well. Because of the very excellence of their villainy, Paul Kelly, Jay Novello and Hal Talia-

"Man from Music Mountain." Republic picture directed by Joseph Kane from screen play by Bradford Ropes and J. Benton Cheney. Presented at Brooklyn Strand Theatre. Running time, 1 hour, 11 minutes.

CAST:

Roy	Roy Rogers
Bob Nolan and Sons of the Pioneers	
Laramie Winters	Ruth Terry
Victor Marsh	Paul Kelly
Penny Winters	Ann Gillis
Sheriff Darcey	George Cleveland
Pat	Pat Brady
Christina Kellogg	Renie Riano
Arthur Davis	Paul Harvey
Dobe Joe	Hank Bell
Barker	Jay Novello
Slade	Hal Taliaferro
Roy's Horse	Trigger

ferro come to a properly bad end after Roy has discovered their scheme of promoting a cattle and sheep ranchers' feud.

Roy has an added incentive in that one of the victims is as pert and pretty as Ruth Terry, who at first shows a curious reluctance to be rescued by the King of Cowboys. With Ann Gillis, who plays Ruth's little sister, it's something else gain. The teen-age crush promotes some real help when the going gets tough for Roy.

New York newspaper reviews *Man from Music Mountain*, October 1, 1943.

Bradford; editor, Russell Kimball; musical director, Morton Scott. CAST: Roy Rogers, Trigger, Bob Nolan and the Sons of the Pioneers, Ruth Terry, Ann Gillis, Paul Kelly, Pat Brady, Paul Harvey, George Cleveland, Renie Riano, Hank Bell, Jay Novello, Hal Taliaferro, I. Stanford Jolley, Jack O'Shea, Tom Smith, Charles Morton. SYNOPSIS: Successful singer and cowboy Roy goes back home to entertain the homefolk. But there's a battle raging. The cattlemen and sheepherders are at it again. Roy agrees to become the law until the mess is cleared up and the villains are where they belong. SONGS: "I'm Beginning to Care," "Wine Women and Song," "Deeper and Deeper," "Song of the Bandit," "After the Rain," "Roses on the Trail," "King of the Cowboys," "Smiles Are Made of Sunshine," "He-Li-O-Yip-I-O-Le-A."

Hands Across the Border (Republic), January 5, 1944 (73 min.), #1227. Filmed at Lone Pine. Producer, Harry Grey; director, Joseph Kane; screenplay, Bradford Ropes and J. Benton Cheney; camera, Reggie Lanning; editor, Tony Martinelli; musical director, Morton Scott; dance director, Dave Gould. CAST: Roy Rogers, Trigger, Bob Nolan and the Sons of the Pioneers, Ruth Terry, Guinn (Big Boy) Williams, Onslow Stevens, Mary Treen, Joseph Crehan, Duncan Renaldo, Frederick Burton, LeRoy Mason, Larry Steers, Julian Rivero, Janet Martin, the Wiere Brothers, Roy Barcroft, Kenne Duncan, Jack Kirk, Jack O'Shea, Curley Dresden. SYNOPSIS: A rancher has been murdered, and his daughter is taking over the raising of a special breed of horses. Roy helps find the murderer, who just happens to be a rival of the girl's father. SONGS:

"When Your Heart Is on Easy Street," "The Girl in the High Buttoned Shoes," "Hands Across the Border," "Cool Water," "Hey, Hey."

Cowboy and the Señorita (Republic), May 12, 1944 (78 min.), #1321. Filmed at Iversons' Ranch. Producer, Harry Grey; director, Joseph Kane; screenplay, Gordon Kahn; original story, Bradford Ropes; camera, Reggie Lanning; editor, Tony Martinelli; musical director, Walter Scharf; dance director, Larry Ceballos; songs, Ned Washington and Phil Ohman. CAST: Roy Rogers, Trigger, Mary Lee, Dale Evans (her debut with Roy in film) John Hubbard, Guinn "Big Boy" Williams, Fuzzy Knight, Dorothy Christy, Lucien Littlefield, Hal Taliaferro, Jack Kirk, Jack O'Shea, Jane Beebe, Ben Rochelle, Bob Nolan and the Sons of the Pioneers, Rex Lease, Lynton Brent, Julian Rivero, Bob Wilke, Wally West, Tito and Corinne Valdes. SYNOPSIS: Roy and his partner are prospecting for gold. A sixteen-year-old girl is to inherit a gold mine left to her by her father, but the greedy gambler who dominates the town is out to find a way to take the gold mine from the girl. Roy puts a halt to the gambler's dastardly deeds. SONGS: "Cowboy and the Señorita," "What'll I Use for Money?" "The Enchilada Man," "Bunk House Bugle Boy," "'Round Her Neck She Wore a Yellow Ribbon."

Yellow Rose of Texas (Republic), June 24, 1944 (69 min.), #1322. Filmed at Iversons' Ranch. Director, Joseph Kane; screenplay, Jack Townley; camera, Jack Marta; editor, Tony Martinelli; musical director, Morton Scott; dance director, Larry Ceballos. CAST: Roy Rogers, Dale Evans, Trigger, George Cleveland, Harry Shannon, Grant Withers, Bob Nolan and the Sons of the Pioneers, William Haade, Weldon Heyburn, Hal Taliaferro, Tom London, Dick Botellier, Janet Martin, Don Kay Reynolds, Bob Wilke, Jack O'Shea, Rex Lease, Emmett Vogan, John Dilson. SYNOPSIS: Roy is working undercover again. This time he's an insurance investigator posing as a singer on a showboat owned by Dale. Dale's father has been framed for a robbery and is in prison. He breaks out, and together, he and Roy catch the villains and find the money from the holdup. SONGS: "I'm Coming Home," "Lucky Me, Unlucky You," "Down in the Old Town Hall," "Down Mexico Way," "Timber Trail," "Show Boat," "Song of the River," "Take It Easy," "Two Seated Saddle and a One Gaited Horse," "Yellow Rose of Texas."

Song of Nevada (Republic), August 5, 1944 (75 min.), #1323. Filmed at Walker Ranch. Director, Joseph Kane; screenplay, Gordon Kahn and Olive Cooper; camera, Jack Marta; editor, Tony Martinelli; musical director, Morton Scott; dance director, Larry Ceballos. CAST: Roy Rogers, Trigger, Dale Evans, Mary Lee, Bob Nolan and the Sons of the Pioneers, Lloyd Corrigan, Thurston Hall, John Eldredge, Forrest Taylor, George Meeker, Emmett Vogan, Le-Roy Mason, William Davidson, Kenne Duncan, Si Jenks, Frank McCarroll, Henry Wills, Jack O'Shea, Helen Talbot. SYNOPSIS: Roy agrees to help a friend teach some manners to his sophisticated, snobby daughter. The daughter is coming out West to sell daddy's ranch after he has died. She later learns that daddy didn't die, he hid out until her attitude improved. SONGS: "Nevada," "It's Love, Love, Love," "There's a New Moon Over Nevada," "Hi Ho Little Dogies," "What Are We Gonna Do?" "Harum Scarum Baron of the Harmonium," "A Cowboy Has to Yodel in the Morning," "The Wigwam Song," "Sweet Betsy from Pike," "Golden Hair Hanging Down Her Back."

San Fernando Valley (Republic), September 15, 1944 (74 min.), #1325. Filmed at Iversons' Ranch. Producer, Edward J. White; director, John English; screenplay, Dorrell McGowan, Stuart McGowan; camera, William Bradford; editor, Ralph Dixon; songs, Gordon Jenkins, Ken Carson, Tim Spencer, Charles Henderson, William Lava, Alyce Walker. CAST: Roy Rogers, Trigger, Dale Evans, Jean Porter, Andrew Toombes, Bob Nolan and the Sons of the Pioneers, Edward Gargan, Dot Farley, LeRoy Mason, Charles Smith, Pierce Lyden, Maxine Doyle, Helen Talbot, Pat Sterling, Kay Forrester, Marguerite Blount, Mary Kenyon, Hank Bell, Vernon and Draper, Morell Trio. SYNOPSIS: Dale is a bit snippy, and Roy seems to be the only one who'll stand up to the female ranch owner. Songs: "San Fernando Valley," "I Drottled a Drit Drit," "Sweeter Than You," "My Hobby Is Love," "They Went That-a-Way," "Days of '49," "Over the Rainbow Trail We'll Ride."

Lights of Old Santa Fe (Republic), November 6, 1944 (76 min.), #1326. Producer, Harry Grey; director, Frank McDonald; screenplay, Gordon Kahn, Bob Williams; camera, Reggie Lanning; editor, Ralph Dixon; musical director, Morton Scott; dance director, Larry Ceballos. Cast: Roy Rogers, Trigger, George Hayes, Dale Evans, Bob Nolan and the Sons of the Pioneers, Lloyd Corrigan, Richard Powers (Tom Keene), Claire DuBrey, Arthur Loft, Roy Barcroft, Lucien Littlefield, Sam Flint, Jack Kirk. Synopsis: Two rodeos are competitive, but one is owned by a crook. Roy gets involved in their problems, and eventually, Dale gets involved with Roy. Songs: "Amour, Amour," "Lights of Old Santa Fe," "The Cowboy Polka," "Cowboy Jubilee," "I'm Happy in My Levi Britches," "Trigger Hasn't Got a Pretty Figure," "The Nerve of Some People," "Ride 'Em Cowboy."

Utah (Republic), March 21, 1945 (78 min.), #1329. Filmed at Iversons' Ranch. Producer, Donald H. Brown; director, John English; screenplay, Jack Townley and John K. Butler; original story, Gilbert Wright and Betty Burbridge; camera, William Bradford; musical director, Morton Scott; dance director, Larry Ceballos; songs, Charles Henderson, Dave Franklin, Bob Palmer, Glenn Spencer, Tim Spencer, Bob Nolan, Ken Carson. Cast: Roy Rogers, Trigger, George Hayes, Dale Evans, Peggy Stewart, Beverly Loyd, Grant Withers, Jill Browning, Vivien Oakland, Hal Taliaferro, Jack Rutherford, Emmett Vogan, Edward Cassidy, Ralph Colby, Bob Nolan and the Sons of the Pioneers. Synopsis: Dale is an Eastern musical star who needs cash to keep the show afloat in Chicago. Her only hope is to sell the ranch she owns in Utah. Roy is foreman of the ranch and doesn't want it sold. Roy and Gabby conspire to keep Dale from selling. Songs: "Utah," "Thank Dixie for Me," "Utah Trail," "Beneath a Utah Sky," "Wild and Wooly Cowgirls," "Five Little Miles," "Welcome Home Miss Bryant," "Cowboy Blues."

Bells of Rosarita (Republic), June 19, 1945 (68 min.), #1324. Filmed at Iversons' Ranch. Producer, Edward J. White; director, Frank McDonald; screenplay, Jack Townley; camera, Ernest Miller; musical director, Morton Scott. Cast: Roy Rogers, Trigger, George Hayes, Dale Evans, Adele Mara, Grant Withers, Janet Martin, Syd Saylor, Addison Richards, Edward Cassidy, Roy Barcroft, Kenne Duncan, Rex Lease, Earle Hodgins, Bob Wilke, Ted Adams, Wally West, Bob Nolan and the Sons of the Pioneers, Robert Mitchell Boy Choir. Poodles Hanneford, Helen Talbot, Charles Sullivan, Hank Bell, Forbes Murray, Eddie Kane, Tom London, Marin Sais, Rosemond James, Marian Kerrigan, Sam Ash, Craig Lawrence, Barbara Elliott, Mary McCarty, Tom Plank, George Barton. Special Guests: Bill Elliott, Allan Lane, Don Barry, Robert Livingston, Sunset Carson. Synopsis: Roy and Bob Nolan play themselves in this one. A villainous coyote is trying to cheat Dale out of the circus she inherited. Roy and his crew are filming close to the location of the circus and find out about the nefarious deeds. Roy calls together all his Republic cowboy friends and stops the evils of the crook. Songs: "Bells of Rosarita," "Bugler's Lullaby," "I'm Gonna Build a Fence Around Texas," "Trail Herdin' Cowboy," "Singin' Down the Road," "Under a Blanket of Blue," "When the Circus Comes to Town," "Michael Finnegan," "Aloha."

Man from Oklahoma (Republic), August 1, 1945 (68 min.), #1328. Filmed at Vasquez Rocks. Producer, Louis Gray; director, Frank McDonald; screenplay, John K. Butler; camera, William Bradford; musical director, Morton Scott. Cast: Roy Rogers, Trigger, Dale Evans, George Hayes, Bob Nolan and the Sons of the Pioneers, Roger Pryor, Arthur Loft, Maude Eburne, Sam Flint, Si Jenks, June Bryde, Elaine Lange, Charles Soldant, Edmund Cobb, George Sherwood, Eddie Kane, George Chandler, Wally West, Tex Terry, Bob Wilke, Bobbie Priest, Dorothy Bailer, Rosamond James, Melva Anstead, Beverly Reedy, Geraldine Farnum. Synopsis: Someone is always giving Dale problems, and Roy is always on hand to solve the problems and punch out the bad guys to blame. Songs: "I'm

Beginning to See the Light," "The Martins and the Coys," "I'm Gonna Have a Cowboy Wedding," "Prairie Mary," "Draggin' the Wagon," "Cherro Cherro Cherokee," "For You and Me," "Skies Are Bluer," "Finale," "Square Dance," "Yes, My Darling."

Sunset in El Dorado (Republic), September 29, 1945 (65 min.), #1421. Filmed at Iversons' Ranch. Producer, Louis Gray; director, Frank McDonald; screenplay, John K. Butler; original story, Leon Abrams; camera, William Bradford; editor, Tony Martinelli. CAST: Roy Rogers, Trigger, George Hayes, Dale Evans, Hardie Albright, Margaret Dumont, Roy Barcroft, Tom London, Stanley Price, Bob Wilke, Ed Cassidy, Dorothy Granger, Bob Nolan and the Sons of the Pioneers, Edmund Cobb, Hank Bell, Jack Kirk, Gino Corrado, Frank Ellis, Tex Cooper, Bert Morehouse, Joe McGuinn, Tex Terry, Bud Osborne. SYNOPSIS: Dale's in Kansas, dreaming that she's her late grandmother, when grandmother was quite the infamous lady, "Kansas Kate." Roy appears in Dale's dream as grandmother's beau. SONGS: "I'm Awfully Glad I Met You," "Belle of the El Dorado," "Lady Who Wouldn't Say Yes," "Go West Young Man," "Call of the Prairie," "The Quilting Party," "T'ain't No Use," "Be My Little Bumble Bee."

Don't Fence Me In (Republic), October 20, 1945 (71 min.), #1327. Filmed at Big Bear. Director, John English; screenplay, Dorrell McGowan, Stuart McGowan; camera, William Bradford; editor, Charles Craft; musical directors, Morton Scott and Dale Butts; dance director, Larry Ceballos; songs, Cole Porter, Morton Shore, Zeke Manners, Jack Scholl, M. K. Kerome, Billy Hill, Larry Marks, Dick Charles, Eddie DeLange, Freddie Slack, F. Victor, R. Herman, Bob Nolan. CAST: Roy Rogers, Trigger, Dale Evans, George Hayes, Bob Nolan and the Sons of the Pioneers, Robert Livingston, Moroni Olson, Marc Lawrence, Lucille Gleason, Andrew Toombes, Paul Harvey, Douglas Fowley, Stephen Barclay, Edgar Dearing, Helen Talbot. SYNOPSIS: Dale's playing a magazine reporter heading West to seek out the true story of Wildcat Kelly (who's been dead for more years than Dale's been alive). In her quest for the truth, she runs into evil

villains, and Roy has to show the bums up. SONGS: "Don't Fence Me In," "A Kiss Goodnight," "Tumbling Tumbleweeds," "Cho Cho Polka," "Along the Navajo Trail," "My Little Buckaroo," "The Last Roundup."

Along the Navajo Trail (Republic), December 15, 1945 (66 min.), #1425. Filmed at Corriganville. Producer, Edward J. White; director, Frank McDonald; screenplay, Gerald Geraghty (based on a novel by William C. McDonald); camera, William Bradford; editor, Tony Martinelli; musical director, Morton Scott; dance director, Larry Ceballos; songs, Larry Markes, Dick Charter, Eddie DeLange, Charles Newman, Arthur Altman, Bob Nolan, Gordon Forster, Jack Elliott. CAST: Roy Rogers, Trigger, George Hayes, Dale Evans, Estelita Rodriguez, Douglas Fowley, Nestor Paiva, Sam Flint, Emmett Vogan, Roy Barcroft, David Cota, Bob Nolan, Pat Brady, Edward Cassidy, Poppy Del Vando, Rosemond James, Tex Terry, Budd Buster, Sons of the Pioneers. SYNOPSIS: Organized crime rears its ugly head when the members learn that there's oil beneath a ranch. The pressure is on to make the owners (Dale and her father) sell the property. When a government agent turns up missing, Roy is called in as a U.S. Deputy Marshal to investigate the foul deeds. SONGS: "How Are You Doing in the Heart Department?" "Cool Water," "Along the Navajo Trail."

Song of Arizona (Republic), March 9, 1946 (68 min.), #1422. Producer, Edward J. White; director, Frank McDonald; screenplay, M. Coates Webster; original story, Bradford Ropes; camera, Reggie Lanning; editor, Arthur Roberts; songs, Jack Elliott, Ira Schuster, Larry Stock, J. Cavanaugh, Mary Ann Owens, Bob Nolan, Gordon Forster. CAST: Roy Rogers, Trigger, George Hayes, Dale Evans, Bob Nolan and the Sons of the Pioneers, Lyle Talbot, Tommy Cook, Johnny Calkins, Sarah Edwards, Tommy Ivo, Michael Chapin, Dick Curtis, Edmund Cobb, Tom Quinn, Kid Chissell, Robert Mitchell Boy Choir. SYNOPSIS: Mean, nasty villains are out to get a boy whose father left money with him from a bank holdup. The boy is living at a boys' home provided by Gabby, after his father dies. Gabby has to call in Roy and his buddies to keep the evil doers from killing the boy. SONGS: "Song of Arizona," "Way Out There," "Round and Round—The Lariat Song," "Did You Ever Get That Feeling in the Moon Light," "Will You Be My Darling?" "Michael O'Leary O'Brian O'Toole," "Half a Chance Ranch," "Mr. Spook Steps Out."

Rainbow Over Texas (Republic), May 9, 1946 (65 min.), #1428. Filmed at Big Bear. Producer, Edward J. White; director, Frank McDonald; screenplay, Gerald Geraghty (based on a story by Max Brand); musical director, Morton Scott. CAST: Roy Rogers, Trigger, George Hayes, Dale Evans, Bob Nolan and the Sons of the Pioneers, Sheldon Leonard, Robert Emmett Keane, Gerald Oliver Smith, Minerva Urecal, George J. Lewis, Kenne Duncan, Pierce Lyden, Dick Elliott, Jo Ann Dean, Bud Osborne, George Chesebro. SYNOPSIS: Bad guys conspire to keep Roy from participating in a Pony Express race being held in his Texas hometown. SONGS: "Rainbow Over Texas," "Cowboy Camp Meeting," "Smile for Me Señorita (Little Señorita)," "Texas U.S.A.," "Lights of Old Santa Fe."

My Pal Trigger (Republic), July 10, 1946 (79 min.), #1427. Filmed at Iversons' Ranch. Copyright: Republic Productions, Inc., Reg, # L353, June 4, 1946, no renewal. Producer, Armand Schaefer; director, Frank McDonald; screenplay, Jack Townley and John K. Butler; camera, William Bradford; editor, Harry Keller; special effects, Howard and Theodore Lyndecker; musical director, Morton Scott. CAST: Roy Rogers, Trigger, George Hayes, Dale Evans, Jack Holt, Bob Nolan and the Sons of the Pioneers, LeRoy Mason, Roy Barcroft, Sam Flint, Kenne Duncan, Ralph Sanford, Francis McDonald, Harlan Briggs, William Haade, Alan Bridge, Paul E. Burns, Frank Reicher, Fred Graham, Ted Mapes. SYNOPSIS: Roy and a not-so-honest-gambler both have ideas of breeding Gabby's palomino stud to their mares. But the gambler (crook that he is) steals the stud, and the stud gets loose and breeds with Roy's mares. Then the gambler accidently shoots the stud, and Roy goes to jail for it. But all's well that ends well, when the gambler slips and tells on himself. SONGS: "Living Western Style," "All the Cowhands Want to Marry Harriett," "El Rancho Grande," "Old Faithful," "Long Long Ago."

Under Nevada Skies (Republic), August 26, 1946 (69 min.), #1429. Filmed at Corriganville. Producer, Edward J. White; director, Frank McDonald; screenplay, Paul Gangelin, J. Benton Cheney; original story, M. Coates Webster; camera, William Bradford; editor, Edward Mann; musical director, Dale Butts; assistant director, Yakima Canutt. CAST: Roy Rogers, Trigger, George Hayes, Dale Evans, Bob Nolan and the Sons of the Pioneers, Douglass Dumbrille, Leyland Hodgson, Tris Coffin, Rudolph Anders, LeRoy Mason, Peter George Lynn, George J. Lewis, Iron Eyes Cody. SYNOPSIS: Roy, Gabby, and Dale are trying to locate a jeweled crest that has a map inside telling about a mineral deposit that's vital in the use of uranium. The bad guys have it, and Roy leads a band of Indians in hot pursuit. SONGS: "Under Nevada Skies," "I Want to Go West," "Sea Going Cowboy," "Ne-Hah-Nee," "That Pioneer Mother of Mine," "Anytime That I'm With You," "Clear Water."

Roll On Texas Moon (Republic), September 12, 1946 (68 min.), #1523. Producer, Edward J. White; director, William Witney; screenplay, Paul Gangelin, Mauri Grashin; original story, Jean Murray; camera, William Bradford; editor, Lester Orlebeck; musical director, Dale Butts; songs, Jack Elliott, Tim Spencer. CAST: Roy Rogers, Trigger, George Hayes, Dale Evans, Bob Nolan and the Sons of the Pioneers, Dennis Hoey, Elizabeth Risdon, Francis McDonald, Edward Keane, Kenne Duncan, Tom London, Harry Strang, Edward Cassidy, Lee Shumway, Steve Darrell, Pierce Lyden. SYNOPSIS: Roy is trying to bring peace between the cattlemen and the sheepers. Gabby owns a cattle ranch, Dale owns the sheep. SONGS: "The Jumping Bean," "Roll On Texas Moon," "Won't 'Cha Be a Friend of Mine?" "What's Doing Tonight in Dreamland?"

Home in Oklahoma (Republic), November 8, 1946 (72 mins.), #1523. Filmed at Bill Licken's Flying L Ranch, near Dougherty and Davis, Oklahoma. Producer, Edward J. White; director, William Witney; screenplay, Gerald Geraghty; camera, William

Bradford; editor, Lester Orlebeck; songs, Jack Elliott, Tim Spencer. CAST: Roy Rogers, Trigger, George Hayes, Dale Evans, Carol Hughes, Bob Nolan and the Sons of the Pioneers, George Meeker, Lanny Rees, Ruby Dandridge, George Lloyd, Arthur Space, Frank Reicher, George Carleton. SYNOPSIS: Small-town editor Rogers teams up with big city newswoman Evans. Together, amongst the shooting, the singing, and the fist fights, they find the killer of a rancher. SONGS: "Miguelito," "Home in Oklahoma," "I Wish I Was a Kid Again," "Everlasting Hills of Oklahoma," "Cowboy Ham and Eggs," "Hereford Heaven."

Heldorado (Republic), December 15, 1946 (70 min.), #1534. Filmed at Las Vegas and Hoover Dam, Nevada. Copyright: Republic Productions Inc., Reg. # L 744, December 11, 1946, no renewal. Producer, Edward J. White; director, William Witney; screenplay, Gerald Geraghty and Julian Zimet; camera, William Bradford; editor, Lester Orlebeck; songs, Jack Elliott, Denver Darling, Roy Rogers and Bob Nolan. CAST: Roy Rogers, Trigger, George Hayes, Dale Evans, Paul Harvey, Barry Mitchell, John Bagni, John Phillips, James Taggert, Rex Lease, Steve Darrell, Doye O'Dell, LeRoy Mason, Charlie Williams, Eddie Acuff, Bob Nolan and the Sons of the Pioneers. SYNOPSIS: Roy's at the annual Heldorado Parade in Las Vegas. The local gambling houses are having problems with black market bad guys, and Roy steps in to lasso the villains. SONGS: "Heldorado," "My Saddle Pals and I," "Good Neighbor," "Silver Stars Purple Sage Eyes of Blue," "You Ain't Heard Nothin' Till You Heard Him Roar," "Amigo."

Apache Rose (Republic), February 15, 1947 (75 min.), Trucolor, #1526. Filmed at Vasquez Rocks. Producer, Edward J. White; director, William Witney; screenplay, Gerald Geraghty; camera, Jack Marta; editor, Lester Orlebeck; songs, Jack Elliott, Tim Spencer, Glenn Spencer. CAST: Roy Rogers, Trigger, Dale Evans, Olin Howlin, Bob Nolan and the Sons of the Pioneers, George Meeker, John Laurenz, Russ Vincent, Minerva Urecal, LeRoy Mason, Donna DeMario, Terry Frost, Conchita Lemus, Tex Terry. SYNOPSIS: Honest Roy is searching for oil. Dishonest gamblers have found

oil, but it belongs to someone else. They try to force the owner to pay his gambling debts with oil land. SONGS: "Apache Rose," "Ride Vaqueros Ride," "Don Jose," "Make a Wish at the Wishing Well," "Nothing Like Coffee in the Morning."

Bells of San Angelo (Republic), April 15, 1947 (78 min.), Trucolor, #1525. Filmed at Red Rock Canyon. Producer, Edward J. White; director, William Witney; screenplay, Sloan Nibley; musical director, Morton Scott; director of photography, Jack Marta. CAST: Roy Rogers, Trigger, Dale Evans, Andy Devine (his debut as Cookie Bullfincher), John McGuire, Olaf Hytten, David Sharpe, Fritz Leiber, Hank Patterson, Fred Toones, Eddie Acuff, Dale Van Sickel, Bob Nolan and the Sons of the Pioneers, Silver Harr, Buck Bucko. SYNOPSIS: Roy is looking for smugglers on the Mexican border, Dale writes Western novels. Together they find the smugglers at a silver mine, but Roy is royally flogged, before coming up with the evidence to put the sneaky, silver smugglers behind bars. SONGS: "Bells of San Angelo," "Hot Lead," "I Like to Get Up Early in the Morning," "A Cowboy's Dream of Heaven," "I Love the West," "Lazy Days."

Springtime in the Sierras (Republic), July 15, 1947 (75 min.), Trucolor, #1529. Filmed at Walker Ranch. Producer, Edward J. White; director, William Witney; screenplay, Sloan Nibley; camera, Jack Marta; editor, Tony Martinelli; musical director, Morton Scott; songs, Jack Elliott, Bob Nolan, Tim Spencer. CAST: Roy Rogers, Trigger, Jane Frazee, Andy Devine, Stephanie Bachelor, Hal Landon, Harry V. Cheshire, Roy Barcroft, Chester Conklin, Hank Patterson, Whitey Christy, Pascale Perry, Bob Woodward, Bob Nolan and the Sons of the Pioneers. SYNOPSIS: The poachers, headed by a lady villain, are hunting out of season animals. Roy is out to stop them and is viciously tossed into a meat freezer. But he thaws out in time to catch the bad guys, and the bad girl too. SONGS: "Springtime in the Sierras," "A Cowboy Has to Sing," "Imagine Me—What a Picture I Would Make," "Seeing Nellie Home (Quilting Party)," "What Are You Going to Do When I Get Old and Gray?" "Pedro from Acapulco."

This publicity photo for *On the Old Spanish Trail* has Roy cheek-to-cheek with Jane Frazee.

On the Old Spanish Trail (Republic), October 15, 1947 (75 min.), Trucolor, #1527. Filmed at Kernville, California. Producer, Edward J. White; director, William Witney; screenplay, Sloan Nibley; original story, Gerald Geraghty; camera, Jack Marta; editor, Tony Martinelli; musical director, Morton Scott. CAST: Roy Rogers, Trigger, Jane Frazee, Andy Devine, Tito Guizar, Estelita Rodriguez, Bob Nolan and the Sons of the Pioneers, Charles McGraw, Fred Graham, Steve Darrell, Marshall Reed, Wheaton Chambers. SYNOPSIS: Roy has to pay his mortgage, and the only way he can raise the money is to capture the bandits who have been robbing oil companies. The wrong man is accused of the robberies and jailed by Sheriff Cookie Bullfincher, but Roy finds the real culprits, gets the innocent man out of jail, collects the reward, and pays his mortgage. SONGS: "Here Is My Helping Hand," "I'll Never Love Again," "My Adobe Hacienda," "On the Old Spanish Trail."

Gay Ranchero (Republic), January 10, 1948 (72 min.), Trucolor, #1528. Producer, Edward J. White; director, William Witney; screenplay, Sloan Nibley; camera, Jack Marta; editor, Tony Martinelli; songs, Abe Tuvim, Francia Luban, J. J. Espinosa, Harry Glick, Jimmy Lambert, Dave Olsen, Augustin Lara, and Ray Gilbert. CAST: Roy Rogers, Trigger, Tito Guizar, Jane Frazee, Andy Devine, Estelita Rodriguez, George Meeker, LeRoy Mason, Dennis Moore, Keith Richards, Betty Gagnon, Robert Rose, Ken Terrell, Bob Nolan and the Sons of the Pioneers. SYNOPSIS: The local airport is in danger of being taken over by thugs and thieves. They're sabotaging the airplanes, and Roy is the sheriff who rides in on horseback with six-guns blazing to halt these uncouth acts. SONGS: "The Gay Ranchero," "Cowboy Country," "Wait'll I Get My Sunshine in the Moonlight," "Granda," "You Belong to My Heart."

Under California Stars (Republic), May 1, 1948 (70 min.), Trucolor, #1621. Producer, Edward J. White; director, William Witney; screenplay, Sloan Nibley and Paul Gangelin; original story, Paul Gangelin; camera, Jack Marta; editor, Tony Martinelli. CAST: Roy Rogers, Trigger, Jane Frazee, Andy Devine, Michael Chapin, Wade Crosby, George Lloyd, House Peters, Jr., Steve Clark, Joseph Carro, Paul Powers, John Wald, Bob Nolan and the Sons of the Pioneers. SYNOPSIS: Trigger is horsenapped, and Roy leaves no stone unturned in finding him. SONGS: "Under California Stars," "Roy Rogers, King of the Cowboys," "Serenade to a Coyote," "Dust," "Little Saddle Pal."

Eyes of Texas (Republic), July 15, 1948 (70 min.), Trucolor, #1623. Filmed at Walker Ranch. Producer, Edward J. White; director, William Witney; screenplay, Sloan Nib-

ley; camera, Jack Marta; editor, Tony Martinelli. CAST: Roy Rogers, Trigger, Lynne Roberts, Andy Devine, Nana Bryant, Roy Barcroft, Danny Morton, Francis Ford, Pascale Perry, Stanley Blystone, Bob Nolan and the Sons of the Pioneers. SYNOPSIS: The lady is a villain, trying to rule the range by the use of a pack of highly trained, killer canines. It's up to U.S. Marshal Roy to discourage such behavior by putting the evil lady in jail and putting the killer canines in a kennel. SONGS: "The Padre of Old San Antone," "Texas Trails," "Graveyard Filler of the West," "Blue Shadows on the Trail," "Pecos Bill."

Night Time in Nevada (Republic), September 5, 1948 (67 min.), Trucolor, #1624. Producer, Edward J. White; director, William Witney; screenplay, Sloan Nibley; camera, Jack Marta; editor, Tony Martinelli; musical director, Dale Butts; songs, Richard W. Pascoe, Will E. Dulmage, H. O'Reilly Clint, Tim Spencer, Edward Morrissey, Bob Nolan. CAST: Roy Rogers, Trigger, Andy Devine, Adele Mara, Grant Withers, Marie Harmond (Harmon), Joseph Crehan, George Carleton, Holly Bane, Steve Darrell, Hank Patterson, Jim Nolan, Bob Nolan and the Sons of the Pioneers. SYNOPSIS: Obnoxious outlaws are on the loose and purloin a train load of cattle that's on the way to Roy's ranch. Roy talks Sheriff Bullfincher into deputizing him so that he can find the beef snatchers. SONGS: "Night Time in Nevada," "Sweet Laredo Lou," "Big Rock Candy Mountain," "Over Nevada."

Grand Canyon Trail (Republic), November 5, 1948 (67 min.), Trucolor, #1625. Filmed at Red Rock Canyon. Producer, Edward J. White; director, William Witney; screenplay, Gerald Geraghty; camera, Reggie Lanning; editor, Tony Martinelli; musical director, Nathan Scott; songs, Jack Elliott, Foy Willing. CAST: Roy Rogers, Trigger, Andy Devine, Jane Frazee, Robert Livingston, Roy Barcroft, Charles Coleman, Emmett Lynn, Ken Terell, James Finlayson, Tommy Coats, Zon Murray, Foy Willing and the Riders of the Purple Sage. SYNOPSIS: Roy is up to his ears in debt because of his silver mine that stubbornly refuses to pay off. But Roy is persistent and keeps digging.

A swindling mining engineer happens upon the scene and tries to convince Roy that there is no silver so that he can get the mine, knowing that just below the surface lurks riches. (Foy Willing and the Riders of the Purple Sage make their debut.) Songs: "Everything's Going My Way," "Ridin' Ropin' Cowboy," "Down the Grand Canyon Trail."

Far Frontier (Republic), December 29, 1948 (67 min.), Trucolor, #1626. Filmed at Walker Ranch. Producer, Edward J. White; director, William Witney; screenplay, Sloan Nibley; camera, Jack Marta; editor, Tony Martinelli; musical director, Dale Butts. Cast: Roy Rogers, Trigger, Andy Devine, Gail Davis, Francis Ford, Roy Barcroft, Clayton Moore, Robert Strange, Holly Bane, Lane Bradford, John Bagni, Clarence Straight, Edmund Cobb, Tom London, Foy Willing and the Riders of the Purple Sage. Synopsis: Roy is working with the border patrol to help arrest American outlaws who keep sneaking back across the border. Songs: "I Love the West," "Far Frontier," "Hittin' the Trail to Monterrey," "Sunset in the West."

Susanna Pass (Republic), April 29, 1949 (67 min.), Trucolor, #1627. Filmed at Corriganville. Cast: Roy Rogers, Trigger, Dale Evans, Estelita Rodriguez, Martin Garralaga, Robert Emmett Keane, Lucien Littlefield, Douglas Fowley, David Sharpe, Robert Bice, Foy Willing and the Riders of the Purple Sage. Synopsis: Game Warden Roy is upset because someone is blowing his fish out of the water with dynamite. Little does he know that the fishy fiends just want the oil that's under the river. But he gets a line on them and with the help of friends, sends them up without that proverbial paddle. (Dale Evans is back in the saddle with Roy after a long absence.) Songs: "Susanna Pass," "A Good Good Morning," "Brush Those Tears from Your Eyes," "Two Gun Rita."

Down Dakota Way (Republic), September 9, 1949 (67 min.), Trucolor, #1628. Filmed at Corriganville. Producer, Edward J. White; director, William Witney; screenplay, John K. Butler and Sloan Nibley; camera, Reggie Lanning; editor, Tony Martinelli; musical director, Dale Butts; songs, Sloan Nibley, Dale Butts, Sid Robin, Foy Willing, George Morgan. Cast: Roy Rogers, Trigger, Dale Evans, Pat Brady, Monte Montana, Elizabeth Risdon, Byron Barr, James Cardwell, Roy Barcroft, Emmett Vogan, Foy Willing and the Riders of the Purple Sage. Synopsis: A less than honest cattle rancher is trying to foist his sick cattle to market, before anyone realizes that they all have hoof and mouth disease. He kills the local vet so that he won't tattle. Total stranger Roy rides in, pistols and guitar working overtime, to stop the fiendish swindler. Songs: "ABC," "Candy Kisses," "Roll on Little Dogies."

Golden Stallion (Republic), November 15, 1949 (67 min.), Trucolor, #1830. Filmed at Iversons' Ranch. Producer, Edward J. White; director, William Witney; screenplay, Sloan Nibley; camera, Jack Marta; editor, Tony Martinelli; musical director, Nathan Scott; songs, Sid Robin, Foy Willing, Nathan Glick, Anne Parentean, Eddie Cherkose, Sol Meyer, Jule Styne. Cast: Roy Rogers, Trigger, Dale Evans, Pat Brady, Estelita Rodriguez, Chester Conklin, Douglas Evans, Greg McClure, Frank Fenton, Dale Van Sickel, Clarence Straight, Karl Hackett, Foy Willing and the Riders of the Purple Sage. Synopsis: A golden mare is trained to smuggle diamonds across the U.S. border and is caught by Roy. He just doesn't know that she's an equestrian smuggler. Trigger has an affair with the mare, and the inevitable happens. Roy uses Trigger's offspring to help capture the smuggling skunks. Songs: "The Golden Stallion," "There's Always Time for a Song," "Bird in a Cage" (Square Dance Tune), "Take a Chance and Learn to Dance," "Dreaming of You."

Bells of Coronado (Republic), January 8, 1950 (67 min.), Trucolor, #1629. Producer, Edward J. White; director, William Witney; screenplay, Sloan Nibley; musical director, R. Dale Butts; photography, John MacBurnie. Cast: Roy Rogers, Trigger, Dale Evans, Pat Brady, Grant Withers, Leo Cleary, Clifton Young, Robert Bice, Stuart Randall, John Hamilton, Edmund Cobb, Eddie Lee, Rex Lease, Lane Bradford, Foy Willing and the Riders of the Purple Sage. Synopsis: Espionage is lurking in the wings, and Roy is an undercover investigator for an insurance company. Foreign agents have been stealing uranium, and Roy uses fists and pistols to keep them from leaving with the stolen goods. Songs: "Bells of Coronado," "Save a Smile for a Rainy Day," "Got No Time for the Blues."

Twilight in the Sierras (Republic), March 22, 1950 (67 min.), Trucolor, #1831. Filmed at Iversons' Ranch. Producer, Edward J. White; director, William Witney; screenplay, Sloan Nibley; camera, John MacBurnie; editor, Tony Martinelli; musical director, Stanley Wilson; songs, Sid Robin, Foy Willing. CAST: Roy Rogers, Trigger, Dale Evans, Estelita Rodriguez, Pat Brady, Ross Vincent, George Meeker, Fred Kohler, Jr., Edward Keane, House Peters, Jr., Pierce Lyden, Don Frost, Joseph Carro, William Lester, Bob Burns, Bob Wilke, Foy Willing and the Riders of the Purple Sage. SYNOPSIS: Greed gets the best of the goons, and they begin making their own money. Roy is the U.S. Marshal who is bent on stopping such counterfeit activity. SONGS: "When It's Twilight in the Sierras," "Rootin' Tootin' Cowboy from the West," "It's One Wonderful Day," "Pancho's Rancho."

Trigger Jr. (Republic), June 30, 1950 (68 min.), Trucolor, #1834. Filmed at Lone Pine. Producer, Edward J. White; director, William Witney; screenplay, Gerald Geraghty; camera, Jack Marta; editor, Tony Martinelli; musical director, Dale Butts; songs, Peter Tinturin, Foy Willing, Carol Rice. CAST: Roy Rogers, Trigger, Dale Evans, Pat Brady, Gordon Jones, Grant Withers, Peter Miles, George Cleveland, Frank Fenton, I. Stanford Jolley, Stanley Andrews, the Reynor Lehr Circus, Foy Willing and the Riders of the Purple Sage, Little Trigger. SYNOPSIS: It's the old "protection racket" that the villain is trying to sell to the ranchers. To make his point, he turns loose a specially trained killer stallion to kill the good horses. Roy saves the day after a young boy helps save Roy. SONGS: "May the Good Lord Take a Likin' to You," "The Big Rodeo," "Stampede."

Sunset in the West (Republic), September 25, 1950 (67 min.), Trucolor, #1832. Filmed at Walker Ranch. Producer, Edward J. White; director, William Witney; screenplay, Gerald Geraghty; camera, Jack Marta; editor, Tony Martinelli; special effects, Howard and Theodore Lydecker; songs, Jack Elliott, Foy Willing, Aaron Gonzales. CAST: Roy Rogers, Trigger, Estelita Rodriguez, Penny Edwards, Gordon Jones, Will Wright, Pierre Watkin, Charles LaTorre, William J. Tannen, Gaylord Pendleton, Paul E. Burns, Dorothy Ann White, Foy Willing and the Riders of the Purple Sage. SYNOPSIS: A train is stolen, and Roy offers his services to the sheriff to help locate the missing locomotive and find out who killed the crew. Gunrunners are using the train to take guns to the beach, where they're shipped to foreign countries. SONGS: "Sunset in the West," "When a Pretty Girl Passes By," "Rollin' Wheels."

North of the Great Divide (Republic), November 15, 1950 (67 min.), Trucolor, #1836. Filmed at Big Bear. Producer, Edward J. White; director, William Witney; screenplay, Eric Taylor; camera, Jack Marta; editor, Tony Martinelli; songs, Jack Elliott. CAST: Roy Rogers, Trigger, Penny Edwards, Gordon Jones, Roy Barcroft, Jack Lambert, Douglas Evans, Keith Richards, Noble Johnson, Iron Eyes Cody, Foy Willing and the Riders of the Purple Sage. SYNOPSIS: First they killed the buffalo to starve the Indians, now the nasty things are choking off the salmon and creating hungry Indians that threaten to go on the warpath. Roy must put a stop to the chicanery at the cannery. SONGS: "North of the Great Divide," "By the Laughing Spring," "Just Keep a Movin'."

Trail of Robin Hood (Republic), December 23, 1950 (67 min.), Trucolor, #1836. Filmed at Big Bear. Producer, Edward J. White; director, William Witney; screenplay, Gerald Geraghty; camera, John MacBurnie; editor, Tony Martinelli; songs, Jack Elliott, Foy Willing. CAST: Roy Rogers, Trigger, Penny Edwards, Gordon Jones, Jack Holt, Emory Parnell, Clifton Young, James Magill, Carol Nugent, George Chesbro, Edward Cassidy, Foy Willing and the Riders of the Purple Sage. GUEST STARS: Tom Tyler, Kermit Maynard, Tom Keene, Monte Hale, Rex Allen, Allan Lane, William Farnum. SYNOPSIS: A kind-hearted pseudo–Santa is growing Christmas trees, which he sells to the poor for a mere pittance. But there's a Scrooge in the woodpile who is routing the trees and hindering the harvest, until Roy and friends step in to help the good guy. SONGS: "Every Day Is Christmas in the West," "Get a Christmas Tree for Johnny," "Home Town Jubilee."

Spoilers of the Plains (Republic), February 2, 1951 (68 min.), #1838. Filmed at Corriganville. Producer, Edward J. White; director, William Witney; screenplay, Sloan Nibley; camera, Jack Marta; editor, Tony Martinelli; songs, Jack Elliott, Aaron Gonzales, Foy Willing. CAST: Roy Rogers, Trigger, Penny Edwards, Gordon Jones, Grant Withers, Fred Kohler, Jr., William Forrest, Don Haggerty, House Peters, Jr., George Meeker, Keith Richards, Foy Willing and the Riders of the Purple Sage. SYNOPSIS: Foreign spies are threatening American security again, and who best to halt the nefarious schemes? Why Roy, of course. He punches one of them into oblivion atop an oil derrick. (Bullet joins Roy's growing corral of wonder animals.) SONGS: "There's a Rainbow Over Texas," "Happy Trails in Sunshine Valley."

Heart of the Rockies (Republic), March 30, 1951 (67 min.), #1837. Filmed at Iversons' Ranch. Producer, Edward J. White; director, William Witney; screenplay, Eric Taylor; camera, Reggie Lanning; editor, Tony Martinelli; musical director, Dale Butts; songs, Jack Elliott, Foy Willing, Geri Gallian. CAST: Roy Rogers, Trigger, Penny Edwards, Gordon Jones, Ralph Morgan, Fred Graham, Mira McKinney, Robert "Buzz" Henry, William Gould, Pete Hern, Rand Brooks, Foy Willing and the Riders of the Purple Sage. SYNOPSIS: A rancher has a dirty little secret, and he's afraid that construction foreman Roy will uncover his dishonest dealings, if Roy continues to build the highway across the ranchers' property. But thugs and henchmen could never stop Roy. SONGS: "In the Heart of the Rockies," "Rodeo Square Dance," "Wanderin'," "Prairie Country."

In Old Amarillo (Republic), May 25, 1951 (67 min.), #1839. Producer, Edward J. White; director, William Witney; screenplay, Sloan Nibley; camera, Jack Marta; editor, Tony Martinelli; songs, Jack Elliott, Foy Willing. CAST: Roy Rogers, Trigger, Estelita Rodriguez, Penny Edwards, Pinky Lee, Roy Barcroft, Pierre Watkin, Ken Howell, Elizabeth Risdon, William Holmes, Kermit Maynard, Alan Bridge, Roy Rogers Riders. SYNOPSIS: Cattle are dying of thirst; there's a drought and no rain in sight. And when there's trouble, there's always a sinister scoundrel around. He's sabotaging all efforts to get water for the cattle so that he can buy them at low cost for his new canning plant. Roy stops the canned cattle caper, and helps get rain to the area. (Pinky Lee makes his first Roy Rogers film.) SONGS: "If I Ever Fall in Love," "In Old Amarillo," "Wasteland," "Under the Lone Star Moon."

South of Caliente (Republic), October 15, 1951 (67 min.), #1840. Producer, Edward J. White; director, William Witney; screenplay, Eric Taylor; camera, Jack Marta; editor, Harold Minter; musical director, Dale Butts; songs, Jack Elliott, Lee Wainer. CAST: Roy Rogers, Trigger, Dale Evans, Pinky Lee, Douglas Fowley, Pat Brady, Charlita, Rick Roman, Leonard Penn, Willie Best, Frank Richards, Lillian Molieri, George J. Lewis, Marguerite McGill, Roy Rogers Riders. SYNOPSIS: Dale's racehorse is stolen by none other than the trainer. Roy has to punch out the rowdy racehorse rustler and return the horse to Dale. SONGS: "My Home Is Over Yonder," "Gypsy Trail," "Won'tcha Be a Friend of Mine," "Yascha the Gypsy."

Pals of the Golden West (Republic), December 15, 1951 (68 min.), #1841. Filmed at Red Rock Canyon. Producer, Edward J. White; director, William Witney; screenplay, Albert DeMond, Eric Taylor; story, Sloan Nibley; camera, Jack Marta; editor, Harold Minter; songs, Jack Elliott, Aaron Gonzales, Jordan Smith. CAST: Roy Rogers, Trigger, Dale Evans, Estelita Rodriguez, Pinky Lee, Roy Barcroft, Anthony Caruso, Edwardo Jiminez, Ken Terrell, Emmett Vogan, Maurice Jara, Roy Rogers Riders. SYNOPSIS: An outbreak of hoof and mouth disease in Mexico has cattle ranchers in the states all in a dither. Border Patrolman Rogers has to battle nature and two legged swine to keep the disease from crossing the border. SONGS: "Pals of the Golden West,"

SPECIAL
"KIDDIE" MATINEE
ARMISTICE DAY NOV. 11
AT 2:00 P. M. ONLY

Roy ROGERS
and TRIGGER

...BATTLES
MODERN-DAY
HORSE
THIEVES
IN A
NEW
ACTION-
PACKED
HIT!

South of Caliente

with
DALE   PINKY
EVANS · LEE

Plus

10-CARTOONS

2 1/2 HOURS OF FUN AND ADVENTURE !
ALL SEATS - 25¢.........

Theater handout promotes upcoming *South of Caliente* in 1951.

In the early 1950s, Roy's films were rereleased, and the original promotional materials were doctored up with photos from a later period. Note the mixture of the old and new Roy in the lobby card for *In Old Caliente.*

"You Never Know When Love May Come Along," "Slumber Trail," "Beyond the Great Divide."

Other Films

Meet Roy Rogers (Republic), June 24, 1941 (10 min. short). Produced and directed by Harriett Parsons. CAST: Roy Rogers, Gene Autry, Judy Canova, Bill Elliott, George "Gabby" Hayes, Billy Gilbert, Bob Baker, Roscoe Ates, Mary Lee.

Son of Paleface (Paramount), August 1, 1952 (95 min.), Technicolor, #10104. Filmed at Iversons' Ranch. Producer, Robert L. Welch; director, Frank Tashlin; screenplay, Frank Tashlin, Robert L. Welch, and Joseph Quillan. CAST: Bob Hope, Jane Russell, Roy Rogers, Bill Williams, Lloyd Corrigan, Paul E. Burns, Douglass Dumbrille, Iron Eyes

Cody, Harry Von Zell, Wee Willie Davis, Charley Cooley, Hank Mann, Chester Conklin, Johnathan Hale, Oliver Blake, Cecil B. DeMille, Bing Crosby, Trigger. SYNOPSIS: Roy is once more a secret agent working for the government to rout out a band of outlaws led by the voluptuous Jane Russell. Bob Hope provides the comedy as Junior, the man that all the town is waiting for, so that he can pick up his inheritance and pay off his father's debts. SONGS: "Am I in Love?" "A Four Legged Friend," "California Rose," "Wing Ding Tonight," "There's a Cloud in My Valley of Sunshine," "What a Dirty Shame," "Buttons and Bows."

Alias Jesse James (United Artists), April 2, 1959 (92 min.), Technicolor, #JJR/516. Producer, Jack Hope; director, Norman Z. McLeod; screenplay, William D. Bowers, Daniel D. Beauchamp; original story, Robert St. Aubrey, Bert Lawrence. CAST:

Bob Hope, Rhonda Fleming, Wendell Corey, Jim Davis, Gloria Talbot, Will Wright, Mary Young. Cameo appearance, Roy Rogers. SYNOPSIS: Bob Hope is an insurance salesman who sells a policy to Jesse James and has to hang around to assure the safety of his client.

Mackintosh & T.J. (Penland Productions) February 5, 1976 (96 min.), Technicolor. Producer, Tim Penland; director, Marvin J. Chomsky; screenplay, Paul Savage; camera, Terry Mead; editor, Howard Smith; art director, Alan Smith; assistant director, Claude Binyon, Jr.; music composed and performed by Waylon Jennings. CAST: Roy Rogers, Clay O'Brien, Billy Green Bush, Andrew Robinson, Joan Hackett, James Hampton, Walter Barnes, Dean Smith, Larry Mahan. SYNOPSIS: Rogers, a drifter and ranch hand, "adopts" a young boy and helps him through adolescence.

Documentary Films

Roy Rogers — King of the Cowboys, Republic Pictures/AMC/Galen Films, 1992 (60 min.). *Roy Rogers — King of the Cowboys*, Scorpio Film Productions, 1992 (80 min.). Excerpts from Roy's films; Roy and Dale narrate and show home movies.

Opposite, Top: **Roy, "Trigger," and Jane Russell in publicity still for** *Son of Paleface.* **This is not the original Trigger, nor even "Little Trigger."** *Opposite, Bottom:* **Roy made a film comeback in** *Mackintosh & T. J.* **in 1976.**

Chapter 6

TELEVISION HISTORY

Had Republic Productions won the first round with Roy Rogers in federal court in 1951, his career would have undergone a major change. He might have retired from show business, as had others when television came along. Instead, he developed a television series and secured a sponsor. The series played a tremendous role in his popularity and transformed a mere merchandising program into a virtual bonanza. It was the series-related merchandise and media coverage that made "Roy and Dale" a part of every American household. As a Western duo, they were unique.

My gratitude to others, such as David Rothel, who have produced an episode log of the 1951–57 series. I have referenced Rothel's material as well as many of the episodes in my collection, and certain novelized episodes included in 1950s television magazines and 1950s TV Guides, in order to present this listing of Roy Rogers' television history. My research and video collection has yielded a record of many of his television guest appearances.

The Roy Rogers Show

One-half hour, NBC, Dec. 30, 1951, to June 23, 1957. Sunday—5:30 to 6:00 P.M. (CST). Mid-1957, episodes leased to Nestle Company for six years. Between 1958 and 1961, show was syndicated in 130 markets, playing mostly on NBC and affiliate stations on Saturday mornings. January 1961 to September 1964 CBS began airing the reruns, again Saturday mornings, sponsored by Nestle Co. and Ideal Toy Co. Pat Brady plays Roy's comic sidekick as a diner cook in Dale's Eureka Cafe in Mineral City, Paradise Valley, Mineral County. Ralph Cotton, the mayor, is played by Harry Lauter, Sheriff Potter by Harry Harvey, Sr. Bullet, "the wonder dog," adds kid appeal to the episodes. TYPICAL PRODUCTION EPISODE CREDITS: Produced by Jack Lacey, Bob Henry, Roy Rogers, and Leslie H. Martinson. Leslie Martinson directs. Supervisor of editing, Fred Peitshanz, A.C.E.; special effects editors, Marshall Pollack, Rex Lipton; music editor, Helen Sneddon; asst. director, Roy Wade; production coordinator, Jerome A. Stanley; set continuity, Bill

Hole; lighting, Wilbur Kinnett; makeup, Ray Stork; hair styling, Mildred Burns; properties, Robert Eaton; special effects, Ivan Arnold; sound, John Kean; costumes, Tommy Thompson; management, W. Arthur Rush, Larry Kent. EPISODES: The premier episode was one hour. The first half was a variety show featuring guest star Bob Hope. Episodes were filmed at Iversons' Ranch and Hertz Ranch, outside Hollywood. Roy chose a Western street located on the Goldwyn lot for the town of Mineral City.

Jailbreak (December 30, 1951). Director, John English; screenplay, Al DeMond and Riley Wilson. CAST: Roy Rogers, Dale Evans, Pat Brady, Steve Clark, Rand Brooks, Terry Frost, Riley Hill, Harry Harvey, Nan Leslie, Douglas Evans, Gregg Barton, Trigger. SYNOPSIS: Falsely accused of murdering his prospective father-in-law, a man escapes jail, with a little help from Dale.

The Set Up (January 20, 1952). Director, Robert G. Walker; screenplay, Eric Taylor. CAST: Roy Rogers, Dale Evans, Pat Brady, Hallene Hill, Harry Harvey, Wheaton

Roy and Dale in *Pals of the Golden West*. When this was being filmed, Roy already had his sights on the television market.

Chambers, Zon Murray, Boyd "Red" Morgan, Trigger. SYNOPSIS: The bad guys are out to get the land that an elderly lady doesn't want to sell. The crooks plan the old lady's murder, and she joins forces with Roy and Dale to stop the evil plots.

Treasure of Howling Dog Canyon (January 27, 1952). Director, Robert G. Walker; screenplay, Al DeMond and Ray Wilson. CAST: Roy Rogers, Dale Evans, Pat Brady, Dorothy Crider, Carl "Alfalfa" Switzer, Don D. Harvey, Denver Pyle, Boyd "Red" Morgan, Chief Yowlachie, Trigger. SYNOPSIS: A femme fatale marries a miner for his treasure map, then has him killed. His son has part of the map, and she's terrorizing him.

The Train Robbery (February 3, 1952). Director, Robert G. Walker; screenplay, Milton M. Raison. CAST: Roy Rogers, Dale Evans, Pat Brady, Reed Howes, William Fawcett, Bob Wilke, Mike Ragan, Charles M.

Heard, Trigger. SYNOPSIS: The postmaster is a crook and hires his buddies to rob the train.

Badman's Brother (February 10, 1952). Director, Robert G. Walker; screenplay, Dwight Babcock. CAST: Roy Rogers, Dale Evans, Pat Brady, Francis McDonald, Minerva Urecal, Bobby Hyatt, Harry Macklin, Riley Hill, Sandy Sanders, Harry Harvey, Trigger. SYNOPSIS: A sinister saddlebum robs and kills, then uses his eleven-year-old brother to cover for him.

Outlaw's Girl (February 17, 1952). Director, Robert G. Walker; screenplay, Dwight Babcock. CAST: Roy Rogers, Dale Evans, Pat Brady, Brett King, Reed Howes, Tom Tyler, John Crawford, Bill Tannen, Rocky Stanton, Art Dillard, Trigger. SYNOPSIS: Dale and a diner waitress are kidnapped by the waitress' outlaw boyfriend.

The Desert Fugitive (February 24, 1952). Director, John English; screenplay, Al De-

General Foods with its line of Post's cereals brought Roy and the gang into our homes weekly for seven years. Used with permission. Courtesy Kraft/General Foods.

Mond and Ray Wilson. CAST: Roy Rogers, Dale Evans, Pat Brady, Rand Brooks, Stephen Chase, Virginia Carroll, Terry Frost, Gregg Barton, Harry Harvey, Riley Hill, Chuck Roberson, Trigger. SYNOPSIS: The good twin is mistaken for the bad twin, who was convicted of swiping vital government documents.

Outlaw's Town (March 1, 1952). Director, Robert G. Walker; screenplay, Dwight Babcock. CAST: Roy Rogers, Dale Evans, Pat Brady, Reed Howes, Ferris Taylor, William Tannen, John Crawford, Tom Tyler, Hank Patterson, Brett King, Art Dillard, Trigger. SYNOPSIS: Roy and Pat Brady go undercover to bring the bad guys to justice from a "no man's land" where the law can't go in after them.

The Unwilling Outlaw (March 8, 1952). Director, Robert G. Walker; screenplay, Virginia M. Cooke. CAST: Roy Rogers, Dale Evans, Pat Brady, Dale Van Sickle, George J. Lewis, Reed Howes, William Fawcett, I. Stanford Jolley, Sherry Jackson, Trigger. SYNOPSIS: The bookkeeper at the bank is embezzling funds and splitting the take with outlaw pals, but the blame is going to another employee, who has a young daughter.

Dead Men's Hills (March 15, 1952). Director, Robert G. Walker; screenplay, Dwight Cummins. CAST: Roy Rogers, Dale Evans, Pat Brady, Forrest Taylor, Richard Emory, Larry Hudson, George Slocum, Steve Raines, Stuart Whitman, Sandy Sanders, Trigger. SYNOPSIS: Mineral City's sheriff is wounded, and it's up to Roy, Dale, and Pat to be sure that the gang doesn't escape from a desert town.

The Minister's Son (March 23, 1952). Director, John English; screenplay, Al DeMond and Ray Wilson. CAST: Roy Rogers, Dale Evans, Pat Brady, Keith Richards, Raymond Hatton, Riley Hill, Terry Frost, Stephen Chase, Harry Harvey, Chuck Roberson, Gregg Barton, Douglas Evans, Ferris Taylor, Lonnie Burr, Trigger. SYNOPSIS: He's not a minister's son, he's a government agent working undercover to catch counterfeiters.

Ghost Gulch (March 30, 1952). Director, Robert G. Walker; screenplay, Virginia M. Cooke. CAST: Roy Rogers, Dale Evans, Pat

Brady, Peggy Stewart, Zelda Cleaver, William Fawcett, George J. Lewis, Dale Van Sickle, Reed Howes, I. Stanford Jolley, Trigger. SYNOPSIS: There's gold on the ranch, and the rancher is taken by a greedy, fellow rancher who wants his gold.

Ride in the Death Wagon (April 6, 1952). Director, Robert G. Walker; screenplay, Ray Wilson. CAST: Roy Rogers, Dale Evans, Pat Brady, Forrest Taylor, George Slocum, Richard Emory, Bee Humphries, Larry Hudson, Trigger. SYNOPSIS: A benevolent elderly lady gives cash to build a clinic, but she gives it to a crook posing as a guard. Roy and Dale have to go after the felon and the cash.

Peril from the Past (April 13, 1952). Director, Robert G. Walker; screenplay, Dwight Babcock. CAST: Roy Rogers, Dale Evans, Pat Brady, John Doucette, Pierre Watkin, Ann Doran, Lee Roberts, Harry Harvey, Bill Catching, Paul Fierro, Russ Scott, Trigger. SYNOPSIS: Two grievous gangsters arrive in town and threaten to tell of the bank teller's record of murder and prison sentences unless he helps them carry out robbery plans.

The Ride of the Ranchers (April 20, 1952). Director, Robert G. Walker; screenplay, Milton M. Raison. CAST: Roy Rogers, Dale Evans, Pat Brady, Fred Cummins, Jim Diehl, Steve Raines, Pedro Regas, Millicent Patrick, Tina Menaro, Russ Scott, Harry Harvey, Augie Gomez, Trigger. SYNOPSIS: A rancher is out of town, and a gang of outlaws is ravaging his home and terrorizing his womenfolk. Roy intervenes before they can ravage his strongbox.

Shoot to Kill (April 27, 1952). Director, Robert G. Walker; screenplay, Dwight Cummins. CAST: Roy Rogers, Dale Evans, Pat Brady, Lee Roberts, John Doucette, Carl "Alfafa" Switzer, Dick Reeves, Sandy Sanders, Trigger. SYNOPSIS: An unscrupulous photographer cons Pat Brady into posing as an outlaw for a picture, then tells everyone that Pat really is an outlaw on the "wanted" list.

The Hermit's Secret (May 4, 1952). Director, Robert G. Walker; screenplay, Dwight Babcock. CAST: Roy Rogers, Dale Evans, Pat

A little mystery in every episode, as Roy and Dale decided upon the action they would take to get the varmints.

Brady, Fred Graham, Evelyn Finley, Gloria Williams, Hank Patterson, Harry Harvey, Henry Wills, James Kirkwood, Stanley Blystone, Trigger. SYNOPSIS: A supposedly benign invalid has killed a man and framed the man's uncle-in-law. But he's not an invalid, after all. Roy and Dale get the evidence, clear the uncle, and put the phony away.

Haunted Mine of Paradise Valley (May 18, 1952). Director, Robert G. Walker; screenplay, Milton M. Raison. CAST: Roy Rogers, Dale Evans, Pat Brady, Frank Jacquet, Harry Harvey, Fred Graham, Jean Harvey, Henry Wills, Bull Brady, Sandy Sanders, Nolan Leary, Tommy Coleman, Hank Patterson, Trigger. SYNOPSIS: An old prospector tells Roy the location of the map to his mine. When his widow arrives, Roy and Dale help her locate it.

Ghost Town Gold (May 25, 1952). Director, Robert G. Walker; screenplay, Dwight Bab-

cock. CAST: Roy Rogers, Dale Evans, Pat Brady, Tom London, Don C. Harvey, Carl "Alfafa" Switzer, Trigger. SYNOPSIS: Pat Brady buys a ghost town whose only resident is a desert dweller who has found counterfeit gold.

The Doublecrosser (June 1, 1952). Director, Robert G. Walker; screenplay, Al DeMond. CAST: Roy Rogers, Dale Evans, Pat Brady, Dorothy Vaughn, Denver Pyle, Harry Lauter, Don C. Harvey, Boyd "Red" Morgan, Trigger. SYNOPSIS: Mayor Cotton is being blackmailed into covering for a gang of outlaws.

Carnival Killer (June 8, 1952). Director, Robert G. Walker; screenplay, Milton M. Raison. CAST: Roy Rogers, Dale Evans, Pat Brady, Rand Brooks, Tom London, Don C. Harvey, Marshall Reed, Harry Harvey, Jeanne Dean, Russ Scott, Trigger. SYNOPSIS: The carnival whip-cracker is framed for the death his boss.

Flying Bullets (June 15, 1952). Director, Robert G. Walker; screenplay, Dwight Cummins. CAST: Roy Rogers, Dale Evans, Pat Brady, Denver Pyle, Harry Harvey, Herman Levitt, Steve Pendleton, George Douglas, Russ Scott, Trigger. SYNOPSIS: Pat Brady becomes sheriff and catches the man who shot a mountaineer.

Death Medicine (September 7, 1952). Director, Robert G. Walker; screenplay, Ray Wilson. CAST: Roy Rogers, Dale Evans, Pat Brady, Ray Bennett, Roy Mallinso, Bill George, Fred Graham, Burt LeBaron, Bill McCormick, Trigger. SYNOPSIS: Wrong-doing wranglers kidnap an old man who is a diabetic. Roy and Dale have to find him in time to give him the life-saving insulin shot.

Outlaw's Return (September 28, 1952). Director, Robert G. Walker; screenplay, Dwight Cummins. CAST: Roy Rogers, Dale Evans, Pat Brady, John Doucette, Myron Healey, Tom London, Fred Graham, Steve Pendleton, Russ Scott, Trigger. SYNOPSIS: An ex-convict's arrival in the area gives cover to outlaws who want a scapegoat for their foul misdeeds.

Hunting for Trouble (October 5, 1952). Director, Robert G. Walker; screenplay, Dwight Cummins. CAST: Roy Rogers, Dale Evans, Pat Brady, Myron Healey, John Doucette, Steve Pendleton, Tom London, Kim Walker, Richard Eyer, Russ Scott, Trigger. SYNOPSIS: Roy is kidnapped by a gang whose leader has mumps. When the gang is quarantined, the law is able to catch them.

The Feud (November 16, 1952). Director, Robert G. Walker; screenplay, Dwight Cummins. CAST: Roy Rogers, Dale Evans, Pat Brady, William Fawcett, Sydney Mason, Ed Hinkle, Stuart Whitman, Gloria Eaton, Pierce Lyden, Ruth Lee, Russ Scott, Harry Harvey, Trigger. SYNOPSIS: A bride is left standing at the altar when the groom, Andy Norton, is informed that his father's murderer is in town.

Go for Your Guns (November 23, 1952). Director, Robert G. Walker; screenplay, Dwight Cummins. CAST: Roy Rogers, Dale Evans, Pat Brady, Carl "Alfafa" Switzer, James Diehl, Bob Wilke, Reed Howes,

Michael Ragan, George J. Lewis, William Fawcett, Trigger. SYNOPSIS: Adolescent boys love infamous gunfighters, and Dale's nephew is no exception.

The Mayor of Ghost Town (November 30, 1952). Director, Robert G. Walker; screenplay, Milton M. Raison. CAST: Roy Rogers, Dale Evans, Pat Brady, Lane Bradford, Zon Murray, Harry Harvey, Frances Conley, Hal Price, Boyd "Red" Morgan, James Diehl, Russ Scott, Trigger. SYNOPSIS: The town of Red Dog has been a ghost town for years, but undue interest gets Roy and Dale shot at and the mayor of Red Dog shot.

Blind Justice (December 14, 1952). Director, Robert G. Walker; screenplay, William Lively. CAST: Roy Rogers, Dale Evans, Pat Brady, James Kirkwood, Bill Tannen, Terry Frost, Stanley Blystone, Russ Scott, Trigger. SYNOPSIS: A blind prospector is using Bullet as a guide to his mine. A felonious veterinarian plans the old man's untimely demise.

The Knockout (December 28, 1952). Director, Robert G. Walker; screenplay, Dwight Cummins. CAST: Roy Rogers, Dale Evans, Pat Brady, Sarah Padden, Charles Bronson, Leonard Penn, Frank Jenks, Wally West, Roy Brent, Trigger. SYNOPSIS: Grandma Conley is in town searching for her grandson, a prize fighter. But he's being controlled by an unsavory trio, and Grandma asks for help from Roy, Dale, and Pat.

The Run-a-Round (February 22, 1953). Director, Robert G. Walker; screenplay, Dwight Cummins. CAST: Roy Rogers, Dale Evans, Pat Brady, Pierce Lyden, Sydney Mason, Ed Hinkle, Stuart Whitman, Harry Harvey, Russ Scott, Trigger. SYNOPSIS: An unsuspecting Easterner is talked into purchasing Dale's ranch after Dale is conned into signing the bill of sale.

Loaded Guns (April 12, 1953). Director, Christian Nyby; screenplay, Barry Shipman. CAST: Roy Rogers, Dale Evans, Pat Brady, Denver Pyle, Lyle Talbot, Evan Loew, George Douglas, Steve Pendleton, Russ Scott, Trigger. SYNOPSIS: An innocent man's gun was used in a murder, but Roy believes in the man's innocence.

The Silver Fox Hunt (April 19, 1953). Director, Robert G. Walker; screenplay, Milton

Ol' Roy might have to whip out his six-shooter and wing a bad guy. From "Huntin' for Trouble" episode, aired October 1952.

M. Raison. CAST: Roy Rogers, Dale Evans, Pat Brady, Leonard Penn, Frank Lackteen, Herbert Wyndham, Roy Brent, Wally West, Russ Scott, Augie Gomez, Trigger. SYNOPSIS: The Acuna Indian chief is murdered and his body left beside the silver mine that belongs to the tribe.

The Mingo Kid (April 26, 1953). Director, Robert G. Walker; screenplay, William Lively. CAST: Roy Rogers, Dale Evans, Pat Brady, Terry Frost, William Tannen, Stanley Blystone, Russ Scott, Trigger. SYNOPSIS: Roy is mugged by an outlaw who steals his clothes. Then he's taken hostage by another outlaw who is using him to rob the town bank.

The Long Chance (May 24, 1953). Director, Robert G. Walker; screenplay, Dwight Cummins. CAST: Roy Rogers, Dale Evans, Pat Brady, Henry Rowland, Myron Healey, Bob Wilke, Sandy Sanders, William Fawcett, Harry Harvey, Trigger. SYNOPSIS: A moral outlaw robs and rustles, but he didn't take the money from the school, so he's looking for the guilty dog who did it.

Money to Burn (June 28, 1953). Director, Robert G. Walker; screenplay, Dwight Cummins. CAST: Roy Rogers, Dale Evans, Pat Brady, Dub Taylor, Harry Harvey, Jr., John L. Cason, Jack O'Shea, Boyd "Red" Morgan, Russ Scott, Trigger. SYNOPSIS: Dale unwittingly buys a stove that has money from a payroll robbery inside. The vile bandits will stop at nothing to get it back.

The Milliner from Medicine Creek (October 11, 1953). Director, Robert G. Walker; screenplay, Milton M. Raison. CAST: Roy Rogers, Dale Evans, Pat Brady, Frances Conley, Hal Price, James Diehl, Zon Murray, Boyd "Red" Morgan, Harry Harvey, Lane Bradford, Russ Scott, Trigger. SYNOPSIS: There's a plot to rob the local Wells Fargo office, and a milliner and her grandfather are suspected of the nefarious deed.

Pat's Inheritance (November 1, 1953). Director, Leslie H. Martinson; screenplay, Milton M. Raison. CAST: Roy Rogers, Dale Evans, Pat Brady, Mary Ellen Kay, Gregg Barton, Terry Frost, Tom London, Myron Healey, Trigger. SYNOPSIS: Pat and his cousin inherit a ranch, and as usual, the bad guys want to take it away.

Outlaws of Paradise Valley (November 8, 1953). Director, Leslie H. Martinson; screenplay, Milton M. Raison. CAST: Roy Rogers, Dale Evans, Pat Brady, Rick Vallin, Pamela Duncan, Pierre Watkin, Jack O'Shea, Harry Harvey, Sandy Sanders, Dick Avonde, Rusty Westcoatt, Russ Scott, Cheryl Rogers, Trigger. SYNOPSIS: Vile villains capture college students on an archeological dig and take them hostage.

Bullets and a Burro (November 15, 1953). Director, John English; screenplay, Al De-Mond and Ray Wilson. CAST: Roy Rogers, Dale Evans, Pat Brady, Raymond Hatton, Chuck Roberson, Norman Levitt, Terry Frost, Gregg Barton, Trigger. SYNOPSIS: The sheriff's brother is controlling a gang of outlaws that is about to steal money from a prospector.

Gun Trouble (November 22, 1953). Director, Robert G. Walker; screenplay, Dwight Cummins. CAST: Roy Rogers, Dale Evans, Pat Brady, Harry Harvey, Jr., John Carson, Dub Taylor, Boyd "Red" Morgan, Russ Scott, Trigger. SYNOPSIS: A teenager gets involved with bad guys who persuade him to kill Roy. But Roy convinces him to return to the side of the law.

"M" Stands for Murder (December 6, 1953). Director, Robert G. Walker; screenplay, Dwight Cummins. CAST: Roy Rogers, Dale Evans, Pat Brady, Myron Healey, Bob Wilke, Harry Harvey, Henry Rowland, Sydney Mason, Trigger. SYNOPSIS: Roy is trying to disprove a local legend that says anyone seen by "One Arm Johnny" (a ghost) will be murdered.

The Peddler from Pecos (December 13, 1953). Director, Leslie H. Martinson; screenplay, Milton M. Raison. CAST: Roy Rogers, Dale Evans, Pat Brady, Dub Taylor, Rusty Westcoatt, Ray Whitley, Harry Harvey, Dick Reeves, Russ Scott, Jack O'Shea, Trigger. SYNOPSIS: Beaver poachers kill a government agent when he tells them to stop poaching pelts.

Bad Company (December 27, 1954). Director, Leslie H. Martinson; screenplay, Dwight Cummins. CAST: Roy Rogers, Dale Evans, Pat Brady, Fred Sherman, Jim Hayward, Dick Reeves, Mike Ragan, Jack O'Shea, Harry Harvey, Wally West, Trigger. SYNOPSIS: Two varmints are responsible for the robbery of their own company, but the hired hands swipe Nellybelle to carry the haul.

Little Dynamite (January 3, 1954). Director, Leslie H. Martinson; screenplay, Dwight Cummins. CAST: Roy Rogers, Dale Evans, Pat Brady, Dub Taylor, Ray Whitley, Harry Harvey, Dick Reeves, Rusty Westcoatt, Russ Scott, Dodie "Little Doe" Rogers, Trigger. SYNOPSIS: The taxes are robbed, and the culprits escape in Dale's wagon, which is holding a small baby.

The Kid from Silver City (January 17, 1954). Director, Leslie H. Martinson; screenplay, Milton M. Raison. CAST: Roy Rogers, Dale Evans, Pat Brady, Francis McDonald, Ray Whitley, Harry Harvey, Dick Avonda, Russ Scott, Charles Tannen, Bill Tannen, Trigger. SYNOPSIS: The storekeeper's son returns, and being a crazed villain, he ambushes the marshal and plots to rid the town of Roy.

The Secret of Indian Camp (January 24, 1954). Director, Leslie H. Martinson; screenplay, Milton M. Raison. CAST: Roy Rogers, Dale Evans, Pat Brady, B. G. Norman, Myron Healey, Harry Strang, Russ Scott, Trigger. SYNOPSIS: A sinister sidewinder uses a ten-year-old orphan with a rifle to frighten Roy and Dale away from a gold mine that he's operating on government land.

Deputy Sheriff (February 7, 1954). Director, Leslie H. Martinson; screenplay, Milton M. Raison. CAST: Roy Rogers, Dale Evans, Pat Brady, Harry Harvey, Tom London, Gregg Barton, Myron Healey, Terry Frost, Trigger. SYNOPSIS: The sheriff is shot, and his deputy is covering for the shooter. Roy, Dale, and Pat get involved and then are trapped by the gang, but they are rescued by Nellybelle.

Highgraders of Paradise Valley (February 28, 1954). Director, Leslie H. Martinson; screenplay, Milton M. Raison. CAST: Roy Rogers, Dale Evans, Pat Brady, Myron Healey, Harry Strang, Ruta Lee, Jack O'Shea, Trigger. SYNOPSIS: The lady who runs the laundry is working with a dishonest ore grader.

The Land Swindle (March 14, 1954). Director, Leslie H. Martinson; screenplay, Milton M. Raison. CAST: Roy Rogers, Dale Evans, Pat Brady, Harry Harvey, Mike Ragan, Fred Sherman, Jim Hayward, Dick Reeves, Sam Flint, Gloria Talbot, Trigger. SYNOPSIS: The town newspaper thinks there is something fishy about the sale of a piece of property. Roy investigates and splits the gang involved in the scam.

The Lady Killer (September 12, 1954). Director, Leslie H. Martinson; screenplay, James Diehl. CAST: Roy Rogers, Dale Evans, Pat Brady, Pamela Duncan, Peter Votrian, Charles Tannen, William Tannen, Richard Avonda, Francis McDonald, Russ Scott, Harry Harvey, Trigger. SYNOPSIS: The banker is a lady who murders the ranchers in order to get their land. Roy stops the felonious felon before she's able to kill an eight-year-old boy.

The Young Defenders (October 3, 1954). Director, Donald McDougall; screenplay, Milton M. Raison. CAST: Roy Rogers, Dale Evans, Pat Brady, B. G. Norman, Norale Norman, Hank Patterson, Rex Lease, John Cason, Don C. Harvey, Barry Regan, Trigger. SYNOPSIS: Pugnacious purloiners out to pilfer pelts hold captive a fur-trappng father, not realizing their captive has two children left alone in a cabin.

Backfire (October 10, 1954). Director, Donald McDougall; screenplay, Dwight Cummins. CAST: Roy Rogers, Dale Evans, Pat Brady, John Doucette, Henry Rowland, Sydney Mason, Brad Mora (Bradley Morrow), Helena Burnett, Trigger. SYNOPSIS: The bogus Reverend Brown and friend pounce on Parson Loomis and steel the payroll that he's been petitioned to carry to the mine.

Last of the Larabee Kid (October 17, 1954). Director, Donald McDougall; screenplay, Milton M. Raison. CAST: Roy Rogers, Dale Evans, Pat Brady, Sarah Padden, Bill George, John Merton, John Cason, Harry Harvey, Don C. Harvey, Jack O'Shea, Fred Sherman, Trigger. SYNOPSIS: The Larabee Kid is the son of a murdered marshal and is out to wreak vengeance on outlandish outlaws who slew his father. He's stealing the stolen money they stole from the stagecoach.

The Highjackers (October 24, 1954). Director, Robert G. Walker; screenplay, William Lively. CAST: Roy Rogers, Dale Evans, Pat Brady, Fred Graham, Forrest Taylor, James Diehl, Steve Raines, Wally West, Russ Scott, Trigger. SYNOPSIS: A young man owes money to the bad guys for gambling debts and is forced to steal fur pelts from his grandfather to pay the bills.

Hard Luck Story (October 31, 1954). Director, Donald McDougall; screenplay, Dwight Cummins. CAST: Roy Rogers, Dale Evans, Pat Brady, Bert LeBaron, John Cason, Rex Lease, Don C. Harvey, Virginia Carroll, Barry Regan, Trigger. SYNOPSIS: Just one premium payment, and any rancher can be insured for the rest of his life — so says the "Hard Luck Insurance Company." But Roy thinks the company is a scam.

Boy's Day in Paradise Valley (November 7, 1954). Director, Donald McDougall; screenplay, Milton M. Raison. CAST: Roy Rogers, Dale Evans, Pat Brady, Dick Shackleton, Don C. Harvey, John Cason, John Merton, George Pembroke, Sarah Padden, Harry Harvey, Trigger. SYNOPSIS: The boys of the town get to be the public officials on Boy's Day. Young Bob Miner gets to be sheriff, and his villainous uncle uses the change of the day to latch onto the property of an elderly man.

Bad Neighbors (November 21, 1954). Director, Donald McDougall; screenplay, Dwight Cummins. CAST: Roy Rogers, Dale Evans, Pat Brady, Forrest Taylor, Alan Wells, Jean Howell, Reyford Barnes, Harry Harvey, Trigger. SYNOPSIS: Homesteaders and cattle ranchers are fighting over land again. Roy and Dale are in the middle.

Strangers (December 5, 1954). Director, Donald McDougall; screenplay, Dwight Cummins. CAST: Roy Rogers, Dale Evans,

Pat Brady, Francis McDonald, John Doucette, David Bair, Henry Rowland, Russ Scott, Harry Harvey, Wally West, Trigger. SYNOPSIS: A talented teenage artist moves with his father to Paradise Valley and is disappointed when no one seems to notice. The only recognition is from fiendish felons, who, under the guise of being surveyors, ask for lodging.

Hidden Treasure (December 19, 1954). Director, Donald McDougall; screenplay, Dwight Cummins. CAST: Roy Rogers, Dale Evans, Pat Brady, Harry Lauter, Dub Taylor, Rusty Westcoatt, William Fawcett, Harry Harvey, Trigger. SYNOPSIS: Rakish rogues overhear Roy and Dale discussing "the key to the great treasure being in a book" and decide to stop at nothing to obtain the book.

Outcasts of Paradise Valley (January 9, 1955). Director, Donald McDougall; screenplay, Milton M. Raison. CAST: Roy Rogers, Dale Evans, Pat Brady, Forrest Taylor, Reyford Barnes, Alan Wells, Margaret Bert, Harry Harvey, Jack O'Shea, Trigger. SYNOPSIS: The inability to find gainful employment causes two young boys to indulge in criminal activities.

The Big Chance (January 23, 1955). Director, Donald McDougall; screenplay, Milton M. Raison. CAST: Roy Rogers, Dale Evans, Pat Brady, Harry Carey, Harry Lauter, Rusty Westcoatt, Dub Taylor, Trigger. SYNOPSIS: Nellybelle is jeepnapped, along with Pat Brady, and both are held captive by a band of blazing bandits.

Uncle Steve's Finish (February 3, 1955). Director, Donald McDougall; screenplay, Milton M. Raison. CAST: Roy Rogers, Dale Evans, Pat Brady, Bill Tannen, Virginia Carroll, Louis Lettieri, Myron Healey, Harry Harvey, Earl Hodgins, Trigger. SYNOPSIS: The stagecoach is robbed, and the schoolteacher is making everyone suspicious by being so nervous.

Dead End Trail (February 20, 1955). Director, Donald McDougall; screenplay, Dwight Cummins. CAST: Roy Rogers, Dale Evans, Pat Brady, Harry Hickok, Carl "Alfalfa" Switzer, Don C. Harvey, Russ Scott, Trigger. SYNOPSIS: A less-than-understanding father is giving his son some heavy problems. The boy is bent on leaving home and joining an outlaw gang.

Quick Draw (March 20, 1955). Director, Donald McDougall; screenplay, Milton M. Raison. CAST: Roy Rogers, Dale Evans, Pat Brady, Don C. Harvey, Carl "Alfalfa" Switzer, Harry Harvey, Louis Lettieri, Virginia Carroll, Russ Scott, Trigger. SYNOPSIS: The stage is held up, and a sheep rancher joins the posse in order to have the opportunity to legally shoot his brother-in-law, who happens to be the robber.

The Ginger Horse (March 27, 1955). Director, Donald McDougall; screenplay, Milton M. Raison. CAST: Roy Rogers, Dale Evans, Pat Brady, Don C. Harvey, Harry Harvey, Frances Karath, Harry Hickok, Trigger. SYNOPSIS: A little girl's horse has been stolen by the outlaw who framed her father on a robbery charge.

The Showdown (May 22, 1955). Director, Donald McDougall; screenplay, David Nowinson and Karl Schlichter. CAST: Roy Rogers, Dale Evans, Pat Brady, Ralph Sanford, Harry Harvey, Ewing Mitchell, Claudia Barrett, Fred Coby, Trigger. SYNOPSIS: A Eureka Cafe waitress and her father's ex-partner are both awaiting the release of the waitress' father from prison. The waitress is happy; but the ex-partner wants to terrorize the father.

And Sudden Death (October 9, 1955). Director, Donald McDougall; screenplay, Dwight Cummins. CAST: Roy Rogers, Dale Evans, Pat Brady, Gene Roth, Myron Healey, Louis Lettieri, Carl "Alfalfa" Switzer (Alfy Switzer), Russ Scott, Bill Tannen, Trigger. SYNOPSIS: Mineral City's mayoral candidate is knifed by the leader of the Shadow Gang, who is posing as a mentally incompetent tinker.

Ranch War (October 23, 1955). Director, Donald McDougall; screenplay, Milton M. Raison. CAST: Roy Rogers, Dale Evans, Pat Brady, Ralph Sanford, Harry Harvey, Sr., Harry Harvey, Jr., Claudia Barrett, Ewing Mitchell, Fred Coby, Russ Scott, Trigger. SYNOPSIS: A greedy rancher employs treachery to force a young couple from their property.

Violence in Paradise Valley (November 2, 1955). Director, Robert G. Walker; screenplay, Eric Taylor. CAST: Roy Rogers, Dale Evans, Pat Brady, Ray Bennett, Bill George, Rory Mallinson, Fred Graham, Bert Le-Baron, Bill McCormick, Harry Harvey, Trigger. SYNOPSIS: No information available on the plot.

The Brothers O'Dell (November 20, 1955). Director, George Blair; screenplay, Milton M. Raison. CAST: Roy Rogers, Dale Evans, Pat Brady, Reed Howes, Henry Rowland, Robert Bice, Paul Harvey, Dan Barton, Dennis Moore, George Eldredge, Trigger. SYNOPSIS: Good guy, bad guy brothers. The bad one robs the express where the good one works. The good one refuses to rat on the bad one.

The Scavenger (November 27, 1955). Director, Donald McDougall; screenplay, William Lively. CAST: Roy Rogers, Dale Evans, Pat Brady, Britt Wood, Rand Brooks, Harry Harvey, Wayne Mallory, Trigger. SYNOPSIS: Counterfeiters hide their stash of phony money, and it's found by an old man. Roy has to provide protection for the elderly gent when the crooks return looking for the loot.

Treasure of Paradise Valley (December 11, 1955). Director, Donald McDougall; screenplay, Milton M. Raison. CAST: Roy Rogers, Dale Evans, Pat Brady, Britt Wood, Claudia Barrett, Rand Brooks, Bud Osborne, Tom London, Wayne Mallory, Jack O'Shea, Trigger. SYNOPSIS: Unable to make mining pay off, an old miner swindles the town by trading stock in the nonexistent mine for food.

Three Masked Men (December 18, 1955). Director, George Blair; screenplay, Dwight Cummins. CAST: Roy Rogers, Dale Evans, Pat Brady, Paul Harvey, Robert Bice, Reed Howes, Henry Rowland, Dennis Moore, Louise Venier, John Hamilton, Dusty Rogers, Trigger. SYNOPSIS: It's Mineral City's 75th anniversary. During the celebration, the mayor of the town is kidnapped in an attempt to keep outlaw Luke Taylor from hanging.

Ambush (January 15, 1956). Director, George Blair; screenplay, Dwight Cummins.

CAST: Roy Rogers, Dale Evans, Pat Brady, Paul Harvey, Dan Barton, Dennis Moore, Henry Rowland, Rosemary Bertrand, Bob Bice, Trigger. SYNOPSIS: A young prospector finds the mother lode and is bushwhacked by the assaulting assayer.

Money Is Dangerous (January 29, 1956). Director, George Blair; screenplay, Dwight Cummins. CAST: Roy Rogers, Dale Evans, Pat Brady, Harry Harvey, Lucien Littlefield, John Truax, Craig Duncan, James Macklin, Trigger. SYNOPSIS: A rancher cum miser is robbed by the man he hired as his bodyguard.

False Faces (February 5, 1956). Director, George Blair; screenplay, Dwight Cummins. CAST: Roy Rogers, Dale Evans, Pat Brady, Harry Shannon, Keith Richards, Ralph Moody, Joe Bassett, Dorothy Andre, Wally West, Trigger. SYNOPSIS: The mayor of Mineral County is a crook who is trying to pin a series of killings on the Indians. Roy and Chief Gray Hawk combine forces to prevent the framing of innocent Indians.

Horse Crazy (February 26, 1956). Director, George Blair; screenplay, Dwight Cummins. CAST: Roy Rogers, Dale Evans, Pat Brady, John Truaz, Harry Harvey, Craig Duncan, James Macklin, Trigger. SYNOPSIS: A bad bandit holds Roy captive and forces him to track his missing horse. Roy finds the horse, then gets control of the bandit.

Smoking Guns (March 3, 1956). Director, George Blair; screenplay, Milton M. Raison. CAST: Roy Rogers, Dale Evans, Pat Brady, Harry Shannon, Harry Harvey, Ralph Moody, Keith Richards, Joe Bassett, Jack O'Shea, Russ Scott, Trigger. SYNOPSIS: A prospector is stealing gold from Chief Kumaska's salt mine. He kills the Indian agent when his nasty little secret is discovered.

Empty Saddles (March 10, 1956). Director, Christian Nyby; screenplay, Dwight Cummins. CAST: Roy Rogers, Dale Evans, Pat Brady, Reed Howes, Paul Harvey, Dennis Moore, Henry Rowland, Bob Bice, Dan Barton, Trigger. SYNOPSIS: The ranchers are ready to take their cattle to market, but rustlers are trying to take them instead.

Sheriff Missing (March 17, 1956). Director,

George Blair; screenplay, William Lively. CAST: Roy Rogers, Dale Evans, Pat Brady, Harry Harvey, Helen Spring, Howard Negley, Keith Richards, Troy Melton, Russ Scott, Trigger. SYNOPSIS: Mineral City's banker wants legal gambling and hires hoods to force the honest sheriff out of town while he tends to dishonest details. Roy goes undercover to capture the creeps.

The Morse Mixup, aka *The Horse Mixup* (March 24, 1956). Director, George Blair; screenplay, Polly James. CAST: Roy Rogers, Dale Evans, Pat Brady, Howard Negley, Harry Harvey, Sr., Harry Harvey, Jr., Keith Richards, Troy Melton, Russ Scott, George Eldredge, Steve Raines, Trigger. SYNOPSIS: Roy is jailed for murder and must find the real killer in order to prove his innocence.

Head for Cover (October 21, 1956). Director, Leslie H. Martinson; screenplay, Dwight Cummins. CAST: Roy Rogers, Dale Evans, Pat Brady, Ellen Corby, Byron Foulger, Robert Knapp, Troy Melton, Les Mitchell, Harry Strang, Trigger. SYNOPSIS: Revenge-seeking robbers blast into town looking for their double-dealing boss.

Mountain Pirates (November 4, 1956). Director, Christian Nyby; screenplay, Eric Taylor. CAST: Roy Rogers, Dale Evans, Pat Brady, Steve Pendleton, Fred Sherman, John McKee, Russ Scott, Trigger. SYNOPSIS: A witness to fish poaching is intimidated by the poachers and refuses to remember anything. Roy gets to chase the bandits with Trigger and with a motorboat.

His Weight in Wildcats (November 11, 1956). Director, Christian Nyby; screenplay, Wells Root. CAST: Roy Rogers, Dale Evans, Pat Brady, Steve Stevens, House Peters, Jr., Pierce Lyden, John L. Cason, Harry Harvey, I. Stanford Jolley, Virginia Carroll, Russ Scott, Wally West, Trigger. SYNOPSIS: Outlaws are converging on the town, looking for money that was long since hidden. Roy turns to an ex-cop for help when the sheriff goes out of town.

Paleface Justice (November 18, 1956). Director, Leslie H. Martinson; screenplay, Al Martin. CAST: Roy Rogers, Dale Evans, Pat Brady, Bobby Blake, Robert Knapp, Troy Melton, Les Mitchell, Bob Bice, John War Eagle, Russ Scott, Anna Marie Majalca, Jack O'Shea, Trigger. SYNOPSIS: A young Indian boy is accused of killing the blacksmith, and the town wants him lynched. Roy is the only one who believes in his innocence.

Tossup (December 2, 1956). Director, Christian Nyby; screenplay, Barry Shipman. CAST: Roy Rogers, Dale Evans, Pat Brady, Gay Goodwin, House Peters, Jr., George DeNormand, Charles Anthony Hughes, George Mather, Bill Catching, Steve Raines, Russ Scott, Wally West, Jack Trent, Trigger. SYNOPSIS: The dispute over a silver mine's ownership places a little girl with the unlikely name of "Tossup" in the middle.

Fighting Sire (December 16, 1956). Director, Leslie H. Martinson; screenplay, Sam Newman. CAST: Roy Rogers, Dale Evans, Pat Brady, Harry Landers, Robert Knapp, Troy Melton, Les Mitchell, Bob Bice, John Meek, Trigger. SYNOPSIS: Gangsters appear in Paradise Valley when ex-pugilist King Kady witnesses a murder. While Roy is protecting the witness, the boxer's son is captured by the mob.

Deadlock at Dark Canyon (January 6, 1957). Director, Christian Nyby; screenplay, Wallace Bosco. CAST: Roy Rogers, Dale Evans, Pat Brady, Harry Harvey, John L. Cason, Nolan Leary, Troy Melton, Steve Pendleton, Trigger. SYNOPSIS: Col. Mattock is not only a cattle baron and activist, he's ready to "git them nesters outta Pinto Basin." His foreman is using his own means of protest to assist the old colonel.

End of the Trail (January 27, 1957). Director, Donald McDougall; screenplay, Al Martin. CAST: Roy Rogers, Dale Evans, Pat Brady, Gregg Barton, Terry Frost, Troy Melton, Harry Tyler, Wally West, Russ Scott, Trigger. SYNOPSIS: An escaped convict is killed on the way to Paradise Valley. Roy agrees to assist in the capture of his partner.

Junior Outlaw (February 10, 1957). Director, Donald McDougall; screenplay, Polly James. CAST: Roy Rogers, Dale Evans, Pat Brady, Speer Martin, Scotty Morrow (Mora), Mel Stevens, Terry Frost, Rusty Westcoatt, Harry Harvey, Bob Bice, Russ Scott, Jack

Roy talking a plan over with yet another of the show's stars, Bullet.

O'Shea, Roy (Dusty) Rogers, Jr., Trigger. A misguided teenager falls in with bad outlaws who are looking for stolen money on Roy's property.

High Stakes (February 24, 1957). Director, Donald McDougall; screenplay, Dwight Cummins. CAST: Roy Rogers, Dale Evans, Pat Brady, Bob Bice, Ed Hinton, J. Harris Howell, Bill Catching, Harry Tyler, Helen Brown, Trigger. The varmint says he's a marshal taking a criminal to trial, but Roy discovers that he's not a marshal but is instead out to kill the key witness.

The King of the Cowboys and the Queen of the West never looked better.

Accessory to Crime (March 3, 1957). Director, Donald McDougall; screenplay Anne Dalyn and Pearl Carr. CAST: Roy Rogers, Dale Evans, Pat Brady, Harry Harvey, Jr., Bob Bice, Ewing Mitchell, Bill George, Bill Catching, Loann Morgan, Wally West, Trigger. SYNOPSIS: The store clerk can't send his son to college unless he joins a smuggling ring and gets the money.

Portrait of Murder (March 17, 1957). Director, Donald McDougall; screenplay, Sam Newman. CAST: Roy Rogers, Dale Evans,

Pat Brady, House Peters, Jr., Ewing Mitchell, Rusty Westcoatt, Edgar Dearing, Trigger. SYNOPSIS: When the vet orders a rancher's cattle killed because of the dreaded hoof and mouth disease, the rancher kills the vet and tries to frame a mute artist.

Brady's Bonanza (March 31, 1957). Director, Donald McDougall; screenplay, Wallace Boscoe. CAST: Roy Rogers, Dale Evans, Pat Brady, Rick Vallin, Harry Tyler, Gregg Barton, Troy Melton. SYNOPSIS: Pat has a uranium mine that he sells for two dollars.

Johnny Rover (June 9, 1957). Director, George Blair; screenplay, Dwight Cummins. CAST: Roy Rogers, Dale Evans, Pat Brady, Reed Howes, Paul Harvey, Dennis Moore, Henry Rowland, Bob Bice, Dan Barton, Trigger. SYNOPSIS: A son goes west to prove to his father that he is self-sufficient. Dad doesn't believe it and goes to visit.

No air dates available on the following:

Fishing for Fingerprints. Director, Christian Nyby; screenplay, Ellis Marcus. CAST: Roy Rogers, Dale Evans, Pat Brady, Francis McDonald, Steve Pendleton, Fred Sherman, Harry Harvey, John McKee, Russ Scott, Trigger. SYNOPSIS: A friend of Pat is charged with robbery, and Roy and Bullet fish for evidence to prove the real culprit is an ex-convict.

Phantom Rustlers. Director, Robert G. Walker; screenplay, Wallace Bosco. CAST: Roy Rogers, Dale Evans, Pat Brady, Minerva Urecal, Harry Harvey, Francis McDonald, Bobby Hyatt, Riley Hill, Harry Mackin, Sandy Sanders, Trigger. SYNOPSIS: Rampaging rustlers are rustling, then hustling the stolen beef into trucks, thwarting apprehension efforts.

Doc Stevens' Traveling Store. Director, Robert G. Walker; screenplay, Milton M. Raison. CAST: Roy Rogers, Dale Evans, Pat Brady, Ferris Taylor, Peggy Stewart, Zon Murray, Stanley Andrews, Harry Harvey, Boyd "Red" Morgan, Trigger. SYNOPSIS: The Traveling Store provides cover for a gang of crooks. Doc Stevens transmits information to them.

Born Fugitive. Director, Donald McDougall; screenplay, William Lively. CAST: Roy Rogers, Dale Evans, Pat Brady, Don C. Harvey, Frances Karath, Harry Hickok, Jean Harvey. SYNOPSIS: An outlaw is killed by his gang, leaving his young daughter with no friends except Dale.

Four more shows were planned, but not produced. *Note:* Some episodes were copyrighted in 1984 by Frontiers, Inc.

Roy and Dale also starred in fourteen television specials sponsored by Chevrolet from 1958 to 1960. In 1962 both of them starred in ABC's hour long variety show "The Roy Rogers and Dale Evans Show."

Other Shows

Hollywood Bronc Busters (Columbia), 1956 (9 min.). Hosted by Jack Lemmon and Ralph Staub. Featuring film clips of Gene Autry, Roy Rogers, Tom Mix, William Boyd, William S. Hart, Buck Jones, Hoot Gibson, Charles Starrett. Produced and directed by Ralph Staub.

Miscellaneous Television Appearances

1950
The Gabby Hayes Show (NBC), Saturday mornings, children's show. *Hollywood Christmas Parade*; Roy Rogers appearance, news clip.

1953
This Is Your Life; hosted by Ralph Edwards.

1954
Cavalcade of America (ABC), Tuesday, 7–8 P.M. (60 min.); "A Medal for Miss Walker"; an anthology series with dramatizations.

1956
The Perry Como Show (NBC), Saturday, 8–9 P.M. (60 min.), weekly musical variety show; Roy and Dale make guest appearance. *The Dinah Shore Chevy Show* (NBC), Friday, 9–10 P.M. (60 min.), weekly musical variety show; Roy and Dale make guest appearance.

1957
The Perry Como Show (NBC), Saturday, 8–9 P.M., December 7 (60 min.), weekly musical variety show; Roy and Dale make guest appearance.

1958
Matinee Theatre (NBC); "Anxious Night" (anthology series; dramatizations); Dale makes appearance. *Bold Journey* (ABC), Monday, 7:30–8 P.M. (30 min.); "I Follow the Western Star" (adventure series, travel documentary); Roy makes appearance. *I've Got a Secret* (CBS), Wednesday, 8:30–9 P.M. (30 min.); Garry Moore, host; (game show); Roy makes appearance. *The Chevy Show* (NBC), Sunday, 8–9 P.M. (1958–1960), (60

NEW from Nestlé's
STRAWBERRY FLAVOR*QUIK

Roy Rogers says:

"KEEPS YOU IN THE PINK!"

- *Makes luscious pink strawberry flavor milk.*

- *Makes glorious pink sodas and floats, too!*

- *Fortified with Vitamins C, B₁, and Iron to keep you in the pink of health.*

* *Great imitation strawberry flavor, tastes just like real strawberries.*

MIXES INSTANTLY WITH MILK

See Roy Rogers, Dale Evans and Trigger on Television every week.

Copyright 1960, The Nestlé Company, Inc.

min.); Roy and Dale hosted fourteen of the special variety shows sponsored by Chevrolet.

1961

I've Got a Secret (CBS), late week-night, Monday or Wednesday (30 min.); Garry Moore, host (game show); Roy makes guest appearance.

1964

The Beverly Hillbillies (CBS), Wednesday P.M. (30 min.); "Dr. Jed Clampett" (comedy); Roy makes appearance. *Hollywood Palace* (ABC), Saturday 8–9 P.M. (60 min.); variety show; Roy and Dale make guest appearance. *The Andy Williams Show* (NBC), Monday or Tuesday, late P.M. (60 min.); variety show; Roy and Dale make guest appearance.

1965

The Telephone Hour (60 min.); "American Song"; Debbie Reynolds, hostess; special presentation; Roy, Dale and others, guest stars. *Hollywood Palace*, February 27; Roy and Dale make guest appearance. *The Tonight Show* (NBC), Saturday or Sunday, 10:15–midnight (105 min.); Johnny Carson, host; variety show; Roy and Dale make guest appearance. *The Andy Williams Show* (NBC), Monday, 8–9 P.M. (60 min.); variety show; Roy and Dale make guest appearance.

1966

The Andy Williams Show (NBC), Monday 8–9 P.M. (60 min.); variety show; Roy and Dale make guest appearance.

1968

Kraft Music Hall (NBC), Wednesday, 8–9 P.M. (60 min.); variety show; Roy and Dale make guest appearance.

1969

Hollywood Palace (ABC), Saturday, 8:30–9:30 P.M. (60 min.); variety show; Roy and Dale make guest appearance. *A Community Happening* (NBC), September 8; pilot comedy variety show with country and western music; Roy and Dale host; guest singers appeared; exec. producer, Greg Garrison; exec. producer, Don Van Atta; producer, Jonathan Lucas; director and writers, Al Rogers, Bernard Rothman, Rich Eustis.

1970

The Ed Sullivan Show (CBS), Sunday, 7–8 P.M. (60 min.); variety show; Roy and Dale make guest appearance. *The Dean Martin Show* (NBC, 60 min.); Roy and Dale make guest appearance; Roy in skit with Dean Martin, Don Rickles; Dale sings "A Good Man Is Hard to Find."

1972

Hee-Haw (syndicated, 60 min.); musical, variety show; Roy and Dale make guest appearance.

1976

Music Hall America (syndicated); Roy sings "Hoppy, Gene and Me." *The Dinah Shore Show* (60 min.); musical variety show; Roy makes guest appearance with Robert Fuller, George Montgomery. Roy sings "Texas Plains" and "Happy Trails."

1977

Wonder Woman (ABC, circa 1976–77), Saturday, 8–9 P.M. (60 min.); superhero series, starring Lynda Carter as Diana Prince/Wonder Woman. Roy plays a rancher raising beef for the government. He's also a widower raising a multicultural family. His natural son is experiencing a bad case of sibling rivalry. When he falls under the influence of bad guys, he betrays his father to a crooked deputy sheriff. He tells them all the moves of his rancher father and about the government contract. The cattle begin to vanish at the rate of a hundred at a time. Roy becomes worried and phones Washington to an old friend from the army. The friend sends Major Trevor to investigate. And wherever Maj. Trevor goes, so goes Diana Prince/Wonder Woman. In the midst of the investigation, the natural son, Jeff, feels the pangs of guilt and confesses his disloyalty and indiscretion with the bad guys. Wonder Woman does most of the fighting, but Roy makes a good showing (without the benefit

Opposite: **In 1960, Roy and Dale were seen plugging a different product on television, as this clipping from the** *Sunday News* **(New York) illustrates.**

of a double). He plants a good right hook into the jaw of the rustling rabble and comes out the victor. (Rebroadcast in some viewing areas February 25, 1989.) *Hee-Haw* (musical, variety show); Roy and Dale make guest appearance. *The Mike Douglas Show*, July or August (60 min.); variety show; Roy makes guest appearance. *Donny and Marie Show* (ABC), Wednesday, 8–9 P.M. (60 min.); Donny and Marie Osmond, hosts (musical variety show); Roy and Dale make guest appearance.

1978
Over Easy (Hugh Downs, host); Roy Rogers guest appearance. *Hee-Haw* (syndicated), February (60 min.); musical variety show; Roy and Dale make guest appearance. *The Merv Griffin Show* (CBS), Monday–Friday, 11:30 P.M.–1:00 A.M. (90 min.); variety show; Roy and Dale make guest appearance. *Country Christmas,* December (60 min.); country music variety special; Roy and Dale are guest stars.

1979
The Muppets Show (syndicated, 30 min.); variety show featuring Jim Henson's Muppets; Roy makes guest appearance. *You Are Loved;* Roy and Dale make guest appearance. *The Phil Donahue Show* (NBC, 60 min.); talk show; Roy makes guest appearance. *Christmas Songs*; Roy and Dale. *PTL Club (Praise the Lord),* syndicated (60 min.); Pat Robertson, host (religious variety show); Roy and Dale make guest appearance.

1980
The Steve Allen Show (NBC), Tuesday 10–11 P.M. (60 min.); comedy, variety show; interview with Roy and Dale. *Come Love the Children,* August; charity fund-raising show featuring Roy and Dale. *PM Magazine*, December (60 min.); news magazine show; interview with Roy and Dale. *The Mike Douglas Show*, March (60 min.); guest appearance by Roy and Dale.

1981
President Ronald Reagan Inaugural, January 20; Roy and Dale participated in festivities before and after inaugural. *Barbara Mandrell and the Mandrell Sisters* (NBC),

Saturday 7–8 P.M. (60 min.); musical variety show; Roy and Dale guest appearance. *Marriott Inc. Roy Rogers Restaurant Opening* (KTLA) February; News program, Los Angeles. *Hollywood Christmas Parade*, December; Roy and Dale, grand marshals of parade. *Today Show*, February; news, variety, broadcast. Subject: "B" Westerns. Roy Rogers film clip. *Good Morning America*, June 24; interview with Roy and Dale. *Wonderful World of Animals. The Tommy Hunter Show. People Are Talking* (Oprah Winfrey, co-host). *Love Is a Neighborhood*, July. *AM Philadelphia*, August, Roy is guest. *Nashville Palace*, November; Roy and Dale guest appearance; Roy sings "When Payday Rolls Around." *Good Morning Washington*, April. *Cherry Blossom Festival.*

1982
The Merv Griffin Show (NBC, 60 min.). *American Rifleman;* interview with Roy Rogers and Rex Allen. *Oral Roberts*, April.

1983
Country Comes Home, May. *CBS Morning News*, June 22. *David Letterman Show*, June 22; filmed live in New York. *CNN News*, August; Golden Boot Awards. *Entertainment Tonight*, August; Golden Boot Awards Show; Roy and Dale guest appearance. *Entertainment Tonight*, September. *Marriott Corp.* (television news piece); Roy presents gift horse to Philadelphia police. *The Fall Guy* (ABC), Wednesday 8–9 P.M. (60 min.); starring Lee Majors as part-time stunt man, part-time bounty hunter in Hollywood; Roy Rogers plays himself. *Happy Trails* (ABC), Wednesday, 8–9 P.M. (60 min.) (adventure series); guest stars: Pat Buttram, James Drury, Jack Kelly, Doug McClure, Roy (Dusty) Rogers, Jr., Sons of the Pioneers, Roy H. Lanham, Vernon Dale Morris, Luther Nallie, Arthur Parker, Rusty Richards, and Dale H. Warren; background music: "Roy Rogers Is Ridin' Tonight"; songs: "Texas Plains," "Cool Water," "Tumbling Tumbleweeds," "Happy Trails."

1984
Fan Fare (Futura Productions), November; activities surrounding Roy and Dale's visit to Portsmouth, Ohio, in conjunction with his birthday, the festivities related to the "Roy Rogers Hometown Exhibit," and the Roy

Roy and Dale began appearing frequently on all types of variety shows and even did one of their own.

Rogers–Dale Evans Convention, were filmed for this television show. *The Fall Guy* (ABC) Wednesday 8–9 P.M. (60 min.); starring Lee Majors as Colt Sievers, stunt man/bounty hunter; Roy Rogers plays himself. *King of the Cowboys* (ABC) Wednesday 7–8 P.M. (60 min.); guests are Dusty Rogers and his band The High Riders, Jock Mahoney, John Russell, Peter Breck, Sons of the Pioneers. The last episode is shown in clips, with a medley of the songs repeated. Roy adds to the medley with "Sons of the Western Soil,"

"Don't Fence Me In," and "Stampede." *Entertainment Tonight* (CBS, 60 min.); "Fall Guy" wrap party. *Entertainment Tonight* (CBS), October (60 min.); Golden Boot Awards. *National Rifle Association*, June; Roy hosts show.

1985

Billy Graham Crusade, September; Roy and Dale appear on show. *Entertainment Tonight* (CBS), August (60 min.); Golden Boot Awards.

1986

A Date with Dale (Trinity Broadcast Network), January. *USO Awards Show*, January. *Entertainment Tonight* (CBS, 60 min.); Golden Boot Awards show. *Hour Magazine,* September (60 min.); Dale Evans appears.

1987

Good Morning America, May; Roy and Dale with Gene Autry, on Nashville Network. *Entertainment Tonight*, September (60 min.); Roy and Gene on Nashville Network. *Trinity Broadcasting Corp.,* November; interview with Roy and Dale.

1988

Gene Autry Museum Opening, November 22. *22nd Annual Country Music Awards:* Roy is elected into the Country Music Hall of Fame. Award presented to Roy Rogers. Roy makes an entrance to thundering applause in the Opry House, Grand Ole Opry, Nashville, Tennessee. The occasion is formal, and Roy is dressed in formal, yet traditional attire: white shirt with ruffles, a Western-cut, grey jacket with black trim, and slash pockets. The bolo tie (usually worn at a more casual level) is tucked close to the neck. He tips his trademark, white Stetson, with the silver band. As he steps up to the podium, he remarks to his many fans, "Boy, these steps get higher, and my bowling ball gets heavier, and my horse gets taller, every year." "I feel like I've grown up with everybody." "I'm sorry Dale couldn't be with me, but I told her she had to stay home and clean the house." "That'll be the day." (Dale is attending a meeting in Victorville at this time.) He accepts the award, and thanks everyone, amidst more deafening applause.

1989

Academy Awards, March 29. *Entertainment Tonight* (CBS), August 7 (60 min.); Golden Boot Awards. *Lone Pine Film Festival*; Roy gives dedication speech. *Celebration Off Stage,* March 24. *American Music Awards. Country Music Awards Show*, October 8.

1990

Video AM. Jane Pauley—Real Life, Spring. *Crook and Chase Show* (TNN). *Good Morning America. 700 Club*, October 4. *Maryland Harbor*; interview. *One on One*, October 18. *Randy Travis–Happy Trails* (TNN, 60 min.); special guest, Roy Rogers. Roy does some riding for the first time since the "Fall Guy" television series. The young palomino that he has chosen to ride is wearing a stock Western saddle (rather unusual for Roy). He looks great atop the mighty steed, his clothing reminiscent of the glorious days in the films and on the fronts of his comic book covers. His white Stetson hat and twin six-shooters in tooled leather holsters show us the Roy that chased the bad guys out of town in each episode. Then the scene shifts to a campfire with the gang gathered to sing Western songs—Roy, Randy, Holly Dunn, Denver Pyle, Michael Martin Murphy, and others. *Republic Pictures Story* (AMC, 60 min.); special presentation. The film history of Republic Pictures is shown with many clips from Roy's films. Interviews with Roy and Dale and others who appeared in his films. *AMC Salutes Texas* (AMC), documentary (60 min.); special presentation. The history of Texas is shown in relation to its contribution to the movie industry. Some of the film clips are of Roy and Dale, in the "B" Western heyday. Dale is a native Texan, and Texas was a central theme in many of the cowboy's Republic films, such as *Rainbow Over Texas. Country Music Awards Show*; Roy sings "Hold on Partner" with Clint Black. *CBS Morning Show* (CBS), November 16. *Cherry Blossom Special.*

1992

Hot Country Nights, February 2; Roy Rogers tribute; Roy appears. *Grammy Awards*, February. *Country Music Awards Show*, February. *CBS Morning News*, April 13. *Country Music Hall of Fame Awards Show,*

They would also appear on talk shows, and they usually got to sing on these as well.

May 20. *Music City News County Awards Show*, June: "Living Legend"; interview with Roy by satellite, July 8. *News Broadcast,* April 28, Anderson, Indiana. *News Broadcast*, May 13; announcing Dale's heart attack. *Crook and Chase Show* (TNN), November 5. *Roy Rogers "King of the Cowboys"*(AMC), December 3 (60 min.); American Movie Classics/Republic Pictures/Galen Films, Inc. Documentary with most of the narrative done by Roy. Includes old 16mm home movies taken by Roy throughout his career. *Hollywood Greetings from Ed Sullivan* (CBS) December 20; Roy and Dale sing "Christmas on the Plains."

1993
Arkansas Educational TV, February 5; Ray Neilson interviews Roy.

Dates not available:

"When It Was a Game," news clip of Roy and Gabby at 1940s Tigers/Reds game (HBO)
Here's Life Houston
Tonight Show (with Burt Reynolds)

Mel Torme Show
Milton Berle Show
700 Club Telethon (early 1980s)

Television Commercials

At one time, the stars of a show did the commercials also. Not just on radio, but on television as well. This practice was very common with the television cowboys and cowgirls selling the sponsor's product, which was usually a cereal or item for the kids.

One such sponsor was Nestle's Quik. Below is the scene and dialogue from the commercial that presented the "Roy Rogers Show" on CBS on Saturday mornings.

Dale is taking items out of the picnic basket as Roy rides up on Trigger (actually Trigger, Jr.). Roy's decked out in standard television attire, plaid shirt, etc. And Trigger is wearing the red, white, and blue show saddle and tack.

Roy: Okay Trigger, let's ask Dale real nice. (Trigger does a little dance routine, and takes a bow.)

DALE: Roy Rogers, you'd do anything to get Nestle's real strawberry-flavored Quik.

ROY: Dale, nothing quenches a thirst like strawberry-flavored Quik. It really keeps you in the pink!

DALE: Strawberry pink color, and luscious pink flavor. That great imitation strawberry flavor tastes just like real strawberries.

ROY: And it's got vitamins and iron too. Keeps you in the pink of health. (Dale mixes a glass before the camera.)

DALE: Just two teaspoons in milk, Quik as a wink, Strawberry Quik, ready to drink. (Roy turns up glass and drinks.)

ROY: Tastes so good, you'll want plenty.

DALE: It's so good you can have plenty.

ROY: Keep in the pink with Nestle's new strawberry-flavored Quik. Right Trigger? (Trigger nods affirmatively, and Roy and Dale nod.)

Other

Ideal Toys Roy Rogers Merchandise. CBS reruns of television series episodes, early 1960s.

Roy Rogers Restaurants (Marriott Corp. 1986). Thirty-second commercials with Roy advertising the food.

Chapter 7
COMICOGRAPHY

The following is a history and analysis of the many appearances of Roy Rogers in comics over the years, based largely on a scrutiny of all of the comics themselves. The fact that Gaylord DuBois was the writer of nearly all of the stories is demonstrated by his original handwritten accounting on deposit at Michigan State University, copies of which are in the collection of this writer, courtesy Ray White and Randall Scott.[1] Other original titles of stories, as submitted by DuBois prior to editing, are shown. The day the story was submitted is also shown.

Dell Publishing Company's Western Comics History

Dell Publishing was founded in 1921, when George T. Delacorte had the good fortune to be fired for making the purchase of too much paper for a company at which he was employed. The good fortune for this young man lay in the fact that he was very ambitious and along with the firing came ten thousand dollars' severance pay.

Delacorte took that money and turned it into a virtual gold mine within a few years. He managed to find a little two-room place on New York City's West 23rd Street to begin his publishing operation, and one of his first customers was the *New York Times*. Before the decade was over, he had some help from an equally ambitious woman, who was instrumental in a lot of successful moves for the publishing concern in the years that lay ahead. Her beginning tasks were working the road as a representative, working as a clerk, and eventually handling the secretarial chores. The way company reps put it in 1987, "She would change not only Delacorte's life, but publishing for the next fifty years. Helen Mayer's impact has been legendary.[2]

Dell Publishing, Inc., was the third comic book publisher to enter the field, doing so in February 1936 with *Popular Comics*, No. 1, the second anthology format title wherein the format was a continuous series

of comic strip reprints. The characters were Dick Tracy, Little Orphan Annie, and Terry and the Pirates.[3]

George Delacorte was involved in drawing comics at least as early as 1929 (*The Funnies*). In October 1936, *The Funnies*, No. 1, appeared in comic book format; it was Dell's second comic book title.

In March 1937, *The Comics* #1, Dell's third comic book title appeared, a milestone in the history of Western comic books. This marked one of the many "firsts" of Dell Publishing in this field, and it would set a trend that would remain an important part of the Dell story, the practice of debuting already popular Western stars into this medium. This issue marked the first appearance in comic books of Tom Mix.[4] The Arizona Kid and Prairie Bill, purely fictional cowboys, were also introduced. Tom Mix was the first really big Western star with full benefit of commercial tie-ins. In April 1937, Dell's *Western Action Thrillers* presented in the third Western comic book title to be published the comic exploits of six cowboys: Buffalo Bill, Texas Kid, Laramie Joe, Two Gun Thompson, Wild West Bill, and Rimrock O'Reilly.[5]

In 1937, Dell issued its second title in a 100-page format with a Western cover, *100 Pages of Comics*, and introduced Two Gun Montana.

In June 1938, Dell issued *Crackajack*

Funnies and added another famous cowboy star and soon to be real-life hero, Buck Jones, to its roster. Buck Jones made his debut into this medium either in *Crackajack Funnies* #1 or in Dell's 1938 *Famous Feature Stories*, depending on which title was first issued.[6] Jones, handsome and rugged looking, made many top-notch Western films in the style introduced by silent-screen legend William S. Hart. In March 1939, Dell issued #9 of *Crackajack Funnies* and in doing so, debuted yet another highly popular Western film hero, Red Ryder. Ryder was somewhat more fictionalized because he only existed in film through portrayals by several actors over the years. The character would sell millions of BB rifles, however, as the Daisy Manufacturing Company's most popular and legendary spokesman.

Dell had some geniuses in its marketing department and was lassoing practically every major Western film star with comic book appeal and commercial tie-ins.

In 1939, Dell issued its first *Large Feature Comic* with black and white artwork, the beginning of a new concept that had been tried before for other companies but met with failure. For Dell, it was the innovation that would make comic book history, providing them with a launching pad for their many characters to come, and especially for the many sagebrush heroes they would be utilizing. This series, their predecessor to "Four-Color Comics," would last for four years.

In issue #3 of *Large Feature Comics,* a cowboy rode in who had gained quite a following and would become one of the all-time legendary greats. The story was *Heigh-Yo Silver*, and the cowboy was "The Lone Ranger," another fictional Western hero who would be portrayed by a host of actors down through the years, until one young Republic Studio star's name would become synonymous with the character for the 1950s set of youngsters.[7] This was the first cowboy in the Dell corral who had debuted elsewhere. He had appeared twice before in a "Lone Ranger Ice Cream Cone, giveaway comic," and in David McKay's *Feature Comic* #21, June 1939.[8] In September 1939, the move came that would soon bring dominance for Dell in the comic book publishing field.

Dell probably didn't have cowboys in mind for immediate titles in the near future, but when one cowboy was crowned "king" by his studio in a massive publicity campaign, that all changed. Roy Rogers was the sudden rage after number one cowpoke Gene Autry went off to fly planes in the war, and Dell managed to stake Roy out in its corral, just as they'd snagged the other top moneymakers.

Four-Color Comics originated with a series #1 of twenty-five issues, beginning with Dick Tracy. The words "Four-Color" did not appear on the cover until issue #19, a Barney Google comic. By the end of 1939, between its Disney titles and those belonging to Warner Brothers, another big contract, Dell was issuing over 100 million magazines and doing it all with a staff of nine workers. Their slogan, "Dell Comics Are Good Comics," practically became a household phrase, as comic books alone were selling 300 million copies per year, "with only a ten percent return."

In August 1941, the *King of the Royal Mounted*, a Dell title for a good while, was part of the Red Ryder Comics.[9] This character was drawn by artist Charles Flanders, but when he took over the Lone Ranger chores, artist Jim Gary took his place. In the decade of the forties, the newest invention to find its way into nearly every home and workplace (it had been around since the mid–1920s) was radio. After Dell Publishing entered the comic book field, the company soon became the number one publisher in that medium and offered radio some competition. By special arrangement, Western Printing and Lithographing Company took over the operation of Dell's Book Division. The distributor was American News. By the end of World War II, paperbacks were a permanent part of American literature, not just a passing fancy. Dell became number two in the paperback field. The first ten titles published by Dell were mysteries by writers like Rex Stout and Agatha Christie.

Dell got involved in just about every genre, including history, romance, and Westerns.[10]

By 1942, series #2, Four-Color Comics had begun. Issue #1 of the second series, *Little Joe*, carried a Western cartoon cover. Issue #36, *Smilin' Jack*, was the first Dell comic to actually bear the familiar Dell logo.

In April 1944, thirty-eight issues into this new "one-shot" series, *Roy Rogers Comics* was issued by Dell. It was produced by Western Printing and Lithographing Company.[11]

With the Roy Rogers title came several important "firsts." This issue marked not only the first Western title of the new Four-Color series, but also the first Western comic with a color photo cover produced by the industry.[12] Dell couldn't have chosen a better name for a ticket to success in Western comic books. Roy was hot at this time, and his name meant money in the bank. It has been reported that this first issue sold a million copies in the first twenty-four hours.[13] Roy Rogers was now to Western film what Walt Disney was to animated cartoons, and the Western influence would even show up in many of the cartoon character issues, especially on covers.[14] The artists housed by Western Printing did justice to the likeness of the recently crowned "King of the Cowboys." They were about to get a lot of practice from Dell Publishing, as many new cowboys entered the folds.

Western Printing and Lithographing Company

1907: Western Publishing bought West Side Printing Co.

1909: Their address became State St., Racine, Wisconsin.

1910: The company assumed the name "Western Publishing."

1915: Western Publishing became the parent company, taking in as a subsidiary Hamming-Whitman Publishing, which dropped the name "Hamming." Whitman was operating at the time out of Chicago.

1930s: Western began an association with Dell Publishing and Simon and Schuster, Inc. At some point the name became Western Printing and Lithographing Co.

Western Printing did all the printing and the production work for everything that Whitman Publishing, Dell Publishing, and Simon and Schuster Co. published on Roy Rogers.

1930s–early 1950s: One of Whitman's chief artists was Henry Vallely.

Early 1940s: Western began producing all of Dell Publishing's comic book material.

Some of the artists whose work appeared in the comics apparently were employed by Western, while others were referred to as "Whitman artists."

1962: Dell Publishing severed its relationship with Western Printing and Lithographing Co.

In 1944, Roy Rogers, the "King of the Cowboys," and Trigger, his golden palomino, made their appearance in Dell's Four-Color series, which was about to further the comic career of Gene Autry. Roy appeared on the first Western photo cover of the Four-Color series, which was distributed at newsstands and sold for ten cents. No other Western comic could match the appearance of the Roy Rogers comic. Trigger was a very handsome palomino and he was used to full advantage in promoting the cowboy. Trigger was used more often than not in the beautiful color photos that adorned both the front and back covers. In most of the photos without Trigger, Roy would be accompanied by his two young daughters, Cheryl and Linda, adding family appeal to the issues. The *Roy Rogers' Trigger Comics* alone reportedly accounted for earnings of $10,000 in 1950.[15] It was reported in 1957 that each of his comic book issues was selling at the rate of two million copies. In 1961, reports stated that the comics were approved by the Parent Teacher Association and were selling 25 million annually and had 66 million readers.[16]

The Dell Western Product

Dell was the publishing company whose logo appeared on the cover, and whose advertising appeared heavily throughout the series. This work encompasses all of the Western comics related to Roy that were produced by Western Printing and Lithographing Co.; 95 percent of the Western Co. Product carries the Dell brand. It is believed that Dell secured the contracts of the licensors for the characters in order to publish their adventures in pulp. It is known that Dell supplied the photos of the characters to Western for the covers and inside covers. A number of photos from Dell's files are in this researcher's personal collection. The details of the arrangements between the two companies may never be known, and it has been the experience of this writer that neither company is willing to provide any information pertaining to the arrangements, and efforts to provide the reader/researcher with such information have been fruitless so far, in spite of numerous pleas. Indeed, only Dell Publishing Co. was willing to share some of the company's history. The copyrights to the characters belonged either to that character or a copyright holding company related to the character. In my research, I have determined that most have fallen into public domain under the copyright laws of the United States because the companies failed to renew their registration after the first twenty-eight-year term. Copyrights of other features in the comics besides the stories directly related to the subject characters originally belonged to Western Printing and Lithographing Co. This company and its artists produced the comics, packaged them, and probably even distributed them. This history and study of these comics is based almost entirely upon my own original research into the series and these titles. It is but a mere portion of a much larger study covering all of the titles produced by Dell/Western. The conclusion drawn about the artists who were involved in the production of these comics has come about through careful, painstaking, comparative analysis with other more documented work produced by them. In the case of those who did not sign in an obvious manner, I have made an educated guess about the artist's identity based upon the styles that I have learned to recognize and associate with many of them. I do not hesitate to use the words "possibly" or "probably" in such attributions. This research will continue indefinitely, and I offer no absolute conclusion that any particular artist was responsible for any particular work. In the case of many of the artists, this work will credit them for the first time in any published scholarly book and provide future researchers with unlimited possibilities. I would encourage and welcome any evidence differing with or supporting my findings.

This study of Roy Rogers in the comic art form in the Roy Rogers series, Four-Color and Regular, involves essentially four periods of time.

1. *The Micale Period.* In this period, there were a few "stray" artists that occa-sionally stepped in to draw Roy, and the stories show evidence of the "bullpen" effect of mixed likenesses from the pens of several artists, but the majority of the drawn Roy Rogers output is by one artist, Albert Micale. This period is essentially covered by issues #1 through 23. Practically all the stories were written by Gaylord DuBois.

2. *The Micale-McKimson Period.* Micale was joined in December 1949 by artists "Al" McKimson (two artists/art director brothers), Peter Alvarado, Randy Steffen, Andrew Bensen, Tony Sgroi, and others. As a result, there were at least several distinctively different likenesses of Roy in each issue by artists whose styles and signing were apparent, in addition to likenesses from several "stray" artists whose contribution was less significant. It was distinctly confusing to have different likenesses of what was supposed to be the same character appear in a single issue of the Roy Rogers comics. Much of this effect was the result of the "bullpen" method of art common to comic book production, wherein the pens and pencils of numerous artists are applied to the work in a large room setting, or at any rate, prior to completion of the product. It is believed that this method was employed in order to step up production because of the large volume of Roy Rogers comics and other titles selling in the late 1940s to mid 1950s. About the time the comics' sales began to show some decline, the artwork was again handled primarily (but not entirely) by one artist, John Buscema. Practically all the stories were written by DuBois.

3. *The Buscema Period.* Begins with issue #74, February 1954. During this period, artist John Buscema stepped in and carried the heaviest amount of work in the entire issue, with only one basic likeness per comic (with the exception of advertising) for a couple of years. Even during this period, however, slight variations appeared from time to time, as other artists contributed to some degree. Buscema's work was usually very dominant. Practically all stories were by DuBois.

4. *The Edson Period.* Begins with issue #109, January 1957. Nat Edson produced the likeness for the majority of the comic stories, keeping the likeness of the character Roy Rogers still somewhat consistent, though he was assisted with a stray artist or two in the regular comic series. From time to time, however, the contributions of the other artists became quite significant. See Chapter 9 for detail on artwork, artist information, etc. The Roy Rogers stories in the *Western Roundup* series were drawn by various artists, including John Ushler, Michael Arens, and Robert Myers, some of whom contributed to the regular series and some who did not.

All titles are *Roy Rogers Comics* unless, as with related titles, they are otherwise noted. The first thirteen are Dell's Four-Color series, with numbers related to that series. All others are Dell's regular series, unless otherwise noted. The covers are referred to as front / inside front / inside back / back. See Chapter 8 for detailed photograph information. The issue number appears on the inside front cover, or first page, and is matched with the code on the first page. Copyright information appears on the inside front cover, or first page, and is noted only as it changes. Copyrights were for twenty-eight years, at which time they could be renewed for an additional twenty-eight years. Based upon my research with the Copyright Office, certain ones were renewed (at least one), while most were not, and my research indicates the majority are in public domain. I note this information on the ones for which I have thus far received it. The story title is taken directly from the title page. S1, S2 denotes first story, second story. Writer(s) information is taken directly from documents previously noted. The term "features" refers to additional stories that become a regular part of the comic or in some instances, are a "one-shot." The term "filler" refers to short stories, usually one to two pages, with limited illustrations, usually one or two. I have avoided headings and subtopic abbreviations as much as possible to conserve space. This work is not intended to be a price guide, with future updates. The values are shown only to enable the student/collector/ researcher to see the impact that the character and this medium have had on our culture—their collectibility. The highest prices at which the comics have been seen are used, and all such prices take into consideration that the comic is in good to mint condition. There is no guarantee that the comics can be found at these prices, as the market fluctuates day to day, and there are appreciable differences in price from one geographical locale to another and among the various places where these comics can be found. Recently the first issues of many Western comics have nearly tripled in value.

Roy Rogers Comics

Four-Color Series

Thirteen issues of this Dell series, begun in 1939 and believed to have been produced by Western Printing and Lithographing Co. (though no company name is shown) featured Roy Rogers. The signatures of the artists of the majority of this work are buried in the detail of the art, as noted on occasion. Traditional Old West themes were utilized. DuBois submitted his work directly to Western and was paid $220 per 48-page story, or about $4.50 per page.

The series used the same format as Single Series (UFS Pub.) in 1938, wherein each issue is a "one shot" devoted to a single character. They began in black and white, then went to a color format as "Single Series," then went on for many years as "Four-Color," when Dell picked up on the idea, providing a testing place and launching pad for new characters. From 1948 to 1962, all titles issued used the same numbering system: 1-1354. The words "Four-Color" appear only on issues 19 through 102. The name however, lasted throughout the entire run.[17]

#38, April 1944. Original copyright by Don Milsop. February 15, 1944. No. AA 450120. Expired February 1972. No code number shown. No copyright notice. Covers: Roy, publicity photo, posed by tree stump/ drawings of Trigger, pieces of Roy's and Trigger's "trademark" attire/continuation of story/ Roy astride Trigger in rocks. S1, Roy Rogers in "Blazing Guns": Gaylord DuBois/Erwin Hess, also possibly Henry Vallely. Originally not titled. Submission date not noted. Roy comes close to a panel kiss, holding the pretty girl in his arms but duty calls at the last moment. The pose takes place of Roy rearing on Trigger. (The pose was already recognized as his "trademark" pose.) Trigger is drawn with four white stockings, indicating that the artist had seen Little Trigger, or another of the doubles. 52 pages. $100–$1,000.

#63, January 1945. Covers: Roy, publicity close-up/Roy, guitar, publicity/reversed negative photo shows Roy and the original Trigger examining a hay wagon/reversed negative shows Roy rearing original Trigger. S1, Roy Rogers in "Robber's Roundup": DuBois/ Micale (signed last panel), possibly Irwin Myers. Panel embrace. DuBois was paid April 12, 1944. Roy relieves Medicine Belt from a reign of terror. Only comic with four full-color photos. Artist changes to post–"Apache Rose" hat for one panel. Roy comes very close to panel kiss. 52 pages. $37– $250.

#86, October 1945. Covers: Roy, Trigger, Jr., or other Trigger double standing outdoors/Roy, publicity close-up/Roy, Trigger, Jr.(?), rearing pose/Roy with guitar, singing to Cheryl. S1, Roy Rogers in "Deadly Treasure": DuBois/Micale (signed last panel). Submitted September 18 and November 27, 1944 (twenty-five pages each time). Roy gets tied up, tossed into a cave, thrown down a waterfall, and narrowly misses connecting head to head with a mountain cat, but emerges from everything without a scratch. This story, artwork and all, was reproduced in a different format in the Whitman Better Little Book #1437. The title name on the cover now appears in a writing style like that of a signature and will remain like this through issue #34, October 1950. The square Dell logo appears in the lower righthand corner. 52 pages. $29–$200.

#95, February 1946. Covers: Reversed negative photo shows Roy with guns drawn/Roy sitting on fence, publicity photo/Roy sitting, playing guitar, publicity photo/Roy, in barn, gun drawn, tinted photo. S1, Roy Rogers in "King of the Cowboys": DuBois/Micale. Original title was "Roy Rogers and the Wolves of the Corozon." Submitted from January 1 to April 27, 1945, in five installments. This is the largest, most paneled story in the series. S2, "Roy Rogers Finds Blood in the Badlands": DuBois/Micale. Submitted September 24, 1945. Roy helps a young lad find his dad's murderer and comes close to a necktie party himself in doing so. Initials "TM" are seen, probably for Tom McKimson, an art director for Western, and "Gaylord" shows in the 26th panel for the writer. Saddle and tapaderos are tooled but no initials appear yet. 52 pages. $29–$200.

#109, June 1946. Covers: Roy, standing in rocks, aiming gun/Roy, Little Trigger, possibly at a personal appearance, shot at night/Roy, Little Trigger who is sitting/Roy playing guitar, singing to Little Trigger, facsimile signature. S1, Roy Rogers and the "Towers of Gold": DuBois/Micale, possibly Erwin Hess, Dan Spiegle. Submitted November 24, 1945. Roy sings an original song here, playing the guitar as he rides along. S2, "Trigger Trails the Herd": DuBois/Micale. Submitted January 12, 1946. First Trigger story and only one in which Roy appears. 52 pages. $22–$150.

#117, September 1946. Covers: Reversed negative shows Roy, original Trigger/Roy in rocks, aiming rifle/Roy, Little Trigger, action photo/Roy looking at his first comic with daughters Cheryl and Linda at home. S1, Roy Rogers and "The Spooks of Howling Mesa": Original title was "Roy Rogers and Howling Mesa." DuBois/Micale. Submitted April 20, 1946. In the beginning of practically every story, Roy comes upon an injured human or animal. Here it's an old man, and Roy gets caught up in an avalanche and flying bats. Roy must solve the mystery of the spooks that are frightening the cattle at night, causing stampedes. Occasionally, Roy's watch, or a fraction thereof, can be seen in photos. 52 pages. $16–$110.

#124, November 1946. Covers: Roy astride original Trigger/Roy astride unknown horse in corral, waving hat/Roy standing, guns in air, publicity photo, facsimile signature/Roy tucking Cheryl and Linda Lou into bed. S1, Roy Rogers in "Raiders from the Sea": Du-Bois/(probably) Erwin Hess, also Jesse Marsh. Billed December 3, 1945. Roy battles an ingenious gang of rustlers. 52 pages. $16–$110.

#137, February 1947. Covers: Roy leaning on fence, gun on hand, first post–"Apache Rose," new attire photo/Roy and Dale, rearing on original Trigger/Roy, original Trigger, possibly film still/Roy behind fence, wagon wheel, gun drawn, publicity pose. Photo of Dale was one of the very few to appear in Roy's comics. S₁, Roy Rogers and "Dead Men's Gold": DuBois/Micale. Billed December 3, 1945. Roy gets the goods on a crooked lawyer. 52 pages. $16–$110.

Early Rogers artist Erwin Hess used large likenesses, showing Roy as a friendly, smiling cowboy in uncluttered panels. Copyright 1946 by Roy Rogers.

Rogers artist Albert Micale would set the pace for the series and establish how Roy should look in the comics. This image began in the Four-Color series and stayed around for ten years. These scenes are taken from Four-Color issue # 153. Copyright 1947 by Roy Rogers.

#144, April 1947. Covers: Reversed negative shows Roy posing beside original Trigger/Roy, possibly original Trigger, in corral, possibly film still/Roy, astride possibly original Trigger/reversed negative shows Roy playing guitar. S1, Roy Rogers in "On the Apache Trail": (probably) Erwin Hess, Jesse Marsh. Possible Myers contribution, Myers' signature, last panel. Submitted June 21, 1946. Roy interrupts Apache train robbers. 52 pages. $16–$110.

#153, June 1947. Covers: Roy in familiar "boots shirt," astride original Trigger, publicity photo/Roy in campfire scene, publicity photo/Roy behind window, rifle at the ready/Roy at home, eating breakfast. S1, Roy Rogers and "The Mad Marksman": DuBois/Micale. Submitted June 21, 1946. Roy plays detective, gets sworn in as a deputy U.S. Marshal, and solves a murder case. 52 pages. $6.50–$45.

#160, August 1947. Covers: Roy, in new attire, specially posed publicity photo, gun drawn/Roy and Dale strolling hand in hand/reversed negative shows Roy and Dale astride original Trigger/Roy, original Trigger, in shot from same series used for cover of #124. S1, Roy Rogers and "The Guns of Mystery Mountain": DuBois/Hess, Marsh. Submitted September 9, 1946. Roy and leading lady Kay Roberts spend a lot of time underground while dealing with cattle rustlers. 52 pages. $12–$85.

#166, October 1947. Covers: Roy in old attire, close-up, publicity photo/Roy, posed photo in barn, looking at "wanted poster" (belongs to earlier series)/Roy posed aiming rifle over saddle/black-hatted Roy sitting on couch with daughters on lap. More contrast in photos used here than in any other single issue.[18] S1, Roy Rogers in "Basin Ranch Mystery": DuBois/Micale. Submitted September 11, 1946. Roy goes looking for the murderer of the son of a good friend. 52 pages. $12–$85.

#177, December 1947. (Original copyright: October 28, 1947, by Roy Rogers, No. AA 69967. Expired October 1, 1975.) Covers: Roy in new attire, astride original Trigger, publicity photo/Roy playing with owl on filming location/Roy cleaning rifle on film location/Roy on original Trigger in another

shot from series used for front cover. S1, Roy Rogers and "The Wolves of the Little Moab": DuBois/Harry Parks. Submitted October 28, 1946. Roy helps an old friend solve a $7,500 robbery. 36 pages. $12–$85.

The Micale Period

#1, January 1948. (Original copyright: November 28, 1947, by Roy Rogers, No. B 109939. Expired November 1975.) Covers: Roy, close-up publicity photo (note the gold saddle ring and the wristwatch)/Roy, original Trigger, probably on filming location/Roy posing in action on film location (note one of the crew strolling across the set)/black-hatted Roy in shot from earlier series, showing lariat to daughters. S1, Roy Rogers in "The Secret of Thunder River": DuBois/Micale. Submitted November 4, 1946. By the 53d panel, Roy has, in classic Western fashion, beaten a bully who far outsizes him in fisticuffs. History feature begins: "Great Lawmen of the Old West." This one is "John Slaughter of Tombstone." Submitted June 13, 1947. Feature called "Chuck Wagon Charley's Tales" begins. DuBois/Harry Parks. The original copyright on this piece is by Oskar Lebeck (Western Company editor). This one is subtitled "Brownie." 36 pages. $47–$325. *Note:* It is believed that the first three "Chuck Wagon Charley's Tales" were either submitted as "Bunkhouse Harmonies" or the first four "Charley's" were not produced by DuBois and his "Bunkhouse Harmonies" were not used. If the former is correct, there is only one Charley story unaccounted for, as he submitted three "Bunkhouse Harmonies" and fifteen "Chuck Wagon Charley's Tales" between June 13 and November 27, 1948. Yet he is credited with having drawn the illustration for *Animal Comics*, and it is noted by Randall W. Scott, Michigan State University Libraries, that it appears that the stories were moved to the Roy Rogers series after eight episodes.[19]

#2, February 1948. Original copyright will remain in Roy Rogers' name until issue #34. Covers: Roy in new attire, about to saddle Little Trigger with silver saddle/Roy, walking on film location, crewman in background/Andy Devine, Cheryl, Roy, probably on film location/Roy, squatting, examining spur. S1, Roy Rogers in "The Tiger of the Hills": DuBois/Micale. Submitted February 10, 1947. Roy rescues the damsel in distress, a Mexican señorita named Rosita. "Great Lawmen of the Old West—Sgt. James R. Gillett of the Texas Rangers." Submitted August 21, 1947. "Chuck Wagon Charley's Tales": DuBois/Micale. 36 pages. $22–$150.

#3, March 1948. Covers: Roy publicity photo, posing over silver saddle/Roy, unknown horse in corral/Roy with unknown horse, stables/Roy about to throw lariat in special pose. S1, Roy Rogers in "Death Warrant for Five": DuBois/Micale. June 11, 1947. Roy receives kiss from leading lady in text, but it's omitted in the art at end of story. Trigger takes a bow in this story, something he gets to do a lot in real life. "Great Lawmen of the Old West—The Martyr of Abilene." Submitted July 17, 1947. "Chuck Wagon Charley's Tales": DuBois/Parks. 36 pages. $17–$120.

#4, April 1948. Covers: Roy, behind fence, gun drawn, in specially posed photo (note chrome-plated .45s)/first subscription page with small publicity photo of Roy astride Little Trigger/Roy playing with unidentifiable Trigger/Roy blowing in chamber of gun in specially posed photo. *Note:* A one year subscription to the comic is $1.00; two years, $1.75. S1, Roy Rogers and the "Ghost of the Lost Galleon": DuBois/Micale. This story is centered around the ghost of an old prospector. "Great Lawmen of the Old West—Johnny Owens, Poison to Outlaws": DuBois/Micale. Submitted July 18, 1947. "Chuck Wagon Charley's Tales": DuBois/Parks. *Note:* Begin only one b&w inside full-sized photo. 36 pages. $17–$120.

#5, May 1948. Covers: Roy, Little Trigger, and unknown horse, posing at stables (note: only two right, white stockings)/same subscription page/black-hatted Roy beside unknown horse, stables/Roy astride Little Trigger (or unidentifiable other Trigger) wearing silver saddle; the rear stockings do not match the horse on the front cover. S1, Roy Rogers in "Badland Bullets": DuBois/Micale. Submitted September 15, 1947. Roy is shot at right away (8th panel) by an owlhoot and shot again by a female in the 14th panel. The brand name "Stetson" had already become synonymous with the cowboy hat. "Great Lawmen of the Old West—Bat Masterson": DuBois. Submitted July 28, 1947. "Chuck Wagon Charley's Tales": DuBois/Parks. Submitted October 27, 1947. 36 pages. $17–$120.[20]

#6, June 1948. Cover: Reversed negative shows Roy in old attire, publicity/same subscription page/Roy tying up bad guy in specially posed photo/Roy and cast in color film still from "On the Old Spanish Trail." S1, "Roy Rogers Rides the River": DuBois/Micale. Submitted December 15, 1947. Roy gets ambushed before unlocking the mystery of the howler in the tunnel. "Great Lawmen of the Old West—William M. Breakenridge, the Straight-Shooting Deputy, Pt. 1": DuBois/Micale. Submitted September 1, 1947. "Chuck Wagon Charley's Tales": DuBois/Parks. Submitted October 27, 1947. 36 pages. $12–$85.

#7, July 1948. Covers: reversed negative shows Roy, hand on gun, standing beside original Trigger in shot from earlier photo series/same subscription page/Roy behind previous unknown horse/reversed negative shows Roy, guns drawn, by stables, gate, specially posed photo. S1, Roy Rogers in "Dead Man's Canyon": DuBois/Micale, Bensen. Submitted January 13, 1948. Roy helps a girl find her missing father. "Great Lawmen of the Old West—William M. Breakenridge, the Straight-Shooting Deputy, Pt. 2": Dubois/Micale. Submitted September 1, 1947. "Chuck Wagon Charley's Tales": DuBois/Parks. Submitted January 14, 1948. 36 pages. $12–$85.

#8, August 1948. Covers: Roy loading six-shooter in specially posed photo/same subscription page/Roy, close-up with Linda, Cheryl/black-hatted Roy from earlier photo series watches daughters sit on ponies. S1, Roy Rogers and "The Headless Horseman": DuBois/Micale (signed). Submitted February 4, 1948. "Great Lawmen of the Old West—McDonald and the Rangers": DuBois/Spiegle. Submitted September 1, 1947. "Chuck Wagon Charley's Tales": DuBois/Parks. Submitted January 26, 1948. 36 pages. $12–$85. *Note:* Dell Publishing address changes to 251 Fifth Avenue, New York.

#9, September 1948. Covers: Roy in Ramon Freulich photo, posing beside original Trigger/same subscription page/Roy drawing guns in publicity photo/ Roy in shot from same series used for front cover. S1, Roy Rogers and the "Baron of Skull Mesa": DuBois/Micale, Steffen, possibly Bensen. (AL, first panel; RS, 16th panel). Submitted March 6, 1948. Roy battles superstition and outlaws. "Great Lawmen of the Old West — Lt. Lee Hall": DuBois/Micale. Submitted September 1, 1947. "Chuck Wagon Charley's Tales": DuBois/ possibly Steffen. Submitted February 14, 1948. 36 pages. $12–$85.

#10, October 1948. Covers: Reversed negative shows Roy in close-up from earlier publicity photo series/Roy mounting Little Trigger in specially posed photo/Roy, close-up publicity photo (note Republic Pictures credit line)/new subscription page placed on back, with encircled color photo of Roy, Little Trigger, from earlier series. S1, Roy Rogers in "War at Indian Creek": DuBois/Micale. Original title: "Roy Rogers at Indian Creek." Submitted April 3, 1948. Roy has gone to work for the Cattlemen's Association and gets caught up in a feuding family. "Great Lawmen of the Old West — Arranged by the Rangers": Submitted September 1, 1947. "Chuck Wagon Charley's Tales": DuBois/ Parks. Submitted March 10, 1948. 36 pages. $12–$85.

#11, November 1948. Covers: Roy on cowcatcher of train engine/same earlier subscription page/Roy kneeling in earlier period publicity photo/Roy reading his comic #6 to Cheryl and Linda. S1, Roy Rogers and the "Guardians of the Malpais": DuBois/Micale, Randy Steffen. Submitted May 7, 1948. Roy keeps a boy from losing his map to the Lost Dutchman Mine to crooks. Two-page story heading becomes "Pioneers of the Old West"; this one is "Col. Ezekiel Williams": DuBois. Submitted April 24, 1948. "Chuck Wagon Charley's Tales": DuBois/Parks. Submitted March 10, 1948. (Now originally copyrighted by Western Printing and Lithographing Co.) 36 pages. $12–$85.

#12, December 1948. (Original copyright: October 29, 1947, by Roy Rogers, No. B 177481. Expired October 1975.) Covers: Roy, dog, Spur (first appearance), in trees, publicity photo/subscription page, Santa Claus, no photo/Roy at home, bathing baby Dusty (first appearance)/Roy, horse, possibly Trigger, Jr., stables. S1, Roy Rogers in "Smuggler's Ford": DuBois/Micale, Steffen, Spiegle. Submitted May 28, 1948. Roy comes to the aid of sheepherders again. "Pioneers of the Old West": DuBois. Submitted April 26, 1948. "Chuck Wagon Charley's Tales — Brownie": DuBois/Parks. Submitted June 13, 1948. 36 pages. $8.50–$60.

#13, January 1949. Covers: Roy standing next to original Trigger on film set/same Christmas subscription page/Roy snoozing on hedge at home, before Dale, Linda, and Cheryl/Roy, Pat Brady, Andy Devine, film still. S1, "Roy Rogers Rides for a Windmill": DuBois/Micale, Steffen. Submitted June 29, 1948. Roy helps a child whose father is a rodeo rider who has been beaten and robbed. "Pioneers of the Old West": DuBois. Submitted July 30, 1948. "Chuck Wagon Charley's Tales — Ginger and Her Puppies": DuBois/Parks. Submitted June 26, 1948. 36 pages. $8.50–$60.

#14, February 1949. Covers: Roy standing between boxcars, gun drawn/original subscription page/Dusty in Roy's lap, playing daddy's guitar/Roy, Dale, close-up color publicity photo. S1, "Roy Rogers on Poacher's Island": DuBois/Micale, Steffen. Submitted August 18, 1948. Roy aids a rancher friend. "Pioneers of the Old West — The Runestone." Submitted August 1, 1948. "Chuck Wagon Charley's Tales" : DuBois/Parks. Submitted August 5, 1948. $8.50–$60.

#15, March 1949. Cover: Roy, original Trigger, close-up publicity photo by Freulich/subscription, no photo/original Trigger, close-up publicity photo/Roy, Cheryl, Linda (in their Roy Rogers outfits), close-up photo. S1, Roy Rogers in "The White Peril": DuBois/Micale (signed), Steffen. Submitted August 26, 1948. Roy gets caught up in a blizzard while on a cattle drive, then encounters a murder situation. Trigger takes a bow. "Pioneers of the Old West — The Challenger of the Ice Floes." Submitted September 8, 1948. "Chuck Wagon Charley's Tales": DuBois/Parks. Submitted August 30, 1948. 36 pages. $8.50–$60.

#16, April 1948. Covers: Roy, Spur, sitting on rock, close-up publicity photo/new subscription page, photo of Roy in square/Roy and dog, probably on location/Roy and cast in film still. S1, Roy Rogers in "Rangeland Refuge": DuBois/Micale (signed), Steffen. Submitted October 30, 1948. Roy takes to the air in this adventure, parachutes, and rides Trigger through a forest fire. "Pioneers of the Old West": DuBois. Submitted October 16, 1948. "Chuck Wagon Charley's Tales": DuBois/Parks. Submitted September 2, 1948. 36 pages. $8.50–$60.

#17, May 1949. Covers: Roy, chin on hand, close-up, publicity photo/2d subscription page/Roy in cap, boat with string of fish/ Roy, close-up publicity photo, Republic Pictures credit line. S1, Roy Rogers and "The Haunted Cliffs": DuBois/Micale (signed). Submitted November 17, 1948. Roy helps a sick Indian boy against the beliefs of his people. "Pioneers of the Old West — Jed Smith, Mountain Man": DuBois. Submitted October 22, 1948. "Chuck Wagon Charley's Tales": DuBois/Parks. Submitted October 5, 1948. 36 pages. $8.50–$60.

#18, June 1949. (Original copyright: April 19, 1949, by Roy Rogers, No. B 197332. Expired April 1977.) Covers: Roy, gun drawn, peers over rocks/illustrated Roy rearing on Trigger, by Micale, on subscription page/Roy at home, looking at Trigger trophy/Roy, extreme close-up, publicity photo. S1, Roy Rogers in "Buried Brands": DuBois/Micale. Submitted November 27, 1948. Roy comes to the aid of a man wrongly accused of stealing cattle. "Pioneers of the Old West": DuBois/Spiegle. Submitted December 4, 1948. "Chuck Wagon Charley's Tales": DuBois/ Parks. Submitted October 10, 1948. 36 pages. $8.50–$60.

#19, July 1949. Covers: Reversed negative shows Roy, original Trigger, from "boots" attire series/subscription page with second illustrated Roy on Trigger, by Micale/Roy squatting with guitar, dog, original Trigger, probably film location/Roy, close-up at home, sitting against door, aiming gun. S1, Roy Rogers and "The High Graders": DuBois/Micale (signed). Submitted January 3, 1949. Roy wages war against high-graders, while helping a young man and his wife.

"Pioneers of the Old West": DuBois. Submitted December 4, 1948. "Chuck Wagon Charley's Tales": DuBois/Parks. Submitted November 27, 1948. 36 pages. $8.50–$60.

#20, August 1949. Covers: Roy, close-up, action photo/subscription page with publicity photo of Roy, Trigger/Roy, action photo/Roy, publicity photo. S1, Roy Rogers and "The 'Lost Partner' Mine": DuBois/ Micale. Submitted February 12, 1949. Roy is trapped in a mine cave-in. S2, "Roy Rogers Does Business in Brimstone": DuBois/ Micale. Submitted February 26, 1949. Roy takes on the job of town marshal, bringing law and order to Brimstone. DuBois/Micale. "Pioneers of the Old West — The Hero of Donner's Pass": DuBois. Submitted February 23, 1949. First Trigger story (untitled): DuBois/Micale. Submitted February 2, 1949. 52 pages. $8.50–$60.

#21, September 1949. Covers: Roy rearing on original Trigger/small photo of Roy from issue #4, used on subscription page/one of the many specially posed studio photos of Roy, entering building, gun drawn/Roy, close-up Republic Pictures publicity photo. S1, Roy Rogers in "Canyon Gold": DuBois/ Micale. Submitted March 30, 1949. Roy helps reunite a father and daughter. S2, Roy Rogers in "Wasted Water": DuBois/Micale. Submitted April 12, 1949. Roy is caught between warring ranchers and farmers. "Trigger": DuBois/Parks. Submitted April 5, 1949. 52 pages. $7–$50.

#22, October 1949. Covers: Roy, in a badly lighted photo, is entering door, gun in hand/ photo of Roy and dog from earlier series (issue #19) used on subscription page/Roy, in photo from previously used series, playing guitar to Dusty/reversed negative shows dog, Roy, original Trigger, at stables. S1, Roy Rogers in "Rustler's Trap": DuBois/ Micale. Submitted May 2, 1949. Roy is filling in for a range detective for the Cattlemen's Association, and goes after rustlers. S2, Roy Rogers and "The Horse Hunters": DuBois/ Micale. Submitted May 11, 1949. A man, mean by nature, hunts wild horses for the sake of abusing them, until Roy enters the scene. "Pioneers of the Old West — A Woman on the Warpath": DuBois. Submitted April 28, 1949. "Trigger": DuBois/Parks. Submitted April 22, 1949. 52 pages. $7–50.

#23, November 1949. Covers: Roy, publicity photo with original Trigger, from "boots attire" series/Roy astride horse, gun drawn; either film still or film location/same subscription page with Roy photo ad/Roy playing guitar, sitting at table. S1, Roy Rogers in "The Rocking B Tally": DuBois/Micale ("Al," several places, splash panel.) Submitted June 18, 1949. A boy's pet bear is accused of killing a man. S2, "Roy Rogers Rounds up a Dude": DuBois/Micale (signed). "Pioneers of the Old West": DuBois/Micale. Submitted June 8, 1949. "Trigger": DuBois/ Parks. Submitted June 3, 1949. 52 pages. $7–$50.

#24, December 1949. New artists' influence shows more in this issue. Heavily mixed likenesses of Roy in most issues from this one forward. It is now believed that from about issue #40 on, one of those artists was Tony Sgroi. Covers: Roy kneeling beside boxcar, specially posed photo, gun in hand/Christmas subscription page with small encircled picture of Roy (new)/Roy on original Trigger, in film still/original Trigger, with Roy in Republic Pictures publicity photo. S1, Roy Rogers in "The Roaring River": DuBois/ Micale. Submitted July 18, 1949. A "Muleface Maggie O'Toole" story. S2, Roy Rogers and "The Silver Spider": DuBois/McKimson, Steffen, Peter Alvarado (signed 2d panel), possibly Bensen. Submitted July 29, 1949. Roy goes after a cold-blooded killer known as the "Silver Spider." "Pioneers of the Old West": DuBois/Micale. Submitted July 24, 1949. "Trigger": DuBois/Parks. Submitted July 23, 1949. 52 pages. $7–$50.

#25, January 1950. Covers: Roy sitting against stump, wearing new gun set (gold plated, first appearance), Spur in lap/Christmas subscription page with different (older) photo of Roy in circle/Roy riding original Trigger, film still/Roy is standing at fence, back to camera, specially posed photo. S1, Roy Rogers and "The Lady Marshal": DuBois/Micale, Steffen. Submitted August 5, 1949. Roy locks horns with a lady peace officer. S2, "Roy Rogers Trades Lead": DuBois/McKimson, Steffen, possibly Bensen, Alvarado, Sgroi. Submitted August 11, 1949. Roy goes searching in rugged country for a man's lost son. "Pioneers of the Old West": DuBois. Submitted August 5, 1949. "Trigger": DuBois/Parks. Submitted July 29, 1949. 52 pages. $7–$50.

#26, February 1950. Covers: Roy, gun in hand, looking over fence/illustrated Roy on subscription page/Roy twirling his trick lasso on film set/Roy astride original Trigger. S1, Roy Rogers and "The Claim Jumpers": DuBois/Micale. Submitted August 20, 1949. Scheming varmints tar and feather a fellow prospector to keep him from the mother lode. S2, Roy Rogers and "Jerkline Feud": DuBois/McKimson, Steffen, possibly Bensen. Submitted September 2, 1949. It's Roy to the rescue when two kids try to save their father's freight business. "Pioneers of the Old West": DuBois/Micale. Submitted August 29, 1949. "Trigger": DuBois/Parks. Submitted August 24, 1949. 52 pages. $7–$50.

#27, March 1950: Covers: Older publicity photo from the round hat days, with original Trigger/Roy and Trigger in film still/subscription page advertising Roy's photos, one shown/current photo of Roy about to use lariat, Spur at his side, facsimile signature. S1, Roy Rogers in "Bears or Branding Irons": DuBois/Micale (signed). Submitted September 18, 1949. Thieving rustlers are blaming the bears for their dirty work. S2, Roy Rogers in "Mustang Mountain": DuBois/ McKimson, Steffen, possibly Bensen. Submitted September 24, 1949. Roy helps a rancher find his sons, while along the way the rancher adopts a boy with a bull. "Pioneers of the Old West": DuBois/Micale. Submitted September 8, 1949. "Trigger": DuBois/Parks. Submitted September 2, 1949. 52 pages. $7–$50.

#28, April 1950. Covers: Roy, in earlier series photo, kneeling beside desert brush/ publicity photo of Roy with original Trigger with plastic saddle/same subscription photo/ Roy on a fence whittling. Photo is an unusual combination; he is wearing a shirt in an earlier style, heavily ornamented with green cactus and brown saddles, that was seldom if ever worn with the new hat. S1, Roy Rogers in "Wolves of Hunger Pass": DuBois/Micale. Submitted September 22, 1949. Sheepherders, goatherders, and sheep-rustling kidnappers keep Roy busy. S2, Roy Rogers in "Apache Blood" DuBois/ McKimson, Steffen, Bensen. Submitted September 12, 1949. Babies switched at birth create hate and discontent. (Roy wears a black hat in this story.) "Pioneers of the Old West": DuBois/Micale. Submitted September 8, 1949. "Trigger": DuBois/Parks. Submitted September 22, 1949. Horse outfitted in rodeo tack. 52 pages. $7–$50.

#29, May 1950. Covers: Roy, close-up, gun in hand, leaning on fence/Roy and original Trigger in plastic rodeo tack/same subscription page/black-hatted Roy and original Trigger in film still. Roy is poking his finger through bullet hole in black hat. S1, Roy Rogers and the "Guardian of the Caves": DuBois/Micale. Submitted October 10, 1949. Just try hunting for gold and dinosaurs in "Jurassic Park" and the bad guys will show every time. S2, Roy Rogers in "A Gift to Grandma": DuBois/McKimson, Steffen, possibly Bensen. Submitted September 26, 1949. A mangy critter, Jughead Dean, is out to rustle cattle and mortgages from honest, hard-working Johnny Long. Roy with blue hat. "Pioneers of the Old West": DuBois/Micale. Submitted October 3, 1949. "Trigger": DuBois/Parks. Submitted September 29, 1949. 52 pages. $7–$50.

#30, June 1950. Covers: Roy standing beside original Trigger, close-up, gold suede fringe/Roy sitting on haystack reading magazine to original Trigger/same subscription page; the photo used is that which was used for the color back cover of issue #21/Roy feeding original Trigger from his hat, probably at his ranch home or the ranch where Trigger and the other entertainment horses were kept/facsimile signature. S1, Roy Rogers and the "Secret of the Valley": DuBois/Micale. Submitted November 14, 1949. El Blanco, the pink-eyed outlaw, has captured the silver mine and is forcing the silversmiths to make jewelry for his gang. S2, "Roy Rogers Toughs It Out": DuBois/Bensen, Steffen, possibly Alvarado, Arens, Sgroi. Submitted October 31, 1949. Roy rides in a helicopter to chase outlaws Mosey Long and Green Elmo. "Pioneers of the Old West—Kit Carson Fights a War, Pt. 1": DuBois/Micale. Submitted December 8, 1949. "Trigger": DuBois/Parks (signed HP). Submitted October 10, 1949. 52 pages. $7–$50.

#31, July 1950. Covers: Roy in a shot from series used for back of issue #25, leaning against fence, arms folded/heavily used older publicity photo of Roy rearing on original Trigger about 1946/different photos used on subscription page/Roy sits astride original Trigger, gold-plated gun in hand, facsimile signature. Trigger in the infrequent plastic saddlery. Roy has new holsters and guns. "Pioneers of the Old West—Kit Carson Fights a War, Pt. 2": DuBois. Submitted December 8, 1949. S1, Roy Rogers and "The Knight Errant": DuBois/Micale. Submitted November 27, 1949. Roy assists an English dude and stumbles upon a cattle rustler. S2, Roy Rogers in "Dangerous Loot": DuBois/McKimson, Steffen, Alvarado, Sgroi. Submitted December 19, 1949. A dishonest banker robs his own bank, then when the get-a-way plane crashes, he kidnaps the stewardess. "Trigger": DuBois/Parks. Submitted October 24, 1949. 52 pages. $5.30–$38.

#32, August 1950. Covers: Roy, wearing the Hyer stovepipe boots, is possibly in front of the same haystack used in the *Dale Evans Comics* #10, here with Spur/b&w of Roy and Trigger from movie still/Roy riding original Trigger in film still/same subscription page/Roy in publicity photo, leaning on fence; new gun set showing. S1, Roy Rogers in "Lynching Moon"; DuBois/Micale signed. Submitted December 17, 1949. A conniving cowpoke steals Roy's clothes to do his dastardly deeds. S2, Roy Rogers in "Thirsty Creek": DuBois/Micale. Submitted January 7, 1950. Cussed outlaws are trying to keep thirsty ranchers and cattle from water. "Pioneers of the Old West": DuBois/Micale. Submitted January 14, 1950. "Trigger": DuBois/Parks. Submitted January 7, 1950. 52 pages. $5.30–$38.

#33, September 1950. Covers: Roy is leaning on the fence rail just posing. For some reason the publishers have dropped the real action poses in the issues numbered in the low twenties and are just using publicity poses/Roy at home reading comic #26 to Dusty/same subscription page/Roy in stable area, about to throw lariat. S1, Roy Rogers and "The Hairy Fugitive": DuBois/Micale (signed). Submitted January 9, 1950. An escaped gorilla kidnaps a little boy. S2, Roy Rogers and "The Man in the Serape": DuBois/Micale, possibly Bensen. Submitted February 19, 1950. Cattle ranchers and sheepherders just can't get along. S3, Roy Rogers in "Circumstantial Evidence": DuBois/Micale. Submitted January 14, 1950. Homesteaders and cattle ranchers battle over land rights; there's a Romeo and Juliet scenario to complete the saga. "Pioneers of the Old West": DuBois/Micale. Submitted February 26, 1950. "Trigger": DuBois/Randy Steffen. Submitted January 14, 1950. 52 pages. $5.30–$38.

#34, October 1950. (Original copyright by Roy Rogers.) Covers: Roy in rough-out boots, jeans, squatting beside three hunting dogs/Roy and original Trigger, probably on film location/same subscription page/large close-up of Roy, Republic Pictures publicity, facsimile signed. S1, Roy Rogers in "Shortcut to Showdown": DuBois/Micale (signed). Submitted January 29, 1950. Bad guys rob the mail, and it takes Roy to stamp out their dishonest dealings. S2, Roy Rogers in "Man's Oldest Weapon": DuBois/Micale (signed "AM," splash panel). Submitted February 19, 1950. Roy and a stone-tossing buddy help the border patrol capture foreign agents. S3, Roy Rogers and "The Boomtown Boss": DuBois/McKimson, Steffen (signed 17th panel), Alvarado. Submitted February 12, 1950. Oilmen try to rig the local election to gain control over the cattle ranchers. "Pioneers of the Old West": DuBois/Micale (signed). Submitted February 3, 1950. "Trigger": DuBois/Parks (signed). Submitted February 3, 1950. Inside b&w photos switch back and forth from earlier shots to current ones. 52 pages. $5.30–$38. *Note:* Dubois submitted "Medicine Trail" on February 5 as a fourth story for this issue, but it was not used.

#35, November 1950. (Original copyright, the Rohr Co.) Covers: Close-up of Roy/close-up publicity, guns drawn/same subscription, photo ad page/Roy and Dale (her final photo in the series) at rodeo appearance, both mounted. Roy is on original Trigger, Dale on closely matched palomino. S1, Roy Rogers and "The Squaw Creek Rustlers": DuBois/Micale (signed). Original title "Cow Creek Rustler." Submitted February 19, 1950. Outlaws are rustling mustangs and using rattlesnakes as guards. S2, Roy Rogers at "Avalanche Pass": DuBois/Micale (signed). Submitted January 14, 1950.

Roy captures cattle rustlers and rescues a man and his son from an avalanche. S3, Roy Rogers and "The Gun Shy Gent": DuBois/McKimson, Alvarado. Submitted May 3, 1950. Larcenous lobos are out to steal a ranch. "Pioneers of the Old West": DuBois. Submitted January 29, 1950. "Trigger": DuBois/Parks. Submitted February 26, 1950. 52 pages. $5.30–$38.

#36, December 1950. Cover: This cover is almost a duplicate of an earlier cover (see issue #21). Roy is rearing a little higher on the horse, and the attire is the same style, though a different design and color. The pose is the same, wave and all; some believe this is a paste-up photo, and that the head doesn't go with the body/Roy and Little Trigger in older photo, in the stables/half-page photo appears to be a movie still, has Roy shooting from a train, on subscription page/no photo, Christmas subscription. S1, Roy Rogers in "Christmas at Colt's Foot Canyon": DuBois/Micale (signed). Submitted May 29, 1950. Roy is in green shirt, blue hat. Horse thieves are blaming their felonious skullduggery on the Indians. S2, "Roy Shoots the Works": DuBois/Micale. Submitted July 1, 1950. Safe crackers, nitro-tossers, and counterfeiters cause an innocent man to be jailed. Roy arrives to set things straight. S3, Roy Rogers in "The Terror of the Mesquite": DuBois/McKimson, Steffen, Alvarado, Sgroi. Submitted May 15, 1950. Tiger Cole is counterfeiting and Lt. Tarbell seeks Roy's help in capturing him. "Pioneers of the Old West": DuBois/Micale. Submitted June 27, 1950. "Trigger": DuBois/Parks. Submitted June 5, 1950. 52 pages. $5.30–$38.

#37, January 1951. Covers: Roy framed in brown Western decorations with "Merry Christmas" under picture/Roy appears to be feeding same colt that is in photo with Dale on cover of *Dale Evans Comics*, issue #11/Roy on original Trigger in movie still, used on subscription page/Dell Comics Club membership, Dell Characters group picture, both have illustrated Roy Rogers. S1, Roy Rogers and "Broken Boundaries": DuBois/Micale (signed). Submitted July 24, 1950. It's range war with electric fences and crooked foremen until Roy rides in. S2, Roy Rogers in "The Trade Rat's Treasure": DuBois/Mc-

Kimson, Steffen, possibly Bensen, Alvarado contributions. Submitted July 17, 1950. Grandpa is murdered for his money by a gambling relative. "Pioneers of the Old West": DuBois/Micale. Submitted July 26, 1950. "Trigger": DuBois/Parks. The title art on the cover undergoes a drastic change but reverses with the next issue. Submitted July 3, 1950. 52 pages. $5.30–$38.

#38, February 1951. Covers: Covers change to color photos combined with artwork. Close-up of Roy, illustrated Indians in background/Roy is reading a "wanted poster," a shot from an earlier series of photos/new subscription page has large photo of Roy, with one of the free photos shown/Roy is kneeling down, giving the dog water from his hat, facsimile signed, first and last name are joined for the first time. S1, Roy Rogers and "Boss of the Unagalla": DuBois/Micale (signed). Submitted August 14, 1950. Roy is a cattle detective called in to help the sheriff. S2, Roy Rogers at "Owlhoot Cabin": DuBois/Micale (signed). Submitted August 22, 1950. (Black-hatted Roy.) Muleface Maggie sold the ranch and owlhoots are out to get her cash. S3, Roy Rogers in "Horse Thief Canyon": DuBois/McKimson, Steffen. (Mostly a Trigger story.) There seems to be less and less evidence of Alvarado being involved now. Close inspection reveals tiny "RR" initials on the tapaderos. Trigger, Jr., is horsenapped. Submitted August 14, 1950. Trigger battles black bronc while Roy battles rustlers. "Pioneers of the Old West": DuBois/Micale (signed). Submitted August 7, 1950. "Trigger": DuBois/Micale (signed). Submitted August 7, 1950. 52 pages. $5.30–$38.

#39, March 1951. Covers: New technique this month, with a scene from one of Roy's films in the background, as Roy is shown in close-up with pistol drawn. Particularly interesting is the fact that the color photo of Roy is current, and the film scene used is from the 1940s/Roy rearing on Trigger at what appears to be fairgrounds or rodeo. Trigger is standing almost perfectly vertical/subscription page with photo/photo appears to be a b&w of Roy and original Trigger in plastic saddlery that has been tinted. S1, Roy Rogers in "Rifles at Black Butte": DuBois/Micale (signed). Submitted September 5,

1950. Robbers are out to get the gold that's hidden in the wool of a lamb. S2, Roy Rogers in "Death Is the Pilot": DuBois/McKimson, Steffen. Submitted September 9, 1950. Roy has to stop dealers who have stolen drugs from a hospital. S3, Roy Rogers at "Thunder Mesa": DuBois/Micale (signed). Submitted September 15, 1950. A plane crash has Roy searching for a friend's daughter and her dude boyfriend. "Pioneers of the Old West": DuBois/Micale. Submitted September 13, 1950. "Trigger": DuBois/Parks. Submitted August 28, 1959. 52 pages. $5.30–$38.

#40, April 1951. Covers: Back to mixed photos and art. Art believed to be from Alvarado. The illustrated background is a posse that Roy is apparently leading; close-up of Roy in action pose/Roy in a new-styled fringed outfit (first appearance) astride original Trigger, evidently at home because dog also on Trigger happens to be one of his hunting dogs/Roy rubbing noses with unidentifiable Trigger double, facsimile signed "Roy Rogers & Trigger" (first appearance). S1, Roy Rogers in "The Red Hand": DuBois/Micale (signed). Submitted September 18, 1950. The town doctor has been murdered and the sheriff poisoned, and the town is trying to arrest the wrong man. S2, Roy Rogers in "Murder at Wetstone": Unknown/Micale (signed). (Black-hatted Roy.) This story does not appear in DuBois account. This could be the first story in the series not written by him. Land grabbers take advantage of the drought to buy land cheap and kill whoever gets in their way. S3, Roy Rogers in "Doctor from Jack Pine": DuBois/McKimson, Alvarado, Sgroi. "M.D. Peso" signing. Submitted September 9, 1950. Diphtheria has appeared in the town, and the lady doctor has to convince the Navajos to be inoculated. "Pioneers of the Old West": DuBois/Micale. Submitted September 20, 1950. "Trigger": DuBois/Richard Moore, Hiram Mankin (signed "Hi"). Submitted November 1, 1950. 52 pages. $5.30–$38.

#41, May 1951. Covers: Roy and original Trigger before an illustrated mountain background/Roy explaining parts of pistol to two children, both of whom are wearing "Roy Rogers and Trigger" sweaters/subscription page carrying new photo of Roy and Bullet (probably first appearance)/Roy squatting while examining a spur, duplicate of an earlier shot, closer up. Major new attire change showing in most photos. S1, Roy Rogers and the "Jinx of Headless Valley": DuBois/Micale (signed). Submitted September 25, 1950. Roy rescues a miner and his daughter from head-hunting Nakannie. S2, "Roy Reads the Signs": DuBois/Micale (signed). Submitted November 1, 1950. A lawyer is murdered, and the wrong man is accused. S3, Roy Rogers and "The Orange Nuggets": unknown/McKimson, Steffen. Claim jumpers are out to steal the gold found by an old prospector. "Trigger": DuBois/Moore, Mankin (signed "Hi"). Submitted October 5, 1950. 52 pages. $5.30–$38.

#42, June 1951. Covers: Roy and Spur, close-up publicity shot/"Cowboy's Rain Slicker": Till Goodan, art/subscription page/facsimile signed publicity pose of Roy sitting on fence. S1, "Roy Rogers and the Return of John Jay": Micale. (Roy in green hat.) A rancher's son returns home in time to help save the ranch from the Crayle gang. S2, Roy Rogers in "Roy Springs a Trap": DuBois/McKimson, Alvarado, Steffen, signed by all. Submitted November 13, 1950. The FBI needs Roy's assistance in a diamond scam. "Pioneers of the Old West": Micale. "Trigger": DuBois/Moore. Submitted November 9, 1950. 52 pages. $5.30–$38.

#43, July 1951. Covers: Roy and original Trigger. Roy's wearing a deputy sheriff's badge in one of the few pictures showing a badge/"Cowboy Chaps": Robert Jenny, art/same subscription page/Roy, in specially posed photo, is looking over bullseye with gold-plated gun in hand, facsimile signed. S1, Roy Rogers and "The Bone Hunter": DuBois/Micale. Submitted October 2, 1950. Villains rob the bank and take hostages, one of whom is a bone-hunting doctor. S2, Roy Rogers in "Tiger Trail": DuBois/Micale. Submitted November 30, 1950. A truck wreck leaves two Bengal tigers on the loose. S3, Roy Rogers in "Die or Drink": DuBois/McKimson, Steffen, possible Alvarado, Sgroi. Submitted November 20, 1950. They're fighting over water rights. "Pioneers of the Old West": DuBois/Micale. Submitted November 30, 1950. "Trigger": DuBois/Moore,

possibly Mankin. Submitted November 21, 1950. 52 pages. $5.30–$38.

#44, August 1951. Original copyright changes to Roy Rogers Enterprises through issue #84. Covers: Roy is blowing the smoke from his recently fired golden six-shooter/"Popular Handguns," which is almost totally out of sync with a Western comic book; the publishers could have easily done the piece on Western guns, i.e., the Colt .45/subscription page/Roy about to throw his lariat, facsimile signed. S1, Roy Rogers and the "Lobos of Live Oak Valley": DuBois/Micale. Submitted November 27, 1950. Cattlemen versus the goat ranchers. S2, Roy Rogers in "Bullets from Nowhere": DuBois/Micale. Submitted January 6, 1951. Buckskin Bullard has snatched Muleface Maggie's adopted daughter. S3, Roy Rogers in "Island Ambush": DuBois/McKimson, Steffen. Submitted November 27, 1950. Don Arturo's cattle are being rustled away on a ship. "Longhorns and Gunsmoke": DuBois. (Original copyright 1951, by Western Printing and Lithographing Co.) This one featured "Billy the Kid." Submitted February 2, 1951. "Trigger": DuBois/new artist, unknown at this time, Moore (signed). Submitted January 6, 1951. 52 pages. $5.30–$38.

#45, September 1951. Covers: Roy is kneeling in action pose, gun drawn, illustrated horseback riders amongst some brush (Alvardo)/"American Horse": Jenny, art/subscription page/Roy waving on Trigger in corral, facsimile signature. S1, Roy Rogers and the "Range Orphan": DuBois/Micale. Submitted January 22, 1951. Gold miner Grandpa is killed, leaving Billy a gold dust orphan. S2, Roy Rogers and the "Lost Payroll": unknown/Micale. The payroll is stolen, and Roy is asked to help find it. S3, Roy Rogers and the "Badlands Bandit": DuBois/McKimson, Steffen, possibly Alvarado, Sgroi. Submitted January 27, 1951. A resigned sheriff sends for Roy to help bring in Scarface Clay's gang. "The End of the Wolf Pack": DuBois/Micale. Submitted February 8, 1951. "Trigger": DuBois/Parks. Submitted January 22, 1951. 52 pages. $5.30–$38.

#46, October 1951. Covers: Roy is crouched down behind fence, golden gun drawn, illustrated background of mountains/"Rope Artists": Jenny, art/new subscription page photo from earlier series/Roy sitting on fence, playing guitar and singing to original Trigger, facsimile signature. S1, "Roy Rogers Finds the Tiger's Lair": DuBois/Micale. Original title: "Roy Finds Tiger's Lair": Submitted February 22, 28, 1951. Apache Joe Sandal is in love with Tom Maine's daughter and makes life tough until Tom allows the courtship. (Artist incorporates colorful shirt.) S2, Roy Rogers in "Raider's Reward": DuBois/Micale (signed). Submitted April 2, 1951. Honey Bock hires hoodlums to force small ranchers off their land. S3, Roy Rogers and the "Madman of Grizzly Peak": DuBois/McKimson, Steffen, Alvarado, Sgroi. Submitted March 26, 1951. A steer-eating grizzly mauls a rancher, and Roy uses doctoring skills to save the man's life. "Outlaws of the Old West—Outlaw's Promise"; DuBois/Micale. Submitted February 10, 1951. "Trigger": DuBois. Submitted February 24, 1951. 52 pages. $5.30–$38. *Note:* DuBois submitted "Pioneer Prophet" on February 10, 1951, as a filler story in this issue, but it wasn't used.

#47, November 1951. Covers: Roy standing beside original Trigger, illustrated ranch in background/"Slowin' 'Em Down on the Range"; Jenny, art/subscription page/Roy sitting on a bench with a German shepherd pup who resembles young Bullet. S1, Roy Rogers and the "Golden Tin": unknown/Micale (signed). Outlaws use the town rodeo to cover their gold robbery. S2, "Roy Hunts for Strays": DuBois/McKimson, Steffen. Submitted February 10, 1951. Muleface Maggie's cattle are straying, with the help of varmints on horseback. "Pioneers of the Old West—Johnny Appleseed": unknown/Micale. "Chuck Wagon Charley's Tales": DuBois/ drawn by unidentified artist who has been working on the Trigger stories the past few issues. Submitted April 23, 1951. "Trigger" feature is out until issue #100. 52 pages. $4.50–$30.

#48, December 1951. (Original copyright: October 23, 1951, by Roy Rogers Enterprises, No. B 330840. Expired: October 1979.) Covers: Roy peers up toward the sun, hand shading his eyes/subscription page with new Roy, Trigger photo from previous series/ "Boots and Spurs"/Roy on bicycle, with

original Trigger acting unimpressed. S1, Roy Rogers and the "River of Gold": DuBois/ McKimson. Submitted April 30, 1951. Roy helps the FBI stop a range war and has to tangle with Louie the Goon. "The Breed of the Pioneers": DuBois/Micale. Submitted May 28, 1951. In a photo on the back of issue #35, November 1950, the two "R"s appeared on the plastic rodeo saddle, for the first time. In this shot, the two "R"s appear on the black leather ornamented saddle. Comic reverts to 36 pages. $4.30–$30. *Note:* On March 26, 1951, DuBois submitted "Little Hunter and the Cougar's Cub" as a filler story for this issue; it was not used. *Note:* It is believed that the editor for 1952-1957 was Kellogg Adams, and he could have been responsible for any stories not written by DuBois.

#49, January 1952. Covers: Christmas cover has Roy decorating tree/same subscription page/illustration of Roy on subscription page: Al Micale, from one of the "Muleface Maggie O'Toole" stories/Roy is rubbing noses with Little Trigger, or look alike (older photo). "King of the Cowboys" is added under Roy's name beginning with this story. S1, Roy Rogers and the "Mystery of Circle Lake": DuBois/McKimson, Steffen, Alvarado, Sgroi. Submitted May 21, 1951. A friend of Roy dies under mysterious circumstances, and Roy is deputized to assist in solving the mystery. "Breed of the Pioneers": DuBois/Moore. Submitted May 21, 1951. "Bowlegs": Jenny, art. 36 pages. $4.30–$30.

#50, February 1952. Covers: Close-up of Roy leaning forward on fence, illustrated background of town/"Boom Towns and Ghost Towns": Jenny, art/new subscription page photo taken from bullseye photo/Roy cleaning Trigger's shoe. S1, Roy Rogers in "The Stroke of Twelve": Dubois/Micale. Submitted June 25, 1951. Roy searches for the son of his dying friend, but a greedy nephew doesn't want him found in time. S2, Roy Rogers in "The Fast Game": unknown/ Micale. Busher strikes gold, which is taken by his former partner, who in turn is fleeced in a crooked card game. "Breed of the Pioneers": DuBois/Micale. Submitted July 30, 1951. "Chuck Wagon Charley's Tales": DuBois/McKimson, possibly Alvarado, Sgroi. Submitted July 5, 1951. 36 pages. $4.30–$30.

#51, March 1952. Covers: Roy leaning forward on Trigger in publicity pose/"Multishot Weapons of Yesteryear": Jenny, art/same subscription page/Roy standing on Trigger, Jr., or other Trigger double's back. S1, Roy Rogers in "Roy Takes a Prisoner": DuBois/ Micale. Submitted June 25, 1951. Muleface Maggie is elected sheriff. S2, Roy Rogers in "One Man's Poison": DuBois/Micale. Submitted August 6, 1951. Roy's good deeds convince Apache Tom to follow the straight and narrow. "Breed of the Pioneers": DuBois/Micale. Submitted July 31, 1951. "Chuck Wagon Charley's Tales": DuBois. Submitted July 28, 1951. 36 pages. $4.30– $30.

#52, April 1952. Covers: Reversed negative shows Roy leaning against tree stump, lariat in hand, illustrated background of cowboy who looks like Roy, roping calf (Alvarado)/new subscription page, small photo/"Hunting the Coyote": Jenny, art/Roy reprimanding Bullet, outdoor scene. S1, Roy Rogers and "The Man Who Tried to Buy Happiness": unknown/Micale. Roy is trying to raise money to save the ranch and the rancher's son. S2, Roy Rogers in "Nester or Neighbor": DuBois/McKimson, possibly Steffen, Alvarado, Mankin, Sgroi. Submitted August 25, 1951. It's war between the ranchers and nesters. "The Swimming Cat": believed to be by Dubois/Micale. Submitted August 30, 1951, as "Breed of The Pioneers" story. "Chuck Wagon Charley's Tales": DuBois. Submitted August 28, 1951. "Range War." 36 pages. $4.30–$30.

#53, May 1952. Covers: Roy sits on the back of a circus wagon/subscription page, photo/"The First Commandos": Jenny, art/Roy, hand on gun, behind circus wagon (note gold-plated spurs). S1, Roy Rogers and the "Portrait of Uncle Ezra": DuBois/Micale (signed). Submitted May 7, 1951. A young lady sketches the wrong person. S2, Roy Rogers in "Red Clay": DuBois/Micale (signed). Submitted September 20, 1951. Roy battles Speed Gatlin for the lady at Diamond M Ranch. "Range Orphan": Believed to be DuBois/Micale. Submitted October 6, 1951, a "Breed of the Pioneers" story. "Chuck Wagon Charley's Tales": DuBois. Submitted October 6, 1951. 36 pages. $4.30–$30.

#54, June 1952. (Original copyright: April 22, 1952, by Roy Rogers Enterprises, No. B 360393. Expired, April 1980.) Roy's cradling a couple of puppies (new sterling silver hatband showing)/new photo on subscription page/"Tracking the Range Killer": Jenny (signed)/Roy, publicity pose, sitting on wagon wheel, facsimile signature has dropped the "& Trigger." S1, Roy Rogers in "Roy Buys into Trouble": DuBois/Micale. Submitted June 4, 1951. Affairs of the heart and cattle rustling make up this tumbleweed tale. S2, Roy Roygers and the "Missing Deputy": DuBois/Micale. (Black-hatted Roy, actually shaded). Submitted October 6, 1951. Ned Raines has been robbed and murdered, and the sheriff's son is accused. "Radio Ranger": Believed to be DuBois/Micale. Submitted October 6, 1951, as a "Breed of the Pioneers" story. "Chuck Wagon Charley's Tales": DuBois. Submitted October 6, 1951. 36 pages. $4.30–$30.

#55, July 1952. Covers: Roy, gun in hand, aiming out the back of a covered wagon/subscription page/"Bill Cody–Pony Express Rider": Jenny, art/Roy, standing tall in original Trigger's stirrups, facsimile signed "& Trigger." S1, Roy Rogers in "Freight Failure": unknown/McKimson, Alvarado, possibly Steffen, Sgroi. The freight hauler's nephew is in cahoots with the bad guys. S2, Roy Rogers in "Calamity Camp": DuBois/Micale (signed). Roy thwarts a would-be murderer. Submitted November 16, 1951. "The Cougar": Micale. "Chuck Wagon Charley's Tales": DuBois. Submitted December 1, 1951. (Last color photo back.) 36 pages. $5– $36.

#56, August 1952. Covers: Roy, close-up, smiling, illustrated background of cowboys/new photo of Roy and original Trigger on subscription page, with illustrated Roys by Micale/"The Trail Thief": Jenny, art (signed full name)/The photo backs are gone, never to return in the original series. Baseball story in first advertisement, Wheaties cereal. S1, "Roy Rogers on the Horse Thief's Trail": DuBois/Micale (signed). Original title: "Roy Rogers on Horse Thief's Trail." Submitted November 25, 1951. Roy puts on tennis shoes to go after Corse Raemer, bank robber and horse thief. S2, "Roy Rogers in Windigo

Valley": Dubois/McKimson. Submitted December 8, 1951. The hunt is on for the half-spook, half-bear that terrorizes the citizens. "Wonders of the West—Death Valley," "Old Two Toes": Micale. "Chuck Wagon Charley's Tales": DuBois. Submitted December 1, 1951. 36 pages. $5–$35.

#57, September 1952. Covers: Roy tying calf, illustrated mountains in background/new subscription page photo from series, previously used/"Barbed Wire": Jenny, art/Wheaties cereal ad, baseball story. S1, Roy Rogers in "Poisoned Water": DuBois/Micale (signed). Submitted February 10, 1952. Subversives have poisoned the waterhole with anthrax bacteria. S2, Roy Rogers in "A Challenge in the Big Bend": DuBois/Micale. Submitted February 10, 1952. Foreign agents subvert American citizens with heroin smuggling and distribution. S3, Roy Rogers in "Coward's Cache": DuBois/McKimson, Alvarado, Sgroi, Mankin contribution (signed). Submitted January 15, 1952. The silver mine payroll is robbed and an honest man framed. S4, Roy Rogers in "Roy Plays a Hunch": Dubois/Alvarado, Sgroi, Mankin contribution (signed). Submitted January 31, 1952. The crooks rob the bank, wound the teller, and threaten to shoot Bullet. "The Oregon Trail": Micale. "Chuck Wagon Charley's Tales": DuBois. Submitted December 10, 1951. 52 pages. $5–$35.

#58, October 1952. Covers: Roy lying behind tree, rifle in hand, illustrated background, mountains/subscription page, photo/"The Schofield-Smith and Wesson Army Revolver": Jenny, art/Wheaties cereal ad, baseball story. S1, Roy Rogers in "Roy Plays for High Stakes": DuBois/Micale (signatures, unknown "MB"). Submitted February 16, 1952. The senator's son is hooked on heroin and helping smugglers at the family's dude ranch. S2, Roy Rogers in "Wolf Trap": DuBois/Micale. Submitted August 6, 1951: Roy's friend is falsely accused of murder. "The Sheep Wagon": McKimson. "Chuck Wagon Charley's Tales": DuBois. Submitted January 31, 1952. 52 pages. $3.70–$26.

#59, November 1952. Covers: Roy playing guitar, singing/same subscription page/Wheaties cereal ad. S1, Roy Rogers in "Tickets to Destruction": DuBois/Micale.

Submitted March 3, 1952. An elderly couple, miniature bombs, and a gent named "Smelly Gookin" all appear in this story about subversives out to destroy the government. S2, Roy Rogers in "Gun Talk in Ghost Town": DuBois/Micale. Submitted March 3, 1952. Roy teams with the feds to stop the flow of illegal aliens. S3, Roy Rogers in "Roy Trails the Black Filly": DuBois/McKimson, Mankin (both signing in the splash panel). Submitted July 9, 1951. "Backwoods Trapper." "Chuck Wagon Charley's Tales": DuBois. Submitted March 3, 1952. $3.70–$26.

#60, December 1952. Covers: Roy is wearing the Hyer stovepipe, double-eagle rodeo boots, and Trigger is wearing the plastic red, white, and blue rodeo saddle, illustrated background/Whitman Book ad/Christmas subscription, photo (last page)/Daisy's BB Red Ryder rifle/Alvarado-illustrated Roy rearing on Trigger in Post's cereal ad, pop-out trading cards. S1, Roy Rogers in "Conclusive Evidence": DuBois/Micale. Submitted April 7, 1952. The sheriff is murdered while looking for poachers. S2, Roy Rogers in "Forgery Farm": DuBois/Alvardo, McKimson, Micale, possibly Bensen, Sgroi. Submitted May 5, 1952. Illegal aliens infiltrate a small town and replace "good girl" Harriet with an evil double. S3, Roy Rogers and "The Killer from Cougar Mountain": DuBois/Micale. Submitted May 14, 1952. A greedy nephew murders his uncle, then tries to make it look like an accident. "Wolf Pack." "Chuck Wagon Charley's Tales": DuBois. Submitted April 14, 1952. 52 pages. $3.70–$26.

#61, January 1953. Covers: Christmas cover shows Roy, arms loaded with Christmas gifts, illustrated background/Whitman Book ad. S1, Roy Rogers in "Christmas at Corbett's Curve": DuBois/Micale (signed). Submitted April 6, 1952. Roy and the feds go after saboteurs. S2, Roy Rogers in "Mountain Mystery": DuBois/Alvarado, Micale, McKimson, possibly Bensen, Sgroi. Submitted May 5, 1952. Devious foreign agents rob an armored car and steal weapons. S3, Roy Rogers in "Man Hunt": DuBois/Micale (signed). Submitted May 19, 1952. Gook Macon, murderer, is out of prison and killing again. He tries cross-dressing to avoid the wrath of Roy. "Chuck Wagon Charley's Tales." "Highway Robbery." 52 pages. $3.70–$26.

#62, February 1953. Covers: Action pose, Roy leaning over barrels, golden six-shooter in hand/Whitman Book ad/subscription page shows Dell comics/Post cereals ad. S1, Roy Rogers in "The Rustler of Goblin Hill": DuBois/Alvarado, Micale, McKimson, Sgroi. Submitted June 2, 1952. Crooks use a helicopter to rustle cattle and sheep. S2, Roy Rogers in "The Clue of the Spur": DuBois/Micale (signed). Submitted December 8, 1951. A jealous father frames a young man to keep him away from his daughter. "Buffalo Skinners." "Chuck Wagon Charley's Tales": DuBois. Submitted June 26, 1952. 52 pages. $3.70–$26.

#63, March 1953. Covers: Roy, whittling on a piece of wood, illustrated background/Mars Candy ad/Roy Rogers picture puzzle, Whitman Book ad/illustrated Roy, Post's Grape-Nuts Flakes ad, Dale in ad. S1, Roy Rogers in "Mantrap on Longshot Mesa": DuBois/Micale. Submitted July 14, 1952. The feds ask Roy to find a man wrongly convicted of murder. S2, Roy Rogers in "The Rifleman of Boulder Wash": DuBois/Alvarado. Submitted July 22, 1952. Miners are being killed for gold dust. S3, Roy Rogers in "Canyon Burial": DuBois/Alvarado, McKimson. Submitted July 15, 1951. Accused of a crime he didn't commit, an old man hides in the mountains, taking along his orphaned granddaughter. "Ranch Rescue." "Chuck Wagon Charley's Tales": DuBois. Submitted July 26, 1952. 52 pages. $3.70–$26.

#64, April 1953. Covers: Roy polishing his rifle/Mars Candy ad/Whitman Book ad/Post's cereals ad. S1, Roy Rogers in "Mantrap at Broken Butte": DuBois/Micale. Submitted September 21, 1952. Bart Madden is accused of killing Curly Bob Calder, but Roy discovers that the heroin-dealing town pharmacist is guilty of many evil deeds, probably murder too. S2, Roy Rogers in "Trouble at Tanner's Ford": DuBois/Alvarado, McKimson, possibly Bensen. Submitted January 28, 1952. Organized crime boss Nick Koretz is trying to take over the lumber business. S3, Roy Rogers in

"Medicine Smoke": DuBois/Alvarado, McKimson, possibly Bensen. Submitted September 22, 1952. Outlaws are importing hoof and mouth disease across the Mexican border. "Lion Hound." "Chuck Wagon Charley's Tales": DuBois. Submitted September 29, 1952. "Roy Rogers at the Rodeo": Micale (four-panel story). 52 pages. $3.70–$26.

#65, May 1953. Covers: Roy, hand and hat filled with baby chicks/Whitman Book ad/illustrated Roy (Alvarado) subscription page/Roy Rogers Deputy Sheriff outfit. S1, Roy Rogers and the "Mine at Ghost Gulch": DuBois/Micale. Submitted October 8, 1952. Miners are dry-gulched and their gold taken. S2, Roy Rogers and the "Man with Iron Hands": DuBois/Micale. Submitted October 6, 1952. Roy tangles with a giant of a mountain man. S3, Roy Rogers and "The Hermit of Pullin's Pocket": DuBois/Alvarado, McKimson, unknown. Submitted October 13, 1952. A small group of Yaqui Indians escape prison and are on the rampage. "The Twister": DuBois. Submitted November 15, 1952. "Chuck Wagon Charley's Tales": DuBois. Submitted October 13, 1952. "Argentine Gaucho": Till Goodan, art. 52 pages. $3.70–$26.

#66, June 1953. Covers: Roy, ringing dinner bell, illustrated background/Whitman Book ad for "Tell-a-Tale" books/illustrated Roy on Trigger, subscription page/illustrated Roy offers Roy Rogers, Jr., trick Lasso, Post's cereals ad/illustrated Roy, probably by Alvarado. S1, Roy Rogers and the "Strange Manhunt": DuBois/Micale (Sal Buscema's name in background work in the final panel). Submitted November 29, 1952. A scientist disappears, and the race is on to see who gets to him first, Roy or foreign agents. S2, Roy Rogers in "Outlaw's Legacy": DuBois/Mankin, John Steel, possibly Bensen. Sal Buscema backgrounds. (Sal's entire name can be seen with 17× magnification, located about where Roy's seat meets his saddle. "Luhrs," for Henry Luhrs, is seen on occasion, as in panel 1, page 9.) Submitted December 8, 1952. Fleabit Pete is out to steal Bug-eye Borgland's fortune. S3, Roy Rogers in "Bullet Trails a Thief": DuBois/Micale. Submitted December 4, 1952. A villain steals gold from Bullet's friend, and Bullet takes it back. Submitted December 6, 1952. "Chiquita — Brett Harte 1883": Micale. 52 pages. $3.70- $26.

#67, July 1953. Covers: Roy drinking from a canteen, illustrated background/Mars Candy ad/Whitman Book ad; Roy Rogers and Dale Evans coloring books/Roy Rogers Ranch Set premium, Post's cereals. S1, Roy Rogers in "Deadly Ranch": DuBois/Micale. Submitted January 10, 1953. Bullet has his own stories now. Rolly Sayward sells "Rolly's Ranch," but the money is stolen before he can get it home. "Bullet Convicts a Criminal": DuBois. Submitted January 15, 1953. S2, Roy Rogers in "Lost Gulch Cabin": DuBois/Alvarado, possibly Steffen. Original title: "Roy Rogers Meets the Menace of Lost Cabin Gulch." Submitted January 12, 1953. Luke Hornell is knifed in the back, the bank is robbed, and Bullet helps Slim Walker catch the culprit. "Genius at Work." "Chuck Wagon Charley's Tales": DuBois. Submitted December 29, 1952. 52 pages. $3.70-$26.

#68, August 1953. Covers: Roy posing with a calf/subscription page showing various comic covers/Whitman Book ad/Post's cereals ad. S1, Roy Rogers in "Rifles at Piute Wells": DuBois/Micale. Submitted January 27, 1953. Bannerman wants to stampede a herd of buffalo over sheepherder John Thornsen's sheep. S2, Roy Rogers and "The Missing Spinsters": DuBois/Micale. Submitted February 2, 1953. An injured prospector sends for two spinster sisters to care for his granddaughter but gets two felons instead. S3, Roy Rogers in "Bullet Guards a Friend": DuBois/Alvarado. Submitted January 24, 1953. Bullet helps a friend find his cattle, then helps to capture the rustlers. Bullet's story is once again combined wth Roy's. Evidently the dog wasn't strong enough to carry his own story, or the writers didn't want to write the stories. "Prairie Ghost," "Chuck Wagon Charley's Tales": DuBois. Submitted January 22, 1953. "Frontier Merchant." 52 pages. $3.70-$26.

#69, September 1953. Covers: Roy is repairing a fence/an illustrated Roy offering wallet on subscription page/Whitman Books ad/the premiums are genuine Roy Rogers buttons offered in Post's cereals ad. S1, "Roy

Rogers Races Murder in Papoose Pass": DuBois/Micale. Original title: "Roy Races Murder." Submitted February 21, 1953. With Trigger in the shop for repairs, Roy rides a bay to go after Craig Bannerman, fresh out of jail and terrorizing the countryside. S2, Roy Rogers in "High Wind and Gun Smoke": DuBois/Micale. Submitted February 23, 1953. A young man saves the life of a rancher's daughter, but the sheriff finds out the lad is wanted for robbery. S3, Roy Rogers in "Bullet Searches a Crook": DuBois/Steffen, Alvarado, McKimson. Original Title: "Bullet Turns In a Crook." Submitted February 16, 1953. For the first time we get to see in the comics Roy's sidekick from the television series and several movies, Pat Brady, whose likeness is captured pretty well as the comic stories begin to align with the television series. Bullet tracks Leonard Strow, who has stolen his own payroll from jailer Pat Brady. "The Choice of Rory O'Hara": DuBois. Submitted February 18, 1953. "Chuck Wagon Charley's Tales": DuBois. Submitted February 14, 1953. "The Last Boomtown Sheriff." 52 pages. $3.70-$26.

#70, October 1953. Covers: Roy is doing blacksmith work, illustrated background/subscription page, with illustrated Roy by Micale/Schwinn Bikes ad/genuine Roy Rogers buttons premium in Post's cereals ad. S1, Roy Rogers and "The Ravening Pack": DuBois/Micale. Submitted March 17, 1953. Renegade Indian "Mosi the Cat" is playing havoc with the spirits and a pack of coyotes. S2, Roy Rogers in "Burro Business": DuBois/Micale. Submitted March 21, 1953. Jug Hacker kills a man and blames it on a wild burro. S3, Roy Rogers in "Bullet Meets a Test": DuBois/Alvarado, McKimson, Steffen. Submitted March 14, 1953. Slick Slade Chicklow has broken out of prison and kidnapped little Luigi. "Jeremy's Promise." "Chuck Wagon Charley's Tales": DuBois. Submitted March 14, 1953. "The Tonto Basin War": August Lenox, art. 52 pages. $3.70-$26.

#71, November 1953. Covers: Rodeo appearance, Roy on bowing Little Trigger/Mars Candy ad/Lionel trains/illustrated Roy, panel story, subscriptions page: Micale. S1,

Roy, pistol at the ready, is seen in some of his less fancy attire, as he dresses up the cover of *Roy Rogers Comics*, **issue #72, December 1953.**

Roy Rogers and "The Flying Butcher": DuBois/Micale. Submitted April 19, 1953. It's a dogfight with airplanes when Roy agrees to help Ranger Barney catch poachers. S2, Roy Rogers in "Apache Justice": DuBois/Micale. Submitted April 12, 1953. Black Ears robs a store, kills the owner, then steals a horse from the livery. S3, Roy Rogers in "Bullet Holds the Fort": DuBois/Alvarado, Mankin. Submitted April 12, 1953. (Roy doesn't appear; they put Roy title on Bullet story.) Bullet saves a little boy from stampeding horses, deep water, and rampaging wolves. "Partner's Win": DuBois. Submitted April 19, 1953. "Chuck Wagon Charley's Tales": DuBois. Submitted April 19, 1953. (This is the final issue for Al McKimson.) "Mustang Runner — Nevada Wild Horse Hunter": Till Goodan, art. 52 pages. $3.15–$22.

#72, December 1953. (Original copyright: October 20, 1953, by Roy Rogers Enterprises, No B 452052. Expired, October 1981.) Covers: Roy, golden .45 in hand, crouched behind wagon wheel/Lincoln Logs ad/Red Ryder in Daisy Co. ad/Post's cereals ad. S1, Roy Rogers and "The Silent Killers": DuBois/Micale. Submitted May 17, 1953. Bullet is blamed for the untimely demise of a herd of sheep. S2, Roy Rogers in "Bullet Plows Through": DuBois/Micale, Mankin. Submitted May 18, 1953. Bullet saves a small child with pneumonia by taking him to town in a barrel on skis. S3, "Roy Rogers at Trail's End": DuBois/Micale, Mankin. Original title: "Roy Rogers at Trail's End in the Desert." Submitted May 23, 1953. Nucky, the gangster, interrupts Penny and Doug's wedding by brandishing machine guns. "Buck Fever": Hiram Mankin, III (signed). "Chuck Wagon Charley's Tales": DuBois. Submitted May 3, 1953. "Indian Canoes." 52 pages. $3.50–$23.

#73, January 1954. Covers: Christmas, Roy decorating tree/Mars Candy Co. ad/Red Ryder, Daisy BB Rifles ad/illustrated Roy (Alvarado) ad in Roy Rogers 3-Dimensional Pictures, premium, Post's cereals ad. S1, Roy Rogers in "The Bighorn Lode": DuBois/Micale, Mankin (Albert Micale's last issue), the comic enters into a major format change. Submitted June 10, 1953. Skunk-

Eye, Grease-Ball, Ape, and Crow-Bait hijack a group of Roy's friends who are negotiating on a load of tungsten in Big Horn Spring. S2, Roy Rogers in "Nester's Welcome": DuBois/Micale, Mankin. Submitted June 13, 1953. Wildcat and Salty rob the general store in Pronghorn, then head out in a blizzard for Spider Gulch. S3, Roy Rogers in "The Red Raiders": DuBois/Micale, Mankin. Submitted June 14, 1953. Renegade Comanches terrorize citizens of Pronghorn. Roy and Bullet bring the varmints in with fly-paper. "Breed of the Pioneers." "Chuck Wagon Charley's Tales": DuBois. Submitted August 30, 1951. "Indian Words." *Note:* DuBois also submitted on June 22, 1953, "White Wolf Ridge East," but it apparently was not used, at least not by that title. It was purchased as stock. 52 pages. $3.15–$22.

The Buscema Period

#74, February 1954. Covers: Roy looking around door, gold-plated revolver drawn/Hormel Foods ad/illustrated Roy, subscription page/Post's cereals ad. S1, Roy Rogers in "Roy Rides the Danger Trail": DuBois/John Buscema. Submitted July 4, 1953. Craig Bannerman and Cutter Boyle break jail in Longhorn and rob the bank. S2, Roy Rogers in "Tornado Weather": DuBois/Buscema. Submitted July 11, 1953. Joe Two-Hats is released from jail and kills Mike Gumber, then kidnaps Chuck and Martha's son. A tornado lifts the child from Joe. S3, Roy Rogers in "Snow on the Warfield Trail": DuBois/Buscema. Submitted July 8, 1953. Johnny Thorson's herd is sheep-snatched, and Johnny is shot and left for dead. "Man Size": DuBois/Goodan (signed "TG"). Original title: "Man Size for Courage." Submitted July 13, 1953. "Chuck Wagon Charley's Tales": DuBois. July 5, 1953. "On the Trail." 52 pages. $3.15–$22.

#75, March 1954. Covers: Roy is squatting, holding a pan of beans and a tin cup of coffee, illustrated background/Mars Candy ad/Whitman Coloring Books show a Roy Rogers and Dale Evans Ranch Tales Coloring Book/Post's cereals ad. S1, Roy Rogers and "The Thundering Flood": DuBois/Buscema. Submitted August 10, 1953. Land-grabber Greenway is out to get Lear Mason's ranch, and Roy is out to stop him. S2, Roy

Rogers and "The Man Hunt": DuBois/ Buscema. Original title: "Roy Leads the Man Hunt." Submitted August 10, 1953. FBI agents Brant and Humphrey elicit Roy's assistance in the apprehension of Four-Eyes Krait. S3, Roy Rogers in "Roy Meets a Giant": DuBois/Buscema. (Evidence of Alvarado background work, signing first panel.) Original title: "Roy Meets the Axe." Submitted August 17, 1953. Axe Corbeau kills the sheriff of Salt Bush County, then heads for the desert with the Sheriff's widow, and Roy is hot on his trail. "Breed of the Pioneers": DuBois/Mankin. Submitted August 18, 1953. "Chuck Wagon Charley's Tales": DuBois. August 3, 1953. 52 pages. $3.15–$22.

#76, April 1954. Covers: Roy on Little Trigger in dance routine, illustrated background/ Whitman Publishing, Tell-A-Tale Books/ Curtiss Candy ad/Post's cereals ad, illustrated Roy, Dale. S1, Roy Rogers in "Roy Rides a Hunch": DuBois/Buscema. Submitted September 14, 1953. Blake Norman wants all the land in Salt Grass Basin and won't stop at murder to get his way. S2, Roy Rogers in "The Manhunt for Five": DuBois/ Buscema. Original title: "Roy Bags Five." Submitted September 7, 1953. Deputy Roy and Ranger Barney stop a moonshine operation by arresting Burgoo and Monkey and the gang. S3, Roy Rogers in "The Wild Man": DuBois/Buscema, Mankin. Original title: "Roy Becomes Live Bait." Submitted September 7, 1953. Grizzly Robart killed a guard to escape prison, and now he and his trained bear are creating havoc for Roy and hunters around Pronghorn. "Samson": DuBois/McKimson. Submitted October 5, 1953. "Chuck Wagon Charley's Tales": DuBois. Submitted September 14, 1953. 52 pages. $3.50–$23.

#77, May 1954. Covers: Roy is feeding an apple to Trigger, Jr./two of my copies have blank inside front and back covers; the third carries an ad for Mars Candy/Whitman Books ad/subscription page has illustrated Roy by Buscema (last page)/Post's cereals ad. S1, Roy Rogers in "Double Trouble": DuBois/Buscema, Mankin. Submitted October 8, 1953. Bob Whittmore is dead, and the bank has been robbed, but then Whittmore's alive and Torrence is dead. Roy and Slim Walker unravel identities and crooks. S2, Roy Rogers and "The Claim Jumpers":

DuBois/Buscema, Mankin. Submitted October 26, 1953. Galoots are trying to get the deed to the uranium mine. S3, Roy Rogers and "The Silent Guardians": DuBois/ Buscema. Submitted October 19, 1953. Rupert Gaines tries to take Sheila's newly inherited gold mine, even if he has to split with fellow crook, Doctooth Mike. "The White Buck": DuBois. Submitted November 18, 1953. "Chuck Wagon Charley's Tales": DuBois. Submitted October 10, 1953. *Note:* The Roy Rogers premiums have been taking a little rest for a while, after a longtime push in the comics. 52 pages. $3.15–$22.

#78, June 1954. Covers: Roy is on one knee, behind a door, with gold-plated six-shooter at the ready, and his trusty dog Bullet is at his feet/Whitman Books ad/Schwinn Bikes ad/"Win a real jeep" in Post's cereals' Roy Rogers family contest ad, illustrated Roy, Dale. S1, Roy Rogers and "The Red Whirlwind": DuBois/Buscema. Submitted November 2, 1953. Roy serves a court order to Balaan Bender but doesn't expect Bender's reaction. S2, Roy Rogers and "The Golden Calves": DuBois/Buscema, Mankin. Submitted October 26, 1953. Sheriff Roy stows away on a plane to stop the smuggling of sick calves. S2, Roy Rogers and "The Challenges to Danger" DuBois/Buscema. Submitted November 16, 1953. "Wanna-be" sheriff Charro Cogan challenges Roy to sheriffing skills, then doesn't play fair. "Yellow Bear Cub": McKimson. "Chuck Wagon Charley's Tales": DuBois. Submitted October 23, 1953. 52 pages. $3.15–$22.

#79, July 1954. Covers: The high-gloss look that has marked and made beautiful 90 percent of these comics has given way to a washed-out, flat look, similar to the old Fawcett Western Comics, and it could be a cost-cutting move. Roy is beside Bullet and has his golden revolver at the ready, pasture, trees in background/Mars Candy ad (artist, Bemelmous)/ Daisy Mfg. Co. ad/Post's cereals ad. S1, Roy Rogers and "The Ghost Well Mystery": DuBois/Buscema, Mankin. Submitted December 6, 1953. Jim Yellow Horse is shot because of a gold nugget in his pocket. S2, Roy Rogers and "The Cloaked Rider": DuBois/Buscema. Submitted November 30, 1953. Cattle are disappearing into thin air, or perhaps into boxcars. S3, Roy Rogers and

"Bald Lightning": DuBois/ Buscema. Submitted December 11, 1953. Jack Picard, the "Mad Dog Killer," has escaped and is headed for Longhorn County. The FBI and Roy are in hot pursuit. "Jack and Jill." "Chuck Wagon Charley's Tales": DuBois. Submitted December 5, 1953. 52 pages. $3.15–$22.

#80, August 1954. Covers: Roy is throwing horse shoes/Whitman Books ad/Colonial Studios ad/Post's cereals ad. S1, Roy Rogers and "The Savage Portrait": DuBois/Buscema. Submitted January 9, 1954. A renegade Yaqui is murdering ranch families, and the sheriff of Longhorn forms a posse to track him down. S2, Roy Rogers in "Roy Rides the Rim": DuBois/Buscema. Submitted January 18, 1954. Spoiled brat Kurt Trane robs a store, then tries to kill his sister. S3, Roy Rogers and "Hot Lead at Rocklin's": DuBois/Buscema. Submitted January 17, 1954. Roy has changed to a fringed shirt. A wagon load of rocks causes a homesteader to go mad and start shooting at a rancher. "The Lion Hunt." "Chuck Wagon Charley's 52 pages. $2.65–$18. *Note:* This is the last 52-page issue.

#81, September 1954. Covers: Roy as a fisherman/illustrations of sporting gear and tackle in the background/"Bonanza": August Lenox, art/illustrated Roy (Buscema), subscription page/W. A. Sheaffer Pen Co. ad. S1, Roy Rogers and "Gun Flames at Windy Gulch": DuBois/Buscema. Submitted January 26, 1954. Pat Brady is mugged and the bank shipment stolen in broad daylight on the streets of Longhorn. S2, Roy Rogers and "Trail of the Bushwhacker": DuBois/ Buscema. Original title: "Bloodshed on the Trail." Submitted February 15, 1954. Deputy Rogers in a jacket for probably the first time. Sidewinder Rudolph Syndric is up to no good with rancher Sloan's daughter. "Breed of the Pioneers—The Prospector." "Chuck Wagon Charley's Tales": DuBois. January 24, 1954. "Riding Circle": Lenox. 36 pages. $2.65–$18.

#82, October 1954. Covers: Roy wrestles with a bad guy/"Cattle Roundup": Lenox/illustrated Roy on subscription page/Curtiss Candy ad. S1, Roy Rogers and "The Vanished Ore": DuBois/Buscema. Submitted January 23, 1954. The artist forgot to draw

in the badge of deputy sheriff Rogers in the first frame. Piddlin' Pete is cleaning out Longhorn's uranium supply without the owner's permission. S2, Roy Rogers and the "Missing Brother": DuBois. Submitted February 26, 1954. In the comics, Pat is more sidekick and less comic. Belden the claim jumper tries to steal the mine, after dumping one of the owners in a creek. "Breed of the Pioneers—Six Gun Play Actor": McKimson. "Chuck Wagon Charley's Tales": DuBois. Submitted February 26, 1954. "Western Wildlife Facts": Lenox. 36 pages. $2.65–$18.

#83, November 1954. Covers: Roy shooting a bow and arrow; illustrated mountains and desert in background/illustrated Roy (Micale) subscription page/"Wyatt Earp—Fearless Frontier Sheriff and Marshal": Goodan/ Lionel Trains ad. S1, Roy Rogers in "The Vengeance Trail": DuBois/Buscema. Submitted February 6, 1954. Yance Halley's gang robs the bank and takes the Mallory family hostage. S2, Roy Rogers and "The Land Grabber": DuBois/Buscema. Submitted March 1, 1954. Brad Varney and his double-dealing ranch hands steal cattle, cut fences, then buy the land for a song. "Breed of the Pioneers—Attack on Fort Ogden." "Chuck Wagon Charley's Tales": DuBois. Submitted March 1, 1954. "Dude Ranch West": Lenox. 36 pages. $2.65–$18.

#84, December 1954. Covers: Roy standing behind bush with rifle aimed, sky background/Santa Claus subscription page, no Roy/"The Penrose Ranch—One of Wyoming's Greatest": Goodan/illustrated Alan Ladd is in the ad for Tri-State Toys. S1, Roy Rogers in "Cloudburst Gold": DuBois/ Buscema. Submitted February 15, 1954. Charley Main and Walt Sanders are killed after they discover gold. S2, Roy Rogers and "The Man Trap": DuBois/Buscema. Original title: "Man Trap in Indian Breaks." Submitted April 3, 1954. Ranger Barney and Roy parachute into a gully in search of a doctor and his daughter. "Breed of the Pioneers—Frontier Heritage." "Chuck Wagon Charley's Tales": DuBois. Submitted April 3, 1954. "Pat Garrett—Western Sheriff and Texas Ranger": Goodan. 36 pages. $2.65–$18.

#85, January 1955. Covers: An unusual issue showing Christmas more subtly than in the others. Roy is ringing a school bell, while illustrated school kids in background are unloading Christmas packages from a stagecoach/Santa subscription page/Daisy Mfg. Co. ad/Mars Candy ad. S1, Roy Rogers in "Gunman's Trail": DuBois/Buscema. Submitted April 8, 1954. Pat is shot and Nellybelle stolen. Roy tracks the varmint to Crazy Horse Range. S2, Roy Rogers in "Roy Ropes a Tiger": DuBois/Buscema. Original title: "Roy Finds a Tiger on the Trail." Submitted April 11, 1954. Juanito's parents are worried that a cattle-killing cat may have their son. "Breed of the Pioneers — Simple Sam." "Chuck Wagon Charley's Tales": DuBois. April 7, 1954. "Billy Tilghman — Last of the Old-Time Sheriffs": Goodan. 36 pages. $2.56–$18.

#86, February 1955. Covers: Roy is wrestling with a villain, with Bullet helping/"The Arikara Indians"/Cheerful Card Co ad/colored-in illustrated Roy (Buscema) on subscription page. S1, Roy Rogers and "Rider's Hazard": DuBois/Buscema. Submitted May 10, 1954. It's rodeo time and Deuce Mastery is pouring acid on ropes in order to win. S2, Roy Rogers and "The Lost Explorer": DuBois/Buscema. Original title: "The Lost Explorers." Submitted May 21, 1954. Two boys are missing from the campsite, and outlaw Catlin is hiding in the same area. "Breed of the Pioneers — Mustang Stallion": R. Powell. "Chuck Wagon Charley's Tales": DuBois. Submitted May 20, 1954. "Sheep Ranching." 36 pages. $2.65–$18.

#87, March 1955. Covers: Roy is shown with Bullet, holding the dog in the window of a structure/"Indian Names" (cartoon art)/Roy Rogers' Trigger Comics advertised on last page/a colored-in, illustrated Roy (Mankin) on subscription page. S1, Roy Rogers and the "Ghost Town Payoff": DuBois/Buscema. Submitted May 29, 1954. They're supposed to be rebuilding the town of Dalomite for tourists, but Roy and the feds get a whiff of illegal alcohol. S2, Roy Rogers and the "Cougar of Lost Canyon": DuBois/Buscema, Mankin. Submitted May 29, 1954. Rancher Will Downey saves the life of a cougar, and the ungrateful wretch steals his son. "Cottonwood Raid." "Chuck Wagon Charley's Tales": DuBois. Submitted May 23, 1954. "The Assiniboin." "The Comanche Indians." 36 pages. $2.65–$18.

#88, April 1955. Covers: Roy is tacking up a wanted poster of Frank James, using his gold-plated pistol for a hammer/Dell Comics Distinguished Achievement Award/illustrated Roy on subscription page/Curtiss Candy ad. S1, Roy Rogers and "The Search": DuBois/Buscema. Original title: "Roy Rogers in Big New Country." Submitted June 5, 1954. One of those rare occasions when Roy appears on a horse other than Trigger. No deputy badge here. The son of Roy's friend is lost in the desert after his party is wiped out. S2, Roy Rogers in "Red Ledge Gold": DuBois/Buscema. Submitted June 25, 1954. Eli Corn tries to kill his partners after they strike gold. "Breed of the Pioneers — Journey West." "Chuck Wagon Charley's Tales": DuBois. Submitted June 5, 1954. "Moving Day for the Assiniboin." 36 pages. $2.65–$18.

#89, May 1955. Covers: Roy is battling a bad guy/"The Coyote — Prairie Wolf," article/an illustration and colored-in Roy (Buscema) on subscription page. S1, Roy Rogers in "The Cowbell Clue": DuBois/Buscema. Original title: "The Clue to the Cowbell." Submitted June 18, 1954. Roy, Pat, and Ranger Barney follow the trail of rustlers who are smuggling cattle through the river. S2, Roy Rogers in "Trails the Pack": DuBois/Buscema. Submitted June 25, 1954. Roy and Bullet tackle a pack of wolves in the Yukon to save a herd of horses. "Breed of the Pioneers — Sure-Enough Men." "Chuck Wagon Charley's Tales": DuBois. Submitted June 30, 1954. "The Indians of New York State." "The Gourd and Its Value to the Indian." 36 pages. $2.65–$18.

#90, June 1955. Covers: Roy with blue-eyed weimaraner pups/subscription page, illustration of Roy (Buscema) riding Trigger/"Rocky Mountain Canary": Lenox/Schwinn Bike ad. S1, Roy Rogers in "Race with Doom": DuBois/Buscema. Submitted August 4, 1954. A young lady is riding to Longhorn with eighty thousand dollars tucked beneath her saddle. Town outlaws want to help her take care of the money. Trigger is absent, and Roy rides a livery horse. S2, Roy Rogers and "The Lost Spinster": DuBois/Buscema. Submitted August 13, 1954. Aunt Laurie is missing. Roy and her nephew run into villainous con men out to con Laurie out of her "Lost Kitten" Mine. "Breed of the Pioneers—The Return of Jesse Baker." "Chuck Wagon Charley's Tales": DuBois. Submitted July 16, 1954. "Interesting Tribal Names." 36 pages. $2.65–$18.

#91, July 1955. Covers: Roy enjoying coffee and grub/Roy in pin-up pictures on subscription page/"Legends of the Old West—Dodge City, One of the Great Trail Towns"/Daisy Mfg. Co. ad. S1, Roy Rogers in "Gunfire at Dry Gulch": DuBois/Buscema. Submitted July 23, 1954. Roy has taken to the air again; he and Ranger Barney are returning from a successful drug bust, when their plane is buzzed by a renegade plane. "Breed of the Pioneers—Pipsqueak." "Chuck Wagon Charley's Tales": DuBois. Submitted August 6, 1954. "Maguey—Blessing from the Gods." 36 pages. $2.65–$18. *Note:* Title changes from *Roy Rogers Comics* to *Roy Rogers & Trigger*, with issue #92.

#92, August 1955. Covers: Roy stands beside original Trigger/illustrated Roy (Buscema) offers binoculars on subscription page/ "Lost"/Colonial Studios ad. S1, Roy Rogers in "Barranca Trail": DuBois/Buscema. Submitted August 13, 1954. Trigger is absent again. Roy, Pat, and Filipe search for Filipe's brother and niece, who are being held by foreign agents. S2, Roy Rogers in the "Wall of Water": DuBois/Buscema. Original title believed to be "Roy Corners a Border Jumper." Submitted October 24, 1954. Roy takes a party to hunt for tourists missing in the canyon. "Breed of the Pioneers—Gunsmoke Challenge." "Chuck Wagon Charley's Tales": DuBois. Submitted August 28, 1954. "Legends of the Old West—The Mother Lode." 36 pages. $2.65–$18.

#93, September 1955. Covers: Roy, behind plastic saddle, gold-plated six-shooter drawn/Dell Pledge to Parents/Stuart Greetings ad/Post's cereals ad. S1, Roy Rogers and "The Search": DuBois/Buscema. Original title: "Roy Leads a Search." Submitted October 6, 1954. The posse of sorts is look

ing for a cattle-killing jaguar and finds a lost boy as well. S2, Roy Rogers and the "Man from Long Ago": DuBois/Buscema. Submitted November 22, 1954. Bullet not in story. One of the most ornate of Roy's saddles to be undertaken by a comic artist appears in this story. Roy and Pat become involved with feuding mountain men. "Breed of the Pioneers—Razorbacks." "Chuck Wagon Charley's Tales": DuBois. Submitted September 20, 1954. "Animals of the West—The Mule Deer." 36 pages. $2.65–$18.

#94, October 1955. Covers: Roy is carrying the rodeo saddle over his shoulder, illustrated town background. The art department is trying a leader, as was used with the *Roy Rogers' Trigger Comics*, lower right hand corner/Red Goose Shoes ad/Schwinn Bicycle Co. ad/Curtiss Candy Co. S1, Roy Rogers in "Flintlock Feud": DuBois/ Buscema. Original title: "Flintlocks in Canyon." Submitted December 4, 1954. Pat and Roy can't seem to get away from the feuding Purdys and Bannermans. S2, Roy Rogers in "The Rogues of Roaring Canyon": DuBois/ Buscema. Submitted October 19, 1954. Pat takes Trigger home while Roy shoots the rapids with Bud Hackett's boat crew. "The Breed of the Pioneers—A Horse for Pete." "Chuck Wagon Charley's Tales": DuBois. Submitted October 26, 1954. For the first time, story spills over onto the last page. *Dale Evans Comics* advertised. 36 pages. $2.65–$18.

#95, November 1955. Covers: Roy sits outdoors and whittles on a tree limb while Bullet looks on/an illustrated Roy (Buscema) on subscription page/"Ginseng"/The Cracker Jack Co. ad. S1, Roy Rogers in "The Two Strangers": DuBois/Buscema. Submitted January 3, 1955. Rabbit and Charles rob the Bleeker bank, then head for their cabin in Box Canyon Springs. S2, Roy Rogers in "The Horse Thief's Trail": DuBois/Buscema. Submitted December 6, 1954. Trigger is stolen with a herd of other horses. Roy takes a rent-a-horse to track the galoots. "Breed of the Pioneers—Top Hand." "Chuck Wagon Charley's Tales": DuBois. Submitted November 1, 1954. 36 pages. $2.65–$18.

#96, December 1955. Covers: Roy in a shot that belongs to series of photos that includes the one used for the cover of issue #87. He's applying a right cut to the jaw of the commonly used villain on this cover/the Daisy Mfg. Co. ad/Christmas subscription page/ Schwinn Bicycle Co. ad. "& Trigger" is now incorporated into the story titles as well as the title of the comic. S1, Roy Rogers in "Ghost Town Treasure": DuBois/Buscema. Submitted February 15, 1955. Mysterious happenings in a very lively ghost town. S2, Roy Rogers in "A Thief and Santa": DuBois/Buscema. Original title: "Roy Meets a Thief and Santa." Submitted February 14, 1955. What appears to be the same red shirt he has worn for many issues turns out to be a jacket in this story. Some rotten varmint is robbing summer retreats in the snow and will continue unless Roy and Charley Bear can stop him. "Breed of the Pioneers—The Calico Kid." "Chuck Wagon Charley's Tales": DuBois. Submitted December 10, 1954. 36 pages. $2.65–$18.

#97, January 1956. Covers: First year without Christmas cover. "King of the Cowboys" dropped from title. Roy sits astride Trigger in a shot that belongs to a series of photos that includes the cover of issue #92. He has his carbine ready for action/Christmas subscription page/Daisy Mfg. Co./Kool-Aid ad. S1, Roy Rogers in "Two Angry Men": DuBois/Buscema. Original title: "Roy Tames Two Angry Men." Submitted February 21, 1955. Roy, Pat, and Sheriff Bob rush to avert a range war. S2, Roy Rogers in "Shadows in the Canyon": DuBois/Buscema. Submitted February 28, 1955. Roy and young Bobby Ring brave the deep snow to save scared steers. "Tawny." "Chuck Wagon Charley's Tales": DuBois. Submitted January 3, 1955. 36 pages. $2.65–$18.

#98, February 1956. Covers: Roy in shot taken from same series as issue #95 has gold-plated six-shooters drawn, ready for action/ illustrated Roy (Buscema) on subscription page/Cheerful Card Co. ad. S1, Roy Rogers in "Black Lightning": DuBois/Buscema. Submitted March 17, 1955. Roy talks a rancher out of putting a young man in jail. Billy Lang returns the favor by helping Roy catch bandits Chink Marble and Bat Low. S2, Roy Rogers in "A Circus Comes to Town": DuBois/Buscema. Submitted March 18, 1955. Floods wash out the roads on which trucks are carrying circus animals, allowing elephants and tigers to escape. "Chuck Wagon Charley's Tales": DuBois. Submitted March 7, 1955. "The Hunter's Herbs." "Tracking." 36 pages. $2.65–$18.

#99, March 1956. Covers: The third of such issues, showing an improvement in photography and focus for front covers. Roy sitting outdoors putting on red double-eagle boots/"The Porcupine"/illustrated Roy on subscription page/Kool-Aid ad. S1, Roy Rogers in "Bear Justice": DuBois/Buscema. Submitted May 7, 1955. Grizzlies seem to be snacking on beef and possibly some of the citizens. S2, Roy Rogers in "Stolen Meat": DuBois/Buscema. Submitted March 7, 1955. Beef thieves are snatching steers. "Breed of the Pioneers—Lost." "Chuck Wagon Charley's Tales": DuBois/ R.T. (signed) probably for Richard Thomas Moore. Submitted June 2, 1955. "Operation Beaver Lift." 36 pages. $4–$28.

#100, April 1956. Covers: Roy holding binoculars sits astride Little Trigger in the plastic saddle, three illustrated palominos in background/Red Goose Shoes ad/illustrated Roy on subscription page/3-M Co. ad. S1, Roy Rogers in "Strange Tracks": DuBois/ Buscema. Original title: "Strange Tracks on the Range." Submitted June 14, 1955. Izzard and Rolby are stealing uranium, holding it in a pillow-wagon. S2, Roy Rogers in "Roy Ropes a Partner": DuBois/Buscema. Submitted June 6, 1955. No Bullet. Roy and Chuck Daniels chase beaver poachers. Beginning with this issue, Trigger gets his own story for the first time since he had his own comic (other than *Western Roundup Comics*). Trigger stars in "Trigger Keeps His Head": DuBois/Buscema. Submitted October 4, 1955. Not a human in this story; it's all done with panel text. "The Breed of the Pioneers—Horse Shy." "Chuck Wagon Charley's Tales": DuBois. Submitted June 2, 1955. "Operation Beaver Lift." *Western Roundup* comics are advertised. 36 pages. $4–$28.

#101, May 1956. Covers: Roy is sitting on ground drinking coffee with his arm resting on show saddle. It looks almost as if the shirt and neckerchief were painted on after the photos were taken. It was very seldom that he wore a neckerchief without a design, and this one seems to have some design, but around the neck, where it's not readily visible/illustrated Roy on subscription page/Sawyer's, Inc., the maker of View-Masters, and Walt Disney Productions/Aluminum Plans and Patterns Service. S1, Roy Rogers in "The Fight at Bannerman's Gulch": DuBois/Buscema. Original title: "Roy Finds War in Bannerman's." Submitted July 12, 1955. The Bannermans have dammed the water, and the Purdys' cattle are dying of thirst. Trigger stars in "Trigger Finds a Refuge": DuBois/ Buscema. Submitted October 7, 1955. S2, Roy Rogers in "The Outlaw Sign": DuBois/ Buscema. Original title: "Roy Spots Outlaw Signs." Submitted July 16, 1955. No Bullet. Kingwell's mares are missing, and he blames Lang's stallion, Black Lightning. "Breed of the Pioneers—Land Rush." "Chuck Wagon Charley's Tales": DuBois. Submitted July 3, 1955. "The Western Saddle." Ad for *Brave Eagle Comics.* 36 pages. $2.65–$18.

#102, June 1956. Covers: Roy is feeding horse in photo that shows touch-up to make horse look like Trigger/illustrated Roy on subscription page/"The Road Runner"/Schwinn Bicycle Co. ad. S1, Roy Rogers in "Trouble in Wolf's Head Canyon": DuBois/Buscema. Original title: "Roy and the Jaws of the Wolf." Submitted July 25, 1955. Chief John Cloud Mountain wrecked his jeep, and now his nurse, Marie Bluebell, is missing. Roy uses a gyro glider to find her. Trigger appears in "The Camp Robbers": DuBois/Buscema. Submitted October 7, 1955. S2, Roy Rogers in "The Man Hunter": DuBois/Buscema. Tom Brennan is accused of murder, and the deputy of Buck County is in Longhorn to arrest him. "Breed of the Pioneers—Arnie Grows Up." "Chuck Wagon Charley's Tale": DuBois. Submitted July 30, 1955. "Mount Up." 36 pages. $2.65–$18.

#103, July 1956. Covers: Roy is using his gold-plated revolver for a hammer again, this time nailing the wanted poster on a tree. Bullet sits at his feet/illustrated Roy on subscription page/Daisy Mfg. Co. ad/Wrigley's Gum ad. S1: "Trigger Follows Through": DuBois/Buscema. Submitted September 7, 1955. Roy, in real life, has re-

cently come out of a law suit over Trigger. A similar story appears here. The villainous Strickland stampedes the Kellond cattle, so that he can foreclose on their mortgage and take the ranch. Trigger is in "Strange Companions": DuBois/Buscema. Submitted October 29, 1955. His buddy in all his stories is Pinto Jack, another horse. S2: Roy Rogers and "The Charro Rider": DuBois/Buscema. Submitted September 3, 1955. Tom Bull's son Joe is scheduled to ride in the Masonville rodeo, but rowdy ne'er-do-wells plan to stop him. "Breed of the Pioneers—Ex-Hero." "Chuck Wagon Charley's Tales": DuBois. Submitted December 11, 1955. "The Baltimore Oriole": D. L. (signed). 36 pages. $2.65–$18.

#104, August 1956. Covers: Roy is aiming his rifle from behind a tree/Cheerful Card Co. ad/Wrigley's Gum ad/Cracker Jacks Co. ad. S1, Roy Rogers and "The Partner": DuBois/Buscema. Original title: "Red Handed." Submitted October 29, 1955. Darb. Torrence's gunsels, Sig, Zigzag, and Joe, try to kill Lansing's daughter before she tells him about the oil wells that Torrence wants for himself. Trigger appears in "The Day of Danger": unknown/Buscema. S2, Roy Rogers and "The Beef Thieves": DuBois/ Buscema. Original title: "Roy Horns In." Submitted November 12, 1955. Bullet is back. Greasy-sack rancher Dace Runger is selling illegal game, as well as cattle that aren't his. "Breed of the Pioneers—The Choice." "Chuck Wagon Charley's Tales": DuBois. Submitted September 20, 1955. 36 pages. $2.65–$18.

#105, September 1956. Covers: Roy is mounting Trigger/"The Pika": D.L. (signed)/illustrated Roy on subscription page/Wrigley's Gum ad. S1, Roy Rogers in "Ghost Bullets": DuBois/Buscema. Original title: "Roy Faces Ghost Bullets." Submitted November 14, 1955. Henry Clay Bannerman was washed up and didn't know the feud between his family and the Purdys ended. He's trying to continue. Trigger appears in "The Twister": DuBois/Buscema. Submitted November 21, 1955. S2, Roy Rogers in "Hostage": DuBois/ Buscema. Submitted November 19, 1955. Trigger is absent. Roy parachutes from a plane to stop a massacre, but Indians shoot holes in his parachute. "Breed of the Pioneers—The Trail." "Chuck

Wagon Charley's Tales": DuBois. Submitted November 12, 1955. "The Sparrow Hawk": D. L. (signed). 36 pages. $2.65–$18.

#106, October 1956. Covers: Roy, in photography that is out of focus, is rearing on original Trigger/illustrated, inked-in Roy on subscription page/3-M Co. ad with Andy Devine/Schwinn Bicycle Co. ad. S1, Roy Rogers and the "Gold Gulch Stampede": DuBois/Buscema. Submitted March 2, 1956. Bullet is absent. There's gold in Bannerman's Gulch. Prospectors, dry-gulchers, and such rush to get more than their share. Trigger appears in "The Trap": DuBois/ Buscema. Submitted December 5, 1955. Trigger makes a showing, but barely. The poor Purdys are rustling calves from the wealthy Purdys and blaming it on the Bannerman clan. "Bookworm." "Chuck Wagon Charley's Tales": DuBois. Submitted November 28, 1955. "The Blue-Winged Warbler." 36 pages. $2.65–$18.

#107, November 1956. Covers: Roy is laying in grass, looking head on into camera, golden pistol in hand/illustrated Roy (Buscema) on subscription page/"Trees of America — The White Oak"/View-Master Disney ad. S1, Roy Rogers in "The Pack Train Mystery": DuBois/Buscema. Original title: "Roy Ropes a Mystery." Submitted April 9, 1956. The Purdy stage has been robbed and driver Ben Talley killed. Trigger appears in "The Little Wild Colt": Buscema. S2, Roy Rogers in "Leap for Life": DuBois/Buscema. Submitted March 31, 1956. Renegade Indians steal repeating rifles to hunt game, but it's against the law for them to own such a rifle. Roy agrees to replacement and amnesty. "Breed of the Pioneers — Courage." "Chuck Wagon Charley's Tales": DuBois. Submitted April 12, 1956. "Relatives of the Horse." 36 pages. $2.50–$18.

#108, December 1956. Covers: Roy has his gold-plated six-shooter drawn/A. C. Gilbert Co., makers of American Flyer trains, ad/ Daisy Mfg. Co. ad/Schwinn Bicycle Co. ad. S1, Roy Rogers in "The Horseless Wagon": DuBois/Buscema. Submitted May 28, 1956. Pat Brady has to prove the worth of his newfangled contraption, Nellybelle, by rescuing Granny Purdy from a fire. Trigger appears in "The Pygmy Horses." DuBois/

Buscema. Original title: "The Canyon Prison." Submitted May 10, 1956. S2, Roy Rogers in "Stolen Roundup": DuBois/ Buscema. Original title: "Roy Drives to Market." Submitted June 5, 1956. Sidewinder E. Z. Loomis offers to buy calves from Lew Purdy, then rustles the critters instead. "Breed of the Pioneers — The Decision." "Chuck Wagon Charley's Tales": DuBois. Submitted June 16, 1956. "The Crossbill." 36 pages. $2.65–$18. *Note:* Major change coming about again. Buscema's last issue.

The Edson Period

It is interesting that whatever prompted the change in the comic at this time resulted in not only a new artist and setting, but a new writer as well. DuBois would not submit any more stories until March 1959.

#109, January 1957. Covers: The Christmas covers are a thing of the past. Roy is squatting down slightly, coming out of what appears to be a cave, gold-plated gun in hand, with Bullet in front of him. His hands are gloved for the first time in a while/Kool-Aid ad/Gilbert Hall of Science ad/Daisy Mfg. Co. ad. S1, Roy Rogers and "The Telltale Nuggets": unknown/Nat Edson. Roy is shown in a Western suit, likely for the first time. The train is robbed while Roy is on board. "Five Empties." Trigger appears in "The Little Vaquero": unknown/John Edson, Ushler (lead-in artwork is changed). "Chuck Wagon Charley's Tales": unknown/ Dan Spiegle. Title 39, United States Code, Section 233 showing the ownership, management, and circulation of "Roy Rogers and Trigger" comics is printed here. "The Mustangers." 36 pages. $2.65–$18.

#110, February 1957. Covers: Roy is pictured in a shot from the photo series used in issue #108. He's standing behind a wagon wheel with gold-plated pistol drawn, hands gloved/ "Big Medicine"/illustrated Roy, not inked-in, is on the subscription page/Colonial Studios offers greeting cards on the back cover. S1, Roy Rogers in "The Land Grabbers": unknown/Edson, Ushler. Manning contribution, possibly Alvarado. The stories are aligned now with the popular television series. Mineral City is the setting. Cattlemen plan to snatch the land from beneath the feet of the homesteaders. "The Trickster." "Roy Rogers' Horse Trigger" has reverted to just "Trigger" with this issue. The feature is "Ride the Wild Stallion": unknown/Edson. (Entire format is new; there are people in the stories, a Mexican grandfather and grandson.) "Chuck Wagon Charley's Tales": unknown/Spiegle, Jesse Marsh. "The Bull That Stopped an Army." 36 pages. $2.65– $18.

#111, March 1957. Covers: Roy wrestles with owlhoot who has a gun in his hand/Roy in illustration (unkown artist) is inked-in on the subscription page. (This illustration looks less like Roy than any others.)/Smith Bros. Cough Drops ad/Daisy Mfg. Co. ad. S1, Roy Rogers and "The Long Chance": unknown/Edson, possibly Manning, Marsh. Pete Grundy's horse thieves are worried that their reputation might be marred when it is thought they stole money from the school. "Bailey's Cow." "Trigger" is billed as "Roy Rogers' Horse Trigger" in "Saved by a Rope": unknown/Edson, so the lead-in may have been an error in the last issue. "Chuck Wagon Charley's Tales": unknown. "The Meanest Outlaw." 36 pages. $4.35–$30.

#112, April 1957. Covers: The shot is from the series that includes the photos used for the covers of issues #106 and #110. Roy has found the barbed-wire fence cut, and he's about to make the dirty galoot pay. Original Trigger is in the background/"Wrangler"/illustrated Roy, not much closer likeness than the previous one, is on the subscription page/3-M Co. ad. S1, Roy Rogers in "Go for Your Gun": Unknown/Edson, possibly Manning, Marsh, Alavarado contributions. An illiterate gang of outlaws robs a Texas bank and gets only promissory notes. "Mud in His Eye." "Chuck Wagon Charley's Tales." Trigger appears in "Lesson for a Lion": unknown/Edson. "Gun Talk." 36 pages. $4.35–$30.

#113, May 1957. Covers: Roy appears on his knees, behind tree, ready for action, gold-plated six-shooter in hand. Photo appears to be part of a series that will be used in future issue #129/illustrated Roy (Buscema) on the subscription page/"Suspicious Hands"/Sawyer's Inc. ad. S1, Roy Rogers in "Three-Gun Treachery": unknown/Edson. Outlaws rob the stage at Indian wells, with Roy riding shotgun. "Golden Ambush." "Chuck Wagon

Charley's Tales": unknown/Nicholas Firfires. Trigger appears in "The Roundup": unknown/Edson, Ushler. "The Indian Saddle." 36 pages. $4–$28.

#114, June 1957. Covers: Roy in an action pose that includes Bullet. Bullet also appears in *Dale Evans Comics*/Dairy Queen ad/7-Up Co. ad/Schwinn Bicycle Co. ad. S1, Roy Rogers in "Manhunt": unknown/Edson, Ushler. Roy is framed for rustling and murder, then jailed in Mineral City. "A Stitch in Time." "Chuck Wagon Charley's Tales": unknown/Firfires. Trigger appears in "Fisherman's Luck." 36 pages. $4.35–$30.

#115, July 1957. Covers: Roy in an unusual entry; he's wearing a jacket, and the color or lighting is off a little, giving Roy a more aged appearance. This look continues for a few more issues. He has just stepped into the door of a cabin, pistol in hand (it doesn't appear to be the popular gold-plated pistol) and is confronting a bad guy who can barely be seen. The words used as a leader to the story inside are blurring the front cover color shots/7-Up Co. ad/Daisy Mfg. Co. ad/Wrigley's Gum ad. S1, Roy Rogers in "The Invisible Army": unknown/Edson. Hank Gruber and Printis Vane threaten Roy and all the ranchers in Mineral City with the "Plague of the Locusts" if they don't sell all their cattle and land at discount prices. "The Spur." "Chuck Wagon Charley's Tales": Trigger in "Bronc Rider": unknown/Edson. 36 pages. $4.35–$30.

#116, August 1957. Covers: Photo of Roy appears to be from the photo series used for last month's issue. Roy is holding gold-plated revolver among the rocks and trees, gazing upward/7-Up Co. ad/Wrigley's Gum ad/Cracker Jacks ad. S1, Roy Rogers in "The Yellow Raider": unknown/Edson. The Yellow Raider is robbing gold mines and leaving evidence showing Roy to be the villain. "The Silver Snare." "Chuck Wagon Charley's Tales." Trigger appears in "Bull-dogger": unknown/Firfires. 36 pages. $4.35–$30.

#117, September 1957. Covers: Roy has photographed splendidly in this cover photo; with pistol in hand (doesn't appear to be gold-plated), he draws gun as he walks into corral/7-Up Co. ad/3-M Co. ad/Wrigley's Gum ad. S1, Roy Rogers in "Roaring Fork": unknown/Edson, Alvarado, Ushler, Manning. Anarchy reigns in the town of Roaring Fork until Roy arrives to bring law and order. "Journey into Nowhere." "Chuck Wagon Charley's Tales": unknown/Edson. 36 pages. $4.35–$30.

#118, October 1957. Covers: Roy in "trademark" pose on Trigger/ad for Roy Rogers merchandise (first appearance in his own comic)/illustrated Roy on subscription page/Schwinn Bicycle Co. ad. S1, Roy Rogers in "Fury in Snake Canyon": unknown/Edson, Manning, Marsh. A $10,000 bounty is offered for the capture of ex-con Slim Acord, who is supposed to have robbed Buckhorn's bank. "Hand of Guilt." "Chuck Wagon Charley's Tales—O'Banion Meets His Son": unknown/Firfires. Trigger appears in "The Firefighters": unknown/ Michael Arens. "Horse, Plain and Fancy." 36 pages. $4.35–$30.

#119, November 1957. Covers: Roy in an action shot as he is cornered by someone we can't see. This photo belongs to a series which includes those previously seen with the "yellow rose" shirt. The leader for the inside story is pretty much out of the way of the photo, for a change/7-Up Co. ad/illustrated Roy on subscription page/Roy's ad for his own merchandise. S1, Roy Rogers and Bullet in "Tornado": unknown/Alexander Toth. Bullet alerts Roy to a robbery in progress at the Clinton bank. "Roy's Western Scrapbook": unknown/ Spiegle. Trigger appears in "The Captives": unknown/Edson. "Speedboating with Roy": unknown/Alvarado. "Chuck Wagon Charley's Tales": unknown/ Edson, possibly Marsh. S2, Roy Rogers in "The Temptation of Sam McGraw": unknown/Toth. Roy has a tough time holding onto a purchased saddle. It seems a map to buried bank loot is engraved in its silver. "Roy's Western Scrapbook": unknown/ Spiegle. 36 pages. $4.35–$30.

#120, December 1957. Covers: The cover here is washed out and dull in color and contrast. Roy, gun in hand (definitely not the gold plated one), is ready for action/Christmas ad for the Roy Rogers brand of merchandise/Daisy Mfg. Co. ad/Schwinn Bikes ad. S1, Roy Rogers in "Hidden Gold": un-

known/Toth. Grandpa dies, leaving a note telling his daughter where his gold is hidden. Two gents of questionable repute steal the note. "Charlie's Gravy." Trigger appears in "A Race with Guilt": unknown/Edson. "Roy's Real Stories of the Old West": unknown/Edson, Spiegle. "Chuck Wagon Charley's Tales": unknown/Manning. S2, Roy Rogers and Bullet in "Masquerade": unknown/Toth. Billy Drake pulls a "John Dillinger," carving a gun from a bar of soap to escape Silver City's jail. 36 pages. $4.35– $30.

#121, January 1958. Covers: More washed out, flat-looking photography has Roy with gun drawn as he wheels around to face trouble/Christmas subscription page/Daisy Mfg. Co. ad/Roy Rogers merchandise ad. S1, Roy Rogers in "Victory Fists": unknown/ Toth. The town of Sonora lines up to see Roy battling a fighter named Gorilla. "Gram and the Squaw Man." Trigger appears in "The Impossible Race." "Chuck Wagon Charley's Tales": Robert Myers/Olindo Giacomini. S2, Roy Rogers in "Stagecoach Stampede": unknown/Michael Arens. Roy romps after horse thieves, while outlaws rebuild a stolen stage to steal the gold shipment. 36 pages. $4.35–$30.

#122, February 1958. Covers: Roy, all decked out in gold-fringed attire, is stepping out of door, gun in hand/Roy Rogers merchandise ad with child and Trigger or Trigger double (cannot determine if negative was reversed)/ Roy illustrated (Spiegle) on subscription page/7-Up Co. ad. S1, Roy Rogers in "The Clue of the Cryptic Key": unknown/Toth. The Pony Express office is robbed and Roy follows a hunch to catch the bad guys. "The Telltale Roan." Trigger appears in "The Hornet's Nest": unknown/Spiegle. "Chuck Wagon Charley's Tales": unknown/Firfires. S2, Roy Rogers in "Double Danger": unknown/ Spiegle. The annual Benton City rodeo is about to begin when the stage is held up and the prize money is stolen from Mrs. Benton. 36 pages. $4.35–$30.

#123, March 1958. Covers: Roy is fanning his pistol at the bad guys/Art Instruction, Inc., ad/Illustrated Roy (Spiegle) on subscription page/Roy Rogers merchandise ad. S1, Roy Rogers and the "Sign of the Burning Rock": unknown/Toth. At the insistence of

Ned Blake's brother Dan, Roy decides to look into Ned's accidental death. "The Tenderfoot." Trigger appears in "Eye Witness": unknown/Spiegle. "Chuck Wagon Charley's Tales": unknown/Manning. S2, "Roy Rogers in Raid at Pioneer Landing": unknown/Arens. Roy runs into a pack of phony cavalrymen who are out to steal the payroll. "A Thousand Cows — But No Milk." 36 pages. $4.35–$30.

#124, April 1958. Covers: The last of the monthly issues after 15 years. The last ten-cent issue. Roy is standing on a stairway, pistol drawn/Roy Rogers merchandise ad/Sgt. Preston of the Yukon appears in an ad from Quaker Cereals/3-M Co. ad. S1, Roy Rogers in "The Rebel Rider": unknown/Toth. The townfolks are out to lynch Roy when he's mistaken for a man with a price on his head. "The Rescue." Trigger appears in "Wild Horse Windup": unknown/John Ushler. "Chuck Wagon Charley's Tales": unknown/Manning. S2, Roy Rogers in "Outlaw's Reward": unknown/Arens. Wanted outlaw Burke Walker agrees to "die" so that Jud Burton can claim the honors and reward. "Roping Techniques." *Note:* For the first time in years, the title copy has changed on this comic to a different lettering style that takes up nearly one-third of the front cover, extending down into the color photo, ruining it for photo enthusiasts more so than did the smaller writing highlighting a story. This writing also appears in the bottom right-hand corner. 36 pages. $4.35–$30.

#125, May-June 1958. Covers: First bi-monthly issue. The title is kept in the same new letter style, but moved back up to the top and more out of the way again. Its size has also been reduced. Roy astride one of the Trigger doubles. Between the grass and the bit used, it's difficult to tell which/illustrated Roy is on subscription page/photo of Roy in a new ad put together for his merchandise; apparently due to limited space for the caption, the signature, which has been joined together for years now, is separated/7-Up Co. ad. S1, Roy Rogers in "Showdown at Mile-High": unknown/Edson, Manning, Alvarado, Spiegle. Roy teaches Jim Davis some judo so that he can win the "bare-knuckle" contest against a mountain bully. "For Safety's Sake." Trigger appears in "The

Midnight Menace": unknown/Arens. "Chuck Wagon Charley's Tales": unknown/ Arens. S2, Roy Rogers in "Smoke Out": unknown/Manning, Edson, Marsh. The town's nutty professor is robbed of a telescopic gun sight that he planned to donate to the army. "Not Just a Miner." 36 pages. $3–$21.

#126, July-August 1958. Covers: Close-up, specially posed, revolver in hand/Roy Rogers merchandise ad/Daisy Manufacturing Co. ad/Wrigley's Gum ad. S1, Roy Rogers in "Backfire": unknown/Edson, Spiegle. Mineral City's bank is robbed, and Roy and Sheriff Ben pursue the bandits, who start a fire to cover their tracks. "The Braggart." Trigger is in "The Silver Saddle": unknown/Arens (Roy is mentioned in the story.) "Chuck Wagon Charley's Tales": unknown/Edson. S2, Roy Rogers in "Bounty Hunter": unknown/ Edson, Spiegle, Manning. Roy goes looking for a man who can prove Johnny Wilson's innocence in a murder trial. 36 pages. $3– $21.

#127, September-October 1958. Covers: Roy is standing on rooftop with both guns drawn and pointed toward ground/Full-sized b&w photo for the first time since the early issues; this is of Roy and Bullet, facsimile-signed "Happy Trails," Roy Rogers/illustrated Roy on subscription page/Wrigley's Gum ad. S1, Roy Rogers and the "Outlaws of Cougar Canyon": unknown/Edson, Spiegle. The train with the payroll is stolen in Cougar Canyon, and the engineer and fireman are left to walk. "The Courageous Capture." Trigger appears in "Perilous Proof": unknown/ Edson. "Chuck Wagon Charley's Tales": unknown/Ushler. S2, Roy Rogers in "The Greenhorn Kid": unknown/Edson, Alvarado. A prospector turns informant, letting the rest of his gang in on what the sheriff is doing. "Hidatsa War Horse." 36 pages. $3–$21.

#128, November-December 1958. Covers: Roy using his new fast-draw detachable holster, next to original Trigger/7-Up Co. ad/ Mattel Toys ad/Roy Rogers merchandise ad. S1, Roy Rogers and "The Drifter": unknown/Edson. Old friend Rawhide Curry shows up at Sam Bradley's ranch, and mysterious accidents begin to happen. "Flash in the Pan." "Chuck Wagon Charley's Tales": unknown/Myers, Giacomini. Trigger appears in "The Trap": unknown/ Edson. S2, Roy Rogers in "The Pyrite Swindle": unknown/Edson. The town's assayer mixes up the sacks brought to him for testing. Pyrite Pete is told his gold is worthless.

#129, January-February 1959. Covers: Roy appears back on original Trigger again, hand on six-shooter, among rocks, with Bullet at Trigger's feet/subscription page, no Roy/ Giant Dinosaurs ad and "Language Legend." S1, Roy Rogers in "Cave-In": unknown/Edson, Marsh. Silverado's bank will foreclose the mortgage on the gold mine unless Dan can hit the mother lode before Thursday. "The Special Ingredient." "Forgetful Freddy": unknown/Ushler. Trigger appears in "Unheeded Warning": unknown/Ushler. S2, Roy Rogers in "The Search": unknown/Edson. The Wells Fargo stage is robbed by road agents. The young lady on board has an unusual ring, and someone is suddenly eager for her to leave town. "The Calumet." 36 pages. $3-$21.

#130, March-April 1959. Covers: Roy is back in a photo that belongs to the series that also includes the shots used on the cover of issues #115 and #116, as well as one of the ads for his merchandise. He is standing in the doorway, detachable holstered gun in hand/subscription page/Art Instruction, Inc., ad/ Kraft Candy ad. S1, Roy Rogers in "Outlaw Trap": unknown/Edson, Alvarado. Roy is summoned to Paiute Falls by Sheriff John Porter, but he's mistaken for "Roarin' Rogers" by Porter's deputies. "A Little Skullwork." "The War Party": unknown/ Alvarado. Trigger appears in "Special Delivery": unknown/Edson, Alvarado (Roy is mentioned throughout the story). New setting for story with this issue. S2, Roy Rogers in "The Little Lawmen": unknown/Edson. The sheriff of Mineral City has a plan for Roy to help him nab Dallas Slavin's bank robbing gang, but the sheriff's six-year-old nephew overhears the plan and rides out after the outlaws. "Roy Rogers' Burrometer": unknown/Ushler. 36 pages. $3-$21.

#131, May-June 1959. Covers: Another "rearing on Trigger" pose, and this shot belongs to the series which has had quite a few used, the ones with the green and white German Shepherd shirt/Kraft Candy ad/Gamble's store ad with Hiawatha bike/7-Up Co. ad. S1, Roy Rogers in "Dynamite Mountain": unknown/Edson, Manning. The railroad is moving in, but Al Miller will shoot anyone before they take his property. "Billy Be-doggoned' Badgood." "A Change in Plans": Spiegle. Trigger appears in "Stampede Canyon": unknown/Ushler. S2, Roy Rogers and "The Stranger with the Gun": unknown/Edson. The Brady bunch robs the bank at Teepee Springs and then holds a rancher's family hostage. 36 pages. $3-$21. *Note:* This issue marks the end of the comic being a "Western" comic in the sense that it has been since its beginning. With the exception of a couple of covers, the photos used reflect an adventure comic focused upon hunting. Roy's hat, in fact, looks totally out of place with the rest of his attire, and his six-guns have been traded in for a high-powered rifle with scope. The story settings become Africa and South America, and Trigger is left back in the States while Roy flies around in a plane, but his name stays on the cover. Roy, in the comics, that have played such an important role in promoting him as "King of the Cowboys," has abandoned the West.

#132, July-August 1959. Covers: Roy and Dusty together as Dad explains something to son while both are out hunting, attired in heavy wool hunting coats adorned with fringe. Both have their rifles/subscription page/Daisy Manufacturing Co. ad/Kraft Candy ad. S1, Roy Rogers and Roy, Jr., in "Trail of the Kayak": unknown/Edson, Manning, Marsh. Roy and his son fly to Alaska to help Harpoon Harry figure out who is rustling his pelts. "Big Chief Roy Rogers" photo article, Roy and daughters. Dale Evans is in "The Voice of the Eagle": Russ Manning (Dale Evans' 1st story in Roy's comics). "Roping Takes a Lot of Practice" by Dusty Rogers, photo article. S2, Roy Rogers in the "Secret Message": unknown/Edson. A young man falsely accused of murdering his uncle sends Roy a message in a puppy's collar. 36 pages. $3- $21.

#133, September-October 1959. Covers: Roy is evidently going up against wild game rather than the bad guys/subscription page, non–Western, no Roy/Art Instruction, Inc./Kraft Candy. S1, Roy Rogers and Roy,

Jr., in "The Tlingit Totem": unknown/ Edson, possibly Marsh. Roy and his son stop at an Alaskan fishing village and find that the totem and wood carvings of the council Chief Kahraut are missing. "The Man Without a Gun." Dale appears in "The Surprise": Manning. "Herman, the Terrible-Tempered Duck": by Dale, a photo article showing Roy and Dale. "My Boys and the Bandit" by Roy, showing him. S2, Roy Rogers and "The Outcast": unknown/Edson, Marsh. Roy's friend Stoneface steals grain from Roy and is banished from the tribe until he redeems his honor. "Roy's Mailbox": Rogers/Mankin. 36 pages. $3.50–$24.

#134, November-December 1959. Covers: Roy is with Dusty in another hunting scene, and they sit behind rocks apparently eyeing or waiting for game to appear. Dusty doesn't look very enthusiastic/Kraft Candy ad/ Nichols Industries, Inc./7-Up Co. ad. S1, Roy Rogers and Roy, Jr., in "Bushman's Gold": DuBois/Edson, Marsh. Submitted March 7, 1959 (stock) (occasional DuBois stories again). Roy and Dusty have to make an emergency landing in a small African village. Roy rescues a bushman with a broken leg. "The Lancer." Dale appears in "The Friendly Cow-Poke": Manning. "The Family Picnic" by Dale/Edson (the first and only comic illustrations of Dodie and Debbie). "The Day Trigger Ran Away" by Roy. S2, Roy Rogers in "The Man Hunters": DuBois/Edson, possibly Marsh. Original title: "Warrant for John Doe." Submitted March 19, 1959 (stock). Roy finds a dying outlaw who confesses to robbery and murder, but the posse is already looking for Roy's friend by mistake. 36 pages. $3.50–$24.

#135, January-February 1960. Covers: Apparently Roy and Dusty are in Roy's big-game room at home, examining one of his mounted animals. The Dell logo square on the front is now carrying the words "Western Adventure."/Kraft Candy ad/Sawyers, Inc. ad/Daisy Manufacturing Co. Ad. "Roy, Jr." has been dropped from the title page of the first story. S1, Roy Rogers in "The Secret of the Sands": DuBois/Edson. Original title: "The Dark Kings." Submitted April 23, 1959. Roy takes his son along to explore the

ruins in the Kalahari Desert. "War Dancers." Dale appears in "The Turquoise Belt": Manning. "The Night Everything Happened" by Roy/Edson. "Roy's Mailbox": Mankin. S2, Roy Rogers in "The Vanishing Trails": unknown/Edson, possibly Mankin. Thieves are rustling beef out of Valley City. Marshal Trent and Sheriff Gray ask Roy's assistance. 36 pages. $3.50– $24.

#136, March-April 1960. Covers: Roy is in the rocks in a Western setting, six-gun in hand, with Dusty at his side/Kraft Candy ad/Junior Sales Club of America ad/ America Geographical Society ad. S1, Roy Rogers in "Savage Shackles": DuBois/Edson. Submitted September 5, 1959 (replacement, stock). Roy and son happen upon an African village whose tribesmen are holding a doctor hostage. "Let's Go Shooting" by Roy/Mankin. Dale appears in "The Slicker": Manning. "Surprise Show Stopper." S2, Roy Rogers in "The Long Day": unknown/Edson. Roy rides to Clarkville to visit Sam Moore and finds that Moore was murdered. "Roy's Mailbox": Rogers/Mankin. 36 pages. $3.50– $24.

#137, May-June 1960. Covers: Dusty is holding a lantern as Roy loads his gun, and it's a Western scene again, complete with hay/ Gambles store ad/"My Pal Trigger": Edson/Kraft Candy ad. S1, Roy Rogers in "Royal Treasures of Ancient Egypt": unknown/Edson. While Roy and his party visit ancient tombs, their camels are spirited away. "A Narrow Escape": Ushler. Dale appears in "The Old Cowboy": unknown/Manning. S2, Roy Rogers in "Reunion": DuBois/Edson, Alvarado. Original title: "Bandits at Dawn." Submitted October 7, 1959. A gold shipment is being held at the Deer Creek bank and the Morgan Boys are waiting to help unload it. "Roy's Mailbox": Rogers/Mankin. 36 pages. $3.50–$24.

#138, July-August 1960. Covers: Roy in safari attire plus cowboy hat and neckerchief is standing on rocks with Dusty, back in hunting scene. Dusty looks out of place as he is in total Western attire/Gambles store ad/Daisy Manufacturing Co. ad/Roy Rogers Quick Draw marker (Speedry Products) ad, has illustrated Roy (Mankin, last page)/ Kraft Candy ad. S1, Roy Rogers in "Haboob and High Water": DuBois/Edson. Submitted December 12, 1959. Roy's plane catches fire over the Nile, forcing him into the water, where he is attacked by river pirates. "Couriers of the Old West." Dale appears in "Strangers in Rocky Rover": Manning. S2, Roy Rogers in "Revenge at Rim Rock": unknown/Edson, Alvarado, possibly Mankin, Marsh. A slick attorney uses cross examination in a murder trial to get the other half of a map as evidence. "Roy's Mailbox": Rogers/Mankin. "The Indians Had a Name for Everything." 36 pages. $3.50–$24.

#139, September-October 1960. The "Western Adventure" in Dell's logo square has been changed to "Exciting Adventure." Roy and Dusty are back in a foreign country again and trying to communicate with someone who is sharing water in the Sahara Desert/subscription page/Junior Sales Club of America ad/Kraft Candy ad. S1, Roy Rogers in "Desert Duel": DuBois/Edson. Submitted January 30, 1960. Colonel DePuis' guide disobeys orders and takes Roy and his son into the hands of Dag Reli in forbidden territory. "Can a Dog Talk?" by Roy. Dale appears in "The Music Box": Manning. S2, "Outlaw's Deed": unknown/Edson. Roy is dismayed at the change in his old friend Bill Walston. He argues for a fair trial for a robber, instead of a shot in the back. "Roy's Mailbox": Rogers/Mankin. "Traced in Sand." 36 pages. $3.50–$24.

#140, November-December 1960. Covers: Roy and Dusty are back in same locale as that used for photo on cover of issue #136; the lead-in for a story inside is right up in the center of the photo, whereas it was in a safe spot at the bottom some issues back. As Roy cautions Dusty to be quiet, they walk below a rock on which stands an obvious bad guy Mexican, complete with sombrero and gun/Art Institute, Inc./"Roy's Trophy Room" (photo article)/Kraft Candy ad. S1, Roy Rogers in "Spears in the Night": DuBois/Edson, Alvarado. Submitted April 9, 1960. Roy tangles with South American Indians to save a member of the tribe. "The New-Old Way of History" Rogers/Edson. Dale appears in "The Witness": unknown/Warren Tufts. This time there's no Pat, Bullet, or even Curley. S2, Roy Rogers in "Navajo Prize": unknown/Edson, Alvarado. An Indian boy wins first prize in a horse race, and then two rowdies mug him and steal the money. "Roy's Mail Box": Rogers/Mankin. 36 pages. $3.50– $24.

#141, January-February 1961. Covers: Roy is explaining to his son about the use of Bolos. This shot is from a series which includes the photo used for the cover of issue #140 and #143. The date is enclosed in the Dell logo square, and it's shown as February only/subscription page/"My Best Friends" by Roy (photo article)/Daisy Manufacturing Co. ad. S1, Roy Rogers in "The Jaguar Hunt": DuBois/Edson, possibly Alvarado. Original title: "Jaguar Hunt on the Ucayali." Submitted May 13, 1960. While visiting in Peru, Roy and Dusty are set upon by crocodiles, jaguars, and witch doctors. "A Bad Day for Santa Claus." Dale appears in "A Job for Hiram": unknown/Manning. S2, Roy Rogers in the "Day of the Cannon": unknown/Edson, Alvarado. The Dugan gang is set to hit Crooked Creek, and the town has to appoint a new sheriff. "Roy's Mailbox": Rogers/Mankin. "Roy Rogers— Transplanting Roots": unknown/Mankin. 36 pages. $3.50–$24.

#142, March-April 1961. Covers: Roy and Dusty are in rocks, in this shot that is part of a series used for the "Roy & Dusty" covers. The Dell logo square carried the words "Exciting Adventure."/Story on construction of plank roads/Dusty and Sandy's Obstacle Race/General Mills cereal advertisement. "Savage Jungles": DuBois/Edson, possibly Alvarado, Manning. Submitted June 20, 1960. Roy and son's adventure takes place in the Peruvian jungles. "My Most Dangerous Moment" by Roy Rogers, illustrated. Dale Evans in "The Big Chase": unknown/Manning. "The Mystery Letter": unknown/Edson, possibly Alvarado, Manning, Spiegle. "Roy's Mailbox": Mankin. "Rope with a Past," half page illustrated story: Possibly Spiegle. 36 pages. $3.50–$24

#143, May-June 1961. Covers: Roy and Dusty photo taken at the same time as the one used for the cover of issue #140. Here Roy is squatted down behind some rocks in the same terrain, with pistol drawn and cocked. Dusty is kneeling at his side/the General Tire & Rubber Company ad/General Foods,

Inc., Kool-Aid ad/General Mills cereals ad. S1, Roy Rogers in "Guardians of the Canyon": DuBois/Edson. Submitted August 10, 1960. When the train derails in Mexico, Roy, Dusty, Bullet and friend Manuel have an adventurous journey through the jungle. The story is interrupted after two pages for a page of advertisement for a Dell Comics Contest. "My First Dog" Rogers/Edson. Dale appears in "A Clean Sweep": unknown/Manning (story interrupted with Dell Comics ad). S2, Roy Rogers in "Little Man's Day": unknown/Edson. Roy helps Abner become a hero to his domineering wife Maude. "Too Tough to Die." 36 pages. $3.50–$24.

#144, July-August 1961. Covers: The photo used here of Roy and Dusty is part of a series which includes the one used for the cover of issue #137. The two are standing in the opening of what appears to be the stables, and Roy has his .45 at the ready. All of the photos in these particular issues of the two together are ruined for the photo collector as the publisher maintains a leader right on the photo./ "Roy Rogers—Small but Important"/Daisy Manufacturing Co. ad/Kraft Candy ad. S1, Roy Rogers in "Black Dynamite': unknown/Edson. Roy teaches a man the fine art of training a black stallion (story interrupted with Dell Comics ad). Dale appears in "The Guilty Man": unknown/Manning (story interrupted by Dell Comics ads). "The Mystery of Foolish Horse" by Roy. S2, Roy Rogers in "The Long Dark Trail": unknown/Edson. Dusty may be in danger after witnessing the murder of Ben Jackson. 36 pages. $3.50–$24.

#145, September-October 1961. Covers: This is the final issue of a *Roy Rogers Comic* of the regular series by Dell Publishing. The cover of this issue is cluttered up with leads and print advertising contests. Roy and Dusty appear tied to a large tree together, in another scene related to their hunting trips./Art Institute, Inc. ad/Junior Sales Club of America ad/Kellog's cereals ad. S1, Roy Rogers in "Wanted ... Two Nameless Gunmen": unknown/Edson. Sam Moore witnessed the robbery of the Elktown bank. Now he and his daughter are hiding to keep the robbers from seeking vengeance (story interrupted for Dell Comics ad). Dale appears in "The Heiress": unknown/Manning.

A story by this same title apears in her second Dell comic, Four-Color #528. S2, Roy Rogers in "The Kid from Dallas": unknown/Edson. A known gunslinger saves Roy's life, and the sheriff of Mineral City wants to know why the "Kid from Dallas" came to town. "Desert Rat." "Fortunes of Gold." 36 pages. $4.30– $30.

Special Comics

It Really Happened Comics, #8, April 1947. Copyright under B66547 following publication February 11, 1947. No renewal found. William H. Wise Co. (Visual Editions, Inc.). Cover: Includes line-drawn picture of Roy. S1, The Roy Rogers life story under title "Roy Rogers, King of the Cowboys": unknown/possibly Parks contribution. Line-drawn cover, no photos. $6.50–$45.

Real Fact Comics, #13, March-April 1948. National Comics Publications, Inc., 480 Lexington Avenue, New York, NY. Dale Evans makes her debut in comic books with this publication. Covers: Dale is line-drawn on the cover, à la Roy Rogers, as she rears on her white horse, waving her hat. S1, "Dale Evans—Hollywood's Number One Stunt Girl and Rodeo Star": J. N. McArdle. 52 pages. $25–$150.

Boy Commandos Comics, #32, March-April, 1949. Dell Comics. Cover: Line-drawn Dale Evans. In this one-shot appearance, Dale is seen in the company of kids in an outdoor illustrated setting, as she rears up on a brown horse, waving her hat. S1, Dale Evans and the Boy Commandos in "Queen of the Western": probably J. N. McArdle. $8.50– $60.

True Movie and Television, #4, January 1951. Toby Press. 52 pages. Roy Rogers featured. $5–$35.

Roy Rogers Riders Club Comic, 1952. Copyright by Roy Rogers Enterprises, under AA211806, following publication April 1, 1952. No renewal found. Special fan club "giveaway" comic, only one issue. Covers: Line-drawn Roy and Bullet: John Steel (signed). Roy leaning on fence petting a dog which is certainly Bullet at this time period, however brown the animal is colored. Trig-

Riders Club Rules and Creed

1. BE NEAT AND CLEAN.

At our house Dale and I are pretty strict about Cheryl, Linda and Dusty keeping their rooms in neat order, putting away their toys when they've finished playing and hanging up their clothes. Remember, your mother is a busy person and just think of how much you can help if you keep your own things neat.

2. BE COURTEOUS AND POLITE.

Saying "please" and "thank you" may not seem too important, but the boys and girls who always remember to be polite to their parents, teachers and friends are the ones I always feel make the best Riders Club members.

3. ALWAYS OBEY YOUR PARENTS.

Sometimes you might think your parents are asking you to do something you feel isn't necessary or they may refuse to let you have your own way. Believe me, pardners, your parents are just doing what they feel will be best for you—remember, they were young once too and maybe felt the same way you do.

4. PROTECT THE WEAK AND HELP THEM.

A true Riders Club member never tries to "bully" anyone, especially someone smaller or weaker than himself, instead he tries to do whatever he can to help them grow stronger.

5. BE BRAVE BUT NEVER TAKE CHANCES.

Just remember the fellow who takes a "dare" isn't always the "hero." Bravery means doing whatever you can to help someone in trouble, but not taking reckless chances where you yourself might get hurt.

6. STUDY HARD AND LEARN ALL YOU CAN.

Everyone has a job to do all his life, and when you're young, school is your "office" and your lessons are your "work." And, the work you do in school pays off with the best jobs when you grow older.

7. BE KIND TO ANIMALS AND CARE FOR THEM.

No matter what kind of a pet you have, always be sure to take good care of it, because that animal looks to you for protection and love. Animals are man's best friends and to keep our friends we have to show them how much we care for them.

8. EAT ALL YOUR FOOD AND NEVER WASTE ANY.

Boys and girls in this country are the luckiest in the world. We have so many hundreds of foods to choose from that we can have anything we want to eat. Thousands of youngsters in Asia and Europe hardly have anything to eat and often have to go hungry. So, never waste any of your food, and then America will have food to share with the less fortunate in other countries.

9. LOVE GOD AND GO TO SUNDAY SCHOOL REGULARLY.

I hope all my Riders Club members go to Sunday School regularly, just like our own children do. Cheryl, Linda and Dusty know that going to church in the morning is the most important part of every Sunday.

10. ALWAYS RESPECT OUR FLAG AND OUR COUNTRY.

We live in the greatest country in the world and it's up to all of us to do everything we can to show our love for America. Doing all we can to protect our freedom and honoring the laws of our country is one of the best ways in which we can show our love and respect.

Roy's rules for "Roy Rogers Riders" were printed on the inside of the Rider's Club comic. Original copyright 1952 by Roy Rogers Enterprises.

ger stands beside Roy, colored excellently./ Roy Rogers and Trigger welcoming the reader as a member of the Roy Rogers Riders Club/story continues/the Riders Club Rules and Creed. S1, Roy Rogers and Trigger in "Ghost Town Jamboree": unknown/ Moore, Mankin. Roy, Bullet, and Trigger wrestle with rustlers. 16 pages. $11–$75.

Roy Rogers, the Man from Dodge City, 1954. Original copyright by Frontiers, Inc. Special "giveaway" comic for Dodge Motors (radio show sponsor). Western Printing and Lithographing Co. Code: R. R. Dodge G.A. Covers: Painting of Roy, Dale, Bullet, Pat Brady, and Trigger in and around Dodge Royal Lancer, desert scene by Peter Alvarado. (Tiny "PA" in lower right hand corner can be seen under magnification; also on rock on left side.)/Dodge ad/Painting of Roy and Dale in Dodge ad/continuation of front cover painting, and '55 Dodge ad. S1, Roy Rogers and "The Man from Dodge City": unknown/ Arens. Dale is in story with Roy and Pat Brady. Roy is transporting the prize money that Dodge is sure to win, and crooks are waiting in the shadows to take the money. Oblong, 7¼" × 4 13/16". 20 pages. $50–$250.

Roy Rogers and Trigger, #1, April 1967. Gold Key 10205-707. K. K. Publications, Inc., a publishing company belonging to Western Printing and Lithographing Co. One issue only. Probably an attempt to revive the comic in 1967 by using reprints. The comic is a reprint of various covers and stories. Covers: Roy Rogers and Trigger #125; the art layout on top is changed with the title appearing on a solid background, out of photo./b&w full-sized photo of Roy and Bullet signed "Happy Trails"/"The Owlhoot Trail"/same photo as front. S1, "The Rebel Rider," issue #124. "Victory Fists," issue #121. "The Courageous Capture" is a one-page short taken from issue #127. The remainder of the comic is several games pages, etc., that have absolutely nothing to do with Roy Rogers, et al, or the West. 36 pages. $2.65–$18.

March of Comics

March of Comics featuring Roy Rogers. K. K. Publications produced by Western Printing and Lithograph Co. Sent to stores with an extra cover of slick stock, the cover of a current Roy Rogers comic, and the pulp cover would be printed up using the company's logo. Their advertising would also often appear on the back cover. Commonly found are: Sears & Roebuck (Roy Rogers Corral ads), Dr. Posner's Shoes, Weatherbird Shoes, Buster Brown Shoes. Give-aways. In additon to stories, there are word games and puzzles. Illustrated covers (majority by Micale) become photo covers. Full-sized, 24 pages, pulp cover, and 5 ⅛" × 7¼". $40–$140. File copies have been seen at $200 plus. When the artist is listed as "unknown" this is because I have not seen this entire comic.

#17, 1948. Original copyright by Roy Rogers. Cover: Line-drawing of Roy and Trigger: Micale. S1, Roy Rogers and the "Kings of the Sand Country": DuBois/unknown. Submitted June 30, 1947. All pulp. 8" × 10". 24 pages. $45–$170.

#35, 1948. Original copyright 1948 by Roy Rogers. Under AA114369, following publication December 21, 1948. No renewal found. Cover: Line-drawing of Roy waving, on Trigger: Micale/Kenny's Shoes ad/ Poll Parrot Shoes ad. S1, Roy Rogers and the "Hard Luck Kid": DuBois/Micale (signed). Submitted July 21, 1948. All pulp. 8" × 10". 24 pages. $45–$170.

#47, 1949. Covers: Line-drawing of Roy waving hat, rearing on Trigger: Micale/ Weather Bird Shoes ad/ads. S1, Roy Rogers in "Bush Peril": DuBois/unknown. Submitted July 27, 1949. All pulp. 8" x 10". 24 pages. $35–$160.

#62, 1950. Covers: Line-drawing of Roy on Trigger: Micale/Childlife Show ad/ads. S1, Roy Rogers and "Quaker John's Revenge": DuBois/McKimson. Submitted October 17, 1949. All pulp. 8" × 10". 24 pages. $35–$160.

#68, 1950. Covers: Line-drawing of Roy firing his six-shooter, on Trigger: Micale (signed)./ story begins/game page: Micale art/ Sears Roebuck and Co. Roy Rogers merchandise ad: Micale art. S1, Roy Rogers in "Feuding Guns": DuBois/Harry Parks. Submitted October 9, 1950. Roy is mistaken for a hired gunfighter. All pulp. 8" × 10". 24 pages. $25–$125.

#73, 1950. Original copyright by Roy Rogers Enterprises. Covers: line-drawing of Roy on

Trigger: Micale/story begins/game page: Micale art/Sears Roy Rogers Corral ad. S1, Roy Rogers in "Guns at Thunder Gap": DuBois/Steffen, Parks, Micale. Submitted December 4, 1950. Cattle ranchers and homesteaders are at it tooth and nail, and one of the victims is widow Irons. Seven puzzles, other illustrations of Roy by Micale. All pulp. 8″ × 10″. 24 pages. $25–$125.

#77, 1951. Covers: Line-drawing of Roy on Trigger and horseback Santa Claus: Micale/Sears Roebuck & Co. ads. S1, Roy Rogers in "Bushwacker's Payoff": DuBois/unknown. Submitted June 11, 1951. S2, Roy Rogers and "The Condor of Kingman's Cray": unknown/artist (R.T.) who has contributed much to the "Chuck Wagon Charley's Tales" features in regular series. All pulp. 8″ × 10″. 24 pages. $25–$125.

#86, August 1952. Covers: Photo of Roy beside fence (top half of color photo that appears on back of *Roy Rogers Comics* issue #32)./Sears Roebuck & Co. ads: Roy Rogers merchandise. S1, Roy Rogers in "Hideout Ranch": unknown/Arens, McKimson. Signed 1st panel, by both, along with other numerous places. Bank robbery, cattle rustling, and Morse code by flashlight. Thank goodness Roy is on hand to stop the chaos. Micale art on three of four puzzle pages. *Note:* Inside front cover is blank on many copies. Oblong, horizontal 5⅛″ × 7¼″. 36 pages. $20–$100.

#91, 1952. Covers: Photo/art mix has Roy helping Santa with gifts/unknown ads. S1, Roy Rogers in "A Test of Courage": unknown. Oblong, horizontal 5⅛″ × 7¼″. 36 pages. $20–$100.

#100, 1952. Covers: Photo of Roy, leaning on saddle, gun in hand/Kali-Sten-Icks Shoes ad. S1, Roy Rogers in "Cabin Death Trap": DuBois/unknown. Submitted November 17, 1952. Oblong, horizontal 5⅛″ × 7¼″. 36 pages. $15–$85.

#105, 1953. Covers: Photo/art mix has Roy and two dogs combined with Santa Claus and chimney scene/Blue Bird Shoes ad. S1, "Roy Rogers, King of the Cowboys": unknown. Oblong, horizontal 5⅛″ × 7¼″. 36 pages. $15–$85.

#116, 1954. Covers: Roy is waving in this photo/Carrier Drug Centers ad. S1, Roy Rog-ers at "Rustler's Gap": DuBois/unknown. Submitted May 23, 1953. Oblong, horizontal 5⅛″ × 7¼″. 36 pages. $15–$85.

#121, 1954. Covers: Photo has Roy carrying Christmas presents/Sears Roebuck & Co. ads. S1, Roy Rogers in "Christmas at Tanner's Ranch": DuBois/Buscema. Submitted March 19, 1954. Oblong, horizontal 5⅛″ × 7¼″. 36 pages. $15–$85.

#131, 1955. Covers: Roy is toting his saddle in this photo/Peter Rabbit Shoes ad. S1, Roy Rogers and the "Secret of the Rocks": DuBois/Buscema/game pages: Buscema art. Submitted December 20, 1954. Oblong, horizontal 5⅛″ × 7¼″. 36 pages. $15–$85.

#136, 1955. Original copyright by Frontiers, Inc. Covers: Roy is decorating a Christmas tree in this photo/Sears Roebuck & Co. ad. S1, Roy Rogers and "The Other Christmas Tree": DuBois/Buscema. Submitted December 18, 1954. Ex-con Nat Kellem is prospecting for uranium, but the ranchers think he's prospecting for their cattle. The code found at the bottom of the first page (as always) is (in this case) K.K. G.A. #136-5512. "Dot-to-dot" puzzle, with a drawing of Roy, "follow the trail" puzzle: Buscema. Oblong, horizontal 5⅛″ × 7¼″. 36 pages. $15–$85.

#146, 1956. Covers: Roy and Bullet sitting on a rock in this photo/Hack Shoe Co. ad. S1, Roy Rogers and "Yaqui Vengeance": DuBois/unknown. Submitted January 9, 1956. Oblong, horizontal 5⅛″ × 7¼″. 36 pages. $15–$85.

#151, 1956. Covers: Photo/art mix. Roy ringing school bell, snow scene/Sears Roebuck & Co. ads. S1, Roy Rogers in "Gunplay at Black Canyon": DuBois/probably Edson or Arens. Submitted June 20, 1956. Oblong, horizontal 5⅛″ × 7¼″. 36 pages. $15–$65.

#161, 1957. Covers: Roy and Trigger photo/Poll Parrot Shoes ad. S1, Roy Rogers in "Avenue of Escape": unknown/probably Edson or Arens. Oblong, horizontal 5⅛″ × 7¼″. 36 pages. $15–$65.

#167, 1957. Photo of Roy under Christmas tree/Sears Roebuck & Co. ads. S1, Roy Rogers in "No Christmas for Gibbsville": unknown/probably Edson or Arens. Oblong, horizontal 5⅛″ × 7¼″. 36 pages. $15– $65.

The special store "giveaway" *March of Comics* **issue began in regular-sized format, with line-drawn covers by Micale. This is issue #35, from 1948. Original copyright 1948 by Roy Rogers. Copyright expired.**

#176, 1958. Covers: Photo, Roy rearing on Trigger/Hahn Shoe stores ad. S1, Roy Rogers in "Reign of Terror": unknown/probably Edson or Arens. Oblong, horizontal 5⅛" × 7¼". 36 pages. $12–$55.

#191, 1959. Covers: Photo, Roy firing rifle, Bullet at his side/unknown ads. S1, Roy Rogers in "Treacherous Crossing": unknown/probably Edson. Oblong, horizontal 5⅛" × 7¼". 20 pages. $12–$55.

#206, 1960. Original copyright by Roy Rogers–Frontiers, Inc. Covers: Roy beside lantern, gun in hand; yellow trading stamps ad./ Blank/Blank/Pennsauken (N.J.) and Montgomery (N.J.) Merchandise Marts ads; very strange-looking illustrated Roy and Trigger. S1, Roy Rogers in "Boots and Bullets": unknown/Edson. The train is robbed with Roy on board, along with an elderly lady he agreed to protect. "Chuck Wagon Lingo" puzzle. "Count the Horseshoes" puzzle, featuring an illustrated Roy. Vertical 5⅛" × 7¼". 20 pages. $12–$55.

#221, 1961. The first Roy and Dale issue. For the first time since the 1954 Dodge giveaway and the second time in comics history (outside the newspaper strips), Roy and Dale are together in a story. Covers: Photo, Roy and Dale, with Bullet/Gimble's Children's Shoes ad. S1, Roy and Dale in "Riddle on the Ridge": unknown/probably Edson. Vertical 5⅛" × 7¼". 20 pages. $12–$40.

#236, 1962. Covers: Photo, Roy and Dale, Trigger/Gimble's Children's Shoes ad. S1, Roy and Dale in "The Lost Stallion": unknown/probably Edson. Vertical 5⅛" × 7¼". 20 pages. $10–$35.

#250, 1963. Covers: Photo, Roy and Dale decorating for party/unknown ads. S1, Roy and Dale in "The Sunset of Thunder Hills": unknown/probably Edson. $10–$35.

Western Roundup Comics

These were 100-page comic magazines featuring compilations of original stories of numerous screen and television cowboys, identical in concept to their independent series. Different ones were featured throughout the series run, but Roy and Gene domi-

nated the series. Their photos alternated in the prominent position on the cover and the inside front and back, and the number one story alternated between the two. Only story titles related to Roy will be shown here, aside from features. Many of the Western Co. artists contributed to the artwork. Original copyrights are shown in the individual subjects' names or companies. The price of the bimonthly issues was 25 cents. The features were all educational and or historical, with an abundance of material on Indian customs and lore. There was much artwork by renowned Western artists such as Tillman Goodan and August Lenox. The photo covers featured small pictures of the stars of the comic, such as Roy, Gene, Rex Allen, Johnny Mack Brown, the Range Rider, Wild Bill Elliott, and Dale Evans. Dale became part of the series in issue #10. The cover photos were incorporated into artwork. The series began with b&w photos on inside covers. With issue #15, the photos were substituted with Western artwork.

#1, June 1952. Covers: Rider on bucking horse over photos/Gene and Champ/Roy and Little Trigger, rodeo appearance/Color rodeo scene. Roy Rogers in "Gunfighter's Retreat": Mankin, unknown. Ma Stebbins has opened a home for geriatric gunfighters, but Toothpick Tolin is trying to foreclose on the mortgage. "Dictionary of Western Terms." Trigger appears in "The Mustangers": Sgroi, Moore. "Horses of the West": Lenox. Song, "Red River Valley." "Let's Go to the Rodeo," "Bronc Riding, Bareback," "Riding Rodeo Style," eight pages on rodeo events: Till Goodan. "Swing Your Partner": Alvarado. Songs, "She'll Be Comin' 'Round the Mountain," "Sweet Betsy from Pike." "Brands and Their History." Boot puzzle. Other artwork by Alvarado, Firfires, John Steel, Mankin. 100 pages. $11–$110.

#2, February 1953. Covers: Photos in lariat circles, green background/Bullet, original Trigger, Roy/Gene and Champ/color rodeo scene. Roy Rogers and the "Graveyard of Stagecoaches": Arens. Owlhoots are snatching stagecoaches, leaving the driver and passengers to walk. "The Bear Claw Necklace." Song, "Goin' to Leave Ol' Texas": Alvarado. "The Great Buffalo Hunt." "Indian Knife Sheath": Lenox. Trigger and

Bullet appear in "Plenty of Savvy": Sgroi, Moore. "A Portfolio of Famous Bucking Horses": Goodan. "The Fifth Cavalry's Epic Ride": Lenox. Song, "Put Your Little Foot." "Fabulous Lost Gold Mines of the West": Lenox. "Great Indian War Chiefs": Lenox. Other artwork by Firfires, Alvarado, Mankin, and Al Gleicher. 100 pages. $7–$70.

#3, July-September 1953. Covers: Cartoon art has cowboy on bucking horse, surrounded by photos/Gene/Trigger, Jr., and Roy/cattle grazing scene. Roy Rogers in "Plan for Murder": Ushler. Roy and Trigger ride onto an auto "accident." The driver has been shot and robbed, and the clues lead to a service station attendant. Trigger and Bullet appear in "The No-good Brother": Moore, Sgroi, Mankin. "The Cowboy's Rope": Lenox. "Indian Name Writing": Lenox. "Surprise Witness": Alvarado. "An Album of Famous Ranches": Goodan. "Indian Bow and Arrow Making." Song, "Oh Bury Me Not." Additional artwork by Alvarado, Firfires, Mankin, and Arens. 100 pages. $6–$60.

#4, October-December 1953. Covers: Photos on signpost, blue background/Roy, close-up/Gene, close-up/Mountain scene. Song, "As I Went Walking down the Street": Alvarado. Roy Rogers in "The Pussy-Footin' Prowlers": Arens, Mankin. An old-timer named "Pokey" has struck pay dirt, but he's bushwacked on the way to the claims office. Trigger and Bullet appear in "Trap a Trickster": Moore, Sgroi. "The Mysterious Stage Robberies": Alvarado. "Famous Horsemen of the World": Goodan. Song, "Good-Bye Old Paint": Alvarado. Additional artwork by Firfires, Alvarado, Mankin. 100 pages. $6–$60.

#5, January-March 1954. Covers: Photos, prairie at night background/reversed negative, Roy and original Trigger/Gene, Champ, Little Champ/Texas Longhorn steers. Roy Rogers in "The Cover-up": Arens. A bird-watcher with the unlikely name of Bertie is up to foul deeds on the estate of Roy's friend. "Indian Wigwam": Lenox. Trigger and Bullet appear in "Money Buys Trouble": Moore, Mankin, Sgroi. "Indian Sand Paintings." "Gold Is Where You Find It." "Famous Women of the West": Goodan. "An Album of Good Badmen":

Lenox. Song, "Great Grand-Dad." Song, "The Big Rock Candy Mountain." Additional artwork by Firfires, Alvarado, Mankin, and Ushler. 100 pages. $6–$60.

#6, April-June 1954. Covers: Photos on black background/Gene on Champ/Roy/ color rodeo scene. Roy Rogers in "The Cracked-Up Getaway": Arens. Owlhoots Red and Flick are up to no good. First they rob the Indian Trust Co., then they steal an autogiro and crash it. "Indian Picture Writings." "The Indian's Cookout": Lenox. "The Message in the Springs": Firfires. Trigger appears in "Trigger Joins the Boys Club": Sgroi. Eight pages of Indian Dictionary. Song, "The Gal I Left Behind Me." "The Little Mohee." Additional artwork by Alvarado, Moore, Mankin and Ushler. 100 pages. $5.50–$55.

#7, July-September 1954. Copyright 1954 by Western Printing and Lithographing Co. under B490273, following publication May 27, 1954. No renewal found. Covers: Framed photos on side of building/Gene, close-up/ Roy/Mustangs, cowboys. Roy Rogers in "Double for Murder": Arens. Roy is stopped by highwaymen who steal his U.S. Deputy Marshal credentials; then he gets stopped by a sheriff who refuses to believe he's ligit. "Indian Invention": Lenox. Trigger and Bullet appear in "Trouble in Texas": Ushler. "Heroes in Petticoats." "The New Teacher": Marsh. "Colorful National Parks": Goodan. "Indian Inventions": Lenox. Additional artwork by Firfires, Moore, Sgroi, and Ushler. 100 pages. $5.50–$55.

#8, October-December 1954. Covers: Illustrated rifles separate photos on black background/Roy doing a running mount upon original Trigger/Gene/cowboy watching over cattle. Roy Rogers, "Trouble on the Line": Ushler. Chris Wilkes has struck uranium, and his ranch foreman is trying to do him in. "Indian Guess Game": Lenox. "Indian Quiz": Lenox. "When Gramps Was a Boy." Trigger and Bullet appear in "Trigger and Bullet Trap a Wild One": Moore, Sgroi. "A Picture Map of Western History": Lenox. "Indian Wildlife Homes Game": Lenox. Additional artwork by Firfires, Alvarado, Moore, Mankin. 100 pages. $5–$55.

#9, January-March 1955. Covers: photos on side of train depot/Gene/Roy battling bad guy/rodeo action scene. Roy Rogers and "The Golden Scar": Arens. Young Bruce Winslow is fishing with Roy when he sees Hardrock drop a canvas package in the river. Now Bruce's continued good health is in question. "Indian Quiz": Lenox. Trigger and Bullet appear in "The Eagle's Prey": Moore, Sgroi. "Indian Strategy." "So Blamed Ignorant." "Ghost Towns of the West": Lenox. "Rangeland Puzzlers": Lenox. "Indian Canoe Travois." Additional artwork by Firfires, Alvarado, Mankin. 100 pages. $5.50–$55.

#10, April-June 1955. Covers: pocketwatches open to reveal photos/Roy, Bullet/Gene, Champ/cowboy watching over cattle. Roy Rogers and "The Outlaws of Cougar Gulch": Edson, Sgroi, Buscema. The Ringer Twins gang has taken over Cougar Gulch, and they're robbing and rustling in surrounding counties. "The Friendly Witness." Trigger and Bullet appear in "Stranger on the Range": Moore, Sgroi. "Famous Indian Battles": Lenox. "Cowboy Cut-Ups." Additional artwork by Firfires, Moore, Mankin. 100 pages. $5.50–$55.

#11, July-September 1955. Covers: photos around a wagon wheel/Gene/Roy/mountain scene. Roy Rogers in "The Riddle of the Prestons": Edson, Manning, Sgroi. A crooked lawyer and mirror-image twins create confusion in the town of Powderhorn. "Montana Cowboy of Seventy Years Ago": Goodan. "Indian Track Lore." "Indian Hunting Lore." "The Doctor's Mistake." "Strange Names of the West": Lenox. "Mussolini": Goodan. Additional artwork by Firfires, Manning, Moore, and Alvarado.

#12, October-December 1955. Covers: Photos on fence posts/Roy, Bullet/Gene, Champ/Desert, cactus scene. Roy Rogers, "The Boom-Town Mystery": Mankin, Marsh, Sgroi, Alvarado, Edson, possibly Buscema, Manning. Con men are at work in Crystal City. They've replaced the county recorder with a crook so that they can get the information on claims. "Superstition Mountains": Lenox. "Indian Quiz": Lenox. "Luke Sherman's Fortune." "Thumbnail Westerns": Lenox. "The Amazin' Mind Reader Trick." Additional artwork by Firfires, Alvarado, Ushler. 100 pages. $5.50–$55.

#13, January-March 1956. Covers: A lariat passes around photos, red background/Roy, badge being pinned on/Gene/Western scene. Roy Rogers and "The End of the Running Rope": Arens. Old Jim Clay dies before he can reveal where the fortune that he left to his nephew is located. Crooks replace the nephew with one of their own. "Oddities of the Wild": Lenox. Dale Evans: "Silent Clue": Manning. "Honest Injun." "The Man Who Outsmarted Himself." "An Album of Maps to Lost Treasure": Lenox. "Nature's Pre-Cooked Fish": Lenox. Additional artwork by Firfires, Edson, Alvarado, Sgroi. 100 pages. $4.50–$45.

#14, April-June 1956. Covers: A Western hotel front is designed with the photos of the cowboys and Dale/no inside photos any longer; "Angel's Camp—Heart of the Mother Lode"/"A Shady Wager." Roy Rogers and "The Phantom Bandit": Arens. Linc, a quiet outlaw, uses a slingshot at a distance to rob his victims. Trigger and Bullet appear in "The Desert's Secret": Arens. "Glory Hole." "Indian Quiz": Lenox. "Demonico's Downfall." "The Red Man's Calendar." "Coup Counting." "Fort Fizzle." Dale appears in "The Edge of Doubt": Firfires. Additional artwork by Firfires, Arens, Sgroi and Edson. 100 pages. $4.50– $45.

#15, July-September 1956. Covers: Artwork showing a train and sun surrounds the photos/"Roaring Camps of the West-Downieville"/"Downieville"/Wrigley's Gum ad. Roy Rogers and Trigger: "Crossed Trails": Edson, Sgroi, possibly some Buscema contribution. Honest Ben Nye doesn't want dishonest ex-con Ghost Carr to move to Mineral City and goes to great lengths to keep him away. "The Trap Within a Trap." Dale appears in "A Visit from Danger": Edson. "Western Scrapbook." "The Figure Eight." "The Frontiersmen—Joe Meek": Micale. "The Comanche." "A Quiet Victory." Additional artwork by Firfires, Edson, Alvarado. 100 pages. $4.50– $45.

#16, October-December 1956. Covers: Painting of cowboy roping calf is bordered by photos/"The Ghost Comes Back"/"Placer Prank"/color photo of Dale sitting on fence. Roy Rogers in "Deadly Destination": Arens. Roy is bushwacked and his money and

A number of the *Western Roundup* series Roy Rogers stories were drawn by Michael Arens, who also drew the newspaper comic strip in the 1950s. Copyright 1956 by Western Printing and Lithographing Co.

papers are stolen by outlaws who want to do his job with a professor who has the secret to a fortune. Trigger and Bullet appear in "Teamwork": Arens. "The Indian's Wireless." "Two-Scalper's Great Coup." "The Frontiersmen — Jim Beckworth": Ushler. "The Buffalo." "Why Animals Buck." Dale is featured in "The Courage of Benny Bowen," with Pat and Buttermilk: Manning. Additional artwork by Spiegle, Alvarado, Sgroi, and Manning. $4.50–$45.

#17, January-March 1957. Covers: Painting of cowboy on foot, roping horse, above photos/"Randsburg — The Town That Wouldn't Die"/"Randsburg" story continued/Monsanto Co. ad. Roy Rogers in "Gun Trouble": Edson, Alvarado, Sgroi, possibly Mankin, Manning. Colt Egger has a young man befriend Roy so that his gang can kill him. "Iron Shirt — Warrior or Legend." Dale rides the comic trail here in "High-Riding Danger": Manning, possible Mankin. "The End of the Open Range." "The Wild Arrow." "The Frontiersmen — Isaac Galbraith, the Indestructible Man." "The Grizzly." Additional artwork by Edson, Myers, Giacomini, Alvarado, others. 100 pages. $4.50–$45.

#18, April-June 1957. Covers: Painting of a cowboy on a bucking horse surrounded by the photos/"Virginia City — Queen of the Ghost Towns"/"Virginia City" story continued/color photo of Roy holding plastic saddle. "The Panic at Como." Roy Rogers in "The Man Hunt": Sgroi, unknown (some landscapes appear to be Toth). There's a large reward offered for Bart Stone, and the citizens of Mineral City see a "Bart Stone" under every rock. Bullet and Trigger appear in "Double Delivery": Firfires. "The Chisholm Trail." "The Medicine Shield." "Law Man." "The Frontiersmen — Buffalo Jones": Ushler. "The Gray Wolf." "The Toughest Cowboy That Ever Lived." Dale Evans appears in "A Fool's Gold": Firfires. Additional artwork by Alvarado, possibly some Toth, Edson. 100 pages. $5–$50.

#19, July-September 1957. Covers: End of photo covers. Western painting shows cowboy being thrown from bronc/"Cowboy Crossword"/"Gopher Gold Strike"/Daisy Manufacturing Co. ad. Roy Rogers and

Trigger in "The Shadow of Totem Rock": Myers, Giacomini. Jim King returns to Totem Rock to look for the strongbox his father buried just before he was killed by bandits twenty years ago. "The Fabulous Wind-Wagon." Dale appears in "Ladie's Day": Manning. "Days of Wells Fargo." "The Western Vignette — Reach!": Firfires. "The Grizzly Tamers." "The Frontiersmen — Jacob Van Renssler." "The Pronghorn." Additional art by Firfires, Arens, Sgroi, Giacomini. 100 pages. $4–$40.

#20, October-December 1957. Covers: Painting of cowboys herding mustangs/"Cowboy Crossword"/"They Called Him Nighthawk"/Wrigley's Gum ad. Roy Rogers and Trigger in "A Test of Speed": Arens. The towns of Black Rock and Arapahoe are vying for a $10,000 dollar purse in a horse race, but Black Rock doesn't play fair. "Rangeland Winters." Bullet and Trigger appear in "Horse of Another Color": Mankin (Roy is mentioned in the story). "Ghost Camp." "The First Law." "Sonora Gold." "Tales of the Overland Stage." "The Frontiersmen — Bill Williams." "Tracking." "The Telegraph." Dale appears in "Cry Wolf": Manning. Additional artwork by Spiegle, Myers, Giacomini, others. $4–$40.

#21, January-March 1958. Painting of cowboy on horse, throwing out lariat/"Lone Star Puzzler"/"Animal Weathermen"/"Demon Horses": Spiegle. Roy Rogers in "Roundup at Redrock": Arens. Lucky Long and his gang have taken over the town of Red Rock, calling themselves the "Citizen's Protective Committee." "Markmanship." "The Coyote — Vagabond Singer." "Early Postal Offices." "Navajo Blankets." "White Hawk's Challenge." "Tales of the Roaring West": Edson. "The Frontiersmen — John Colter, the Dread of the Blackfeet." "Frontier Courts." "Claim Jumping." Dale appears in "Harvest of Hate": Manning. Additional artwork by Firfires, Ushler, Giacomini, Sgroi, Manning. 100 pages. $4–$40.

#22, April-June 1958. Covers: Painting of bandit chasing stagecoach: Ken Sawyer (signed)/crossword puzzle/"The Comanche Sleeper"/"The Land-Lookers." Roy Rogers and Trigger in "Test of Courage": Ushler, Alvarado contribution. Roy is driving beef to Fort Moccasin, and pseudo-outlaws are trying to stop the drive. "Telltale Tracks." "The Road Runner." "The Gold Freight." "Duel in the Desert." "Frontier Banks." "Indian Gold." "The Frontiersmen — George Rogers Clark": Toth (signed). "Exploration." Dale appears in "The Fugitive": Manning. Additional artwork by Spiegle, Edson, Giacomini, Mankin, Firfires. 100 pages. $4–$40.

#23, July-September 1958. Painting of three cowboys chasing another, possibly Alvarado/"Cowpuncher's Crossword"/ Daisy Manufacturing Co. ad/Wrigley's Gum ad. "Tales of Wells Fargo" has taken the number one position away from Roy, a sign of the impact of the "adult" television Westerns. In fact, Roy comes third, after "Wagon Train" even. "2000 Mile Walk." "The Burro." "Living Clouds." Roy Rogers and Trigger in "The Trail of Terror": Edson, Spiegle, Alvarado, Sgroi. Greedy land grabbers try to stop a wagon train to keep homesteaders from participating in the land rush. "Nothing but Good." "The Battling Bulls." "The Frontiersmen — Bad Heart": Arens. "Chuck Wagon Lingo." Dale appears in "Ghost Town Gold": Manning (signed "Doe"). Additional artwork by Spiegle, Firfires, Mankin, others. 100 pages. $4–$40.

#24, October-December 1958. Covers: Painting of mustanger being thrown, possibly Spiegle/"Armored Stage"/"Range Vernacular"/Wrigley's Gum ad. "A Medium of Exchange." "Passing the Hat." "The Walking Boats." "Ramrod — The Cattle Trail Game." Roy Rogers and Trigger in "Storm Witness": Arens. A young boy witnesses a crime, but the victim says he's wrong. "The Railroad." "Sound Judgment." "Quicksilver Justice." "Silent Signals of the Range." Dale appears in "Joker's Reward": Spiegle. Additional artwork by Firfires, Mankin, Edson, Tufts, Spiegle. 100 pages. $4–$40.

#25, January-March 1959. Covers: Painting of a train holdup/"Abandoned Ships of the American Desert"/Giant Dinosaurs ad; "The Old West Talks"/Daisy Manufacturing Co. ad. Roy Rogers name has fallen to fifth position in the lineup. "The Wood Stones." Roy Rogers in "Troublesome Traders": Edson. All the horse ranchers are

trying to sell their stock to the army, but Captain Black has less than honest intentions when he criticizes the offerings. "Campfire Crossword" puzzle. "Claim Staker's Race." "3 Clues to Place the Bad Man" puzzle. "The Frontiersmen — The Rabbit's Foot." "A Will to Live": Ushler. "The Round House Raid." "Brand the Breed." Dale appears in "The Guilty One": Myers and or Giacomini. Additional artwork by Firfires, Edson, Alvarado, Mankin. $4.50–$45.

Roy Rogers' Trigger Comics

It is believed that Morris Gollub is the artist reponsible for many of the paintings on the covers and some of the artwork in the series; he may be the first artist. All covers carry a small photo of Roy in the upper right-hand corner. There were three photos used, two of which are almost identical. The first photo used is from a reversed negative. The apostrophe on Roy's name is omitted on issues 1, 3, 9, and 16. Original Trigger and Trigger doubles inspired art.

#329, Four-Color (#1) May 1951. Original copyright 1951, by Rohr Company. The cover title has the apostrophe omitted. Covers: Painting of Trigger jumping a fence, with a youngster riding and holding onto his mane: Gollub/photo of original Triger, unsaddled and rearing/photo has Trigger all rigged out in the Roy Rogers saddle and tack, bowing/painting of Trigger and colt: DeSoto (signed). Trigger is on a ranch with "Uncle Mike," nephew and niece Pete and Pat, and "Curly," the foreman. "Trigger": DuBois/possibly Gollub, Moore possible "Zimmerman" signing. Submitted August 21, 1950. 36 pages. $8–$55.

#2, September-November 1951. Original copyright 1951 by Roy Rogers Enterprises. Whether this cover is a photo or painted likeness of the horse has long been a matter of controversy: magnificent golden palomino standing on a rock, with blue sky background; not original Trigger, at any rate./ "Horses of History": Jenny/"Fast on their Hoofs": Jenny/painting of Trigger standing in stream: Gollub (signed). S1, "Trigger and the Drygulcher of Gunsight Notch": DuBois/Moore. Submitted September 25,

1950. S2, "Trigger Junior Meets the Test": DuBois/A Moore signing in 1st panel. Submitted October 9, 1950. During this time, Roy Rogers' Trigger was originally copyrighted by Roy Rogers Enterprises, but Dale Evans was not. 36 pages. $5–$35.

#3, December 1951–February 1952. Covers: Painting has Trigger climbing brushy cliff as some hombres are in pursuit/"Cow Camp Cookery"/story continues over both sides of back cover. S1, "Trigger Tackles a Sidewinder": DuBois/probably Moore, unknown. Submitted March 12, 1951. S2, "Trigger and the Underground Railway": DuBois/Randy Steffen. Submitted March 29, 1951. 36 pages. $2–$14.

#4, March-May 1952. Covers: Trigger battles with a big black horse in this painting: Gollub (signed)/"Survivor of the 7th": Jenny (signed)/story/story. S1, "Trigger Fights for Life": DuBois/Steffen. Submitted August 20, 1951. S2, "Weetamah's Bridle": Steffen. S3, "Trigger Trails the Lost": DuBois/possibly Moore. Submitted August 25, 1951. 36 pages. $2–$14.

#5, June-August 1952. Cover: Trigger is rearing up, leading a herd of mustangs, with stormy skies overhead in this painting/"The Army's Last Mounts": Jenny (signed)/story/story. S1, "Trigger Wins a Warrior's Plume": DuBois/probably Moore. Submitted October 14, 1951. S2, "Trigger Shares Danger on the Dark Continent": DuBois/Steffen, original title, "Trigger Shares Danger." Submitted October 13, 1951. 36 pages. $2–$14.

#6, September-November 1952. Covers: Trigger is accompanied by a small white dog in this painting/"The Pocket Pacifier"/story/story. S1, "Trigger Beats the Gun": DuBois/Moore. Submitted January 10, 1952. S2, "Trigger Runs the Gauntlet": DuBois/Steffen. Submitted January 26, 1952. 36 pages. $1.90–$9.

#7, December 1952–February 1953. Covers: In this painting, Trigger is attempting to elude some varmints by crossing a tree felled across a ravine, and, in an unusual move, he is saddled/"The Gentle Art of Roping"/story/story. S1, "Trigger Takes to the Wild": DuBois/Steffen. Submitted April 28, 1952. "Trigger Outruns a Robber": DuBois/Steffen, possible Moore contribution ("RTM" in splash panel). Submitted April 28, 1952. 36 pages. $1.30–$9.

#8, March-May 1953. Covers: Painting of Trigger looking after newborn; dapple in background, storm clouds overhead/"Old Man Porcupine"/story/story. S1, Trigger in "Horse Thief Cove": DuBois/third artist enters fold, unknown, possibly Joe Russo, but there appears to be a small Micale contribution. Submitted September 15, 1952. S2, Trigger and the "Red Renegade": DuBois/Steffen. Submitted September 9, 1952. 36 pages. $1.90–$9.

#9, June-August 1953. Covers: Painting has Trigger staring down into a poisoned water hole/"Famous Indian Chiefs—Quanah Parker": Till Goodan (signed)/story/story. S1, "Trigger Fights for Two": DuBois/third artist. Submitted December 23, 1952. S2, Trigger and the "River's Secret": DuBois/Steffen. Submitted December 19, 1952. 36 pages. $1.90–$9.

#10, September-November 1953. Covers: Painting shows Trigger is losing ground, trying to make it up a mountain: Steffen (signed)/"The Mountain Lion." S1, Trigger in "Killer Cat": unknown/Steffen. S2, "Trigger Turns Detective": unknown/Steffen. 36 pages. $1.90–$9.

#11, December 1953–February 1954. Covers: Painting of Trigger barely escaping the path of a locomotive as he is pursued/"The Development of the Western Saddle": Till Goodan (signed)/story/story. S1, Trigger and the "Carnival Killer": unknown/possibly Joe Russo (signed, last panel). Trigger and the "Milk Run": unknown/same as S1. The development of the Western saddle. 36 pages. $1.30–$9.

#12, March-May 1954. Covers: Painting shows Trigger harnessed to a jeep with chains, pulling it uphill out of the mud: Steffen (signed)/"The Wolf"/story/story. S1, Trigger in "Peril Rides the Storm": unknown/Steffen (signed, splash panel). S2, Trigger in "Deep-Water Rustlers": unknown/Steffen. 36 pages. $1.30–$9.

#13, June-August 1954. Covers: Painting shows Trigger about to fall backwards as he ascends a steep cliff/The "Mustangers": Steffen/story/story. S1, Trigger in "Timberland Terror": unknown/Steffen. S2, "Trigger to the Rescue": unknown/Steffen. *Note:* This story title was worked into a Whitman Cozy Corner Book and used as a Roy Rogers comics story in England. 36 pages. $1.30–$9.

#14, September-November 1954. Covers: Painting of Trigger jumping through broken down fence/"The Pony Express"/story/story. S1, Trigger in "Tide of Peril": unknown/Steffen. S2, Trigger and "The Moaning Cave": unknown/Steffen (signed). 36 pages. $1.30–$9.

#15, December 1954–February 1955. Covers: Painting shows Trigger trying to keep his balance as he walks logs in river/"The American Buffalo"/story/story. S1, Trigger in "Challenge of the Wolf Pack": unknown/Steffen. S2, Trigger in "Journey of Peril": unknown/Steffen. 36 pages. $1.30–$9.

#16, March-May 1955. Original copyright 1955 by Frontiers, Inc. Covers: Painting of Trigger leading a herd of mustangs. The company is using a leader on the cover: "They both knew only one could be king of the herd"/"Wild Horses"/story/story. S1, "Trigger, King of the Herd": unknown/Steffen. S2, Trigger and the "Morongo Roundup": unknown/Steffen. 36 pages. $1.30–$9.

#17, June-August 1955. Covers: Painting of Trigger about to be saddled; leader: "Trigger Comes Home"/Dell Comics Distinguished Achievement Award/story/story. S1, Trigger in "Rangeland Rescue": unknown/Steffen. S2, "Trigger Comes Home": unknown/Steffen. Trigger will soon be a part of Roy's comics. $1.30–$9.

Dale Evans Comics

Publisher: National Comics Publications, Inc., 430 Lexington Ave., New York. Logo: "DC." Each issue features several Dale stories, a "Sierra Smith" feature story, and filler stories. The filler stories are interesting tidbits of history and contain information on rodeo stars, etc. The plots of the Dale Evans stories are incredible, as if they had been written by the writer of Superman stories. The real quality of this magazine lies in the other features. "Dale Evans Roundup" is a feature wherein Dale addresses the readers, and Roy is mentioned often. The information in these first-hand type of articles is often not factual, however. Dale, in her first comic, doesn't have the frills of all the gloss later used by Dell Comics, but she was given a photo cover with her debut issue. It is possible that Jean Klinordlinger wrote some of the stories shown here.

#1, September-October 1948. Covers: Photo of Dale and "Pal." She looks like a mere kid here, cute, but there is no comparison with any later photos, not even those in the next issue./letter from Dale/DC ad/Schwinn Bikes ad. S1, "Secret of Ghost Town Greed": Susie Day/Jack Farr, Ray Burnley. Whatever may be said for the artwork, and it is fine, much can be said about the likeness of the subject. The comic should have read "based on the character, Dale Evans," as there is no resemblance to the real-life subject at all. At this point there was no Dale Evans Enterprises or any Roy Rogers company holding a license to her name or likeness that is shown in the publisher's copyright statement. S2, "Readin', Robbin', and Six-Gun 'Rithmetic": Day/Farr, Burnley. S3, "The Spirit of Annie Oakley": Day/Farr. "The Dude Meets Dale." "Sierra Smith": Alex Toth (signed). "Rodeo King": Frank Bolle (?). 52 pages. $25–$180.

#2, November-December 1948. Covers: Photo of Dale, close-up, smiling/DC ad/Daisy Manufacturing Co. ad/Eveready ad. S1, "Roughneck Romeos": Day/Jim McArdle. Dale's riding a solid brown horse with no identity before Pal comes along in the stories. S2, "The Evil Eye of Eagle Eye": Day/McArdle. Dale is now on a white unidentified horse. S3, "The Rodeo Hat": Day/McArdle. "Prospector—Arizona Bill": Stookie Allen. "Cowboy Artist—Charlie Russell": Allen. "Sierra Smith": Toth. 52 pages. $17–$115.

#3, January-February 1949. Covers: Line-drawn. Dale on a white horse, is closer to her likeness than the story art has been: Stookie Allen./DC ad/National Radio Institute ad/Eveready ad. S1, "Diamonds Ain't Hay": unknown/McArdle. Pal is her horse here. "Dale Meets the Stalker." "Sierra Smith": Toth.

S2, "Two-Ton Crime Wave"/unknown/ McArdle. S3, "The River of Never Return": unknown/McArdle. 52 pages. $13–$95.

#4, March-April 1949. Covers: Photo of Dale taken during a personal appearance with Roy/Kodak ad/National Radio Institute ad/Daisy Manufacturing Co. ad. S1, "Phantom of Cactus Canyon": unknown/ McArdle. "Sierra Smith": Toth. S2, "Mere Slip of the Gun": unknown/McArdle. S3, "A Dead Man's Life": McArdle. "Cougar!": Jimmy Fitch. "Pawnee Bill–Major Gordon Lillie." "Indian Facts." "Super Scout—Dan Beard." "Roller Skate Facts." "Dale Evans Round-up." (Roy is mentioned in Dale's comics, but Dale is never mentioned in Roy's comics.) 52 pages. $13–$95.

#5, May-June 1949. Covers: Photo cover from previous series of photos,, this one showing Dale tightening the cinch strap of the rodeo saddle, on her horse. This horse has on the plastic Roy Rogers rodeo red, white, and blue saddle and tack. S1, "The Thin Air Disappearances": unknown/McArdle. Pal is identified in the first story. S2, "Those Deadly Dreams": unknown/Lew Schwartz. "Sierra Smith": Toth. S3, "Dale Evans of the Pony Express": unknown/McArdle. She is identified in the story as a "movie star, and Queen of the Westerns." "Beacon of Peril." "From Rags to Riches." "Texas High School Rodeos." 52 pages. $13.50–$90.

#6, July-August 1949. Covers: Photo cover of Dale posing aboard a wagon/Kodak ad/DC ad/B. F. Goodrich ad. S1, "The Horse Thief Catcher": unknown/Lew Schwartz. "Sierra Smith": Toth. "The Alibi Bandit": unknown/ Schwartz. "Sagebrush Sam." "Dale Evans Roundup." S3, "Riot at the Roughhouse Rancho": unknown/ Schwartz. $13.50–$90.

#7, September-October 1949. Covers: Photo cover of Dale standing out at the stables feeding carrots to her horse/Kodak ad/ Charles Atlas ad/Daisy Manufacturing Co. ad. S1, "The Belles of Buffalo Wallow": unknown/McArdle. S2, "City of Dreadful Dust": unknown/McArdle. "Sierra Smith": Toth. "Sagebrush Sam." "Dale Evans Roundup." S3, "Canyon of Disaster": unknown/McArdle. "Flyin' Cowboy, Ken Boem." 52 pages. $13.50–$95.

#8, November-December 1949. Covers: Photo cover of Dale sitting astride her bowing horse. If you will look really close, you will see Roy's initials, the famous trademark-like "RR," appearing on the tapaderos. The producer has whited the initials out, as Roy's initials cannot be allowed to appear on the cover. Roy's name does not appear in Dale's comic at all, except in "Dale Evans Roundup," and then he's only identified as "Roy." They did a better job of whiting out the initials on the cover of #4./Kodak ad/Daisy Manufacturing Co./Electric Game Co. ad. S1, "Gobblers and Gold Dust": unknown/McArdle. "Dale Evans: The East Goes West." "Sierra Smith": Toth. "Dale Evans Roundup." S2, "Oil Is Where You Find It": unknown/ McArdle. "Shirt Maker-Bob Gwynn." 52 pages. $13–$95.

#9, January-February 1950. Covers: Photo cover of Dale sitting on silver-laden horse, talking to cowboy/Kodak ad/National Radio Institute ad/Daisy Manufacturing Co. ad. S1, "The Ship of the Desert": unknown/McArdle. "Dale Evans Roundup." "Sierra Smith": Toth. "Sagebrush Sam." "Letter to Fans." S2, "On the Merry-Go-Round": unknown/McArdle. S3, "The Money Tree": unknown/McArdle. 52 pages. Alex Toth art. $13.50–$95.

#10, March-April 1950. Covers: Photo cover of Dale sitting on a haystack, playing the guitar/Kodak ad/National Radio Institute/ Daisy Manufacturing Co. ad. S1, "Mining Engineer": unknown/McArdle. S2, "The Senator Goes West": unknown/McArdle. "Sierra Smith": Toth. "Dale Evans Round-up." S3, "The Prince of Bangistan": unknown/McArdle. Tom Mix, long since deceased but still around in comics, is shown here in a Ralston cereal ad, and Whip Wilson, another sagebrush hero, is shown in a Bazooka gum ad, both drawn. Silver-screen cowboy Jimmy Wakely shows up drawn, in an ad for his comics. "Schoolboy Rodeo—Booger Red Nixon." Roy Rogers cap pistol is advertised by American Seed Co. 52 pages. $13–$95.

#11, May-June 1950. Covers: Photo cover of Dale with a young colt/Kodak ad/Daisy Manufacturing Co. ad/Hollywood Film Studios ad. S1, "Talent Scout for Danger": un-

When DC's artist J. N. McArdle drew Dale for her first comic book series, she became the only full-time Western comic book heroine, but she didn't look like the Dale Evans fans knew from her pictures with Roy. This is from issue #16. Copyright 1951 by National Comics Publications, Inc.

known/McArdle. "Bullets and Balloons": unknown/McArdle. "Sierra Smith": Toth. "Dale Evans Roundup." "Protector." "Leave It to Binky." S3, "The Snow Broncos of Pride Mountain": unknown/McArdle. 52 pages. $13.50–$95.

#12, July-August 1950. Covers: Photo cover of Dale shown as the bull's-eye in a target. She is called here "America's Favorite Cowgirl Movie Star" and "Queen of the Westerns." Her horse is "Pal, the Wonder Horse."/Kodak ad/DC Comics ad/Peter Pan peanut butter ad. S1, "The Horse That Forgot to Remember": unknown/McArdle. S2, "The State Fair Fraud": unknown/McArdle. "Sierra Smith Roundup": Allen Ulmer. "Dale Evans Roundup." "Buzzy Says Balance Your Fun Diet." "No Foolin'." S3, "Fancy Footwork": unknown/McArdle. 52 pages. $13.50–$95.

#13, September-October 1950. Covers: Photo cover of Dale, brim of her hat tied back with chin-string, standing beside her horse/DC Comics ad/Novelty Mart Toys ad/Daisy Manufacturing Co. ad. S1, "Castle of Golden Deams": unknown/McArdle. "Sierra Smith": Ulmer. S2, "Carmen Ropes 'Em In": unknown/McArdle. "It's Rough" (Jim Shoulders, etc.). "The Midnight Marauders." "No Foolin'." "Tom Mix" Ralston ad. S3, "Monkey Business": unknown/McArdle. "Dale Evans Roundup." 52 pages. $7–$50.

#14, November-December 1950. Covers: Photo cover of what could be the same haystack, but our cowgirl has herself decked out in different attire this issue/DC Comics ad/Daisy Manufacturing Co. ad/Hollywood Film Studios ad. S1, "The Wagon Train from the Past": unknown/McArdle. S2, "Suitors and Looters": unknown. "Sierra Smith": Ulmer. "The Gauntlet of Death." "Dale Evans Roundup." S2, "The Nemesis of the Deerslayers": unknown/McArdle. "The White Ranch—Cal Thomson" (spelled Thompson in the text). "Longhorns—Val Kimbrough." 52 pages. $7–$50.

#15, January-February 1951. Covers: A sad time for these issues as they move from color photo covers to an illustrated cover, and unrealistic illustrations at that. Line drawing has Dale riding the back of the wheelchair of

her "Uncle Six"'s wheelchair down a pipeline: McArdle/ Kodak ad/National Radio Institute ad/ Hollywood Film Studios ad. S1, "The Watermelon Trail": unknown/McArdle. S2, "The Oil Rustlers": unknown/McArdle. "Sierra Smith": Ulmer. "Andy Womack—Rich Clown." "Pete Crump—Brahma Buster." "Cactus Charley's Scrambled Squares." "Dale Evans Roundup." S3, "A Cowgirl's Holiday": unknown/McArdle. 52 pages. $7–$50.

#16, March-April 1951. Covers: Line-drawing of Dale riding an ostrich: McArdle/DC Comics ad/National Radio Institute ad/Daisy Manufacturing Co. ad. S1, "Cowgirl of the Pampas": unknown/McArdle. S2, "The Highwayman": unknown/McArdle. "Sierra Smith": Ulmer. "Sagebrush Sam." "Dale Evans Roundup." S3, "The Sheriff of Sangamo County": unknown/McArdle. 52 pages. $7–$50.

#17, May-June 1951. Covers: Line-drawing by McArdle of Dale with long red hair, swooping down on the villains in a parachute/DC Comics/Daisy Manufacturing Co. ad/U.S. Royal ad. S1, "The Town That Couldn't Be Captured": unknown/McArdle. S2, "Uncle Six's Ward": unknown/McArdle. "Sierra Smith": Ulmer. "Chief Hot Foot." "The Hoofs of the White Stallion": Bill Ely. S3, "Great Land Race": unknown/ McArdle. Dale's horse Pal has turned from solid white to solid gold. "Dale Evans Roundup." "The Original Hit and Run": Al McClean. "Presenting Buffalo Briefs." 52 pages. $7–$50.

#18, July-August 1951. Covers: Line-drawing by McArdle of a pretty Indian girl who is chasing Dale, shooting a bow in which the artist apparently forgot to place an arrow/DC Comics ad/"Leave It to Blinky"/P-F Shoes ad. S1, "The Bagpipe Rustlers": unknown/McArdle. S2, "The Wagons That Vanished": unknown/McArdle. "Sierra Smith": Ulmer. "Dale Evans Roundup." S3, "Buffalo Buckaroo": unknown/McArdle. "Indian Oddities." "Pat Garrett." "The Golden Rock." 52 pages. $7–$50.

#19, September-October 1951. Covers: Line-drawing by McArdle of Dale atop an elephant, attacking the badguys/Kodak ad/Charles Atlas ad/Daisy Manufacturing Co. ad. S1, "Jumbo on the Range": unknown/

McArdle. S2, "The Box of Death": unknown/McArdle. "Indian Dances." "Dale Evans Roundup." S3, "The Stolen Wampum Belt": unknown/McArdle. "Indian Lore." "Sierra Smith": Ulmer. 52 pages. $7–$50.

#20, November-December 1951. Covers: Line-drawing by McArdle of a scene in which outlaws (and the old man in a wheel chair) look on as Dale's horse hits a trip rope, throwing her off/public service ad/Daisy Manufacturing Co. ad/Wheaties cereal ad. S1, "The Outlaws of Big Nugget Butte": unknown/McArdle. "The Accursed Canoe": Leonard Starr. "Ticks of Disaster." "Indian Headress." S2, "Indian Warpath": unknown/McArdle. 36 pages. $7–$50.

#21, January-February 1952. Covers: In a line drawing by McArdle, the stagecoach driver seems to have been shot off his seat, and the shotgun rider is wounded. Dale has apparently happened along and mounted one of the lead horses, bringing them to a halt/Kodak ad/public service ad/Daisy Manufacturing Co. ad. S1, "The Bullridge Bandit": unknown/McArdle. S2, "Cowgirl Schoolmarm": unknown/McArdle. "Sierra Smith": Ulmer. "Dale Evans Roundup." "The Warbag." "Western Wonders." "Indian Time." 36 pages. $7–$50.

#22, March-April 1952. Covers: Line-drawing by unknown/McArdle of Dale trying to break up a horse fight/"Leave It to Blinky"/National Radio Institute ad/Daisy Manufacturing Co. ad. S1, "The Challenge of the Cheyenne Princess": unknown/McArdle. "Sierra Smith": Ulmer. "Indian Bronco Busting." "The Snake Dance of the Hopis." S2, "Pal's Last Ride": unknown/McArdle. Art is imitating life here, as Dale gets a new horse, but instead of it being named "Buttermilk," it's "Soda." 36 pages. $7–$50.

#23, May-June 1952. Covers: Line-drawing by McArdle of Dale watching a kangaroo beat up the bad guys/public service ad/Daisy Manufacturing Co. ad/Sheaffer's Ink ad. S1, "The Kangaroo Cowboy": unknown/McArdle. S2, "The Salted Gold Mine": unknown/McArdle. "Sierra Smith": Ulmer. "Indian Customs." "The Bravest Pioneers." S3, "The King of the Grizzlies": unknown/McArdle. 36 pages. $7–$50.

#24, July-August 1952. Covers: Line-drawing by McArdle of Dale battling tigers in a cage/public service ad/DC Comics ad/Wheaties cereal ad. S1, "Wildcat Round-up": unknown/McArdle. S2, "The Tenderfoot Redskins": unknown/McArdle. "Sagebrush Sam." "Dale Writes a Shooting Script." S3, "The Crimes of the Ex-Owlhoots": unknown/McArdle. This is the final issue of this series. 36 pages. $7–$50.

Queen of the West Dale Evans Comics

The writer of the Dale Evans stories in this series is unknown, but there is a possibility that Eric Freiwald and Jean Klinordlinger contributed. "Queen of the West" appears after Dale's name in the story titles. The stories are aligned, in setting, with the television series. Pat Brady is included, but Roy is not.

#479, Four-Color (#1) July 1953. Original copyright 1953 by Dale Evans Enterprises. Dell Publishing Co. Produced by Western Printing and Lithographing Co. Covers: Dale's hair is short and red, and she's in a solid green blouse with embroidery and has little gold boots for earrings. (These earrings will become a trademark of Manning's depictions of Dale.) She stands next to her new horse Buttermilk/photo taken at home, with Dusty, Dodie, and Sandy; Dale's holding the baby up out of the playpen/story/story. S1, Dale Evans and "The Gent from Laredo": Hi Mankin. Dale's cafe is held up, but when she catches up with the crooks, they have become jewel thieves. S2, Dale Evans in "Bandit Bait": Hi Mankin. (Artist doesn't catch the real Dale likeness the way it will be captured later by Russ Manning.) Dale and Pat chase robbers and get a lot of assistance from Buttermilk and Bullet. (Buttermilk is a white horse here.) 36 pages. $10–$65.

#528, Four-Color (#2) October-December 1953. Covers: Photo cover of Dale painting a wagon wheel. Her hair is very short now, and she's in a cowgirl hat and a plaid flannel shirt. (Roy was actually in photo but was cut out here.)/photo of Dale in the kitchen letting daughter Linda Lou sample some cooking/story/story. S1, Dale Evans and "The Heiress": unknown, Mankin. Dale does some super sleuthing to find the missing heiress daughter of an old man. S2, Dale Evans and the "Man in the Red Suspenders": unknown, Mankin. The bank is robbed, and the crook's suspenders are Dale's only real clue in finding him. *Note:* Mankin is probably responsible for most of the Bullet likenesses in these stories. 36 pages. $5.70–$40.

#3, April-June 1954. Covers: Photo, mixed with art, of Dale looking great with a rich California tan, complementing the Roy Rogers package. She is in nice but fairly conservative Western attire and has a big steak about ready to come off the grill. The hat she wears for the rodeo, or was wearing at one time, closely matches Roy's hat and was, in this writer's opinion, much more becoming to her than the one worn in most of her comic photos, which seems somewhat small. Her hair is dark brown and very short now./ photo of Dale with Bullet, taken at home, where they're sitting on a haystack/story/ story. S1, Dale Evans in "Little Dog Lost": Mankin (signed, last panel). Crooks are after a diagram for a man's invention, and it's hid in a dog collar in Dale's possession. S2, Dale Evans and the "Ring of Guilt": Manning, Marsh, "D.L." (signed). Dale is a riding instructor in a girl's summer boarding school. She has her hands full attempting to prove a girl innocent of stealing a valuable ring. 36 pages. $6–$45.

#4, July-September 1954. Covers: Photo of Dale displaying a Japanese lantern/photo of Dale standing to the left of Buttermilk/ "Reading Western Brands": Lenox/color shot of Dale with arrows and target. S1, "Dale Evans": Ushler. Roy is mentioned in this outing where Dale goes up against bad guys to compete in a shooting contest in order to use the money to pay for a child's operation. S2, "Dale Evans": Manning (signed). Bullet is believed to be by Mankin, other possible artist is Bennett. Dale gets involved when crooks are out to blackmail Princess Neva of Sulania. 36 pages. $6–$45.

#5, October-December 1954. Covers: Photo of Dale in blue jean Western outfit with rifle in hand, joined by Bullet, outdoor setting/

photo of Dale sitting outdoors (probably at home) in buckskin jacket/"Cowboy Cut-Ups"/color shot of Dale with Indian doll. S1, Dale Evans and "The Hide-Out": Jesse Marsh. (Bullet by different artist as well.) Dale does some roping and fancy shooting to apprehend some escaped cons and the parole violator to whom they owe money, who's pretending to be a detective. S2, Dale Evans and "The Million Dollar Kid": Manning. Other possible contributions: Bennett, Jacobs. This issue is probably as much as Roy will ever appear in a Dale Evans comic. He is mentioned, his movies are mentioned by a fan, and it's stated that he does come into the cafe (a regular customer), but he's out of town at the moment. The Double-R-Bar Ranch is worked into the story. 36 pages. $4.30–$30.

#6, January-March 1955. Covers: Photo of Dale astride the horse, bending over to have a chat with the animal. She is in a leather blue/brown fringed outfit. Buttermilk's tact is really conservative compared with Trigger's/photo of Dale, in more conservative attire, with Bullet outdoors/"Western Party Pranks"/color shot of Dale, rifle under her arm. S1, Dale Evans and "The Doll with Green Eyes": Manning, possibly Mankin. Crooks are attempting to scare a girl from her ranch. S2, Dale Evans and "The Midnight Visitor": Manning, possible Mankin. The bad guys are making it look like their dirty work was done by a youngster. 36 pages. $4.30–$30.

#7, April-June 1955. Covers: Dale's decked out in green Winter attire here, displaying a very serious expression as she stands behind a fence with her gun on someone/one of her rodeo pictures, with Buttermilk in the RR plastic saddlery/full-sized drawing of Dale rearing on her horse: Mankin. S1, Dale Evans in "The Crossroads": Mankin. Crooks have hidden diamonds in a Primrose plant which Dale has purchased. Roy is mentioned in this story. S2, Dale Evans and "The Dangerous Trail": Manning. Dale is dry-gulched by "Bat" and "Nails," but John Tall Horse comes to her aid. 36 pages. $4.30–$13.

#8, July-September 1955. Covers: Dale appears here attired in a red and white candy-striped blouse, with long red string tie, and

Dale finally wound up with a comic company geared to the kind of cowgirl she was when she rode her horse into the Dell/Western corral. Her covers were every bit as impressive as Roy's, as can be seen here with issue #5.

also has on a skirt and holster. The gun she has in her hand is probably the .38 that Roy gave her for the television series. It looks a little more ladylike than the big Western .45, as she holds it on the bad guy here/Dell Comics' Distinguished Achievement Award/ Dale in long-fringed outfit, outdoors/color shot has her and Bullet before cafe menu sign. S1, Dale Evans in "The Treasure of Butterfly Rock": Edson. Crooks on the run from a posse seek a sanctuary in some ruins being worked by geologists. S2, Dale Evans in "Trial and Error": Manning, Marsh. Other possible artist: Rotsler. Dale must stop an angry bunch of vigilantes from breaking a man out of the calaboose. 36 pages. $4–$30.

#9, October–December 1955. Covers: Photo of Dale in same plaid outfit that she was in on the back of issue #6. Here she's holding onto Bullet with one white-gloved hand, while she aims her pistol toward some unknown danger./Dell's Pledge to Parents/ story/story. S1, Dale Evans and "Black Star": Manning. Dale finds a little Indian girl who has run off from the reservation after being accused of stealing. "Jeb's Big Idea." Bullet is in "The Stealthy Stranger": Mankin. S2, Dale Evans in "Ghost Town Intruders": Manning, Mankin. Crooks have stolen money from Dale that was earmarked for building a children's clinic. 36 pages. $4.30–$30.

#10, January–March 1956. Covers: Photo of Dale, really looking like her character as "Queen of the West." She is wearing a blue and white striped blouse, blue jean vest with conchas, red string tie, blue jean skirt, gun belt and holster, and the hat with the chin string, as she stands next to Buttermilk./ photo from the series which includes several other inside photos (i.e., from issues 3, 4), wearing her leather jacket with fringe and sitting on a haystack/story/story. S1, Dale Evans in "Killer at Large": Manning, Toth. Dale and Pat look for the killer of Judge Martin, and Dale sets herself up as bait for the capture. "The Heroic Coward": Manning. "Western Vignettes—Star Witness": Mankin (signed, splash panel). "A Bridge for the Navajo." S2, Dale Evans in "The Heroic Coward": Manning, Toth. A stage performance becomes a real-life adventure for Dale and Pat. 36 pages. $4–$30.

#11, April–June 1956. Covers: Photo close-up of Dale in a very attractive pose, reading "Good Manners for Dogs" to Bullet/"Outstanding Award for Dale Comics"/story/ story. S1, Dale Evans and "The Secret of Last Chance": Arens. A ghost town has been rebuilt, and one of the attractions is fake holdups for show. The "actors" overplay their parts. "Amity Goes Overboard." Western Vignettes—Doomed Witness": Mankin (signed). S2, Dale Evans in "Swarm of Trouble": Firfires. A foreman of a honeybee farm tries to get his boss out of the way so he can take over the operation. His tactic is provoking the bees to sting an innocent passerby. 36 pages. $3.50–$24.

#12, July–September 1956. Covers: Photo of Dale with Bullet, sitting in what is apparently "Nellybelle." She's decked out in a white suit with red, yellow, and blue Indian designs, pistol in hand, ready for the bad guys./"A Question of Nerve"/story/Wrigley's gum ad. S1, Dale Evans "Secret in the Hills": Manning, Toth contribution, small. An old woman becomes irrational after her murderer son dies. S2, Dale Evans in "Tomahawk Trail": Dan Spiegle. Dale is framed after owlhoots make a plaster impression of Buttermilk's shoes. "Western Vignettes— The Bandit's Mistake": Ushler. 36 pages. $4–$28.

#13, October–December 1956. Covers: photo of Dale talking on an old telephone/"The Oldest Street in America"/story/story. S1, Dale Evans in "Trouble at the J-Bar-M": Manning. Bullet is absent from her story this time. Dale must find a locket to prove which girl is the heiress daughter and which is the imposter. "The Taming of Cimmaron." "Western Vignettes—Message at the Fort": Spiegle. "The Strangest Roundup in History." S2, Dale Evans in the "Decoy Robbery": Manning, Mankin. Dale and Pat foil bank robbers. 36 pages. $3.50–$24.

#14, January–March 1957. Covers: Photo of Dale all decked out in brown Western outfit with blue jacket, standing beside Buttermilk at what is probably their ranch home/"The Legend of the Great American Desert"/sub-

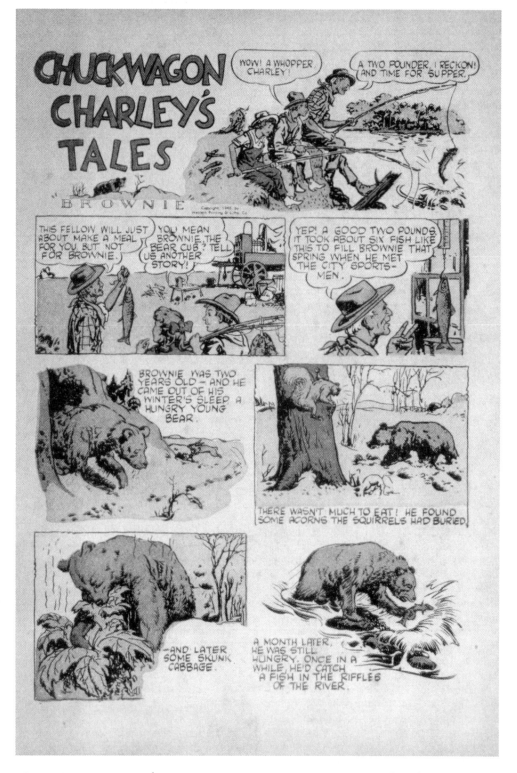

"Chuck Wagon Charley's Tales" had taken on quite a different appearance. Here, in a 1948 issue, Harry Parks lent his talents to the feature. *Roy Rogers Comics* #12. Copyright expired.

scription page/Monsanto ad. S1, Dale Evans and "The Frame-Up": Toth (signed), Manning. A subject's name is Al Taylor, which accommodates the artist's initials for signing. A nephew, about to inherit a ranch, is framed. "The Youngest Prospector." "Western Vignettes—The Lost Bounty": Spiegle, unknown. S2, Dale Evans and "Whistling Wind Cave": Mankin (signed). Dale must deal with crooks who are passing themselves off as out-of-town lawmen. 36 pages. $3.50–$24.

#15, April-June 1957. Covers: A leader appears that ruins the full-sized color photos of the subject. Here Dale appears in a photo that probably belongs to a series that includes the shot used on the back cover of *Western Roundup Comics*, issue #16, wherein she's decked out in the red outfit with hers and Roy's initials. She appears with pistol in hand and Bullet at her side/"The Homing Pigeon": Mankin (signed)/"Western Wonder"/color shot of Dale astride Buttermilk at filming location. The horse is in the RR plastic saddlery. (*Note* the beat-up straw hat.) S1, Dale Evans and "The Sky Raiders": Manning, Mankin. A crook is posing as a "sales representative." "A Quick-witted Miss." "Western Vignettes— A Slip of the Tongue": Spiegle, unknown. S2, Dale Evans "The Jinx": Manning, Mankin. 36 pages. $4.30–$30.

#16, July-September 1957. Covers: Photo of Dale astride Buttermilk in an action sequence/Roy Rogers merchandise ad/Daisy Manufacturing Co./Wrigley's gum ad. S1, Dale Evans in "The Code": Mankin. The victim of a shooting uses the arm of a phonograph to tap out a Morse code message. "Shiny Top." "Western Vignettes — The Silver Saddle": Firfires. S2, Dale Evans, "The Poetic Barber of Mineral City": Mankin. A gent has been lying in letters to his mail-order-bride-to-be, and now she's arriving in town. 36 pages. $3.50–$24.

#17, October-December 1957. Original copyright changes to Roy Rogers–Frontiers, Inc. Covers: Photo cover action pose of Dale, pistol in hand, next to Bullet/Blue Bell, Inc. ad (Jim Shoulders for Wrangler jeans)/subscription page/Wrigley's gum ad. S1, Dale Evans "The Mark of Guilt": Spiegle. Trouble

awaits a man returning home from prison to clear his name. "The Sheriff's Game." "Quick Sand Crisis." S2, Dale Evans: "Slip Egan's Mistake": Manning, Mankin. Dale makes use of horses to catch a bank robber and horse thief. 36 pages. $3.50–$24.

#18, January-March 1958. Covers: Photo of Dale in a bright green outfit and a long white string tie, sitting up on Buttermilk and drawing her six-shooter. For photo collectors, the cover is ruined by the leader./subscription page/"The Snipe Hunt": Mankin/Monsanto ad. S1, Dale Evans in "The Fatal Error": Mankin, Manning. A boy who has lost his job goes berserk, and Dale goes to his rescue. "Silent Partner." "The Magnificent Cannon": Ushler. S2, Dale Evans "Twister Trouble": Manning, Mankin, unknown. The most attractive Dale to appear in the series shows up in a few panels here. Dale comes to the rescue of a child who gets caught up in a tornado while going for a doctor. 36 pages. $3.50–$24.

#19, April-June 1958. Covers: Dale, in this photo, is coming out of a stall, her gun drawn and Bullet at her side/"Famous Women of the West—Unsung Heroine": Mankin/"Clown of the Desert"/subscription page. S1, Dale Evans: "The Legend of Lost Valley": Firfires. Dale and Pat discover hidden jewels in the desert. "Muley and the Mirage." "Western Vignettes—A Lucky Break": Moore, Spiegle, S2, Dale Evans in "The Girl from Thunder River": Moore, possibly Spiegle. Dale comes to the aid of a runaway girl from an orphanage. (The "Thunder River" name was used once before in a story title: "Secret of Thunder River," Roy's first story in the first issue of the regular series by DuBois/Micale.) 36 pages. $3.50–$24.

#20, July-September 1958. Covers: Photo of Dale in the red and white star–adorned outfit with initials, standing beside Buttermilk, just posing/subscription page/Daisy Manufacturing Co. ad/Wrigley's gum ad. S1, Dale Evans in "Stagecoach to Nowhere": Manning. Pat Brady has been replaced by "Curley." Dale and Curley use her delivery wagon to catch crooks. "The Secret Weapon." "Repetitious Sam": Moore, Spiegle. S2, Dale Evans: "Bandits in Blue": Firfires. Outlaws ambush soldiers and steal their credentials in order to get their hands on gold bullion scheduled for pickup. 36 pages. $4–$28.

#21, October-December 1958. Covers: Photo has Dale sitting among rocks, gun in hand and Bullet at her side, and she's appearing in attractive grey and black outfit/photo of Dale and Bullet, facsimile signed/subscription page/7-Up Co. ad. Dale Evans in "Bait for a Bandit": Warren Tufts, Spiegle. A very different looking likeness of Dale from this artist, with a much lower cut neckline, and the hat often hangs down her back from the chinstrap. An outlaw steals Buttermilk after Dale refuses his offer to buy the horse. "The Invisible Brands." "The Slick Operator": Edson. S2, Dale Evans "Strike at Chichimocho": Tufts. A gent is fueling tensions against the Indians. 36 pages. $3.50–$24.

#22, January-March 1959. Covers: An era of fine Western comics is drawing to a close. This is the final issue of Dale's comic. Photo of Dale, in attractive black and white outfit, adjusting the saddle on Buttermilk/subscription page/"The Fishpole Tree"/Daisy Manufacturing Co. ad. S1, Dale Evans in "Hidden Guns": Manning (signed). Dale must dampen the spirits of wild trail hands. "The Useful Tree." "Western Vignettes—Smiley's War": Ushler. S2, Dale Evans in "Trouble at Clay's Corners": Manning. Dale gets caught up in a dispute over who gets the ranch after the grandfather dies. 36 pages. $4–$28.

Roy Rogers Western Classics

Reprints in the 1980s–1990s. Americomics/Paragon Comics. Lakewood, Florida. Covers are Roy Rogers publicity photos, some of which were comic covers in the 1950s. Reprints of 1950s stories from regular series, re-inked. Also current and old photos of Roy, news stories. The comic stories used are all from the John Buscema work on Roy and the Russ Manning period for Dale. Gabby Hayes stories are included, mostly ones by artist Leonard Frank. Some colorizing of b&w photos. There were five issues. Bill Black, AC editor, contributed to artwork.

The Great American Western, Special Limited Edition

1980s. Americomics. Roy on cover of #3, along with the Durango Kid and Tom Mix. Comic includes article on "The Trail of Robin Hood" by editor and publisher Bill Black. $1–$4.

Chapter 8

Photographic History

My research has indicated that Roy Rogers is definitely the most photographed of all Hollywood Western stars and is one of the most photographed of all Hollywood stars in general because of his impact on so many media and the fact that such photos were necessary to market him in many different ways. There were constant sessions by Republic's publicity crew to promote him as a Republic star and to promote his films.

The artwork on posters and other movie materials was inspired by the photos. There were sessions by Roy's publicity folks to produce photos that would have to be used to feed a myriad of interests from comic books to magazines to merchandise to fan club materials. There were sessions with the photographers sent out from the many magazines which covered him constantly and vigorously for two decades. Many of these most precious negatives, transparencies, and original prints are still in the files and warehouses of the companies that used them. Many have, however, emerged from such places, especially during the past couple of decades, and have been sold to dealers who in turn make tons of prints, or limited prints, from an original negative or from a second generation negative produced from an original print. There are dealers who have bought out "lots" of celebrity negatives from publishing, merchandise production, and other companies; prints from these negatives often have not been issued since the original use. I have one dealer friend who has many Roy Rogers negatives of this type, and he is not even considering making prints for another ten years.

Photos are used in this section solely to illustrate various points, and no attempt is made to override the copyrights of any other individual, such as the photographer, or any companies, such as the Roy Rogers companies, or the publishing companies having originally published the photos. My research has indicated that in some instances such photos might have been copyrighted by the photographer, but in most instances they were protected originally in copyrights by the publishers, Republic Productions, Inc., other film companies, or the Roy Rogers companies. They belong to their respective copyright holders.

My research has further indicated that in many instances the magazines (including film magazines and comic books) that used many of the photos failed to renew the copyrights upon the expiration of the original copyright registrations, and therefore, these photos fall in the public domain. Each and every photo and publication or item upon which a photo appeared would have to be researched individually through the U.S. Copyright Office in Washington, D.C., as I have done in many instances. Suffice it to say, they are movie memorabilia collectibles. One of the essential keys to dating photographs of Roy Rogers lies in a thorough understanding of the history of his attire (see Chapter 10).

Roy Rogers' family has probably been the most photographed in Hollywood history, especially after he and Dale became the most popular Western couple in Hollywood. This resulted from the close association of Roy and Dale in films, etc., after 1944. Arline seldom, if ever, looked the part of the cowgirl. Most of the Roy

Rogers photos after 1946 contain either Dale or one of his many leading ladies from the films.

Photograph sessions did understandably let up after the heaviest part of Roy's film career had passed, and decreased further with each medium that faded as time marched on, i.e., television, then comics, then rodeo appearances. The majority of the publicity photos are from 1938 to 1962. Most of the photos that have been taken since that time have been either candid shots or were taken during personal appearances at special events, such as charity functions or openings of Roy Rogers Restaurants. From the 1970s to the present, there appears to be as many films shot of Roy as there are still photos, owing to technology and the accessibility of home video cameras. He has also made a multitude of guest appearances on television, on both music and talk shows. Many people have acquired a significant collection of these "clips" and have assembled them onto VHS tapes. "Still" photos are being made from these by collectors, and they are usually offered for sale or trade between collectors. The quality of many of these is generally poor, however.

Individuals also are making still photos from frames of the old television series episodes. These are usually offered for sale fairly inexpensively, but the quality seems to run from poor to fair. As the enterprises bearing his name continue to become involved in merchandise production, especially since the nostalgia craze and Western craze have swept the country, recent publicity photos pop up now and then, often in the form of merchandise-related advertising. It can be a little difficult to distinguish the 1970s photos from those taken in the 1980s. The same holds true of the 1980s and 1990s. Roy has held up to aging very well and is trim and fit, looking as though he could still do a quick mount and chase the bad guys out of town.

There are literally thousands of Roy Rogers photos in existence that move from one collector to another. There are thousands of negatives from which prints have been mass-produced and are continuing to be produced. Thousands more negatives are likely in safe-keeping with the companies, and as many have been bought by dealers who are just not ready to release prints yet. "New" or rarely seen prints will continue to surface throughout the future. For every commercial photo that you see, there should be many from the same session in existence. During a session, photographers would take scores of photos from which to select. Sometimes one would be used in one medium and others would find their way into use in another medium. Careful examination will reveal that they are from a single session. Celebrity photo companies were very big business in the 1940s and still are today. They contributed to much of the advertising found in the old film magazines. Most of these companies at that time mass-produced close-up and portrait-type photos, mostly black and white, some color, ranging in size from wallet-sized to 8" × 10". The earliest prints can command high prices in mint condition. Photos were sent out to news agencies such as Acme Newspictures, a division of NEA Service, Inc., 331 Fifth Ave., New York. These prints, when they can be found, are generally of the highest quality, as they were intended for reproduction, usually one time, by whichever company received them. On the ones that were in the hands of news agencies, a vanilla-like paper glued to the backs carried all information to be used with photo. This paper is coded with a number (for example, SF 901683 could have been sent from a San Francisco service) and shows the bureau to which it is sent, along with the date, with the initials in parentheses. Also shown is who is to be credited (Acme in this case). Such photos were often rubber-stamped on back with such notices as "This picture is sold to you for your publication only and must not be loaned, syndicated or used for advertising purposes without written permission from Acme. By accepting this picture you agree to hold Acme harmless from any loss or damage arising by reason of your use or publication of this picture." Any negatives command a very high price in the marketplace. Dealers are reluctant to sell them because of the number of prints that can be made and sold. Prints from original

1427-74. For *My Pal Trigger*, **1946. This was used on a magazine cover as well.**

negatives command a higher price in the marketplace than those that are mass-produced from second generation negatives. Although thousands of every type commercial photo were once in existence, the numbers of these and the mediums in which many were used, i.e., comics and magazines, have diminished significantly because of the paper drives during the 1940s for the war effort.

Comics

Family-type photos appeared on some backs and insides through issue #33 of *Roy Rogers Comics*. Photos of Roy on the cover go back and forth from pre–*Apache Rose* attire (1946) to then current attire, through issue #36. The photography went through many phases and turned out products ranging from extraordinary to poor. Either Roy's health or the photographer and the lighting, or a combination of both, caused him to look especially ill in the photos used for issues #115–131, between 1957 and 1959.

Magazines

Photos from magazine publishing company files. Many are candid-like. Magazine articles would feature from one to a dozen photos, both color and black and white. A tremendous amount of "at home" or informal appearing photos would be utilized here.

Candid

Usually taken by an amateur photographer at events that featured Roy, especially rodeos and parades. Tens of thousands of these exist, taken with every type of camera imaginable. Numerous photos of this type were taken by magazine publishers or Roy's publicity department as well and found their way into magazines. The true candid photos taken by amateur photographers are the last to make it into the marketplace. Sometimes an individual will still have the negatives and will make prints for a collector, perhaps in trade for other Roy Rogers collectibles. For nearly thirty years, fans and tourists in general have stopped by the Roy Rogers (later Roy Rogers–Dale Evans) Museum in California and have had the opportunity to photograph Roy in those now familiar surroundings. Photos of Dale at the museum are far less common. There are many thousands of amateur photos of Roy in existence from the decades of personal appearances, many of which will continue to emerge as the years pass. They are some of the most interesting.

Negative Reversals

Many of the photographs that exist of Roy in every medium are what I call "negative reversals." This is a practice that has taken place since the beginning of photography. For many years, historians and others including filmmakers, were convinced that William "Billy the Kid" Bonney was left-handed. Then it was discovered that the familiar photo of him was made in this manner. Those not familiar with Roy or simply careless in their work have produced hundreds of photos of him with reversed image. These have appeared on magazine covers, comics covers, and merchandise. There are several all-important clues to recognizing reversed photos. Which side the neckerchief hangs down on, with any cowboy, is a matter of preference or tradition. Roy kept his neckerchief hanging on his left side throughout his career. On men's belt buckles, the belt end with the tip passes through the buckle and points to the wearer's left. And for every left-handed guitar picker running around the West, there are at least several hundred right-handed ones. And a man customarily wears his watch on the arm of the hand he uses the least, which in Roy's case is his left. Negatives reversed during processing have turned the King of the Cowboys into a southpaw. Rings, especially wedding bands on the wrong hand, can also readily indicate that the negative was reversed in the machine prior to photo reproduction. The part of the shirt that holds the female part of the snap, the part which is pearl-covered, should be on the wearer's left. Even a pistol, when only one is drawn, would more than likely appear in the right hand of a right-handed subject with correct negative position. More often than not, the cowboy will stand to the left side of his horse, the proper mounting side.

The following are examples chosen from hundreds of "negative reversals": Cover, *Jack and Jill*, 1961/ Cover, *Movie Thrills/* Thermos, Aladdin Thermos Co. lithograph, artist: Ed Wexler/ Jigsaw puzzle #2628:29, Whitman Pub. Co. (some of these have been "doctored," i.e., the neckerchief painted in)/Jigsaw puzzle #2982/ Jigsaw puzzle #2610:29/ Cover photo, "Brasada Bandits," novel, Whitman Pub. Co./ Photo, *TV Guide*

1022-1. From *Young Bill Hickok*, 1941.

article: "And He's Not Even Dreaming."/ Cover, *Movie Life*/ Cover, 78 RPM story-book record album, *Lore of the West*, RCA Victor/ Photo, magazine article: "How Roy Rogers Changed My Life/ Photo, article: Swedish publication/ Cover, songbook *Roy Rogers Album of Cowboy Songs*, Robbins Music/ Book: *Roy Rogers and Dale Evans Cut-Out Dolls*, 1952, Whitman Pub. Co./ Photo, Meyercord Decal/ Republic color publicity "Roy Rogers, King of the Cowboys, and Trigger, Smartest Horse in the Movies"/ Cover, *Modern Screen*, August 1945/ Roy Rogers Comics, Four-Color issues 95, 117, 144/ *Roy Rogers Comics*, regular Dell series issues 7, 10, 12, 19, 21, 24, 28, 75, 99/ Photo, packaging, VHS video cassette tape: *My Pal Trigger*, Video Classics Co./ Cover, *Western Stars*/ Cover, *Western Hollywood Pictorial*/ Cover, *Movie Fan*, November-December 1950.

Republic, Film Related

Stills are 8″ × 10″ photograph prints of the scenes from a film, often the same as are used on the lobby cards. Most are slightly sepia-colored, if original, and they often have some degree of brittleness or cracks. Photo duplication these days is so easy that it can require some amount of experience to be able to tell the difference. Generally the more yellow photos appear (this is especially visible on the back side), the older a print. Know your dealer and study the paper, finish, etc.

Most photos related to Republic studios, either film stills or publicity stills, were originally identified with a number in the lower right- or left-hand corner. These numbers have often been removed in the reproduction process, however. This was done for two reasons: They distract from the image, and less experienced dealers might be concerned with copyright problems. Most photographs did not bear any separate registration and even when they did, they have long since lapsed into public domain. The numbers, when present, can be useful in identifying the photo. RRDECA and many other concerns have distributed 8″ × 10″ publicity prints made up on heavier stock.

Roy Rogers Publicity Department

To answer millions of pieces of fan mail, most of which requested a photo, a reproduction of Roy's signature was mass-produced on the photos. There was often a greeting attached, such as "Many Happy Trails." Originals of these photos are relatively scarce. Other "facsimile" signed photos were heavily used by magazines, celebrity photo companies, and, for a while, by the comics publisher and some merchandisers. The signature added a little personal touch, the next best thing to getting a photo autographed.

Autographed

Collectors are slow to relinquish negatives and original prints of their candid photos. Such items often change hands only when a collector dies and the family steps in, takes over the estate, and calls a dealer. Autographed photos from Roy, usually at personal appearances, are much slower to surface on the market, as they are even more special to the fans who obtained them.

Film Print Chart

Many merely collect photos of their favorite stars and have no concern for the age of the print, while others desire only original prints, or ones that are very old. The majority of photos have numbers assigned by Republic and other studios which serve to identify them with particular films. Numbers were also assigned to publicity photos, public appearance photos, and even informal photos once they were accepted for use in publicity. After a film was shot, the leading actors and actresses would report to the still department to have publicity photos taken that would be released to promote the film. These are "still publicity photos" and are posed, sometimes in the same attire as that worn in the film, but often the studio opted for a flashier style. Film stills, on the other hand, usually indicate actual scenes from the film, and they were used in the glass display cases outside the theaters, as well as in the lobbies, to promote the film. Movie material stores and dealers have made negatives from most photos that pass through their hands, and from that point on they are produced in mass quantity as they are sold at retail outlets, shows, and by mail order. Many negatives have been badly overworked, resulting in a cloudy print that is no longer full of contrast. Original prints have a tendency to turn brown over a period of time, and companies have been known to create the brownish color for effect. If you are truly interested in original prints, beware of the paper being too slick and in good condition, even though it is brown. The aging process is usually not even, unlike deliberate tinting. Beware of the words "Kodak Paper" showing on the backside. Newer prints often show these words. Careful scrutiny, common sense, and knowing your dealers are the key factors here. So long as you're paying in the neighborhood of $3 to $5, don't worry about it. This is the going rate for dealers who sell prints with no regard to the age. Sometimes you can stumble across a very old print in good condition for this price. In distinguishing the new from old, the borders and backs should show age right along with the area of the image. There are literally millions of prints that were made in each decade from the 1940s and the 1950s through the present day, so it can be very difficult to tell what you have. Even rubber stamps, in the hands of less than honest dealers, have been applied. Study the prints intently, and in time you can become very comfortable in your selections. This list will help identify the master photo and the source of the photo. Some prints have had their numbers removed in the duplication process, and some must be studied under a magnifying glass in order to make out the number. In the instance of the Republic photos, the first part of the number relates to the source film. The part of the number appearing after the dash designates the individual print number. Any main number can have literally scores of prints, each a different image, or still. In fact, they can still be made, but these usually won't carry any sort of markings. Publicity stills, on the other hand, are limited to a specific number of negatives. Often in studying the overall history of the photos, one can determine that a particular photo session produced many photos, and they were used in many different mediums. The information pre-

1841-27. From *Pals of the Golden West*, 1951. Roy administers a little justice.

sented is taken from photos in the author's personal collection and the collections of others. Only one photo of a kind will be shown, especially per film. The -# in parenthesis indicates a number in my collection, and indicates at least that many different prints exist. A -58 indicates that at least 58 different prints exist. It is no indicator of the maximum number in existence.

HP   *Slightly Static* (-A3 scene)
L11   *The Old Homestead*, 1935 (Liberty) (-4 scene)
1615   *Rhythm on the Range*, 1936 (Paramount) (-167 scene)
603   *The Old Corral*, 1936 (Republic) (-1 scene)
302   *The Old Wyoming Trail*, 1937 (Columbia) (-20 scene)
MT   *Melody Time*, 1948 (RKO Radio) (P-74 scene/ Pub 59 publicity)

R Numbers

Early stills from films that were also used for publicity.

R-1   *Billy the Kid Returns*, 1938 (Republic) (-97 scene)
R-2   *Come On Rangers*, 1938 (Republic) (-35 scene)
R-3   *Shine On Harvest Moon*, 1939 (Republic)
R-4   *Rough Riders Roundup*, 1939 (Republic) (-40 publicity, three of the cast)
R-6   *Southward Ho*, 1939 (Republic) (-58 publicity, Roy, Gabby)
R-7   *Frontier Pony Express*, 1939 (Republic)
R-8   *In Old Caliente*, 1939 (Republic) (-46 scene)
R-9   *Wall Street Cowboy*, 1939 (Republic) (-1 scene/ R 9H publicity)
R-507   Publicity shot (see 1323-55)

Regular Series Republic Stills

704   *Under Western Stars* 1938 (-8 publicity/ -210 publicity, Roy, lady)

Dale tending to the mail, circa 1948.

707   *The Old Barn Dance*, 1938 (Republic)
713   *Wild Horse Rodeo*, 1937 (Republic)
921   *Arizona Kid*, 1939 (Republic)
922   *Saga of Death Valley*, 1939 (Republic) (-10 scene)
923   *Days of Jesse James*, 1939 (Republic) (-13 scene)
No # *Man of Conquest*, still, group. Len wearing tuxlike suit, big bow tie (cut from film.)
924   *Young Buffalo Bill*, 1940 (Republic) (-43 scene)
925   *In Old Cheyenne*, 1941 (Republic) (-22 scene)

A favorite publicity stunt has Roy riding Trigger into a hotel, circa 1942.

1022   *Young Bill Hickok,* 1941 (Republic) (-1 scene/-18 scene)

1023   *Robin Hood of the Pecos,* 1941 (Republic) (-18 publicity, Roy, leading lady)

1024   *Badmen of Deadwood,* 1941 (Republic) (-13 scene)

1025   *Sheriff of Tombstone,* 1941 (Republic) (-29 scene)

1026   *Nevada City,* 1941 (Republic) (-23 scene)

1121   *Jesse James at Bay,* 1941 (Republic) (-20 scene/-44 publicity, Roy, three of cast)

1122   *Red River Valley,* 1941 (Republic) (-22A publicity, Roy, Trigger/ -31 scene)

1123   *Man from Cheyenne,* 1942 (Republic) (-29 publicity, Roy, Gale Storm)

1124   *South of Santa Fe,* 1942 (Republic) (-46 scene)

1125   *Sunset on the Desert,* 1942 (Republic) (-49 publicity, Roy, Gabby, leading lady)

1126   *Romance on the Range,* 1942 (Republic) (-34 scene)

1127   *Sons of the Pioneers,* 1942 (Republic) (-46 scene)

1128   *Sunset Serenade,* 1942 (Republic) (-36 scene)

1129   *Heart of the Golden West,* 1942 (Republic) (-36 scene)

1129-38-INF   Publicity

1193   *Brazil*

1204   *King of the Cowboys,* 1943 (Republic) (-52 scene)

1221   *Ridin' Down the Canyon,* 1942 (Republic) (-15 scene/-37 publicity, Roy, Lorna Gray)

1222   *Idaho,* 1943 (Republic) (-77 scene)

1223   *Song of Texas,* 1943 (Republic)

1224   *Silver Spurs,* 1943 (Republic) (-44 scene)

1226   *Man from Music Mountain (Texas Legionaire),* 1943 (Republic) (-60 scene)

1227   *Hands Across the Border,* 1944 (Republic) (-111 scene/-114 publicity, Roy, leading lady)

1247   *Lake Placid Serenade,* 1944 (Republic)

1321   *The Cowboy and the Señorita,* 1944 (Republic) (-64 scene)

1322   *Yellow Rose of Texas,* 1944 (Republic) (-24 publicity, Roy and Dale/-57 scene)

1323   *Song of Nevada,* 1944 (Republic) (-55 publicity) (also seen as: RR-508)

1324   *Bells of Rosarita,* 1945 (Republic) (-48 scene/-66 publicity, six cowboys/-PA 125 publicity, Dale)

1325   *San Fernando Valley,* 1944 (Republic) (-62 publicity, Roy, Dale)

1326   *Lights of Old Santa Fe,* 1944 (Republic) (-95 publicity, Roy, Dale)

1327   *Don't Fence Me In,* 1945 (Republic) (-31 scene/-PA-90 same as 1328-PA-90)

1328   *Man from Oklahoma,* 1945 (Republic) (-46 scene/-PA-90 publicity, Roy and Dale)

1329   *Utah,* 1945 (Republic)

1421   *Sunset in El Dorado,* 1945 (Republic) (-26 scene)

1422   *Song of Arizona,* 1946 (Republic) (-84 publicity, Roy, Sons of the Pioneers)

1425   *Along the Navajo Trail,* 1945 (Republic) (-28 scene/-PA-121 publicity, Roy, Dale)

1427   *My Pal Trigger,* 1946 (Republic) (-19 scene/-74 publicity)

1428   *Rainbow Over Texas,* 1946 (Republic) (-61 scene)

1429   *Under Nevada Skies,* 1946 (Republic) (-28 scene)

1491   *Hit Parade of 1947* (-9, Roy)

1520   *Home in Oklahoma,* 1946 (Republic) (-11 scene/-62 publicity)

1523   *Roll On Texas Moon,* 1946 (Republic) (-17 scene)

1524   *Heldorado,* 1946 (Republic) (-85 publicity close-up)

1525   *Bells of San Angelo,* (Republic) (-74 scene)

1526   *Apache Rose,* 1947 (Republic) (-31 scene)

1527   *On the Old Spanish Trail,* 1947 (Republic) (-72 publicity, main four of the cast)

1528   *Gay Ranchero,* 1948 (Republic) (P-1528-44 publicity/-47 scene /-53 publicity, Roy, Jane Frazee)

Roy, on one of the touring Triggers. Used for general publicity, 1944.

1529   *Springtime in the Sierras*, 1947 (Republic) (-64 publicity, Roy, Jane)

1587   *Out California Way*, 1946 (Republic)

1621   *Under California Stars*, 1948 (Republic) (-46 publicity, Roy, Jane)

1623   *Eyes of Texas*, 1948 (Republic) (-16 publicity, Roy, leading lady)

1624   *Night Time in Nevada*, 1948 (Republic) (-1 scene)

1625   *Grand Canyon Trail*, 1948 (Republic) (-54 publicity, Roy, Jane)

1626   *Far Frontier*, 1948 (Republic) (-35 publicity, Roy, leading lady)

1627   *Susanna Pass*, 1949 (Republic) (-7 scene/-44 publicity, Roy and Dale)

1628   *Down Dakota Way*, 1949 (Republic) (-11 scene)

1629   *Bells of Coronado*, 1950 (Republic (-40 scene/-51 publicity)

1830   *Golden Stallion*, 1949 (Republic) (-34 scene/-70 publicity, Roy, Dale)

1831   *Twilight in the Sierras*, 1950 (Republic) (-28 scene/-48 publicity, Roy and Dale)

1832   *Sunset in the West*, 1950 (Republic) (-39 publicity, Roy, leading lady)

1834   *Trigger, Jr.*, 1950 (Republic) (-43 publicity)

1835   *Trail of Robin Hood*, 1950 (Republic) (-48 publicity, Roy, leading lady)

1836   *North of the Great Divide*, 1950 (Republic) (-39 publicity)

1837   *Heart of the Rockies*, 1951 (Republic) (-45 publicity, Roy, leading lady)

1838   *Spoilers of the Plains*, 1951 (Republic) (-34 scene/-47 publicity, Roy, leading lady)

1839   *In Old Amarillo*, 1951 (Republic) (-34 scene/-42 publicity, Roy, leading lady)

This photo is from a session that produced the one used for the cover of *Roy Rogers Comics* #20, August 1949.

1840   *South of Caliente*, 1951 (Republic) (-29 scene/-52 publicity)

1841   *Pals of the Golden West*, 1951 (Republic) (-27 scene)

10104   *Son of Paleface* (-2/106 scene/-179 publicity, Roy, Jane Russell)

JJR 516   *Alias Jesse James*

MTS   *Mackintosh & TJ*

Roy grabbing a few winks between shows. Illinois State Fair, Springfield, 1946.

IRR Numbers

These are informal and formal shots taken mostly at the Rogers home and used for publicity. Most appeared in magazines and comics. There are close to 600 of these.

IRR-130/IRR-300: Dusty in master bedroom
IRR-312: Dale in robe at home, reading mail
IRR-427: publicity, Roy, Dale, Trigger
IRR-?: Roy, Dale, next to tree.
IRR-578/ORR-202: Only one ORR# seen

RR Numbers

Publicity photos include those taken on tour. There appear to be more than 1,115 of these.

RR 1: First Republic publicity shot
RR-In-1/RR-INF-2: Roy, Cheryl on sofa
RR-OH/RR-M-4: Roy, Dale at event

RR-XX4: 1942 tour. On lawn across from nation's capitol
RR 5H/RR 9H: Black-hatted Roy, publicity
RR-INF-18/RR-19: Personal appearance
RR-INF-20: Roy, Cheryl, in home
RR-INF-41/RR INF-46: At home publicity, Arline, Cheryl, Roy
RR INF-51: At home publicity shot, Roy, Cheryl
No # Bow and arrow, at home
No # Mowing yard, at home
No # Pigeon pen, at home
RR-INF-65: Roy with gun at home
RR-81/RR-94/RR-101/RR114: Personal appearance
RR-115: Personal appearance
RR-122: Publicity
RR-134/RR-165/RR-180/RR-198: Publicity shot, Trigger, Roy
RR-209: Publicity
RR-218/RR-231/RR-232/RR-244: Publicity
RR-249: Publicity, late 1940s

A fan had this still that was autographed by Roy probably sometime after 1950, as first and last names are joined.

RR-255/RR-262: publicity

RR-390/RR-501/RR-502/RR-503/RR-508: Publicity

RR 1323-55/RR-512/RR-514/RR 1115-2: Family pose

RR-G-2: I have seen one of these

RR-W1: c. 1941, Wheatie cereal endorsement

RR W-85: Wedding pictures (used in magazines)

Dale Evans

Film Stills (Republic)

1089 *Here Comes Elmer*/ 1135 *West Side Kid*/ 1139 *In Old Oklahoma*/ 1178 *Swing Your Partner*/ 1182 *Hoosier Holiday*/ 1236 *Casanova in Burlesque*/ 1461 *Hitch Hike to Happiness*/ 1568 *The Trespasser*/ 1641 *Slippy McGee*

Publicity Stills, Etc.

DE-1, DE-2x, DE-14, DE-140, DE-195, DE-201 (*Song of Arizona*), DE-205, DE-214, DE-229, DE-233 through 234, DE-501 through 503, 1322-9 PA (*Yellow Rose of Texas*), 1422-110 PA (*Song of Arizona*), 1425-P3 (*Under Nevada Skies*)

Miscellaneous

P-1835-8: Informal, Roy and Rocky Lane on set of *Trail of Robin Hood*
No number, Dale and Lou Costello

Chapter 9

ROY ROGERS
AND DALE EVANS
IN COMMERCIAL ART

Roy Rogers has had more impact on merchandising and marketing, not only in America, but around the world, than any other American Hollywood Western star. In merchandising and advertising, it was often more practical to use an image of Roy in the commercial art form, as opposed to a photograph, and sometimes this was the only possibility. In this art form, Roy has appeared many thousands of times, taking in most every type media, and scores of artists were instrumental in bringing this about. This chapter concerns itself with discussing many of the hundreds of different likenesses found of Rogers, his wife Dale, and his horse and dog, "Rogers and Co." so to speak, and with identifying many of the artists whose work has been highly visible and served to promote Roy as the King of the Cowboys. Roy Rogers was introduced to many youngsters in this form, and the form was popular enough to support product merchandising for nearly fifty years, a comic book run of nearly twenty years, plus scattered additional issues, and a comic strip with a run of twelve years, in addition to other media.

No attempt is made to violate the rights of any individuals, such as artists or any company through the use of illustrations in this chapter. The copyrights, and any other rights that exist, belong to their respective holders, and are shown where known. My research has indicated that most of the artwork of the Roy Rogers (and Dale Evans, Trigger, Bullet, etc.) likeness, has been done on a "for hire" basis and has not been copy-righted by the artist, but rather, in many instances, has been copyrighted by one of several Roy Rogers companies. The present status of the copyright must be researched through the Copyright Office in Washington, D.C., as I have done, for a complete knowledge of the status. My research has further indicated that many copyrights on items containing or displaying this artwork have not been renewed after the expiration of the original registration.

Information presented on the character in all mediums of art includes comic strips, comic books, film posters and related materials, merchandising, and sponsor's products and associated advertising. Information on the artists is also shown where it was attainable. Roy went through a lot of different appearances at the mercy of the numerous artists that drew him in the comics through nearly two decades. The "bullpen" effect is seen from the beginning, with several artists contributing enough that the Rogers appearance changes back and forth, panel to panel, in the 13 Four-Color issues. Everyone seems to have their favorite Roy. Longtime collector Colin Jellicoe of England has shared with me that he likes the Micale Rogers. Bill Black, friend and comics publisher who produced the recent *Roy Rogers Western Classics* comics, believes that John Buscema was the cream of the crop and has patterned some of his own original Rogers likenesses after Buscema's. A longtime collector in Texas prefers Peter Alvarado's Rogers over most. I personally prefer the likenesses created by a number of artists including Alvarado, Mike Arens, Andrew Bensen, Randy Steffen, and Toni Sgroi.

The Artists

Many of these artists will have their Roy Rogers and Dell Western comic work documented for the first time with this text, while in the case of others, this will be the most extensive amount of information about them to be published. This work will shed light on a long overlooked area, and I hope that those who can either support or take issue with the findings presented here will do so. On a number of these artists, there simply was no published information to be found.

Kellog Adams. Artist/writer/editor. Schooling: Art Center School, Los Angeles. Adventure Comics: *3-D Comics* (Cheerios cereal), The Lone Ranger, Bozo, Kite Fun, et al. Work in comic books: Western Printing and Lithographing Co.: 1952–1957. Writer/illustrator: Donald Duck, Bugs Bunny, Mickey Mouse, Mary Jane, Porky Pig, Daffy Duck, Tweety and Sylvester. Writer/editor: Lassie, Red Ryder, Rin Tin Tin, Roy Rogers, the Lone Ranger, Gene Autry, and others.[1] I have discovered his name, and also what appear to be his initials and fragmented pieces of his name, buried in some artwork in the *Western Roundup* series. It is hoped that, in the future, his accounting might be made available, should such exist. He could be responsible for a number of the Roy Rogers stories outside the works of Gaylord DuBois, as well as the *Western Roundup* titles. I regret that his specific titles cannot be shown at this time.

Stookie Allen. Pulps. Credits: Dell Publishing, 1929, "Bug Movies" in *The Funnies*. Western Printing and Lithographing Co. (1930s): fillers. Eastern Color (late 1940s): fillers. National (DC Comics, late 1940s): filler, etc. Allen drew Dale Evans for the cover of her DC series issue #3, January-February, 1949. He also drew filler work for her DC series.

Peter Alvarado. Syndicated work: Alvarado drew the Roy Rogers comic strip for King Features Syndicate, daily and Sunday, for 2½ years, 1949–1952, working closely with fellow artist John Ushler. He drew the Gene Autry daily strip in its first two months (a short-lived strip). Drew Mr. Magoo, 1964–1966. Spare time: fine arts painter. Comic book work: Jacquet Shop, 1939–1940. Worth Co.: Shock Gibson, 1939–1940. Novelty Co.: Blue Bolt, Dick Cole, 1940. Western Printing and Lithograph Co.: drew practically all of Western's characters, including Roy Rogers, Gene Autry, Red Ryder, Annie Oakley, and the Range Rider. Drew various characters, series features, and contributed to much filler material in the *Western Roundup* comics, from 1948 to the 1950s. Little Hiawatha, Barney Bear, all Walt Disney, MGM and Hanna-Barbera characters. He drew one of the better likenesses of Roy, as can be witnessed in the Big Golden Book *Roy Rogers, King of the Cowboys.* Much of his work in the Rogers comics series I have discovered the hard way, through examination of artwork under heavy magnification, discovering "buried" signings and making comparisons with credited work for the Western company, including Whitman products. My conclusion is that Alvardo contributed heavily not only to the Dell/Western product but also to likenesses of Roy and Dale used in advertising, possibly in sponsors' products themselves, and in Roy Rogers merchandise. I have discovered evidence of his work in the Rogers film posters. I have also discovered what appears to be his work prior to his association with Western in and on the covers of comics by National Periodicals such as the Hopalong Cassidy series. I believe, by virtue of having discovered signings of art used for covers of the Dell series, that there was some contribution in this area. The covers of *Roy Rogers Comics* that mix photos of Roy with artwork backgrounds appear to be Alvarado's work. He employed a lot of blacks and dark colors, and one of the finest examples can be found in an entire comic, *Ernest Haycox's Western Marshal*, February 1954, in which his characters are present in a story by primary artist Raymond Kinstler. See also Gene Autry's "Nickel Plated Pay-off," *Western Roundup* #1, and the Rex Allen story in *Western Roundup* #7. Peter Alvarado produced more varied likenesses of Roy throughout many years than any other artist. He always emphasized the squinting facial appearance and could render

As Alvarado's and Ushler's likenesses of Roy filled the daily newspaper comic strips, Alvarado's Roy took the close-ups on December 30, 1949. Copyright expired.

some of the more realistic Rogers images, but they did not always resemble one another. His Roy was always the right size and weight, and one of the characteristics of his work was the action of the figures, usually emphasized with motion lines. His Roy, along with John Uslher's, dominated the early comic strips. Peter Alvarado used both his scrawled first name, more often his scrawled last name, and nearly always a buried "PA" in various sizes.

Al Andersen. Artist. Credits: painting, cover of Dale Evans Whitman novel, *Danger in Crooked Canyon*, Whitman #1506, 1958. Painted a very attractive Dale and very good likeness of her as well. Other painted covers for Whitman: *Bat Masterson*, 1960, signed work.

Michael Arens. Artist. Credits: Western Printing and Lithographing Co., 1950s. Drew most of Western's characters in their regular issues and in the *Western Roundup* title. Drew Roy and Dale in King Features Syndicate's "Al McKimson's Roy Rogers" comic strip, 1950s, and some of his finest work can be seen in the Sunday printings. Other credits: 1954 Roy Rogers' Dodge giveaway comic. Roy Rogers Whitman book *Roy Rogers and the Brasada Bandits*, 1953. Produced one of the best likenesses of Roy found in the history. Mike Arens' Rogers was probably the most consistent realistic likeness of Roy produced for the comics. He captured the physical proportions and the personality that were very true to the Roy seen in film and in other mediums. In the Roy Rogers newspaper strip, Arens was doing anonymous work, ghosting for "Al" McKimson at first; later, in the 1950s, he was

able to sign this work. Arens signed his work "MA," with the letters joined, but these initials can only rarely be seen by the naked eye. I have discovered many of his signings. His stories often included a pipe smoker, and he favored portly sheriffs and other heavy-set and often bearded characters. He was contributing to the Trigger stories in Roy's comics in 1957 and 1958. His last Rogers work appears to be a Trigger feature in #126, June 1958. He produced numerous Dale Evans stories. What appear to be his buried signings have been discovered by this writer as early as issue #25, January 1950.

Stephen Bennett. Bennett rendered fine likenesses of Roy, Dale, and Gabby for the prestigious Victorian Gallery series of English trading cards (see Chapter 12).

Andrew Bensen. Bensen drew Roy for the 1950 Whitman novel *Roy Rogers and the Ghost of Mystery Rancho* and drew Gene Autry for the 1950 Whitman novel *Gene Autry and the Golden Ladder Gang*. It is believed that he contributed to the drawing of Roy in the comics series from issue #24 through #108. If not, his likeness of Roy had certainly influenced the work of other artists, as comparative analysis suggests his work in this area. Andrew Bensen's Roy was proportionally correct, and he could get very close to Arens' face for Rogers, producing very realistic images, but not consistently. On occasion, the cowboy would look too hardened.

Bill Black. When AC Comics began reprinting the Roy Rogers comic stories from the Dell series, Black's wife Rebecca re-inked them. Then when his company produced the first "giveaway" to come along with original

Arens gave us numerous Roys in the *Western Roundup* series, as seen here in the title page to "Double for Murder," issue #7. Copyright 1954, Western Printing and Lithographing Co. Copyright expired.

art since 1954, the "Hardee's Giveaway," he drew Roy for the cover, the coloring page centerfold, and the puzzle page. He is a great admirer of Buscema's work in the Rogers series during the mid–1950s, and his Roy definitely takes on the Buscema likeness.

Frank Bolle. Widely published drawing for adventure stories, including Dr. Solar. Known for Tim Holt comic book series work. Drew Roy on occasion, i.e. *Sunday Pix*, April 7, 1957. Signed work "FWB."

Ray Burnley. Burnley has been credited by other researchers as a possible artist of Dale Evans in her DC series.

John Buscema. Born in 1927, this New York City native began comic work in 1948 with Marvel/Timely/Atlas. He did a variety of love, crime, and western strips, working for Orbit along the way, until 1955, when he went to Charlton for a very short time. Then it was on to Western Printing and Lithographing Co. There he got heavily involved with the Roy Rogers series, providing the character with a whole new facelift in a distinctive uncluttered setting out West that would last through issue #108. Buscema was particularly adept at drawing the movie characters for comics. The Trigger stories in Roy's comics featuring Trigger's horse-buddy Pinto Jack (9 issues, 1956) appear to show contributions from Buscema, along with Randy Steffen. He left the Dell characters about 1958, going back to Marvel in 1966 and getting involved in drawing superheroes like Capt. Marvel. But when Buscema entered the Rogers series, he brought with him a streamlined King of the Cowboys, creating for Roy in the comic books a more contemporary though totally unrealistic image. The character would remain consistent in likeness as long as Buscema was holding the reins, as would the settings and supporting cast. It is believed that the sparse landscapes and background work during the Buscema period were produced by his brother Sal and that Sal was contributing to the stories, especially backgrounds, long before John entered the picture. I have discovered what appear to be his signings and his style much earlier. The entire John Buscema work in Roy's series appears to be a house-cleaning effort for the Rogers comics, and in spite of gross overstatements in the artwork itself, this effort was badly needed just for the sake of presenting one

Roy Rogers in this media form, more or less, eliminating a practice that had gone on far too long. Buscema's Roy Rogers was too tall in comparison with the real-life subject and was muscular, broad-shouldered, and in general a perfect physical specimen. He walked, even ran, in an unnatural, straight-as-an-arrow posture. He was a perfect model for a Roy Rogers statue or cardboard stand-up display. He carried to extremes Roy's appearance in the television series and on the comic book covers, the two main areas in which Roy was seen at this time. This character looked in action the same way the real-life subject did in poses for the camera, except for his attire. On television, Roy was usually seen in plaids, but on the comic's covers, he was shown in the flashy attire of personal appearances. Buscema used neither. He outfitted Roy in immaculate, perfectly tailored solid colored shirts and trousers that hinted at a lot of starch. What few wrinkles were used in the obviously skin-tight attire almost seem part of the design. This Roy, along with all the supporting characters, especially the females and on occasion even the villains, put one in mind immediately of images found in romance comics. Beauty for the girls, rugged, wholesome handsomeness for the men. And nothing rustled Buscema's Roy away from that appearance. Not wind, not rain, not even a blizzard. His shirts seem to be the pull-over type, showing neither snaps or buttons and closely resembling sports shirts found in the mid–1950s. There is only a hint of yoke or Western style. The pants would appear much the same except for the legs tucked into the boots, which, interestingly enough, were devoid of the double-eagle or thunderbird designs common to the real Rogers appearance. Occasionally some fringe was used, but there would be no contrast with shirt designs regardless. A solid-color neckerchief was used throughout the Buscema issues, usually yellow to match the ever-present gloves. Wide-open spaciousness, some rocks and boulders that even looked clean, and a lot of sky. Buscema didn't detail the tooled Western-designed saddle and tack for Trigger, another trademark associated with the real Roy Rogers. John Buscema signed his work with a very tiny "JB" that can be difficult to find.

Richard Case. Case was producing work

John Buscema drew a very handsome Roy and "Trigger," but often got carried away with his subject's size, as evidenced here, where the head is almost dwarfed in panel three. Buscema's entire name is written on Roy, astride "Trigger," in panel five, seen under 17 power magnification. Copyright 1954 by Roy Rogers Enterprises, Inc.

for Whitman in the 1950s, and it is believed that he may be responsible for some contribution to the Rogers comics. His work can be seen in books such as *Gene Autry Makes a New Friend*, a Whitman Tell-A-Tale Book, 1952.

Mel Crawford. Crawford drew Roy and Dale for Simon and Schuster from 1953 to 1956, producing the likenesses that would be seen in numerous Little Golden Books such as *Roy Rogers and the New Cowboy* (1953), and *Dale Evans and the Lost Gold Mine*, (1954). All of the work that I have been able to document thus far appears to be tailored for this outlet, drawn for children with a slight cartoon effect.

Roland Davies. Drew Roy for original stories in British comics annuals such as *Roy Rogers Adventures*. Used very rough lines, moreso than even John Ushler.

Wynne Davis. Produced excellent likenesses of Roy, based upon publicity photos, for covers of Australian Roy Rogers comics, 1950s. Also did the background artwork for these covers in the Peter Alvarado style.[2]

DeSoto. Produced paintings of Trigger for *Roy Rogers' Trigger* comics, and some of his work is clearly signed (see Chapter 7).

E. Joseph Dreany. Produced painted likenesses of Roy for dustcover of Whitman Book *Roy Rogers and the Ghost of Mystery Rancho* (1950) and *Roy Rogers and the Trail of the Zeroes* (1954). Drew Dale in *Dale Evans and the Coyote* (1956), a Little Golden Book. His Dale likeness was fine, but he did not capture the true likeness of Roy, albeit he produced great Western character art.

Nat Edson. Nat Edson drew Tim Tyler for a period of time before moving to Western Printing and Lithographing Co., where he worked on a number of titles. He contributed a considerable output to the Rogers series, beginning most noticeably when he drew Roy from the end of the Buscema period to the end of the series. His style can on occasion resemble that of Arens. Nat Edson's Roy was very clean cut, as much so as Buscema's, and he delivered up Roy in correct proportions. He was often dressed more nattily, and Edson did especially well with the face. All the age that had been applied by numerous artists in recent history had been removed. There is also some resemblance to Alvarado's Roy on occasion. Nat Edson

would sometimes write his last name but so small that a magnifying glass must be used to discover it. It can be very difficult to locate, but I have discovered several. His style is mostly recognizable in the youthful appearance of his subjects, especially in the eyes.

Bill Ely. Ely has been credited by other researchers as a possible artist for Dale in her DC Series. His work also appears in filler for her comics in this series. Ely contributed to the Dell Westerns, and his work can be seen signed in feature stories of *Red Ryder Comics*. An example is *The Kiyotee Kids* (original copyright 1949 by Stephen Slesinger, Inc.) in issue #73, August 1949.

Jack Farr. Farr has been credited with possibly having drawn Dale for her DC series.

Nicholas S. Firfires. Firfires, son-in-law of the legendary Western star Buck Jones, drew for the Trigger comics and drew Dale for her Dell comics. He drew most of Dell Western's characters in their individual series and produced a heavy amount of volume for the *Western Roundup* title. His work can be seen in quantity as well in the contents and painted covers of Dell Western's *Zane Grey's Western Magazine*. 1940s–1950s, where his work is signed. Firfires produced painted covers for Dell Western comic books, especially those of Buck Jones, and some of these are signed. Although he drew Dale and Trigger, I have not been able to determine any contribution to a Roy likeness.

Reg Forster. Forster drew Roy for original stories in the British-published *Big Golden Book* and contributed to the Roy likenesses in the comic stories found in the British *Wonder Comics* of the 1950s. His Roy appears to have been drawn for children.

Olindo Giacomini. Along with Robert Myers, Giacomini provided illustrations for such Whitman hardback novels as *Timber Trail Riders—The Long Trail North* (a Mike Casey story). It is believed that one of the pair of artists, or both working together, are responsible for artwork in Dell's *Western Roundup* comics as well as numerous stories in various titles of Dell's Western comics. It is felt that some of their work appears in "The Shadow of Totem Rock," the Rogers outing in *Western Roundup* #19. The art-

Nat Edson introduced a new Roy likeness that was far removed from the Buscema work and captured a more realistic appearance in his subject's physical stature, while maintaining a fair one so far as the facial characteristics went. Copyright 1957 by Roy Rogers Frontiers, Inc.

work is filled with wild scribblings, especially with landscape, smoke, clouds, wind, or dust being kicked up by animals.

Gus Denis Gifford. Gifford drew Roy for *The Sheriff Comics* in Great Britain, 1950s. His likenesses could approach very close to the American ones produced by Harry Parks.[3]

Al Gleicher. Gleicher drew a fine mid-fifties Roy for Whitman in *Roy Rogers and the Trail of the Zeroes*, a likeness that was in many ways better than those produced by several of the artists working on the comic book stories full-time. His work at times, however, resembles some of Peter Alvarado's. It is believed that he contributed to some of the Rogers stories in the comics, especially the *Western Roundup* comics where he drew Rex Allen, among others. There is the possibility that he might have drawn some of the Rogers likenesses that were scattered throughout the comics in ad spots, subscription pages, etc. His art for Whitman was later used by Roy Rogers Enterprises in merchandise such as neck-scarfs in 1986.

Morris Gollub. Gollub produced painted covers for Dell comics, *Roy Rogers' Trigger* among these, and it is likely that he was responsible for the artwork in the stories of that series, in and around the Randy Steffen work.

Tillman Goodan. Goodan drew for Western for a number of years and is recognized for his covers and Gene Autry likenesses in Autry's early comics. He supplied many Western scene drawings for *Western Roundup* comics that featured Roy and Dale stories. It has been reported that it was Goodan who drew the Western designs that were hand-tooled into one of Roy's famous silver and jewel inlaid leather saddles and into some of his accessories. Tillman's wife drew backgrounds and scenery in the stories he drew for Western.[4] It was his drawings that graced the now famous Ranch Brand Dinnerware of the 1940s. There is a slight possibility that he contributed to some of the artwork in the early issues of the Rogers series, as there are a few likenesses, both human and equine, that take on his style.

Leon Gregori. Gregori painted the fine likeness of Roy and Dale and horses for the inside covers of the book club edition of Elise Miller Davis' 1955 book *The Answer Is God*.

Hap Hadley. Hadley produced the huge Roy Rogers likeness for the billboards during the 1943 Republic Productions Roy Rogers publicity campaign. These were reproduced on various publications such as 1940s rodeo magazines.

Mark G. Heike. Associate editor for AC Comics, he drew Roy for the story portion of the Hardee's give-away Roy Rogers comic. The likeness was far removed from any of the 1940s–1960s Roys in the comics, and he favored a much larger-than-life likeness, no doubt influenced somewhat by John Buscema's and Bill Black's work. This Roy was inked-in with a color that ran more toward brown than flesh color.

Hans Helweg. It is difficult to judge his work, as the one example is a combined effort with another artist, Crawford, in *Roy Rogers and the New Cowboy* (1953) by Simon and Schuster.

Erwin L. Hess. Hess drew Roy for Whitman in the 1940s in *Gopher Creek Gunman* and then in the Four-Color *Roy Rogers Comics* (see Chapter 6). Hess is believed to have contributed to comics artwork for a number of years. He delivered the physical proportions correctly, perhaps a little on the short side, but emphasized the young, naive looks of the real subject. His Roy could never be mistaken for the bad guy.

John Higgs. Higgs drew for Whitman in *Trigger to the Rescue* as fine a likeness of Trigger as that done by any of the artists.

Walt Howarth. Howarth drew Roy for covers and contents of British Roy Rogers comic stories in the numerous annuals and for the Roy Rogers stories in some 1950s British *Wonder Comics*. It is the opinion of this researcher that he was their finest Roy Rogers artist, capturing an incredible realistic likeness of Roy and producing some exceptionally fine action paintings of Roy on Trigger. It is obvious in his work that he was not merely drawing for the juvenile audience.

John Jameson. Jameson drew Roy for original stories in British published *Big Golden Books*.

Mel Keefer. Keefer has been credited with drawing Dale for her Dell Comics series in 1954, but I have yet to find his work.[5]

Spencer Kimball. Kimball painted likenesses of Roy, Dale, and their attire in signed prints of cut-out dolls art. He came from Santa Fe, New Mexico. A framed piece seen in a collectibles show in New York in 1992 shows Roy in undershorts and Dale in slip and bra, surrounded by different pieces of their famous trademark attire. Good likenesses of each, c. 1950s.

Everett R. Kinstler. Kinstler is a long-time comic book artist whose work has been highly praised. Although his comic work never included Roy and Dale, so far as I have been able to document, Kinstler did a painting of them which is now hanging in the National Cowboy Hall of Fame in Oklahoma City.

J. M. LaGrotta. LaGrotta painted and drew one of the finest likenesses of Roy and Trigger to appear in publishing history. This artist's work can be seen in *Roy Rogers at the Lane Ranch*, the 1950 Whitman Tell-A-Tale Book. He even used the original Trigger in his work. It is possibly his work that appears in the painting on the cover of the Whitman *King of the Cowboys* Big Golden Book, and there are some similarities with a few paintings used on the covers of Simon and Schuster Little Golden Records. His name appears in artwork and Roy's likenesses on movie posters, such as for the film *In Old Amarillo*. There is a possibility of some contribution from him, however slight, in Roy's comics during the Edson period and in Roy's stories in the *Western Roundup* title.

August Lenox. This noted Western artist, who manages to capture much realism in his work, made a heavy contribution to the filler material in the *Western Roundup* series. He also drew Bullet and Trigger, plus other characters in the 1953 Whitman Cozy Corner Book, *Roy Rogers' Bullet and Trigger—Wild Horse Rodeo*. It is believed that his signing is seen in some characters' *Western Roundup* stories, especially in those done by Firfires.

Al Lewin. Lewin drew Gene Autry for Big Little Book, in 1939, written by Gaylord DuBois. It is believed that he contributed in a limited amount to *Roy Rogers Comics* between issues #24 and #73.

Henry Luhrs. Luhrs drew Dale for Whitman novel *Danger in Crooked Canyon*. He possibly drew Dale in the Dell series, and it is believed his work can be found in titles of *Jace Pearson's Tales of the Texas Rangers* and *The Rifleman*.

James Nivison McArdle. McArdle attended Fordham University and the Academy of Design. He was an illustrator for *Collier's*, Fairchild Publications, and *Liberty* magazines. Most of the artwork in Dale's early comics, the DC series, is by McArdle, both in the stories and covers. He has received credit in Ron Goulart's book *American Comics*, and *Who's Who of American Comics* (1974). He is another artist about whom little has been offered. (It is possible that DC Comics had a policy that artwork go unsigned, but Alex Toth's work in Dale's comics was signed.) McArdle's signings can be found under magnification. He draws an attractive cowgirl, but does not really capture Dale's likeness, as little attempt was made by artists and writers of her DC stories to do so. After leaving DC, McArdle worked on the syndicated Davy Crockett, 1955–1959.

Al McKimson/The McKimson Bros.: Chuck, Tom. The McKimson brothers were art directors at Western, 1940s–1970s. "Al" was the pen name for both Chuck and Tom, and there was a third brother, Robert, an animator. The King Features Syndicate's Roy Rogers newspaper strip (1949–1961) carried the Al McKimson name beginning Sunday, December 5, 1950, for the Sunday editions, and January 1, 1952, on the dailies. Other artists such as Peter Alvarado, John Ushler, and Michael Arens were involved in drawing the strip, but "Al McKimson" was used in most instances. This could apply as well to the comic book stories, as part of the work appears to be fairly consistent, while other likenesses crop up, sometimes in the same story. In one story of McKimson's, there are three different artists' pens applied to Roy. "Al" McKimson had several ways of signing. One was using his initials in the tiniest print, mixed into the artwork, and barely large enough to find with the magnifying glass. Signings of "AM" and "TM" are quite common, usually in a written style. (Micale's was practically always printed, and the two are really easy to distinguish.) The McKimsons would use scrawled signatures, making them appear somewhat blotched and hiding them in, or more to the point, disguising them as grass or weeds. McKimson signings were often disguised, as in *Mustang Mountain*, issue #27, March 1950. Examine the lower right-hand corner of the last panel for "Al M." Al McKimson did some ghosting as well in some of Fred Harman's Red Ryder stories. McKimson work appears signed in a one-page comic story in *Wyatt Earp* #921 (1958). It is believed that the McKimson name appears on the likeness of Roy on the movie poster for *Idaho*, as well as others. The work that I attribute to "Al" McKimson resembles that of Arens somewhat; it is proportionately correct and close in facial likeness. The essential difference was the characteristic face that served to identify his work. Thomas McKimson directed the production of the Whitman children's books, including the activity books. He drew "Bugs Bunny" for the Dell Comics, 1945–1949, and for Little Golden Books.

Hiram Julian Mankin, III. Mankin attended Chouinard Art Institute in L.A., then did syndicated work with Zack Mosley on "Smilin' Jack." From there, he assisted Jerry Siegel with "Superman" in the comics in 1941. Then he worked with George McManus in "Bringing Up Father" in 1942. He assisted Don Heilman on "American Adventure" in 1949 and that same year worked with Buford Tune on "Dottie Dripple." Mankin worked on "Bugs Bunny" for the newspaper strip, 1950–1951. He illustrated the Dell comic "I Met a Handsome Cowboy." Then he contributed to the Roy Rogers syndicated newspaper strip, 1953–1958, as a principal artist. He was an artist who did a very good job of capturing the likeness of Roy and generally kept the cowboy with a worried look on his face in order to maintain the "squinty eyes" characteristic. His work can be seen in the Whitman novel *King of the Cowboys*. It is believed that he contributed to the comics stories as early as April 1951, with a contribution to about December 1953. He drew many Roy and Dale stories including "Little Dog Lost" in *Queen of the West—Dale Evans* issue #3. He also contributed to many stories with another principal artist. Mankin drew some one-page comic stories for Rex Allen Comics (issue #27, December-February 1958). Mankin did a considerable amount of work in the *Western Roundup* series, drawing, besides Roy in issue #1, other characters such as Wild Bill Elliott. He drew a number of the Trigger, and Trigger and Bullet stories for *Western Roundup*.

The Bullet character appears to be his in almost all of the stories. He is believed to be the creator of the Roy likeness on the poster for the film *Heart of the Rockies*. Mankin signed almost all of his work with everything from his full name, including the "III," to his nickname "Hi," which is much more commonly found. From Western Co. work, he went into animation layout and design and was working for Hanna-Barbera in 1964.[6]

Russell Manning. Manning was born in Van Nuys, California, and attended L.A. County Art Institute and New York School of Visual Arts. Jesse Marsh got him on at Dell in 1953, and he worked on the entire Dell line. He drew Dale in her comic and rendered the most attractive likeness of the cowgirl. He drew characters that are exceptionally handsome compared to those of most other artists. His Rogers likeness is particularly handsome as well. Manning found a way to sign almost all of his output by printing his name, his initials, or his wife Dodie's name (as "Doe") or her initials, often in signs on buildings. He spent more than fifteen years at Western. In 1965 Manning replaced Jessie Marsh in drawing Tarzan. He made a heavy contribution to Dell's "Wyatt Earp" title and to the "Rex Allen," "Rawhide," and "Gene Autry" characters. Some of his signed work shows "Russ." He did work in "Korak" and "Tarzan" stories. His Roy often reflects the image of Clint Walker or a movie cowboy much larger in physical size than Roy, muscular, and with the high cheekbones present.

John Mariani. Mariani was a Western illustrator who did heavy work for *The Western Horseman* beginning in 1944. He is believed at this time to have contributed in a small way to Roy stories beginning in 1949, when artist Micale was joined by a host of others. Marinari's Roy wore a crumpled hat over too fat a face. There is much signed work for *The Western Horseman* for comparison.

Jesse Marsh. Marsh drew Tarzan for Dell from 1947 until 1965. His work was much admired by Alex Toth and Russ Manning. His Roy Rogers work can be seen in the early Four-Color series. He lived in the L.A. area and worked for Disney from 1939 to 1948. Marsh began drawing for comic books in 1946, making his debut in Gene Autry's

Dale Evans from the pens of Jesse Marsh, found in her Dell Comics series, issue #5. Copyright expired.

series. He did a large volume of work for Dell and Whitman in Southern California; these Western titles covered Gene Autry, Roy Rogers, Rex Allen, and Annie Oakley. He excelled in drawing outdoor terrain and settings and drawing his subject involved in everyday tasks. Practically all of the *Western Roundup* comics contain his work, and he contributed to most of the characters' stories. His characters often appeared well into a story being drawn by other artists. Jesse Marsh produced very muscular cowboys with very hard features who were sometimes ape-like in appearance. Although this resulted in great villains, his Roy would not have been identifiable at all, had the name not been printed. Aside from the distinguishable eyes of his subjects, often the lush jungle-type terrain is the first clue to his work.

Albert Micale. Micale was also known as "Al Mack." He attended Pratt Institute and then illustrated for Street and Smith, Popular Pulps, and various Western magazines and books. He was a Western Co. artist. Little if anything has been written in any detail on Micale. This subject is much deserving of a study. Micale drew Roy for the *Roy Rogers Comics*, beginning with the Four-Colors, and for ten years thereafter, 1944–1954. His Rogers was the introduction to Roy in the comics for many youngsters, and today he is the artist behind the most expensive comics collectibles, in the Rogers series. He also drew Roy for the Dell Comics subscription ads. Micale drew illustrations for some of the comics' accompanying features, such as "Pioneers of the Old West." He drew Roy in the Whitman Better Little Book *Deadly Treasure* (1945), and Tall Better Little Book *Snowbound Outlaws* (1949), and *The Range Detective* (1950). Albert Micale was still drawing for Western in 1959, as evidenced by Dell Western comics in my personal collection, titles including "Ben Bowie and his Mountain Men" and "Boots and Saddles." Albert Micale's Roy was one that would be recognizable to many, as he had the longest running consistent Roy, and it was his Roy that dominated the comics in the early years. His likeness could have been one of the best, and at times was very realistic, but too often his Roy was overly tall and broad-shouldered. He was a very friendly, likeable Rogers, whose sense

of humor shone, and he was close to the personality seen in the Roy Rogers films, as DuBois and Micale were perfectly matched. Also, on the positive side, Micale is one artist who often went to a lot of trouble to detail the tooled leather holsters and saddlery and changed Roy's attire frequently, especially in the latter part of his work. In physical size, his Roy would compare with Buscema's versions, however.

Richard T. Moore. Moore attended the Art Center in L.A. His nickname was "Sparky." He credited Charles Russell, Will James, and Alex Toth as his influences.[7] After heavy work in children's art for Hanna-Barbera and Flintstones, where he did animation layouts, etc., he settled at Western Printing and Lithographing Co., contributing to almost all of their cowboy characters, as can be evidenced especially in the *Western Roundup* titles. It is believed that Moore drew Roy for one story in *Western Roundup* comics, but his heaviest contribution was with Trigger in the Roy Rogers series (after Gollub and Steffen) and Trigger and Bullet in the *Western Roundup* series. In the 1960s, he had ventured into non–Western characters such as "Secret Agent" and "Korak."

Feg Murray. Murray had a regular syndicated newspaper comic panel, and Roy was one of his favorite subjects over the years, resulting in his appearance in many of the large-sized colored Sunday editions. Murray produced what is likely the first drawing of Roy and Trigger to appear nationwide in his "Seein' Stars" in 1938, an original of which is in this researcher's collection. He drew a very realistic Roy and Trigger, often inspired from film stills and publicity photos.

Irwin Myers (see the Big Little Book #1476, *King of the Cowboys*). Myers also contributed to comics as early as 1945, Four-Color #63. He drew Roy without the youthful appearance associated with the work of most artists. Myers drew hard, calloused-looking subjects, especially good villains. He often showed them with faces shaded, side views, or heads lowered. Irwin Myers' Roy simply did not resemble the "King of the Cowboys" but did resemble the work of artist Harry Parks at times. The Rogers likeness ran closer to that of Gene Autry, whom Myers drew more effectively.

This opening page to "Roy Rogers Rounds Up a Dude," in _Roy Rogers Comics_ #23 shows a typical full name signing of Albert Micale, one of the few artists who was able to get away with that. Copyright 1949 by Rogers.

Harry Parks produced Roy for Four-Color Comics #177, the only time the artist would give us a full story of Roy's. He captured a fairly realistic likeness of Roy at the time, but one totally different from Micale's work. Copyright expired.

Robert Myers *see* Olindo Giacomini.

Ernest Nordli. Nordli produced painted covers for Dell Comics and is believed to have done some of the ones for the *Roy Rogers' Trigger* series. He drew Roy for Simon and Schuster in *Roy Rogers on the Double-R-Bar.*

Harry Parks. Parks is another artist about whom little has been written, but he produced very interesting work. The panels contain rather rugged-looking individuals and are fairly cluttered with a lot of sharp lines. His likeness of Roy carried a very good resemblance to the subject at the time, although he is a little on the heavy side. Harry Parks' Roy was almost comical at times. He captured the youthful appearance but in a less handsome and less consistent fashion, even in the space of one story. He shows the cowboy in fringe and with the pre–*Apache Rose* hat, which seldom was seen with the real Roy. (Roy had, at the time of the printing, just begun to display the fringe with any frequency.) Parks gives Roy a realistically colored gunbelt and holster, rather than copying Micale's yellow pattern. Beginning with issue #1, he began drawing the "Chuck Wagon Charley's Tales." He drew small subjects generally but used a lot of lines in the panels, showing almost no dead space. He drew many of the Trigger features.

M. D. Peso. This may be the name of an artist contributing to Roy's stories in the McKimson period comics. See splash panel, issue #40.

Leo Rawlings. Rawlings drew Roy for original stories in British comic books and annuals.

Ken Sawyer. Sawyer produced painted covers for Dell Westerns, and at least one *Western Roundup* cover is signed. Any work specifically on Roy and Dale is undocumented at this time. Sawyers' signed work was used on various Whitman hardback novels.

Roy Schroeder. Schroeder was an artist who sporadically captured the personality of Roy in his illustrations. When he was on target, he was good. When he missed, it was by a mile. In *Roy Rogers and the Enchanted Canyon*, the Whitman Roy Rogers novel, one of the better likenesses was repeated several times.

Lew Schwartz. Schwartz has been credited by other researchers for having contributed to the Dale likenesses in her DC series. He was reportedly responsible for drawing Dale in at least four of her stories (see Chapter 7).

Tony Sgroi. I first came across Sgroi's work in credited Whitman children's hardcover novels and recognized the possibility of his contribution to the Western characters in the Dell series, including Roy. I then learned of his work in Fawcett's Lash LaRue series through artist and comic publisher Bill Black. Making comparisons with all of this known work enabled me to come to the conclusions I have drawn pertaining to Sgroi's contribution to the Rogers comics. I have found much of his work in other Dell Western characters, including the Flying A's Range Rider, and he did quite a few of the Whitman books, including the Annie Oakley and Jim Bowie titles. I believe at this time that his contribution to the Rogers comics began about issue #25 and continued to some degree until the Buscema period. Sgroi drew especially clean-cut figures that are rather handsome and realistic in appearance, and often his style can be detected in the manner in which he drew his characters running. There seems to be some Jesse Marsh influence to Sgroi's work that results in subjects that resemble Marsh's Tarzan.

Jon Small. Small produced art for Dell Western titles, especially stories having to do with the American Indians. Any specific Roy and Dale contributions are undocumented at this time.

Paul Souza. In 1954, Souza painted an extremely fine likeness of Roy and Trigger for the lithographed cover of the Whitman hardback novel *Roy Rogers and the Enchanted Canyon*. That same year he produced fair to excellent likenesses of Roy in the Whitman Cozy Corner Book *Roy Rogers and the Desert Treasure*. He may have contributed to the comics stories of Roy and or Dale.

Dan Spiegle. Spiegle's characters seem to appear in early Roy Rogers comics, such as Four-Color #63, 1945, and it is believed that one of the Roys in these early issues is from his pens. In 1949, he met Bill Boyd, and that same year he began drawing the Hopalong Cassidy newspaper strip (Los Angeles Mirror Syndicate). King Features bought the strip in 1951. Spiegle drew Hoppy until the strips ended in 1955. Entering the comic book field in 1956 with Dell, he worked on a variety of titles, including the Western ones. He drew some of the finest mean and villainous faces, but did not do this consistently.

Randy Steffen. Steffen was a very popular Western artist, and his work was used by many in the world of publishing. He drew Roy for the Whitman Tell-A-Tale Book *Sure 'Nough Cowpoke*. He contributed heavily to *Roy Rogers Comics*, issues #25–73. His characters often take on a slight Spanish appearance, and this did not result in a realistic likeness of Roy. Steffen's Roy was superb in size and movement. His Roy likeness is much better in the Tell-A-Tale work. Steffen's work can also be found in Dell's *Zane Grey's Western Magazine*, 1940s–1950s, and heavily in *Western Horseman Magazine*, beginning March 1948, covers and inside art. Randy Steffen signed in full much of this work used for comparative analysis, but in the comics stories, one must look for small initials. On occasion the last name can be found scrawled and buried in the art. He illustrated books such as *Stagecoach Days* by Vickie Hunter and Elizabeth Hamma (Menlo Park, CA.: Lane Book Co.).

Alexander Toth. Toth was known for pro-ducing excellent work, but changing styles, which, especially when the work is unsigned, makes it extremely tough to follow his history and to positively identify it. He worked for DC beginning in 1947 and did the "Sierra Smith" stories found in the early Dale Evans comics. He went over to Dell in the mid–1950s, working on a variety of titles, including *Zorro, Rio Bravo, Western Roundup*, and television titles such as *Frontier Doctor*. He favored a lot of black ink and emphasized much hair on his subjects—bushy eyebrows, mustaches, unkempt hair—in addition to lined and weathered-looking faces; this made for characters who appeared sinister. He later went to a smooth, clean-cut style that can make his unsigned work with Western/Dell hard to identify for the person not a "Toth" expert. He drew Roy for over a half dozen stories, issues #119 through #124. Although Toth is an artist of legendary status for many, his Rogers was simply unique. He rendered a totally unrealistic Rogers, from the craggy, bushy eyebrowed, worried face approaching cartoon art at times to the really disheveled physical appearance—baggy shirt, crumpled hat and all. For most of the Rogers stories, he used a small symbol that resembles a coat of arms which he always placed in a very inconspicuous place, usually in the first panel. He also wrote his name on the sides of rocks, etc., in the landscape in a size that requires a magnifying glass to detect. One can also sometimes find his initials worked together, disguised in the artwork.

Warren Tufts. In 1949 Tufts debuted the *Casey Ruggles* Western comic strip. About 1954, he created *The Lone Spaceman* and the following year *Lance*, which he distributed himself. He worked for Hanna-Barbera doing television animation and became part of the *Johnny Quest Team*. In the 1950s he drew for the Western Co., depicting Dale in several stories in her comics series, and also worked on other titles such as *Rawhide* and *The Rifleman*.

John Ushler. Ushler's likeness of Roy ran to above average, mostly fair-plus. The book *Roy Rogers' Favorite Western Stories* actually carries few illustrations of Roy. However, the ones that are there are by Ushler and are well executed. He drew Roy in the early newspaper comic strips, sharing panel space with artist Peter Alvarado. Some of his best Roy Rogers work is found in the *Western Roundup* comics, in which he drew about a half dozen Rogers entries and numerous other characters' stories. He also drew at least one Trigger outing. Other examples of his work can be found in the comics of Johnny Mack Brown, Rex Allen, and Buffalo Bill, Jr., and in various other Whitman hardback novels, including *Fury*. His kind of character had a tendency, especially the villains, to be on the thin, wiry side, with a good crop of hair. They seem to reflect rough-edged, hard-living country folks or sun-dried Westerners. But these villains are the first thing one notices about Ushler's work. Among his work for Whitman was the Roy Rogers novel *Roy Rogers and the Rimrod Renegades*. John Ushler scrawled his last name, and often all that can be made out is the first three letters, disguised in the work.

John Ushler's Roy from *Western Roundup* comics story in issue #3. Copyright 1953 by Western Printing & Lithographing Co., Inc.

Henry E. Vallely. Vallely worked for Whitman and turned out nice illustrations. He drew Roy but just failed to capture the Rogers likeness. Roy comes out looking heavier-set, more along the lines of Buck Jones. Vallely drew tall, broad-shouldered cowboys with a rugged Jones, Ken Maynard, or Tom Mix appearance, which didn't do Roy justice. He drew Roy for the novel *Raiders of Sawtooth Ridge*, and it is believed that he contributed to at least the first Roy Rogers comic book, Four-Color #38, 1944. Henry was one of Whitman's finest and most productive artists and drew the Lone Ranger in an early book.

Nicholas Viscardi (Nick Cardy). Some of the Dale Evans output in her DC series has been attributed to this artist. He drew the character Batlash in the 1960s for the comic of that title.

Helmuth G. Wegner. Wegner drew Dale in *Dale Evans and Buttermilk* for Whitman. A nice-looking cowgirl, but not the Dale Evans we know.

Ed Wexler. Much of Wexler's drawing of Roy for use on his merchandising line was some of the best of the likenesses, overall, and his work included the series of school lunch kits, saddlebags, chuckwagons, etc. Wexler was the first artist to draw Roy for these items, as he was an illustrator for the American Can Co. when the American Thermos Co. (later King Seely Thermos Co.) had them create the first fully lithographed steel lunch box and bottle. This 1953 Roy Rogers set shows Roy on Trigger, while Dale waves from under the Double R Bar gate. Working as an artist for American Can, Wexler created the artwork for the company until 1964.

"One-Shots"

At one time or another, these artists have rendered a likeness of Roy and or Dale, many for commercial products and packaging, others to illustrate magazine and newspaper articles.

Nicholas Alascia. Various commercial forms.

Biro. Various commercial forms.

Cherokee. Real name Clyde H. Elder. Signs work "Mr. Chero." Artist whose drawings of Western stars have received a lot of recognition; his portrait of Roy was used with an article from this writer in *Classic Images* 203 (May 1992). Numerous works of his are on display in the Gene Autry Oklahoma Museum of Local History, at Gene Autry, Oklahoma.[8] Known by friends as "Cherokee."

Mark Christianer. Illustrator who drew very good 1950s likenesses of Roy and Dale for Smoky Mountain Knife Co.'s "Riders of the Silver Screen" novelty character knives, 1990.

Don Cook. His excellent likeness of Roy appeared in a 1991 article in the *Fort Worth Star-Telegram*.

J. Cornell. Various commercial forms, including likeness of hatless Roy and Dale on cover of RCA Camdem LP record jacket *Jesus Loves Me*.

Mario Demarco. Artist who has made many fine pencil drawings of legendary film cowboys, including Roy, and has published on his own press many books on these subjects. Works from photos, and many of his drawings can be linked with particular publicity stills.

John Hagner. Artist who has drawn most of the cowboy heroes, and whose works of Roy and others, have been seen as very realistic. They have appeared in *Double R Bar Ranch News*.

JNO. Various commercial forms; including a pinback button of the 1980s.

Dave LaFleur. Drew Roy for commemorative poster prints in 1990s.

Lamwinih. Various commercial forms.

Loniro. Caricaturist from Argentina. Drew large caricature portrait of Roy for Argentina television guide *Canal TV*, 1962.

Bill Maunder. His drawings of Roy often take on a Spiegle appearance and have appeared in various published materials, including the Roy Rogers–Dale Evans Collectors Association Newsletters.

David Miller. Miller painted a portrait of Roy and Trigger, for Prell shampoo. It was presented to Roy on the *This Is Your Life* television series, 1953, by host Ralph Edwards.

A. NN. Various commercial forms; these initials have also been discovered by this researcher in likenesses of Roy on General Foods Post's cereal ads.

Pecoraro. Produced excellent painted

likeness of Roy for packaging of video tape "Rough Rider's Roundup," produced by All Occasion Video.

Petrizo. Various commercial forms.

Robert Phillips, Jr. Phillips' fine drawing of Roy, influenced by a publicity still, appears in *Roy Rogers–Dale Evans Collectors Association Newsletter*.

Armand Polverari. This artist's drawings of Roy have appeared in recent years in publications such as *Roy Rogers–Dale Evans Collectors Association Newsletter* and have been used in the Roy Rogers Festival event. He signs his work "Mondo." Possibly the Roy likeness used in the Marriot Corporations Roy Rogers restaurants advertising. An excellent likeness of aged Rogers, jovial expression, but a little heavy in the face.

Pauline Pruitt. Roy Rogers fan from Bluefield, West Virginia, who became inspired to paint a portrait of Roy and donate it to the Roy Rogers Hometown Exhibit in Portsmouth, Ohio. In an impressive work, she captured a considerable amount of that which is "pure Roy" in her likeness of the "King."

Dick Rockwell. Various commercial forms.

Rosario. Various commercial forms.

Bob Sallee. Sallee drew fine likenesses of 1950s Roy and Dale for Smoky Mountain Knife Works for their tin decorator signs (1991) and "Sunset Barlow" character knife series, 1991. He lives in Georgia.

Warren Satter. Various commercial forms.

Don Sherwood. "Famed American Illustrator"[9] Sherwood drew good likenesses of Roy and Dale for character pocket knives (Camillus Cutlery, for Smoky Mountain Knife Works, 1991) and decorator tin signs offered by Smoky Mountain Knife Works, 1991. Also drew Roy and Dale for associated full color poster. Background includes a comic strip "Dan Flagg."

Elvira, Tony Tallarko. Drew Dale for cartoon panel appearing in newspapers, reprinted in fan publications.

Tayenbaum. Various commercial forms including drawing of Roy for RCA LP APL1-1520, record jacket *Mackintosh and T.J.*

Tom Tridico. Produced nice likeness of Roy and Trigger for Portsmouth, Ohio, Chamber of Commerce brochures.

Byron Warren. Produced Roy likeness for cover of August 1980 *Rob Tucker's Memory Lane* magazine, inspired by 1940s Republic Pictures promo picture.

S. J. Woolf. Produced portrait of Roy that captured his appearance, but not his personality. Published in film magazine, *Motion Picture*, October 1945.

Unknown Artists, Miscellaneous Likenesses

1960s Nestle's ads. Several different artists.

Ranch Romances magazines, 1950s.

1960s Speedry Products Co. items, ads, and packaging.

1950s Roy Rogers merchandise ads in Sears and Roebuck catalogues.

1950s View-Master ads, Canada.

50th Anniversary Roy Rogers Belt Buckle. Aged likeness, but well executed.

Much merchandise from the 1950s carries what is usually a fair likeness of Roy and or Dale, Trigger, and Bullet. I am in the process of attempting to identify some of this, which includes neckerchiefs, bandannas, wallets, belt buckles, etc.

Roy Rogers and the Deadly Treasure. Big Little Book, 1940s. Cover.

Roy Rogers, King of the Cowboys. Big Little Book, 1940s. Cover likeness is excellent.

Dust jacket illustration, *Roy Rogers and the Gopher Creek Gunman*, Whitman hardback novel, 1940s. One likeness is by Dreany, while the artist who produced the other likeness, which bears no resemblance to Roy, is unknown.

Mexican lobby card *"Crepusculo en las Sierras"* ("Twilight in the Sierras"), 1950s, bears a very good photo-inspired likeness of Roy.

Cover drawing, *Roy Rogers and the Sons of the Pioneers; King of the Cowboys*, LP record, Bear Family BFX 15124. Film and publicity photo–inspired work, one excellent, one fair.

The Comic Book Roy Rogers

The Four-Color Series took in the work of several artists, the "bullpen" effect showing right away in such early stories as "Apache Blood," but the number one artist who would help carry Roy to prominence in this medium, and so add to the overall popularity of the "King of the Cowboys," was introduced here and was able to sign some of his work "Albert Micale."

In issue number one of the regular series, January 1948, Micale would, with just a little help from various artists who would lend their talents in scattered panels, and in perhaps, inking, carry the series single-handedly through issue #23. It was with #24, December 1949, that artists started pouring out of the woodwork to lend their contributions to the stories, and there would be many artists doing this through issue #73, January 1954. The majority of what I see as "Al" McKimson, which could be editing and occasional contributions to the artwork, which produces a certain effect, ends about issue #71, November 1953, after about 45 entries.

Steffen and Arens probably produced the best likenesses and most consistently good work for Roy's image. Western Printing and Lithographing Co. would not provide any information in this area (they provided little information in any area), but it is probable there were many new artists at the time, and they would begin working in the bullpen, in sort of an apprenticeship, adding to whatever was being worked on at the time. Initials of an artist will show up in work considerably ahead of the time that he assumes a more prominent position in the series.

A single story might contain as many as a half dozen likenesses of Roy by as many different artists. Yet, in most issues, a story would appear by Micale, who totaled about 100. In issue #74, Buscema took over Micale's duties and, with help in small ways from various artists, he would carry the issues through #108, about 70 stories.

At this point, the bullpen process was back in order, with various artists dropping in and out of stories principally drawn by Arens, Toth, and Edson. Arens would move over to the *Western Roundup* Roy stories, while Toth would drop out for the most part after a few stories, leaving the bulk of the output to Edson. Edson would be joined by various artists who contributed to the stories,

and, in the case of Spiegle, even held the reins in one. Nat Edson and Russ Manning seem to be two artists who were contributing on a small scale to the early Edson outings. Edson would, however, carry the load as principal artist to the end of the series. Manning came in full-time with the Dale Evans feature in #124, then #132 through #144, and it is here, rather than with Roy likenesses, that one can see his style best. Arens, over at *Western Roundup*, was joined by Ushler, Mankin, Moore, and others. I believe there is a possibility that Gleicher, LaGrotta, and even Steel made some contribution, however slight, in these stories.

The Carbon Copy Likeness Artists

When one artist apparently took a break in the middle of a story, and his chair was filled with a fellow artist who might draw a few panels or the rest of the story, any number of likenesses were likely to come about. He might be in the mood, or simply elect to, draw out the strip in the style of the artist he's filling in for. Most were very gifted at being able to draw in the style of another, and besides it could be fun, a way of breaking monotony with artistic license. This makes it at times impossible to determine who drew what. In this case there might be subtle changes in the likeness, but generally the new likeness would closely resemble the previous one.

Renegade Artists' Likenesses

On the other hand, should the new artist choose to be a renegade and draw with no regard for the overall appearance of the strip, rendering his very own unique Roy interpretation, right next to the Roy from the pens of the guy who went to lunch abruptly, we wind up with a "renegade likeness," one different for the sake of being different. Should this artist only draw a few panels and then a third artist fill the chair, you can imagine what the overall strip looks like. This situation took place in a number of issues prior to John Buscema's entering the corral, and it happened a few times after John left for other pastures. These likenesses are just likenesses resulting from artistic expression and the individual artist's interpretation of the subject. The artist would step in and draw Roy for a number of stories, in a number of issues. At this time, if he was going to be handling the reins, he would be driving the team his way. The thing that is better with renegade likenesses over carbon-copy likenesses is their consistency. When a researcher comes along years later to study the likeness, there are plenty of examples to study. The panels are consistent, as are the likenesses in the stories, issues after issue. Work is there that the researcher can get a handle on. With the carbon copy artists, switching back and forth from copying the style of an artist who might even himself be copying the style of another artist, it is almost impossible to identify the artists involved.

Composite Likenesses

What is equally difficult are the composite likenesses. One artist draws the outline of a face, and perhaps the eyes. Another comes along and does the ears, hair, hat, nose. Another comes along and draws the body. Next time around, which might be the next panel or the next story, positions are switched. The guy that drew the eyes now draws the nose and ears. And then another drops by and does the body. Each artist, a panel at a time, might attempt to draw in the style of the other, adding even more confusion to the overall likeness. There are a number of stories in the *Roy Rogers Comics* that are made up of panels where you witness the familiar work of several different artists, sometimes in the same figure. You cannot testify without a doubt about the identity of any one of the artists, however.

Comparison Works

At times, as in the case of Joe Musial, a highly prolific artist at Western, the "ghost" artist could and did attempt to duplicate the style of the one of whom they were drawing (Musial was particularly adept at this), but others would just jump in with their own unique styles. Either way, the issues were clouded for future comics historians and researchers. It is interesting that several of the artists managed to sign their work, albeit buried in the artwork. Some of these signatures have been discovered and some not. One story is drawn with small, far-away figures who seldom have their face toward the reader. Overall the biggest problem for research was the mixing of several likenesses in as many stories.

Another point of interest in Roy's comics is that except for advertisements, Dale Evans was kept completely out of them. She was in the films, though always portraying another character rather than Dale Evans. She shared radio and television programs in her own name. And she shared the comic strips as drawn by Al McKimson in the syndicated King Features newspaper comics. She shared lunch boxes, with artist Al Wexler doing her justice with his pen, and she was on toys and coloring books. In the comics, however, there were only a few appearances in photos in the earlier issues, and she never appeared in the stories.

Roy Rogers the character was the same no matter where you encountered him. Some of the comic artists were just not able to capture that character, but some got unbelievably close. We often look at two different and distinct Rogers' likenesses, each perfect in its own way. This leads to much confusion in the appearance of the comic overall. Part of Roy's image and his overall characteristics carried over into all the mediums in which he was presented. The most outlandish instances, which occurred far into the issues, were hats inked in, in black, red and, even green. Trigger showed up in perfect palomino gold and white, went to yellow at times, and on an occasion or two showed up all gold, with no white tail, mane, or face. On at least one occasion, he was all brown. Roy's hair throughout the series went from brown to black to yellow to white. Bullet was drawn in a likeness that was always realistic (surely a dog is easier to deal with), but serious students will even find exceptions here. In certain instances in comic art, as in the case of the cowboy heroes of the 1940s–1950s films and television, a likeness to the image seemed to take precedence over a likeness to the person in real life or even the character as seen in the other media forms. There were almost as many likenesses as there were artists involved in producing the cowboy in the comic art form. It may never be possible to produce a count of the number of "Roy Rogers" that have existed in the comic art form since 1938. On film, we were offered one major likeness of Roy. In art, there were many, many distinctively different likenesses of Roy. It has been reported that one of Roy Rogers' favorite likenesses was by John Buscema. That might be why those were chosen for the 1980s–1990s reprints by AC Comics. When Buscema entered the bullpen, the comics straightened out again, for better or worse, depending on opinion. Roy was, at least, rescued from a comic with as many Roy Rogers likenesses in it as the real character had bullets in his six-guns.

The Landscapes

In the majority of comics produced by other publishers, the essence of the real Western landscape, all that mysterious beauty so long identified with the terrain, is buried in a maze of lines from the central illustrator's or inker's pens. The very setting that made the story immediately identifiable as a Western and much of the intrigue that kept Easterners attached to this type of adventure in the first place simply wasn't there. It was the unique talents of the individual artists and their ability to transfer the wide-open spaces, canyons, mesas, arroyos, cliffs, and cacti to the pulp page that made the Dell Westerns what they were, and that overall clean, uncluttered appearance so necessary to the telling of stories depicted in that rugged country was consistent throughout the series, naturally more so with certain artists than others. But, by and large, the Western Co.'s artists did not waste ink or lines in their panels, and the effect was that the landscape was as large on pulp as it was in reality. It did not subtract from the central "larger-than-life" characters, however.

It is unknown just how much influence and control was exerted by Dell Publishing, if any, in producing this unique quality that allowed the company to stand way out front in Western comics. These contents and the occasional advertising that eventually came along, which was generally Western in theme and uncluttered in appearance, greatly complemented the splendid high-gloss color photo covers and vice versa. Comics pro-

duced around the same characters, but for another publisher, i.e., K. K. Publishing, maintained the same appearance in the contents, so it is believed that this quality and uniqueness was brought about essentially by the Western Co. and its artists. There is much to be said about the comparisons of work between artists such as Nicholas Firfires and John Buscema, two outstanding men whose talents produced the appearance described above. Nothing is conclusive in the analysis of panels, and we may never have all the answers about who drew what in the panels of the classics, so we must trudge on down the trail, revealing what we know or assume at the time.

In many instances, one artist drew landscapes, while another drew the figures. It has been reported that Sal Buscema drew the landscapes for brother John at Western and that Mrs. Goodan drew the landscapes for her husband Till. At this time, I have no information to document any teamwork in the Firfires landscapes, but it may perhaps be produced one of these days through continued research. The stories drawn by Mike Arens also carry a very distinctive landscape. Some comics produced by other publishers would, on occasion, come close to the appearance that became a trademark of Dell Western, as can be witnessed in some Hopalong Cassidy and Monte Hale stories, both from Fawcett Publishing, but all in all, no other publisher/producer managed to serve the cowboy and his environment as well as the product from these two companies, Dell and Western Printing.

The Illustrated Trigger

After the Four-Color period for Roy, when he was awarded his first regular comic in its own series, his magnificent steed would be right by his side, just as in every other phase of his show business career. With *Roy Rogers Comics*, issue #20, August 1949, "Trigger" became a regular feature at the back of the "Roy" stories, where he had just appeared with his master. Artist Harry Parks had drawn Roy for at least one issue (Four-Color #177), and had really gotten his pens exercised in Roy's comics with the "Chuck Wagon Charley" feature, issues #1–19. Roy's main artist, Albert Micale, drew Trigger for his first solo outing to get him off and running, but then he became the work of Parks in issue #2. He drew nineteen stories, throughout a year and a half, uninterrupted, until issue #40. For that issue, in April 1951, just eight months before Roy's television series was launched, an artist stepped into Roy's comics and drew Trigger one time in work and a setting that was worlds apart from Parks'. Then in the next month, with #41, it is difficult to tell what happened. The artist whose work would now show in the "Trigger" features for a long time to come definitely had a different way with a set of pens than Parks, and his work resembled nothing found in the Rogers stories throughout their entire run, nor anything found in any other comics. Trigger was drawn in fine style by Parks, and I must say resembled more closely the Trigger being drawn by artist Micale, whose work was always right next door for comparison, than the Roy likenesses of other artists resembled the real cowboy when several of them started drawing him for different stories in the same issue. Perhaps the best renditions of Trigger were the likenesses created by John Buscema, 1955–1956, and the images used by General Foods in their Post cereals advertisements and by Ed Wexler in his work on the lunch kits.

The Illustrated Dale Evans

Roy's career as a cowboy was years ahead of Dale's as a cowgirl. After they married in December 1947, when they were still years away from merchandise and a television series proclaiming them "America's Favorite Western Couple," she was not even seen in his films for a while and her highest profile was on the road, at rodeos and in various other personal appearances. National Periodicals decided, however, that the latter exposure, combined with her recent Western film history, was enough to launch a comic book series. It was a company known for its "Superman" comics and those of various cartoon characters, film comedians such as Martin and Lewis, and cowboys who were pure fiction, with an exception or two such as Hopalong Cassidy. In the viewpoint of most fans today, she was ill-

placed with this company, as they just couldn't do her justice compared to the treatment Roy had long been getting at Dell Publishing. But it was a start. The writers wrote incredible stories for her that were more suited for Superman, and the artists overplayed her sex appeal in a unique DC comics way, which always seemed to produce a comic likeness bordering on cartoon art that didn't resemble the real Dale Evans as she had been seen and would be seen in the future in shoot-'em-up films and on television. She was "Queen of the Westerns" at DC. By that time the television series was really pounding the image of "Roy and Dale" into America's living rooms in early 1953, and everyone had witnessed for several seasons the "new" Dale Evans and knew that she, beside husband Roy Rogers, was the "Queen of the West."

Dell Comics was ready to give her a chance in their special try-out series, Four-Color Comics. They had the Roy and Dale merchandise as well as the television show to lean on for promotional support, and they probably considered a Dale comic to be not much of a gamble, especially given Roy's track record for nearly a decade of issues. They chose as well to lean somewhat on artwork showing a very attractive (which she really was) lady detective first and a cowgirl second. The big plus in knowing how to handle her was with the high gloss photo covers and the spacious, clean artwork. Her comics stood out every bit as much as Roy's. After an artist whom I haven't been able to identify yet teamed with Hi Mankin to produce the first adventures of Dale, they let Mankin at the wheel to more or less solo, and he quickly showed Dale in the stories very close to the way she was seen on television weekly. The hair got shorter, yet he drew her as sexy as a cowgirl should be and attractive, but not to a degree that would overshadow her stories. Pat Brady was given the beefy comic part totally in line with the television series, and she was portraying the Dale Evans everyone was accustomed to. The stories were realistic. She was not "Super Cowgirl"; she was just a super cowgirl who went about helping those in need. Bullet and her horse "Buttermilk" were with her, as in the television series. The comic's inside pages would contain the same type of photos often seen in film magazines, the "at home" pictures of her and the kids, and her animals. Occasionally Roy's name would be mentioned, and the Double R Bar Ranch, or one with a name close to that, would be used, as well as Mineral City, and her cafe, just as on television. Overall, with a few exceptions, she was drawn more average attractive, than sexy attractive. On one or two occasions when Mankin or Manning, the pair that did the majority of her stories, got sidetracked, she would find herself in the hands of artists such as Jesse Marsh, John Ushler, Dan Spiegle, Richard Moore, Nicholas Firfires, Nat Edson, or Mike Arens. Marsh, Firfires, Edson and Arens tended to draw her as an average pretty cowgirl to an even greater degree. The others produced a Dale that bordered on cartoon art. As is the case with Roy in the comics, everyone has their favorite Dale, and mine would have to be from the pens of Manning, Arens, and Marsh.

The Comic Strips

Americans, young and old alike, kept up with Roy's (and later Dale's) adventures by means of the daily and Sunday comics for many years, twelve as a matter of fact, from 1949 to 1961. Peter Alvarado and John Ushler introduced Roy in this medium but it was some time before the Sunday editions were produced. In the daily papers there would be an ongoing story carried out in four to eight panels that emphasized action involving good guys and bad guys. The limitations were found in the size of the panels and the fact that they were usually in black and white. A number of Western Printing and Lithographing Co. artists would drop in and out of the strip, drawing Roy for two comics series. Mike Arens produced some great likenesses of Roy and Dale for the Sunday issues, and so did Hi Mankin, who worked on the strip for about five years.

The Books

There were a number of artists whose contribution was greater in books than in the comics, and a few artists contributed little, if

anything at all, to the comics. Irwin Myers, Joseph Dreany, J. M. LaGrotta, John Higgs, Ernest Nordli, Hans Helweg, Mel Crawford, August Lenox, Al Gleicher, Roy Schroeder, John Steel, Helmuth Wegner, Paul Souza, and Henry Luhrs made their real contributions to Roy and Dale, et al., in the books issued by Whitman and Simon and Schuster. A few of these artists probably made a slight contribution to the comics stories of the couple, but when it is that slight, it is often very difficult to document. The artists were able to stretch out and take every liberty with Roy and Dale's likenesses in the books, and some of the best likenesses of either can be found here. As a result, they are excellent for use in comparative analysis in attempting to identify the artists of the comics works. On the other hand, some of the very poorest likenesses are probably to be found in the coloring books, where few lines were used in rendering a likeness in order to leave plenty of area to color. Some of these likenesses bear no resemblance at all to the real life subjects. Painted covers, which were often used, offered much better likenesses and made for a very attractive package. The book format, which allowed Mike Arens to use a considerable amount of room in displaying his likenesses of Roy, resulted in the production of some of the finest likenesses of Roy in the entire commercial art form history.

Advertising

General Foods' Post Cereal boxes and related advertising copy. I find the likenesses here to be the cream of the crop really. It appears that the artists studied certain photographs of Roy (Republic publicity) and rendered about as good a likeness of him, and even of Dale, as could be achieved. Considering that a giant of a cereal manufacturer was involved here, it is not a surprise. It is my personal belief that Peter Alvarado and John Ushler contributed significantly to this work and that Hi Mankin did some work here as well. I have discovered what appear to be their initials in the artwork, and I have spent many hours studying and comparing the works. In some instances, one finds oneself looking twice to see if it is a painting or a

Artist Joyce Deck's painting of Roy and Dale captures much of what the stars have contributed to Hollywood cowboy history and American popular culture.

photo. Without any reservations, I believe that the best likeness, taking into consideration everything I have seen, is that found on the magazine ad for General Foods' "Name the Pony" contest. Post's cereals offered the best likenesses overall of Roy and Dale, while certain smaller companies did a rather poor job of producing realistic likenesses. One exception is the ad for Roy Rogers merchandise ran by Hickok Co. in a Fawcett comic.

Merchandise

One can get caught up in the Roy Rogers and Trigger of 1952–1955 and wonder if the horse ever spent any time on all fours. Whoever decided upon using Roy rearing on Trigger for a trademark pose exhibited a streak of genius for creating a high-profile trademark. In 1953 the pose was used by Al Wexler on a thermos that was part of the

Roy Rogers and Dale Evans lunch kits, and it served to help sell 2½ million lunch sets. It is unknown who came first, Steel or Wexler, but probably Wexler did. I assume the lunch kits' success led the management team to lean to a great degree on the unofficial trademark pose. It was John Steel, in my estimation, who produced a painted likeness very close to that used by Wexler. The Steel work appeared on merchandise in its original state, and prints were made from this likeness that rendered it to a simple drawing used to accommodate other types of merchandise. The painted likeness can be found as late as 1992 on the front of the box for the Comic Book Trading Cards. The drawing can also be found on the box for the Roy Rogers spurs made by Classy Products in 1954. Of all the merchandise and packaging on which the painted likeness of Roy appeared, the lithographed school lunch kits of the original 1953 issue probably take the honors.

Chapter 10

ROY ROGERS' ATTIRE

The history of colorful, fringed West-ern attire can be traced back to the Indian-made items, such as buckskin jackets, that appeared in the 1800s. Many were worn by whites.[1] The history of the more spectacular cowboy attire can be traced back to the items worn by the original cowboys, the Spanish vaqueros, and to the Wild West shows of Buffalo Bill, Pawnee Bill, and others. Sil-ver conchas, or pieces of silver plate, were common, as was leather tooling. The really showy attire, with its roots in Old West his-tory, was put to use by the film cowboy be-ginning with Tom Mix. It had an immediate impact on Western fashion for all cowboys and those aligning themselves with the cowboy or "Old West" idealogy, heritage, and traditions.[2]

The attire being marketed in stores and catalogues in the 1920s–1930s ranged from practical styles to styles bearing the Holly-wood influence, mostly in the order of pip-ing and the "slash" or "half moon" pockets. Most of the styles from that period forward have been a mixture of the two.[3] One of the mediums serving to keep plenty of demand alive has been the rodeo. Roy spent much of his film career working these events as a special attraction. Although he started out fairly conservative, by 1942 Roy had adopted attire with a real flair and rode into the Madison Square Garden Rodeo arena in a snow-white outfit highlighted with bright red boots. He established trends, and he was constantly exposed to the industry and the trends set by others.

The film cowboy's attire, along with his horse's attire, was used primarily to adopt a trademark-like appearance that would allow him to distinguish himself from his competi-tion, while giving the fans the show they paid to see. Not one of the many cowboys riding out of Hollywood used these items more effectively than Roy. There seemed no end to his imagination, nor that of his designers. No matter what the item of wearing apparel was, he would go a step farther in showiness and design. There is no better example serv-ing to illustrate the wide variety of his attire than the photographs that were part of the monthly comic books from 1944 to 1962. Those photographs, along with a few others from before and after the comics, account for the entire attire history of Roy Rogers. He was the king of Hollywood cowboy at-tire, the model supreme.

It should be noted here that by and large, the attire will serve to identify the period of the photo. In the case of photos used in the comic books, the comic's issue date is useless much of the time because in the early years of the comics, Roy's publicity department and that of Republic Produc-tions, Inc., sent Dell Publishing Co. photos of Roy in attire that was already obsolete. In the 1950s, Dell Publishing was sending West-ern Printing and Lithographing Co. photos of Roy taken in the 1940s. Perhaps Dell re-ceived them occasionally, stockpiled them in its files, and then sent them to Western in-discriminately. There are certain issues that show Roy in fairly current attire, from per-haps only months before, but there are many that show a Roy from an earlier period.

The study of the attire is an interesting one because the direction of the star can be seen as he progresses from just another of the film cowboys in the Hollywood corral to one of the most popular ones, to the most popular, and on to an American institution in all media.

Tailor's flocked to Hollywood to open businesses catering to the needs of the Holly-wood cowboy, and many used their skills of designing and custom tailoring to become very successful. Some even became legends. Roy spent a great amount of time in New York because of the Madison Square Garden Rodeo, his many other personal appearances, and the companies associated with his publishing ventures and merchandising. There were numerous East Coast tailors who had a wide reputation and catered to the needs of the rodeo and Hollywood cowboys.[4]

In the 1940s and 1950s, Roy's primary tailors were Nathan Turk, who had a business in Sherman Oaks,[5] a suburb of L.A., and Ben, the Rodeo Tailor, of Philadelphia.[6] In the 1950s, Roy also used "Nudie" Cohen, whose operation was in L.A.[7] Cowboy couturier Turk studied tailoring in Europe, and in 1943 he was employing nine men in his Hollywood shop.[8] In 1949, Western designer Bob Gwynn was making shirts for Dale, but it is not known at this time if he also produced some for Roy. Roy would take all of the honors in consistent, overall unique, and highly spectacular attire. The only other star to come close to matching Roy's appearance was Rex Allen, and that was for a relatively brief period of time. In 1948 Roy and his new bride Dale Evans were appearing at functions in matching whipcord suits made by Turk.[9] When they joined their careers, they began a Hollywood Western film practice of cowboy and wife in matching outfits that would not only last throughout their careers, but would also have an impact on Western fashion for the populace. It wasn't long before these matching outfits were a fairly common sight at rodeos.

In Hollywood, however, Roy and Dale had a monopoly on this practice. They were known as "Hollywood's Favorite Western Couple." In fact, they were Hollywood's only Western couple, and the attire helped to keep that foremost in everyone's minds. Most of their less formal outfits were gabardine with suede fringe. In 1943, Roy's outfit cost was $700.[10] He reportedly owned 100 twill, gabardine, and whipcord suits ($150 each), 200 gabardine shirts ($50 each), silk bandannas, hand-tooled leather belts, gold-trimmed silver buckles, and scores of Stetson hats. His custom-made boots carried the design that he adopted, which Roy himself

and most magazine writers called the "thunderbird"; according to his bootmaker, however, this was an incorrect name.[11] (This term would eventually be replaced in most articles by the term "double-eagle.")

Roy's favorite colors were said to be yellow and brown, blue and grey, and snowy white.[12] It was reported that at first Roy wasn't all that crazy about the fancy attire, but the fans found it to their liking and they won out.[13] In 1961, it was reported that he was spending well over $10,000 a year on clothes.[14]

Shirts

The number one piece of attire, and in most instances, the piece that lent itself to the most variation in style, was the Western shirt. Roy began with fairly simple shirts, showing a custom-made look, for his first feature film and publicity photos. In publicity photos associated with his first feature film *Under Western Stars*, he is seen in a no-frills outfit, the piping being the main feature.[15] Then he went to striped, lace-up shirts, with up to five buttons on extra long cuffs, button-down pocket, and piping. Patterned material for shirts was common even back in the 1800s, but without the frills, or even collars. Floral designs, embroidered collars, fringe, and other ornaments were a part of Buffalo Bill's attire. It wasn't long before Roy's attire would be custom designed and tailored, and it became considerably more elaborate than any attire the Wild West shows, or the Hollywood West for that matter, had ever seen.

Several basic styles were prominent right away. The simple Western piping separated the yoke from the main body of the shirt and appeared on the pockets on an otherwise solid-color shirt. Plaids, checks, or stripes and solids were mixed with piping. These materials would normally make up the yoke and the cuffs and the area above the cuffs. Then the collar would often contain a design, such as a tree leaf. Every combination imaginable was used, even the mixture of plaids and stripes. And little things to further enhance the trademark quality were employed, such as a large number of mother-of-pearl snaps on the cuffs. Most Western

With the Texas Highway Patrol and soldiers during a 1942 Army base tour. Note all the flowers and the "thunderbird" boots.

shirts of the day would have three or four snaps on the cuffs, but Roy's would be seen with as many as seven or more. Then there were the solid plaids, checks, or stripes, with simple Western tailoring, namely the three-point yoke. Every occasion would seem to call for a different style shirt, be it films, comic book photos, merchandise photos, personal appearances, both rodeo and other, television series, and television guest shots. Naturally, the personal appearances were marked with the most spectacular ones. The shirts began with brightly colored simple styles, mixing two tones, or solids with plaids, checks, and stripes. They soon took in fringe upon a vast array of pattern mixtures, and before long one could count on long fringe (about eight inches hanging from the yoke and about four inches coming off the sleeves), sequins, and embroidery, all on contrasting colors and patterns of material, much of it shiny gabardine that would reflect the bright lights under which Roy often worked. There is little doubt that he used hundreds of shirts.

About 1949 it was reported a shirt cost from $30 to $150, depending on how elaborate it was. The great majority of styles worn by Roy were duplicated in various color combinations, and the patterns were switched about often. The particular shirts, along with neckerchief, hat, trouser, and holster combinations, provide one key to determining photos that were produced from a single session and used in various mediums.

In the competition department, Gene Autry would come nearest Roy in the use of embroidered shirts. Rocky Lane was fond of solid-color striped shirts, some similar to Roy's.

The embroidery on Roy's shirts eventually went to the max in the early 1950s. On one really elaborate shirt, the embroidery covered nearly every inch of the shirt: cactus and saddles in the sleeves, with large animal heads on the front and an even larger one covering most of the back. Roy was not one for bib shirts, the kind Monte Hale and Wild Bill Elliott wore, but there were a few occasions when he would don one. In the late

1940s, all of the stops were pulled out, and the shirts ranged from subdued plaids and stripes, mostly for film work, to the most flamboyant Western styles ever created. The latter departed from the single layer of suede fringe to encompass three overlapping layers of very long suede fringe, that encircled the yoke, front and back, over embroidered designs. Suede collars with steer skulls and lace-up fronts with large horseshoe designs completed the style. The designer from this point on was limited only by his imagination. Variations of this basic style used designs of not only horseshoes, but also deer, eagles, dogs, etc. There were heavy quilted shirts for the winter and lighter weight ones for the summer, another factor that helps place a photo with a given year, but they all appear somewhat on the heavy side. It would be interesting to know just how much one of Roy's outfits would weigh, especially the ones designed for the cooler months.

Trousers

In Roy's early films, he was going back and forth from wearing jeans (dungarees then) to wearing what appears to be custom-made trousers, but plain ones. Did you ever notice that despite all the running, mounting, fighting, and various acrobatic acts, Roy never had to stop and tuck his trouser legs back into his boots? Anyone who has ever worn his pants stuck into his boots knows that all his time would be spent doing just that, were it not for one important concept of the tailored trousers, stirrups sewn onto the end of the leg to hold the trouser leg in the boot. It was relatively simple but very innovative and all-important concept. These stirrups can be seen in certain photos of Roy removing his boots, but I have discovered that few are aware of their existence. Right after his initial trousers with a simple Western cut that is most significant in the shape of pockets and belt loops, Roy went to the striped trousers, which would be worn with any style shirt. They would often as well contain piping down the outer leg, from the belt to the stirrup. The trousers were seldom as loud as the shirts, except when an entire outfit approach was used; brown with thin white stripes and piping was common. The

trousers were made to provide a lot of room in the seat area because much time was spent in the saddle, and material that offered a lot of stretch was utilized. Several of the Western stars wore jeans much of the time, and few wore custom-made trousers with a really unique look. In 1949, a pair of the trousers was costing Roy $65.

Neckerchiefs

The bandanna of the working cowboy appeared in a variety of print patterns, with red being the predominant color. Its sister silk neckerchief of the Old West days was used for special occasions, such a dances,[16] and that neckerchief or scarf gave rise to the fancy Hollywood versions that were another piece of apparel that could complement the overall attire. Odd as it may seem, this neckerchief usually came in contrasting colors. Roy began with fairly simple prints (bandanna-type)[17]; a center-tied short silk neckerchief, with no print; neckerchiefs with polka-dots, bandannas worn cavalry style; and string ties. After 1941 and the film *Nevada City*, he acquired something different, a multi-colored, longer silk neckerchief. On most occasions, the color of the neckerchief or scarf had little to do with the colors or style of shirt, and it stood out entirely on its own. The new and elaborate print scarves that Roy went to by 1941 were seldom available to the cowboy public at large. They were a little more than the average cowpoke would wear, even to a rodeo. Roy used hundreds of neckerchiefs. Rex Allen would come nearest Roy in showing off colorful neckerchiefs.

Hat

Roy's hats appear to be customized from the beginning of his film career. The large black one with about a 5″ brim that he wore as a member of the Sons of the Pioneers might have been a store shelf one. But by 1941, hat designer Byon-Polnick's company was handling Roy's unique style.[18] Roy began with a fairly common rancher-style hat, insofar as the crease was concerned, but it usally had a higher crown and or wider

The famous "Boots and Cactus" shirt is seen in about 1945, as Roy is experimenting with much heavier ornamentation. This was used for photos for many magazines and comics.

brim than a working cowboy or rodeo cowboy would select. Roy was building on a tradition firmly rooted in the styles created or adopted by Tom Mix and Buck Jones, only to lesser extremes. His first hatband was a tooled leather one. Other hats with styles closer to traditions linked with the real Old West decorated Roy's head in the films until the end of the historical ones. He had these in tan and black colors. He also had a certain black hat he wore on occasion before the white hat/good guy, black hat/bad guy

Attire by Nathan Turk, 1940s. Made for Lucky Carson, one of Roy's doubles, according to George E. Pitman, collector. Courtesy George E. Pitman.

image was ingrained into the American consciousness. That hat was along the lines of the white one he would begin wearing in 1946 and adopt permanently by 1947, with the film *Apache Rose*. A similar hat was still seen on occasion as late as 1952, but Roy in general used it only at home.[19] Because the hat was the most characteristic item of the cowboy attire, Roy designed, or had designed for him, a hat with a totally new concept in styling as far as Hollywood was concerned. The hat had a diamond crease that was used at least as early as 1890[20] and a front roll on the brim, which resulted in a more streamlined and pointed approach to crowns that had long been seen as round. This basic style crease was known as the "Denton Pinch" when it was marketed to the general public. (It was probably named after Denton, Texas, or John B. Denton, for whom the town was named.) Roy would shape the crown so that it was higher in front and lower in back than was usually the case. This particular style never seemed to catch on all that much in

standard fashion, and this worked to Roy's advantage.[21] He set his unique hat style off even further in the mid–1950s by replacing a more traditional hatband by an engraved sterling-silver one. And, he went to an even more unique double inch-wide crease in the crown that goes unobserved unless you see the top of the hat.

Belt

The Western belt is one of the least likely items to stand out because the showiness has traditionally been pretty much held to different designs tooled into the leather. Most photographs do not reveal much that could be viewed as unique, just Western floral patterns tooled into 2″ wide leather that are typical of store-bought belts. The obvious difference lies in the buckle. Here is an object that can be ornate and, if desired, flashy. Roy seemed to prefer the more traditional style over the larger square or rectangular

This 1946 publicity photo introduces us to the fringed style that would be the basis for many of his shirts, mixing plaids and solids with the oak leaf collar.

plate ones that became popular during the 1940s–1950s and soon, in much enlarged versions, came to dominate the rodeo scene. He was seen occasionally with one of these, however.[22] Roy's earliest buckles were engraved, probably German silver, and by 1939, one was sporting his name and would be seen often through 1947. He was fond of having silver work done that showed designs of objects like longhorns, his initials, or a cowboy on a bucking bronco. He would switch buckles between his regular belt and his

In 1982, Roy demonstrates to Jack Lambert, New York Stetson dealer, just how he fashions his "trademark" crease. Used with permission. Courtesy Jack Lambert.

gunbelt, and 1948 saw the appearance of a new buckle, with a place for the name not yet engraved, surrounded by a floral design.[23] Another silver buckle carried his initials inside a diamond shape surrounded by a floral pattern.[24] He must have been very busy or for some reason did not want the unengraved one personalized, for by 1954, it still had not been done. By 1955, similar buckles were being switched about almost as much as the gunbelts and various other items of attire.

Gunbelt and Holsters

Again, early in Roy's career, there was nothing fancy about his gunbelt and holsters, but as this was an item that really stood out with the film cowboys, that soon changed. You had single-gun cowboys in the films and two-gun cowboys, and Roy was always the two-gun variety. He went back and forth between a couple of dark brown hand-tooled jobs, but before long adopted a very elaborate, lighter brown rig that really showed off the tooling. There would be certain ones that were used far more than others, but many can be documented by studying the photos down through the years. Going a step farther than any of his competition, he went from bone-grip, nickel-plated six-guns in the 1940s to those and white-gripped ones in the early 1950s (probably 5½″ barrels) to gold-plated ones with pearl grips (probably 7½″ barrels) in the mid–1950s and back to more conservative ones. Roy would also adopt in the 1950s the break-away holster, which eliminated removing the gun from the holster during drawing. He would come to wear very elaborately tooled leather rigs, and they inspired a set of toy replicas, sans the tooled leather.

Still from *Apache Rose*, the film that celebrated the new image of a "King of the Cowboys." Most of the elements are present that would last throughout his career. Note the white hat.

Boots

Early in Roy's career, they were simply-stitched top boots with a wingtip of extra skin, probably store shelf ones,[25] but by 1942 they became very elaborate with inlay and overlay designs and "thunderbird" or "double eagles" became the first and constant essential design.[26] Tom Mix got the public used to the cowboy's pants being tucked into heavily inlaid, high profile, high top boots, and Roy adopted this practice as one of his personal "trademarks." There were many pairs because next to his shirt, they were the most showy part of his attire. Multicolored with the eagles always prominent, they became an essential "trademark" piece of attire, and although the eagles could be seen on occasion in store-bought boots, they were not all that common.[27] Once Roy adopted them for his own, none of the other stars really copied him. Some of the boots

even showed fancy inlay work in wingtips. Colorful beading was employed. In 1952, he was seen wearing a pair of red, white, and blue boots made by C. H. Hyer and Sons of Olathe, Kansas.[28] The boots have a 14″ top, which was higher than those he normally wore, and they were in the stovepipe style. They were further set off with fancy spurs, a less visible adornment, but very audible in the television series of the 1950s. The spur straps were wide and heavily tooled, as were the heel bands. The spurs were engraved, as were the buckles and conchas on the leathers. Whereas many chose the shorter topped boots, such as the Pee-Wees worn by Gene Autry, Roy went for the taller ones, some even the stovepipe style. According to author/boot collector Tyler Beard in *The Cowboy Boot Book*, Roy "wore out hundreds of inlaid eagle boots over the years." In 1949 a pair of the boots were running him about $75.

Trigger's Attire

Judging from most published accounts, Roy didn't acquire his number one horse until at least after the completion of his first feature film, *Under Western Stars*, but in that film he had already acquired a fancy show saddle that was made of tooled leather and adorned with silver. These saddles would become extremely popular during the 1940s and were primarily used for showy events such as rodeo parades. Few of the Western stars went so far as to acquire one, and cost was surely a primary factor here. Almost every saddle company offered one in its line, and California was home to many companies such as Edward Bohlin.[29] It is believed at this time that Bohlin made at least one of several heavily adorned saddles used by Roy in the 1940s–1960s. Another likelihood is that the Bona-Allen Co. of Buford, Georgia, produced one of Roy's main saddles, as they were the company that produced the child's Roy Rogers saddle that was sold through Sears and Roebuck Co. in the early 1950s. This company has been around since 1873.[30] On personal appearance tours, Trigger shone as brightly as his rider.[31] Magazine articles state that the saddles cost $150 in 1943. Renowned artists such as Till Goodan and Bob Brown drew patterns that would be tooled into Roy's leather items, such as the saddles. In 1953 it was reported that one of Roy's silver, ruby, and gold inlaid saddles was insured for $50,000 and that it took sixteen men six months to tool the designs into the leather. One saddle held 1.36 ounces of gold, 1,400 ounces of silver, and 1,500 rubies. Each silver and gold ornament carried an individual design.[32]

Beginning in 1947, Roy also acquired several lightweight, colorful, plastic saddles, at least one of which was made by All-Western Plastics Co.

Changes in Styles

An understanding of Roy Rogers' attire during the heyday of his career is the primary key to being able to date any one of thousands of Roy Rogers photographs or to relate an illustration to a particular "Roy Rogers," i.e., the Roy of the 1940s, the Roy of the 1950s, etc.

As complicated as it might appear because of the hundreds of different costumes involved, it is not too difficult, once you become familiar with the basic attire, to identify the periods in which that attire was worn.

Basically, the periods are pre–1946, post–1946, and 1960s–1990s. However, that broad a division won't allow for very much accuracy. It is also interesting to look more closely within these periods.

In 1941 multicolored silk neckerchiefs were introduced and the last stringed hat. Heavy embroidery of flowers and roses began in 1942, when "thunderbird" or "double-eagle" boots were adopted.

The key to the period is the conventional Hollywood-styled round crowned hat. The film *Apache Rose* (released February 1947, probably filmed late 1946 to early 1947) pretty much marked the end of Roy being seen in the old style hat. The new hat made its first appearance on a comic book photograph with Four-Color issue #137, which was also issued in February 1947. There are a few photos from late 1946 that show the new hat.

Along with the old style hat, we have lace-up shirts in stripes, solids, and two-tones or plaid, checks or stripes over solids; there are also embroidered button and snap shirts. The very heavy embroidered designs that began to appear in 1944 were of cactus, desert plants, stars, flowers, roses, boots, "thunderbirds," and saddles. The pockets were usually "slash" or "half-moon" until 1946 when Longhorn pockets were introduced. The collars were usually either plain or embroidered. Fringe first appeared during a tour in October 1944. This was on a solid shirt, and by 1946 it would be used heavily with two-toned solids and then dark solids over plaid designs.

Naturally there are photos from the period extending through most of 1941 that show Roy in Old West–style period attire, Hollywood version, from his historical setting films. A black hat was seen on occasion, basically the same style as the white or tan hats. There are a few photos that were taken at home, usually with the kids, with Roy in the first new hat with the diamond-shaped crown, and it is black.

The oak-leaf collar made its first appear-

Roy even went with shiny fringe, and much longer, as seen in this publicity still with Dale, for *Golden Stallion*. **Note shiny oak leaf collar as well.**

ance on a mixed solid and plaid shirt (see Four-Color Comics #86, October 1945). Then in June 1946, the collar appeared on a plaid shirt with fringe and a solid shirt with fringe (see Four-Color Comics #109).

Through 1945 the majority of shirts were embroidered. In 1946, those shirts were mixed with several fringe styles, either solid, all plaid, or all stripes. The new hat appeared in late 1946. These new hats were light in color, either browns, tans, or off-whites. They had a diamond-shaped crown, creased vertically in front to allow for a point.

Several more fringe styles were introduced. Fringe was in and would stay in throughout the 1950s. It was almost always a suede leather fringe that set Roy totally apart in appearance from his competition. Pre–1946 fringe was relatively short (several inches in length); it hung from the yoke surrounding the shirt and ran from the elbow to the wrist portion of the sleeves.

One particular embroidered shirt really stands out. It was covered with cactus, desert plants, and boots, and would be used in a photo session yielding many prints that would be used essentially for comic book and magazine covers.

In 1947 the oak leaf collar was here to stay with the introduction of a shirt style that would be made in many variations: plaid over solid (complimentary or same colors) on yoke, collar, and cuffs (running from elbow to wrist), one tier of suede fringe as described above. The first time this shirt was seen in a comic book photo was in Four-Color issue #137, February 1947. The embroidered styles continued during this period, as did all stripe, checked, and plaid styles with no fringe. This shirt is seen in publicity photos associated with the film *Springtime in the Sierras*, released July 1947. The first plastic saddles made their appearance at this time.

Late in 1949, Roy got some boots from a different bootmaker, and they appear to be from the Hyer Co. The first appear to have about a 12″ top, and they are identified by the stovepipe top and the line of stars around the very top. They showed up on the cover of the comics issue #25, January 1950. They were seen again on the cover of the April issue, on the back of issue #52, April 1952, and, with about a 14″ top, on the cover of issue #60, December 1952.

Through 1948 and most of 1949, Roy was using single-action .45 Cal. "Peacemaker" or "Frontier" six-guns with stag grips, of several barrel lengths, including 5½″ and 7½″. The holster and gunbelt were very dark brown tooled leather. In the Roy Rogers Comics, a photo used in January 1950 shows us his new gold-plated guns with at least 7½″ barrel length and with pearl

or ivory grips with a horse's head. The new belt and holsters were a much lighter, more mahogany color, showing off to better effect the elaborate tooling and frills including large studs and buckles. They may be seen in the publicity still #1832-39, associated with the film *Sunset in the West*, released September 1950.

In late 1949, after all the tans, grays, and off-white hats, Roy was seen in a very white one, and they would get even whiter in the ensuing years.

In mid–1950, another major change in the fringed shirt styles came about. It is seen in photos with a magazine article about Alan Ladd's birthday party published in August. It is seen in a September publicity photo (same as above) for *Sunset in the West*, in photos used for a school writing tablet, and in *Roy Rogers Comics*, issue #37, January 1951. Heavy flannel plaid or plain quilted material was used for the yoke, with three overlapping tiers of long suede fringe. The yoke material was used for the collar and cuffs. The body of the shirt was a solid lace-up, with a huge embroidered horseshoe on front. The collar had steer heads. The first steer heads were shorthorns, then came the longhorn steers, and at least one shirt was made with the steer heads upside down. There would be many color combinations used in this style. Basically, they employed three colors. The embroidered shirts that Roy has held on to all along became far more elaborate in design. The first of these more elaborate shirts appeared on a comic book photo in April 1950 and was apparently by the same designer who produced the 1946 cactus and boots shirt. This one contained two huge horse's heads, almost cartoonlike in appearance, inside two huge horseshoes for the front. The remainder was covered with cacti, desert plants, and saddles. Photos of Roy in this shirt were used for school writing tablets, magazines, and comics covers. It was also seen on the front of comics issue #44, August 1951. All of the embroidery work was done in colorful bright gold, brown, and green. There would be many variations in this style.

In early to mid–1951, Roy decided to set his hat off even more with an engraved sterling silver hat band about ½″ wide. It actually had a buckle, like a small belt, but was

The Longhorn version shirt collar can be seen in this publicity still with Penny Edwards for *Spoilers of the Plains*, **1951.**

fastened to the side so that the camera did not pick it up.

The next major shirt change to take place in Roy's fashion came about in 1955. The new design was seen for the first time in a comic book photo in issue #95, in November. The shirts were a heavy material, so it is likely that they were not used until the fall. The basic pattern was a solid color, lace-up affair, heavily embroidered with huge designs all over, including the sleeves and back, with one tier of extra long suede fringe. One pattern with numerous variations would be Indian designs, while another showed dogs. The collar appeared to have a sequin or rhinestone stitch. The fringe ran around the yoke and all the way down the sleeves. One unusual shirt had only three snaps on the cuffs. A few more conservative ones were made with simply a striped yoke and cuffs, with a huge horseshoe front and back plus the fringe. And a few shirts with more sparkle than ever were turned out by using rhinestones all over the body of the shirt, topped off with glittering fringe. The new break away holster came about, and the hat band was seen in gold as well.

Keep in mind that these were the major styles, of which Roy had many different designs and color combinations. It would have taken a 40-foot trailer to haul all of his wardrobe in the 1950s. He had shirts alone

In the mid to late 1950s, Roy went all out with huge designs and a single layer of suede fringe, longer than ever. Note the decorated trousers and extra wide gunbelt with the "Fast Draw" holster.

for every imaginable function. In addition to these major styles discussed, there were shirts which appear to be one or two of a kind, possibly made for a special occasion. Then there were scores of conservative, basic Western shirts used throughout this entire period. The simple plaids, stripes, checks, and solid over stripes or vice-versa that Roy started out with were also maintained and used heavily.

One can imagine this scenario for the year is 1950: Roy was on location filming *Sunset in the West*, wearing plaid shirts. He attended a ribbon-cutting ceremony during the week wearing a heavily embroidered shirt with no fringe. He performed at a rodeo at week's end and was seen in the plaid over solid job with the oak leaf collar and one tier of fringe. Upon completion of the filming, he went to the still studio to have publicity photos taken to promote the film. He chose the new shirts with the three tiers of fringe and the steers on the collar. Then at home there was a photo session, the results of which would be sent to magazines and the comic book publisher. Roy chose a checked shirt for romping with the dogs, then one with plaid over solids for action photos out by the corral. He left on tour and took a wide assortment of embroidered and heavily fringed shirts for three weeks on the road. So it was throughout his career. When a new style was introduced, it pretty much replaced the old, but each of the major styles — embroidered, fringed, and conservative — were constantly mixed, depending upon the function. Any particular shirt was generally confined to a given period, but would show up on occasion at any time thereafter. You didn't see the bright red shirt with the Indian heads after he went to the new hat in 1946, however. And seldom did you see the cactus and boots shirt worn with the new hat. Knowing the shirts, the major style changes that took place, and when they were introduced can be a great tool in identifying the periods of most photos in the attire history.

Chapter 11

"TRIGGER"

In this chapter the word Trigger, without quotation marks, refers to the actual horse by that name, the original Trigger. "Trigger" in quotation marks refers to the character Trigger, which, in actuality, might be any one of numerous doubles.

Important information pertaining to "Trigger" has been generated in the past 55 years from four main sources: 1. publicity, media; 2. Roy Rogers; 3. Glenn Randall, who trained "Trigger" from 1941 through 1965, and gave interviews in the 1980s; 4. William Witney, the director of Roy and Trigger films, 1946-1951.

These sources differ with one another on many points. Each one will be examined. Because of practical limitations of space in this book only a portion of my overall study may be shown. Everything to do with "Trigger" is show business, pure and simple. It is not the most honest thing in the world, but honesty is not an issue. If it were, you wouldn't have pure publicity, and without the publicity, there would be no stars. Fiction is the key word, as in good novels, plays, films, or live shows. The purpose of all these mediums is to entertain. It's not a scam. We Americans spend a large portion of our lifetime wages on entertainment, and if it's good entertainment, we get our money's worth.

Roy Rogers and "Trigger" were one of America's most top-notch acts for over two decades. They entertained us so well they became legends and idols in our eyes, our hearts, and our imaginations. "Trigger" became a legendary star in his own right, getting much press, publicity, and media attention. My research indicates that "Trigger" the character horse was portrayed on film and in photos and live appearances by whichever horse was necessary and available at any given time, and I doubt that this revelation will come as much of a surprise to anyone. Whenever the subject is brought up

among true-blue-cowboy-hero-worshippers, a class in which I have held a lifelong membership, most readily admit that they are aware there were numerous "Triggers."

The films and shows were a result of hardworking and skilled people and animals. Roy and "Trigger" were out front, but up ahead, perhaps days ahead, in the background and on the sidelines, many other talented people were required to make the show go on. People and horses cannot be in two different places at the same time. And when shows are being scheduled miles apart and time is tight and physical endurance gets pushed to the max, whether it be films being made or shows being put on, the only solution is backups, or "doubles" as they're called in the business. With a person, distance and camera angles are employed to create the illusion necessary to trick the eye of the beholder. This isn't necsessarily true with a horse, unless the observer is very familiar with horses. Most of the observers that will say that they can tell one "Trigger" from another were fans of Roy and "Trigger." And the legend was created for, and has been maintained for, those fans.

It does not appear that Roy Rogers is going to change the way he refers to "Trigger." It is clear to me after studying the many interviews and conflicting statements made over the years, that when Roy says, "Trigger," the name is always in quotations marks. The "Trigger" he will refer to is whichever one the question most readily applies to, or whichever one he is thinking of at the time. This is publicity thinking, and he has done it throughout his career. It has

Trigger is seen in this still from *Don't Fence Me In*, 1945.

maintained the legend of "Trigger" ever since the horse first rode into our lives. For the most part, when Roy rode out on his horse, the horse was advertised and promoted as "Trigger," just as the man born Leonard Frank Sly, even prior to the name change, was advertised and promoted as "Roy Rogers."

Roy Rogers had numerous doubles, as legions of grown-up fans now know. The doubles kept Republic with a star cowboy by preventing Roy from getting injured or killed while filming stunts. The same was true for the horses Trigger, Little Trigger, Trigger, Jr., and other "Triggers," and different horses would be particularly good at certain feats or tricks.

Roy's filming alone would have worn out the finest horse specimen in the world in short time. The road work, that is, tours, rodeos, stage performances, etc., was more exhausting than anyone not in the Rogers entourage will ever know. The filming and road work obviously required a large number

of horses. This is not to say that in either medium there were not certain ones "up front" at any given time. There were several such horses over the course of Roy's career. The following information is based upon the very earliest palomino in Roy's career that was much more prominent than any other. In my research, I have studied thousands of photos, as well as the published accounts of numerous individuals. My research will continue indefinitely, and I hope that others will be devoted enough to carry on additional research.

The original Trigger was very likely present in most, perhaps even all, of the feature Republic films and the six years of weekly broadcast television episodes. He also appeared in a multitude of the photos used for comic books, magazines, and advertising. It appears that he might have made a tour, perhaps Roy's first, and evidence seems to indicate that it was he who appeared at events in and around Los Angeles. It must be kept in mind, however, that the majority of what

The original Trigger in a publicity still for *Melody Time*, 1948.

came out of the Rogers camp and was published in any form, regardless of who was talking, had publicity as its purpose. Roy and Dale's lives were oriented to writing and talking in a publicity fashion, so when one reads that Trigger, Trigger, Jr., and even Buttermilk are touring the country with Randall in the specially equipped trailer, it is anybody's guess which horses are out there. Magazine articles, as well as Dale's books, kept Trigger touring even in 1956-1957 writings. There are three important things to bear in mind in analyzing this situation:

1. Every palomino horse has his or her

own unique markings. Many horses resemble each other closely, but not identically.

2. Many photographs are doctored for a variety of reasons, from creating an illusion to producing an eye-appealing product.

3. Photographs often do not lend themselves well to study at all because of the photography, the conditions at the time, or, the angle of the subject to the camera.

I have been frustrated to find many photographs that fall into this category. Often, only one particular distinctive marking can be seen in a given photo.

The study of the publicity associated with "Trigger" over the years can be very interesting to sort through, for sometimes it doubled back on itself, producing some interesting revelations. It is important to keep in mind that in the early years, the golden palomino that was with Roy was "Trigger." Later on, a "Trigger, Jr.," was introduced. But, although Trigger, Jr., was a real horse, he was also a character, as was "Trigger." I believe it would be reasonable to assume that the corrals and trailers contained numerous golden palominos who could be "Trigger," or "Trigger, Jr.," or a horse by any other name, or a horse by no particular name.

I believe Glenn Randall knew much more than he ever told, and I believe William Witney knows more than he has told. Some persons, such as trainers or film producers who were very close to the subjects, have shed some light on the mysteries, enough to make us all the more curious. Many of these people are no longer around, however. I have studied the publicity and information pertaining to "Trigger," as well as the photographs and films containing information, especially the markings on the horses, and have drawn many conclusions.

My study of the hundreds of photos indicates that there were at least three principal horses that were "Trigger" in all the mediums. Then there were many others that were shown anywhere from once to a half dozen times in all mediums. All of this is in addition to any "Triggers" in distant film shots. This discussion focuses entirely upon high profile "Triggers." People who were closely involved with the films have admitted to a half dozen or more "doubles" for Trigger in that medium. It has been shown that Trigger was relied upon for years to get Roy

and the producers out of tough filming situations. They would have the doubles on the scenes for certain stunts, but there were some stunts that they just couldn't film, despite numerous attempts, because the horses were afraid of whatever objects were employed. They could always depend on the "Old Man" as they called him, to bail them out, however. The horse had quite a reputation with everyone on the set for being fearless.[1] How much of this is fact and how much publicity, we will probably never know, but it's a beautiful story.

The Original Trigger

Birth: My research has determined that the original Trigger was foaled on a ranch in Santa Cietro, California, part-owned by film star Bing Crosby, and managed by Roy Cloud, a horse breeder formerly of Nobelsville, Indiana. Mr. Cloud bred horses, raced horses, and entered his horses in parades. One of these horses was "Golden Cloud," a palomino later sold to Hudkins Stables. It is possible that Mr. Cloud bred some of the "Trigger" doubles as well. (See Notes–Chapter 1, reference 69.)

Description: Blaze extends from left side of face, jutting out over left eye with a notch cut out, to right face, covering entire right nostril and top part of mouth only. Above left eye, in that area usually covered by mane, the blaze returns, with a jagged edge, to center of face, resulting in very large white area on forehead. On right side of face, blaze runs straight up, considerably away from eye, to high part of forehead, where it turns in. The white area, well below the right nostril, makes a 90 degree right turn and, with a jagged edge, continues toward the mouth. Without being able to see this side of the face, or the part of the blaze extending toward the left eye, it is impossible to make a positive identification. Horse has only one white stocking, his left rear. One must make a decision based on this, and perhaps the right side of the face. Often in photos, and on film, the stockings appear blurred or discolored, and the mane obstructs the blaze near the eye. The more of the three distinguishable markings one can see, the better the chance for a positive identification. Eye

The original Trigger having his hoof print placed in cement at Grauman's Chinese Theater in Holly-wood, 1949.

marking visible: near positive identification, if paid attention to in detail, i.e., under magnification. Mouth marking visible: same applies. Stocking visible: assumption only. Any two markings together are conclusive in this study.

Size: 1100 pounds (*The Western Horse-*

man, April 1961; *Movie Fan*, March 1953). In 1976, an article describing Trigger in the museum states his height to be 15.3 hands.

Purchase: Roy's version: In *Liberty*, December 14, 1946, Roy is quoted as saying he bought Trigger in 1937, on the installment plan. In an article by Roy, in *American Magazine*, August 1949, he states that he purchased Trigger for three hundred dollars, and had to "do it on time" (installments).

Witney's version: After returning from the three-month tour following the release of *Under Western Stars* (April 1938), Roy went to Hudkins Stables to talk about buying Trigger. Witney relates that there was a handshake and a time payment plan for $2500.

Scripps-Howard News Service: A story reprinted in the Roy Rogers–Dale Evans Collectors Newsletter, 5, no. 30 (1986) mentions an installment plan with several hundred dollars down. In *The Western Horseman*, April 1961, Duane Valentry states that $1,000 was paid down and the remainder of $2500 was paid in installments.

Randall's version: In an interview conducted by David Rothel, Randall stated that this transaction meeting didn't take place until 1941, after a string of films had been made. In this version Roy sent Randall to buy the horse, at the latter's suggestions. Roy put up the money and Randall did the negotiating.

According to numerous articles, Roy promised as part of the deal that only Hudkins' horses would be used in his Republic films.[2]

In *The Mountain Broadcast and Prairie Recorder*, March 1946, writer Frame Henderson states, "Roy raised Trigger from a colt, and scrimped and saved to buy him, feed him and train him, when in his early days with the Sons of the Pioneers, his earnings were comparatively small." Numerous published articles state that Roy used a guitar as part or all of the down payment.

According to most sources, Roy didn't actually buy Trigger until after his first feature film. This is credible from a strictly economic point of view. He used a fancy, silver adorned, tooled-leather saddle, a "Dick Dixon" model, or one similar to it, in the film, however. One might wonder why he would own such an expensive saddle, if he did not even own a horse and was having trouble making ends meet and paying to handle fan mail.

Another version to the Trigger story was related by Ray "Crash" Corrigan in the Pontes article in *Westerns and Serials*. The description he gives applies to Little Trigger and not the original Trigger, however.

In the film *Under Western Stars*, close observation of the close-up running scenes reveals that there were at least two different horses used for shots only seconds apart, one view from the front, another from the side.

Age: In interviews, Roy gave Trigger's age as 25 in 1957 and 33 in 1965, which places the horse's birthdate in 1932. In his book, William Witney states Trigger was 14 years old when he began working with him in 1946, which would also place the date of birth in 1932. A 1962 article (probably written in 1961) states that Trigger was 29 years old, was retired, and had six doubles to do what show business work there was to be done (this article also placed birth in 1932).

A *Movie Collector's World*, August 1992, article by Mario Demarco places birth in 1933, when compared with Rothel's accounting. It has often been reported or indicated in articles and books that Trigger was four years old when he appeared in the Errol Flynn film, right before Len met him.

In an article called "My Television Adventures" in *Jack and Jill*, May 1961, Roy says, "Trigger is 27 years old this spring" (places birth in 1933 or 1934). According to a Rothel interview in *The Singing Cowboys*, Trigger was three years old at the time of the Robin Hood film (1937), which places the birth in 1934. Witney indicates that he was 3–4 years old during the filming of *Under Western Stars*, 1937, which places the birth in 1934–1935.

According to *Movie Life*, 1943, at Roy's first appearance at Madison Square Garden Rodeo in 1942, Trigger's seventh birthday was celebrated (places birth at 1935). *Movie Fan*, March 1953, said that Trigger was 18 years old (places birth at 1934–1935).

Name: In a Rothel interview in *The Singing Cowboys*, Roy states that he was getting ready to film *Under Western Stars* when Smiley Burnette suggested "Trigger" as a name. According to a quotation in Witney's book, the horse was named "Trigger" the same day that Len's name was changed to "Roy." (That would be in 1937, before *Under Western Stars* was filmed.) In Witney's version, a wrangler at Hudkins told Len the horse's name was "Pistol." Len told him he was going to name him "Trigger," and the wrangler noted he didn't care what he was called, so long as the name on the rental check was correct.

Training: According to Roy in *The Great Show Business Animals* and *The Singing Cowboys*, Trigger was used for close-ups and special scenes, including chase scenes. Randall says that Trigger came first and was used for pictures. Based upon this author's study of photographs, it does not appear that the horse seen racing at breakneck speed in film still number 704-114 from *Under Western Stars* is the original Trigger or the horse most commonly referred to as Trigger. One has white stockings (front view), and the other is a darker color horse (side view). Still photo #704-114 shows a Trigger with blaze face running from the right side of the face to the left side, like "Little Trigger," and also shows some white stockings, but not four. Publicity photos #704-8 and #704-79 for the film show the original Trigger. The blaze on the face and the white stockings suggest that the running horse was another horse. According to Witney, the first trainer/wrangler for Trigger was Jimmy Griffin. From the time Roy took possession of Trigger right after *Under Western Stars*, Jimmy took care of, trained, and transported Trigger and another horse, "Little Trigger." Randall says he began training Trigger in 1941 and trained him for 24 years. A *Movie Fan* article, March 1953, states that Trigger had been trained by Roy since the age of five. Magazines began reporting on Trigger's tricks right away and through the years offered every number imaginable. For a long period of time, the tricks numbered more than 60. In *The Western Horseman* article, April 1961, they hit 100, and in *Jack and Jill*, May 1961, they hit 101. One example of a trick: patting him under the mane caused him to rear.

Contracts: In *Liberty*, 1946, Roy states that the "Trick Trigger" has a contract providing him equal screen billing. Many articles and published and taped interviews relate that Trigger never had a contract. This researcher's study indicates that the original Trigger definitely appeared in these films among others: *Billy the Kid Returns* (1938), still of Roy playing guitar to horse and R-1-47; *Wall Street Cowboy* (1939), #R9-1; *Don't Fence Me In* (1945), lobby card with seven of the cast on horses; *Eyes of Texas* (1948), #1623-37; *Susanna Pass* (1949), #1627-53, front view of Trigger racing after truck; *Bells of Coronado* (1950), where Roy is doing the running mount, in front of doctor's home; *Spoilers of the Plains* (1951), still #1838-8; *Heart of the Rockies* (1951), leading the band of men scene.

Personal appearances: Witney states that the original Trigger was taken on the 1938 tour. The film was released in April 1938. Roy and Trigger made almost every major city in the United States and were gone about three months. It appears that the horse was as big a hit as Roy.

Magazine articles from New York City (1942) covered Roy at the rodeo, where horse looks like the original Trigger. In photos taken at the Stage Door Canteen on Eighth Avenue (New York City), however, there is no blaze showing on right side of face. The same is true of photos of the birthday celebration, which may show the Stage Door horse, with long narrow face and blaze running down center of face only. Photos taken the same year at the New York Infirmary for Women and Children reveal what appears to be a third horse. Back at the rodeo, in a different performance, the horse has four white stockings. Dixie Hotel event photos show a horse with four white stockings, and a blaze that runs from right to left on face, as with Little Trigger. A magazine article from this period, "Roy and Trigger Thrill New York," shows one of the first primary Trigger doubles used for personal appearances, probably Little Trigger.

Siring: Roy has been quoted in interviews as saying that "Trigger" never sired. *The Mountain Broadcast and Prairie Recorder*, March 1946, states: "However Roy is planning on going into the horse breeding business, and has purchased a string of palominos with this [mating Trigger] in mind."

In *Liberty*, 1946, Roy mentions 24 wives, and 17 in foal, and says he has gone into the "colts by Trigger" business, which will bring in a thousand dollars a foal. In magazine or filmed interviews, he states that he bred Trigger one time, to produce a colt for a little girl in Pennsylvania.

The Western Horseman, April 1961, states that J. B. Ferguson, the Texas oilman who offered to buy Trigger in the 1950s, gave Roy a sorrel that he bred with Trigger, producing a foal for Ferguson as a consolation. Quaker Cereals ran newspaper ads about 1949 for a contest to "name the son of

The original Trigger with Roy in publicity still for film *Billy the Kid Returns*, 1938.

Trigger." The 1st prize was a week spent with Roy. In *Roy Rogers and Trigger Comics*, January-February 1960, an article by Roy to readers states that Trigger sired a colt and the mother was Buttermilk. (Buttermilk, according to Roy in *Happy Trails*, was a buckskin gelding.) In 1963, Roy was quoted as saying that Trigger never sired any foals as far as he knew.

According to a 1979 report, Roy had some descendents of Trigger on the ranch and was raising horses. In 1980s interviews, Roy said that Trigger never sired a foal and never had a contract. Such information as the *Liberty* article can be put down as pure publicity. *Pulse*, 1990, states that Randy Travis purchased a horse from Roy named "Trigger, Jr.," who is the "grandson" of Trigger. *The Mountain Broadcast and Prairie Recorder*, March 1946, states "he has never been mated."

Falling: In *The Answer Is God*, Elise Miller Davis describes Roy's first appearance at Madison Square Garden Rodeo in 1942. Trigger slipped and fell in the mushy turf, throwing Roy, and another time he slipped going around the arena, causing Roy to be thrown from the saddle and dragged until he was saved by two rodeo wranglers. All of this apparently was due to the turf conditions and the concrete underneath.[3] Roy stated in published and filmed interviews in later years that Trigger never once fell with him during his career.

Trigger's home: Randall, who lived in North Hollywood, as did Roy, says he kept Trigger in stables at back of his house for many years. Some articles state that Trigger was kept at a Van Nuys ranch with the other performing horses. Other sources show "Thousand Trails" ranch as the place Trigger was kept. A 1956 source varies this slightly, saying Trigger was kept at "Thousand Oaks." According to Witney, circa 1963, Roy and Dale gave up the ranch at Chatsworth and moved to the green hills of

Hidden Valley, close to Hollywood. This was a valley of horse-raising folks, and Trigger had a big comfortable place to live out his retirement.

Death: Roy reported that Trigger died in 1965 at age 33, which is very old for a horse. His heart just finally played out. Roy went over a year without telling anyone. In *The Great Show Business Animals*, Rothel writes, "It was a sad day around the Rogers household when Trigger died."

Horse No. 2
(Probably "Little Trigger")

Very narrow blaze at top of forehead, gradually widens (2″–3″) as it runs downward, along center of face, widening to 3″–4″ at bridle, where it begins angle towards nostril. Only top part of right nostril is covered, as blaze works its way toward center of mouth. There is a noticeable quarter-sized dark spot here that is even with the area just below the top part of the nostril. White area under nose, near top center mouth, has large notch, very visible. Blaze straight up center of face, left side, narrow. Only top part of left nostril covered. Four white stockings near even. Seen in RR XX 4 Pub. (and other photos taken at the time). On lawn across from nation's Capitol, 1942. *American Movie Classics Magazine,* March 1992, cover, 1942 photo. *Roy Rogers Comics* #86 (Four-Color), 1945. Photo #T-12, 8th Service Command tour, Texas, 1942. #B-RR-47, Army base tour, 1942. Texas tour, Alamo photos, 1942. Madison Square Garden Rodeo, 1943. George Hommel photos (Republic Pictures), NBC Studios, Hollywood, 1942, horse is put through dance routine. Photo #45, "Trigger entering hotel" photo, 1942. Cover, *Roy Rogers' Favorite Cowboy Songs* (Washington, D.C., photo), 1942. Photo #112, tour photo, probably Houston. Cover, *Life,* July 12, 1943. Parade, New York City, 1943. Bellevue Hospital (NYC) show, 1944. Madison Square Garden Rodeo, 1945. Photo in *Roy Rogers and Trigger ** Col. Jim Askew's Texas Rodeo Souvenir Program*, Philadelphia, 1946.

It was apparently about 1940 that Roy acquired another palomino, Little Trigger, whose name, for some unknown reason, will not be used and will be kept out of all pub-

lished matter this writer has witnessed throughout the heyday of Roy's career. The horse was 18 months old, chunkier than Trigger, and much more mischievous. This horse had four white stockings, as opposed to Trigger's left rear white stocking. Jimmy Griffin, Trigger's trainer until 1941, also took care of "Little Trigger." Star horse in *Trigger, Jr.* film and *Son of Paleface* film. Randall states that "Little Trigger" came second and was used for personal appearances. Witney writes that Roy couldn't keep the horse (Trigger) couped up in a trailer for weeks on end touring and still use him in films. So the second horse was picked up for personal appearances. He had a bad habit of biting Roy on the back of the neck. Note white stockings at the 1942 New York rodeo. The rodeo went on for several weeks, and the photos that resulted from it show different "Triggers." The one in the hotel room doesn't even appear to be the one shown entering the hotel. Different photos seen in books and magazines, reportedly of the performances this exact year, show different horses. San Antonio: the photograph showing this event is very interesting, in that unless the negative was reversed, this horse is not even one normally photographed during the personal appearances. The blaze on the face runs over the right side, as it would with the original Trigger, but the forefeet are showing stockings. Usually, the horse with the white stockings has the blaze pouring off the left side of the face. In *Movie Shows*, circa 1944, the article "Trigger Tricks" shows horse that in all likelihood is actually "Little Trigger," based upon my study of the horses, and statements made in published works by William Witney and trainer Glenn Randall. Notice in this article the four white stockings, bearing little resemblance to the legs of the horse originally introduced as Trigger. Compare with horse in film still #1327-42 from *Don't Fence Me In*, released October 1945. *Movie Life Yearbook*, 1946, shows Roy holding a seven-day-old colt, and the caption states it is "marked like Trigger" and that "Roy made deposit — may buy him later on."

This discussion seems to make it obvious that even though this horse in New York is being called "Trigger," it is actually "Little Trigger" or "Trigger, Jr.," or some

Roy is putting one of the tour "Trigger's" through a dance routine.

other "Trigger." The horse in the birthday photos is not the horse in the rodeo photos. The rodeo photos do appear to show the original Trigger, but according to many published accounts (Randall, for one), Trigger wasn't used for rodeo and road work during this time. Roy mentions in a televised interview that he purchased "Trigger, Jr.," in Pennsylvania, after he saw him there and had to bargain for a while to get him. Fisher Palomino Farms, in Souderton, Pennsylvania, was having a very highly publicized disposal sale in 1947. Fisher often took his horses to the Madison Square Garden Rodeo to show or sell them. Several horses in particular were advertised individually in various

This "Trigger" is doing some fancy stepping. Probably "Little Trigger."

publications such as *Western Horseman.* Roy stated that it took him six years to buy Trigger, Jr. He was nine years old, placing the birthdate in the early 1940s. Then Roy toured him around the country, as he did a number of tricks—high step dances, things of that sort. I believe it is a very distinct possibility that Roy purchased "Trigger, Jr.," from Fisher Farms, and it is possible that the horse was one highly advertised as "Allen Gold Zephyr" or was another horse similar in markings. I believe this might have been the same place Roy acquired "Little Trigger."[4]

Horse No. 3

Very similar to horse no. 2. Bottom part of right nostril is white, and bottom part of mouth is white. Seen in publicity photo with Roy leaning on fence, *Rainbow Over Texas,* 1946. Same photo appears on "Along the Navajo Trail," sheet music, 1945. Still #1427-19, *My Pal Trigger,* 1946. Exhibit cards, 1947, with photos early to mid-1940s. Apparently not Trigger, Jr. In *Happy Trails,* Roy says that Trigger, Jr. was seven years old in 1952, and this places birth in 1945. "My Television Adventures" by Roy Rogers in *Jack and Jill,* May 1961: "Trigger, Jr., is 12..." (places birth in 1948-1949). Trigger, Jr., went to tea with Roy in the Waldorf-Astoria Hotel, New York City. Trigger, Jr., also made two trips across the ocean, one to England and Ireland (1954?) and one to Honolulu. Practically all photos are of Trigger and Little Trigger in Witney's book. One photo, identified as Trigger, Jr. (circa late 1940s), is difficult to make out, but at least one white stocking shows, on the horse's right rear leg, and there are possibly three others. Blaze either extends down center of face only or runs from horse's right (top right) to left face, as with Little Trigger. If blaze runs down center only, this would explain one horse, with such mark-

WE HAVE SOLD OUR BEAUTIFUL 250 ACRE ESTATE AND HORSE BREEDING FARM

Forced to Sell!

DISPOSAL SALE

of all our horses and ponies

SHOW, PLEASURE and BREEDING STOCK

BROOD MARES, COLTS and STALLIONS

of GRAND CHAMPION BLOOD LINES

No reasonable offer refused

Write for your free, descriptive price list.

FISHER PALOMINO FARMS, Souderton, Pa.

VISITORS ALWAYS WELCOME

Little Trigger in *Son of Paleface*.

ings, that occasionally appears, a horse referred to in this text as Trigger, Jr. See also, cover, *Roy Rogers Comics*, Four-Color #86, October 1945; cover, *Roy Rogers Comics* #2, February 1948; cover, *Roy Rogers Comics* #5, May 1948; cover, *Roy Rogers Comics* #76, April 1954; cover *Roy Rogers Comics* #77, May 1954; cover, *Roy Rogers Comics* #100, April 1956.

Other Horses

In the film *In Old Caliente*, a Trigger double appears in a rearing scene. The comic book covers and inside photos of the entire Roy Rogers series show a number of different horses, and it is obvious that many of these photos have been doctored. However, in one that doesn't appear to have

Opposite, Top: **This is an unidentifiable "Trigger," in a publicity still for *Rainbow Over Texas*, 1949.** *Bottom:* **Fisher Farms ad showing "Alen's Gold Zephyr" appeared in Roy Rogers Championship Rodeo Program, 1947. Note the very high rear stockings, similar to those on horse appearing on back of the William Witney book. Could be Trigger, Jr., or his sire.**

been, Roy sits astride a horse with markings not similar to the main three. See issue #125 and Gold Key #1.

According to an article in *Movie Stars Parade*, 1948, "At Sky Haven, located 55 miles from L.A. Roy raised wheat, grain and fruits as well as palominos like Trigger. The horses were trained like Trigger, to eventually replace the celebrated 15 year old." All information on the primary "Triggers" is abundant with contradictions. Few probably even noticed the difference. I was one of the kids who was so thrilled upon seeing Roy and "Trigger" in the early 1950s that I guarantee I did not. Roy generally commanded more attention than the horse did, as he was the hero and he was dressed in attire that held one spellbound. He was simply bigger than life itself. Together Roy and "Trigger" were a breathtaking spectacle, and I doubt if any except equestrian professionals scrutinized "Trigger." A kid would be lucky to see Roy in person once in his life, perhaps more often in larger cities, but even then, appearances would come a year apart.

Chapter 12

COLLECTIBLES AND MERCHANDISE HISTORY

This is by far the most comprehensive listing and study of merchandise and collectibles ever compiled on any Western star. The goal is total comprehensiveness, but in light of the overwhelming number of items manufactured (probably on the order of 25,000), the absolute achievement of that goal is an impossibility.

The title I use for a collectible is the official/original title as advertised or the best title in lieu of this. As has always been a standard in describing cowboy character collectibles, the most official name of the item is used, which in this instance includes the name "Roy Rogers," "Dale Evans," etc.

Values used are shown only for the purpose of documenting the impact that Roy Rogers and Dale Evans have had on popular culture and how the memorabilia and nostalgia market has been influenced. These values are in no way meant to be an indicator of the price at which the item can be purchased. I have seen, or heard of, the items being displayed or advertised for sale at the values shown and have shown the highest prices observed or have consulted dealers and combined that information with my own experience for estimating the values on items not actually seen. Highest value always represents mint condition item in mint, original packaging. Prices on such items can fluctuate greatly relative to the locale, the event or store at which they are found, and especially the time period. I have witnessed dramatic differences from one week to the next and from one event to the next. It is not known just how many licenses were issued by Roy Rogers companies to foreign manufacturers, nor how much merchandise was produced without any "authorization," but there is evidence of a large number of items appearing over the years. It is possible that Britain rivals the U.S. in production of RR items. Those that have been documented are shown with the domestic items. Prices given for new items and values shown are two different things. The value is based upon the "street" or "market" price and can be higher than the price at which an item is sold in a special place, for instance a museum gift shop or a catalogue of which the average marketplace customer might not even be aware. Essential data are shown when available. The photographs and information used here are solely for the purpose of illustrating this text on Americana collectibles, and no attempt is made to violate any existing copyrights or trademarks on any item appearing. The photos are either of collectibles no longer being produced or permission has been obtained to use the photo of an item currently or recently in production, or the items are in the private collection of the author. The copyrights and trademarks belong to their respective holders and are noted when known.

Vintage Collectibles, 1938–1960s

Ads *(see also* Tear Sheets*)*

Ads, especially for films and merchandise, appeared in many different periodicals and newspapers. They are commonly bought, sold, and traded as "tear sheets," carefully backed with cardboard and sealed in plastic. Examples of those typically found follow.

The Answer Is God. October 16, 1955. McGraw-Hill Publishing Co. Photo of Roy and Dale. Small. $2–$3.

Auto-Lite/Ride Trigger, Me? 1953. *Saturday Evening Post.* Endorsement, Auto-Lite auto products. Full page. Illustrated: b&w photo of Roy lookalike Ken Marvin of New York City. $10.

Auto-Lite/Ride Trigger, Me? 1953. Endorsement, Auto-Lite auto products. Half page. Illustrated: b&w photo of Roy lookalike Ken Marvin. $3–$5.

Back to School with Roy Rogers Guaranteed Products. August 23, 1954. *Life.* One-third page. Photo: Roy, merchandise. $3.

Boston Garden World Championship Rodeo. "King of the Cowboys" 25th Annual (October 1955). Full page. $10.

Boys! Girls! Here's the Safe, Easy Way to "Outdraw" Your Friends. 1960. Speeddry Products, Inc. RR merchandise. Photo of Roy. Partial page. $1–$3.

Brand a Bargain at Your Chevy Dealer's Truck Roundup! Late 1950s. Photo of Roy. Small. $2.

Brand a Bargain at Your Chevy Dealer's Truck Roundup! Circa 1958. Photo of Roy. Full page $3–$6.

California Casual Suit. 1944. Betty Co-Ed of Hollywood Co. Photo: Dale Evans. One-third page. $2.

Canaries Are Wonderful Pets. 1946. Photo: Dale Evans. One-eighth page. $2.

Cardigan Suit. November 1945. Betty Co-Ed Cosmetics. Photo: Dale Evans. One-sixth page. $2.

Causin' All the Talk . . . Sellin' All the Records. May 7, 1955. *Billboard.* Roy Rogers records/RCA Victor. $2–$4.

A Child's Trust Is a Precious Thing. September 9, 1956. *Saturday Evening Post.* RR merchandise. One-fourth page. Illustrated: b&w of Roy with youngster. $3–$5.

Christmas Is Coming. December 5, 1955. *Life.* RR merchandise. Three pages. Illustrated: photos of Roy, Dale, merchandise. $20.

Clothing Pattern. Summer 1947. *McCall's Needlework.* Photo of Roy on an endorsement. Full page. $10.

Come to the Roy Rogers Roundup.

1950s. Used Dependable Cars (probably affiliated with Dodge). Photo of Roy rearing on Trigger. Full page. $4–$7.

Dale Evans Rogers Angel Unaware. 1950s. Boone's Book and Bible Store. Not illustrated. One-sixth page. $1.

Dell Comics. 1950s. Photo: RR family reading comic books. Full page. $3.

Drum Is Mighty Strong for Friskies. January 26, 1948. *Life.* Endorsement, Carnation Co. Half page. Illustrated: b&w photo of Roy and dog Drum. $5–$8.

Fall Days Are Fun Days—Roy Rogers Guaranteed Products. October 18, 1954. *Life.* Photo: Roy, merchandise. One-third page. $3.

Film Star Hair. November 1947. *Photoplay.* Colinated Foam Shampoo. Photo: Dale Evans. One-fourth page. $2.

For Young Cowhands—Roy Rogers Guaranteed Products. April 26, 1954. *Life.* One-third page. Photo: Roy, merchandise. $3–$5.

Free Roy Rogers Western Rings. 1952. Newspaper. General Foods. One-eighth page color. $5–$15.

Go Western in This Swanky Ranch Togs Shirt. December 1944. Ranch Togs of Hollywood Co. One-third page. Photo: Dale Evans. $2.

Golden Stallion. February 1950. *Hit Parader.* (Roy Rogers film) with Roy and Dale songs. Full page. $10.

Hands Across the Border. February 12, 1944. (Roy Rogers film.) Full page. $10.

Havin' Fun the Real Roy Rogers Way. July-August 1958; October-November 1958. *Roy Rogers Comics* #126; *Gunsmoke* (Dell Western comic) #11. (RR merchandise). Full page. $5.

Heart of the Golden West. December 1, 1942. *Look.* (Roy Rogers film.) Republic Pictures. One-fourth page. $2–$4.

Hey Kids! It's Fun and Easy. 1956-1957. Baker's Instant Chocoloate Mix. Illustrated Roy. (Same as 1960s Nestle's.) Full page. $3–$6.

Idaho. March 22, 1943. *Life.* (Roy Rogers film.) Republic Pictures. One-fourth page. $3–$5.

I'm a Mercury Man. May 24, 1957. *Life.* Mercury outboard motors, Kiekhaefer Corp. Two photos: Roy, Dale, and family. Full page. $5–$8.

Roy Rogers merchandise ad. *Life* magazine, 1955.

I'm Glad to See You Cowpokes Have Real Roy Rogers Gear. October 1957; April 1958. *Roy Rogers Comics*, #118, 124. RR merchandise. Full page. $5.

Introducing the Brand New Roy Rogers Quick Draw. 1960. Speedry Products, Inc. RR merchandise. Photo of Roy. Full page. $5.

It's Easy to Learn Dancing. January 1945. *Song Hits* magazine. Pioneer Publications, Inc. Photo: Dale Evans. One-fourth page. $2.

"It's Our Brand" Say Roy Rogers and Dale Evans. 1950s. RR merchandise. Photo: Roy, Trigger, Dale. One-third page. $3.

Roy Rogers merchandise ad. Back of "Lassie" title, *Dell Comics*, 1958.

It's Trigger on the Range. March 1952. *Open Road*, vol. 34, no. 3. Endorsement: Mercury outboard motors, Kiekhaefer Corp. Half page. B&w photo of Roy in boat. $3–$5. Also: *Boy's Life*, 1952. $3–$5.

Kahn's Tender, All-Meat Wieners. 1958. Local television sponsor. Partial page. Photo of Roy. $2–$4.

Kids You Can Meet Roy Rogers. September 26–October 2, 1952. *TV Guide*. Contest in New York City area. (For naming television series episode of September 28, 1952.) $3–$5.

Look at These Real Roy Rogers Toys for Christmas. November-December 1957. *Roy Rogers Comics*, #119, 120. RR merchandise. Full page. Illustrated: specially posed color photo of Roy with youngsters. $5–$8.

Magic Chef. September 1940. *Better Homes and Gardens.* Endorsement. Full page. $10. *See also* Displays.

Magic Chef. September 7, 1940. *Saturday Evening Post.* Full page. $10.

Magic Chef. September 1940. *Ladies Home Journal.* Endorsement. Half page. $3–$5.

Man from Music Mountain. September 6, 1943. *Life.* (Roy Rogers film.) Republic Pictures. One-fourth page. $3–$5.

Movie Star Portraits. December 1948. Irving Klaw Co. Photo: Roy. One-fifth page. $2.

Movie Star Portraits. 1940s. Movie Star News Co. Photo: Roy. Full page. $2.

My Spiritual Diary. 1955. By Dale Evans Rogers. Baptist Book Store, Jackson, Miss. $2–$3.

Name the Pony Contest. 1960. Nestle's Quik. Illustrated Roy. Full page. $2–$5.

Nestle's Strawberry Flavored Quik Keeps You in the Pink. June 19, 1960. Major newspapers. (In collection: *New York Sunday News*.) Sponsor: Nestle's Foods. Half page. Specially posed photo of Roy, b&w. $10–$15.

Now These Feature Pictures Never Before on Television. May 7, 1955. *Billboard.* Roy Rogers films/MCA-TV. Full two pages. Illustrated: photo of Roy, rearing on Trigger. $20. (This came about when Republic Pictures finally won the years-long court battle to edit films and sell to television.)

The Pick of America's Most Famous Gifts at Western Auto. December 6, 1954. *Life.* RR merchandise. One RR item on full page, color. $3.

Post's Sugar Crisp. 1950s. Various World Championship Rodeo magazines/programs. Sponsor: General Foods, Post Cereals. Two full pages. Illustrated: drawings of Roy, Trigger, and Bullet. $10–$15.

Roy and Dale on NBC Radio and Television. *Coronet*, August 1953. $4.

Roy and His Son Say It's the Real Thing. 1950s. Photo: Roy, Roy, Jr. One-eighth page. RR merchandise (lamp). $3.

Roy Rogers Crackin' Good Gun/Roy Rogers Cookies. Early 1951. Newspaper. Carr-Consolidated Biscuit Co. Half page color. $12–$20.

Roy Rogers Deputy Sheriff's Badge. Early 1950. Newspaper. Quaker Oats. Half page color. $12–$20.

Roy Rogers Family Contest. June 1, 1954. *Look.* Post's Sugar Crisp cereal. Full page. Illustrated. $5.

Roy Rogers Favorite Cowboy Songs. September 1945. *Song Hits.* Photo: Roy. One-twentieth page. $2.

Roy Rogers Favorite Cowboy Songs. November 1945. *Hit Parader.* Photo: Roy. One-twentieth page. $2.

Roy Rogers Frontier Shirts by Rob Roy. November 27, 1950. *Life.* Endorsement, RR merchandise. One-fourth page. $3.

Roy Rogers Merchandise. July 1950. *Gabby Hayes Western Comic* #20. RR merchandise: Hickok Mfg. Co. Full page. Illustrated: drawing of Roy. $5–$10.

Roy Rogers Merchandise. Christmas ad, 1954. Seven full-sized pages. Illustrated: b&w photos of Roy, Trigger, Dale and youngsters, specially posed. $15–$20 (full set). $3–$5 per page.

Roy Rogers Microscope Ring. Early 1949. Newspaper. Quaker Oats. Half page color. $12–$20.

Roy Rogers Quick Draw Handbook. 1960. Speedry products, Inc. RR merchandise. Photo of Roy. Partial page. $1–$3.

Roy Rogers Quick Draw Marker. July-August 1961. *Roy Rogers Comics* #138. RR merchandise. $2–$4.

Roy Rogers Rodeo Ad. 1950s. Madison Square Garden Rodeo. Stiff cardboard. Large photo of Roy. $200–$400.

Roy Rogers Rodeo Appearance. October 4–29, 1944. Madison Square Garden Rodeo. Newspaper. One-eighth page. $3–$5.

Roy Rogers Says: "It's a Cinch to Take Kodacolor Snapshots Like These!" September 7, 1959. *Life.* Endorsement. Eastman Kodak Co. Color photos: Roy, Trigger, Dale, family. Full page. $10–$20.

Roy Rogers Shoots for Santa. November 16, 1953. *Life.* RR merchandise. Four pages. Illustrated: b&w photos, specially taken for ad. $20 (full set). $3–$5 per page.

Roy Rogers 3 Power Binoculars, Roy Rogers Wrist Watch. December 1951–January 1952. Bill Boyd Western comic #20. RR merchandise. $2–$4.

Roy Rogers Thrill Circus. July 7–13, 1947. Newspaper, Cincinnati, Ohio. Roy Rogers Circus: Thomas H. Packs. 3¾″ × 6¾″. Illustrated: b&w publicity photo of Roy and Trigger. $5.

Roy Rogers Toys-Clothes Are Tested by Our Children for Your Children. November 1954. *Ladies' Home Journal.* RR merchandise. Photo: Roy, Dale, family. Half page. $4–$7.

Roy Rogers–Dale Evans Art-O-Magic Round-Up. 1960. Speedry Products, Inc. RR merchandise. Photo of Roy, Dale, family. Full page. $3–$5.

Roy Rogers/Dale Evans Merchandise. 1952. Sears and Roebuck Catalog. Five pages. Illustrated. $10–$20 set. $2–$5 per page.

Roy's Own Trick Lasso. 1952. *27th Annual Rodeo Magazine*, Madison Square Garden. One full page. Knox-Reese Co. $4–$8.

Roy's Own Trick Lasso. 1952. *The American Magazine.* $4.

San Fernando Valley. October 25, 1944. *New York Daily News.* Brooklyn Strand Theater. (Roy Rogers film.) $3–$5.

Santa's Most Famous Gifts. December 6, 1954. *Life.* RR merchandise. $2.

See Trigger and Me in Real-as-Life Action Shots. 1950s. Uncle John's Hobby Shop, Edmonton, Alberta, Canada/Viewmaster Stereo Stores. (Probably newspaper.) Illustrated Roy and Trigger. $4.

64 Actual Photos of the Favorite Western Stars. June 1948. *Motion Picture.* Stewart-Croxton Studios. Photo: Roy. $2.

Son of Paleface. July 12, 1952. *Box Office Magazine.* Film advertisement. Photo: Roy rearing on Trigger. $3–$5.

Songs of the Soil. 1940s. Western Music Mail Order Supply. Photo: Roy. One-eighth page. $2.

Songs of the Soil. 1940s. Western Music Publishing Co. Photo: Roy. One-third page. $2.

Start Collecting Roy Rogers King of the Cowboys Pop-Out Trading Cards. *27th Annual Rodeo Magazine*, Madison Square Garden. One full page. $5–$8.

"Straight Talk About Good Health Care and What It Costs." 1960s. St. Louis Post-Dispatch. Seven photos: Roy and Dale. Two full pages. $6 set. $2–$4 per page.

Stratford Celebrity Ball Pens. 1947. Endorsement. 12½″ × 2⅝″. $2–$3.

A Summer of Fun. 1954. *Life.* RR merchandise. Half page. Illustrated: photo of Roy, merchandise. $5–$7.

Sunset in El Dorado. 1945. (Roy Rogers film.) 5¼″ × 11¼″. $3.

Take Command, Get the First Thrill, New '55 Dodge. 1954. *Roy Rogers and the Man from Dodge City,* giveaway comic, back. Color painted likeness: Roy, Dale. $5.

They Got What They Wanted ... A Real Roy Rogers Christmas. December 1957. *Ladies' Home Journal.* RR merchandise. Photo of merchandise. Full page. $5–$8.

Trigger Meets a Real Roy Rogers Cowboy. March 1958. *Roy Rogers Comics*, #123. RR merchandise. Illustrated: color photo of Trigger and youngster, specially posed. Full page. $5.

'Twas the Night After Christmas—A Real Roy Rogers Christmas. December 1958. *Ladies' Home Journal.* RR merchandise. Photo: Roy, merchandise. Two pages. $8–$12 set. $3–$5 per page.

"We Never Carry More Than $50 in Cash." Circa 1960. American Express Co. Two photos: Roy and Dale. Full page. $3.

When They Said "Roy Rogers," They Meant Roy Rogers. December 1, 1956. *Saturday Evening Post.* RR merchandise. Two full pages. Illustrated: two painted scenes by artist Mayan. $15–$20 set. $5–$10 per page.

Win a Pony. 1960. Nestle's Quik. Illustrated Roy, merchandise. Full page. $3–$6.

Win a Real Jeep in Post Cereals' Roy Rogers Family Contest. June 1954. *Roy Rogers Comics* #78. Sponsor: General Mills' Post Cereals. Full page. Illustrated: drawing of Roy, Dale, Pat Brady probably by artist Hiram Julian Mankin. $5–$8.

Win a Wee Trigger. 1947. *Movie Stars Parade.* Full page. $10.

Win a Week with Roy Rogers/Name the Son of Trigger. (See Chapter 11.) 1948. Newspaper ad. Sponsor: Quaker Oats/Mother's Oats. Full page. $30–$50. (Also appeared as **"Win a Vacation with Me in Hollywood."**)

Win This Big Chance to Be in My Next

Movie. Late 1940s. Newspapers. Quaker Oats. Full page. $15.

Win Your Own Pony. May 2, 1955. *Life.* Sponsor: General Foods, Post Cereals. Full page. Color portrait of Roy, believed to be by artist Peter Alvarado. $12–$20.

The World's Finest ... Made in America. 1953. Endorsement, Schwinn Bicycles. Roy riding bike beside Trigger. Half page. $5–$7.

Yippee ... Says Dale. It's Roy and Trigger. Circa 1948. Yan-Paul Fashions, Inc. Photo: Roy, Dale. One-eighth page. $2.

Yipeeeeeeeee Ride with Roy Rogers. Circa 1950s. *Sunday Advertiser.* Roy Rogers comic strip. Photo: Roy and Trigger. Partial page. $5.

Merchandise

R.R. **ALARM CLOCK.** 1950s. No manufacturer shown. Unknown marketing. Possible 1950s unauthorized. Approx. 2″ × 6″ × 6″. Beige plastic case, clear cover. Picture of Roy and Trigger on black background, gold alarm and second hand, black hands. $75–$125. (Little is known about this item. Seen one time at a flea market, in rough condition, for $100.)

R. R. AND TRIGGER ANIMATED WIND-UP **ALARM CLOCK.** 1952. E. Ingraham Company, Bristol, CT, distributed by Carmody Products, New York. Retail stores, catalogues. 40-hour clock. 1½″ × 4″ × 4½″. Enameled metal case with brass frame comes in cactus (pale green), saddle (dark brown), sky (light blue), or desert sand (tan and ivory). Illustrated face, Roy riding Trigger across desert. Small inscription "Roy Rogers and Trigger" near center. (Doesn't appear on all versions.) Sears and Roebuck #4 G 7306E. "Watch Roy and Trigger gallop at every tick!" "Roy and Trigger actually gallop on gorgeous desert scene dial that has all the rich colors of the West!" according to ad. Originally $3.28. $125–$400. Version without Roy name on face is valued $85–$150. Case does not have stand attached. Both are 1951-1952.

R. R. 40-HOUR ANIMATED WINDUP **ALARM CLOCK.** 1954. Bradley Time. Retail stores, catalogues. Same size as above. Similar to the one by Ingraham. There are, however, numerous differences in the painted scene, although each clock shows Roy riding Trigger in a desert scene with mountains in background. Roy sits straight up in the saddle in this painting, but leans forward in the product of some manufacturing runs in the Ingraham version. "Roy and Trigger gallop at each second's tick" used in ad. Advertised in *Life.* Originally $3.95. $125–$400.

AMERICAN DAILY STRIPS. Great Britain. 1950s. Believed to be foreign printings, by arrangement, of King Features Syndicated Roy Rogers strip. Known to exist 1956-1960, with Hi Mankin's work. $15–$45.

R. R. RADIO SHOW **ANNOUNCEMENT FOLDER.** 1944. Includes 8″ × 10″ glossy photo. $200–$400.

R.R. **ARCHERY SET.** 1953–1956. Ben Pearson, Inc. Retail stores. 16″ suedene quiver, paper target on green board. 4½ foot hickory bow, brass-tipped cedar arrows. Armguard, fingertab has Roy's name. Box carries photos of Roy. Comes with Roy Rogers Archery Booklet, Roy photo on cover. RR brand on "suedene" quiver. Original price $6.95. $75–$125.

R. R. JUNIOR **ARCHERY SET.** 1953-1956. Ben Pearson, Inc. Retail stores. Smaller than the one shown above. Three sizes. Box shows mountain cat perched on tree limb, sheep below. 49″ hardwood bow, 39″ bow, or 38″ bow, depending on set. Rubber-tipped cedar arrows, 20″, 18″, or 15″ for safe indoor use. Original price: $1-$3.95. $50–$100.

R. R.-DALE EVANS **ART-O-MATIC ROUNDUP.** 1960. Speedry Products. Set #875. Five markers, 15 Western pictures to draw, tracer, nine cattle brand stencils, personally autographed full color Roy and Dale picture (likely facsimile signatures). Box shows illustrated Roy rearing on Trigger, desert scene background. Photo of Dale, Dodie, and Debbie on box. Originally $3.98. $50–$80.

R. R. **ATHLETIC SHIRTS.** Early 1950s. E-Z Mills, Inc., New York. Underwear type shirts. $45–$100.

R. R. "DEPUTY SHERIFF" **BADGE.** 1950s. Radio show premium. It is believed that many such tin items were manufactured by various plants in Long Island City, NY, and Providence, RI. On the air advertising, cereal boxes. Possibly several versions, including: (a) 2¼″ × 2¼″. Gold-colored metal. Raised "Roy Rogers" name on banner across top. Raised horse's head, star, six-guns, and word "Deputy." Original cost was 25 cents and one label from cereal box. Value $15–$30. (b) Same description but possibly from 1948-1950. Raised Roy likeness in circle, surrounded by words "Roy Rogers Deputy Sheriff." $30–$50.

R. R. "DEPUTY SHERIFF" **BADGE**. January 1950. Radio show premium. The Roy Rogers Show. Quaker Oats/Mother's Oats. On the air, cereal boxes, newspaper advertisements, 2½" across, six points. Raised Roy face, beside Trigger. "14 K. gold-plated" used in advertisement. Built-in mirror, secret compartment, whistle on back. Originally 35 cents and one trademark. $40–$75.

R. R. SIGNAL **BADGE**. Radio show premium. Quaker Oats/Mother's Oats. Some of the badges may have been made by Hickok Manufacturing Co. of New York. Advertised on the air, on cereal boxes. Drawing of Roy and Trigger is by different artist from the one who's work was used for the above badge. The signal badge has been witnessed in more than one form and size. $70–$100.

R. R. **BADGES** (MISC.). 1940s–1960s. Some badges came on attire, especially belts. Some contain a cut-out through which the belt passed. Others were clothing ornaments. $10–$30.

R. R. STRIKING **BAG**. 1955–1956. J. A. Dubow Sporting Goods Corporation. Leather, lined, six-panel pattern. Taped seams, valve-type bladder. Laced. Picture of Roy, Trigger on sides. Originally $4.25. $40–$75.

R. R. **BALLOONS**. Early 1950s. Pioneer Rubber Co., Willard, OH. $10–$15.

R. R. STERLING SILVER EXPANSION **BAND**. 1952. Carmody Products, Ltd., New York. Sold separately. Lariat link design with saddle buckle ends. Stainless steel back. Sears NO. 4 G 1876E. Originally $2.95. $25–$60.

R. R. COWBOY **BAND SET**. 1950s. Retail stores. Illustrated Roy and Roy photo on box, with campfire scene. Four plastic wind instruments and banjo. $65–$85.

R. R. AND TRIGGER **BANDANA**. 1950s. Retail stores. Variety of colors: red, yellow, etc. (red with white art most common). Cotton. Artwork includes brands, facsimile signature, Roy rearing on Trigger, and "Many Happy Trails." Made in USA, fast color.

Note: Western Art Manufacturing Co. may have made these bandanas. $35–$75.

R. R. AND TRIGGER CHINA **BANK**. 7½" tall. Roy rearing on Trigger. Blended colors finish. $35–$150.

R. R. BOOT **BANK**. Almar Metal Arts Co., Point Marion, PA. White metal. Also copper finish. 3½" × 4½". $25–$50.

R. R. BOOT **BANK**. Circa 1950s. Retail stores. Plastic. $20–$30.

R. R. BOOT **BANK**. 1950s. Fosta Co. 4¾" × 1¾". Plastic. Red, with black painted cowboy, horse, lariat overhead/cowgirl, horse, lariat overhead. Obvious Roy and Dale piece, possibly unauthorized, as names are not used. $5–$10.

R. R. HORSESHOE **BANK**. Circa 1950s. Metal, plastic. Wall mount. $70–$100.

R. R. AND TRIGGER SAVINGS **BANK**. 1950s. Ohio Art Co. Lithographed tin. For wall mounting. Red, yellow, blue. Picture of Roy, Trigger inside horseshoe. $100–$200.

R. R. **BASKETBALL**. 1955–1956. J. A. Dubow Sporting Goods Corporation. Natural crude rubber, abrasive-proof. High tensile strength. Four-piece pattern. Miniature. 21½" circumference. Finished with black seams, rubberlike lacquer. Originally $1.50. $45–$80.

R. R. **BED**. 1950s. Belvedere Manfacturing Co., Inc., Los Angeles. Retail stores, catalogues. No other information. $400–$1,000.

R. R. CHENILLE **BEDROOM ENSEMBLES**. 1953. Polly Prentiss Co. Retail, catalogues. Full, twin, youth. Variety of colors. Roy rearing on Trigger under Double R Bar gate. Matching rug in three sizes, with nonskid rubberized Latex back. (Roy rearing on Trigger in opposite direction.) Matching drapes 36" × 90". Bedspreads originally $6.95–$9.95, drapes originally $6.95, rugs originally $3.98–$8.98. Entire set: $100–$500.

ROY/DALE CHENILLE **BEDROOM ENSEMBLES**. 1954. Polly Prentiss Co. Retail, catalogues. Bedspreads in three sizes, rugs in various sizes. Five colors. Roy or Dale designs, two qualities. Matching rug. Drapes designed with lariat, horseshoe (not matching other items.) Design same as for 1950s set. Same design applies to rug (Trigger rearing in opposite direction.) Spread originally $6.98–$10.98, drapes originally

$6.98–$7.98, rugs originally $3.98–$11.98. Entire set $100–$500.

R. R. **BEDROOM ENSEMBLES.** 1950s. Monument Mills Corp., New York. Retail, catalogues. Sears and Roebuck #24 G 2556 M, full-size 88″ × 105″ spread; 24 G 2672M, twin-size 74″ × 105″ spread; 24 G 2673M youth-size 74″ × 90″ spread; 24 G 2674M, matching draperies. Spice beige, mint green, or cherry red. One row has Roy rearing on Trigger, lariat in hand, Bullet at horse's feet, name "Roy Rogers" written above. Second row has Roy holding Bullet, "Trigger" in writing, and third row has Roy and two others in scene that appears to be cowboys playing guitars. Heavy woven cotton. Drapes unlined. "Simpleat tops." Tie-backs. (No information regarding rugs.) Items originally cost $4.49–$4.98 in 1952. Entire set $100–$300.

R. R. **BEDSPREAD.** 1950s. Beige cotton. 55″ × 69″. No other information. $75–$125.

R. R. **BEDSPREAD.** 1954. Fieldcrest. Large 66″ × 80″ hemmed, double-woven cotton and rayon Jacquard. Contrasting two color mural designs. Originally $4.98. $100–$200.

R. R. **BEDSPREADS AND DRAPES.** 1954–1956. Monument Mills Corp. Retail stores, catalogues. Two sizes. "Distinctive colors." Double R Bar ranch gate, Roy rearing on Trigger, Bullet running, "RR" brand. All-cotton washable. Beige or grey with multicolored design. Matching drapes. Spreads and pair of drapes each originally cost $7.95. $100–$200.

R. R. **RANCH BEDSPREADS AND DRAPES.** 1955–1956. Monument Mills, Inc. Roy Rogers cowboy motif. Three sizes. Colors: gulf blue, emerald green, scarlet red, tan. Draperies, tie-backs to match. Originally $6.50. $100–$200.

R. R. STEERHIDE COWBOY **BELT.** 1952. D. H. Neumann Co. Also Boyville Co. Retail, catalogues, magazine ads. 1″ wide. Sizes 22–32. Tan or black. "Studs and jewels give it a festive rodeo air" used in ads. "Roy Rogers" inscribed on both sides. Ornate buckle set. Eagle engraved on buckle. Sears and Roebuck #43 G 365. Originally $0.97. $50–$80.

R. R. STEERHIDE **BELT.** 1953. D. H. Neumann Co. Retail stores, catalogues. Sizes 22–32. Different from one above.

"Tooled, studded and jeweled with multi-colored stones." At least four different designs. Roy Rogers name appears on all in two places (what appear to be attached plates). "Embossed designs on silver or gold colored buckles." Originally $1–$1.95. $50–$80.

R. R. BIKE-TYPE **BELT.** 1953. Retail stores, catalogues. Two conchos in back. Roy Rogers' name twice on back. Originally $1.98. $40–$70.

R. R. STEERHIDE **BELT.** Circa 1954. D. H. Neumann. Retail stores, catalogues. Sizes: 22–32. "Embossed, studded with colored stones." "Silver or gold colored buckles." Different from ones above. One has large oblong buckle showing Roy rearing on Trigger, name "Roy Rogers." Other has badge attached, Roy Rogers name on belt. Originally $1–$1.95. $50–$80.

R. R. SHERIFF'S BADGE **BELT.** 1949. Hickok Mfg. Co., Rochester, NY. Retail stores. No sizes given. Inscribed with Roy's signature; color pictures of Roy and Trigger all around. Genuine leather. "Man-sized cowpuncher's buckle." Instead of a standard tip, it has a smaller badge for a tip, with the initials RR. Originally $1.50. $50–$80. *See also* R. R. Badges (Misc.).

R. R. **BELT BUCKLE.** 1950s. Retail stores. 3½″ × 3⅞″ steel plate. Designed layer cast upon plate. Design: all raised, Roy bust (hat, neckerchief, shirt) on right in horseshoe containing laurel design; underneath "RR" in small square; left side has "Roy Rogers and Trigger" in rectangle, running at angle. Underneath is cowboy on bucking horse. Each of four corners has wagon wheel, all connected by border of S shapes, facing opposite directions. Horizontal striations background, solid. Receiver, hook riveted on C-shaped piece riveted onto back of plate. $75–$125.

R. R. **BICYCLE.** I have only seen one reference to this item existing. If it does indeed exist, it would fall into the $1,000–$4,000 range. If it existed, surely it would have been manufactured by Schwinn or another maker of fine bikes. Schwinn advertised in the *Roy Rogers Comics* in 1956.

R. R. 3-POWER **BINOCULARS.** 1951–1953. Herbert-George Co., Chicago. Retail stores, mail order. Black. Color decals.

Metal, large. Three-power American Optical lens. Strap. Originally $2.98. $65–$100. *See also* Camera and Binocular for additional information on similar item.

R. R. **BIRTHDAY CARD**. 1950s. Waldorf Greeting Cards, England. 5″ × 6″. Color drawings of Roy and Trigger. $35–$75.

R. R. **BLANKET**. 1950s. Fieldcrest Co. Retail stores, catalogues. 66″ × 80″. "Contrasting two color." Designs of ranch fence, gate, Roy rearing on Trigger, larger Roy standing, Roy Rogers name on end. "Large, hemmed, double wove cotton and rayon Jacquard." $80–$125.

R. R. HORSE **BLANKET**. 1952. Troy Blanket Mills, New York. Retail stores, catalogues. 24″ × 46″. 44 percent wool, 36 percent rayon, 20 percent cotton. Black, white, red striped saddle blanket. Sears # 10 H 8487M. Originally $2.89. $80–$150.

BOOKS

King of the Cowboys Presenting Roy Rogers. 1947. Edited by David Rodney. Beveney Publishing Co., London. Printed by Welberson Press. Cover: b&w photo of Roy and Trigger on red background, black binding. $30–$50.

R. R. Rodeo Programs. 1940s-1950s. Produced by Roy's companies for his rodeo. (Rohr Co.) Many slightly different printings. Photo covers, contestant line-up, articles. $30–$75.

Program for Profit: Roy Rogers, "King of the Cowboys" Manual. 1953. Elliott Bogeer. Roy Rogers Enterprises, CA. 19 pages. All other details same as above. Catalogue and merchandise manual. $100–$150. Rare.

Roy Rogers Catalogue and Merchandising Manual. 1953. Elliott Bogeer. Roy Rogers Enterprises, CA. 19 pages. Supposedly sent to prospective retailers for Roy Rogers merchandise. A letter to the author from Frances Williams, personal secretary to Roy Rogers and general manager of the Roy Rogers–Dale Evans Museum, stated that Roy's manager, Art Rush, had all of these catalogues and that after his death on January 1, 1989, cartons of materials were brought from his office to the museum. The catalogues were not in the

files, however. Rare. $100–$150. (Photocopies of these manuals have sold for $50.)

Program for Profit: Roy Rogers, "King of the Cowboys" Manual. 1954. Elliott Bogeer. Roy Rogers Enterprises, CA. 16 pages. All other details same as above.

The Answer Is God. 1955. Elise Miller Davis. McGraw-Hill, New York, NY. Book stores, book clubs. Small hardcover. The regular printing was issued with black and white photo dust cover and with childhood through career photos. Biographical. The book club printing was issued with a painted scene of Roy and Dale by Leon Gregori on the dust jacket and the inside hardcovers (painted rodeo appearance scene here) but contained no photos. $10–$15. *Note:* The lack of a dust jacket on many copies found in old book stores in the South/Southwest, and the title, keeps the value down. I have found on several occasions that book dealers did not know that the subjects of the book were Roy and Dale. The book is most often found in religious sections of stores.

Roy Rogers—King of the Cowboys. 1955. Frank Rasky. Julian Messner Co., unknown location. Second printing, 1958. $10–$30.

The Angel Spreads Her Wings. 1956. Maxine Garrison. Revell Publishing, Westwood, NJ. Book stores. Hardback. No photos inside, b&w photos on dust jacket. Includes Roy and Dale biographical information. Ms. Garrison was once an employee of Roy Rogers Enterprises. $10–$20.

Roy Rogers–Dale Evans Catalogue. 1955–1956. Picture of Roy, Trigger, Dale on cover. RR Plus Brand merchandise. 35 pages. $60–$100.

Follow Your Star. 1957. Dana Reed. Teenage Books, New York. $25–$45.

Roy Rogers Souvenir Program. 1957. Roy Rogers Show (personal appearances). Sold at performances. 8½″ × 11″. Color photos on cover, b&w inside. Numerous printings. Slight variation in this and similar ones, apparently for same year. Contains John Ushler art. Originally 50 cents. $30–$75. These type books were constantly produced and reprinted, with variations year after year. Special printings exist for certain appearances.

The values shown on the following books are for the hardback editions. Many have been printed in softcover and pocketbook editions. These can usually be found for $1–$5.

Angel Unaware. 1953. Dale Evans Rogers. Revell Publishing, Westwood, NJ. Book stores, clubs, personal appearances. Most of the small hardbacks have a b&w photo of Roy and Dale, and Robin on the dust jacket. The book went into dozens of printings and may be found with a variety of photo dust jackets. 63 pages. $5–$25 depending upon printing. (Often found without dust jacket $3–$10.)

My Spiritual Diary. 1955. Dale Evans Rogers. Revell Publishing, Westwood, NJ. Book stores, clubs, personal appearances. 144 pages. Some dust jackets have a photo of Dale on the back holding a bible. $5–$25.

To My Son—Faith at Our House. 1957. Dale Evans Rogers. Revell Publishing, Westwood, NJ. Book stores, clubs, personal appearances. 142 pages. B&w photo of Dale in Western attire on dust jacket cover. Many printings. 60,000 copies sold at fifth printing. $5–$25.

My Favorite Christmas Story by Roy Rogers. 1960. Roy Rogers with Frank S. Mead. Revell Publishing, Westwood, NJ. Retail stores. 64 pages. Solid red hardback, with facsimile signature on front. Dust jacket has bust photo of Roy. Photo of Roy (profile portrait) on cover. $10–$30.

No Two Ways About It. 1963. Dale Evans Rogers. Revell Publishing, Westwood, NJ. Book stores, clubs, personal appearances. 64 pages. Photo of Dale on dust jacket front by Bany Martin. Originally $1.50. $5–$8.

Dearest Debbie. 1965. Dale Evans Rogers. Revell Publishing, Old Tappan, NJ. Book stores, clubs, personal appearances. 62 pages. B&w photo of Debbie on front, Dale on back. $5–$15.

A series of Roy Rogers stories was published by Whitman Publishing Co. and Simon and Schuster. Whitman was owned by Western Printing and Lithographing Co. Simon and Schuster's books were produced by Sandpiper Press and Artists and Writers Guild, printed by Western Printing and Lithographing Co., and published simultaneously in Toronto, Canada, by Musson Book Co. The books were sold in retail stores, including five-and-dime stores. Writer/illustrator noted. It is believed that the first printings of the hardback novels, were issued with dust jackets, and subsequent printings as well as special printings (i.e., book club) were often not. Abbreviations will be used for the following items. WP: Whitman Publishing Co.; S&S: Simon and Schuster; DJ: dust jacket.

Roy Rogers, Robinhood of the Range. 1942. WP #1460. Better Little Book. Illustrator: Erwin Hess. 3½″ × 4½″ × 1″. 432 pages. Painted likeness of Roy and Trigger on cover. $15–$50.

Roy Rogers, King of the Cowboys. 1943. WP #1476. Better Little Book. Elizabeth Beecher/Irwin Myers. 3½″ × 4½″ × 1″. 352 pages. Painted likeness of Roy on cover: possible Nordli art. $15–$50.

Roy Rogers and the Gopher Creek Gunman. 1945. WP #2309. Hardback novel. DJ: Photo of Roy in circle, drawn prairie town, mountains scene, large cowboy on white horse. Don Middleton/Erwin L. Hess. Middleton was a pen name for famed writer Fran Striker, co-creator of *The Lone Ranger.* One sentence in this book was used here for the third time, having appeared first in Striker's *The Lone Ranger* pulp magazine (story "Valley of Shadows") and later in *The Lone Ranger and the Mystery Ranch.* A character in *Gopher Creek Gunman,* Luther Abercrombie, was first introduced December 2, 1935, in a *Lone Ranger* radio broadcast. What is believed to be the first printing has a blue cover with the title encircled by a lariat above a six-gun and holster in a red square. The dust jacket shows Roy on Trigger in an oil well fire scene, painted by artist Joseph Dreany. A photo of Roy appears in a circle in the right-hand corner. What are believed to be subsequent printings were issued without art in a solid brown hard cover with the title in red. Other Whitman books are advertised in the blue edition but not in the brown. 5¼″ × 8″ × 1¼″. 248 pages. $15–$50.

Roy Rogers at the Crossed Feathers Ranch. 1945. WP #1494. Better Little Book. Illus-

Roy Rogers and Trigger Belt Buckle. From toy gun set, 1950s. Author's collection.

BOOKS, continued

trator: Erwin Hess. 320 pages. Drawn likeness of Roy, Trigger on cover. $15–$50.

Roy Rogers and the Raiders of Sawtooth Ridge. 1946. WP #2329. Hardback novel. Snowden Miller/Henry E. Vallely. What is believed to be original printing was issued with red cover, and designed with the title (Roy Rogers' name in yellow) above badge and smoking six-gun (gun in yellow). Subsequent printings, some possibly issued by book clubs, appear to be those issued with brown cover and no artwork. Back pages of contents (Whitman ads) different. The story in this book is also that of *Roy Rogers Comics* Four-Color #86. 246 pages. $15–$50.

Roy Rogers Coloring Book. 1946. WP #1006. Activity. Mixed art: Alvarado, Parks. 7⅞" × 10⅞". Line-drawn cover of Roy rearing on Trigger, same front and back, believed to be by Harry Parks. 60 pages. $25–$65.

Roy Rogers and the Dwarf-Cattle Ranch. 1947. WP #1421. Better Little Book. Illustrator: Henry E. Vallely. 352 pages. Drawn likeness of Roy, Trigger on cover. $15–$50.

Roy Rogers and the Deadly Treasure. 1947. WP #1437. Better Little Book. Writer: Gaylord DuBois. Illustrator: Albert Micale (frames from the comic strip). 288 pages. Drawn likeness of Roy, Trigger on cover by Vallely. $15–$50.

Roy Rogers and the Mystery of Howling Mesa. 1948. WP #1448. Better Little Book. 288 pages. Drawn likeness of Roy, Trigger on cover. Illustrated. $15–$50.

Roy Rogers and Robbers Roost. 1948. WP #1452. Better Little Book. 288 pages. Drawn likeness of Roy, Trigger on cover. Illustrated. $15–$50.

Roy Rogers and the Snowbound Outlaws. 1948. WP #701-10. Tall Better Little Book. 3³⁄₁₆" × 5⁷⁄₁₆" × ¾". Illustrator: Albert Micale. 182 pages. Drawn likeness of Roy, Trigger on cover. Possibly went into second printing. $15–$50.

Roy Rogers Paint Book. 1948. WP #1158. Activity. 11" × 15". 48 pages. Photo front: Roy and Trigger. Inside art by Harry Parks. $40–$65.

Roy Rogers and Dale Evans Paper Doll Book. 1948. WP #995. Activity. $25–$65.

Roy Rogers and the Mystery of the Lazy M. 1949. WP #1462. Better Little Book. Drawn likeness of Roy, Trigger on cover. Illustrated. $15–$50.

Roy Rogers and the Ghost of Mystery Rancho. 1950. WP #2348. Hardback novel.

Dust jacket has photo of Roy with artwork background; back has painted likeness of Roy and Trigger by E. Joseph Dreany. What is believed to be the original printing has a tan cover with "Roy Rogers" in white, and the rest of the title in dark blue, above and below ghost figure in dark blue. Subsequent printings are likely solid color, no artwork. Walker A. Tompkins/Andrew Bensen. 250 pages. $15–$50.

Roy Rogers and the Outlaws of Sundown Valley. 1950. WP #2347 Hardback novel. DJ. Illustrator: John Ushler. $15–$50.

Roy Rogers Range Detective. 1950 (some printings show 1949). WP #715-10. Tall Better Little Book. Illustrator: Albert Micale. 186 pages. Drawn likeness of Roy on cover: Micale. Possibly went into second printing. $15–$50.

Roy Rogers at the Lane Ranch. 1950. WP #811-15. Tell-A-Tale Book. Illustrator: J. M. La Grotta. 28 pages. Laminated litho photo cover of Roy. $15–$45.

Roy Rogers' Trigger to the Rescue. 1950. WP #2038-25. Cozy Corner Book. Illustrator: John Higgs. $15–$45.

Roy Rogers and Dale Evans Cut-out Book. 1950. WP #1186. Activity. Drawn likeness of Roy, Dale on cover, frontier town background. Roy's facsimile signature. $25–$65.

Roy Rogers and Dale Evans Cut-Out Dolls Book. 1950. WP Activity. Roy and Dale photos cover. (Color publicity photo from film "Grand Canyon Trail.") $25–$65. Uncut: $100–$150.

Roy Rogers and Dale Evans Paper Doll Book. 1950. WP. No other information $25–$65.

Roy Rogers on the Double-R Ranch. 1951. S&S #S7/SA1070. Sandpiper Books. Elizabeth Beecher/Ernest Nordli. 78 pages. $15–$45.

Roy Rogers and Dale Evans (and Trigger) Coloring Book. 1951. WP Activity. 8½" × 11". Photo cover has Dale (long hair), Trigger, Roy in heavy fringe over Indian designs attire. $25–$65.

Roy Rogers Coloring Book. 1951. WP. No other information. $25–$65.

Roy Rogers and the Sure 'Nough Cowpoke. 1952. WP #801:15. Tell-A-Tale Book. Elizabeth Beecher/Randy Steffen. 5½" × 6½". 28 pages. Laminated lithographed photo cover of Roy. Illustrated. $15–$45.

Roy Rogers and the Rimrod Renegades. 1952. WP #2305. Hardback novel. Snowden Miller/John Ushler. 250 pages. $15–$50.

Roy Rogers and Dale Evans Cut-Out Dolls Book. 1952. WP Activity. Drawn likeness of Roy and Dale together rearing on Trigger on cover; also Roy, Dale small photos. $25–$65. Uncut: $100–$150.

Roy Rogers and Dale Evans Punch-Out Book. 1952. WP Activity. 10" × 15". Drawn likeness of Roy and Dale on cover (both in sitting position). Covers plus six pages all heavy cardboard. Roy, Dale punch-out front; Trigger, Buttermilk punch-out back. $25–$65. Unpunched: $100–$150.

Roy Rogers, King of the Cowboys. 1953. S&S #575. Big Golden Book. Elizabeth Beecher/Peter Alvarado. Painting of Roy on Trigger on cover: Alvarado. This painting was altered and used on unauthorized R. R. items. *See* R. R. and Trigger Comic Book Holder. 94 pages. $15–$75.

Roy Rogers and the New Cowboy. 1953. S&S #177/LE1770. Little Golden Book. A. N. Bedford/Hans Helweg, Mel Crawford. (A. N. Bedford is pseudonym for Jane Werner Watson.) 6⅛" × 7⅞". 28 pages. $15–$45.

Roy Rogers' Bullet and Trigger Wild Horse Roundup. 1953. WP #2152:25. A Cozy Corner Book. Elizabeth Beecher/August Lenox. 7⅜" × 8³⁄₁₆". 28 pages. $15–$45.

Roy, Dale and Dusty Coloring Book. 1953. WP. Photos of Roy, Dale, Dusty on cover. $25–$65.

Roy Rogers and Dale Evans Coloring Book. 1953. WP #1027. Activity. Illustrator: Peter Alvarado (signed). Photo cover of Roy, Bullet, and Dale. (Negative reversal.) $25–$65.

Roy Rogers and Dale Evans Rodeo Sticker Fun Book. 1953 WP #2161. Activity. Illustrator: Peter Alvarado. 10⅜" × 12". Painted likeness of Roy, Trigger, Dale, Buttermilk, Bullet on cover. $25–$65.

Roy Rogers and Dale Evans Cut-Out Dolls Book. 1953. WP Activity. $25–$65. Uncut: $100–$150.

Roy Rogers' Bullet Leads the Way. 1953. WP #2567:15. Tell-A-Tale book. 28 pages.

BOOKS, continued

Photo of Bullet on cover. Frances Wood/Bart Doe. Frances Wood believed to be pseudonym for Dale Evans. Art is actually by Alvarado, so Bart Doe is a pseudonym. $15–$45.

Roy Rogers', Dale Evans' Big Book to Color. 1954. WP #1184:25. Activity. Illustrator: John Ushler. Cover photo of Roy in plaid shirt and Dale in brown and white outfit, decorating with pumpkins, streamers. $25–$75.

Roy Rogers Annual. 1954. WP #4058:496. Activity. Illustrator: Hi Mankin. Photo cover: Roy, Trigger, and hunting dog. Original copyright. Published May 12, 1954. Registered by Roy Rogers Enterprises, under A 146327. No renewal found. $25–$75.

Roy Rogers and the Trail of the Zeroes. 1954. WP #1501:49. Hardback novel. Packer Elton/Al Gleicher. 5½″ × 8½″. 282 pages. Laminated lithographed photo cover: Roy, Trigger. Back has artwork by E. Joseph Dreany. $15–$50.

Roy Rogers and the Desert Treasure. 1954. WP #2063:25. Cozy Corner Book. Photo cover. Alice Sankey/Paul Souza. 28 pages. $15–$45.

Roy Rogers in Surprise for Donnie. 1954. WP #2657:15. Tell-A-Tale Book. Alice Sankey/John Steel. 28 pages. Drawn likeness of Roy on cover, laminated. $15–$45.

Roy Rogers and the Enchanted Canyon. 1954. WP #1502:49. Hardback novel. Jim Rivers/Roy Schroeder. 282 pages. Painted likeness of Roy, Trigger on cover (front, back) by Souza. $15–$50.

Roy Rogers and Cowboy Toby. 1954. S&S #195.25/LE1950. Little Golden Book. Elizabeth Beecher/Mel Crawford. 28 pages. Drawn likeness of Roy on cover by Crawford, laminated. $15–$45.

Dale Evans and the Lost Gold Mine. 1954. S&S #213/LE2130. Little Golden Book. Monica Hill/Mel Crawford. Monica Hill is a pseudonym for Jane Werner Watson. 28 pages. Drawn likeness of Dale on cover by Crawford, laminated. $15–$45.

Roy Rogers and Dale Evans Cut-Out Dolls Book. 1954 WP #1950. Activity. Drawn likeness of Roy and Dale with colt and calf on cover. $25–$65. Uncut: $75–$100.

Roy Rogers and Dale Evans Cut-Out Dolls Book. 1954. WP #1950 (this number is used on numerous such books). Activity. 10½″ × 12″ cardboard folder with inside pockets with standup Roy (fringed attire, no hat); Dale (halter/short set) dolls. Clothing in paper sheets. Photo of Roy, Dale on cover. Originally 29 cents. $25–$65.

Roy Rogers and Dale Evans Cowtown Punch-Out Book. 1954. WP Activity. Drawn likeness of Roy, Trigger, and Bullet on cover; also Roy, Dale photos set in horseshoes on cover. $25–$65.

Roy Rogers–Dale Evans Ranch Tales. 1954. WP Activity (Coloring) Book. $25–$65.

Roy Rogers' Trigger and Bullet Coloring Book. 1954. WP #1315. Activity. Originally 10 cents. $25–$65.

Roy Rogers and Dale Evans 2 Statuette Dolls and Clothes. 1954. WP Activity. Photos of Roy and Dale, cactus, town background cover. $25–$65.

Roy Rogers' Pal Pat Brady Coloring Book. 1955. WP #1256. Activity. $25–$65.

Roy Rogers and the Brasada Bandits. 1955. WP #1500:49. Hardback novel. Cole Fannin/Michael Arens. 282 pages. Laminated lithograph photo cover of Roy, Trigger (reversed negative). $15–$50.

Roy Rogers and the Mountain Lion. 1955. S&S #231/LE2310. Little Golden Book. Ann McGovern/Mel Crawford. Painted likeness of Roy, Trigger on cover. Illustrated. 28 pages. $15–$45.

Roy Rogers, King of the Cowboys. 1955. S&S BB3470/reprint. Big Golden Book (same as above: #575, 1953). 94 pages. $15–$65.

Roy Rogers' Favorite Western Stories. 1956. WP. Hardcover, oversized. 252 pages. Photo of Roy on cover. $15–$75. In box: $125.

Roy Rogers' Trigger and Bullet Coloring Book. 1956. WP Activity. Illustrated cover. $20–$65.

Dale Evans and Buttermilk. 1956. WP #2570:15. Tell-A-Tale Book. Rose Welden/Helmuth G. Wegner. 28 pages. Laminated photo cover: Dale, Buttermilk. $15–$45.

Roy Rogers King of the Cowboys. 1956. WP #1503:44. Hardback novel. Cole Fannin/Hi Mankin. 282 pages. Laminated lithograph photo cover: Roy, Trigger. $15–$50.

Dale Evans and the Coyote. 1956. S&S #253/LE2530. Little Golden Book. Gladys Wyatt/E. Joseph Dreany. 24 pages. Drawn likeness of Dale, Buttermilk on cover by Dreany, laminated. $15–$45.

Roy Rogers and the Indian Sign. 1956. S&S #259/LE2590. Little Golden Book. Gladys Wyatt/Mel Crawford. 24 pages. Painted likeness of Roy, Trigger on cover, laminated. $15–$45.

Prayer Book for Children. 1956. S&S #BB3350. Big Golden Book. Dale Evans Rogers/Eleanor Dart. $20–$75.

Roy Rogers' Pal Pat Brady Coloring Book. 1956. WP Activity. Illustrated cover. $20–$65.

Roy Rogers and Dale Evans Cut-Out Doll Book. 1956. WP Activity. $25–$65. Uncut: $75–$100.

Roy Rogers–Dale Evans Big Toppers Book. 1956. WP #2407:25. Cozy Corner Book. Roy, Trigger, Dale on front, red-fringed attire, Dale sitting on fence. $15–$45.

Roy Rogers Double-R-Bar Ranch Coloring Book. 1956. WP Activity. Photo of Roy, Dale, pointing out carvings on tree. $25–$65.

Roy Rogers and Dale Evans in River of Peril. 1957. WP #1504. Hardback novel. Cole Fannin/Michael Arens. 282 pages. Drawn likeness of Roy, Dale, Trigger on cover, laminated; also small photo of Roy. $15–$50.

Roy, Dale and Dusty Cut-Out Dolls Book. 1957. WP #1950. Activity. Large photo of Roy, Dale, Dusty on cover. "And the Double-R-Bar Ranch" at bottom. $20–$55. Uncut: $65–$90.

Dale Evans and Danger in Crooked Canyon. 1958. WP #1506. Hardback novel. Helen Hale/Henry Luhrs. 282 pages. Drawn likeness of Dale on cover by Al Andersen, laminated. $15–$50.

Roy Rogers and Dale Evans Coloring Book. 1958. WP #1027. Activity. Reprint of 1953 activity book. Copyright Roy Rogers-Frontiers, Inc. (For unknown reason, same 39 cent price is shown on cover.) $20–$65.

Roy Rogers and Dale Evans Coloring Book. 1959. WP Activity. Photo cover, Roy and Dale. Roy with bow and arrow. $20–$65.

Trigger and Bullet Coloring Book. 1959. WP #2958. Activity. 6½" × 7½". $20–$55.

Dale Evans' Bible Stories. No information. $30–$60.

BOOKS (FOREIGN)

Abbreviations are used in this section to indicate publishers. WDL: World Distributors, Ltd. (WPL): By arrangement with Western Printing and Lithographing Co./ Reprints of American *Roy Rogers Comics* stories. P&S: Purnell and Sons, London, England. D: Dean. T: *Roy Rogers' Trigger Comics.* The number in parentheses is that of the *Roy Rogers Comic* issue from which reprint was made.

Roy Rogers Adventures #1. 1958. D. Six text stories by Arthur Groom. Illustrator: Roland Davies. Painting of Dale, Trigger, Roy (inside horseshoe) on cover. 79 pages. $30–$50.

Roy Rogers Adventures #2. D. 1959. Same as above. Illustrator: Leo Rawlings. Painted likenesses of Trigger, Roy, Bullet, Pat, and Dale on cover. 79 pages. $30–$50.

Roy Rogers Adventures #3. 1960. D. Eight text stories. Writer, illustrator same as #2. Some full-color illustrations and cover. 93 pages. $30–$50.

Roy Rogers Comic Album #1. 1952. WDL (WPL). Cover: Roy with pistol, looking out of wagon (55). Contents: "Jinx of the Headless Valley" (41), "Roy Springs a Trap" (42), "Die or Drink" (43), "Thirsty Creek" (32), "Dangerous Loot" (31). Six Trigger stories. "Pioneers of the Old West" feature. $30–$60.

Roy Rogers Comic Album #2. 1953. WDL (WPL). Cover: Roy lying in grass with calf (68). Contents: "Mantrap on Longshot Mesa" (63), "Man Hunt" (61), "Clue of the Spur" (62), "The Rustler on Goblin Hill" (62), "The Rifleman of Boulder Wash" (63), "Canyon Burial" (63). "Chuckwagon Charley's Tales" feature. $30–$60.

Roy Rogers Comic Album #3. 1954. WDL (WPL). Cover: Roy in doorway, pistol in hand, Bullet at feet (78). Contents: "The Big Horn Lode" (73), "Nester's Welcome" (73), "The Red Raiders" (73), "Roy Rides the Danger Trail" (74), "Tornado Weather" (74), "Snow on the Warfield Trail" (74).

BOOKS (FOREIGN), continued

"Chuckwagon Charley's Tales" feature. $30–$60.

Roy Rogers Comic Album #4. 1955. WDL (WPL). Cover: Roy behind fence, pistol in hand, Bullet at his side (79). Contents: "River of Gold" (48), "Trail of the Bushwacker" (81), "The Thundering Flood" (75), "One Man's Poison" (51), "Red Clay" (53), "Bullet Meets a Test" (70), "Roy Buys into Trouble" (54). $30–$60.

Roy Rogers Comic Album #5. 1956. WDL (WPL). Cover: Artist's portrait of Roy and Trigger from 1940s photo which was printed as a reversed negative on the British *Roy Rogers Cowboy Annual* in 1952. Contents: "The Stroke of Twelve" (50), "The Fast Game" (50), "Mystery of Circle Lake" (49), "Portrait of Uncle Ezra" (53), "Roy Takes a Prisoner" (51), "Bullet Guards a Friend" (68). "Chuckwagon Charley's Tales" feature. $30–$60.

Roy Rogers Comic Album #6. 1957. WDL (WPL). Cover: Walt Howarth painting of Roy and Trigger. Contents: "In Poisoned Water" (57), "A Challenge in the Big Bend" (57), "The Missing Deputy" (54), "Wolf Trap" (54), "Coward's Cache" (57), "Roy Plays a Hunch" (57). "Chuckwagon Charley's Tales" feature. $30–$60.

Roy Rogers Comic Album #7. 1958. WDL (WPL). Cover: Walt Howarth's drawing of Roy based on concept used for American comic covers produced by the Western Co. Contents: "Tickets to Destruction" (59), "Trigger Fights for Two" (T-9), "Gun Talk in Ghost Town" (59), "Trigger and the Carnival Killer" (T-11), "The Hermit of Pullin's Pocket" (65), "Backwoods Trapper" (unknown), "Trigger and the Milk Run" (T-11). $30–$60.

Roy Rogers at the Lane Ranch. 1951. WDL. British reprint of 1950 American Whitman Tell-A-Tale Book. Illustrator: J. M. La-Grotta. 20 pages. More reprints of these type of books may exist. $15–$45.

Roy Rogers Number Book. 1954. Purnell and Sons. Mostly puzzles and games. Illustrated. $20–$65.

Roy Rogers Bumper Book. 1955. Adprint-P/C. All text features: 9 text stories. Some with color illustrations. Unknown art. 79 pages. $20–$65.

Roy Rogers Big Golden Book #1. Unknown date and publisher, probably P&S, 1950s, perhaps 1954. Contents: "Roy Rogers and the Hungry Indian," "The Hard Way," "The Freight Train Holdup," "A Friend in Need," "Charlie MacDowell's Lucky Day," "A Good Night's Work," "The Moon Rock Robberies," "The Dynamited Dam," "The Big Storm." *Note:* Only one R. R. Big Golden Book was produced in the United States. $20–$75.

Roy Rogers Big Golden Book #2. 1955. P&S. Contents: "Roy Rogers, King of the Cowboys," "Dynamite," "Trigger to the Rescue," "The Affair at Black Rock," "No Gold at Buffalo Creek," "Big Bill and the Indians," "Snow," "The Forgers," "Bullet Takes a Hand," "Dust Storm," "Trouble Times Two," "One Good Dog," "One Way Out," "A Man-Sized Job," "The Dam." $20–$75.

Roy Rogers Big Golden Book #3. 1954. P&S. 93 pages. Contents: Purnell all text features (12 text stories take material from Roy Rogers #2, 1954, plus new material written by Elizabeth Beecher). Not known exactly which book this is referring to. Beecher is a writer for Simon & Schuster. $20–$75.

Roy Rogers Big Golden Book #4. 1959. P&S. Original art. Jameson/Forster. 79 pages. All text features, 9 text stories. $20–$65.

Roy Rogers Stories #1. 1953. Adprint/LTA Robinson, London. 79 pages. All text features, 2 text stories, illustrated. Contents: "Roy Rogers and the Hungry Indian," "The Hard Way," "The Freight Train Holdup," "A Friend in Need," "Charlie MacDowell's Lucky Day," "A Good Night's Work," "The Moon Rock Robberies," "The Dynamited Dam," "The Big Storm." This is probably another printing of Big Golden Book #1, with a different cover. "The Big Storm," with the exception of the title page, is a direct reprint of American material. The rest is original artwork. $30–$60.

Roy Rogers Stories #2. Adprint/LTA Robinson, London. 79 pages. Painted cover same as American Big Golden Book, Unknown stories. $30–$60.

Roy Rogers Cowboy Annual #1. September 1951. WDL. Cover: Photo of Roy on Trigger (31). Contents: "Gun Shy Gent" (35), "Terror of the Mesquite" (36), "At Owlhoot Cabin" (38), and Trigger story. One color photo of Roy and Bullet, another of Trigger. Several stories on Western characters. $30–$60.

Roy Rogers Cowboy Annual #2. September 1952. Adprint/LTA Robinson, London. Cover: Color photo of Roy and Trigger (reversed negative [7]; photo is from same series). Contents: "Mustang Mountain" (27), color photo captioned "Roy on His Ranch" (see back, *Roy Rogers Comics* #32, August 1950), "The Roy Rogers Story," "Rodeo," "The Trail of Tears," "Yellow River Seige," "Bears or Branding Irons" (27), "Trigger" (27), "They Died with Their Boots On," "Who Is the Mysterious Cowboy?" (Roy Rogers connect-the-dots puzzle), "The Chums of Roaring Creek," "Indian Gold" (path puzzle). Back cover: Colorized Republic Pictures photo of Roy on Trigger (reversed negative). $30–$60.

Roy Rogers Cowboy Annual #3. 1953. Adprint/LTA Robinson, London. Cover: Painting of Roy rearing on Trigger. Contents: "Roy Hunts for Strays" (47), "Roy Rogers and the Man Who Tried to Buy Happiness" (52), "Nester or Neighbor" (52), "North of the Great Divide," "South of Caliente," "Pals of the Golden West," article on Roy's sidekicks. "Chuckwagon Charley's Tales" feature. $30–$60.

Roy Rogers Cowboy Annual #4. 1954. Adprint/LTA Robinson, London. Cover: Photo of Roy with Christmas presents (61). Contents: "Adventures of Papoose Pass" (title change from story in *Roy Rogers Comics* #69), "Bullet Searches a Crook" (69), "Roy Trails the Black Filly" (59), "Manhunt for Five" (76), "Mountain Mystery" (61), "The Killer from Cougar Mountain" (60), "High Wind and Gunsmoke" (69). $30–$60.

Roy Rogers Cowboy Annual #5. 1955. Adprint/LTA Robinson, London. Cover: Roy and Little Trigger (79). Contents: "The Red Whirlwind" (78), "The Golden Calves" (78), "The Challenge to Danger" (78), "The Silent Guardians" (believed to be "The Silent Killers" [72]), "Double Trouble" (77), "The Claim Jumpers" (26), "The Manhunt" (75), "Roy Meets a Giant" (75). $30–$60.

Roy Rogers Cowboy Annual #6. 1956. Ad-

print/LTA Robinson, London. Cover: Roy and Trigger. Contents: "Savage Portrait" (80), "Roy Rides the Rim" (80), "Hot Lead" (80) ["Hot Lead at Rocklins"], "The Cloaked Rider" (79), "Bald Lightning" (79), "The Ghost Well Mystery" (79). Back photo is from a series which includes the one used for *Roy Rogers Comics* #75, March 1954. Value $30–$60.

Roy Rogers Cowboy Annual #7. 1957. Adprint/LTA Robinson, London. Cover: Walt Howarth painting of Roy and Trigger, based on a Republic Pictures still. Contents: "Apache Blood" (28), "A Gift to Grandma" (29), "Wolves of Hunger Pass" (28), "Rangeland Rescue" (T-17), "Trigger Comes Home" (T-17). $30–$60.

Roy Rogers Cowboy Annual #8. 1958. Adprint/LTA Robinson, London. Cover: Walt Howarth painting of Roy and Trigger. Contents: "Backfire" (126), "Silver Saddle" (126), "Bounty Killer" (126), "Perilous Proof" (127), "Outlaws of Cougar Canyon" (127), "The Trap" (128), "The Green Horn Kid" (127), "The Drifter" (128), "The Pyrite Swindle" (128). "Chuckwagon Charley's Tales" feature, Geronimo story. $30–$60.

Roy Rogers Cowboy Annual #9. 1959. Adprint/LTA Robinson, London. Cover: Walt Howarth painting of Roy. Contents: "Guardian of the Caves" (29), "Roy Toughs It Out" (30), "The Secret of the Valley" (30). Trigger stories, other stories. $30–$60.

Roy Rogers Cowboy Annual #10. 1960. Adprint/LTA Robinson, London. Cover: Color photo of Roy (130). Contents: "Dynamite Mountain" (131), "Stranger with a Gun" (131), "Secret Message" (132), "Outlaw Trap" (130), "The Little Lawman" (130), "Trail of the Kayak" (132), "Stampede Canyon" (131). $30–$50.

Roy Rogers Cowboy Annual #11. 1961. Adprint/LTA Robinson, London. Cover: Roy and Dusty (143). Contents: "Cave-In" (129), "The Long Day" (136), "The Vanishing Trails" (135), "Savage Shackles" (136), "The Secret of the Sands" (135), "The Turquoise Belt," "The Unheeded Warning" (129). Three short stories on Roy: "The Night Everything Happened," "Let's Go Shooting" (136), "Surprise Show Stopper" (136). $30–$50.

BOOKS (FOREIGN), continued

Roy Rogers and Dale Evans Coloring Book.
Late 1950s. Unknown publisher. Painting
of Roy, Dale on cover, possibly by Howarth. Dale is waving hat. $30–$50.

Radio Fun Annual. (Roy Rogers stories.)
1940s–1950s. England. Unknown number
of volumes. The following Roy Rogers
stories, with original British artwork, are
taken from these annuals. "Traitor to his
Tribe" 1940s. Unknown artist. 24-panel
story. "RF" appears at page bottom, also
"E." $5–$10. "The Gold Train Goes
Through" 1940s. Unknown artist. "Tom"
shows as buried signing on intro panel,
but not same artist as story. 23-panel story
("Meet Roy Rogers and his Wonder Horse
Trigger). $5–$10. "Redskin Vengeance"
1950s. 23-panel story. Artists: Probably
Walt Howarth/Reg Forster. (Roy is called
the "King of the Range." Victim rancher in
story is named Rocky Lane.) $5–$10. "The
Treachery of Black Snake" 1950s. 39-panel
story. Artwork: Appears to be Reg For-
ster, shows influence of Peter Alvarado.
Intro panel appears to be Walt Howarth.
Oversized panels $30–$60.

R. R. "KING OF THE COWBOYS"
BOOTS. 1952. Description probably applies
to boots made by Ranger Boot and Shoe
Co., Terrell, TX. Retail stores, catalogues.
Sears and Roebuck #15 G 1259. Brown, tan.
Half sizes, 8½–3. Leather. Fancy inlay and
stitching, leather vamp. Roy rearing on
Trigger in front of ranch gate. Roy Rogers
name across top. "Searosole" with rubber
heel used in advertisements. Originally $7.65
(other brands, such as "Range Riders" sold
for $3.98). In box, mint, $100–$200.

R. R. OVERSHOE **BOOTS**. 1952. This
description probably applies to boots made
by Converse Co., Malden, MA. Retail
stores, catalogues. Sears and Roebuck #76 G
9858. Galoshes type. Tan top over brown
vamp. Sizes 13, 1, 2, 3; no half sizes. "Thick
rubber, 100% water-proof," "cotton-net lining," "Non-slip sole and heel," "Roy Rogers"
and "Trigger" on sides, with drawing of Roy
riding Trigger, looking back over shoulder.
Same design as sweatshirt. "Hero Roy
Rogers and Trigger 'dude-up' this overshoe
boot" used in ads. Originally $3.35. In box,
mint, $75–$150.

BOOTS LIKE ROY'S AND DALE'S. Early
1950s. Tex Tan Leather Co., Yoakum, TX.
Retail stores, catalogues. Sizes 8½–3. Rubber heels, pull straps. Dale Evans' "Star
style" $10.95, Roy's "Thunderbird style" used
in ad. $12.95. Advertised in *Life*. 1954: $7.95
up. $100–$200.

R. R. **BOOTS**. 1954. S. Goldberg and Co.
Roy rearing on Trigger, in front of ranch gate.
Believed to be felt material. Fringed tops.
Advertised in *Life*. 1954: $1.99. $100–$200.

R. R. WESTERN **BOOTS**. 1955–1956.
Acrobat Shoe Co. (General Shoe Corp.) Retail stores, catalogues. Overlays, inlays, or
embossing in color. Fancy stitching. High
and low heel models, round and sharp toes.
Four styles: 1. picture of Roy and Trigger
embossed on sides, Roy Rogers name across
top (low heel) 2. eagle or "thunderbird" overlay design, Roy Rogers name on pull-straps
3. three styles, generic-styled inlay Western
designed, Roy name on pull-straps 4. Roy
rearing on Trigger embossed, Roy name in
lariat writing overhead, name also on pull-
straps. Originally $7.95–$9.95. $100–$200.

R. R./DALE EVANS INFANT **BOOTS**.
1955–1956. Acrobat Shoe Co. Retail stoes,
catalogues. All leather. Roy/Dale on horseback on sides. Originally $4.95. $75–$150.

R. R. BUNKHOUSE **BOOTS**. 1955–1956.
Ripon Knitting Works, Ripon, WI. Retail
stores. Sizes: 5–12. Brown, red, royal blue.
Roy's "thunderbird" design in red, green,
royal blue with "Catspaw" Softee moccasin-
type sole, glove-leather sides, sizes: 5–10.
(Also with horseshoe pattern/steerhorn ornament.) Originally $2.50–$2.95 a pair.
$100–$200.

R. R. DOUBLE-R-BAR BUNKHOUSE
BOOTS. 1955–1956. Ripon Knitting Works.
"RR" brand, thunderbird design. "Catspaw"
Softee soles. Glove leather sidewalls. Colors:
Red, green, royal, blue. Originally $2.95 a
pair. $75–$150.

R. R. BUNKHOUSE **BOOTS**. 1956. Illinois Glove Co., Champaign, IL. Retail
stores. Same sizes. "Thunderbird Metallic
Yarn" used in advertisements. Similar to
above. Originally $2.95 a pair. $75–$150.

R. R. DOUBLE R BAR BRAND **BOOTS**.
1956. Unknown company. Thunderbird
design. Advertisement in *Saturday Evening
Post*, December 1956. Originally $9.95. $100–
$200.

Roy Rogers Cuffs as shown in advertising of the Boot-Ster Co. 1950s. Personal photo used with permission. Courtesy Jack Miller.

R. R. RUBBER COWBOY **BOOTS**. 1950. Quaker Oats–sponsored Roy Rogers contest prize. For boys only. Radio announced. $75–$150.

R. R. **BOOT-STERS**, CUFFS. 1948. Boot-ster Manufacturing Co., Clarksville, TN. These were made to wear on the ankles, at the top of shoes, providing the appearance of a boot, for those parents who chose not to buy boots for the youngster. Approximately 4″–5″ tall. Artwork of Roy rearing on Trigger on sides. The matching artwork on the wrists patterned after real cowboy equipment. $75–$200.

GENERAL FOODS, POST CEREALS **BOXES**. Illustrated with likenesses of Roy, Trigger, Dale; Roy Rogers premiums often inside. 1953–1955. Unknown printing co. Some artwork appears to be that of Peter Alvarado. Backs and or fronts show Roy, advertise Roy Rogers premiums: *Roy Rogers*

3-D Photos, Glasses, 1953. *Roy Rogers Pop-Out Cards*, Post Raisin Bran. *Roy Rogers and Dale Evans Golden Records*, Post Sugar Crisp. *Roy Rogers Western Medals*, Post Sugar Krinkles. *Roy Rogers Pin-back Set,* Post cereals, 1953. *Roy Rogers Ranch Set*, Post Toasties, 1957. No premiums inside: Roy's head, front; Roy rearing on Trigger, back, Post Grape-Nuts Flakes. Intact, mint, premium enclosed $200–$350. Box, assembled or flat: $75–$125.

QUAKER OATS/MOTHER'S OATS **BOXES**. Circa 1948–1951. Quaker Oats Canister with Roy Rogers premium ad. On lithographed paper label. *Roy Rogers Ring*, Quaker Oats. *Roy Rogers Autographed Souvenir Cup*, Mother's Oats (same company as Quaker). *Roy Rogers Deputy Sheriff's Badge*, Mother's Oats. Complete $250–$400. Otherwise: $100–$150.

R. R. COOKIE **BOXES**. 1940s. Carr-Consolidated Biscuit Co. 1948–1951. (This box has been mistakenly identified as a Quaker Oats box; the cookies were made with Quaker Oats and their trademark appears on box.) Illustrated Roy and Trigger on 2¼ × 5½ × 7¾ box. Rare. Box alone: $50–$100. *See also* R. R. Cookies.

R. R. **BOXING GLOVES**. 1955–1956. J. A. Dubow Sporting Goods Corporation. Ages to eight years. Sturdy leather with canvas lining. Filled with boxing glove hair. Set of four. Originally $5.50. $100–$150.

R. R. **BOXING GLOVES**. 1955–1956. J. A. Dubow. Ages to 14 years. Originally $7. $100–$150.

R. R. I.D. **BRACELET**. Early 1950s. Micron Manufacturing Corporation. $45–$75.

DALE EVANS I.D. **BRACELET**. Early 1950s. Micron Manufacturing Corporation. $45–$75.

R. R. BOY'S **BRACES**. 1954. D. H. Neumann. Suspenders. All elastic with badge-type adjustments. Designs on elastic. On colorful display card with illustrations of Roy and Trigger. Original price in 1954: 89 cents. (These are similar in design to those manufactured in 1948 by Hickok.) $50–$100.

R. R. COWBOY **BRANDING IRON** SET. 1950s. Knox-Reese Co. Believed to be retail stores. Miniature branding iron with ink pad. $75–$150.

R. R. **BRIDLE**. 1953. Bona-Allen, Inc., Buford, GA. Retail stores, catalogues. Natural russet—"matches everything." 4″ mouth port bit. "Roy Rogers" embossed on brow band. Metal bit, buckles. Sears No. 10 H 8162M. Shipping weight 1 pound, 4 ounces. Originally $5.49. $100–$200.

R. R. **BRIEFS**. Early 1950s. E-Z Mills. Underwear shorts. $45–$100.

R. R. **BUBBLE GUM**. Early 1950s. The Times Confectionery Co., London. 5¼″ × 6¾″. Red, green and yellow wrapper has illustration of Roy and Trigger. Wrapper also covered with trivia. Package contained photo trading cards (see entry below). $35–$60. *See also* R. R. Picture Card Album. (The wrapper alone has been seen at $5–$8.

R. R. **BUBBLE GUM CARDS**. Early 1950s. Roy Rogers Bubble Gum. The Times Confectionary Co., London. *See also* R. R. Bubble Gum. Set of 24 miniature movie stills. 2½″ × 1¾″. There were numerous

sets, some containing text on reverse, some not. "Roy Rogers," and "Trading Card No. ____" on top, "presented with Roy Rogers Bubble Gum" at bottom. Set $35–$100.

R. R. **BUCKBOARD**. 1950s. Ideal Toy Co. Retail stores. 16″ long. $85–$125.

R. R. **BUNKHOUSE**. 1955. Unknown company. Television show premium. General Foods, Post Cereals. The "Roy Rogers Show." "Name the Pony" contest. (Entry blank and one boxtop from Post Toasties.) "Roy Rogers Bunkhouse" writing on top. $40–$75.

R. R. **BUSINESS CARD** CASE. Late 1950s. Aristocrat Manufacturing Co. Cowhide. 4″ × 7″. Floral border, stipling. "RR" brand in center. *See also* Leather Stamping Plates. $65–$85.

R. R. PIN-BACK **BUTTONS**. Three categories of Roy Rogers buttons: Original 1940s–1950s; "Fantasy" or reproductions (usually passed off as originals); and New (1965–present day). The later day buttons are shown under "Later Collectibles." There are at least 40 of the original buttons. Many were obtained as premiums, either in cereal boxes or by mailing in one or more box-tops for one button or a complete set. The Post Cereals premiums and other originals can be recognized by the one-piece litho construction. The later versions are two-piece construction, one set over the other. Few buttons, if any, contain identifying marks showing a manufacturer. Much of this type of material was made in metal plants in Long Island City, NY, and Providence RI. 1. *Roy Rogers*. 1940s. B&w. Roy, in flowery design decorated shirt, pre-1947 hat, next to Trigger. Name appears at bottom in white lettering. $25–$50. 2. *Roy Rogers*. 1940s. B&w, pre-1947 hat, bust shot with Roy leaning slightly forward, smiling. Name at bottom, black lettering on white scroll. $25–$50. 3. *Roy Rogers*. 1950s. Pre-1947 hat. B&w bust shot on yellow background. Roy looking to his left smiling. Name at bottom, black lettering on white strip. $15–$25. 4. *Roy Rogers and Trigger*. 1950s. Roy in pre-1947 attire. B&w on yellow background. Roy looking at Trigger, who is holding head slightly up. Names at bottom, black lettering on white strip. $15–$25. 5. *My Pal Trigger* and *My Pal Roy Rogers*. 1950s. 1950s attire and hat.

B&w photo on red background, or reversed. Roy, head tilted slightly to his left, smiling. Name under photo. Small print on pin's bottom reads: "Copyright Roy Rogers, Made in USA by Ideal Novelty & Toy Co., Hollis 7, New York." "My Pal" on top. All white lettering. 1¾". (Originally issued with Roy Rogers doll by Ideal.) $50–$80. 6. *Roy Rogers Fan Club Reception.* 1940s. Extra large. Words appear across top in large back lettering. Pre-1947 attire, hat. Three lines, the top one reading "Chicago, October, 1948." B&w bust shot of Roy (same photo as #17) on yellow background. Name at bottom of photo, black lettering on white strip. $40–$80. 7. *Dale Evans Fan Club.* 1950s. Black hat tossed back, long hair, and 1940s attire, b&w bust shot. Various colors used. "Member" at top. "Dale Evans Fan Club" at bottom. Black lettering on white strips. $25–$50. 8. *Roy Rogers Riders.* 1950s. B&w photo on red background, or reverse. Roy in fringed outfit, next to original Trigger in rodeo tack. Common pose used in association with Riders Club. "Sears Corral" at top. Black lettering on white strips. $25–$55. 9. *Roy Rogers and Trigger.* 1950s. Large. 1⅝". Basically same button as #8, with different printing. Name at bottom: Black lettering on white strips. Black bust photo on yellow background. $15–$25. 10. *Roy Rogers Riders.* 1950s. Basically the same button as the two previously shown, but different writing. "Mortan's" at top, rest at bottom. Black lettering on white strip. Same colors. $25–$50. 11. *"For Democracy 100%."* 1940s. Small. 1940s hat and attire. Black and white. Bust shot, signature on right side, names separated. A star on each side. All lettering, designs are white on black background. $75–$100. 12. *Roy Rogers.* 1940s. Small. B&w bust photo on white background. Large black lettering on white background. "Republic's Singing Western Star" on bottom. One little star, left side. $75– $100. 13. *Roy Rogers.* 1940s. Small. 1¼". B&w photo on grey background. Roy, pre- 1947 attire, sitting facing left, looking toward camera, smiling. Black lettering at bottom. Possibly attached to fabric. $25–$50. 14. *Roy Rogers.* 1950s. Small. 1¼". B&w bust shot, dark background. Roy, pre-1947 hat, attire, looking to his right, smiling. Name, black lettering on white

strip at bottom. $10–$25. 15. *Roy Rogers.* 1940s. Small. 1¼". B&w bust shot, on dark background. Pre-1947 hat. Black lettering outlined in white at bottom. $15–$25. 16. *Roy Rogers.* 1950s. Small. Green. 1950s photo, bust shot. Name at bottom. Black lettering on white strip. $15–$25. 17. *Roy Rogers.* 1950s. Small 1¼". Pre-1947 attire, hat. B&w bust shot on yellow background. Name at bottom: black lettering on white strip. $25–$50. 18. *Roy Rogers.* 1950s. Small. 1¼". Premium related. B&w bust photo on blue background. Roy in fringed attire, smiling, looking to his right. $25–$50. (This 1¼" button was issued with Roy Rogers Republic Pictures publicity photo.) 19. *Dale Evans.* 1950s. Small. Green. 1940s b&w photo, same as that used for #7. 1¼". $20–$45. 20. *King of the Cowboys Roy Rogers.* (Jumbo Roy Rogers Button) 1953. 1⅝". General Foods premium. 1950s photo, head shot, smiling. Multicolor. Lithographed metal. Title on top, red lettering, white background. Name on bottom, black lettering, yellow background. Originally from Post's Grape-Nuts Flakes set of 15 offered in 1953. Original cost with Super Beanie: 20 cents and 1 box top. $15–$40. 21. *King of the Cowboys Roy Rogers.* 1953. Smaller version of #20. Multicolor. Lithographed tin. Offered with set of 15 above. These smaller ones were in the boxes of cereal. $15–$40. 22. *Roy Rogers "Happy Trails."* 1950s. $10–$20. 23. *Roy Rogers.* 1950s. Small. 1¼". B&w bust shot on yellow background. Roy, eyes looking very slightly to his left, smiling. Lettering in black print on white strip. $10–$20. 24. *Roy Rogers.* 1950s. Small 1¼". B&w photo of Roy, fringed attire, smiling, looking up and to his left. Blue background. $10–$20.

GENUINE R. R. **BUTTONS** were issued in September 1953 as premiums associated with the radio and television shows. Sponsor: General Foods, Post's Grape-Nuts Flakes. The "Roy Rogers Show"–Radio. Fifteen different small tin litho buttons with drawings, photos. ¾". Advertising in back, along with "R.R." and "1953." Individual $12–$25, set $100–$300. 1. *Dale Evans.* Multi-colored photo. Name in black print at bottom. 2. *Pat Brady.* Multicolored painted likeness. Name in black print at bottom. 3. *Trigger.* Realistically colored.

Name in black print at bottom. 4. *Bullet.* Name in black print at bottom. 5. *Nellybelle.* Realistically colored illustration. Name at bottom in red print. 6. *Roy's Guns.* Belt, one holster, two guns, drawn. Black print at bottom. 7. *Roy's Boots.* Red, white, and blue thunderbird design boots. Print at bottom in red. 8. *Roy Rogers' Saddle.* Drawn, silver ornamented saddle. Print in red at bottom. Yellow background. 9. *Roy Rogers Sheriff.* Yellow star on red background. Six-guns, scroll. Name at top, black print. 10. *Roy's Brand.* Red and black R's surrounded by yellow on red background. Print at bottom in black. 11. *Dale's Brand.* "DE" on end of branding iron, in yellow on white background. Name top and bottom in red. 12. *Roy Rogers Junior Deputy.* Spread-eagle shield badge, name and title on badge. Name on top in black print. Title center red print. 13. *Buttermilk.* Horse's head facing opposite direction (left) than that of Trigger. Realistically colored. Name in black print at bottom. 14. Unknown. 15. Unknown.

R. R. **BUTTONS.** 1950s. 1¼". Photo of Roy (bust shot) smiling, looking to his right. Name printed at bottom. Possible three-colored ribbon, steer head attached. $30–$50.

R. R. AND TRIGGER **BUTTONS.** 1950s. 1¾". Photo of Roy looking at Trigger. "Roy Rogers and Trigger" at bottom. Ribbon and small horse figure attached. $40–$50.

SUPER BEANIE AND JUMBO R. R. **BUTTONS.** 1950/1953. Radio-television show premiums. Post's Grape-Nuts Flakes. The "Roy Rogers Show." Color button with bust shot likeness. "King of the Cowboys" on top, "Roy Rogers" on bottom. (Beanie carries no Roy identification.) $30–$50.

R. R. RANCH **CALENDAR.** 1959. $40–$60.

R. R. AND TRIGGER **CAMERA.** Late 1940s. Herbert-George Co. 620 snap-shot camera. 3½" × 3" × 2¾". Black with silver face. Drawing: Roy rearing on Trigger, upper left-hand corner, lariat encircling face, writing Roy Rogers name at bottom. Vinyl strap. Originally $4.49. $55–$150.

R. R. AND TRIGGER **CAMERA** (and Binoculars). 1950s. I have only seen the Herbert-George camera. Occasionally another one such as this one is reported, but no manufacturing information is given. This could possibly be one seen advertised in comic books by greeting card companies, a much more inexpensive unit. Often sold with binoculars. Set intact: $75–$125.

R. R. **CANTEEN.** 1950s. Probably piece of camping set. $45–$75.

R. R. **CARD GAME.** Early 1950s. Herbert of Hollywood. $45–$75.

R. R. **CEREAL BOWL.** 1950s. Universal Co. 7". China. Roy on Trigger, waving. $40–$60. *See also* Chinaware Set.

TRIGGER **CERTIFICATE** OF HONORARY OWNERSHIP. 1950s. Large likeness of Trigger's head, on paper, probably 8" × 10". Bordered by spiral marking, with the RR brand at each corner. The brands on the left are reversed. Roy Rogers facsimile signature. Issued in recognition for fan's devotion, recipient is named honorary shareholder in horse. $25–$50.

R. R. **CHAPS AND VEST** SET. 1956. Attached to display cardboard with illustrated likeness or photo of Roy. "Roy Rogers and Trigger" on front, with picture of Roy on Trigger. $100–$250.

R. R. **CHAPS AND VEST** SETS. Early 1950s. Sackman Brothers. No additional information. $150–$250. *See also* Vests.

R. R./DALE EVANS **CHAPS, SKIRT, VEST SETS.** 1954. Angelus Souvenir. Leather, corduroy, "suedene," or twill. Trimmed in Roy and Dale's personal brands. These bear no resemblance to those offered in Sears, Roebuck catalogues. Here, Roy's brand "RR" is on sides of chaps, encircled in lariat. Also on chaps belt and on vest. Girl's outfits have white waistband, bottom trim, brand "DE" on vest. White pockets on skirt. Sizes 2–12. Originally $2.95–$8.95. $175–$300.

R. R., DALE EVANS PLASTIC **CHARM.** 1950s. $15–$25.

ROY AND TRIGGER **CHARM.** Early 1950. The "Roy Rogers Show"—radio. ⅝" × ⅞". Blue plastic frame holds b&w photo. Example: 1940s Roy standing beside Trigger in publicity shot related to film. $25–$50.

R. R. **CHARM BRACELET.** Circa 1950. 6" length. $50–$75. (Many jewelry items were manufactured in plants in Rhode Island.)

R. R. **CHINAWARE** SET. 1950s. Universal Co. Four pieces. Entire set: $200–$300. *See also* Plates, Bowls, etc.

ROY AND DALE **CHOW** SET. 1955 Hettrick Co. Painted, illustrated picnic table with attached bench seats. $300–$1,000.

PERSONAL **CHRISTMAS CARD** FROM R. R. Early 1940s radio premium. "Mailed directly from Hollywood." $30–$60.

R. R. **CHUCKWAGON**. 1950s. Possibly Ideal Toy Co. 13″ long. $60–$120. *See also* Wagons.

R. R. **CHUCKWAGON**. Early 1950s. Steger Products Manufacturing Corp., Steger, IL. No other information. $60–$120.

R. R. FIX-IT **CHUCKWAGON AND JEEP**. Mid-1950s. Ideal Toys. Plastic set. Scale model. Carton: 4½″ × 7½″ × 24″. Roy, Dale, and Pat Brady, 3″ seated figures. Roy is driving team, Dale is waving, as is Brady. Horse-drawn chuckwagon with accessories. Nellybelle jeep replica. Bullet figure, cooking equipment, bucket, storage chest, team of horses. Sixty different parts to assemble. "A wagon full of Do-It-Yourself fun!" $100–$250.

R. R. THEATER **CIRCULARS**. 1938–1952. Theaters often had their own circulars printed and often used press book materials for reproduction. $10–$30.

R. R. **CLAY MODELING SET**. Early 1950s. Standard Toykraft Company, Brooklyn, NY. $45–$100.

R. R. **CLOTHES TREE**. Early 1950s. The Westerner Co., Los Alamitios, CA. $100–$200.

R. R. JEANS 'N' RIDER **COAT**. Early 1950s. Part of set. $100–$300. *See also* Jeans, Pants, Slacks.

R. R. WESTERN RIDER **COAT**. Early 1950s. Roy's own leather label in front. Sears No. 50 G 9131M. Original price, 1952: $2.09. $100–$300.

R. R. STORM **COAT**. Early 1950s. Champ Manufacturing Co. No description. $100–$200.

R. R. JACQUARD KNITTED-IN DESIGN **COAT-SWEATER**. Early 1950s. "Roy" on side of front, "Rogers" the other side. In green and blue. Heavy cotton, button front. Ribbed cuffs, hemmed bottom. "R-R" appears on cloth patch on front, both sides. Roy is on Trigger running down slope. Original price, 1953: $1.89. $100–$300. 1955–1956: Same as above, various Western designs, colors, Roy Rogers Double R Bar Plus brand. Pauker Boyswear Corp. Also available in cotton links. $100–$300.

R. R. **COLORING SETS**. 1949. Quaker Oats–sponsored Roy Rogers contest prize. Radio-announced. No other information. One thousand were offered. $50–$100.

R. R. **COMB**. Early 1950s. Standard Pyroxoloid Corporation. $25–$45.

COMIC BOOKS (*See also* Chapter 6)

Four-Color Series. New York: Dell Publishing Co., 1944–1947. Thirteen issues. All color photo front, back. Many with full-sized sepia or b&w photos on inside covers. No. 63 has color photos inside. Artists include Albert Micale, Harry Parks, Henry Vallely, Erwin Hess, Dan Spiegle, Jesse Marsh. Numbers are those of Four-Color Series, which includes many other characters. Thirteen Roy Rogers issues: #s 38, 63, 86, 95, 109, 117, 124, 137, 144, 153, 160, 166, 177. Originally 10 cents. $50–$200. #38 $200–$1,000. Increased from $400 maximum value in 1994.

Roy Rogers Comics. New York: Dell Publishing Co., 1948–1961. 145 issues. Produced by Western Printing and Lithographing Co., New York. Color photo front, back: 1–55. Earlier issues have b&w photos inside. Artists include Albert Micale (1–73), "Al" McKimson, Randy Steffen, Andrew Bensen, Peter Alvarado (24–36), Hi Mankin, Richard Moore (43–72), McKimson (37–62), John Buscema, Sal Buscema (74–108), Nat Edson, Russ Manning (109–118, 125–145), Alex Toth (119–124), Michael Arens (121, 123), among many others. Monthly #1 (January 1948) through #124 (April 1958). Bimonthly to #145 (September–October 1961). Originally 10 cents (to 15 cents in 1961). $5–$350.

March of Comics, Featuring Roy Rogers. 1948–1963. 25 issues: #s 17, 35, 47, 62, 68, 73, 77, 86, 91, 100, 105, 116, 121, 131, 136, 146, 151, 161, 167, 176, 191, 206, 221, 236, 250. $50–$170. (One report of $250.)

Special Comics. Various titles (8 issues), *"Give-Aways"* (3 issues), *Roy Rogers' Trigger* (17 issues), *Dale Evans Comics*, 1st Series (24 issues), 2d series (22 issues), *Western Roundup Comics* (25 issues).

Foreign Comics (by arrangement, Great Britain, France, Canada, other countries). Most of the foreign counterparts are interesting in that the reproduction of the photo covers offers a contrast to the U.S. versions, not really running inferior, but using a process that is a combination between a photo reproduction and a painted likeness. Buried signings of the artists can be found in the work. In the contents artwork, re-inking is often apparent with colors heavier and more vibrant. Most often the covers of the comics are the same as U.S. versions, with a different contents and with a different issue number used, but in some instances they are supplied with a different photo, one that never appeared on the domestic version, as in the case of the English version of Roy Rogers and Trigger #70. The English versions were published by Pemberton's of Manchester, distributed by World Distributors, authorized by Roy Rogers Publishers (no such company known, although shown as such), and printed by Co-Operative W. Society (CWS) of Reddish. Believed to have begun with American issue #36 in 1950 (English #1). American issue #23 is the earliest documented (unknown English number). Some English versions were issued un-inked, which indicates that they received the artwork prior to inking. Modifications were also made in the text. "Christmas at" was dropped from "Christmas at Colt's Foot Canyon" in their #1 (American #36). The English issue dropped the third story, but used the "Pioneers of the Old West" and "Trigger" features and then assembled various b&w photos for the inside front, inside back covers, and back covers, some never used in American issues. *Note:* Old Mexico versions have superior art (cover) graphics to many of the U.S. products. Painted likenesses of Roy on covers inspired by Alex Toth likeness of Roy. Letters "EN" appear as Logo, top left corner. Stands for "Organizacion Editorial Novaro, S.A." (publisher). Printed by arrangement with The Western Co. Text is in Spanish. Price shown in circle under eagle's head, bottom of cover. $35–$100.

Roy Rogers Comics/Super-Comics Series. 1950s. Monthly. Distributed by Consolidated Press. Registered for transmission by post in Australia as a periodical. Price: 8D. The covers appear to be part lithograph printing and artwork is based upon Roy Rogers publicity photos. The concept is that of the mixed photo/artwork covers of the American series in the 1950s. Here the artwork is by Wynne Davies, and his name appears. The stories are American reprints. #39, May 1951. Cover based on publicity photos taken for film *Trigger, Jr.,* and *Roy Rogers Comics*, February 1951. #42, August 1951. Based on publicity photos from same film. #45, November 1951. Based upon post-*Apache Rose* film still. #51, May 1952. Unknown inspiration, but pre-*Apache Rose* Roy is shown, about to whale bad guy. #60, February 1953. Unknown inspiration, but probably film still. Title, issue no. and date appears across top of cover. $20–$50.

The Sheriff Comics. Roy Rogers stories. Possibly Australia. Price: 3D. 1950s. Original stories, artwork. "True Tales of the West." Comic story novelization of films of Roy, Gene Autry, and Bill Boyd. Artist: Gus Denis Gifford. #2, *Apache Rose.* $10–$20.

TV Comics. Roy Rogers stories. Great Britain. Mid–1950s. $10–$20.

Wonder Comics. Roy Rogers stories. 1940s–1950s. Printed in England. The Amalgamated Press, London. Registered for transmission by Canadian magazine post. Sole agents for Australia and New Zealand: Messrs. Gordon and Gotch, Ltd. Original Roy Rogers comics stories in newspaper form published every alternate Friday. Colors on stories I have seen are limited to red and black. Wonder name at top of page, then "Roy Rogers in . . . [story title]." Intro panel has photo of Roy, caption speaking to readers: "Howdy Wonder chums" and continues to introduce story; Facsimile signature. In film fashion, the next adventure is advertised at bottom of page. Nine to twelve panels contain entire story. Unknown artist of 1940s stories has likeness totally off, Roy resembling Tom Mix. 1950s stories offer much improvement with artist rendering good likeness. 1950s stories are numbered into the thousands, i.e., 1,688, appearing near title. $10–$20 (American). Samples (*1940s*): "Rustler's Roundup," "Comanche War Drums," "Mike Lanagan's Treasure," "Masked Man," "The Red River Con Runners," "Peril at Sundown," "The Servants of Wildcat," "The Return of the Barson Brothers," "Clever Ruse," "Black Barton's Last Ride," "Kidnapped Sheriff," "Jed Carson Pays His Debt," "The Rustler's of the

Border," "Redskins on the Warpath," "Wolves at Bay," "Face from the Past," "Old Jeb Caston's Past," "Danger Tribe." (*1950s*): No. 1, 667 "Trigger to the Rescue." No date shown. No. 1, 686 "The Siege of Fort Grayson." September 1, 1951. No. 1, 687 "Dangerous Chase." September 15, 1951. No. 1, 688 "The Hostages." September 29, 1951. No. 1, 691 "The Medicine Man's Escape." November 10, 1951. No. 1, 696 "Attack in the Night" January 19, 1952. No. 1, 697 "The Battle of the Blizzard." February 2, 1952. No. 1, 700 "Stampede." March 15, 1952. No. 1, 705 "A Desperate Duel." May 24, 1952.

R. R. **COMIC STRIPS**. 1949–1961. Often found as tear sheets. Original copyright, December 31, 1949, by King Features Syndicate, following publication in *New York Journal-American*, registration #B5-12668. Registration not renewed. According to one source, King Features Syndicate began publishing and distributing the strip to newspapers on December 2, 1949. "Tear Sheets," pages of this comic removed from the newspaper and generally displayed in protective covering, are highly collectible. When newspapers were read, they usually went straight to the trash. Those that did happen to be saved inasmuch as they were printed in color the paper turned yellow and deteriorated quickly because of the chemicals in the inks and paper. The strip was signed "Al McKimson." "Al" was actually two brothers, Chuck and Tom. See Chapter 9. "Ghost" artists were used, two being Michael Arens (early 1950s) and Hi Mankin (by 1956). Circulation of 63 million was reached. 1957: Carried in 186 newspapers across the country. Values: first strip tear sheet, Dec. 2, 1949, $100–$200; 1950s tear sheets, $20–$50; 1960–1961 tear sheets, $10–$20. Entire comic sections of newspapers, usually much handled, generally the later years, can be found for less than the tear sheet. These should be examined once, photocopied, and sealed permanently and tightly in an oil-free, protective covering. Examples: Daily editions, 1/1/52–1/10/52: Artist Peter Alvarado. 1/11/52–3/5/52: Artist John Ushler. Possibly Mike Arens' work here and there. "King of the Cowboys" dropped in title 2/16/52. Sunday edition, September 30, 1956, artist Mike Arens.

R. R. **CONCHAS**. Early 1950s. Rauf Fastener Co., Providence, RI. Several sizes. One popular size: 2″ diameter. Lariat stamped raised edge. "RR" brand on separate gold colored piece, attached. Originally used on holster sets, spurs, etc. $5–$10.

R. R. **COOKIES**. Early 1950s. Carr-Consolidated Biscuit Co. Made with Quaker Oats, honey, cashew nuts, raisins, flour, milk and creamy butter. Box contains "crackin' good gun" premium offer. Photo or painted likeness of Roy and Trigger on box. Cookies, complete with premium: $200–$500.

R. R. **COVERED WAGON**. 1955–1956. The N.N. Hill Brass Co. Canvaslike top. Pulled by horse. Four red-enameled steel wheels with nickel-plated gongs. 19¾″ long, 10¾″ high, 7″ wide. Originally $2. $75–$150.

R. R. SPECIAL **"CRACKIN' GOOD GUN."** Early 1951. (Also known as "Bang Gun.") Roy Rogers Cookies. Carr-Consolidated Biscuit Co. The "Roy Rogers Show"–Radio, television, late 1940s–early 1950s. Premium. 8″ stiff paper fold-out pop gun with illustration of Roy (bust) and facsimile signature printed each side (pistol grips). Originally free in box. $55–$85.

R. R. DE LUXE **CRAYON BOX**. 1952. Sears No. 3 G 4902. Action picture of Roy and Trigger (rearing pose) on cover, inside on papers. 60 quality wax crayons. 24 pictures to color, 5 stencils. 4 sheets drawing paper, color guidance picture. Originally $1.87. $55–$90. (Pictures alone $3–$5.)

R. R. **CRAYON BOX** (small). 1952. Sears No. 3 G 4906. 36 crayons, 18 Western pictures to color, 3 Western stencils, 3 sheets of paper and guidance picture. Roy rearing on Trigger (same illustration) on cover. Photo of Roy and Trigger on papers inside, different pose, nonrearing. Facsimile signature upper left corner. Originally 91 cents. $45–$75.

R. R. **CRAYON SET**. Early 1950s. Standard Toykraft Co. Roy stencils, art materials. $45–$150.

R. R. AUTOGRAPHED SOUVENIR **CUP**. October–December 1950. Quaker Oats Co. premium. The "Roy Rogers Show"–Radio. Also advertised by company with store signs and on Mother's Oats and Quaker Oats cereal box labels. 4.5″ Roy's head with hat, painted on Lustrox cup. Inscribed "Roy Rogers" (facsimile signature) and "King of the Cowboys" on hatband. Possibly more than one manufacturer. One is the F and F Mold and Die Works, Dayton, OH. (Described in some collectibles books as "Toby Mug" or "plastic premium mug." The Toby mug was a different type mug offered by Quaker Oats over the radio show October-November 1949 and was a sixteenth century style having nothing to do with Roy Rogers.) Original price was one label and thirty-five cents. $40–$75.

R. R. **CURTAINS**. 1950s. Cotton. Long. Illustrations show Roy rearing on Trigger with lariat in hand forming Roy Rogers name. Also written on curtains is "Trigger." Other illustrations of calves, cowboys. $85–$150. *See also* Bedroom ensembles.

R. R. **DARTBOARD**. Early 1950s. Dartboard Equipment Co., Philadelphia. No additional information. $85–$150.

D. E. STAR-CAL **DECAL**. 1950. $30–$50.

R. R. AND TRIGGER **DECAL APPLIQUÉ**. 1950–1952. Meyercord Co. No. 517-A. Photo of Roy standing beside Trigger produced from a reversed negative. 6½" × 8". Originally 29 cents. $15–$45.

OFFICIAL R. R. WESTERN **DENIMS**. Early 1950s. Designed exclusively for "King of the Cowboys." Sanforized. Roy Rogers leather label in back. Sears No. 50 G 9129M. Originally $2.14. $70–$150.

R. R. **DESSERT DISH**. 1950s. Universal Co. 5¼". China. Illustration of horse's head. $25–$50. *See also* Chinaware Set.

R. R. CHILDREN'S **DINNERWARE**. Early 1950s. Universal Potteries Company, Cambridge, OH. $75–$300.

"ROY ROGERS SAYS 'I WAS RAISED ON QUAKER OATS'" **DISPLAY**. 1950. Quaker Oats Co. 5' full-color photo, diecut cardboard store display. Roy in fringed attire, free-standing. $500–$2,500.

"GET YOUR ROY ROGERS AUTOGRAPHED SOUVENIR CUP" **DISPLAY**. 1950. Quaker Oats Co. 15" × 22". Store sign. "Roy Rogers, Box G, Dept. 5, Chicago 77, Illinois." Full color, paper. $100–$300.

R. R. QUICK DRAW MAGIC MARKER **DISPLAY**. 1960. Cardboard display box to hold markers. Two sizes. Has photo of Roy's face, hat. Outside borders on one formed by illustrated six-guns. This one holds two sets of 6 markers. The smaller one (no six-gun art) holds a straight 12 markers. $75–$150.

R. R. "WIN YOUR OWN PONY" **DISPLAY**. 1955. Post's cereals. Large cardboard merchandise display sign with Roy photo or painted likeness, right-hand side. Approximately 3' × 2'. Came with two hanging paper banners, one Roy, one Dale, drawn likenesses, approximately 2' × 1'. $300–$1,500.

R. R. STORE **DISPLAY**. 1949. Unknown merchandise, possible Roy Rogers Corral. Likeness of Roy (neckerchief on wrong side) on wood grain effect, surrounded by lariat pieces tied on both sides. $1,000–$1,500.

R. R. SOCKS, MICKEY MOUSE **DISPLAY**. 1950s. Mickey in painted likeness on top of approximately 1' × 3' metal sign, Roy's painted likeness (face only) on bottom. "Roy Rogers Socks" in block lettering. Yellow painted background. Likeness matches that found in advertising used with his "Pledge to Parents" on merchandise and is professionally done. Not known which store used this. Found at NYC Gallagher memorabilia show. $100–$200.

THE NEW 1941 ALL-AMERICAN MAGIC CHEF **DISPLAY**. 1941. Magic Chef Ranges. Approximately 3' × 1'. Photo of Roy rearing on Trigger. $100–$150.

R. R. TRICK LASSO **DISPLAY**. 1952. Knox Reese Co. Company sent display to dealers who ordered as many as three dozen lassos. Near life-size cut out of Roy. $500–$800.

R. R. TRICK LASSO **DISPLAY**. 1952. Knox Reese Co. Approximately 12" × 18". Cardboard. Roy in maroon shirt. Brush background. $60–$150.

R. R. **DIXIE CUP PHOTO LIDS**. 1930s–1950s. Showing many different dairies' advertising on reverse side and publicity still photo, some sepia-toned, from many of Roy's films. One in particular shows *Rough Riders Roundup*. Sizes: both 2½" and 2¾" diameter. 1930s: $25–$50. Examples: 1940s, Hoodsie Ice Cream Co. $15–$35. 1950s, Perfection Ice Cream Co. $15–$35.

DALE EVANS **DIXIE CUP PHOTO LIDS**. 1946. Same as above. Individual Drinking Cup Co., Easton, Pennsylvania. Pat. No. 1273891. Wiseman Farms. $15–$25.

DALE EVANS **DOLLS**. 1950. Quaker Oats–sponsored Roy Rogers contest prize. Radio-announced. For girls only. 500 offered. $175–$250.

R. R. "MY PAL" **DOLLS**. Early 1950s. Ideal Novelty and Toy Co., New York. 22" tall. Stuffed fabric. *See also* Pin-back Buttons. $100–$600.

R. R.-DALE EVANS WESTERN COS-TUME **DOLLS**. 1955–1956. Nancy Ann Storybook Dolls, Inc. "They stand, sit and watch!" Roy Rogers catalogue numbers 4R/4D, "Parade Wardrobe Dolls." Assorted colors, sequins, jewels (Dale's); dress-up cord pants, fancy shirts (Roy's). Numbers 3R/3D, "Rodeo Wardrobe" with holsters, guns; Numbers 2R/2D, "Roundup Wardrobe," leather chaps/skirt, holsters and guns, plaid shirt. All are eight inches tall. Individual Western motif boxes. Originally $2.50 each, each style. $125–$200 set.

R. R. **DRAWING BOX**. Early 1950s. The Westerner Co. No additional information. $40–$65.

R. R. **ENGRAV-O-TINTS**. 1940s–1950s. Peerless Wghg. & Vendg. Mch. Corp., NY. "Portraits of Movie Stars." 1" × 2" b&w photo cards. Coin-operated scales provided these; the person's weight appeared stamped on reverse, below company identification and fortune. 1/16" thick cardboard. Very old-style portrait effect. No number, identifying mark. "Roy Rogers" in script type at bottom ⅓ white area long with "Republic Pictures." Back reads "Collect Engrav-o-tints Portraits of Movie Stars" at top. Bottom (reversed) "You are frank in your opinions, but are careful to express them diplomatically." $8–$12.

R. R. **EXHIBIT CARDS**. 1940s–1950s. (Also called arcade cards and arcade pictures.) Exhibit Supply Co., Chicago. According to Exhibitor's Price List, 1946, "All our cards are produced right in our own factory and printed on cardboard milled especially for us." 3½" × 5½" photo cards, produced in two colors (black and white, green and white, etc.) and sold in vending machines, as found in penny arcades, sportslands, carnivals, and amusement parks. Many with facsimile signatures (FS henceforth). These exist on Roy, Dale, Gabby Hayes, Pat Brady, more. Originally (1946) $3.85 per thousand (dealers price). One cent to the public. 32 different Roy Rogers cards. Ad for Roy Rogers cards: "Big sellers to young and old." During 1946, "Roy Rogers"/

"Buckaroo" cards ranked fourth in sales out of ten types. $15–$40.

Series One. Early 1940s. FS. Full-length shot. 1. Roy, distant, using lariat, on rearing Trigger. Western suit, facing observer's right. FS, lower right-hand corner in white. 2. Close-up of #1. Cut off midway of Trigger. FS across saddle area. 3. Distant, rearing on Trigger. Waving. Rifle scabbard appears. Roy in vest, gloves. Facing observer's right. FS, lower left-hand corner. 4. Trigger, Roy side by side. Three-fourths full figure. FS, lower left-hand corner. Subject looking to observer's left. 5. Roy, rearing on Trigger, waving hat. Trigger's tail between legs. Two-toned, piped shirt, dark cuffs. FS, center. 6. Close-up, Roy facing observer's right, looking over his shoulder to observer's left. Solid shirt. Smiling. "Cordially Roy Rogers," lower left corner. (*See also* Miniature Size Cards.) 7. Roy, rearing on saddleless horse (Little Trigger or Trigger, Jr., four white stockings). Smiling. Black shirt, sleeves rolled up. FS, lower right-hand corner. Subject facing observer's right. 8. Roy, bust over fancy saddle, hand against head. Ring on both hands. Two-toned solid/plaid shirt. Smiling. "Cordially Roy Rogers," bottom left-hand corner. 9. Close-up of #9. No saddle showing. FS, left center, low. (*See also* Miniature size cards.) 10. Roy sitting in chair playing guitar. Tack hangs on chair. Legs crossed. "Cordially Roy Rogers," lower left-hand corner. Smiling. 11. Close-up #10. Bottom of guitar cut off. 12. Trigger, Roy, side by side, both looking to observer's left. Serious pose. Plaid shirt. Archery bag strap shows across chest. FS, lower left bottom. 13. Close-up of #12. Face to below slash pocket only. "Cordially" added. FS, lower left. 14. Roy sits on Trigger while playing guitar. Leg crossed over saddle. Subject, horse facing observer's left. Grinning. No tapederos on stirrups. FS, lower left corner. 15. Rearing Trigger nearly vertical as Roy waves with gloved hand. No tapederos. FS, lower left. Subject, horse facing observer's right. 16. Roy, half figure, leans over fancy saddle. From series which includes #9, 10. Looking to observer's left, smiling. One hand over saddle, the other over horn. "Cordially Roy Rogers," lower left. 17. Close-up #17. Hat cut off, both sides. "Cordially Roy Rogers," lower left. 18. Roy, ¾ figure, hands on guns, partly raised out of holsters. Solid over plaid shirt, black hat. Serious pose. "Cordially Roy Rogers," lower left-hand corner. 19. Close-up of #19. "Cordially Roy Rogers," lower left-hand under slash pocket. 20. Photos from same series. Roy, facing observer's left, looking to observer's right. Gun drawn, other hand on belt. "Cordially Roy Rogers," bottom center. 21. Close-up of #21. "Cordially Roy Rogers," left lower center. 22. From series including ones above employing fancy saddle. Hands are crossed here, lariat in hand. Grinning, looking slightly left center. "Cordially Roy Rogers," bottom right. 23. Close-up of #23. "Cordially Roy Rogers" moved to lower left. 24. Roy sits astride Trigger, facing observers right, playing guitar, leg over saddle. Looking down at guitar, smiling. FS signature higher than normal, left. 25. Roy, Trigger come to abrupt halt, Trigger's head back. No tapederos. FS, lower left. 26. Close-up, looking up and to observer's right. Chin string pulled tight. Slight smile. "Cordially Roy Rogers," lower left. 27. Distant view of above shot. Details unverified but should be one of the shots with the fancy saddle. 28. Variation of #5. Only difference is Spanish-architecture structure in background. 29. Roy, clad in fringed buckskin attire, black hat, is astride Trigger, who is drinking from a water hole. FS, left center. Roy facing observer's right, looking back over his shoulder. Plain saddle, no tapaderos. 30–32. Unknown.

Series Two. Mid–1940s. 1. Green, white card. Bust shot, Roy smiling. Facing observer's left, looking straight at camera. Flowery designed shirt, polka dot neckerchief. "Howdy Friend, Roy Rogers," bottom center. 2. Black, white. Part of series including green, white card. Roy, facing right, flowery shirt, polka dot neckerchief. Smiling, looking straight into camera. "Sincerely Yours, Roy Rogers," bottom center. 3. Roy, both guns drawn and aimed over drawn-in tree. Aimed at observer. Serious pose. Newer series, similar hat to #29. "Cordially Roy Rogers," lower left.

Series Three. Early to mid–1940s. Mixed cowboys. These could possibly be from the "Buckaroos" set mentioned above. 1. Fred Humes, Roy Rogers, Ken Curtis, Jimmy

Wakely. Photo of Roy same as green, white above (#1). Sepia-toned. 2. Blue, white. Jack Padjeon, James Warner, Roy Rogers, Monte Hale. Roy is standing, plaid lace-up shirt, hands on guns, serious pose. Black hat. Facing oberver's left. "Yours Roy Rogers," bottom center.

Series Four. Late 1940s, early 1950s. Movie stills. Designated "Western 112." 1. Circa 1947. Roy, Andy Devine, Tito Guizar from film *On the Old Spanish Trail*. 2. Roy and Dale circa 1951. In this photo from NBC, Roy is adjusting Dale's string tie. Both facsimile photos. $15–$25.

Western Aces. Circa late 1940s. Pre-1947 photo of Roy in center of card designed as playing card. Words "Western Aces" read both ways on sides. FS. Probably one of a series using many stars.

Other. #1. Green, white. Pat Brady. Comical sad pose. Looking to observer's lower left. "Roundup Greetings Pat Brady," lower right.

1950s cards reported: 1. Miniature-sized, same company as series one. Miniatures of series one's #6 and #10 exist. Probably all of that series exist in this size. 1½″ × 2½″. Reproductions of these cards are fairly common and sell at prices of from $1 to $2 each, to $5 for a set, which can include up to 20 cards. They generally look new, especially the backs. Most often the backs of the originals are found at least slightly brown to yellow from age.

R. R. **FAN CLUB** MEMBERSHIP CARD. 1940s. Large photo. Fan club address: P.O. Box 283, Station G, New York 19, New York. $40–$70.

R. R. **FAN CLUB** CARD. 1950s. Photo of Roy and Dale. Brown (sepia) and white. The cards indicate any of hundreds of U.S. fan clubs. Approximately 4″ × 5″. Facsimile signatures. $40–$60. ($1 = six journals and one 8″ × 10″ photo of Roy and Dale. *See also* Rider's Club items.

R. R. **FAN CLUB** MEMBERSHIP CARD. 1951. Holland. 3½″ × 5½″. B&w photo of Roy holding guitar. $40–$60.

R. R. AND TRIGGER ACETATE **FIGURE**. 1960. Hartland Plastics Co./Roy Rogers Enterprises. Unbreakable. "Roy Rogers Plus Brand." Roy in white shirt, red yoke. Black gun belt, boots, white hat. Black saddle on Trigger. Subject has right hand in air; horse has right foot raised. On 7″ × 11½″ card, blister packed. $70–$175.

R. R. AND TRIGGER REPLICA PLASTIC **FIGURE**. 1950s. Hartland Plastics Co. Approximately 8¼″ long × 10″ high. Outfit: Blue, red. White hat. Originally $3.98. $100–$150. This is the larger and more common. Rare to find with guns. They were tiny, detachable, and generally have become lost. This has been seen with new guns fashioned. Commonly found without hat or guns. Beware of horse switching on these figures. $70–$175. Boxed $250.

DALE EVANS AND BUTTERMILK REPLICA PLASTIC **FIGURE**. 1950s. Hartland Plastics Co. Same measurements as Roy and Trigger, above. Mate of above. Same applies for hat and gun. Painted olive green; white hat. Originally $3.98. $75–$100. Boxed $200.

DALE EVANS AND BUTTERMILK REPLICA PLASTIC **FIGURE**. 1950s. Hartland Plastics Co. This is a second version. White hat, white shirt with blue collar, yellow neckerchief, black belt, blue riding pants. Off-white colored horse with brown mane, tail, tack saddle. Dale has right hand in air, left hand on hip. $75–$100. Boxed $200.

BULLET REPLICA PLASTIC **FIGURE**. 1950s. Hartland Plastics Co. Height: The dog's ears come to Roy's boot-tops when placed along side. White, black. Originally 49 cents. $40–$100.

R. R. AND TRIGGER REPLICA PLASTIC **FIGURE**. Circa 1960. Hartland Plastics Co. Small size. $75–$100.

R. R. BOBBING HEAD **FIGURE**. 1962. Composition figure. 6½″. Spring-mounted head. Painted outfit, square green base. Aqua/dark/red/white. Facsimile signature decal at base. $65–$125.

R. R. **FILM INFORMATION SHEET**. 1938–1951. Republic Studios. Film publicity department released to magazine publishers, etc., all details on a film, including information on the cast, production crew, and a lengthy synopsis typed on 8½″ × 14″ paper. Often found with library stamp showing files of publisher to whom it was submitted. $20–$50.

R. R. **FILMS**. A number of publications advertise films at the prices shown: 16mm films/Original, uncut. Examples: *West of the Badlands, Bells of San Angelo, Song of Texas, Hands Across the Border, North of*

the Great Divide. $100–$150. 16mm prints. TV edited 54 min. versions.

> *Under Western Stars*. Near mint: $150–$200
> *Arizona Kid*. Excellent: $125–$175
> *South of Santa Fe*. Excellent: $125–$175
> *Song of Texas*. Very good: $100–$150
> *Man from Oklahoma*. Excellent: $130–$160
> *Don't Fence Me In*. Good: $120–$145.
> *Roy Rogers 8mm Films*. Advertised on Super 8 film: *South of Santa Fe, Heart of the Golden West*, etc., $89 (60 min.).

R. R. BANTAM **FLASHLIGHT**. 1950. Bantam-Lite, Inc., New York. Quaker Oats–sponsored Roy Rogers contest. Radio announced. 10,000 offered. $50–$100.

R. R. POCKET **FLASHLIGHT**. 1950s. Unknown manufacturer. Art has Roy on rearing Trigger, hat in hand. Name encircled in lariat underneath drawing. $50–$75.

R. R. LARIAT **FLASHLIGHT**. 1950s. Unknown manufacturer. $50–$100.

R. R. SIGNAL SIREN **FLASHLIGHT**. 1950s. Usalite (United States Electric Mfg. Corp.). Signal button, 3-way switch, siren in cap. Full color metal case, plastic head. Roy rearing on Trigger, lariat above head. Roy Rogers Secret Code Book. Roy and Trigger in circle on box. Original (1954) price: 98 cents. Intact: $50–$100.

R. R. PAPER **FOLD-OUT**. Dell Publishing Co. Early 1950s. Premium. 6½″ × 7½″, opens to 33″ length. Five color photos. $65–$125.

R. R. INTERMEDIATE **FOOTBALL**. 1955–1956. J. A. Dubow Sporting Goods Corporation. Strong sidewall, pebble-grained. Official two-piece valve. White with black lace, bands/tan with white lace, bands. Picture of Roy, Trigger on sides. Originally $2. $100–$200.

R. R. **FOOTBALL**. 1955–1956. J. A. Dubow Sporting Goods Corporation. Moulded rubber. White with black lace, bands. Originally $1.20. $100–$200.

R. R. JUVENILE **FURNITURE**. Early 1950s. The Westerner Co. No additional information. See individual furniture listings.

R. R. HEALTH **GLASSES**. Early 1950s. Federal Glass Company, Columbus, OH. Drinking glass contains measurements for encouraging kids to drink all of their milk. $60–$85.

R. R. WESTERN **GLOVES**. 1954. Illinois Glove Co. Top grain horsehide, goatskin, fabric. Lined or unlined. Fringe, Roy Rogers signature, studded horseshoe designs on cuffs. Sizes 5–8. (Roy Rogers gloves first appeared in Sears and Roebuck catalogue in 1953 as "gauntlet" gloves.) Originally $0.89–$2.95 a pair. $65–$100.

R. R. GAUNTLET **GLOVES**. 1955–1956. Illinois Glove Co. Lined deerskin with Roy Rogers metal signature, brand. Simulated hand stitch. Sizes: 5–8. Color: saddle. Originally $4.95. $65–$100.

R. R. SUEDE GAUNTLET **GLOVES**. 1955–1956. Illinois Glove Co. Sueded calf, hand portion. Garment-suede cuff and fringe. Roy signature and brand in metal attached to cuff. Color: Russet/beige. Originally $1.98. $65–$100.

R. R. HORSEHIDE GAUNTLET **GLOVES**. 1955–1956. Illinois Glove Co. Front quarter horsehide, hand portion. Garment-suede gauntlet. Roy's name and brand in metal. Leather fringe. Colors: black, brown, cork. Originally $2.95. $65–$100.

R. R. CUFF **GLOVES**. 1955–1956. Illinois Glove Co. Same as above, but with scalloped band. $65–$100.

R. R. AND TRIGGER **GLOVES**. 1950s. Unknown manufacturer. Fabric glove, vinyl gauntlets, fringed. Roy Rogers/Trigger names printed. A large star is on gauntlet with names. $50–$100.

R. R. **GLOVES**. 1955–1956. Illinois Glove Co. 25 percent wool, 75 percent estron. Leatherette cuff has picture of Roy, Trigger, Double-R-Bar brand, star. (Star removable.) Sizes 4–7. Colors: black, brown, green, burgundy. Originally 98 cents. $65–$100.

R. R. FABRIC **GLOVES**. 1952. 13 percent wool, 41 percent rayon. Design with Roy and Trigger on artificial-leather flared cuffs, fringed to give authentic cowboy appearance. Sears No. 43 G 875. Originally 79 cents. $65–$100.

R. R. WARMTH ON HAND **GLOVES**. 1952. Illinois Glove Co. Metal Roy Rogers signature on cuff. Some cuffs studded and jeweled. Originally $1.95–$2.95. $65–$100.

R. R. BUCKSKIN **GLOVES**. 1952. Sueded buckskin. Decorated with smart "Roy 'N' Trigger" design. Roy rearing on Trigger. (All advertising states "Roy 'N' Trigger" on items, but "Roy and Trigger" often appears.) Horseshoe designs with metal studs. Flared cuffs or simulated leather. Cotton fleece lined. Color: buck (med.) tan. Sears No. 43 G 874. Originally $1.75. $75–$125.

R. R. **GLOVES AND MUFFLER SET**. 1955–1956. Illinois Glove Co. American knit for boys. Individual gift box. Sizes 4–6. Ages: 5–10. Colors: navy, brown, maize, red. Originally $2.95. $85–$150.

R. R. AND TRIGGER TOY **GUITAR**. 1955–1963. Jefferson Co., Philadelphia, PA. Also called "Sunburst" guitar. 26″ long. Large illustration of Roy on Trigger covers bottom half of body. Small illustration of Roy and Dale on top face. "Roy Rogers Plus Brand" below where neck attaches to body. "Roy Rogers" written by illustrated Roy. "And Trigger" printed under sound hole. White lariat encircles face. $200–$300.

R. R. AND TRIGGER **GUITAR**. 1950s. Jefferson Co. Identical to above guitar, except for small differences. Tailpiece does not extend up as far into Roy's illustration, and "RR" brand is not partially covered by neck, where it joins body. $200–$300.

R. R. AND TRIGGER **GUITAR**. 1955–1963. Jefferson Co. Similar to above guitars, with different illustrations. Large Roy (to waist) standing next to Trigger on lower half. Dale's face top left, Plus brand top right. $200–$300.

R. R. **GUITAR**. 1950s. Small version. Facsimile signature, outline of head and hat on guitar head (neckerchief on wrong side). Signature also under tailpiece. Drawing of Roy sitting on ground, playing guitar beside campfire. Horse, pine trees, mountains in background. $250–$350.

R. R. **GUITAR**. 1950s. Larger version of above guitar. $300–$400.

R. R. **GUITAR**. 1950s. Rich Toys/Ranch Rhythm Toys, Tupelo, MS. Red, with white rope painted around face, illustrations of Roy rearing on Trigger, Double RR Bar Ranch gate, in white. 30″ long. Cardboard and wood. Photo leaflet included. (Leaflet: $10–$20.) Roy Rogers facsimile signature. $175–$250.

R. R. CAP **GUN**. 1950s. Unknown manufacturer. 9″ long. Marble and pearl-type handles. $35–$85.

R. R. DEPUTY SHERIFF **GUN**. 1953. Unknown manufacturer. 10″ long. $55–$95.

See also Roy Rogers Deputy Sheriff Outfit, under Outfits.

R. R. TUCK AWAY **GUN**. Early 1950s. Unknown manufacturer 2½″ derringer. Cap gun. $35–$75.

R. R. SIGNAL **GUN**. Early 1950s. Langson Manufacturing Co., Chicago. 7″ long. Battery operated. $100–$300.

R. R. MINIATURE **GUN**. 1940s–1950s. Made in U.S.A. Unknown manufacturer. Several sizes and colors exist. Smaller ones have "RR" in circle stamped on grip. Some have elaborate designs, detailed flower inlays in metal. All metal, metal color, cock and fire. Size: 2¾″ long × 1⅛″ high. $5–$10 each. Size: 5⅜″ long × 2⅜″ high. Designs on cylinders, adjoining part. "RR" and "Roy Rogers" facsimile signature on both side of barrel. $8–$12 each. Size: 2¾″ long × 1⅛″ high. Gold-painted, with tiny leather holster. $15–$25.

R. R. KEYCHAIN PUZZLE **GUN**. Early 1950s. Unknown manufacturer. 2½″ long. Plastic. $30–$50.

R. R. **GUN**. 1940s–1950s. Unknown manufacturer, Colt possibly included. Cal. 44 "Peacemaker," single-action. 5½″ barrel. Blued steel. Stag handle grips. Used by Roy in films, personal appearances, television, etc. Impossible to place a value on, but would bring in the thousands.

R. R. **GUN**. 1940s–1950s. Unknown manufacturer, Colt possibly included. Similar firearm with 7½″ barrel, gold-plated. White handle grips with design. Used by Roy in numerous photos for comics, publicity. Impossible to place a value on, but would bring in the thousands.

R. R. SINGLE **GUN AND HOLSTER SET**. 1953. 1″ wide cowhide black belt, holster with Roy's name in wide, bold letters on belt. "R" on holster, surrounded by metal in sunburst pattern. Cap firing and nonfiring. Three wooden bullets. Gun: 8″ nickel-plated. Sears No. 43 H 4990/91. Initials on gun. Originally $1.98. $100–$300.

R. R. QUICK DRAW IDEAS **HAND-BOOK**. 1960. Speedry Products, Inc. Richmond Hill, New York. With marker. Photo of Roy on cover. $8–$15. *See also* Roy Rogers Quick Draw Marker and Art-O-Matic Roundup.

R. R. **HANDOUT**. 1948. *Melody Time* film advertisement, world premiere. $20–$35.

R. R. COWBOY BAND **HARMONICA**. 1950. Unknown manufacturer. Quaker Oats–sponsored Roy Rogers contest prize. Radio-announced. 2,000 offered. Solid brass plate, precision tuned. 1″ × 1¼″ × 4″. $60–$100.

R. R. RIDERS CLUB **HARMONICA**. 1950s. Harmonic Reed Corp., Philadelphia. 4½″ long. Metal, engraved. Typical Pat. No. 2, 317, 425. $45–$65.

R. R. RIDERS CLUB **HARMONICA**. 1950s. Same size as above. Variation in artwork on sides, different from version above. $45–$65.

DALE EVANS BOXED **HAT** AND OUTFIT. 1950s. $100–$300.

R. R. "THROW AWAY" **HAT**. 1950s. "Roy Rogers hats" were on occasion the prize for area contests and were also tossed out to the youngsters at appearances. These were similar in design to his custom design, but especially made for publicity "give-aways," charity event donations, contest prizes, etc. They are not beaver felt. Some were probably autographed, as opposed to a facsimile signature. $150–$300.

R. R. RODEO **HAT**. 1953. Unknown manufacturer. Roy's name on lustrous rayon band. Edges of white brim are whip-laced in authentic cowboy style. Strong rayon chin cord with adjustable bead. Preshaped for lasting fit, retains it's smart looks. "A hat that any good cowpoke will be proud to wear." Red, black, tan. Small (6½″–6⅝″); medium (6¾″–6⅞″); large (7″–7⅛″). Sears Cat. No. 43 G 531. Originally $1.94. $60–$90.

ROY AND DALE **HAT**. 1950s. Sackman Brothers Co., New York. In felt and straw. Five colors, eight styles (including typical cattleman's type, and Denton Pitch type, similar to both styles worn by Roy, pre– and post–*Apache Rose* period; see Chapter 10). Laced brims, adjustable chin straps. Roy Rogers and Trigger/Dale Evans name on band. All sizes. Originally $0.98–$1.98. Advertised in *Life*, 1954; $1.98. $60–$100.

R. R./DALE EVANS STRAW **HAT**. 1955–1956. Sackman Brothers Co. Colors: red, black, green, gold, buckskin. Bands, chin cords, slides. Originally 98 cents. $60–$100.

R. R./DALE EVANS FELT **HAT**. 1955–1956. Sackman Brothers Co. Colors: red, black, green, gold, buckskin, pink, charcoal. Bands, chin cords, slides. $60–$100.

DALE EVANS **HAT**. 1950s. Pla-Master. Red wool felt. "Dale Evans," "RR Plus brand" on outside band. "Play-Master Western" and Good Housekeeping seal on inside band. White lace around brim. $40–$100.

R. R. AND TRIGGER **HAT**. 1954 or later. Red 100 percent wool felt. Inside band shows "Roy Rogers and Trigger," "RR Plus brand," Good Housekeeping Seal. White lace around brim. $40–$100.

R. R. QUICKSHOOTER **HAT**. 1950s. Possibly Mattel. This is a hat that Roy made televised commercials for in the 1950s. Gun pops out of hat. $100–$200.

R. R. RAIN CAP STYLE **HAT**. 1952. With visor. Yellow/black and gray colors. Sears No. 40 G 644/45 M. Originally 59 cents. $40–$90.

R. R. **HAULER AND TRAILER**. 1955–1956. Louis Marx and Company No. 768. All-steel truck and trailer with lithograph Roy Rogers motif. Figures include Roy, Dale, Pat, Bullet, two horses, three saddle/bridle sets. Doors open on trailer to form ramps. Boxed. 15½″ × 3½″ × 4½″. Originally $1.98. $150–$400.

R. R. **HAULER AND VAN TRAILER**. 1957. Line Mar Co. Carton: 4″ × 6½″ × 11″. Lithographed metal van, metal cab hauler. Cord goes to remote control unit. Operates forward, reverse. Total length: 13″. Van side, rear doors open. Side reads: "Roy Rogers and Trigger" and "Trigger, Jr." Illustration of Roy on rearing horse on side of van. $150–$400.

R. R. **HERALDS**. (Movie materials.) 1938–1952. One- to two-color poster artwork on pulp paper. Photocopy reproductions are now very common. Average $20–$40.

R. R. **HOLSTER AND GUN**. 1950s. Brown leather holster with Roy, drawn in white, holds brown plastic gun. Overall length about 4″. $75–$150.

R. R. **HOLSTER OUTFIT**. 1955–1956. Classy Products Corporation. "Texan" three-piece holster in black, natural top-grain cowhide. Nickel "RR" Western buckle. Nickel-plated plastic bullets. Leather leg ties. Originally $4.95. $150–$350.

R. R. **HOLSTER OUTFIT**. 1955–1956. Classy Products Corporation. Natural and aniline finish top-grain cowhide. "RR"

nickel conchas, studs. Hand-tooled effect, embossed. Four bullets. Originally $2.98. $150–$350.

R. R. **HOLSTER OUTFIT**. 1955–56. Classy Products Corporation. Same, but has Roy's signature embossed on belt. Leather leg ties. Originally $3.98. $150–$350.

R. R. **HOLSTER OUTFIT**. 1955–1956. Classy Products Corporation. Miniature double holster, cowhide, three-piece "Texan" style pocket. Trimmed with "RR" brand. Nickel-plated tongue buckle. Originally $1.98. $100–$200.

R. R. AND TRIGGER OFFICIAL **HOLSTER OUTFIT**. 1950s. Classy Products. No other information. $150–$350.

R. R. OFFICIAL FLASH-DRAW **HOLSTER OUTFIT**. 1950s. Swivel-Hip firing action. "RR" brand on genuine cowhide holsters and guns. Illustrated Roy on colorful box. "Roy Rogers Plus Brand." Two different designs. $150–$350.

DALE EVANS **HOLSTER OUTFIT**. 1950s. No other information. $100 minimum.

R. R. 2 **HOLSTER OUTFIT**/R.R. "CLICKER" GUNS. Part of Western outfit. Plain leather, four metal studs, no design apparent. These might be found separately. $75–$125.

R. R. OFFICIAL **HOLSTER SET**. 1955–1956. Classy Products Co., New York. Box: 2″ × 13″ × 13″. Roy Rogers Plus Brand. Roy rearing on Trigger on cover (facing observer's right). Leather belt, holsters, with two 10½″ silvered metal cap pistols with white-painted metal grips. Roll caps. "RR" brand on each side of pistols, along with "Roy Rogers" in script. Belt, holsters: numerous silvered brass rivets. Belt: 4″ wide at front, tapers to back. Two belt pieces joined by rawhide at back. Originally $4.95. $150–$400. (In box.)

R. R. **HOLSTER SET**. 1955–1956. Classy Products Corporation. Box: 13″ square, 2″ deep. Illustrations seem to be identical to above box. Brown leather belt, holsters, with design of silver foil stamped "RR," and horseshoe and name outlined in red cut-glass stones. Silvered metal guns with various Roy brands/symbols on barrels. Pistol grips: gray plastic with horsehead design, with "RR." Name on one side of each gun. Originally $4.95. $150–$400. (In box.)

DALE EVANS **HOLSTER SET.** 1955–1956. Classy Products Corporation. Embossed butterfly design on belt, holsters. Nickel-plated plastic bullets. Nickel stud trim, Western buckle. Originally $4.95. $150–$350.

R. R. DOUBLE **HOLSTER SET.** 1954. Classy Products. Two-tone leather. Double strap. Roy's name on belt. Wooden bullets. Studs around top grain leather holster pockets. Regular and Deluxe sets. Advertised in *Life*, 1954: $4.95/$10.95. $150–$350.

R. R. DOUBLE **HOLSTER SET.** 1954. Classy products. Tooled leather with strap buckle across holsters. Studded in two rows. "RR" at holster's bottom. Larger number of bullets. Originally $10.95. $150–$350.

OFFICIAL R. R. **HOLSTER SET.** 1952. Roy and Trigger (rearing pose) embossed on antique finish, 10″ studded holsters, split cowhide leather. Plastic leg ties. Two official Roy Rogers 9″ break-barrel six shooters with "jeweled" handles. Embossed "Roy Rogers" at top of each holster and on belt. (*See also* Snaps; Studs; Conchas.) Sears No. 49 G 2658: non-firing guns; 49 G 2650: cap-firing guns. Originally $3.98. (Gene Autry brand was going $2.79.) Guns are often found separately, generally in the $40–$70 range. $150–$350.

OFFICIAL R. R. **HOLSTER SET.** 1952. George Schmidt. Dark brown steerhide holsters, belt. Whip-laced with gray lace, edges. Holsters: 10″ × 4½″, metal studs (Rauf Fastener Co.), 2″ RR metal conchas on attached leather strip. Belt: 2¾″ × 29″, Roy's name embossed in silver, embossed buckle, keeper. Six gray wooden bullets. $50–$150.

R. R. ROCKING **HORSE.** 1955–1956. The N.N. Hill Brass Co. American Eagle saddle. Steel legs, metal saddlelike seat. Hand grips. Reins with nickel-plated jingle bells. 12″ wide, 17″ high. 25½″ long. Seat: 6″ × 6″. Originally $4. $100–$200.

R. R. TRIGGER **HORSE TRAILER, AND JEEP.** 1950s. Ideal Toy Co. With Nellybelle jeep and Pat Brady, Roy and Trigger figures. All plastic. Trailer and jeep equal 15″ long. $100–$300. Jeep only $25–$40.

TRIGGER'S LUCKY **HORSESHOE.** 1950s. Unknown manufacturer. Full size, black rubber. $45–$65.

R. R. **HORSESHOE PITCHING SET.** Early 1950s. Knox-Reese Manufacturers. $100–$160.

R. R. AND TRIGGER **HORSESHOE PLAQUE.** Late 1940s. Wooden plaque has photo of Roy and Trigger inside horseshoe. Roy's name on top, Trigger's on bottom. $75–$150.

R. R. **HORSESHOE SET.** 1950s. Ohio Art Co. Hard rubber. Inscribed. In box, $80–$160.

R. R. **HORSESHOE SET.** 1950s. Ohio Art Co. Four hard rubber shoes. Metal parts with lithographed artwork of Roy, Trigger, Double R Bar gate. $80–$160.

HORSESHOE WORN BY TRIGGER. 1950s. Mounted on solid walnut base, shaped like a shield. Gold-plated inscription with certification. Prize in October, 1952, New York City area contest. One was also donated by Roy to 6th Annual Charity Horse Show in Portsmouth, 1955. Advertised in *TV Guide* (September-October 1952). Only one existed for this contest, but duplicates were probably used for others. $300–$500.

R. R. OFFICIAL DEPUTY SHERIFF **I.D.** 1953. $25–$45. See also Roy Rogers Official Deputy Sheriff's Outfit.

INSERTS. 1938-1952, 1976. Movie materials. Size: 14″ × 36″. Roughly found at the same price range as half-sheets. $35–$50. (1945 film.)

R. R. **IRON-ONS** *see* Transfers.

R. R. GENUINE SUEDE LEATHER **JACKET.** 1956. Collar stitch bordered. Arrow pockets. Long fringe. Advertised in *Saturday Evening Post*, December 1956. Originally $12.98. $100–$300. *See also* Jeans 'n' Jackets, Pants and Jackets, Outfits.

R. R. **JACKET.** Early 1950s. Irvin B. Foster Sportswear Co., New York. No additional information. $100–$300. *See also* Rodeo Suits.

R. R. **JACKET.** Early 1950s. Rob Roy Co., New York. No additional information. $100–$300.

R. R. WESTERN **JACKET.** 1955–1956. Wm. Schwartz and Company. Cotton Cavalry twill; Roy and Trigger screened on rayon lining. Suede fringe on yoke, sleeves. Colors: brown, charcoal, green, red, black. Sizes 2–7/4–12. Originally $8.95/$9.95. $100–$300.

R. R. "CORRAL" LEATHER **JACKET.** 1955–1956. Wm. Schwartz and Co. Imported suede with calfskin yoke. Roy rearing Trigger on yoke. Lined. Zipper front. Colors: spice, sand. Sizes 2-7/4-12. Originally $16.95/$17.95. $100-$300.

R. R. "TRIGGER" LEATHER JACKET. 1955-1956. Wm. Schwartz and Co. Same description as above. Colors: spice, sand, palomino. Sizes 2-7/4-12. (Also wool quilt lining, at more expense.) Originally $14.95/$15.95. $100-$300.

R. R. "ROUNDUP" LEATHER JACKET. 1955-1956. Wm. Schwartz and Co. Calfskin. Rayon lined. Zipper front. Colors: palomino, white, red, cork. (Also with wool quilt lining, at more expense.) Originally $14.95-$16.95. $100-$300.

R. R. "CHEYENNE" LEATHER JACKET. 1955-1956. Wm. Schwartz and Co. Imported suede, calfskin trim. Colors: Charcoal, spice, palomino, sand. Originally $16.95-$17.95. $100-$300.

DALE EVANS JAMA-JEANS. 1954. NiteKraft. Cotton flannel. Sizes 4-8. Originally $2.95. Sizes 8-16: $3.95. $65-$150.

R. R. JEANS. 1953, 1954. Blue Ridge Manufacturers, Inc., New York. Retail stores, catalogues. Sears #50 G 5129M. "Sunfast white-back, Deeptone blue." Sizes 4, 6, 8, 10, 12, 14, 16. "Extra heavy, extra tough 9-oz. super twist Sanforized denim fabric," "copper-riveted," "thread bartacks in back," "long Western-cut legs with large cuff turn-up." "Every seam triple stitched," "2 front swing pockets," "2 back patch pockets," "button or zipper fly." "Roy Rogers leather label in back." Part of set. See also Jeans 'N' Rider Coat. Originally $2.14. Advertised in Life, 1954: $2.79. $70-$150.

R. R. "DEPUTY SHERIFF" JEANS. 1955-1956. Blue Ridge Manufacturers. Retail stores, catalogues. Roy Rogers Catalogue #409B. Brown denim, 8 oz. Embroidered pocket emblem. Sizes 4, 6, 8, 10, 12, 14, 16. Originally $2.49. Kiddie's sizes 2, 4, 6, 6X. Originally $1.98. $70-$150.

R. R. JEANS. Early 1950s. Rob Roy Co. No additional information. $70-$150.

R. R. FRONTIER 45 DENIM JEANS AND JACKETS. 1950s. Blue Ridge Co. Advertised in Life, 1954: $2.79. $100-$400. (For both.)

R. R. JEANS 'N' JACKET. 1952. "Authentic Roy Rogers denims! Approved by Roy. Sold Exclusively at Sears." 8 oz.

Sanforized blue denim. Roy's own special emblem in front. Imitation leather patch in back "branded" by Roy. Back patch pockets have embroidered loop design. Matching jacket. Jeans: 50 G 9136M, $1.98. Jacket: 50 G 9137, $1.98. (Regular Sears brands sell for $1.89 each.) $100-$400.

NELLYBELLE JEEP WITH FIGURES. Mid-1950s. Marx Toys. Gray pressed steel with blue wheels, yellow "Nellybelle" name decal both sides. Jeep: 5" × 5" × 11". Hood raises, detailed engine. Windshield raises, side panels removable, plus roll bar. Three hard plastic off-white color figures of Dale, Pat, Bullet. In carton: $150-$250. Figures alone: $5-$10 each.

NELLYBELLE JEEP. 1954. Sherwood Toys, Walden, NY. Heavy gauge steel replica. Ball bearing rear axle and push rods. Pedals. Semipneumatic tires. Decal picture: Roy rearing on Trigger, on Jeep's doors. Originally $24. $500-$800. See also Horse Trailer and Jeep.

R. R. JEWELRY. Early 1950s. Hickok Manufacturing Co. No additional information. See individual items, i.e., necklaces, charms, etc.

R. R. MULTICOLORED SATIN 25" KERCHIEF. 1955-1956. Western Art Manufacturing Co., Denver. Roy Rogers, Trigger, Bullet design. Colors: Blue, red, gold. Originally $1. $65-$100.

R. R. KEY CASE. Early 1950s. Aristocrat Manufacturing Co. No picture of Roy, but "RR" brand is stamped into cowhide, surrounded with floral pattern. See also Leather Stamping Plates. $50-$75.

R. R. TRICK KEY CHAIN. Early 1950s. The Plas-Trix Co., Brooklyn, NY. $25-$50.

R. R. LUCKY COIN KEY RING. November 1950. Advertised in RR comics. Offered in Movie Fan magazine for joining fan club. $25-$50.

ROY AND DALE COLORFORM DRESS-UP KIT. 1960. Prizes in RR Nestle's contest. Drawing of chuckwagon, Roy on boy's box, Dale on girl's box. $75-$125.

R. R. KIT BAG. Early 1950s. Acme Brief Case Co. No additional information. $100 minimum.

R. R. HUNTING KNIFE. 1953. Ulster Co. Artwork same as above. 7¼" long. With leather sheath, has compass attached. Drawing of Roy (head), facsimile signature. Originally $2.98. $75–$150.

R. R. **KNIFE**. Early 1950s. Colonial Knife Co., Inc., Providence, RI. $65–$125.

R. R./DALE EVANS/TRIGGER MINIATURE CHARACTER **KNIVES**. 1940s–1950s. Sold in penny bubble gum machines. $30–$65.

ROY AND TRIGGER PLASTER **LAMP**. 1950s. 8″ high. Engraved signatures. Painted scene on shade. Figure is Roy rearing on Trigger. Full color. $100–$250.

R. R. ON TRIGGER **LAMP**. 1950s. Plasto Mfg. Co., Chicago. 11″ tall. Painted plaster, rearing on Trigger. Facsimile signature on base. $100–$250.

R. R. **LAMP**. 1950s. Unknown company. 24″ tall. Plaster cast. $100–$250.

R. R. MECHANICAL **LAMP**. 1949. Pearson Industries, Chicago. Two revolving drums, one inner, one outer, with pictures. $1,000 minimum.

R. R. RANCH **LANTERN**. 1950s. Ohio Art Co. #90. Metal. Hurricane type with plastic chimney. 7¾″ tall. Battery operated. Horseshoe encircling chimney. "RR" brands, arrowheads, steerheads, etc. In box, $60–$180.

R. R. RANCH **LANTERN**. 1950s. 8½″ tall. Lithographed metal with clear plastic center chimney. Bright red, blue, yellow. Roy portrait and other symbols. Battery operated. $60–$180.

R. R. HUMMING **LARIAT**. 1951. Carr Biscuits. Premium. The "Roy Rogers Show," radio. $75–$125.

R. R. DELUXE TRICK **LASSO**. 1947. Knox-Reese Manufacturers, Philadelphia. Originally 98 cents. $50–$100.

R. R. TRICK **LASSO**. 1952. Knox-Reese. Entirely new. Glows in the dark. Offered as prize in October 1952 *TV Guide* contest for NYC area. Also sold with colorful contestant seal, with drawing of Roy, for 1952 National Lasso Contest. Sold at rodeos, etc. Drawings of Roy, Trigger on package. $75–$125, complete.

R. R. TRICK **LASSO/SWIVEL LASSO**. Mid-1950s. Classy Products Co. RR Plus Brand. Has belt clip. Doubles as dog leash. $50–$100.

R. R. JUNIOR TRICK **LASSO**. 1950s. Post's Grape-Nuts Flakes (General Foods). "Roy Rogers Show," radio-TV. Originally 25 cents plus one box top. $50–$100.

R. R. **LINCOLN LOG SET**. 1950s. No further information. $75 minimum.

R. R. LIFE SIZE PROMOTIONAL **LITHOGRAPH**. 1957. Life Size Studios, Redstone, NH. 24″ × 67½″. Roy, fringed attire, standing beside Trigger. Licensed by Frontiers, Inc., 1957. $500–$1,000.

R. R. **LOBBY CARDS**. 1938–1952. Possibly American Lithograph Co. and or Morgan Litho. Co., and or Allied Printing Co. Republic Productions, Inc., movie materials. No separate registration shown for movie materials. Copyright notice sometimes appeared on these materials for the film. For registration on films, see Chapter 5. Usually offset process using mixed scenes from film stills. 11″ × 14″/12½″ × 16″. Original lobby cards were normally issued in set of eight. According to information contained in 1950s rerelease Roy Rogers Press books, upon the films rerelease there might be only four cards available. One title card emphasizes the major character and is the most valuable or collectible. The other seven are scene cards and normally show a scene from the film. Individual cards have been seen in the neighborhood of $30–$40 for scene cards, depending upon condition, with title cards at $50 or more, especially when found with a dealer who specializes in these cards. Title cards average $40–$70. Examples of scene cards: *Arizona Kid*, $50; *Carson City Kid*, $35; *Don't Fence Me In*, $25; *Frontier Pony Express*, $50; *Heart of the Golden West*, $25; *Man from Music Mountain*, $25; *On the Old Spanish Trail*, $25; *Ridin' Down the Canyon*, $25; *San Fernando Valley*, $25; *Shine On Harvest Moon*, $50; *Trail of Robin Hood*, $35; *Trigger, Jr.*, $25–$50; *Melody Time*, $75. Many of the Rogers films were rereleased, and in most cases, the original material was updated with the then present day Rogers photo, either publicity shots or stills from later films, and the word "Rerelease" shows in very small print. If the film is pre-*Apache Rose* (1938 through early 1947) and Roy appears in his post-*Apache Rose* attire (the fringed shirts, and or the pointed crown "South-Western," "Denton Pitch," or "California-styled" hat, that is the first and foremost clue to the material being later than the original release. This is particularly striking when seen on the first feature film *Under Western Stars* material. There is a large degree of contrast in the two different Rogers' appearances in the photos. The rerelease material will have its own value, as now that material is over forty years old. It is much more commonly seen than the original release material on his earlier films, and one must decide what it is worth to one's collection. The important thing is to be able to recognize the difference. For instance, the film *Song of Arizona* was first released in 1946 but was rereleased complete with new paper, press books, et al., during the early to mid-1950s. Commonly seen prices: *Song of Nevada,* $15-$20; *Hands Across the Border,* $15-$20; *Heldorado,* $15-$20; *Shine On Harvest Moon,* $15-$20. *Note:* Research into the files at the Library of Congress reveals no separate copyright registration for paper movie materials related to the films. The copyright for the film itself is usually first claimed on the press sheets or production sheets. A search of particular titles shows that the registrations were not renewed when they expired. Examples follow: *Heldorado.* 7 Reels. Original copyright: December 11, 1946, by Republic Productions, No. L 744. Expired: December 1974. No renewal found. *My Pal Trigger.* 8 Reels. Original copyright: June 4, 1946, by Republic Productions, No. L 353. Expired: June 1974. No renewal found.

R. R. **LOBBY CARDS (FOREIGN).** *Old Mexico.* 12½" × 16¼". Produced on very good heavy stock, with excellent large- and small-sized "still" photos reproduced. Everything is, of course, printed in Spanish, with the film title in very small print in English under the main Spanish print. Republic's logo. Distributed by Republic Pictures de Mexico, Inc. The words "Jose Emparan 48," or "Jose Emparan No. 48 Mex D.F." appear in small print. All of the surrounding artwork, including likenesses of Roy taken from publicity photos and stills, is drawn by Mexican artist. "King of the Cowboys" is omitted for Roy, but "Smartest Horse in the Movies" appears for Trigger. Among those in the writer's personal collection are *Twilight in the Sierras, Apache Rose,* and *Roll On Texas Moon.* A lot of Mexicans are in the still reproduced for the first, and Mexican (probably Mexican-American) actress/comedienne Estelita Rodriguez is in the latter shot. Both are in two-color format:

blue/white or turquoise/white. $20-$40.

R. R. **LOBBY CARDS (MINI).** Domestic and foreign, some produced in recent years. Domestic ones of title and scene cards are very well produced and have been found as high as $10 each.

R. R. **LUCKY PIECE** *see* **RIDERS LUCKY PIECE**

Note: R. R. **LUNCH BOX SETS.** ("Thermos" and "Holtemp" are registered trademarks of the American Thermos/King Seeley Thermos Co.) Three and a half million kids carried their sandwiches and milk to school in a Roy Rogers and Dale Evans lunch box and Thermos set. Roy wasn't the first cowboy television star to appear on a lunch box. Hoppy was, and it was on a decaled job. Roy's marketing people went immediately to the Aladdin folks and proposed a Roy Rogers box. Aladdin had one cowboy character and wasn't interested in doing another. They probably figured the cowboy craze would be just a passing fad. Roy's people, undaunted, went to American Thermos. After three visits, American decided to go with the idea. Instead of using a decal on the flat tin rectangular steel box, they used a different approach. The result was the first fully lithographed steel box, one that carried a message over its entire surface. The artist, Ed Wexler, lent a touch to the likeness of Roy, as only a few artists had done in the past. The cardboard display card was handsomely done and showed Roy in his trademark pose, rearing on Trigger. The first year two and a half million kits were sold, and American Thermos Company's overall sales shot up by 20 percent. American Can Co. in Brooklyn manufactured the boxes for American Thermos until 1964. The Roy Rogers kit quickly became a standard in the industry; there would come to be at least 12 different boxes in nine or more different sets, which set a single series record. In 1961, American Thermos became King Seely Thermos.

R. R. SADDLEBAG TAN VINYL **LUNCH BOX.** 1960. King Seeley Thermos. 1960. Sold in tan and white. Bottle that belongs here has Roy on the rearing Trigger and is similar to the 1955-1956 thermos. This is the most common of the lunch box sets. Box, $100-$200.

TRIGGER FLAT STEEL **LUNCH BOX.** 1957. Sold without Thermos and with generic thermos. Gray band, metal handle. $75–$150.

R. R. AND DALE EVANS DOUBLE R BAR RANCH FLAT STEEL **LUNCH BOX AND THERMOS**. 1953, 1954. American Thermos Co. First issue in series. Lithograph on tin. Narrow box. Back, sides are wood grain design with two brands on back. Ed Wexler art. Thermos #2197. Dale is waving under ranch gate as Roy rides up on Trigger. The half-pint bottle that belongs to this box shows Roy standing beside Trigger, Dale kneeling down in front of him, next to Bullet. Red plastic cup. Lunch boxes have no number stamped in metal. 6⅜″ high × 8⅝″ wide × 3⅝″ deep. White lacquered inside. Originally $2.89 set. Box, $75–$150; bottle, $50–$75; set, $125–$225. The most common set.

R. R. AND DALE EVANS STEEL **LUNCH BOX AND THERMOS**. 1955, 1956. Lithograph on tin. Roy is seen rearing on Trigger and waving. Cattle surround them. Matching Thermos, #2077, yellow sky background. Thermos has Roy rearing on Trigger against yellow sky. Wexler's name buried in prairie grass to the right of the steer in the foreground. Steel/glass, 8″ tall. Red plastic cup. "Polly Red Top" seal. Back: eight scenes of Double R Bar Ranch. "Roy Rogers and Dale Evans Double R Bar Ranch" in center circle. Red band. Originally $2.89 (1955). Box, $60–$125; bottle, $35–$60; set, $100–$200.

R. R. AND DALE EVANS STEEL **LUNCH BOX AND THERMOS**. 1955–1956. Same as above, eight scenes on front. Back: Indian signs on bear rug design, Roy Rogers Double R Bar Ranch printed above art. Ads announce new, bigger 10 oz. Thermos. Valve: Box, $60–$100; bottle, $35–$60; set, $100–$200.

R. R. AND DALE EVANS STEEL **LUNCH BOX AND THERMOS**. 1955, 1956. Variation of above, with blue band. Variation of same Thermos, but with blue sky background, #2097. Value: Box, $60–$100; bottle, $35–$60; set, $100–$200.

R. R. AND DALE EVANS STEEL **LUNCH BOX AND THERMOS**. 1955, 1956. Variation of above, with green band. Same yellow sky background Thermos. Value: Box, $60–$100; bottle, $35–$60; set, $100–$200.

R. R. AND DALE EVANS DOUBLE RR BAR RANCH **LUNCH KIT**. 1954. Variations

of first box, with different colored or designed sides, backs with same fronts. Back has a "My Brand" place for owner's name. Lithograph on tin. Slightly larger in size, red band with Roy brands. Sold with above Thermos. Originally $2.89. Box, $60–$100; bottle, $45–$65; set, $100–$200.

R. R. AND DALE EVANS DOUBLE RR BAR **LUNCH KIT**. 1954. Variation of above box. Red band. Only difference is leather handle. Sold with same Thermos. Value: Box, $60–$100; bottle, $45–$65; set, $100–$200.

R. R. AND DALE EVANS DOUBLE RR BAR **LUNCH KIT**. 1954. Variation of above box. Same Thermos. Blue band, leather handle. Value: Box, $60–$100; bottle, $45–$65; set, $100–$200.

R. R. AND DALE EVANS **LUNCH KIT**. 1955–1956. Lithograph on tin. Eight different small scenes around the face. Same scenes as back of previous box. The back shows a cowhide attached to a log wall. Red band. Thermos same as above, blue sky. Box, $45–$70; bottle, $30–$60.

R. R. AND DALE EVANS **LUNCH KIT**. 1955–1956. Same as above, but with blue band. Same Thermos. Value: Box, $45–$70; bottle, $30–$60.

R. R. AND DALE EVANS LIGHT-WEIGHT **LUNCH KIT**. 1957–1959. $2.49. Blue band. Lithograph on tin. Illustration of Roy, Dale, and dog on one side, Roy in red shirt. Opposite side, Roy and Dale roping calf at rodeo appearance. Reads: "Roy Rogers–Dale Evans Double R Bar Ranch." Thermos #2097. Steel, glass. Red screw-on cup. Flat steel. Metal handle. Issued with 1954 "Roy rearing on Trigger" Thermos. Box, $60–$125; bottle, $35–$60; set, $100–$200. Third most common set, tied with tan saddlebag lunch box. *Note:* This dog has been identified in one source, as "Hot Dog Russell." The dog's color bears no resemblance to Bullet.

R. R. CHOW WAGON **LUNCH KIT**. 1958–1961. King Seeley Thermos after 1960. Lithograph on tin. Ninth box model. Dome type. Roy on side, Dale on end. Thermos is the yellow sky one. Box: $40–$150; bottle, $35–$65. Second most common set.

R. R. SADDLEBAG **LUNCH KIT**. 1961. King Seely Thermos. Cream color vinyl. Creme version is rare. Same thermos as

Roy Rogers Deputy Sheriff Outfit, as advertised on back of *Roy Rogers Comics*, 1950.

above. Artwork: unknown. Box, $150–$450. (Brown version is only $150.) Bottle, $35–$65.

R. R. **LUNCH PAIL**. Early 1950s. Herbert-George Co. No additional information. $60–$100.

MAGAZINES. Roy on cover/magazine articles. (*See* Bibliography.) Clipped articles generally sell for $2 per page, $3 if color photo. Clippings are seen at $1 small, $1.50 medium, $2 large size. Clipped photos fall in the same category. Magazines with Roy, Roy/Dale on cover are seen at $15 to $60. The *Life* magazine with Roy and Trigger cover, July 12, 1943: $35–$60.

R. R. **MAILING BOX**. 1951. Quaker Oats Co. Branding iron ring. Box: $20–$30.

R. R. **MANNEQUIN**. Early 1950s. P. L.

DeLuca Company, Los Angeles. $500–$1500.

R. R. OFFICIAL DEPUTY SHERIFF'S MANUAL. 1953. $25–$65. *See also* Roy Rogers Official Deputy Sheriff Outfit.

R. R. QUICK DRAW MARKER. 1960. Speed-Dry Products, Inc., Richmond Hill, NY. Felt nib marker. Six brilliant certified D and C colors. Advertised in *Roy Rogers Comics*. Originally 57 cents. $25–$50 with handbook. *See also* Handbooks.

R. R. MARTINGALE. 1953. Bona-Allen, Inc. Natural russet with drop ornament of golden palomino with embossed Trigger (head looking to observer's right). Sears No. 10 H 8235M: $4.75. $75–$150.

R. R. MASK. Early 1950s. Frontiers, Inc., Hollywood, CA. No additional information. $60–$150.

R. R. WESTERN MEDALS. 1955. General Foods. 27 different medals. Originally premium inside Post's Raisin Bran box. $15–$25 each. Set: $500.

R. R. MEMBERSHIP CARD. Early 1950s. Sears Back to School Contest. Photo of Roy, reversed negative. Printed horizontally. $25–$45.

INTER-OFFICE MEMOS, RADIO STATION DIRECTIVES. 1941–1947. Mutual Network. The "Roy Rogers Show," radio. Original memos, announcements, etc., from conference calls, etc., can be found typed on standard size typewriter paper. Originals are in the Manuscript Division of the Library of Congress, Washington, D.C. $5–$10 per page.

R. R. MILITARY SET. Early 1950s. Standard Pyroxoloid Corporation, Leominster, MA. $65–$95.

R. R. MINERAL CITY. 1950s. Lithographed tin. Town with hotel, music hall, cafe, bank, barber shop, trade goods. (Unknown manufacturer. Appears to be simpler version of those shown below. Possibly unauthorized.) $100–$300.

R. R. MINERAL CITY SET. 1950s. Louis Marx and Co. No. 4258. Lithographed tin buildings unit. Inside furniture. Figures include cowboys, horses, calves, etc. Post office, barber shop, trade goods, assay office, Fargo express, bank, music hall, hotel. Accessories include saddles, bridles, fence, tree, cactus, buckboard, etc. Boxed. Originally $5.98. $250–$650. It is believed that several versions of this exist, with some variations. They are also found with figures mixed from other Marx Roy Rogers sets and other Marx sets. *See also* Roy Rogers Ranch/Rodeo sets.

R. R. MITTEN AND SCARF SET. 1955–1956. Illinois Glove Co. Sizes: 3–4. Ages 2–5. Colors: navy, brown, maize, red. Originally $1.95. $85–$150.

R. R./DALE EVANS HARD-SOLE MOCCASINS. 1955. Acrobat, Storybook, Family Shoe, all divisions of General Shoe Corp. Fringed. Picture of Roy rearing on Trigger on tops. Originally $3.49. $50–$100.

R. R. COMFORTABLE MOK-SANS. 1954. Tex Tan of Yoakum. Full grain glove leather. Leather insole. Soft or hard soles. Designs of Dale or Roy on tops (rearing on horses). Sizes 8–3. Originally $2.98–$3.79. Advertised in *Life*, 1954: $3.79. $50–$100.

MUFFLERS. *See* Glove and Muffler Sets.

R. R. MUG. China, white. Illustrated. $35–$65.

R. R. PAPER NAPKINS. Early 1950s. Beach Products, Inc., Kalamazoo, MI. $5–$15.

R. R. KING OF THE COWBOYS SILK NECKERCHIEF. 1940s. Yellow, red. Likenesses of Roy, Trigger, Bullet. Printed: "Many Happy Trails, Roy Rogers and Trigger." Roy rearing on Trigger pose. $65–$100.

R. R. NECKERCHIEF. 1950s. "Guandero Tie" by Oasis Frontiers, Phoenix, AZ. Sears No. RN 2785E. 100 percent Polyester. Solid colors, including (author's collection) pale blue. Roy's facsimile signature in white lettering on one side; stone in snowflake design other side. Metal slide with "RR" in star on front; "Roy Rogers" in block print stamped underneath; Roy's facsimile signature engraved both sides, along with numerous small stars. $65–$90. *See also* Scarf.

NESTLE'S QUIK CONTAINER. 1960. 3½″ × 5½″ × 6″. Has Roy Rogers coupon ad with photo. $100–$200.

NEWSLETTERS

Double R Bar Ranch News. 1940–1955(?). Published by the Roy Rogers Fan Club, quarterly (1940s). Free to members. 1951: Eight pages of news/photos. Drawn

Roy, upper left-hand corner (probably artist Alvarado), with lariat surrounding cover photo. (January 1951: cover, Robin). 1955: Eight pages of news/photos of Roy, Dale, family. Front, drawn Roy rearing on Trigger in front of Double-R-Bar Ranch scene; used on merchandise of the period, artist probably John Steel. 9″ × 12″. Published bimonthly in Hollywood, California, in 1950s. Photo covers. $40–$175.

The Evanstar. 1940s(?)–1950s. Published by the Dale Evans Fan Club. President: Lois Blair Johnson. $65–$100.

NEWSPAPER ARTICLES. (*See* Bibliography/Tear Sheets/Magazines.) A multitude of articles have appeared in all newspapers since the 1930s, running into the thousands of clippings. $1 small to $5 full page to $50 full-page color photo to $250 full-page color photo Sunday supplement cover.

INTRODUCING R. R. **NOVELTY CARD.** 1940s. Tiny chain that makes up part of man's face, attached to 3½″ × 6¼″ cardboard. Changes man's expression as it is tapped with finger. Paramount-Publix theater circuit, New York, 1950s. This is not Roy Rogers the cowboy star, but is a very special collectible to any Roy Rogers collection, as it is a piece of memorabilia connected to Roy Rogers the vaudeville actor who brought a suit against Leonard Slye and Republic Productions in 1938 for using his name. $20–$30.

R. R. **OIL PAINTING** SET. Early 1950s. Paint by numbers materials. $100–$200.

R. R. QUAKER OATS **ORDER SHEET.** 1951. Quaker Oats Co. $15–$20.

R. R. APPROVED PONY RIDING OUT-FIT. 1952. Bona-Allen, Inc. "This is it, pardner! A real rough and tough range riding outfit that's backed by the King of the Cowboys, Roy Rogers. It's great for all young cowboys up to 15 years old." Complete outfit has saddle, bridle and martingale. "Roy Rogers" and picture of Roy rearing on Trigger embossed on both fenders in palomino gold. No blanket. 10 G 09509L. Originally $49.50. (*See also* individual items.) $700–$2,500.

R. R. DEPUTY SHERIFF'S **OUTFIT.** 1953. Includes Roy Rogers Official Deputy Sheriff's Manual, Official Roy Rogers Deputy Sheriff I.D., Deputy Sheriff Badge, and 10″

gun. Advertised in May 1953 *Roy Rogers Comics.* $100–$300.

R. R. COWBOY/COWGIRL **OUTFIT.** Early 1950s. Foreign. J. and L. Randall, Potter's Bar, G.B. Includes Hat, tie, shirt, vest, chaps, six-guns/holster set. Vest has action pictures of Roy, Trigger. Tie has picture of Roy rearing on Trigger. Chaps have large name, each leg, over picture of Roy waving, rearing on Trigger. Pictures cover entire bottom halves, to knees. Comes with white thin belt, small lariat. $150–$500.

DALE EVANS **OUTFIT**, GLAMOROUS 6 PIECE. 1952. Bolero, skirt, in mercerized, Sanforized twill, with combed cotton polo shirt. Lariat, kerchief. Plastic clicker gun in holster. Sears No. 29 G 4328. Washable. State size: 3, 4, 5, 6, 6X. 13 oz. Red. Originally $3.98. In box, mint, $150–$400.

DALE EVANS 11-PIECE SET COWGIRL **OUTFIT.** 1952. Dale is rearing on horse, her name written in lariat, on face of skirt. Shirt, tie, slide, and hat matches boy's set. Sears No. 40 G 4549. Originally $4.79. (Other Western sets similar in style, not Roy or Dale: $3.79.) Complete, in box, mint, $150– $500.

R. R. 11-PIECE SET COWBOY **OUTFIT.** 1952. "Sold Only at Sears." Bat wing cotton twill chap front pants with Roy rearing on Trigger designs, two-toned cotton shirt (fringed), Western loop tie and leather slide (steer skull). Roy Rogers name above picture, Trigger below. Cotton hat and leather belt (lace-up) and two holsters. Hats resemble Mountie styles. Two clicker pistols. Lariat. Matches cowgirl outfit. State size: 4, 6, 8, 10, 12. Sears No. 40 G 4548. Originally $4.79. Complete, in box, mint, $150–$500. *See also* Guns.

R. R. 9-PIECE COWBOY **OUTFIT.** 1953. Black corduroy pants with chap front, pink trim. Elastic back waist. Pink and black check embroidered broadcloth shirt. White scarf, belt, holsters, 2 break-barrel guns. RR in lariat loop on holster belt. Sizes: 4, 6, 8, 10, 12. Sears No. 40 H 4530. No hat included. Originally $6.85. $150–$400.

R. R. 9-PIECE SET WESTERN **OUTFIT.** 1953. *See* "11 Piece Set Cowboy Outfit." Steer skull tie slide. Somehow, a year later same outfit was counted as nine pieces. Possibly the two clicker guns were counted earlier. Sears No. 40 H 4552: Originally $4.94. $150–$500.

DALE EVANS 9-PIECE SET WESTERN **OUTFIT**. 1953. Same description as for above Roy Rogers set, 40 H 4522. Sears No. 40 H 4553. Originally $4.94. $150–$400.

DALE EVANS 9-PIECE COWGIRL **OUT-FIT**. 1953. Black corduroy skirt, kick pleat front, pink trim. Pink and black check cotton shirt. Same extras as 40 H 4530, white string tie. Sears No. 40 H 4531. Originally $4.94. $150–$500.

R. R. 9-PIECE COWBOY **OUTFIT**. 1953. Unknown company. Dark brown chap front pants, with pictures of Roy and Trigger in orange and white. Dark brown shirt, cotton, fringed, embroidered front yoke, (flowers), belt, holsters, toy metal clicker pistols. Scarf, lariat. Size: 4, 6, 8, 10, 12. Sears No.: 40 H 4522. Originally $4.85. $150–$500.

ROY/DALE 7-PIECE **OUTFIT**. 1953. Light-colored chap front pants. Pictures of Roy riding Trigger hard. Roy Rogers name on top, Trigger on bottom. Pictured opposite direction on each leg. Same picture on skirt front. Sears and Roebuck. Originally $4.77. $150–$300.

DALE EVANS COWGIRL **OUTFIT**. 1955. Sackman. Complete Dale suits in real Western styles. Includes gun, holster, tie, lariat. Sizes 2–14. Designs on yokes, skirt. Originally $4.95–$5.95. $150–$300.

R. R. COWBOY **OUTFIT**. 1955. Sackman Brothers. Complete Roy and Dale suits in real Western styles. Includes gun, holster, tie, lariat. Sizes 2–14. Designs on yokes, chaplike pants. Originally $4.95–$5.95. $150–$300.

"SUIT 'EM WESTERN" R. R. **OUTFIT**. 1955. Sackman Bros. Outfits with guns, holsters, lariat, tie, shirt, chaps, slacks. Originally $4.95–$5.95. Value: $150–$300.

"SUIT 'EM WESTERN" DALE EVANS **OUTFIT**. 1955. Sackman Bros. Outfits with gun, holster, lariat, tie, shirt, fringed skirt. Originally $4.95–$5.95. Value: $150–$300.

R. R. FESTIVE WESTERN **OUTFIT**. 1955. J Bar T Co. Embroidered yokes. Lace-up look, horseshoes on collars. Originally $10.95. Denim pants with attached holsters: $7.95. $150–$250.

DALE EVANS FESTIVE WESTERN **OUTFIT**. 1955. J Bar T. Embroidered yokes. Lace-up look, horseshoes on collars. Originally $10.95. Denim pants with attached holsters: $7.95. $150–$250.

R. R. **OVERALLS**. Early 1950s. Fargo Manufacturing Co., Philadelphia. No additional information. $75–$150.

R. R. **PAINT BY NUMBER SET**. 1953–1955. General Foods. Premium. Photo of Roy on box. Three different sets. Paints, brush, instruction sheet, paint by number photos of Dale, Roy. $45–$100. *See also* R. R. Watercolor Set.

R. R. BOXED **PAINT SET**. 1950s. 10″ × 14″. $45–$100. (Possibly same as above.) *Note:* Manufacturer of above sets could be Standard Toykraft Company, as they did produce a Roy Rogers paint set in the early 1950s.

R. R. **PAINT SET**. 1957. Offered as prize in Bakers Instant Chocolate contest. 3-D plaques with nine nontoxic paints, paint thinner, and brush. Four pictures include Roy rearing on Trigger, Dale riding Buttermilk, Roy feeding Trigger, and Roy and Bullet. $65–$150.

R. R. AND D. E. **"PAINT THEM YOUR-SELF" SET**. Early 1950s. Crafts Co. Includes six molded plaster figures and paint materials. $150–$300.

R. R. ON TRIGGER **PAINTING**. 1940s. Artist unknown. This painting now hangs in the Roy Rogers–Dale Evans Museum, but it occupied the Rogers homes for many years. Inspired by a scene from Roy's 1947 film *Springtime in the Sierras*. Impossible to determine value.

R. R. TWO-PIECE KNIT **PAJAMAS**. 1952. Softly combed cotton. Western designs printed on pullover top. (Not designs of Roy or Trigger.) Guns, holsters, howling coyotes, branding irons. Words "Roy Rogers and Trigger" appear with designs. Sears No. 43G4635. Original cost: $2.25. (Other brands $2.19.) $65–$150.

R. R. RANCHJAMA **PAJAMAS**. 1954. Allison Co., New York. Color fast cotton knit, two-ply brushed fabrics. Rib cuffs, anklets, waistbands. Fringed. Color picture of Roy or Dale. (Roy rearing on Trigger, encircled by lariat. Signature left side of picture.) Originally $2.59. $65–$150.

R. R. FLANNEL **PAJAMAS** FOR COWBOYS AT CURFEW. 1954. NiteKraft. Sanforized, two-toned cotton flannel, or broadcloth. Sizes 4–12. Originally $2.95. $65–$150.

R. R. "SKI" **PAJAMAS**. 1953. Roy, Trigger, Bullet print. Words "Roy Rogers and

Trigger." Small boy's sizes. Advertised in Sears catalogue: $1.95. $65–$150.

R. R. **PAJAMAS**. 1960. Material printed with holsters, guns. Other print: hats, etc. Prizes in RR Nestle's contest. $55–$100.

R. R. **PAJAMAS**. Early 1950s. Frackville Manufacturing Co., New York. Woven. $65–$150.

R. R. FRONTIER **PANTS AND JACKET**. 1954. Wm. Schwartz and Co., Philadelphia. 1950s. Jacket, suede-fringed. Jacket originally $8.95–$9.95; pants $4.95–$5.95. $150–$400.

R. R. **PARTI-KITS**. Early 1950s. Herbert of Hollywood. No further information. $50–$100.

R. R. **PEN**. Early 1950s. Flo-Ball Pen Corporation, New York. Ball point pen. $35–$100.

OFFICIAL DELUXE R. R. FOUNTAIN **PEN**. 1955–1956. Stratford Pen Corporation. Stainless steel point. Roy's name on barrel. Comes in clear plastic box decorated with Mineral City scene, Roy, Dale, etc. Originally $1. $75–$150.

OFFICIAL DELUXE R. R. **PEN AND PENCIL SET**. 1955–1956. Stratford Pen Corporation. Roy's name on barrels. Same box as above. Originally $1.95. $75–$150.

R. R. **PEN CARRYING CASE**. Early 1950s. Aristocrat Manufacturing Co. Cowhide. 2″ wide. "RR" brand in center, rest is floral design. $60–$150. *See also* Leather Stamping Plates.

R. R. MECHANICAL **PENCIL**. Early 1950s. Flo-Ball Pen Corporation. $45–$100.

R. R. **PENCIL BOX**. 1955–1956. Eagle Pencil Co. Roy, Trigger, Bullet on bright red box, embossed in gold. Two tiers, three colored pencils, eraser, six crayons, Magic Slate. 10¼″ × 4¼″ × 1½″. Originally 75 cents. $75–$150.

R. R./DALE EVANS **PENCIL BOX**. 1955–1956. Eagle Pencil Co., Roy, Dale, Trigger, Bullet on saddle tan box. Top try, drawer hold ruler, three pencils (one no-tip), thick lead pencil, ten crayons, eraser, lettering guide. 8½″ × 4¾″ × 1½″. $75–$150.

R. R. **PENCIL BOX**. 1955–1956. Eagle Pencil Co. Roy and Trigger embossed in silver on bright red box. Sliding tray holds ruler, three pencils, ten crayons, eraser. 8″ × 4½″ × ¾″. Originally 29 cents. $75–$150.

R. R. **PENCIL BOX**, WITH R. R. PEN-CILS. 1952. Hassenfeld Brothers, Pawtucket, RI. Saddle tan. Two drawers with six 7″ Roy Rogers pencils. Pen holder, pen point, ruler, eraser, six crayons, protractor, triangle, six paints, brush, water dish, pennant sheet. 9″ × 4⅞″ × 2⅜″. Sears No. 3G4807. Originally 74 cents. $75–$150.

R. R. **PENCIL BOX**. 1954 or later. Possibly Hassenfeld Brothers. Approximately 4″ × 7″. Illustrated Roy, Trigger, Dale, Bullet on box. "Roy Rogers Plus Brand." $75–$150.

R. R. **PENCIL CASE**. Early 1950s. Unknown manufacturer. Vinyl, snap close. Facsimile stitching. Roy Rogers name in writing. Illustrated Roy rearing on Trigger. $45–$65.

R. R. **PENCIL PACK**. 1955–1956. Eagle Pencil Co. One dozen pencils to package with Roy, Dale, Bullet, and Trigger on front. Originally 39 cents. $50–$85.

R. R. **PENCIL POUCH**. 1955–1956. Eagle Pencil Co. Roy and Trigger in three colors on snap-button pouch. Leatherlike flexible plastic in red, green, or brown. Contains six pencils. Originally 29 cents. $50–$85.

R. R. **PENCILS**. 1955–1956. Eagle Pencil Co. Originally three for 10 cents. $35–$65.

R. R. **PENCILS**. 1950s. Roy's name in wood. $35–$65. *Note:* Could be same pencils as above.

R. R. "SOUVENIR OF THE RODEO" **PENNANT**. 1942. 3½″ × 8½″ blue felt with portrait, trim strip, and inscriptions. Name under drawing misspelled "Rodgers." Purple felt streamers attached. One particular pennant has tag with date: 6/25/42. $60–$90.

R. R. "I WAS AT THE RODEO" **PENNANT**. 1942. 3½″ × 8½″ red felt pennant with portrait, trim strip, and inscriptions. Name under drawing of Roy misspelled "Rodgers." Purple felt streamers attached. $60–$90.

R. R. TEXAS LONGHORN **PENNANT**. 1950s. 11″ long, attached to 13″ plastic horn. Illustrated Roy rearing on Trigger. $75–$125.

R. R. AND TRIGGER **PENNANT**. Late 1940s. 28″ long. Illustrated Roy rearing on Trigger. $50–$100.

PHOTOGRAPH SHEETS. Mixed Western stars, male, female. 8″ × 10″ sheets contain miniature b&w film stills, publicity pictures. One in particular contains Roy publicity photo from *Melody Time*; Dale Evans publicity photo, short fringed skirt, posed with two guns drawn; Jane Frazee publicity photo. $5–$8.

R. R. LARGE SEPIA PHOTOGRAPH. 1950s. 1′ × 2′. Roy eating from can of pork and beans. $10 average.

R. R./DALE EVANS "STILL" PHOTOGRAPHS. 1930s–950s, 1976. (*See* Chapter 8 for in-depth descriptions, tips, etc., on all the following photographs.) Actual action scenes from a film. Original prints will be identified with a number consisting of three to four digits, a hyphen, then one to three digits. 8″ × 10″. Most have exchanged hands many times over the years, and it is unusual to find one naturally yellowed and with a breakdown of materials from age. Used in theaters to promote/advertise film. $10–$30. Subsequent prints: $3–$5. *Note:* At present date, every type photo imaginable, even from comics, merchandise, and in magazines, is being reshot to make a negative; any number of prints are made as they sell. They are worth whatever a person is willing to pay, but generally are found at $3–$5. The quality is usually so poor (because they are several generations removed from the original negatives) that they are seldom passed off as originals. They are even being made into pinback buttons. Stills that never existed originally are also being made from the films and television show episodes.

R. R./DALE EVANS PUBLICITY STILL PHOTOGRAPHS. 1930s–1950s, 1976. Photo taken in stills studio after completion of film. Posed, alone or with cast members, sometimes in different attire from that which was worn in film. 8″ × 10″. Numbers same as "stills" above, and with variation. Same comments as above apply to question of age, etc. $10–$30. Subsequent prints: $3–$5.

R. R./DALE EVANS PUBLICITY PHOTOGRAPHS. 1930s–1990s. Photos were taken expressly for publicity and were used in many media, such as event promotion, magazine articles, comic books, books in general, merchandising, and mail-out by Roy Rogers companies in response to fan letters. 8″ × 10″. Originals carried a number, which generally was not reproduced in media. Often, the backs of photos will have markings by the enterprise that used them, i.e., Dell Library, *Ladies' Home Journal*, etc. Average across years: $5–$10.

R. R./DALE EVANS PUBLICITY PHOTOGRAPHS. 1940s–1950s. Vary in size from 1″ × 2″ to wallet-sized to 4″ × 5″. Mass-produced from original studio prints and sold by the millions by celebrity photo companies for advertising for films, use in magazines, etc. Mostly b&w, some color. Used by sponsors such as Post's Cereals in contests and as premiums; also used by Dell Comics in subscription offers. Printed on regular to heavy stock. Scene stills and publicity stills used. Usually in sets (by Post's cereals/Dell Comics) but rarely found in sets today. Heaviest comic related activity 1949–1956. Many advertised as "autographed." This has little bearing on today's prices, as "autographs" were mass printed facsimile type. Originally the price varied from free to 5 cents; many were 1 cent. $3–$10. Big, full-color "pin-ups" (1952–1954): $10–$20.

R. R./DALE EVANS COMIC BOOK PHOTOGRAPHS. 1940s–1960s. Many photos were especially posed for National Periodical's comics (Dale's first series) and Dell Publishing Co.'s comic books and were used in no other medium. A few were also used on merchandise such as writing tablets and on Whitman Co. books. The Dell photos contain markings on the back identifying Dell Library and usually carry a number used in their filing. $5–$15.

R. R./DALE EVANS CANDID PHOTOGRAPHS. 1911–present. Candid photos have been taken of Roy and Dale since their childhood. The originals from childhood days are probably only in the possession of family members. Candids are common from 1940s to present, taken at every type of event conceivable, especially gala Hollywood events. There are thousands from personal appearances and rodeo tours over the years in the hands of those who took them. Occasionally these get into the marketplace. Any size, 1940s–1950s: $20–$100. Thousands have been taken over the past couple of decades, especially at Golden Boot Awards, Roy Rogers Restaurant openings, and at the Roy Rogers–Dale Evans Museum: $5–$10.

R. R./DALE EVANS MAGAZINE PHOTOGRAPHS. Many resemble candid photos. They were taken during appointments with Roy and Dale by magazine photographers for use in magazines, usually film type. Taken in every possible place, including many at their home. Normally found in 8″ × 10″ size. Often have ruler markings and measurements from layout department showing what was used and cropped. Backs usually identify magazine and file number. $5–$15.

PICTORIAL NEWS OF THE DAY NEWS SERVICE BULLETINS. 1950s. Posted in factories, offices, etc. *Pictorial News of the Day.* Dispatch Photo News Services, Inc. New York City. April 16, 1952: "It's a Boy for Trigger." 17″ high, 14″ wide. Subscription: $52 per year. $30–$100.

R. R. 3-DIMENSION **PICTURES.** September 1953/January 1954. The "Roy Rogers Show"-radio, television. By General Foods. Also known as photo folder. (Inside the Post's Sugar Crisp box.) Two-sided cards. Set of four different ones. 2½″ × 4¼″. Full set with viewer in box. $35–65.

R. R. DIXIE PREMIUM **PICTURE.** 1940. #207. Color photo of Roy waving, rearing on Trigger. Back has four photos. 8″ × 10″. $30–$50.

R. R. DIXIE PREMIUM **PICTURE.** 1940. #208. Color photo of Roy from *Under Western Stars.* Playing guitar beside Trigger. Back has five photos. 8″ × 10″. $30–$85.

R. R. DIXIE PREMIUM **PICTURE.** 1949, 1950. Color photo of Roy and Trigger. Approximately 8″ × 10″. Republic Pictures name, Roy Rogers name on left border. Originally free. $30–$65.

D. E. DIXIE PREMIUM **PICTURE.** 1945. Several different photos. $30–$50.

DELL COMICS FAMILY GROUP **PICTURE.** 1950s. Includes likenesses of Roy, Trigger, the Lone Ranger, Tarzan, Gene Autry, and Lassie among cartoon characters. Photo of boy lying on floor with cocker spaniel dog and reading comic. $20–$45.

SEARS AND ROEBUCK R. R. CHRISTMAS **PICTURE.** 1950s. Giveaway. Value: $30–$50.

R. R. **PICTURE CARD ALBUM.** Early 1950s. The Times Confectionery Co., London. Designed to hold two sets (24 each) of Bubble Gum Trading Cards, showing and telling story of two films (*In Old Amarillo, South of Caliente*). Mail order. Originally given for one Roy Rogers Bubble Gum wrapper and 9 cents worth of stamps. $40–$70 (without cards).

R. R./R. R. AND TRIGGER THEATER GIVEAWAY **PICTURES.** 1940s–1950s. Republic Productions, Inc. Usually 8″ × 10″ color photos. Paper stock. Print under picture identifying subjects and Republic. Provided theaters for promotion. $10–$30. What with today's color laser photocopy quality, items such as this have been/are being mass-produced and at times are passed off as "originals." As a rule of thumb, if such items look too new, be suspicious.

R. R. ON BUCKING HORSE PIN. 1950s. Polished metal. Pin with keeper. "RR" stamped in horse's rump. May have been part of jewelry set or Western attire outfit. $35–$60.

R. R. **PISTOL.** Early 1950s. Leslie Henry Co., Mt. Vernon, NY. No additional information. Could possibly be part of pistol and spurs set. $75–$150.

R. R. CAST IRON CAP **PISTOL.** 1950s. 11″ long. $75–$150.

R. R. FORTY-NINER **PISTOL.** Early 1950s. Leslie-Henry Co. 9″ cap gun. "Puffs smoke." $150–$400.

R. R. FORTY-NINER **PISTOL AND SPURS SET.** 1940s. 8½″ long. $80–$300.

R. R. DISPLAY **PLATE.** 1950s. $65–$100.

R. R. RODEO **PLATE.** 1950s. Universal Co. Oven-proof, 6″. Roy twirling lariat. $45–$100. *See also* Chinaware Set.

R. R. RODEO **PLATE.** 1950s. Universal Co. Different artwork. Roy on rearing Trigger. 9″. $45–$100.

R. R. CERAMIC **PLATE AND MUG SET.** 1950s. $100–$200.

COWBOY STARS **PLAYING CARDS.** 1950s. Unknown company. Cards featured Roy, Rod Cameron, Rex Allen, and Rocky Lane. $30–$75.

R. R. **PLAYING CARDS.** 1960s. Gemaco Co. Made in USA. 52 cards. Black plastic case, clear lid. Same b&w Roy photo every card. "Roy Rogers" and "King of the Cowboys" at top of card. $25–$45.

DALE EVANS **PLAYSUIT.** 1960. Fringed shirt, fringed shorts or skirt. Prize offered in Roy Rogers Nestle's contest. $75–$200.

R. R. **POCKETKNIFE.** 1953. Ulster Co. Drawing of Roy rearing on Trigger, under red plastic of handle. Facsimile signature on top, "Trigger" on bottom. One long blade, one short, plus screwdriver blade. High carbon steel. Ring on end. 3½″ long. Originally $1.98. $60–$100.

R. R. POP-OUT CARDS. 1952–1955. General Foods. Premiums. The "Roy Rogers Show"–Radio, television. 36 different cards. (In Post cereal boxes.) Each card individually numbered. 2¼″ × 3¼″. Excellent art work, likely by Peter Alvarado, and possibly Hi Mankin. $15–$25 each. Entire set (must be unpunched): $500–$1,000. Examples: #1. Double-R-Bar Ranch. Roy and Dale standing behind sign. #2. Trigger rears high in the air. Roy on rearing Trigger. #21. Trigger (Trigger, Jr., type) prancing in corral, with plastic rodeo saddle, tack. #30. Roy stands facing viewer, both guns drawn. #35. Dale applies first aid bandage to Roy's arm. (Initials "RM" and "RLM" are visible on Dale, under magnification, suggesting artwork by Russ Manning. Unknown numbers: Roy, Trigger, and Dale, desert scene, inspired by Republic publicity photo. Roy, Trigger, swimming. Roy, gun in hand, peering over rocks. Roy cleaning Trigger's hoof. Roy, Trigger, swimming. Most of these are paintings inspired by photos that have appeared on or in comic books or on merchandise.

R. R. PORTRAIT. Late 1940s. Cain's Dance Academy/Ballroom. Tulsa, Oklahoma, nightclub which featured prominently in 1930s–1950s Western music, especially Western Swing, has since the late 1940s been the home of a large (approximately 2′ × 3′) tinted portrait (photograph) of Roy, signed. The nightclub displays the portrait on its wall of portraits, signifying that Roy made a personal appearance at this famous historical spot. Items of this nature draw special interest from collectors and do not easily lend themselves to a value, as they are not usually considered to be for sale. When establishments change hands or themes, such work can wind up in private collections, sometimes as part of an auction. Suffice it to say that the value of a one-of-a-kind item such as this, especially one that has occupied a prominent place, is very high.

R. R. PORTRAIT. Unknown company. Likely premium. Illustrated picture of Roy and Trigger. Unknown artist. Facsimile signed. $35–$55.

R. R. AND TRIGGER POSTCARD. 1955. Fan Club related. $15–$25.

ROY AND DALE RELIGIOUS **POST-CARDS.** Post–July 1963 (zip code appears in address on reverse). American Tract Society, New York and Oradell, NJ. "Scriptcards" and "Tracards." High gloss. 5⅜″ × 3⅜″. "King and Queen of the Rodeo." Religious testimony by Roy and Dale beside color photo. $5–$10.

R. R. AND TRIGGER FOUR COLOR POSTERS. 1949. Quaker Oats–sponsored Roy Rogers contest prize. Radio-announced. $40–$100.

R. R. FILM POSTERS. There is theater paper of most every type concerning each of the Rogers films; a book would be required to show just any one item, such as lobby cards, connected with Roy's Republic feature films. Generally, the posters and other memorabilia in the same time period as the ones noted will bring the same price, give or take a few dollars. It is believed that the lithographed posters were produced by the American Lithograph Corporation, Morgan Litho Co., Essex Co., and Allied Printing Co., and the artwork was supplied them by Republic Productions, Inc. The artwork is discussed in Chapter 9. Some of it appears to be by such artists as John Ushler and Peter Alvarado.

"One Sheet" posters (size: 27″ × 41″; 22″ × 28″), 1950s; also: 30″ × 40″, 40″ × 60″. All heavy stock, lithograph process, film or film type scenes depicted in artwork, mixed with generally large pictures of the star by various artists. Generally these are found at about 20 percent more than the "half-sheets," if other factors (the age, condition, etc.) remain constant. Because of the popularity of the stars and the overwhelming, undying loyalty of the "Sagebrush Heroes" fans, as well as the brilliantly colored artwork produced by artists for Republic Productions, most of the Republic "B" Western posters will often bring more money than major film studio's "A" Western posters. They can range anywhere from $75 to $200 plus. They can be seen in the Poster Collection, Prints and Photographs Division, at the Library of Congress. These following prices have been seen recently in auctions and at shows. *Under Western Stars* (1938), $160–$200; *Arizona Kid* (1939), $125–$175 (copyright 1939 by Morgan Litho. Corp., Cleveland, OH); *King of the Cowboys*

(1943), $110–$150; *Man from Oklahoma* (1945), $110–$135; *The Cowboy and the Senorita* (1944), $75; *Song of Arizona* (1946), $100–$125; *The Gay Ranchero* (1948), $95–$125; *Down Dakota Way* (1949), $110–$135; *Susanna Pass* (1949), $75–$100; *Pals of the Golden West* (1951), $85–$115.

"Half Sheet" posters. Also known as "Displays." Printed on heavy stock. (Size: 22″ × 28″). *Under Western Stars* (1938), $120–$160; *Arizona Kid* (1939), $100– $140; *King of the Cowboys* (1943), $90–$120; *Man from Oklahoma* (1945), $90–$110; *Song of Arizona* (1946), $85–$105; *Gay Ranchero* (1948), $80–$100; *Down Dakota Way* (1949), $85–$110; *Susanna Pass* (1949), $100–$135; *Pals of the Golden West* (1951), $65–$95.

R. R. FOREIGN MINIATURE **POSTERS**. 1940s. From Spain by "Graficas Valencia" Valencia. Beautiful color miniature replicas of Spanish Roy Rogers' half sheets, on thin paper, some with much information on reverse in Spanish. 3¼″ × 5″. "Wargui Films Presents." On a particular one, "Republic Pictures International" appears, as well as the names Elizabeth Allan and Wilfrid Lawson. Two in this writer's collection are *Cita en la Frontera (Hands Across the Border)*, Oct. 13, 1946 (possible connection with Cine Oriente theater), $20–$30; *La Cancion de Nevada (Song of Nevada)*, $20–$30.

R. R. **PRESS BOOKS**. 1938–1951. Republic Pictures. Movie materials. Distributed by National Screen Service. Oversized books contain ads for Roy's films that can be sent to local newspapers, with a theater's name inserted in the blank. These were produced for both the first release and rerelease of the films. The rerelease books from the early to mid–1950s are about 5 percent larger than those of the 1940s. $60–$100.

PRICE LISTS, WITH R. R. ITEMS. 1946. Exhibit Supply Co. Exhibit card price list. Four pages. $15–$30.

R. R. HAND **PUPPET**. 1950s. Flesh-colored rubber head in likeness of Roy, hat. Cloth bottom. $75–$150.

R. R. STRAIGHT SHOOTER GUN **PUZZLE**. 1950s. Plastic. $30–$65.

R. R. WOOD PICTURE **PUZZLE**. 1950s. Whitman Publishing Co. It is not known at this time how many were produced. 1. Roy astride Little Trigger, fringed outfit. 2. Roy over the silver saddle. $25–$55.

R. R. PICTURE **PUZZLE**. 1954. Whitman. 4¼″ × 5″ color photo jigsaw puzzle showing Roy with gun in hand. Miniature version of larger types. Photo from session which produced those used for *Roy Rogers Comics* 1957–1959, i.e. #s 119, 130, with Roy in "yellow rose" shirt. $25–$55.

R. R. PICTURE **PUZZLES**. 1953. Whitman Publishing Co. Whitman evidently began issuing these in the late 1940s. The earliest one in this writer's collection is 1948. One identification number for all, in a particular series, regardless of photo. Some of these came with an extra photo enclosed, suitable for framing. The boxed jigsaw type has photo on box of assembled puzzle. Some show original copyright, some do not. These are photo jigsaw puzzles, and the photos are similar to, and in some instances exact copies of, those used for the *Roy Rogers Comics* covers, but appear on the puzzle as much as six months to a year earlier. Many are altered, often with paint, for the puzzles. Originally 29 cents.

Jigsaw 4400 series. Boxed. #4404:29. 1957. 14⅛″ × 18¼″; ⅛″ thick; 63 pieces. Roy, on a staircase, looking back, pistol in hand. Photo also used for *Roy Rogers Comics* #124, April 1958. Originally 29 cents. $25– $65. Roy, Dusty, Dale sitting on fence. $25–$65.

Frame Tray Inlay 4427 Series. #4427:29. 1948. Original copyright: Frontiers, Inc. 11½″ × 14½″; ⅛″ thick. Approximately 29 die-cut pieces, one in the shape of a heart. Title in all block lettering. Year in Roman numerals. This particular puzzle is a copy of the photo used for comic #13, January 1949, enlarged approximately twice the size of the comic. The photo takes on a slight painted effect, so it might have been doctored to offset the loss of definition from the enlarging process. $25–$65. #4427:29. 11½″ × 14½″; ⅛″ thick. Original copyright: 1956, Roy Rogers–Frontiers, Inc. Approximately 48 die-cut pieces. Title in all block lettering. Year in Roman numerals. Photo is used for cover of *Roy Rogers Comics* #109, January 1957. Roy, in green-fringed and red rose-decorated white shirt, is looking around rock, gold-plated six-gun in hand, and Bullet at his feet. $15–$50.

2604 Series. "Roy Rogers" appears written rather than being in block lettering. Year

Roy Rogers Ranch Set advertised on the back of *Roy Rogers Comics*, 1950s. Used with permission. Courtesy Kraft General Foods.

shown in Arabic numbers. There is only one number for identification, and all the puzzles in this series show the number "2604." 11½" × 14⅞"; ⅛" thick. Original copyright: 1952, Roy Rogers Enterprises. Approximately 25 die-cut pieces, one in the shape of a four-leaf clover, another of an airplane. Photo from a series worth some discussion. The same design shirt is employed for the photo used for *Roy Rogers Comics* #63, March 1953 and for this 1952 puzzle. However, although the poses are almost identical, the shirts are different colors. On the comic cover, Roy is whittling toward his body; in the puzzle photo, the knife travel is away from the body. The neckerchief appears to be the same in both shots. The background illustrations for the two are totally different. The puzzle is shown in a Whitman advertisement on the inside back cover of the comic. $30–$65. 2604. 11½" × 14⅞"; ⅛" thick. Original copyright: 1952, Roy Rogers Enterprises. Approximately 25 die-cut pieces cut in the same shape as the above listed. Another interesting shot from a series which includes similar photos used for different mediums. The front cover of *Roy Rogers Comics* #74, February 1954, sports a 1952 photo from the same series as this puzzle. On the comic, there is no painted background, while on the puzzle, there is a considerable background. Roy is behind the same door in each, but looking two different directions; in both cases the gold-plated six-shooter is pointed straight up. The neckerchief is probably the same, except that the doctoring for the puzzle photo, which is very apparent, altered its color. The gun, as well as the fringe on the shirt, appears to have undergone treatment from an artist's brush. $30–$65. 2604. 11½" × 14⅞"; ⅛" thick. Original copyright: 1952, Roy Rogers Enterprises. Approximately 25 die-cut pieces, one in the shape of a heart. Photo used for this one is from a series that includes the one used for the cover of *Roy Rogers Comics* #65, May 1953. Background painted scenery appears to be by artist Peter Alvarado, as his initials shown in an area to the left of subject. $30–$65. 2604. 11½" × 14⅞"; ⅛" thick. Original copyright: 1953, Roy Rogers Enterprises. Approximately 26 die-cut pieces, one in shape of heart, one in shape of airplane, one in shape of four-leaf clover, but the

pieces are smaller and arranged differently from the previously mentioned puzzle with similar pieces. Photo was used for the cover of the 1954 Whitman hardback novel *Trail of the Zeroes*. $30–$65. 2604. 11½" × 14⅞"; ⅛" thick. Original copyright: 1953, Roy Rogers Enterprises. Approximately 26 die-cut pieces, one in the shape of a star. Roy, Dusty, and Dale are sitting on a fence in this one. This photo belongs to a series which includes the shot taken for the cover of *Roy Rogers Comics* #67, September 1953, with Roy in the blue-fringed gold shirt. Dale is in a white-fringed, star-decorated, brown outfit. $30–$65. Unknown number, probably 2604. 1953. Trigger, no saddle and stock harness on, standing to the right of Bullet, as one looks at the photo; the horse is looking down at the dog. This photo might have been used elsewhere earlier in color, but it is a shot that belongs to a series of photos which includes the one used on the inside back cover of *Roy Rogers Comics* #141, January-February 1961. $30–$65.

2600 Series. All block lettering, appearing in bordered area at top; year in Roman numerals. #2610:29. 11⅜" × 14⅞"; ⅛" thick. Original copyright: 1952, Frontiers, Inc. Approximately 26 die-cut pieces, some in the shape of animals: a dog, duck, squirrel, and rabbit. Series number has changed, but everything else remains the same. Photo here is most interesting. By *Roy Rogers Comics* #38, February 1951, the printing company had begun using photos with painted/illustrated background scenes. This one evidently is from a series of shots that included the one used for #57, September 1952. The painted background is totally different, this one showing Trigger rather than pastureland and a barn. The photos are extremely close, with the difference being the pigging rope which is in Roy's mouth here. It was apparently taken moments before or after the one used for the comic, and it's a negative reversal. This photo has been doctored: the neckerchief was painted solid dark blue. In the artwork on the stirrup leathers of Trigger, where there normally appears an "R," there is what resembles a "J." $30–$65. #2628:29. 11⅜" × 14⅞"; ⅛" thick. Original copyright: 1952, Roy Rogers Enterprises. Approximately 30 die-cut pieces, one in the shape of a duck, another of a bell. An exact copy of the photo used for comic #52, April 1952. This one apparently lent itself better to puzzle making. Not only is it not doctored at all, but it looks as natural in color, if not more so, as the copy used for the comic. $30–$65. Unknown number but probably in this 2600 series. 1957. Photo is the exact photo used for *Roy Rogers Comics* #117, September 1957. $30– $65. Some puzzles were packaged in photo slip covers. Slip cover value: $6–$10.

2900 Series. All identification is in very small print at top or bottom of puzzle. Year in Arabic numbers. Smaller puzzles. 2982. 9¼″ × 11½″; ⅛″ thick. Original copyright: 1950, Rohr Co. Inlay tray. Approximately 18 die-cut pieces, one in the shape of a child. Roy, sitting against desert brush holding reins of Trigger, who is all decked out in the rodeo red, white, and blue tack. $30–$65. 2982. 9¼″ × 11½″; ⅛″ thick. Original copyright: 1950, Rohr Co. Approximately 17 die-cut pieces, one in the shape of a fish. Same photo as on one of the Roy Rogers Writing Tablets (Frontiers, Inc.), and the one used (partially) for front cover of *Roy Rogers Comics* #37, January 1951. Roy leans on silver-ornamented saddle, facing camera. $30–$65. #2982. 9¼″ × 11½″; 1950. Roy is sitting astride Trigger, facing camera, left arm crossed, left hand on right arm. Photo appears to be from series which includes shots used for back and front covers of *Roy Rogers Comics* #26, February 1950. 15 die-cut pieces. $30–$65. 2982. 9¼″ × 11½″; ⅛″ thick. Approximately 18 die-cut pieces, one in the shape of a dog, another of a fish. Roy is shown holding two puppies, and this photo is one from a series of shots which includes the one used for the cover of *Roy Rogers Comics* #54, June 1952. $30–$65.

Unknown series. Same large size. Roy standing beside Trigger in a photograph by photographer Ramon Freulich.

R. R. RUBBER **RAIN SET**. 1952. "Designed for the 'King of the Cowboys,' styled especially for you." Colorful contrasting collar, fringed front and back yokes. Two open-through slash pockets with stenciled picture of Roy on one, Trigger on the other. Black with yellow trim; yellow with black trim. (Likeness of Roy is unusual.) Sears No. 40 G 7618/19. Originally $3.88.

(Other brands: $2.94 to $3.69.) $80–$200.

R. R. PLASTIC **RAIN SET**. 1952. "Electronically sealed." "Snap-fastener fronts." Slash openings and comes with plastic case. Yellow/black, gray/yellow, Sears No. 40 G 7644/45. Originally $2.79. $80–$200.

R. R. **RAINCOAT**. 1950. Quaker Oats-sponsored Roy Rogers contest prize. Radio-announced. With helmet. 500 offered. $80–$250.

R. R. RUBBER **RAINCOAT**. 1955–1956. S. Buchsbaum and Co. Clasp fasteners, Western fringe. Stenciled picture of Roy and Trigger. Helmet, visor. Originally $4.50. $80–$200.

R. R. DEPUTY PERSONALIZED PHOTO **RAINCOAT**. 1955–1956. S. Buchsbaum and Co. Bakelite Krene material, Elasti-Glass. Picture of Roy one side. Photo pocket. Includes helmet, visor. Originally $2.98. $80–$200.

R. R. **RAINCOAT**. 1950s. Transparent body with yellow highlights. Roy and logo on badge. Yellow plastic snaps have metal guns inlaid. $80–$200.

R. R. **RAINCOAT**. 1950s. Cable Raincoat Co., Boston. Unknown description. May apply to any of the above-mentioned items which show no manufacturer.

R. R. ELASTI-GLASS **RAINWEAR**. 1955. S. Buchsbaum. $80–$200.

R. R. **RAINWEAR**. 1955. S. Buchsbaum. Rubber raincoat and helmet. Black or yellow with Western trim. Sizes 4–12. Originally $4.50. $80–$200.

R. R. DOUBLE-R-BAR **RANCH SET**. 1950s. Louis Marx and Co. No. 3980. Tin lithographed ranch set. Original is almost a duplicate of the company's "Bar M Ranch," but is modified with different figures, entrance gate. "Bar M Ranch" over bunkhouse door. Figures contain bulky-looking horses, cows. Boxed. "Authorized by Roy Rogers." $100–$400.

R. R. RODEO **RANCH SET**. 1950s. Louis Marx and Co. No. 3985. First set all original Roy Rogers, but still issued with both bunkhouses. Horses have molded saddles. Boxed. $100–$400.

R. R. DOUBLE-R-BAR **RANCH SET**. 1955–1956. Louis Marx and Co. No. 3986. Complete rodeo, three stall chutes, cowboys with lassos, whips. Bucking horses, steers.

Ten-section log fence. Ranch gate. Lithographed metal ranch house. Ranch accessories. Figures are acetate plastic. Tree, cactus, anvil, pump, etc. Originally $3.98. $100–$400.

R. R. RODEO RANCH SET. 1950s. Louis Marx and Co. No. 3990. Finest Roy Rogers set produced. Horses have removable saddles, bridles, etc. Original ranch house furniture excluded. $100–$400.

R. R. RODEO RANCH SET. 1950s. Louis Marx and Co. No. 3995. Same as No. 3990, except fence has changed from white rail to board. $100–$400.

R. R. RODEO RANCH SET. 1950s. Louis Marx and Co. No. 3689. Believed to be set No. 3986, which has been shown in reviews as No. 3689. More rare set which included two figures of Roy, also those of Pat Brady and Jeep Nellybelle. Two versions. One, even more rare, substitutes wagon for jeep and includes no ranch house. $100–$400.

R. R. RODEO RANCH SET. 1950s. Marx Co. Heavy carton 4″ × 9″ × 22″. Full-color lithograph tin ranch house, white plastic rail fence, rodeo chute, and gateway (inscribed "Roy Rogers Double R Bar Ranch"). 2½″ tall figures of Roy, nine other cowboys. Livestock figures, saddles, bridles, tree and cactus, wishing well, wood pile, chopping block, whetstone, anvil, grill, barrel, other items. Roy figure has gun in hand, raised. Authorized by Roy Rogers. $100–$400.

R. R. RANCH SET. 1953. General Foods. The "Roy Rogers Show," radio, television. 23 pieces, some possibly cardboard. Plastic figures. Metal jeep. (50 cents and two Post Cereals box tops.) $100–$200. *Note:* These sets are found with pieces combined from different Ranch/Rodeo sets, versions of sets, and other sets such as the Marx's Mineral City set and the Bar M Ranch set. *See also* Roy Rogers Mineral City Set.

R. R. RANGER SET. 1954. Auburn Rubber Co. Two rubber and vinyl knives, one pistol, one hatchet. Box has illustrated Roy rearing on Trigger. Originally 98 cents. $65–$150.

RECORD JACKET: *Alan McGill Sings (Words and Music by Roy Rogers).* 1950s. Sacred Records, Inc. LP 9040. 12″ LP has picture of Roy and McGill on gold and blue cover. (Only two of the songs are written by

Roy: "Lord, Have Mercy on My Soul" and "Read the Bible and Pray.") $20–$35.

R. R., DALE EVANS RECORD PLAYER. 1959. Detachable speakers have silhouette of Roy and name on one, Dale and name on the other. The classic "rearing on Trigger" pose is on the inside lid of the main body, where Bullet is also shown in desert scene. $150–$300.

R. R. "HAPPY TRAILS" 45 RPM RECORD PLAYER. 1950s. RCA Corporation, Camden, NJ. Hard plastic. Illustrations: Rodeo scenes, six-guns, etc. $150–$300.

RECORDS

See Chapter 3 for more detail. Generally, those LPs from the 1960s to 1990s can be found in the range of $20–$40. This section will deal only with older vintage material.

78 RPM. Decca, RCA Victor labels. Early Sons of the Pioneers, Roy Rogers, Dale Evans. The following represent hundreds of recordings: DECCA: "I've Sold My Saddle for an Old Guitar"/"Think of Me" (both recorded in Dallas), 6092; RCA VICTOR: "I Wish I Had Never Met Sunshine"/ "Rock Me to Sleep in My Saddle," 20-1815; "A Two-Seated Saddle and a One-Gaited Horse"/"Havaii-Na" (both Dale), 21-0360; "Last Night My Heart Crossed the Ocean" (Dale with Roy Rogers Riders)/"Please Send Me Someone to Love" (Dale), 21-0456; "Betsy"/"Hasta La Vista," 20-3059; "Blue Shadows on the Trail"/"(There'll Never Be Another) Pecos Bill," 45-5186/20-2780; "On the Old Spanish Trail" (with Spade Cooley)/ "I've Got a Feelin' (Somebody's Stealin' My Darlin')," 20-2320; "Dangerous Ground"/ "I'm Restless," 20-2236; "Along the Navajo Trail"/"Don't Blame It All on Me," 20-1730; "Make Believe Cowboy"/"Hawaiian Cowboy," 20-2604; "I'm Gonna Gallop, Gallop, Gallop to Gallup, New Mexico"/"Old Fashioned Cowboy," 20-2917. $20–$50.

EPs. Hymns of Faith. (2 record set.) RCA Victor. EPB 3158. 1954. $30–$100. *Pecos Bill.* Bluebird. EYA-5. $30–$100. *Roy Rogers Roundup.* RCA Victor. EPA-253. $30–$100. *Roy Rogers Souvenir Album.* (2 record set.) RCA Victor. EPB-3041. 1952. Exists in 78 RPM record set as well, Musical Smart Set. $30–$100. *Sweet Hour of Prayer.*

RCA Victor. EPA-2-1439. 1957. $30–$100. *The Masked Marauder.* RCA Victor. Early 1950s. $30–$100.

LPs. Dale Evans Sings. Allegro. 4116. 1940s. Elite High Fidelity 10″. B&w photo of Dale on cover, Western attire, on red background. $30–$100. *Hymns of Faith.* (10″ LP) RCA Victor. LPM-3168. 1954. $20–$60. *Lore of the West.* RCA Victor "Little Nipper" series Y-388. Two 78 RPM records, stories, pictures set. 1950s. $50–$125. *Roy Rogers Souvenir Album.* (10″ LP). RCA Victor LPM-3041. 1952. $40–$80. *Roy Rogers Tells and Sings About Pecos Bill.* RCA Victor. "Little Nipper" series. Two 78 RPM records, stories, pictures set. 1950s. $50–$125. *A Child's Introduction to the West.* 1950s. Unknown, possibly Golden Records. Painting, Roy and Dale on horses. LP.

Children's 78s/45s. $25–$40. *Gabby the Gobbler.* 1955. RCA Victor. 45 RPM: 48-0374. 78 RPM:21-0374. *If You Ever Come to Texas/Dusty Skies.* (Dale.) Unknown year. Bel-Tone Records. 78 RPM. E-0263 (Matrix B7 19-½.) *Roy Rogers Square Dance Record Album.* 1950. Quaker Oats–sponsored Roy Rogers contest. Radio-announced. 500 offered. No other information. $40–$60.

Little Golden Records. Produced by the Sandpiper Press, printed in U.S.A. by Western Printing and Lithographing Co. Records made by Bestway Products. 78 RPM/45 RPM. Picture sleeves with painted likenesses. The artwork in some of the paintings appears to be that of Peter Alvarado. $20–$35. "The Night Before Christmas," R 183; "The Little Boy Who Couldn't Find Christmas/The Story of Christmas" (Roy and Dale), R 198; "Daniel the Cocker Spaniel," AV1700/187/186; "Goodnight Prayer/Keep in Touch," AV1705/205/2058/205; "Hoofbeat Serenade" (Roy and Dale)/"A Goodnight Prayer" (Roy), unknown number; "Happy Trails to You"/"A Cowboy Needs a Horse," AV1710/176; "A Cowboy Needs a Horse" (Roy)/"Chuck Wagon Song" (Roy and Dale), unknown number; "The Little Shoemaker," AV1715/196; "The Lord's Prayer" (Roy), "Ave Maria" (Dale), AV1720/240 (R 240); "Cowboys Never Cry" (Roy), "I Love the Outdoors" (Dale), R 255; "Jesus Loves the Little Children"/"The Lord Is Gonna Take Good Care of You," R 256;

"Open Up Your Heart" (Roy and Dale)/ "Friends and Neighbors" (Roy and Dale), AV1725/179; "Roy Rogers Had a Ranch"/ "The Chuck Wagon Song," AV1730/199; "Swedish Rhapsody" (Roy)/"Bamboo Boat" (Roy), AV1735/185; "Thank You God" (Roy and Dale)/"Let There Be Peace on Earth," R 312; "Roy Rogers' Cowboy Songs," AV 3240/324 (EP, 6 songs), 45 RPM; "Dale Evans' Songs of Faith," AV3650/325 (EP, 6 songs), 45 RPM; "Happy Trails" (Roy and Dale)/"The Bible Tells Me So," LG18; "Cowboys Never Cry"/"Hoofbeat Serenade," LGR 8-4.

Bell Records. $25–$40. "Friends and Neighbors" (Roy and Dale)/"The Little Shoemaker" 1050.

Disney Records. "Roy Rogers Talks and Sings About Pecos Bill." (Talking Record Book; two records and a story book.)

R. R. THIRD DIMENSIONAL FILM REELS. 1952. Sawyers, Inc., Portland, OR. Seven pictures on each. Roy and Trigger. Sears catalog no. 3 G 6452. Roy Rogers and Trigger #945 is one reel offered among other titles. Six reels for $2. Another reel is "Dale Evans, Queen of the West." $15–$20.

R. R. SHOW **RESPONSE CARD**. November 1948. Quaker Oats. Radio show, Mutual Network, Chicago, IL. Painted likeness of Roy, Trigger, Dale, and Gabby, encircled by lariat. Facsimile signature "Roy Rogers and Trigger." $25–$40.

R. R. SHOW **RESPONSE CARD**. October 1948. Quaker Oats. Radio show, Mutual Network, Chicago, Illinois. Painted likeness of Roy rearing on Trigger, waving. Facsimile signature. "Many Happy Trails, Roy Rogers." (Front: 1 cent U.S. Postal card.) $25–$40.

R. R.–DALE EVANS **RESPONSE CARD**. Mid–1950s. Roy Rogers Enterprises. From Roy Rogers-Dale Evans Fan Service (1½ cent bulk mail postage). Color photo front, facsimile signature. Opens up. Roy, Dale, six kids photo inside. $25–$45.

R. R. **RIDERS CLUB MEMBERSHIP CARD**. 2½″ × 4″. May 1952. Horizontally printed. $30–$60.

R. R. **RIDERS CLUB MEMBERSHIP CARD**. May 1953. Vertically printed. 2½″ × 4″. May 1953. $30–$60.

R. R. **RIDERS LUCKY PIECE**. May 1952. Small. $20–$50.

R. R. **RIDERS LUCKY PIECE.** 1950s. Large. $30–$75.

R. R. **RIFLE.** 1955–1956. Louis Marx and Co. 35″ long. Moulded stock, grip. Heavy wall acetate plastic. Color: walnut. Peep sight. Steel barrel. Die cast cap housing. Pump lever. Ejects smoke from muzzle. Originally $2.98. $85–$225.

R. R. BIG GAME **RIFLE.** Mid–1950s. Marx Toys. Carton: 2″ × 5″ × 35″. Rifle: 34″ long. Detailed cap-firing replica of .348 caliber game rifle with metal parts (black) and simulated dark red wood stock. Web strap. Roy Rogers facsimile signature on stock. $125–$250.

R. R. CAP SHOOTING CARBINE **RIFLE.** Mid–1950s. Marx Toys. Plastic. 26″ long. Illustrated Roy on box. Barrel smokes. $85–$200.

R. R.-DALE EVANS **RIFLE RACK.** Letters, probably wooden, large, "RR," "DE," spread apart to hold rifle. Horseshoes attached above letters actually hold the rifle. The author has observed this piece used in this way. It might have had another original intended purpose. $100–$200.

R. R. SILVER HAT **RING.** 1950s. Sterling Silver. "Roy Rogers" name in writing style at top, across back of hat brim. Hat band is prominent. This has been reported as being rare. I have heard of prices of several hundred to a thousand dollars.

R. R. SADDLE **RING.** Early 1949. W. G. Simpson Co., Phoenix. Quaker Oats–sponsored, but sold in stores. Roy Rogers radio show. Originally $1. Roy Rogers "signed." $60–$150.

R. R. AND TRIGGER **RING.** 1952. Sterling Silver, oval. Sizes: 3½, 4½, 5½. Sears #4 G 05902E. "SS" shows inside ring. Raised Roy is facing wearer's left, rearing on horse. "Roy Rogers" written at bottom, with Trigger separating the names. Background: sun, mountains, clouds, fence. Possible plain sides. Originally $1.18. $100–$300.

R. R. AND TRIGGER **RING.** 1950s. Premium. Similar to above, but different material, background. $75–$150.

R. R. AND TRIGGER **RING.** 1950s. Silver, octagonal. Raised Roy is facing wearer's left, rearing on horse, waving. "Roy Rogers" written under Trigger. Raised design on sides. $100–$300.

R. R. **RING.** 1950s. Probably a premium.

Marked "sterling" silver. Size 4, nonadjustable. Top has raised image of Roy rearing on Trigger. Surrounded with images of sun, hillsides, fence. Left and right side of band has crossed branding iron designs. This ring is listed as scarce in Hake's Americana and Collectibles bid catalogue #119, May 1992. $100–$300.

R. R. BRANDING IRON **RING.** 1948–1951. Quaker Oats cereal premium, probably manufactured by one of the many companies in Queens, New York, that produced cereal premiums. Roy Rogers radio show, mail-order. Designs on sides. Iron is attached to top, making for a strange-looking piece in photos. Black top. $100–$200.

R. R. BRANDING IRON **RING.** 1948–1951. Quaker Oats cereal premium. Roy Rogers radio show, mail-order. Designs on sides. Same as above, but white cap. $150–$200.

R. R. MICROSCOPE **RING.** 1947–March 1949. Premium. Roy Rogers radio show. Two magnifying lens, folding, mounted on top of ring, making for strange-looking object in photos. 15 power magnification. Embossed with picture of Roy on top, Trigger and Double R Bar Ranch brand on sides. Golden color. Adjusts to any size. Originally 15 cents and a trademark. $75–$150.

R. R. PHOTO **RING.** 1950s. Possible premium. Smiling face of Roy, photo stops below chin. $60–$100.

R. R. PHOTO **RING.** 1940s–1950s. Possible premium or possibly for gum ball machine. Red plastic, perhaps other colors. Bust photo to end of neckerchief. $60–$100.

R. R. **RING.** 1952–1955. General Foods, Post's Raisin Bran. Twelve different rings in cereal boxes. 2½″ wide; lithographed. Roy, sheriff, Dale, six-gun, DE brand, boots, six-gun in holster, RR brand, Trigger, saddle, Bullet. $20–$35. Set: $200–$400. *Note:* Some of the rings above are manufactured by Micron Manufacturing Corporation, Brooklyn, NY.

R. R. **RING BINDER** BOOK. Early 1950s. Feldco Looseleaf Corp., Chicago, IL. $45–$75.

R. R. 'N' TRIGGER **ROBE.** 1952. Boyville. Roy and Trigger pattern on heavy "Beacon" cotton blanket cloth. Shawl collar. Rayon cord trimmed collar, double cuffs, pockets, rayon cord sash. Sizes: 4, 6, 8, 10.

Wine and blue colors. 43 G 48/49. (Different numbers denote different colors.) Originally $3.97. (Other brands $3.37.) $85–$200.

R. R. BATH **ROBES**. 1950s. Auerbach Co. No description. Same as above.

R. R. **RODEO GAME**. Early 1950s. Rogden Co., Chicago. $100–$250.

R. R. **RODEO PLAY SET**. Early 1950s. Marx Co. Fencing, jeep, 9 animals, 6 saddles, 6 reins, flag, 2 cactus plants, 12 cowboys, instruction sheet, Roy, Dale, Bullet and Pat Brady figures. In box, $75–$250. *See also* R. R. Ranch Sets.

MADISON SQUARE GARDEN **RODEO PROGRAMS**. Roy covers: $30–$75. *See also* Books and Magazines.

R. R. **ROUNDUP KIT**. Early 1950s. Knox-Reese Manufacturers. No additional information. *See also* R. R. Lassos.

R. R. "HAPPY TRAILS" **RUBBER STAMP**. 1¼″ × 1¾″ image of Roy rearing Trigger, waving. Fringed attire. White stockings. No "R"s on tapaderos. $40–$70 (provided it's pre-1970s).

R. R. **RUFFERALLS**. Early 1950s. Fargo Manufacturing Co. No additional information. $75–$150.

R. R. **SADDLE**. 1952. Believed to be Bona-Allen Co. For children to age 15. 11″ seat with 8½″ swell fork, 2¼″ cantle. Select leather skirting. ¾ single rigged with 2½″ rings. Natural russet leather, with Roy rearing on horse and name embossed on fenders, in palomino gold color. Rope rolled border, clear lacquer finish. White web cinch with 2¼″ rings, each end. Sears No. 10 H 09508M Originally $39.50. *See also* Pony Riding Outfit. $700–$1,500.

R. R. **SADDLE**. Full-sized, adult. This saddle has been seen on a Video Collectibles Auction tape. Heavily tooled leather. Likenesses of Roy, Trigger. $500–$3,000.

R. R. **SADDLE SEATS**. 1950s. Not documented. If such exists: $85–$150.

ROY AND TRIGGER "PHOTONE" **SCARF**. Late 1940s. Yan-Paul Fashions, Inc. Photo of Roy standing beside Trigger, center; Roy rearing on Trigger outlying areas. 50″ rayon triangular. "Not printed but actual photographs." Blue, brown, and rust colors. Originally 39 cents. $65–$100. *See also* R. R. Neckerchiefs, Bandannas.

R. R. **SCHOOL BAG**. 1952. Acme Brief Case Co., New York. Tan "football grained"

imitation leather; plastic binding. Lifelike picture of Roy on the saddle. Lunch pocket, zipper pencil case. Fringed outfit, gun in air, but this horse looks like a paint; two horses, riders in backgound. 10″ × 14″. Sears No. 3 G 4748/49. With plastic handle or shoulder strap. Originally $1.90. $75–$150.

DALE EVANS QUEEN OF THE WEST **SCHOOL BAG**. 1952. Acme Brief Case Co. With plastic handle plus removable plastic shoulder strap. Lunch pocket is removable. Has Dale riding on horse, to observer's right. Can be carried separately with the strap. Red plaid cotton with red plastic trim. ID holder, name plate. 10″ × 14″. Sears No. 3 G 4747. Originally $1.90; other brands such as "Rough Riders," sold for $1.59. $75–$150.

R. R./DALE EVANS "TEXON" **SCHOOL BAG**. 1955–1956. United Leather Goods Corporation. 14″ × 9″ × 3½″. Metal corners, bell rivets. Shoulder strap or handle style. Roy bag is ginger; Dale bag is red. Picture of Roy/Dale on horseback on front, with name. Originally $1.98. $75–$150.

R. R. **SCHOOL BOOK CARRYING CASE**. Circa 1950. Unknown manufacturer. 11″ × 14″. Simulated leather. Illustrated Roy on Trigger, lariat encircling written name. "King of the Cowboys" printed. Straps, buckles. Lunch compartment. $75–$150.

R. R. **SCRAPBOOKS**. 1950s–1990s. Fan collections. It has been popular, during the past five decades at least, to accumulate newspaper clippings, event tickets, small photos, etc., in protective display scrapbooks, usually in the ring binder type, sometimes consisting of 100 or more pages. These are commonly found in the marketplace today. $100–$400.

R. R. **SCRIPTBOOK**. Republic Productions. These should exist for every film, but they are rarely found. These are the books from which the cast memorized their lines. Several inches thick, on typing-sized paper. Script normally typed, but usually found with many penciled-in notes, and changes. Originally $300–$400. Copies: $10–$30.

ROY AND DALE COLOR PHOTO **SCRIPTCARDS**. 1950s. The American Tract Society. Scriptcard # S 101. 5⅜″ × 3⅜″. Photo of Dale, Trigger, and Roy produced from reversed negative. Correct reproduction appears on Tracard No. 2. (This card is likely also in existence with the correctly reproduced photo.) $10–$20. *See also* Post-cards, Tracards.

R. R. SHOW TV **SCRIPTS**. 1951–1957. Used in 1950s television show production. $200–$300. Copies: $10–$30.

"SEEIN' THE STARS" SYNDICATED CARTOON COLUMN. 1930s–1950s. Feg Murray, artist. King Features Syndicated newspaper cartoon column. Usually found in form of tear sheet. Date printed in numbers/slashes. Murray began featuring Roy in his panel as early as 1938. The likenesses of Roy and Trigger are often excellent, with the drawings, apparently by numerous artists, inspired by film stills and publicity photos. (Many initials, illegible names appear in the artwork, seen under magnification.) Dailies: $5–$10; Sundays: $10–$20. The following examples are from my personal collection:

Dailies. 7/25/38 (Three months after release of first feature Republic film): Roy is in pose that will become a "trademark" for him, rearing on Trigger. This is possibly the first time Roy was seen in the newspapers in comic art form in original work not studio related.

Sundays. 12/14/41: Roy on Trigger. Inspired by film still. 6/27/43: Trigger, shown registering in San Antonio, Texas, hotel, with Roy. 1/2/44: "Trigger and Roy Rogers" (Trigger riding *Roy*) in "Hollywood Vice Versas." *See also* R. R. "Sculptoon." 6/30/44: Roy rearing on Trigger, inspired by publicity photo. 10/27/46: Inspired by commonly seen poses in early 1940s films. 5/25/47: Roy riding Trigger. 7/13/1947: Inspired by still of Roy riding Trigger from 1947 film *Springtime in the Sierras*. 4/25/48: Inspired by photo of Roy on saddleless Trigger used for 1946 exhibit cards.

SHEET MUSIC. Roughly 9″ × 12″. "Texas for Me." 1962. Paramount–Roy Rogers Music, photo front. Roy. $15–$25. "The Bible Tells Me So." 1955. Paramount–Roy Rogers Music, photo front. Roy and Dale. $12–$20. "I Just Kissed Your Picture Goodnight." 1942. Dale Evans. $15–$25. "Jeanie with the Light Brown Hair." 1939. Dale Evans. Calumet Music, photo front. $15–$25. "A Christmas Prayer." 1957. Paramount–Roy Rogers Music, photo front. Roy and Dale. $15–$25. "Along the Navajo Trail." 1945. Leeds

Music, photo front. Roy. $15–$35. "Dust." 1938. Santly Bros. Music, photo front. Roy. $15–$35. "Buckeye Cowboy." 1952. Paramount–Roy Rogers Music. Photo front. Roy. $15–$25. "It's a Sad, Sad Story." 1941. From Republic picture *Robin Hood of the Pecos*. Mills Music. Photo front. Roy. $15–$35. "What a Dirty Shame." 1952. From the Paramount picture *Son of Paleface*. Famous Music Corporation. "Special Picture Release." Roy. $10–$35. "No Letter Today." 1943. Southern Music Pub. Co. Photo front. Roy. $15–$35. "Do Ya or Don't Cha." 1945. Roy. $15–$35. "Corral in the Sky." 1949. Dale Evans. $15–$25. "Hawaiian Cowboy." 1948. Roy. $15–$25. "On the Old Spanish Trail." 1947. Roy. $15–35. "Smiles Are Made Out of Sunshine." 1943. Roy. $15–$35. "When My Blue Moon Turns to Gold Again." 1941. Roy. $15–$35. "When the Desert Sun Goes Down." 1942. Roy. $15–$35.

R. R. **SHIRTS**. Early 1950s. Hallmark Shirt Co., London. Dark yoke over light body. Light collar. Fringe. Lariat encircles picture of Roy and Trigger, bust. Roy is wearing black hat. Dark cuffs. Used in Grand Roy Rogers Competition in association with comics publisher (WDL) and Roy Rogers Fan Clubs. $75–$125.

R. R. **"THROW AWAY" SHIRTS**. 1950s. Facsimile. Shirts, in somewhat similar design to those worn by Roy, were donated as prizes to charity events, etc. It is believed these shirts were specially manufactured for "giveaways" related to contests, charities, etc. Research has not revealed any identical shirt worn by Roy, except in a photo related to the shirt, believed to be part of the promotion. Tree leaf collar, acorn designs on dark yoke, "V" slash pockets. $150–$200, unless shirt happens to be custom made, and so identified, by one of Roy's principal designers. In this case the value is $300–$1,000.

R. R. **SHIRTS**. 1940s. "Worn in Hollywood by Roy Rogers" used in ad. Photo shows Roy wearing an exact style shirt. Lace-up, vat-dyed cotton broadcloth, two button cuffs, one flap pocket, pearl buttons. Horseshoes on collar. Colors: solid red, orange, or blue. Sizes small, medium, large. Sears No. 33 K 1480/81/82. Originally 89 cents. $100–$300.

R. R. SANFORIZED BROADCLOTH

SHIRTS. 1952 Washfast, heavier cotton. Embroidered Western motif on front yoke, horseshoes on collar. Two slash pockets. Loop cord trim at front yoke. Three-button cuffs. Maroon and gray, navy and blue, dark green and light green. Sizes 4–12. Horseshoes on collar, slash pockets. Sears # 43 G 3484 Originally $2.87. $40–$100.

R. R. 'N' TRIGGER COLORFUL KNIT SHIRTS. 1952. Reads "Roy Rogers and Trigger." Appears to be short fringe across top. Long and short sleeves. Portrait close-up, Roy standing beside Trigger. Red and green attire. 43 G 4059, 43 G 4259. Original costing 1953: short sleeves, $1.08; long sleeves, $1.33. $40–$100.

R. R. EXCLUSIVE COTTON KNIT SHIRTS. 1952. Boyville Co. "Day-Glo" design in color. Short sleeves, crew neck. White, blue, or maize. Sizes: 4, 6, 8, 10 and 12. Sears No. 43 H 4054: Two for $1.10. $25–$85.

R. R. WESTERN SHIRTS. 1953. Boyville Co. Embroidered "Roy" in lasso on one collar, "Trigger" on other. Light yoke over dark body. Slash pockets. Sears and Roebuck. Originally $2.87. $40–$100.

R. R. FRONTIER SHIRTS. 1954. Rob Roy Co. Sanforized cotton broadcloth, cotton flannels, rayon gabardines. Contrasting colors. Fringed yokes, with Western designs. Roy's picture on inside tag. Three-button cuffs, piped pockets. Sizes 2–12. Fringeless styles advertised in *Life*, 1954: short-sleeves, $1.95; long sleeves, $2.95. $40–$100.

R. R. KNIT SHIRTS. 1954. Norwich Knitting Co., NY. (Also seen as Norwich Mills.) Contrasting yokes. Lace-up look, fringe. $35–$80.

R. R. NORWICH COWBOY SHIRTS. 1955–1956. Norwich Mills. Combed interlock knit, sizes 4–12; various colors. (Kiddie's sizes 3–6X.) Originally $1.95. $40–$100. Also flatknit. Originally $1.49. $35–$80.

R. R. SHOOTIN' IRON. Early 1950s. Unknown manufacturer. 8″ generic cap pistol. Also 9½″ model. Rogers name only on packaging. $125 in package only.

R. R. SHOOTIN' IRONS. 1953. Kilgore. "Replica's of Roy's own guns." Elaborately etched barrels (RR brand, etc.). Horse's head on grips. Dura-Gleam finish. Revolving cylinder and repeater models in cap and non-firing styles. Facsimile signature under cylinder. Three sizes. Originally $0.79–$1.75.

Two sizes advertised in *Life*, 1954: 79 cents/ $1. $125–$300.

R. R. SHOOT'N IRONS. Early 1950s. George Schmidt Co. 10″ cap pistol. Brown bone plastic grip. Signature under cylinder. $125–$300.

R. R. DE LUXE SHOOTIN' IRONS. 1952. (May be seen as "Shoot'n Irons." Advertised in contest, 1952, *TV Guide*. Chrome-plated. Automatic spring-release for quick, safe reloading, never miss firing mechanism, rustproof construction. Brass bullets. Trophy buckle. Two gun holster, genuine top-grain cowhide. Pockets decorated with nickel-plated studs. Leg ties, "authentic replica of Roy's own equipment." $125–$400.

R. R. SHOOTIN' IRONS AND SPURS. 1950s. George Schmidt, Los Angeles. Guns: Roy's signature below chamber. "RR" on brown bone designed plastic grips. Cap-firing. 8¾″. Originally $1–$1.79. Spurs with real leather straps. Originally $1.49–$1.98. Spurs, $75 on average. Guns: $40–$75 each. (These spurs or guns are often found separately and sometimes as just a single item from a pair.)

R. R. DE LUXE 2 GUN SIX SHOOTER SET. 1952. Beautifully embossed dark tan steerhide holster, belt, whip-laced edges. Roy's initials on both guns, name embossed on belt. Metal pistol grips. Nickel-plated domes, cross strap on holsters, curved belt 4″ at widest point. Six wooden bullets. Fits waist 24″–29″. Sears No. 43 G 4993 nonfiring guns; 43 G 4992: cap-firing guns. Originally $7.98. (Other Western sets, not Roy/Dale, range from $3.69 to $5.79.) Complete, in box, mint, $125–$400. *See also* Snaps.

R. R. TENNIS SHOES. Early 1950s. Converse Rubber Co. No additional information. $75–$150.

R. R. DRESS SHORTS. Early 1950s. B. Schwartz Company/Wm. Schwartz Company. No additional information. $35–$85.

R. R. WESTERN SLACKS. 1955–1956. Wm. Schwartz and Co. Cotton cavalry twill. Zipper fly. Mother of pearl type gripper top closure. Western piping. Colors: brown, charcoal, green, red, black, tan, grey. Sizes 2–7/ 4–12. Originally $4.95/$5.95. $85–$200.

R. R. SLEEPERS. Early 1950s. E-Z Mills. Knit material. Sleeping type night shirt. $50–$150.

R. R. NECKERCHIEF SLIDE. 1950s. Gun-shaped. $25–$65.

R. R. TIE **SLIDE**. Early 1950s. Western Art Manufacturing Co. No additional information. $25–$65.

R. R. COWBOY BOOT **SLIPPERS**. 1952. (This description may apply to slippers by Little Falls Felt Shoe Co., Little Falls, NY.) Retail stores, catalogues. Sears No. 15 G 1986. Red and blue, black and gray. Sizes 8–13, 1, 2. No half sizes. "Warm felt," "Padded sole." Illustrated Roy rearing on Trigger with lariat encircling them, sides. "Waist-high cowhands' first choice" used in advertising. Originally $1.98. In box, mint, $75–$150.

R. R. FELT **SLIPPERS**. 1950s. S. Goldberg and Co. Roy rearing on Trigger, under Roy Rogers name. Several other styles, including picture of Roy and Dale. Advertised in *Life*, 1954: $1.99. $75–$150.

R. R. COWBOY BOOT **SLIPPERS**. 1955–1956. S. Goldberg and Co. Felt upper with multicolor Roy rearing on Trigger print. Fringed felt collar, brass stud ornaments. Pull tabs, spurs. Sizes 5–2. Various two-toned color combinations. Originally $1.99. $75–$150.

R. R. MOCCASIN **SLIPPERS**. 1955–1956. S. Goldberg and Co. Brown suedene upper on brown felt. Fawn suede plug with multicolor Roy and Trigger screen print. Suede leather sole. Originally $1.99. $75–$150.

DALE EVANS MOCCASIN **SLIPPERS**. 1955–1956. S. Goldberg and Co. Same as Roy Rogers Cowboy Boot Slipper, but with Dale Evans screen print. Same.

R. R. COWBOY **SLIPPERS**. 1952. Retail stores, catalogues. Sears No. #15 G 948. Sage green over brown. Sizes 8–13, 1, 2. No half sizes. Picture of Roy rearing on Trigger on tops. "Imitation suede," "padded sole and heel," "for young cowhands" used in advertising. Originally $1.98. In box, mint, $75–$150. *See also* R. R./Dale Evans Moccasins.

R. R. **SNAPS**. Early 1950s. Rauf Fastener Co., Providence, RI. Fastening devices found on clothing, holsters, etc. "RR" brand stamped. Metal. $2–$5.

R. R. **SOAP**. Early 1950s. Monogram Soap Company, Los Angeles. $55–$100.

R. R. **SOCKS**. 1950s. Chester H. Roth Company, Inc., New York. Originally 25 cents. $25–$75.

R. R. **SOCKS**. 1952. Cotton reinforced with nylon at toe and heel. Roy Rogers and Trigger on each sock. Roy rearing on Trigger design. Original package contains four pair in variety of colors. 43 G 1835. Originally 92 cents. Package $25–$75.

R. R. LOAFER **SOCKS**. Early 1950s. Ripon Knitting Works. No additional information. Could resemble the 1952 socks. $25–$75.

R. R. **SOCKS**. 1955–1956. Wrenn Hosiery Co. Halenca stretch nylon. Roy's Double-R-Bar brand on solid colors: navy, brown, green, black, charcoal. Two sizes cover 7–11. Originally 69 cents pair. $25–$75.

R. R. **SOCKS**. 1955–1956. Wrenn Hosiery Co. Combed cotton. Nylon reinforced heel, toe. Sizes: 7–11. Assorted colors. Three pairs to package. Cellophane envelope has official Roy Rogers button. Originally $1 package. $25–$75.

R. R. **SODA CAN**. 1950s. Continental Beverage Corporation. 2¾" diameter, 5" tall, lithographed picture, Roy rearing on Trigger. $150–$250.

SONGBOOKS

Songs of the Soil Songbook. 1948. Photo of Roy, other cowboy singers on cover. $30–$50. *Roy Rogers Album of Cowboy Songs*. 1941. Edward B. Marks Music Corporation, New York. $30–$50. *Bob Nolan's Cowboy Classics No. 1*. 1943. American Music, Inc., Hollywood. (Original songs by Bob Nolan, Tim Spencer, and Roy Rogers.) $30–$50. *Bob Nolan's Cowboy Classics No. 2*. 1943. American Music, Inc. $30–$50. *Tim Spencer's Sagebrush Symphonies No. 1*. 1943. American Music, Inc. $30–$50. *Tim Spencer's Sagebrush Symphonies No. 2*. 1943. American Music, Inc. $30–$50. *The Sons of the Pioneers Song Folio No. 1*. 1943. American Music, Inc. $30–$50. (Len is in photo. Name Vern Spencer appears.) *Original Son of the Pioneers Song Folio No. 2*. 1943. Crown/American Music, Inc. $30–$50. (Len is in cover photo.) *Sons of the Pioneers Original Songs of the Prairie Folio No. 3*. 1943. Crown/American Music, Inc. $30–$50. *Roy Rogers' Own Songs Folio No. 1*. 1943. American Music, Inc. $30–$60. *King of the Cowboys Roy Rogers' Favorite Cowboy Songs*. 1943. Robbins Music, New York. 72 pages. $30–$60.

Roy Rogers Spurs. Classy Products.

Music Folio of Popular Western Songs. 1945. Large Roy Rogers photo cover. Movie Songs, Inc., New York. $30–$60. *King of the Cowboys Roy Rogers Song Folio.* 1952. Paramount–Roy Rogers Music Co. $30–$50. *King of the Cowboys Roy Rogers Guitar Folio.* 1954. Paramount–Roy Rogers Music, Inc., New York. $30–$50. *Roy Rogers' Own Song Collection of Pop New Hits.* 1943. $30–$50. *Music Folio of Popular Western Songs.* 1947. $30–$50. (Dale cover.)

R. R. ALL-SEASONS **SPORTS KIT**. 1955–1956. J. A. Dubow Sporting Goods Co. Football, basketball, baseball, whistle. Carying carton. The balls have a picture of Roy on rearing Trigger. Originally $2.95. $100–$200.

R. R. **SPURS**. 1950s. Jeweled. No other information. $70–$100.

R. R. GOLDEN COLORED **SPURS**. 1950. Quaker Oats–sponsored Roy Rogers contest. Radio-announced. 1000 offered. $100–$200.

R. R. **SPURS**. 1950s. Geo. Schmidt Manufacturing Co., Los Angeles. Roy rearing on Trigger on box photo. "RR" brand on metal attached to leather pieces. $75–$150.

R. R. **SPURS**. 1954. Classy Products Corp., Long Island, NY. "RR the Plus Brand." Yellow and brown box has illus-trated Roy rearing on Trigger. The "RR" brands appear on metal pieces attached to leather parts, three times on each spur. Cast iron with chains. Each box shows serial number. The set in author's personal collection is #552. Roy Rogers "Pledge to Parents" on box. Not registered with copyright office as such. $75–$150.

R. R. **SPURS**. Early 1950s. Leslie Henry Co. No other information. *See also* R. R. Shootin' Irons and Spurs.

R. R. FIX-IT **STAGECOACH**. 1955. Ideal Toy Corporation. Carton: 5½″ × 6½″ × 15″. Plastic set. Hitchable horses, changeable wheels, opening doors, seated Roy figure for driving coach. Detailed unhitchable horses with removable harnesses. Driver holds whip. Plastic rifle. Doors open. Tool box, jack, mallet, wedge bars, wrench. Money chest, rifle, tools. 15″ × 4½″ × 6½″. Roy's photo plus illustration of Roy rearing on Trigger on carton. Originally $3.98. In box, $85–$200.

R. R. **STAGECOACH WAGON TRAIN**. 1950s. Marx Toys. Wind-up. 14″ long. Plastic. Carton: 2½″ × 3″ × 14½″. Single unit stagecoach and horse team, three lithographed metal wagons, joined. Entire unit moves in circular motion when wound. Heavily illustrated carton. $85–$200.

Roy Rogers and Trigger Boy's Suit. Irvin Foster, 1950s. Personal photo used with permission. Courtesy Ray La Briola Collection.

R. R. FIX-IT **STAGECOACH WAGON TRAIN**. Mid–1950s. No other information. Probably same as item above. Marx Toys.

R. R. **STAGECOACH PLAY SET**. 1950s. In box, $40–$80.

R. R. LEATHER **STAMPING PLATES**. 1950s. Originally from Aristocrat Manufacturing Co. Presently owned by Mervin Bendewald, New York City. In recent years, these have surfaced from manufacturing company lots purchased by dealers. They are heavy metal plates that contain the artwork for Roy Rogers wallets, and for the Aristocrat's Roy Rogers key case, pen carrying case, business card case, etc. Made in the 1950s, used in the manufacturing process by Aristocrat Co. The Double R Bar brand is opposite the other figures in an area to itself. $200–$400 each. *Note*: The following process is useful in studying engravings and identifying marks not visible to the naked eye: Photocopy the metal object. The image will be reversed. Hold it before a very bright light and use a normal magnifying glass to read the tiny markings. *See also* Wallets, individual items.

R. R. PHOTO **STAMPS**. Circa 1950s. Picture of Roy's face. No other information. $40–$60.

R. R. TRIGGER GOLD **STATUETTE**. 1950s. Roy Rogers/National Safety Council.

Many of these were made and used as prizes in public school contests sponsored by the National Safety Council/Roy Rogers and for other events. As the result of their being placed permanently in school display cases, they are considered scarce. Undoubtedly, some have made it into circulation or wound up in the possession of private collectors. Several hundred dollars. Could possibly approach four figures, depending upon school and documentation.

R. R. **STUDS**. Early 1950s. Rauf Fastener Co., Providence, RI. Metal decorations, stamped "RR" used on gun holsters, etc. $2–$5. *See also* Snaps, Conchas.

DALE EVANS COWGIRL **SUIT**. 1950. Quaker Oats–sponsored Roy Rogers contest prize. For girls only. Radio announced. $100–$300.

ROY/DALE 2-PIECE **SUIT**. 1953. Dark yoke embroidered with Trigger head one side, boot on other side, over lighter body. One slash pocket. Yoke matching cuffs, three snaps. Pants have white stitch bordered pocket. Sears and Roebuck. Originally $7.74. $100–$300.

ROY/DALE 3-PIECE **SUIT**. 1953. Jacket has cactus embroidered on yoke above fringe. Light-colored cuffs. Pants have embroidery, white border, snap pockets. Either shirt or hat rounds out set. Girl's skirt has fringe. Sears and Roebuck. Originally $5.74. $100–$300.

R. R. WASH **SUIT.** Early 1950s. Strouse-Baer Co., Baltimore. No additional information.

R. R. RODEO **SUIT.** 1950s. Irvin Foster Co. Brown wool gabardine with plaid inserts. Brown/beige leather lanyard trim. Colorful braided embroidery of Trigger with "signature" on right sleeve and Roy rearing on Trigger with facsimile signature on left sleeve. Embroidered label on both jacket and pants, with drawing of Roy standing beside Trigger, facsimile signature, maker's name. Jacket has two-sided copper coin (Roy Rogers Riders Lucky Piece) as zipper pull. Piece has Roy in relief, reverse has "Good Luck Forever," Trigger, and RR brand. $150–$400.

R. R. SHERIFF'S BADGE **SUSPENDERS.** 1948. Hickok Manufacturing Co. Steers head "Klip" on tips. $50–$100.

R. R. **SWEATERS.** 1950. Quaker Oats-sponsored Roy Rogers contest prize. Radio-announced. 500 offered. $75–$200.

R. R. ORLON PULLOVER **SWEATERS.** 1955–1956. Pauker Boyswear Corporation. Sizes 3–12, various colors; Roy's thunderbird design, Double R Bar design. Originally $3.98. $75–$200.

R. R. ORLON COAT **SWEATERS.** 1955–1956. Same, but no thunderbird design. $75–$150.

R. R. WESTERN **SWEATERS AND JACKETS.** 1950s. Pauker Boyswear Corporation, New York. Sweaters: $1.79. Cardigan coat sweaters: $1.95. Jackets with studded yokes: $3.95. Sweaters: $75–$125; jackets: $125–$200.

R. R. **SWEATSHIRT.** 1952. Roy and Trigger on front (Roy riding, shooting behind him). Blue or green. Sears # 43 G 2714. Originally $1.29 or $1.25 in lots of two. $45–$100.

R. R. **SWEATSHIRT.** 1954–1956. Norwich Mills. Same design as T-shirts. Originally $1–$1.39. $35–$75.

R. R. **SWIM TRUNKS.** Early 1950s. Pauker Boyswear Corporation. No additional information. $65–$125.

R. R. COTTON **T-SHIRTS.** 1954. Norwich Mills. Colorful Roy Rogers designs. 1. Roy is riding hard and throwing lariat as he passes through Double R Bar gate. 2. Roy, Trigger, Dale, with Roy's and Dale's names

above image. Sizes 2–12. 1950s. Advertised in *Life*, 1954: 69 cents. *See also* Sweatshirts. $35–$80.

R. R. **T-SHIRTS.** Early 1950s. Pauker Boyswear Corporation. $35–$80.

R. R. **TABLE.** 1950s. Child's table. Card table style, with folding legs. Leather appearance with border stitching. Illustrations of Roy rearing on Trigger, Dale sitting astride Buttermilk, surrounded by lasso. Smaller illustrations in corners. Inside smaller lasso circles are Bullet, Nellybelle with characters, Pat Brady, and RR Plus Brand. From the television series years, 1951–1957. Probably sold at Sears and Roebuck stores. $60–$250.

R. R. WRITING **TABLET.** 1950s. Lakeside Central Co., Chicago/Southern Central Co. Color photo front. $8'' \times 10''$. Made from white high-bulk newsprint. Two sizes: standard and triple page count. Signed "Many Happy Trails," etc. Several different color photos, including those used for comics, magazines, etc. Facsimile signatures. Originally 10–25 cents. $30–$60.

R. R. MERCHANDISE PHOTO **TAGS.** 1950s–present. Some of the merchandise items, perhaps clothing, came with a color photo card. One in personal collection shows Roy, Trigger, and Dale. Measures 2 $7/16'' \times 2\ 9/16''$. The back carries the Roy Rogers "Pledge to Parents." This particular tag was on merchandise manufactured by the Douglas Plymouth Corporation, Mantowoc, WI. 1950s. (This tag appears to have been made circa 1955–56). Another tag has photo of Roy rearing on Trigger. $15–$30.

R. R. **TELEPHONE.** Possibly same phone as below. # 4269-M-1 stamped into plastic inside. "Roy Rogers" on front. Brown plastic, brass-colored metal ringers, black plastic earpiece, mouthpiece.

R. R. WESTERN **TELEPHONE.** 1950s. Ideal Toys. Three actions. 9'' high. $45–$150.

R. R. **TELESCOPE.** Early 1950s. Herbert-George Co. $45–$90.

R. R., JR., AND TRIGGER **TELESCOPE.** 1950s. I have only heard of one of this item. Documented in phone conversation with its owner, Bill Smith of Ohio, who donated it to the Roy Rogers–Dale Evans Museum recently. Black; measures approximately 7–9'' in length collapsed. A decal on the side is of a drawn boy, about teenage, rearing on

Trigger, with lasso dropped encircling both. It would be most difficult to place a price on an item such as this, but it can be extremely valuable because it is so rare. No stampings of manufacturer.

R. R. **TENNIS SHOES** *see also* Shoes.

R. R. TEPEE **TENT**. 1952. Light green tent material decorated with bright red action pictures of Roy and Trigger. Roy rearing on Trigger, with lariat out, forming names. 4′ 6″ × 4′ 6″ at base, 4′ 9″ height. Awning lowers, ties down at doorway. Ropes, poles, stakes. 6 G 07760. Originally $5.98. $100–$300.

R. R. TEPEE **TENT**. 1954. Hettrick. 4′ 6″ × 4′ 6″ base, 4′ 9″ high. Illustrated Roy and Trigger, side (Roy straddling wagon wheel beside horse). Poles, metal stakes. Originally $6.75. $100–$300.

R. R. UMBRELLA **TENT**. 1954. Hettrick. 6′ 9″ × 6′ 9″ base, 5′ high, 4′ wall. Illustrated Roy riding Trigger toward observer's left. Originally $11.95. $100–$300.

R. R. **TENT**. Early 1950s. Hettrick. Illustrated Roy riding Trigger toward observer's right. 4′ × 4′. "Roy Rogers — King of the Cowboys on the Range" printed on side. $100–$200.

R. R. **THEATER PAPER**. 1930s–1950s. Theaters, often using materials supplied in press books, had their own individual advertisements printed, published, and distributed in a variety of ways. These are generally found in small sizes, the height and width of an old *TV Guide* and smaller, and range from one page (usually printed on both sides) to several pages in the form of a small booklet. Generally the films for one or two weeks would be carried at a time. They often produced specialty items to promote films. Examples in my personal collection: *South of Caliente*. 1951. "Plus 10 cartoons; 2½ hours of fun and adventure. All seats — 25 cents." State Theatre, Deposit, NY. (Printed by Cato Show Print, Cato, NY.) $8–$12. *Schine's Theaters, Chicago*. 1950s. "Roy Rogers in a thrilling Western attraction." On 12″ × 8″ paper with Gene Autry. $8–$12. *Home in Oklahoma*. 1946. "Gun-Throwing, Lead-Slinging Outdoor Action." Same theater, printing company as above. $8–$12. *Along the Navajo Trail*. July 21, 1946. (December 1945 film.) Bell Theatre. Roy on cover. 3¼″ × 4⅜″. Sepia toned. $15–$25.

R. R. **TICKETS**. 1940s–1950s. Example: ticket to see Roy in person at Hillsboro High School Athletic Field, July 11, 1947. $20–$50.

R. R. BOLO **TIE**. 1950s. Steer head slide on card. $50–$150. *Note:* It is felt that a dealer's card also exists holding one dozen ties. Ties: $30–$50 each.

R. R. DUDE **TIE**. Late 1950s. Bolero tie with ornament slide. Photo display card holds one dozen ties. Photo of Roy and Trigger. Tie: $30–$50.

R. R. WITH TRIGGER "KING OF THE COWBOYS" DE LUXE CLIP-ON **TIE**. 1950s. Best Clip Co. Dark green, imitation leather fringe on ends. Painting of Trigger and "RR" brand on each side. On card with photo of Roy and Trigger inside good luck horseshoe. $45–$80.

R. R. SATIN CLIP-ON **TIE**. 1955–1956. Western Art Manufacturing Co. Roy and Trigger hand-screened design. Metal clip attached. Colors: blue, yellow, red, green, white, black. Originally 69 cents. $45–$80.

R. R. LEATHER "CHAP" **TIE**. Western Art Manufacturing Co. Clip-on style. "RR" brand burnt on one side. Painted Trigger design on other side. Colors: white, brown, tan, with contrasting belt. Originally $1. $45–$100 complete.

R. R. PLASTIC BRAIDED STRING **TIE**. 1955–1956. Western Art Manufacturing Co. Assorted "RR" brand metal slides attached. Metal tips. Four colors. Originally $1. $45–$80.

R. R. SATIN **TIE**. 1955–1956. Western Art Manufacturing Co. Roy and Trigger hand-screened design. Comes with metal cuff slide. Colors: blue, red, yellow, green, white, black. In acetate window box. Originally 69 cents. $45–$80.

R. R. RAYON CREPE CLIP-ON **TIE**. 1955–1956. Western Art Manufacturing Co. Painted Roy and Trigger design, each side. Leather fringed tips. Colors: gold, red, blue, green, brown, pink, white, black. Originally $1. $45–$80.

R. R. **TIE**. 1950s. Description probably applies to Sackman Bros. Co. Retail stores, catalogues. No color/material given. "Western loop tie, leather slide." In this listing, sold only as part of entire 11 piece Western outfit. The slide is in the shape of a steer head, showing face. Approximately 6″ × 4″, tied. *See also* Bandanas, Neckerchiefs,

Outfits — Cowboy/Cowgirl. $45–$80. (Would have to be matched with photo in catalogue for authenticity.)

R. R. **TIE**. 1950s. Bodner Neckwear Co., Philadelphia. No information available. May apply to any of the above items showing no manufacturer. $45–$80.

R. R. MINIATURE PISTOL/HOLSTER **TIE CLIP**. 1950s. 2¾″ long. $40–$60.

R. R. **TOILETRIES**. Early 1950s. Monogram Soap Co. No additional information. *See also* Soap.

R. R. **TOKEN**. 1950s. Metal. Raised head, hat of Roy, name. $20–$50. *See also* Riders Lucky Piece.

R. R. **TOOTHBRUSH**. Early 1950s. Owens Brush Co., Toledo, OH. $35–$65.

R. R. **TOP**. 1950s. All-Western Plastics Co. Documented only in advertising. $25–$60. *See also* Yo-Yos.

R. R. **TOY CHEST**. Early 1950s. Hazel Novelty and Cabinet Co., St. Louis. $150–$350.

R. R. **TRADER CARDS**. Circa 1950. The Dorne Associates, Hollywood, CA. Series numbers. Packaged sets. $250–$400.

ROY AND DALE COLOR PHOTO **TRA-CARDS**. 1961–1962. The American Tract Society. 2½″ × 3⅜″. $5–$10. Religious testimony of Dale and Roy, along with scripture on back of photos. No. 1: Photo of Roy rearing on Trigger. Back: "Go to Sunday School" by Roy. No. 2: Photo of Dale, Trigger, and Roy. (Same negative reversal mentioned above.) Back: "Royalty of the Rodeo." No. 3: Photo of Roy beside Dale, leaning on fence. Back "King and Queen of the Rodeo." No. 3: Photo of Dale adjusting Roy's neckerchief (correct photo reproduction, bears this series number as well). No. 3: (2nd version) Photo is a negative reversal of that on item 4. No. 4: Same size as first No. 3 above. Roy is putting Trigger through dance routine. Unknown number: Roy and Dale. There are at least three versions of No. 3, two with one photo (one a negative reversal) and one with a different photo. The photos used on all cards seen thus far are circa 1950–1954. Address: W. 46th St., New York 36, NY.

R. R. AND DALE EVANS RELIGIOUS **TRACT**. 1950s. King and Queen of the Cowboys — At the Fork in the Road religious message printed on fold-out tract, with full-color photo front of Dale, Trigger, and Roy.

Photo is from same session that produced the one used for the American Tract Society postcard S 101. $5–$8. *See also* Postcards, Script Cards.

R. R. TRADING CARDS, PHOTO CARDS

Many different sets of photo cards exist, both domestic and foreign. Some of those discovered are:

Kane Cards. 1950s. England. Kane Products. 1½″ × 2½″. Color photos. Complete set is 25 photos. $75–$150 set.

A.B.C. Minors Picture Cards. Series of ten. Premium with cigarettes. Set one: Includes Roy Rogers (No. 1). Notice on reverse states: "Wear your minors badge for a picture card" and "collect the series for a special badge." 1¼″ × 2⅜″. Individual card $8–$20. Unknown set: Probably celebrity oriented, as numbers run high. Particular card numbers for Roy are 23, 117. Black and white, late 1940s to early 1950s. Roy and Trigger cards. 2¼″ × 3⅜″. $8–$20 each. *See also* Postcards. Circa 1940s–early 1950s. Film-photo Service, Amsterdam. Book 14: E 15, Roy Rogers. Other books: Card numbers E-25, F-1 (a, b), F-2, F-16 (Dale), F-16 b, F-19 b, F-24, F-27, and F-29 a, b. The colorized photos on the face of these regular Dutch postcards are larger reproductions of those photos used in the little Holland-produced *Hollywood Strips* and *Hollywood Stars* miniature celebrity photo books. All are Republic or Paramount publicity pictures. All belong to a numbered set (i.e., KF 30 thru KF 50). There is evidence that there are at least 20 Roy Rogers cards, and maybe more. Many of this type of cards are associated with a food product, such as gum. $8–$20 each. *See also* Postcards.

Hollywood Strips. 1940s. Tekenfilms En Hun Meester. Deel 14. Produced in Holland, believed to be by Dandy Gum Co., and sold in Canada and northern United States by Maple Leaf Gum Co. Miniature book with 1⅝″ × 2¾″ color photos, gloss and non-gloss. Most of photos are late 1940s–early 1950s, and some are prints of publicity pictures from *Son of Paleface* film. These are found in the books, which have numbers (i.e, No. 14), and separate from the books, cut into singles (*see* Movie Stars — 4 below). Individual "E" numbers with a star's name (i.e., E 15, Roy) also appear on the card bottom, along with the film company shown abbreviated. Text throughout book in Dutch. Seven pages of text and four photos. Book: $15–$20; individual photos: $3–$10.

Hollywood Stars. 1950s. Identical to above description. Exception: Book and series number (i.e., Series D, No. 31) shown. Holland. Some gloss on cards, though less than in above book. Numerical order of the cards does not relate to order in book. Believed to be produced by same companies mentioned above. No text. This particular book contains two Roy photos (1950s), #195, 196. Book Series D, No. 31 contains 6 photos. #195, 196 are Roy Rogers. (No. 196, exact same card as No. 1, under Movie Stars—4, with exception of identification in white area at bottom. "Roy Rogers," "Series D," "No. 196.") Book: $15–20; individual photos: $3–$7.

Movie Stars—1. No company identification. 5″ × 7″. Large b&w, either a candy store or mail premium. Bears words "Aquatoned in U.S.A." under "Roy Rogers," "Shine On Harvest Moon," and "A Republic Picture." Some have numbers, some do not, indicating two different issues or companies. $4–$15.

Movie Stars—2. No company information. 6″ × 8″. Probably candy store or mail premium. 6-picture sheets, but are found as individual cards as well. Tinted in single color (blue, brown, green) on medium-weight vellum stock. Possibly from same company that produced those shown above. Star's name and studio shown. $15–$25 per sheet. An individual card can be $3–$5.

Movie Stars—3. Maple Leaf Gum Co., Canada. 1 9/16″ × 2¾″. Flat (no gloss). Unknown number of cards in series, as numbers continually climb in collections. One source shows 70, but numbers in my personal collection are running much higher. Prominent identification feature is the number printed in a circle under photo, between star's name and studio name. Nicely colored photos, 1940s and 1950s era, produced in both horizontal and vertical format. I should mention here that the company was probably not using negatives to print their own photos, as I have seen no evidence of a "negative reversal," which is common with companies producing their own prints. The

Roy Rogers cards in my personal collection are: No. 33. Cardboard. 1950 photo, Roy with gloved hands on guns in holster, plaid shirt, colored green. Vertical print. "Roy Rogers," "Centhra." Not known where the company came up with the "Centhra" name for Roy's studio, which was Republic. $5–$8. No. 95. Paper. Roy, Trigger, and Jane Russell photo from film *Son of Paleface* (1952, Paramount). Vertical print. "Roy Rogers," "Jane Russell," "Par." Roy sitting on fence, Russell standing, Trigger behind fence. Yellow/green tint overdone on Roy's attire, which included unrealistic turquoise hat and green and white boots. $5–$8. No. 101. Paper. Roy Rogers. Late 1940s–early 1950s. Vertical print. Photo with Roy's hat tinted green. Roy holding both guns pointed upward, gloved hands. "Roy Rogers," "Rep." $5–$8. No. 102. Paper. Roy Rogers, Trigger with hunting dog on Trigger's back, early 1950s publicity, but using Paramount identification, so probably issued at same time *Son of Paleface* ones issued. Vertical print. Trigger tinted realistically. Roy's heavily fringed shirt tinted unrealistically solid yellow. "Roy Rogers," "Par." $5–$8. No. 105. Cardboard. Early 1940s. Roy and Trigger (horse and saddle colored wagon). Horizontal print. "Roy Rogers," "Rep." $5–$8. No. 140. Cardboard. Bob Hope, Jane Russell, Trigger, Roy Rogers in photo from 1952 Paramount film *Son of Paleface*. Horizontal print. Multicoloring on Roy's shirt, but hat is tinted yellow-green. Trigger is grey in color. "B. Hope, J. Russell, R. Rogers," "Par." $5–$8. No. 163. Cardboard. Roy in 1950s publicity photo, vertical print. Shirt tinted red, white fringe, blue neckerchief. $5–$8.

Movie Stars—4. Believed to be from Dandy Gum Co., produced in Holland, but sold in U.S. and Canada by Maple Leaf Gum Co. (*See also* Hollywood Strips.) Very similar to above cards, but 1⅝″ × 2⅝″, and paper rather than cardboard (at least what has been discovered thus far). Gloss. No numbering, only star's name and studio under color photo. "Roy Rogers," "Rep. Pict." 1. (My number.) Early 1950s publicity photo of Roy putting Trigger through dance routine, with Roy in multicolored attire, Trigger in realistic colors. Reddish-brown/green tints are dominant. $5–$8.

Movie Stars—5. Paper. Believed to be made by Filmphoto Service. Possibility also made in conjunction with Dandy Gum Co., Holland. (*See also* Hollywood Strips.) Very similar to Movie Stars—4, but flat and with identifying "F" numbers and with names in script type, and 1¹¹⁄₁₆″ × 2⁹⁄₁₆″. These cards exist in larger size. (*See also* Movie Stars—6.) No. F-27. Roy in yellow and wine-colored attire with leading lady Jane Frazee in green and white attire in Republic Pictures publicity photo. $5–$8.

Movie Stars—6. Filmphoto Service. Identical in format to above series, but printed on a correspondence-type postcard with company identification on reverse. "KF" numbers in place of "F" numbers, script type. "Pict." remains in common with not only above series, but with "Movie Stars—4" as well. Value (all cards): $5–$8. No. KF 30. Late 1940s–early 1950s. Roy, mostly blue/green tint, plaid shirt, playing guitar. Flesh tones a little dark. Outdoor setting in publicity photo. "Roy Rogers," "Rep. Pict." No. KF 37. Roy, standing with guitar being held, pointed upward. Tint runs heavily toward yellow-green. Shirt yellow-green in this late 1940s–early 1950s publicity photo. Hat tinted gray. Flesh-tones too yellowish. "Roy Rogers," "Rep. Pict." No. KF 38. Roy, in late 1940s–early 1950s publicity photo, striped maroon shirt, realistically colored hat, multicolored neckerchief, flesh tones too rosy-cheeked, lips too red, unnatural. Sky background. No company identification on reverse. "Roy Rogers," "Rep. Pict." No. KF 39. Trigger and Roy, sky, mountain backdrop. Roy has on wine colored/white checked shirt, gloves tinted white, hat white. Trigger appears very natural in color. Boots realistically colored. "Roy Rogers," "Rep. Pict." KF 40. Roy, close-up bust publicity photo, hand up to face, gloves tinted gray. Checked shirt tinted green, multicolored neckerchief really stands out. Flesh tones same as in previous one. Hat realistic beige. "Roy Rogers," "Rep. Pict." No identification on reverse. KF 48. Trigger, Roy, mid-1940s publicity photo. Trigger tinted too brown. Roy in conservative shirt, jeans. Wine-colored neckerchief. "Roy Rogers," "Rep. Pict." Identified on reverse.

Movie Stars—7. No company identification. 1⅞″ × 2¼″. B&w bust publicity photos. Value: $5–$8. 1. (My number.) Late 1940s–early 1950s photo of smiling Roy, checked shirt. Hat doesn't fit all the way into photo area. White area at bottom: "Roy Rogers."

Film Stars. Circa late 1940s–early 1950s. Unknown company. 2¼″ × 3⁷⁄₁₆″. Black and white publicity photos. Name of star and studio at bottom in photo area. White boarded on heavy stock. Thought to be candy store, gum, or mail premium. No. 23. Publicity photos shows Trigger, Roy standing side by side. This time "Rep. Pict." is on the left side with name, number on right. Blank reverse. No. 117. Photo exactly that used for KF 39 above. Blank reverse. "Roy Rogers," "Republic Pictures" in white.

R. R. **TRICYCLE/CHUCKWAGON.** 1950s. Full-sized. $200–$500.

R. R. AND TRIGGER **TRANSFER.** 1950s. Iron-on. Several different pictures. Red and black ink. $25–$45.

R. R. RIDER **TRIGGER** TOY. 1955–1956. The N.N. Hill Brass Co. Lithographed picture of Roy on Trigger, with parts that move as toy is pulled. 9″ long, 8½″ high, 5″ wide. Originally $1. $65–$100.

FAITHFUL **TRIGGER.** 1955. Stern Toy Co. 22″ high. Single piece handle grip extending from top. White hooves, mane, and tail. Rubber-tired wheels. Saddle, bridle. Originally $10. $160–$225.

R. R. STUFFED **TRIGGER.** 1950s. Orange. About 3 feet tall, rearing position. $60–$125.

R. R. **TRIGGER** HOBBY HORSE. 1955–1956. The N.N. Hill Brass Co., Philadelphia. Horsehead mounted on two-piece hardwood stick. Six-inch wheels with chimes. Bullet attached to rear. 39″ long. Originally $2. $60–$125.

R. R. AND **TRIGGER** ANIMATED PULL TOY. 1955. N. N. Hill Co. Small. Roy on Trigger. Wheels, string. Originally $1. $100–$200.

R. R. AND **TRIGGER** PULL TOY. Late 1940s. Unknown manufacturer. 8½″ tall, 9″ long, wood and metal. Musical chimes. $100–$200.

TRIGGER TOY. 1950s. N.N. Hill Brass Co. Wooden, musical toy. 20″ long, 6″ high. With wagon. Painted young cowboy with Roy Rogers type boots, on wood. $60–$150.

GALLOPING FUN ON **TRIGGER.** Exhibit Supply Co. 10 cents for one-minute ride. Not documented. Price unknown.

MUSICAL **TRIGGER**. 1950s. Moulded Products Co. Plays music when rocked. Also comes without music box. Originally $11.95. $60–$125.

R. R. HORSE "**TRIGGER**." Early 1950s. Doughboy Industries, Inc., New Richmond, WI. Inflatable toy. $65–$85.

R. R. HORSE "**TRIGGER**." 1955–1956. Ideal Toy Corporation. No. 5274. Inflatable Trigger toy, silk-screened, simulated saddle/ bridle. Reins. Rust-colored vinyl. 17″ high, 21″ long. Decorated box. Originally $1.98. $65–$100.

R. R. **TRIGGER**. Early 1950s. Van Voorhis and Lower, Inc, Ontario, CA. Stick horse. $70–$150.

R. R. **TRIGGER**. Early 1950s. Unknown manufacturer. 7″ × 18½″ × 23″. Vinyl and plastic. Riding toy. Steel wheel supports. $100–$200.

R. R. **TRIGGER/TRIGGER, JR**, TRACTOR AND TRAILER. 1954. Marx Co. Dodge tractor. $120–$200.

R. R. AND **TRIGGER** METAL CATTLE TRUCK. 1950s. Marx Toys. Tin lithograph. 15″ long. Red tractor, yellow/blue van. Roy, Trigger on sides. $120–$200.

R. R. **TRU-VUE CARD**. Mid-1950s. Tru-Vue Co. Film card. 14 pictures. $30–$60.

R. R. **TV CHAIR**. 1950s. Les Brown. Kiln-dried wood frame. Blonde lacquer finish. Western brands and rearing Trigger design. Seat: 16″ × 16″ with 25″ back. Originally $14.50. $100–$150.

R. R. **TV SEAT**. 1950s. (Possibly same as above or variation.) Leather saddle seat. Three wooden legs. $100–$150.

R. R. **TYKERCHIEF**. Early 1950s. Western Art Manufacturing Co. No additional information. $40–$85. *See also* Ties, Nickerchiefs.

R. R. **UNDERWEAR** *see* individual items: briefs, shirts, etc.

R. R. BOLERO **VEST**. 1955–1956. Western Art Manufacturing Co. Hand-screened Roy and Trigger design on pockets (in horseshoes). Metal deputy sheriff badge attached. Sizes: small, medium, large. Colors: blue, red, black. Originally $1. $100–$200.

R. R. **VIEW-MASTER**. Sawyers, Inc. For 3-D stereoscope pictures. Originally $2. $40–$75. *Note:* For a while, Roy Rogers rearing on Trigger was used in the ads, but the design was later pulled and a generic cowboy and horse were substituted.

R. R. **VIEW-MASTER REELS**. 1956. Sawyers, Inc. Set. $40–$60. Individual reels: $15–$20.

R. R. **VIEWER**. Early 1950s. Comiscope Company of America, New York. Value slightly more than View-Master viewer.

R. R. **VIEWING REELS**. Early 1950s. Comiscope of America. Undocumented. Value slightly more than View-Master reels.

R. R. TOY **WAGON**. 1950s. 16″ × 27″. No other information. $60–$125.

R. R. **WAGON**. Late 1940s. Unknown manufacturer. 7″ long, 12″ tall. Covered metal and wood. Pull toy. $100–$150.

R. R. **WAGON TRAIN**. 1950s. Marx Toys. No other information. $100–$200.

R. R. **WALKIE-TALKIE SET**. 1950s. No other information. $70–$125.

R. R. **WALL PLAQUE**. Early 1950s. Plasto Manufacturing Co. Plastic plaque. $35–$55.

R. R. **WALL PLAQUE**. 1940s. Unknown manufacturer. Laminated color photo on Masonite™ type board 4⁵/₁₆″ × 5¹³/₁₆″. Photo: Roy rearing on "Trigger," likely Little Trigger, white fence in background. Facsimile signed: "Many Happy Trails, Roy Rogers." $20–$50.

R. R. AND TRIGGER **WALL PLAQUE**. 1950s. Unknown manufacturer. Laminated color 8½″ × 11″. Photo: Roy on "Trigger," who is doing dance routine. Probably Little Trigger. Artwork of bullrider in background. Photo used for *Roy Rogers Comics* #76, April 1954. $75–$200.

R. R. 3-D **WALL PLAQUE** SET. 1960. Offered as premium by Nestle's Quik. Four different plastic plaques. $50–$100.

R. R. **WALL PLAQUE AND PISTOL SET**. 1955. Kilgore Co. Three different replicas of Roy's guns. Sold separately without plaque. "Dura-gleam" finish. Elaborately etched barrels. Revolving cylinder, repeating models in cap and nonfiring styles. Originally $0.79–$1.75. Small, $50–$80; medium-sized, $60–$100; large, $70–$150.

R. R. **WALLET**. 1952. "Only at Sears by mail." India calf skin, sunset tan. Roy rearing on Trigger, under name overhead, encircled by lariat. Embossed and hand tinted. Two-toned braid edging and zipper on three sides. Lined bill pocket, snapped coin pocket.

Four swing windows. 3½″ × 4½″ closed. Sears No. 25 G 2850E. $2.50. (Others are $2.39.) $65–$100. *Note:* Name "Peter" appears on Trigger (see below).

R. R. VINYL **WALLET**. 1950s. $55–$80.

R. R. GENUINE LEATHER **WALLET**. 1950. Hickok Mfg. Co. Zipper. Embossed with Roy and Trigger in color. $65–$100. With Roy Rogers Riders Club membership card inside: $75–$125.

R. R. **WALLET**. 1954. D. H. Neumann Co. Plastic, zip-around, picture of Roy and Trigger (rearing pose). Originally $1–$1.50. $50–$100.

R. R. AND TRIGGER LEATHER **WALLET**. 1950s. Aristocrat Co., Newark, NJ. Roy and Trigger stamped into leather. Name in very large cursive style under figures. "RR" with bar underneath. Very scarce. $100–$200.

R. R. LEATHER **WALLET**. 1950s. Aristocrat Co. Roy, Bullet. Lariat writes Roy Rogers name. Name in large writing style, top left side. "RR" with bar underneath. $100–$200. Very scarce.

R. R. AND TRIGGER LEATHER **WALLET**. 1950s. Aristocrat Co. Roy rearing on Trigger. Double R Bar Ranch gate, ranch scene in background. Subjects are facing observer's right. "RR" and bar. $100–$200. *Note:* "Pete" or "Peter" appears on Trigger, suggesting artwork by Peter Alvarado. Very scarce.

R. R. LEATHER **WALLET**. 1950s. Aristocrat Co. Roy waving on Trigger, surrounded by lariat. "RR" and bar. $100–$200. Very scarce.

ROY, TRIGGER AND DALE LEATHER **WALLET**. 1950s. Aristocrat Co. Roy, Trigger, and Dale stamped into leather. "RR" and bar in lariat circle, opposite side. Floral design both sides. $100–$200. *Note:* "Al" (rest illegible) appears on hats of each subject.

R. R. AND DALE EVANS **WALLET**. Early 1950s. Aristocrat Manufacturing Co. Roy, Trigger, Dale in center. "RR" brand. $100–$200.

R. R. AND TRIGGER **WALLET**. Early 1950s. Aristocrat Co. The big Roy Rogers name is in cursive style under Roy rearing on Trigger. To the left is the ranch gate. The right side holds the etched (this time) double R brand. Encircled with lariat. Floral pattern surrounds. $100–$200.

R. R. BORDERPAPER **(WALLPAPER)**. 1950s. Dark green background. Painted scene includes Double R Bar Ranch gate, fence, two cowboys sitting on horses, mountains, desert plats, Roy rearing on Trigger, waving, saddle on fence, two cowboys under gate. Pattern repeats itself every 19″. 9⅛″ wide. Roy in fringed attire, blue bandana. 25′ roll: $70–$100.

R. R. KING OF THE COWBOYS HAND-SHAPED **WASHCLOTH**. 1950s. Roy, both guns drawn, standing in front of fence. $25–$75.

DALE EVANS QUEEN OF THE WEST ⅞″ TERRYCLOTH **WASHING MITT**. Mid-1950s. Design in brown, red, green, blue and flesh. $25–$75.

DALE EVANS **WATCH**. 1951. Ingraham Co. Dale is shown drawn inside horseshoe. Silvered-metal round case. Orange border, black numerals. Celluloid-enclosed pop-up box. $150–$300.

R. R. **WATCH**. 1952–1954. Ingraham Co. Colored dial shows Roy rearing on Trigger, waving. Facsimile signature lower left corner. Red numerals, black hands. Chrome-plated case, stainless steel back. Ingraham movement. Leather band is good quality. Sears No. 4 G 8862. Texas type brand, saddle tooled, silver-color metal buckle, tip. Originally $3.95. $150–$300.

R. R. **WATCH**. 1952–1954. Ingraham Co. Leather band — better quality. Same picture as 4 G 8862. Sears No. 4 G 1869E. Smaller, thinner watch, same style band, buckle, tip. Originally $4.95. $150–$300.

R. R. **WATCH**. 1952–1954. Ingraham Co. Smaller, thinner watch with lariat-like link design, stainless steel expansion band, ID bar engraved: "Roy Rogers and Trigger." Same picture as 4 G 8862. Best quality unit (watch and band). Sears No. 4 G 1865E. Roy Rogers expansion band; identification bar engraved with "Roy Rogers and Trigger." Originally $6.95. $150–$300.

R. R. AND TRIGGER POCKET **WATCH**. 1959. Bradley Time. Stop watch feature. Illustrated Roy portrait (yellow hat, black shirt, red neckerchief, flesh-tone face) and Roy on rearing Trigger at ranch gate on dial face. Facsimile signature "Roy Rogers and Trigger" at bottom. Silvered metal case, clear crystal. $250–$400.

R. R. POCKET **WATCH**. 1960. Ingraham

The Official Roy Rogers Boots. By J.P.'s Custom Handmade Boots. 1990s. Personal photo, used with permission. Courtesy J. F. Patrickus.

Co. Stop watch feature. Background, Roy rearing on Trigger by gate. Foreground, bust shot. Facsimile signature and written Trigger name underneath picture. $250–$400. *Note:* These pocket watches have been reproduced in unauthorized version. The reproduction makes use of a color laser photo copy on dial face. Value is debatable.

R. R. POCKET **WATCH** FOB. Early 1950s. Carmody Products, Ltd. $25–$60.

R. R. **WATERCOLOR SET.** Early 1950s. Paint by number picture panels. Photos show four completed panels. $100–$200.

R. R. **WATERCOLOR SET.** Early 1950s. Avalon Manufacturing Corporation, Brooklyn, NY. Smaller version of above set. $75–$125.

R. R. **WESTERN TOWN.** 1950s. Marx. #4258. Box: 6″ × 10″ × 34″. The majority of the sculpture work for Marx sets was performed by Joe Ferriot of Akron, OH, from the late 1940s until 1976. $200–$600.

WINDOW CARDS. MOVIE MATERIALS. Usually found with several inches of white space above main artwork. This space was used for local theater name imprint. (Size: 14″ × 22″.) Most window cards: $40. *The Cowboy and the Senorita*, $40; *Yellow Rose of Texas*, $40.

R. R. **WOODBURNING SET.** Early 1950s. Rapaport Brothers, Inc., Chicago. No additional information. $150–$300.

R. R. AND TRIGGER **WRISTWATCH.** 1951. Ingraham Co. Rectangular case. Roy, in recent horseshoe-breasted attire, next to Trigger, in circle. Names underneath. $150–$300 (all watch values are for mint, in box).

R. R. AND TRIGGER **WRISTWATCH.** 1951. Ingraham Co. Same picture as above: Roy has hand on Trigger's nose on dial face, green border, black numerals. Names at bottom. Silvered metal round case. Originally given for one order of greeting cards ($4.50), plus $1.75. $150–$300.

DALE EVANS QUEEN OF THE WEST **WRISTWATCH.** 1952–1954. Ingraham Co. Nonshatter crystal. Picture and facsimile signature on brightly colored dial. Dale standing, fringed outfit, waving. Signature is across center. Chrome-plated case, stainless metal back. Cactus flower motif. Sears No. 4 G 1875E. Expansion band with cactus flower motif. Originally $6.95. $70–$100. Same watch with tan "saddle tooled" leather strap (4 G 1869E). Originally $4.95. $150–$300.

R. R. **WRISTWATCH**. 1954. Bradley Time. Same picture of Roy and Trigger, side by side, that was used for the Ingraham versions. Unbreakable crystal, with strap or bracelet bands. Rolled gold or stainless steel back. Advertised in *Life*, 1954: $4.95–$6.95. $150–$300.

DALE EVANS **WRISTWATCH**. 1954. Bradley Time. Picture of Dale next to horse, inside horseshoe. Unbreakable crystal, rolled gold or stainless steel back. Strap or bracelet models. Originally $4.95–$6.95. $150–$300.

R. R. OFFICIAL **WRISTWATCH AND JEWELRY SET**. 1950s. Two saddle cuff links; one saddle tie clasp with stone. Gold colored. Boxloads of these were handed out or sold, without the watches included, during a Roy and Dale appearance at Madison Square Garden Rodeo. Mounted on small cardboard, no pictures. No information on watch for these sets. $30–$50 (without watch).

DALE EVANS OFFICIAL **WRISTWATCH AND JEWELRY SET**. 1950s. One necklace, horseshoe with stones. Silver colored. Same distribution as above. $30–$50 (without watch).

R. R. ROUNDUP KING **YO-YOS**. 1950. All-Western Plastics, Co., Alliance, NE. Face with photo of Roy and Trigger (probably original Trigger). Several colors (red, blue, green, white, yellow, etc.) These would be very valuable had not a warehouse full of them been discovered a few years back by the grandson of the owner. 1986: $6.75 each. 1991: $10 each. Cardboard display boxes sold out by 1990: Double R Bar Ranch gate, photo of Roy (bust shot) speaking in comic balloon. Backs: "Roy Rogers King of the Cowboys is leading a national Roundup to find the King and Queen of Roundup King Top Spinners. Various prizes awarded to runners-up. King and Queen chosen in preliminaries authorized by All-Western Plastics, Inc., will have their expenses paid to the finals at the big corral in Hollywood to choose the National King and Queen and meet Roy and Trigger. Watch newspapers, theatres and corrals for details of authorized contests." A tornado destroyed the factory and mold. 1993: $15–$25. It is believed that this company also produced tops, as Roundup King Top is shown on back. *See also* Tops.

Later Collectibles, 1965–1993

Ads

AC Classics Comics. Late 1980s. Foldout advertisement, b&w photo of Roy, approximately 1′ × 2′. $1–$2.

The Art Merchant. (ad for R. R. Limited Edition Montage Print) March–April 1983. $1–$2.

Cowboy Kings and Classics Westerns. Video Marketplace. January/February 1990. $1–$2.

Dale Evans Handpainted Socks. 1992. Mail-order. Photos, Roy and Dale. Full size. $2.

Digital Word Processor Hearing Instruments from Nu-Ear! July 26, 1992. *The Fresno* (CA) *Bee*. Photo of Roy. $1–$2.

The Drummond Co./Nu-Ear Digital Word Processor Hearing Instruments. July 1992 newspapers (*Fresno Bee*). One-fourth page. $2.

Happy Trails Chocolates. 1992. Mail-order. Colt, Inc., Nashville. Photos of Roy. Full size. Color. $2.

Happy Trails to You. Roy Rogers and Dale Evans Collector Plate. 1991. Brochure. The Hamilton Collection, Jacksonville, FL. Color. Large. $3.

Heart of the Golden West. 1992–1993. Film Prints, Inc., Wichita, KS. *Yippy Yi Yea* magazine. Painted likeness of Roy by Dave LaFleur. Color, full page. $1–$2.

M and S Video Proudly Presents "Triple B Western." 1991. M and S Video. Photo of Roy and Dale. $1–$2.

New Tasty Treats Repel Fleas on Dogs and Cats. May 7, 1978. Jay Norris Corporation, Freeport, NY. Family Weekly Sunday (newspaper) Supplement (in author's collection: *Hutchinson* [KS] *News* ad). Endorsement. Size: One-half page. 1950s b&w photo of Roy and Bullet. $5.

News You'll Like to Hear from "The King of the Cowboys." Nu-Ear Electronics, San Diego. Mail order. Color photos. $1–$2.

The 1991 Dixie Gun Works Catalog. 1991. Photo, Roy, family. Small. $1–$2.

Nostalgic Cowboy Decorator Signs. 1992. Mail order. Smoky Mountain Knife Works, Sevierville, TN. Photos of signs with painted likenesses of Roy and Dale. Color. $2.

The Pick of America. February 1992. *Country America* magazine. $2.

Portsmouth, Ohio. 1990s. Portsmouth Chamber of Commerce mail order. Painted likenesses of Roy and Trigger by Tom Tridico. Full size, color. $4.

Riders of the Silver Screen. 1992. Mail order. Camillus Co. Photos of character knives with Roy, Dale, others. Full size, color. $2.

Riders of the Silver Screen. 1992. Camillus Co. Poster size. Color, with illustrated Roy, Dale, others. $5.

Roy and Dale Invite You to Save at Far West Savings. *Hollywood Studio* vol. 14, no. 10 (May 1981). Endorsement: Far West Savings and Loan. Size: One-half page. B&w photo. $2.

Roy Rogers and Trigger Figure Set. Christmas 1992. J.C. Penney Stores catalogue. Roy Rogers merchandise. Photo of merchandise. $1–$2.

Roy Rogers .45. 1991. Mail order. United States Historical Society, Richmond, VA. Illustration of Roy Rogers six-gun. Large, cardboard. $2.

Roy Rogers .45. June 1991. *Guns and Ammo* magazine. Photos of Roy, guns. Full page. $3.

Roy Rogers Key Ring. 1991. Arvo Ojala Productions, North Hollywood. Color Roy Rogers photo. Handout Advertisement. 1991: $1–$2.

Roy Rogers Roast Beef Sandwich. 1969. Roy Rogers Restaurants: Marriott Corp. One-fourth page. Color photo of Roy, specially posed, color background. $5.

Roy Rogers Roast Beef Sandwich. Roy Rogers Western Foods, Inc., Washington, D.C. One-half page. Color photo. $5.

Roy Rogers Tribute. 1992. Various publications. Color photo of Roy. Full size. $2.

"Three Generations of Rogers Keep Their Guns in a Fort Knox Safe." 1992–1993. Fort Knox Security Products, Orem, UT. Various publications including *Oaktree Express*. Mail order. Photo of Roy, family $2.

U. S. Historical Society Antique Arms Commission Contract. 1991. Roy Rogers .45 Cowboy Edition. $5–$10.

You Grew Up with Them, but You Didn't Out Grow Them. April 1980. *Saturday Evening Post*. Word Publishing Co., Waco, TX. RR books and records. $1–$2.

Merchandise

R. R. ART REPRODUCTIONS. 1980s, 1990s. By artist Mario DeMarco. Commonly found at movie memorabilia shows, etc. $8\frac{1}{2}'' \times 11''$. $1–$2. The originals would be considerably more, but who ever sees these? They lend themselves easily to reproduction.

R. R. FESTIVAL BADGE MAGNET. *See* Magnets.

R. R. MUSEUM BAG. 1960s–1970s. Giveaway at first museum, after visit and purchase. $5–$10.

R. R.-DALE EVANS MUSEUM BAG. 1990s. Complimentary with gift shop purchase.

R. R. CUSTOM BELT BUCKLE. 1986. Maroy Enterprises, Norman, OK. Mail order. Brass or gold and silver plate. Finely crafted, limited edition. Numbered and registered. Name "Roy Rogers," Roy likeness, Bullet, Roy rearing on Trigger and "King of the Cowboys," "Bullet the Wonder Dog," and "Trigger Smartest Horse in the Movies" raised. Back: Short biography and facsimile signature. Described as "beautiful piece of workmanship." Original prices: brass, $25; gold and silver plate, $60. Set of four (with Tex Ritter, Gene Autry, Rex Allen) mounted in solid oak frame.* $125/$225.

R. R. 50TH ANNIVERSARY BELT BUCKLE. 1990. C and J Co. Advertised in various catalogues, magazines. $3\frac{1}{8}'' \times 2\frac{1}{2}''$. Pewter cast in high-relief detail, enameled.

**This buckle, or one identical in design, was also issued as part of the Ruger Super Bearcats Roy Rogers Limited Edition Gun Set, priced at $1100, issued in 1987. (See Guns.) Only 75 of these existed. Buckle number would match gun number. This buckle is silver-plated.*

Raised: Pewter-colored likeness of Roy from artist's portrait, unknown; hat enameled white; "Roy Rogers King of the Cowboys" in red enamel; steer head. Top: "50th Anniversary" engraved on scroll. Spurs (raised) extend out from each end of scroll. Border: Little, raised "RR" brands on red background. Other: Back shows limited edition number out of 10,000. Originally $20. $30–$50.

BOOKS

The Roy Rogers Book. 1987. David Rothel. Empire Publishing: Madison, NC. Mail order sales, magazine advertising 8½″ × 11″, 223 pages. B&w illustrations. Color photos on brown cover. Hard and soft cover. Printed on gloss stock. $10–$30.

Roy Rogers King of the Cowboys—A Film Guide. 1979. Bob Carman and Dan Scapperotti. Privately published. Mail-order sales, magazine advertised. 8½″ × 11″. 196 pages. B&w illustrations. B&w photo on blue cover. Soft cover. Printed on pulp stock. $10–$30.

Trigger Remembered. 1989. William Witney. Earl Blair Ent.: Toney, Alabama. Mail-order sales, magazine advertised. 4¼″ × 5½″. B&w illustrations. Color photos on covers. Soft cover, printed on gloss stock. $10– $15.

The Roy Rogers Story. 1992. (Working manuscript title for the present work.) Robert W. Phillips. Approximately 600-page copy of very early sample draft of manuscript is reported to be displayed at the Roy Rogers–Dale Evans Museum, Victorville, CA. Too early to valuate.

Growing Up with Roy and Dale. 1986. Roy Rogers, Jr., with Karen Ann Wojahn. Regal Publishing: Ventura, CA. Mail order sales, magazine advertised. 4¼″ × 5½″. 206 pages. B&w illustrated. Color dust jacket. $10–$50.

Roy Rogers Hometown Photo Album. 1982. Elmer Sword. Portsmouth Area Recognition Society, Portsmouth, OH. 5⁷⁄₁₆″ × 8⅜″. 48 pages. Mail-order sales, magazine advertisement. Printed on gloss stock with b&w photos. Soft cover. $5–$15.

Roy Rogers—King of the Cowboys. 1971. William L. Roper. T. S. Denison and Co. Minneapolis, MN. $10–$40.

Time Out, Ladies! 1966. Dale Evans Rogers. Revell: Westwood, NJ. Book stores, clubs, personal appearances. (Dollar Book Club, Christian Heritage Reader's Club.) 118 pages. One common version shows a cup of coffee on softcover, another a photo of Dale on paper cover. Many softcover and pocketbook versions are reprinted by other companies, with permission. Seventh printing December 1973. $1–$5.

Salute to Sandy. 1967. Dale Evans Rogers. Revell: Old Tappan, NJ. Book stores, clubs, personal appearances. 117 pages. Photo of Dale, Sandy on front, Roy with Sandy on back. $8–$10.

The Woman at the Well. 1970. Dale Evans Rogers. Revell: Old Tappan, NJ. Book stores, clubs, personal appearances. (Pinebrook Book Club, Good Housekeeping Book Club, Word Book Club, and Guideposts Book Club, in addition to certain ones shown above.) 191 pages. Hardcover has color photo of Dale on front, Roy and Dale on back of dust jacket. Bantam pocketbook has only the Dale photo on front (239 pages). 275,000 copies sold by 1972. Fourteenth printing by March 1972. Also printed by Bantam Books, with permission. $5–$8.

Dale—My Personal Picture Album. 1971. Dale Evans Rogers. Revell: Old Tappan, NJ. Book stores, clubs, personal appearances. 125 pages of photos, family history. Color photo of Dale on dust jacket front cover, Roy on back. $10–$20.

Cool It or Lose It. 1972. Dale Evans Rogers. Revell: Old Tappan, NJ. 96 pages. Color photo of Dale on dust jacket back. $5.

Where He Leads. 1974. Dale Evans Rogers. Revell: Old Tappan, NJ. 125 pages. Color photo of Dale on dust jacket front. $5

Let Freedom Ring. 1975. Dale Evans Rogers with Frank S. Mead. Revell: Old Tappan, NJ. 128 pages. Color photo of Dale on dust jacket front. $5

Trials, Tears and Triumph. 1977. Dale Evans Rogers. Revell: Old Tappan, NJ. 128 pages. Color photo of Dale on dust jacket front. $5.

Hear the Children Crying. 1978. Dale Evans Rogers with Frank S. Mead. Revell: Old Tappan, NJ. 137 pages. Color photo of Dale on back. $5.

The Story of Roy Rogers and Dale Evans—Happy Trails. 1979. Roy and Dale with Carlton Stowers. Word Books: Waco, TX. $15–$20 first printing; less for November 1979 second printing. Additional printings: March 1980. Christian Herald Family Bookshelf edition, January 1980. *Guideposts Magazine* edition, 1979. Pocketbook printing, January 1981. Pocketbook printing, Bantam, 1990s. New version out. All are $1–$3.

Woman, Be All You Can Be. 1980. Dale Evans Rogers with Carole C. Carlson. Revell: Old Tappan, NJ. 127 pages. $3–$5.

Grandparents Can. 1983. Dale Evans Rogers with Carole C. Carlson. Revell: Old Tappan, NJ. 128 pages. Color photo of Dale, Roy on dust jacket front; Dale, Roy, and family on back. $5–$10.

God in the Hard Times. 1984. Dale Evans Rogers with Floyd Thatcher. Word Books: Waco, TX. Drawn portrait of Dale on cover. $3–$5.

The Home Stretch. 1986. Dale Evans Rogers. Word Books: Dallas, TX. $3–$5.

Let Us Love. Circa 1987. Dale Evans Rogers. Word Books: Dallas, TX. $3–$5.

Only One Star. 1988. Dale Evans Rogers, with Fritz Ridenour. Word Books: Dallas, TX. 165 pages. Color photo of Dale on inside back of dust jacket. $3–$5.

Finding the Way. Dale Evans Rogers. Revell: Old Tappan, NJ. $3–$5.

Christmas Is Always. 1958. Dale Evans Rogers. Word Books: Old Tappan, NJ. $3–$5.

Roy Rogers and Dale Evans Coloring Book. #1027. Whitman Publishing Co. Reprint of 1953 activity book. Possible copyright: Roy Rogers Enterprises, Inc. $5.

Roy Rogers King of the Cowboys. 1994. Georgia Morris and Mark Pollard. Collins Publishers of San Francisco. Coffee table size, dust jacket. $24.95. Limited edition also exists; signed by Roy. $75–$100.

Say Yes to Tomorrow. 1994. Dale Evans Rogers. Publisher: Fleming H. Revell (division of Baker Book House Co., Grand Rapids, Michigan). $10.

In the Hands of the Potter. 1994. Dale Evans Rogers with Les Stobbe. Thomas Nelson Publishers: Nashville, TN. $15.00.

Happy Trails: Our Life Story. 1994. Roy and Dale with Jane and Michael Stern. Simon & Schuster. Photo dust jacket. $23.50.

THE OFFICIAL R.R. **BOOTS.** 1986–1992. J. P. Patrickus at J.P.'s Custom Handmade Boots. Also advertised in numerous catalogues, newsletters, etc. All adult sizes. Variety of colors, including red, white, and blue, three tones of grey, three tones of brown, and black/burgundy/gray. Special 50th anniversary edition, black and gold. These are the famous "double-eagle" design and come in all-leather boot. Serialized, collector's box with certificate of authenticity. Original price in 1986 $850. (In the fall of 1987, the price was lowered to $550.) 1993: Price increased to $1850. Informed by company that its license to produce these expired 1992. These will become highly collectible considering that they are "Collector Editions," authenticated with a certificate, made only by order, and are being discontinued.

R. R. EMBOSSED **BOOTS.** 1994. Rocketbuster Boots. Retro of 1950s style: Roy Rogers, Trigger, and Ride'em High with Roy's lariat spelling his name. Sizes 3–12. Catalogue number G0342. $450.

R.R./DALE EVANS ROCKETBUSTER **BOOTS.** 1994. Designed after Roy's and Dale's 1950s boots. Value unknown.

ROGERSDALE ENTERTAINMENT COMPLEX **BROCHURES.** 1995. 25 million dollar entertainment complex in Victorville, California, advertising materials. $3–$5.

R. R.-DALE EVANS COLLECTORS ASSOCIATION **BUMPER STICKER.** 1980s–1990s. RRDECA. 11 7/8″ × 2 7/8″. $1–$2.

PIN-BACK **BUTTONS.** (New or "Post-Era." Generally 1980s–1990s.) 1. *Roy Rogers and Trigger.* 1980s–1990s. 1980s. A reproduction of #9 in the vintage series. The difference is the area covered by the celluloid-covered photo on the button. On the original, the photo covers all the button. On the reproduction, the edge, or part of the edge, is white. $2–$5. 2. *Roy Rogers.* Circa 1980s–1990s. Very similar to #16, vintage series. Face is flesh-toned. Barely covered or not covered at all with celluloid, and lithographed picture wears off tin. 1/16″ smaller. $1–$3. 3. *Roy and Dale.* 1990s. Large. 1½″. 1947 color wedding photo, from film magazine of the period. Roy and Dale cheek-to-cheek. $10– $20. 4. *Roy and Dale.* 1990s.

Large. 2¾" diameter. Late 1940s b&w photo of Dale cheek-to-cheek with Roy. These are sometimes passed off as originals by dealers to unsuspecting buyers. $2–$5. 5. *Happy Trails.* Circa 1970s. Black and white. 1970s photo (bust) of Roy. His name is not on button. Print at top: "Happy Trails" in large black lettering. From Roy Rogers–Dale Evans Museum, 1970s–1980s. $2–$5. 6. *Roy Rogers.* 1990s. Color photo of Roy, smiling, looking up and to his left, gray hat. Grey background. Name "Roy Rogers" in large black print at bottom. Probably sold at RRDE Museum. $2–$5. 7. *Roy Rogers.* Late 1980s–early 1990s. AC Comics, Lakewood, FL. Close-up b&w photo of Roy, 1940s. Face shot, not all of hat is in photo. $1.25–$3. 8. *Roy Rogers.* Late 1980s–early 1990s. AC Comics. B&w photo of Roy, close-up plaid shirt, 1950s. $1.25–$3. 9. *Roy Rogers.* Late 1980s–early 1990s. AC Comics. Drawn color likeness of Roy by artist Bill Black. Close-up, face shot. $1.25–$3. 10. *Roy and Trigger.* Late 1980s–early 1990s. AC Comics. Drawn color likenesses of Roy and Trigger by Black. Name "Roy Rogers" in top right hand corner. $1.25–$3. 11. *Roy Logo.* Late 1980s–early 1990s. AC Comics. Drawing of Roy's head (from "Roy and Trigger" button art) and large name "Roy Rogers." $1.25–$3. 12. *Dale.* No. 1. Late 1980s–early 1990s. AC Comics. Drawing of Dale, close-up of face, by artist Black. $1.25–$3. 13. *Pat Brady.* Late 1980s–early 1990s. AC Comics. B&w photo of Brady, extreme close-up. Not all of hat in photo. $1.25–$3. 14. *Roy Rogers Festival.* 1991. Roy Rogers Festival, Portsmouth, Ohio. 2⅞" diameter. "Roy Rogers Festival" across top, "Portsmouth, Ohio" and "July 4-6, 1992" below. Line for guests or attendee's name. B&w photo of Roy and Dale.

ROY AND DALE "THE GOLDEN YEARS" **CALENDAR**. 1982. Roy Rogers Enterprises. Far West Savings and Loan Association, giveaway. Sold at RRDE Museum, 1990s. 11¹/₁₆" × 8⁹/₁₆". *17" × 11¹/₁₆"* opened. 12 sepia-toned photos of Roy and Dale: movie stills, publicity, candid. "50 Years of Stardom."

WESTERN FILM STARS **CALENDAR**. 1987. Mail-order. 12 pen and ink drawings of Western film and television stars, including Roy and Dale. Cover dedicated to Roy's 75th birthday. Includes Roy Rogers film titles and television series episode titles. 11" × 17". Drawings: 8" × 10". Heavy stock paper, suitable for framing. Limited printing: 300 copies. Some numbered and signed by artist Armand Polverani. Sold through RRDECA, Portsmouth, OH. $10–$20.

R. R. HAPPY TRAILS CHOCOLATE **CANDY**. 1992. Colt, Inc., Nashville, TN. 12-piece collector gift box. Dealers can order a 60-piece counter display. Pure milk chocolate over peanut butter with chunks of pecans, peanuts, raisins, and other "trail mix goodies." Colorful box has early 1950s photo of Roy, playing guitar in front of painted desert scene. Roy's name written on bright red box with lariat. 12-piece box: $10–$20. 60-piece with display: $30–$50. Boxes: $5–$15.

R. R. **CANTEEN**. 1990s. RRDE Museum. Small canteen with cover. Name "Roy Rogers" across front. $10–$20.

R. R. **CAP**. Circa 1990s. Korol Western Corp. Green, perhaps other colors. 100 percent polyester, one size fits all. Made in Taiwan. RRDE Museum. White print on front. $2– $10.

R. R. CORRAL **CAP COLLECTION**. 1993. Arrowcatch Productions. Probably inspired by Dixie Cup lids. Twelve caps in red prismatic foil contain the same basic likeness in several different expressions, all from the McKimson period in *Roy Rogers Comics*, surrounded by gold foil 1½" diameter. Limited to 3400 sets. (Bullpen artwork see Chapter 7.) $11.95.

R. R.–DALE EVANS MUSEUM **CHECK**. Signed: Roy Rogers, Jr. Sample: Written 11/20/91, for return postage of early draft copy of manuscript of this book. Processed Security Pacific National Bank, Los Angeles, 11/22/91. $2–$5. *Note:* Checks signed by Roy, and on original museum, would have significant value, in the range of $30–$50.

R. R. "WELCOME TO COWTOWN, NYC" **CIRCULARS**. 1990. Dusty Trails Western store handout (New York). $2–$5.

R. R.–DALE EVANS MUSEUM **COIN PURSE**. Circa 1990s. Red Rubber. Sold at RRDE Museum. $3–$5.

R. R. COMIC BOOK **COLLECTOR CARDS**. 1992. Arrowcatch Productions,

Yorba Linda, CA. Advertised as being available August 31, 1992. When mailing time drew near again in November 1992, it was announced that further examination after final cutting revealed quality was still not up to par and all cards in this production run were reportedly destroyed. Three test cards were mailed out to those who had ordered sets. First edition. Series 1: 70 cards with the *Roy Rogers Comics* covers #1–70 reproduced on the front and miscellaneous photos, including collectibles, on the reverse. These sold for $15 per set. Full color front, back, high-gloss stock. With initial orders there was a free Special Limited Edition Card in each set. If any of the cards should surface from the early November 1992 production run, they should appear to be of a lower quality and will probably represent more value to the serious collector. Original five test cards have blue borders. Later issues have red borders. Photos originally on writing tablets, rodeo programs, etc. Two card check list is part of the set. Folding heavy cardboard box uses 1950s Roy rearing on Trigger by artist John Steel, sides has Roy from McKimson period comics. In March of 1994, the price had risen to $19 per set. $20–$30.

R. R. COMIC BOOK **COLLECTOR CARDS.** 1994. Arrowcatch Productions, El Cajon, CA. Gold signature series. First 13 four color Rogers comics used. Full color. High gloss. Roy's facsimile signature in gold. Originally $13.95.

R. R. **COOKIE JAR.** 1994. McMe Productions. Authorized limited edition. 11½″ tall. Approximately six pounds. Hand-painted ceramic. Roy signature on back of collar. $129.

R. R. "HAPPY TRAILS" **CUPS.** Circa 1990s. Comet Co., Chelmsford, MA, USA. (Stamped on bottom.) Four in complete set. RRDE Museum. Plastic. Colorful band of artwork around tall white cup (drinking glass shape) with drawing of Roy, words "Happy Trails." Printed at bottom: "America salutes the music, the movies, and the memories that are Roy Rogers." Also stamped on bottom: "Top rack dishwasher safe." Original price unknown. $20–$40.

R. R. TRIBUTE LP **DISPLAY.** 1992. RCA. Free in Tribute LP contest. Approximately 12″ high cutout of Roy, guns in hands. Free standing. $10–$20.

R. R. LIFE-SIZE STANDUP **DISPLAY.** 1994. Advanced Graphics. Full-color Roy has pistols drawn. From 1950s photo. Die-cut and mounted on easel. $25–$50.

R. R. AND TRIGGER **FIGURE SET.** 1992. Hartland Plastics. J. C. Penney stores, catalogue. Roy waving, Trigger in bright blue tack. Face hand-painted. 9″ × 4″ × 11″. Made of acetate. Multicolored. Made in USA. Originally $39.99.

R. R. AND TRIGGER SOUVENIR **GLASS.** Circa 1990s. Drawing of Roy rearing on Trigger, with blue background. Trimmed in gold. "RR" in gold band, top and bottom. Words "Roy Rogers and Trigger." RRDE Museum. $5–$20.

DALE EVANS **GREETING CARDS.** 1990s. These are greeting cards with Dale Evans' inspirational messages and will double for note cards. Desert scenes. A box contains 12 different 5″ × 7″ cards. $12. Sold through Roy Rogers–Dale Evans Collectors Assn., Portsmouth, OH. $10–$20.

R. R. LIMITED EDITION RUGER **GUN/ SET ONE.** 1987. Ruger. 5,000 made. Four models make up set: .22 Cal., .357 Magnum, .44 Magnum, and one to be announced. Customized from Ruger Stainless Steel revolvers. Roy Rogers' signature on the barrel. Edition number appears on the ejector tube (two numbers, dash, and five numbers). Custom grips, other parts, have "RR" (probably all) and scenes such as Roy rearing Trigger (.22 Cal.) and Trigger alone (.357 Magnum). Box: Velvet lined, solid black walnut, with picture of Roy and Trigger laser-engraved on lid. Letter of authenticity. Owners' names maintained in book in RRDE Museum. Bonus: 45 RPM record, *King of the Cowboys*, sung by Roy's son. Originally $850 per gun. These guns, once sold out, will appreciate considerably; prices for the earlier numbers in set are running higher than others.

R. R. LIMITED EDITION RUGER **GUN/ SET TWO.** 1987. Ruger. Customized from Super Bearcat model. 75 made. Stag horn grips, Roy's signature on barrel, edition number on ejector tube. Picture of Roy on Trigger on cylinder. "Metalife" stainless steel–looking finish. Various parts gold plated. Same box, letter of authenticity, and other details apply. Bonus of 45 RPM record. This one comes with gold- and silver-plated Roy Rogers belt buckle. (*See also* Buckles.) Originally $1100. Again, these will probably appreciate considerably.

R. R. LIMITED EDITION COMMEMORATIVE .45 **GUN**. 1991–1992. To celebrate Roy's fifty years riding the Hollywood range, the Roy Rogers–Dale Evans Museum and the United States Historical Society in Richmond, Virginia, have authorized and issued a commemorative numbered and lettered limited edition of 2,500 Roy Rogers Single-Action .45 army revolvers, at the price of $1,350 each.

R. R. BOOT **KEY RING**. 1980s–1990s. Roy Rogers–Dale Evans Collectors Association. 2⅝" × 1⅞". Boot-shaped rubber. Variety of colors. Back identifies association with address. $1–$5.

R. R. NOVELTY CHARACTER **KNIFE**. 1990. Smoky Mountain Knife Works. Part of the "Riders of the Silver Screen" character novelty knife series. Full-color illustration of Roy, sealed under acrylic with a 3½" closed length carbon steel blade. 5¾" opened length. Roy, riding a bucking Trigger (?), while twirling his lariat. Artist Mark Christianer signed work. Backside is plain, black. Made in USA. Original price in 1992: $4.99. $5–$10.

DALE EVANS NOVELTY CHARACTER **KNIFE**. 1990. Part of the above series. Same information applies. Dale riding Buttermilk, Bullet in foreground. Christianer artwork, signed. Originally $4.99. $5–$10.

R. R. CHARACTER BARLOW **KNIFE**. 1990. Barlow and Smoky Mountain Knife Works. Part of the "Sunset Barlow" series. Full-color illustration of Trigger, Dale, and Roy (Roy based on photo used for cover of *Roy Rogers Comics* #59, November 1952) by artist Bob Sallee. 1991. Two-blade Barlow knife with full-color scene on back as well: Roy in the classic "rearing on Trigger" pose, Dale in background on Buttermilk, bidding their farewell "Happy Trails." 3½" closed length. Originally $9.99. $10–$20.

R. R. TRICK **KNIFE**. 1990s. Imperial Co. Ireland. White case with red lettering. Roy's name in lariat circle. $20–$30.

R. R. COLLECTOR SERIES CHARACTER **KNIFE**. 1990. Camillus Cutlery. Built on Camillus pattern #23, deluxe special tribute picture knife from company that produced original 1950s character knives. Artwork by Don Sherwood has Roy in fringed attire in a desert scene, firing both six-shooters, under acrylic. The back side is also illustrated, showing Roy and Dale in montage with nine other "silver screen" characters. Not copies of any originals. "Riders of the Silver Screen" series. 4¾" long. Stainless steel blade, nickel silver pins, brass liners. Originally $49.99. $50–$60.

DALE EVANS COLLECTOR SERIES CHARACTER **KNIFE**. 1990. Same series. All above information applies. Sherwood artwork has Dale on Buttermilk in the background, waving as Roy and Trigger look on. Originally $49.99. $50–$60.

R. R. HORSESHOE **KNIFE**. 1980s. Plastic and metal. Roy on one side. Two blades open on either end. Originally $8. $20–$30.

R. R. FESTIVAL BADGE **MAGNET**. 1980s–1990s. Roy Rogers Festival, Portsmouth, Ohio. 2⅝" sq. Variety of colors. Reads "Roy Rogers Festival, Portsmouth, Ohio." Magnet covers all of reverse. $1–$5.

R. R. **MARBLE**. 1990s. RRDE Museum. Roy's head in a horseshoe. $5–$10.

R. R. **MATCHES**. 1992. Roy and Dale on cover. $2–$3.

R. R.–DALE EVANS MUSEUM **MIRROR**. Circa 1990s. RRDE Museum. $5–$10.

R. R.–DALE EVANS MUSEUM BEVERAGE **NAPKINS**. Circa 1990s. Creative Arts. "Happy Trails" printed on front. 30 in complete set. Sold at RRDECA Museum. $5–$10.

HAPPY TRAILS CHILDREN'S FOUNDATION **NEWSLETTERS**. Apple Valley California foundation newsletter. $3–$5.

R. R. CHRISTMAS **ORNAMENTS**. 1992. Hays & Associates, Hollywood. Limited first edition (in a series), 1992. 3¼". "Color picture of Roy Rogers"; back reads: "Roy Rogers, King of the Cowboys." Ornament is gift boxed. Advertised in various magazines, fall 1992. Ad shows drawing of Roy instead of picture. Originally $8 each or six for $46.

R. R. CHRISTMAS **ORNAMENTS**. 1993. Hays and Associates. Limited Edition. 3¼" white glass bulb, decorative gift box. Limited to 5,000 sets. Six different ones: Roy Rogers and Dale Evans, Roy Rogers and Bullet, Gabby Hayes, Roy Rogers and Roy

Part of the Roy Rogers collection of author.

Rogers, Jr., "Dusty," Dale Evans and Buttermilk, Roy Rogers and Trigger. Original price for six ornaments was $45. $50–$75.

R. R. **PAINTINGS**. 1990s. Spencer Kimball–painted likenesses of Roy, Dale, attire in signed prints of cut-out dolls art. Artist is from Santa Fe, New Mexico. A framed print was seen in a collectibles show in New York in 1992. Roy is in undershorts, Dale in undergarment and bra, and they are surrounded by different pieces of their famous trademark attire. Good likenesses of each, circa 1950s. $40–$60.

R. R. **PAINTINGS**. Colin Jellicoe. 1989. Manchester, England. Oil board. Roy on Trigger. $8'' \times 8''$. Sold. Value unknown.

PORTSMOUTH, OHIO, CHAMBER OF COMMERCE/VISITOR'S BUREAU **PAMPHLET**. 1990. Colorful painting reproduced of Roy and Trigger. Unknown artist. Cover is credited to Tom Tridico. $1–$3.

R. R. **PARTY INVITATION CARD**. May 1990. New York. Publishing party for *Box-Office Buckaroos* book (Robert Heide, John Gilman). Roy on one side surrounded by cattle brands. $2–$5.

R. R. RESTAURANT GRAND OPENING **PARTY INVITATION CARDS**. 1960s–1990s.

Marriott Corp. Hardee's Food Systems. Sample: April 27, 1992. 910 Manhattan Ave., Brooklyn, NY. Heavy beige paper stock with red print. Restaurants are franchise-operated and printing was probably done locally. Limited printing, regionally distributed, old cards destroyed. $2–$10.

R. R.–DALE EVANS MUSEUM **PENNANT**. Circa 1990s. Trigger rearing beside star on left side, words on right side. Names in red, "Museum" in black. Blue background. $5–$10.

"KING OF THE COWBOYS" AT THE HOMETOWN EXHIBIT **PHOTO CARD**. 1980s. RRDECA. Color photo of Roy at exhibit, holding Gabby Hayes comic book. $2–$5.

R. R. COLOR **PHOTO CARD**. 1980s. The American Postcard Co. Usually sold in souvenir/gift shops, newsstands, etc., especially in major cities. 1940s photo of Roy and Trigger. $2–$5.

R. R. B & W **PHOTO CARD**. 1980s–1990s. Postcard size. B&w 1940s picture of Roy over words "Portsmouth, Hometown of Roy Rogers." Festival, newsletter sales. Sold through RRDECA. $1–$2.

R. R. **PILLOWS**. 1994. Dakotah Fabrics.

Leather, jewel-studded, fringe. Facsimile signature. $50–$75.

R. R. **PILLOWS, BEDSPREADS.** 1993. Dakotah Fabrics, NY. Tufted chenille spreads, embroidered pillows, etc. Pillow cases are using the *Roy Rogers Comics* covers photos and old advertising photos, as well as artwork for design. Some of the ad-related photos focus on the trick lasso.

CLASSIC TV WESTERNS **PLATE COLLECTION.** 1991. The Hamilton Collection. It is not known how many are of Roy or Dale. One has beautiful color photo of Roy, Trigger, and Dale reproduced on 8½" diameter plate, with 23k gold rim. Limited to 14 firing days total.

R. R. SOUVENIR **PLATES.** 1980s/1990s. Sold through RRDECA, Portsmouth, OH. Decorative, photographic reproductions permanently molded into 9½" melemine plates, sepia tone. Not a decal, won't wear out, wash out, or fade out. Four illustrations: 1. Roy sitting on fence, beside Trigger. 2. The classic pose "rearing on Trigger." 3. Roy galloping on Trigger. 4. Roy, Trigger, and Dale. Original price in 1986: $11. $25–$45.

R. R./D. E. HAPPY TRAILS TO YOU **PLATES.** 1991. The Hamilton Collection, Jacksonville, FL. Same plate as Classic TV Westerns Roy and Dale. Original price: $29.50. $50–$75.

HAPPY TRAILS TO YOU **PLATES.** 1994. The Crestley Collection. Photo of Roy and Trigger, reversed negative. Roy sitting on wagon wheel. Proceeds went to: Happy Trails Children's Foundation. $19.95.

R. R./DALE EVANS **POEMS.** 1986. Michael Bright. "The Legend of Roy Rogers." "The Legend of Dale Evans." "A Prayer for Roy and Dale." 1987: "Trigger." 1988: "A Little Boy's Dream." Printed on heavy stock. RRDECA, Roy Rogers Festivals, etc. $1–$2.

"PORTRAITS OF THE DEARLY DEPARTED" **PORTRAIT.** Likeness of Roy on Trigger, Trigger being the subject of interest, hanging in art deco nightclub in South Beach, Miami, owned by German multimillionaire Thomas Kramer. Not known if this is painted or photo likeness.

R. R. **PORTRAIT.** Everett Raymond Kinstler. Cowboy Hall of Fame and Museum. Impossible to place a value on such an item. Should it ever be auctioned or sold, it would bring in the thousands.

R. R. **POSTCARD.** 1980s. Ludlow Sales Co., NY. Newsstand sales, souvenir stores. Late 1940s photo of Roy and Trigger. $1–$2.

R. R. **POSTCARD.** 1980s. American Post Card Co. Same marketing. Full colored reproductions of 1940s Roy, Trigger photos. Brilliant color reproduction. $3–$5.

R. R. AND DALE EVANS **POSTCARDS.** 1987. RRDECA. Two oversized postcards, 6" × 9", in color, are available in a set of 12. Original price of each set of six cards was $7.50. Set: $10–$20; individual cards: $2–$5.

RIDERS OF THE SILVER SCREEN **POSTER.** 1991. Camillus. Artwork by Don Sherwood. Full color, 20" × 24". Printed on heavy stock. Free with purchase of Collector Series Character Knives by Camillus. Knives are shown below montage of characters, including Roy and Dale riding in desert scene. Trigger, Jr., is outfitted in the rodeo saddle and tack here. Originally $9.99. (Reduced at time of this writing from earlier price of $19.99.)

R. R. COMMEMORATIVE **POSTERS/ PRINTS.** *Heart of the Golden West.* 1992. Film Prints, Inc. Limited edition of 2,000 prints, all signed by the artist. One-sheet movie poster. Contains original artwork (likenesses of Roy and Trigger) by artist Dave LaFleur. Roy Rogers annual festival June 3–6, 1992, was debut showing. There two of the originals, numbers 1 and 6, were presented to Dusty and the Sons of the Pioneers. Originally $50 each. *Roy Rogers.* 1993. Film Prints, Inc. Half-sheet poster of same film as above. Autographed by Roy Rogers. Limited edition to 500 prints. Originally $100. *All My Heroes Are Cowboys.* 1980s–1990s. Ivan Jesse Curtis. Likenesses of twenty-two of the all-time favorite cowboys. Limited edition of 2,000 prints. *Roy Rogers.* 1990s. American Masters. Lithographed eight-color scenes on fine art paper, 24" × 30". Individually numbered. Hand autographed by Roy: "Happy Trails Roy Rogers and Trigger." *Happy Memories Roy Rogers–Dale Evans Print.* 1993. Artist: Kim Reinmuth. 1,000 prints signed and numbered. $75. *Dale Evans Inspirational Concert Event Poster.* June 5, 1987. Roy Rogers Scholarship Fund, Shawnee State

Merv Bendewald, beside part of the Bendewald Roy Rogers collection, the "Roy Rogers Corner" in his Big Sky Furniture store. Personal photo used with permission. Courtesy Merv Bendewald.

University, Portsmouth, OH. 9 3/16″ × 7 5/16″. Close-up picture of Dale, circa 1960s. $3–$5. *Roy Rogers Festival Event Posters.* 1980s–1990s. Portsmouth Area Recognition Society. Drawing of Roy. $5–$20. *Roy Rogers King of the Cowboys Poster.* 1980s. Republic Pictures. Advertising poster for Roy Rogers films on Republic Home Video VHS tapes. Roy rearing on Trigger. $10–$20. *The Roy Rogers Show Posters.* 1980s. Paramount Pictures. Advertising poster, cardboard, for Roy Rogers television series episodes on VHS tape. $10–20. *Cowboy Collage Poster.* 1980s. Sold in drug stores, etc. Numerous film cowboys, including Tom Mix, Ward Bond. Roy is on top (head and hat picture), John Wayne in center. $10–$20. *Limited Edition Autographed Print.* 1982. The Art Merchant, Hollywood. 24″ × 30″ color montage personally signed by Roy. 1,600 exist. Advertised in magazines. Ad states that according to state law, plates must be destroyed after original print run. Contains eight photos, Republic studios stills, publicity shots. Originally $100. $150–$200; the lower numbers (if numbered) bringing the higher price. *Roy Rogers King of the Cowboys Print.* Circa 1990s. Artist: Joe Glisson. Limited edition of 300 lithographs, Roy rearing on Trigger, waving. Personally autographed by Roy Rogers, signed and numbered by artist. 100 pound Regency coated paper. 16″ × 20″. Accompanied by letter of authenticity. Originally $49.95. (Framed in golden custom-made hardwood, with print under plexiglass, $195.) *Boyhood Home of Roy Rogers in Southern Ohio.* 1982. George Little. Sold at RRDECA, possibly museum. Original painting in museum.

R. R. COWBOY **PRAYER**. 1990s. RRDE Museum. Probably the one written by William Alexander and Dale Evans for the Roy Rogers Riders Club. For unknown reason, it is signed by Dusty instead of Roy Rogers. $2–$10.

R. R. FESTIVAL **PROGRAM**. June 4, 1988. RRDECA. Program of events, luncheon menu, etc. Shawnee State University, Scioto County, OH. $5–$10.

R. R. **RESTAURANT ITEMS**. 1969–1990. Marriott Corp. In the form of standard fast food restaurant items, such as bags, cups, cardboard containers, etc., these are now being treated with some collectible value. Roy's likeness can be seen on some items such as the cardboard placemat. Average value: $5–$20.

R. R. **RESTAURANT ITEMS**. Hardee's Food Systems. Restaurant items are being collected by avid collectors, but it is too early to place a value on the Hardee's Roy Rogers Restaurant items. Items that predate the Hardee's takeover of the chain from Marriott Corp. have attained collectible status. The logo of the rising yellow sun and dark brown mountain is on nearly all items. Takeout bags (several sizes), free item coupon cards (signed and dated), French fry containers (two sizes; typical run number 18/324), fried chicken buckets and boxes (boxes replaced buckets), cups (several sizes), Roy's Roasters cups (one distributor is Fast Food Merchandisers, Rocky Mount, NC.), drink trays (U.S. Pat. No. 4,509,640), paper placemats, etc.

R. R.–DALE EVANS/MUSEUM **SCARVES**. 1980s. Roy Rogers Ent. licensed museum gift shop. Include one of several drawn likenesses of Roy and Trigger, apparently by artists Hi Mankin and Al Gleicher. (One illustration shows background of rocks; another, no background. $5 in light blue or light brown. Discontinued by fall 1987. $10–$20.

R. R. **"SCULPTOON"**: "TRIGGER'S REVENGE". Created, sculptured by Larry Shapiro of Los Angeles, CA. Constructed on life-size scale with moving parts. Coin-operated saddled Roy. For sale in 1987 for $5,000.

R. R. FESTIVAL CONDIMENT **SHAKER**. Circa 1990s. RRDECA. Blue print on glass mason-like jar (miniature) souvenir shaker. Roy Rogers Festival, Portsmouth, OH, 1991. Words "Happy Trails to You." $3–$5.

ROY AND DALE COWBOY DECORATOR **SIGNS**. 1990. Camillus Cutlery. Don Sherwood art. Artist concepts for items that may or may not have been produced. A. *Roy Rogers and Dale Evans Time for Fun Watches.* Artist: Bob Sallee. Smoky Mountain Knife Works. Possibly 12″ × 16″. Paintings by Don Sherwood and Bob Sallee. One of Dale is based on photo of her and Buttermilk on the cover of *Queen of the West, Dale Evans Comics* #22, January–March 1959. Neither these particular items, nor this sign, as depicted in the artwork, ever existed. The watches and their display boxes as they existed in the imagination of Smoky Mountain Knife Works owner Kevin G. Pipes are shown in the artwork. $10–$20. B. *Back to School with Roy and Dale.* Artist: Don Sherwood. Both brilliantly colored, high-embossed tin signs, "reproduced from rare originals." 12″ × 16¼″. 1992 price: $9.99 $10–$20.

R. R./DALE EVANS HANDPAINTED **SOCKS.** 1992. Dale Evans Handpainted Socks, California. Catalogue sales, magazine ads. Ordered by phone: (914)-763-5330. Probably sold at RRDE Museum. 100 percent mercerized cotton. Wearable art. Variety of styles, art. Originally $72 per dozen.

R. R. **SWEATSHIRTS.** "Young Rascals" crew-neck pullover, cotton/poly fleece, long sleeves. These are white with a large photo of Roy in black and signature in red. The original price in 1985 was $18. Sold through RRDECA, Portsmouth, OH.

R. R.–DALE EVANS MUSEUM **T-SHIRT.** Circa 1990s. Fruit of the Loom. Blue, perhaps other colors. Illustration of Roy rearing on Trigger below name. Sky background. RRDE Museum.

R. R.–DALE EVANS MUSEUM **T-SHIRT.** Circa 1990s. Hanes Co. White, perhaps other colors. Illustration of Roy rearing on Trigger, lariat spelling out name above. RRDE Museum.

R. R.–DALE EVANS MUSEUM **T-SHIRT.** Circa 1990s. Fruit of the Loom. Green, perhaps other colors. Illustration of Roy, Trigger, and Dale under names. RRDE Museum.

R. R. CLASSIC COMIC BOOK COVER **T-SHIRTS.** 1992. Artwear Collection. Albuquerque, NM. Sixteen designs. Originally $18.

R. R. AND DALE EVANS ADULT **T-SHIRTS/SWEATSHIRTS.** 1992. Legends Brand, Wichita Falls, TX. Mail-order. Styles/sizes: Short sleeve T-shirts in S, M, L, XL, white/natural. Long sleeve T-shirts in same sizes, white. Youth short sleeve T-shirts in 6–8, 10–12, 14–16, white. Sweatshirt in S, M, L, XL, white. Youth sweatshirt in 6–8, 10–12, 14–16. All shirts heavy weight pre-shrunk 100 percent cotton. (Sweatshirts/youth T-shirts are cotton/synthetic blend.) Youth small, 2–4, no designs. Designs: RR 001–Roy and Trigger; b&w

Republic publicity print, facsimile signature. RR 002–Roy's Trick Lasso 1952; contestant seal photo from 1952 Roy Rogers Trick Lasso contest. RR 003–Dale Evans; b&w Republic publicity print, facsimile signature. RR 004–Roy serenading Trigger; b&w Republic publicity print from 1938 film *Billy the Kid.* RR 005-Singing cowboy picture postcard; reproduction of 1940s postcard. RR 006–Portrait of young Roy, 1938 Republic Studios b&w publicity print # R.R. 1. RR 007-Shoes and Boots; ad for 1950s Roy Rogers merchandise, box front, color, Roy and Trigger. RR 008–Feedin' Trigger; 1940s color publicity print of Roy and Trigger, surrounded by artwork, from advertising on a 1950s Roy Rogers merchandise box. RR 009–*Rainbow Over Texas* movie poster; color reproduction of lobby card from Roy's 1946 film. Shows Trigger, Roy, Dale, and Gabby. RR 010–Saturday morning; color print of children sitting before television in 1950s, watching Roy, close-up of Roy's face. RR 011–Publicity poster; color or colored Republic print of Roy and Trigger, 1940s. RR 012–Settin' pretty with Trigger; 1940s Republic b&w publicity print of Roy sitting on fence, next to Trigger, surrounded with green leaves artwork. RR 013–Roy and Dale; Republic 1940s color publicity print of the pair.

R. R. T-SHIRTS PHOTO **TAG.** 1993. Artwear, Inc. Small card, with hole for attaching to garment. Comic book cover on front. The registered trademarks "Happy Trails" and the Roy Rogers facsimile signature are on back.

TAPES, AUDIO. *See* Chapter 3. $15–$40.

VIDEO/VHS **TAPES.** Republic or Paramount film titles sell for an average of $16. Some of the 1951–1957 episodes from the "Roy Rogers Show" television series can also be found in video stores for an average of $15/two episodes and are commonly seen in collector trade publications for $18–$25/four episodes, on Paramount, Critic's Choice, and other labels. Companies producing the films on VHS format are Republic Pictures, Good Times Home Video, Paramount Pictures, Concord Video, GTK, Kid's Klassics, United American Video, Hollywood Select Video, Viking Video Classics, Burbank Video, MNTex Entertainment,

Inter Global Video, All Occasion Video, the Congress Video Group, Silver Screen Video, Front Row Entertainment, and Parade Video. As previously mentioned, many of the films and television series, like much that has to do with the Roy Rogers of the 1940s–1950s, are in public domain. Some of the tapes are of good quality; some are inferior. Some are the original uncut full-length versions (60–70 plus minutes), while others (most) are the ones Republic trimmed down to 54 minutes for television. Most of the packaging makes for a nice collectible piece, and a few offer very good painted likenesses of Roy or exceptionally nice pictures. In the spring of 1993, Republic marketed a new "All-American Series," which featured twelve Roy Rogers films.

R. R. RESTAURANT BOLO TIE. 1970s. A part of the uniform of restaurant employees. Brown nylon cord with metal disc keeper (slide) with sunset scene logo. $20–$40.

R. R. TISSUE HOLDERS. 1994. No further information.

R. R. TOWELS. 1994. No further information.

HOLLYWOOD WALK OF FAME **TRADING CARDS.** 1990s. Possibly Chamber of Commerce. One card in set shows Dale in blue-fringed Western attire, another has Roy in the yellow/brown blue suede fringed attire. Either card is $2–$5.

U.S. HISTORICAL SOCIETY, ANTIQUE ARMS COMMISSION; COLOR BROCHURE. Roy's picture. 1991. $2–$5.

R R. **WASTE CANS.** No further information.

R. R. **WATCH.** It was reported that these watches were never in production, but samples were made. (This can make them very collectible.) Adults': quartz, with Bullet also appearing, cost $60. Matched goldtone case, quartz, sweep second-hand, water resistant, $30. (Men's: black case, strap; Women's: smaller with white case, strap.) These come in see-through box.

R. R. & TRIGGER "KING OF THE COWBOYS" **WRISTWATCH.** 1993. Fossil Co. Hong Kong. Face artwork is reproduction of 1950s Ingraham watch: Roy next to Trigger, names at bottom. "Vintage Styled Timepiece." Genuine leather band with western style stitching. Limited edition: 10,000. Certificate of authenticity. Fancy display box contains R. R. & Trigger bandanna and pop-up art. *See also* Bandannas. Watch: $75–$100. Box: $10–$20. Bandanna: $10–$20. Set: $100–$150.

R. R. AND DALE EVANS LCD **WRISTWATCH.** 1985. Bradley Time/Elgin National Industries. Licensed by Roy Rogers Enterprises, Victorville, CA. Available from the Roy Rogers–Dale Evans Collectors Association in 1986. Discontinued by spring of 1987. The boys' and girls' watches are digital, with the classic "Roy rearing on Trigger" pose on the face and ran around $20 at that time. (Tan plastic case, matching strap.) The children's watches are digital, metal case and brown strap, with Roy, Dale, and Trigger on face, for $10. These come in blister packaging, with same drawing, Roy rearing on horse.

NOTES

Chapter 1

1. All published materials seen by this writer, except for those originating in Ohio, have used the Slye spelling. Recorded documents as early as 1916 show the Sly spelling. A check of Hamilton County records for the 1920s and 1930s shows Slye, and not Sly, to be a fairly common name. Although it may not apply in this instance, it was a common practice for families to alter the spelling of their name to make it clear that they were not related to others with the name. Birth certificates, state of Ohio. Three out of four of the Womack children's birth records show Carter County, Kentucky. One shows adjacent Boyd County, Kentucky.

2. Birth certificate No. 109946, state of Ohio. Apparently there was no record of the birth in 1906. The court was shown facts that resulted in this birth being recorded April 19, 1943. Elmer Sword, *Roy Rogers Hometown Photo Album* (Portsmouth, Ohio: Portsmouth Area Recognition Society, 1982).

3. Birth certificate No. 6192/27, state of Ohio.

4. Birth certificate No. 6245, state of Ohio. About the time of Leonard's first feature film, Republic Pictures publicity department created Cody, Wyoming, as his birthplace. This story appeared in: *Movies Magazine*, November 1940; *Hollywood Magazine*, December 1941; and *Who's Who in Hollywood Magazine*, 1941. In the early years of Roy Rogers' career, 1912 was given as his birth year, and to this day, this date remains in many reference books. Even the "This Is Your Life" television show on which Roy was honored in 1953 used the erroneous date.

5. Even in later years, there remained an extremely close resemblance. An article "Hook, Line and Snowman" in *TV Pictorial* 2, no. 1 (February 1956) shows the two fishing together circa late 1955. Some articles state the Indian blood was on the father's side. *The Mountain Broadcast and Prairie Recorder*, March 1946, article states that the Indian blood was on the mother's side and that his other early forebears were Irish.

6. *TV Western Roundup* 1, no. 1 (1957) states

that Rogers' great-great-grandmother was a member of the Choctaw Indian tribe.

7. Elise Miller Davis, *The Answer Is God* (New York: McGraw-Hill, 1955).

8. "Hero of the Badlands," *Movies* 5, no. 12 (June 1942). According to another account, Andy had opened his own business close to Cincinnati. Leonard's birth certificate lists his father's occupation as "shoe laster." Rovin, Jeff. *Country Music Babylon* (New York: St. Martin's Press, 1993) Rovin states Andy was a guitar-maker. First time this has been seen in print.

9. Davis, *The Answer Is God*. This was a family residence either at this time or when Andy and Leonard returned here to live in 1928.

10. Davis, *The Answer Is God*. Telephone conversation with friend of Sly family, March 13, 1992, discussing Cleda (Roy's sister) and ideas that some might have gotten about her dad because of these changes in jobs. It is this author's conclusion that the Slys appear to have been a very proud and close family, with a history of hard work during some very tough times. Roy is quoted by Louella Parsons in *Photoplay*, April 1947, as stating that he never had a pair of shoes until he was almost twelve.

11. Anonymous telephone conversation, March 13, 1992. It was amazing what this blind uncle was capable of doing with his hands and tools. Sword, *Hometown Photo Album*, says that Will, also called "Bill," was blinded at age seven when a mixture of dirt and glass was thrown in his eyes.

12. In a Cincinnati, Ohio, radio station interview in late 1991, Roy stated that it was a year and a half before they moved onto the houseboat, which would place this event around the spring of 1913. Published/recorded interviews have produced conflicting statements. Irwin Stambler and Grelun Landon, *The Encyclopedia of Folk, Country and Western Music,* 1969, give Leonard seven years in Cincinnati and then place him on "a farm near Portsmouth," so these authors skip entirely over Portsmouth itself. A Scripps-Howard News Service article, circa 1986, shows five years on the houseboat (one in Cincinnati, four in Portsmouth). After examining scores of published accounts, this author believes that the time

Leonard actually spent on the houseboat was roughly seven years.

13. Birth certificate No. 48, state of Texas. Certificate shows that Lucille was born to F. Hillman Smith and Bettie Sue Wood Smith. See also, Dale Evans Rogers *The Woman at the Well* (Old Tappan, NJ.: Revell, 1970). Roy Rogers and Dale Evans Rogers, with Jane and Michael Stern, *Happy Trails: Our Life Story* (New York: Simon & Schuster, 1994). Book leaves out any reference to Lucille Wood Smith and birthdate of Oct. 30, 1912.

14. Dale Evans Rogers, *Woman at the Well*.

15. Roy Rogers and Dale Evans Rogers, with Carlton Stowers, *The Story of Roy Rogers and Dale Evans–Happy Trails* (Waco, TX: Word Books, 1979).

16. Marriage certificate, Leonard and Arline, 1946. Correct spelling, by her own account, is Arline. Most published sources from 1943 on have shown the spelling as "Arlene," including Roy and Dale's *Happy Trails* book. The "Arlene" spelling may have begun with the July 1943 *Life* magazine article. *Roy Rogers Own Songs*, American Music, 1943, shows proper spelling. Death certificate No. 17402, state of California, shows "Arlene" spelling.

17. Birth certificate No. 48782/352, state of Ohio.

18. According to Rogers and Rogers, *Happy Trails*, the houseboat was moved to Mill Street. During my visit to Portsmouth, however, a longtime resident active in the Roy Rogers hometown activities stated that he had no recollection of the houseboat ever having been on Mill Street. He had never seen it, and fancied himself a local historian. In a telephone conversation on March 23, 1992, an anonymous Portsmouth resident told me that the houseboat remained in this area until about the mid–1960s, when Roy decided to move it to his museum in California. Roy's fans had already discovered it, however, and stripped it for souvenirs. The years had also taken a toll on it. It simply was in no condition to be moved and was subsequently torn down. Len's Uncle Will, who had remained living in it, died in the late 1950s or early 1960s.

19. Sword, *Hometown Photo Album*. The Union Street school burned in 1929 and was replaced with the U.S. Grant School.

20. Feg Murray's "Seein' Stars," June 30, 1940, stated that Roy's ambition was to become a minister.

21. Roy in "Roy Rogers King of the Cowboys" (AMC-TV, 1992.) See also, Rogers and Rogers, *Happy Trails*. Roy's publicity writer describes Duck Run as a "shambles community" in *20th Annual Rodeo Magazine* (Madison Square Garden), vol. 19 (1945) and states that it could not be found on any map. The author has been told that the site of the farm, where the old house still sits, is actually not in Duck Run. The farm is located in a hollow in a rural area surrounded by tiny communities, one of which is Duck Run. See also, Robert Joseph, *Movies Magazine* 5, no. 12 (June 1942). This interesting account skips the move to Portsmouth and has Len moving from Cincinnati to a "small community near Rushtown, Ohio" at the age of two months. According to Douglas Green, *Country Music Magazine*, [The Slys] moved to Portsmouth, and then to Duck Run on the Ohio River." Portsmouth, not Duck Run, is on the Ohio. The *18th Annual Rodeo Magazine* (Madison Square Garden Rodeo) 1943, notes that a nearby neighbor was Branch Rickey, who would later play for the Brooklyn Dodgers.

22. *Roy Rogers: A Man from Duck Run,* Capitol record LP ST-785. According to the liner notes, Roy helped his dad build this house when he was eleven (which would make it the fall of 1922). Davis, *Answer Is God*, places the house building about 1919, when the Slys moved and describes it as a little boxlike, six-room farmhouse. Len would have been eight at this time. According to Rogers and Rogers, *Happy Trails*, they made the move in 1919 and "with the help of relatives and his children," the house was built. According to the author's telephone conversation with an anonymous respondent, a structure existed on this same site when the Slys arrived and they simply built onto it. One must keep in mind, when researching Sly family/Rogers history in the Portsmouth area, that different factions connected with Rogers history/publicity/events, etc., do not get along well with one another, and have been sort of feuding now for several years. This appears to be widely known, and apparently jealousy is involved. As a result of the conflict, a researcher is subject to receiving conflicting information from the various sources. This has been the experience of this researcher. This has also resulted in some informants choosing anonymity, or my choosing to show them as "anonymous."

23. Rogers and Rogers, *Happy Trails*.

24. *Movies*, June 1942.

25. Roy is credited in many published sources with being an expert with a gun, a bow and arrow, or a slingshot. *Movies Magazine,* November 1940, contains an incredible story of a Republic Studios publicity man allowing Roy to shoot an apple off of his head with a bow and arrow. Supposedly, the photographer dared Roy to do this, and then after it was over, the publicity man fainted.

26. Telephone conversation with an anonymous Portsmouth resident, March 1992. Roy, in Griffith interview, places it 1921–1922.

27. According to the Stowell article, "Uncle Bill" taught Andy to play and even performed with him and a couple of others, and Andy passed his teaching on to Len. Laurence Zwisohn, in his article "Roy Rogers" in *The Journal of the American Academy for the Preservation of Old-Time Country Music*, December 1992, says that

Len and the girls used yodeling to call to each other across the fields.

28. Divorce documents, Fox vs. Fox, 1929, state of Tennessee.

29. Davis, *The Answer Is God.*

30. Rogers and Rogers, *Happy Trails.*

31. Rogers, *Woman at the Well.* All published source materials avoided the husband's first name until *Only One Star,* where Dale revealed the full name of her son, which produces the assumption that the father's name was Thomas Frederick Fox. This researcher discovered the name Thomas for the husband for the first time on the divorce petition filed in Memphis. In *Happy Trails: Our Life Story,* 1994, Dale finally names her "first steady boyfriend" as "Thomas Fox." She states that he was 18 years old. Birth certificate no. 61433, state of Tennessee, shows date of birth as April 11, 1909. In "In the Hands of the Potter" (Rogers, 1994), Dale states that this ex-husband later became an alcoholic, married several more times, badly mistreated all of his wives, and eventually committed suicide, when his sister refused to go fishing with him. This is the first time this information has appeared in print. Research continuing.

32. Dale Evans Rogers, with Fritz Ridenour, *Only One Star* (Dallas: Word Books, 1988).

33. The author checked marriage records in a dozen counties in Arkansas, Missouri, and Tennessee, as well as in each state capitol. No record is found of this marriage. It was common then, as today, for couples from Arkansas and Tennessee to go into Missouri to marry, where the laws were less stringent.

34. Birth certificate No. 4192, state of Tennessee. Rogers, *Only One Star.* She is residing at 900 Faxon St.

35. Although music played a large part in family and social life in the hills, Len never really played in a professional sense until he left Ohio, according to numerous print sources, including *DISCoveries* interview, October 1992.

36. Stowell. Uncle Bill is quoted as saying Len's favorite numbers were "Chicken in the Bread Pan, Pickin' Out Dough" and "Granny, Will Your Dog Bite?" Author's note: Some of Len's early musical influences were probably medicine shows. These shows traveled the roads peddling their wares through the more populated areas such as Cincinnati. These minstrels hawked products to the tunes of fiddle, guitar, banjo, and mandolins, playing the latest songs of the day and giving local residents a chance to learn the new songs and buy what they wanted as well.

37. Stowell article quotes Uncle Bill as saying Andy Sly bought Len a saddle horse to ride back and forth to McDermott High School and that he had only ridden mules prior to this time. So we have the saddleless mare in earlier years (about the time of his twelfth birthday) vs. the saddle horse in the high school years 1925–28. The saddle horse will seldom be mentioned in later articles and interviews.

"This Is Your Life" television show, 1953. Robert Joseph, *Movies Magazine,* June 1942, states that Roy bought the guitar from a pawn shop *after* arriving in Los Angeles, using part of his first week's salary as a truck driver. Roy is quoted as saying: "I used to pass it every day in the truck, and the blamed thing shined in the window." As many sources mention the Ohio guitar, if this event transpired, it was his second instrument. It is mentioned in at least one source that the guitar was taken along on the Ohio-California trip. Joseph states Roy took lessons through a correspondence course. *17th Annual Rodeo Magazine* (1942, Roy's publicity department) indicates course was completed in California.

38. Stowell. The Crabtrees remain numerous in the Portsmouth area and still reside in the old homeplace, as witnessed by author in recent visit.

39. Roy is quoted as telling a slightly different story in the Joseph article in *Movies Magazine*: "I left high school and decided to forsake the farm. I loved the country and outdoor life. But I watched my pa work his life away, making a bitter living out of the soil. I decided to hit it out for Cincinnati. I was a gangling kid, too big for my own size. I didn't know a thing about the city. I just knew I wanted to be there. I guess you'd call me a hick." This could be the 1910 Ohio Street address.

40. Petition for divorce No. 27688, Circuit Court of Shelby County, Tennessee. Filed May 4, 1929. Dale states in *Happy Trails* that Tommy was six and a half months old at the time, and that her brother-in-law and his wife took her to Memphis.

41. According to books by Dale Evans Rogers, she pleaded to no avail for him to give the marriage a second chance. In *Happy Trails* Dale describes her husband pleading for her to return, but she refuses.

42. Petition for divorce No. 27688, Circuit Court of Tennessee. Filed May 4, 1929. In Rogers, *Woman at the Well,* Frances Fox appears to move to Memphis after the divorce, but the divorce was filed and granted in Memphis. In Memphis she may have used the stage name "Fanny Fox."

43. "This Is Your Life" television show. Roy has stated often that at the time of their move to California in 1930, they hadn't seen Mary "in six years." Writer David Rothel, who interviewed Roy at the time of his writing *The Singing Cowboys,* used the term "late 1920s" for when Mary married (apparently in Ohio) and moved to California. In a *Photoplay* article, Roy is quoted as saying that his two sisters married at age 14. See also, Cincinnati radio interview.

In *Happy Trails,* Carlton Stowers states that the California trip took place in the spring of 1930. About an equal number of sources, including magazine articles, television shows, books, and recorded and published interviews have used

1929 or 1930. All the above sources also differ on whose idea it was to leave Ohio for California.

44. Some reports say that there were two cars. In *Happy Trails*, Roy refers to the Dodge as a jalopy, and so does Davis in *The Answer Is God*. But Davis goes on to say they used a truck when they were picking peaches. According to Roy and Andy on "This Is Your Life" television show, the drive was made with two vehicles, the "other one" first, possibly the Maxwell, and "this one," the 1923 Dodge pickup truck that was on the show, which was picked up en route after the other one played out. *The Mountain Broadcast and Prairie Recorder,* March 1946, states that Leonard's first trip to California was made in an old jalopy with an uncle. Some pure publicity, *Who's Who in Hollywood* 1, no. 11 (1956), states that "Back in '29, Roy worked his way west as a fruit picker, truck driver, and road builder."

45. Davis, *Answer Is God*, says that in 1954 the Dodge division of the Chrysler Corp. took over the vehicle for museum purposes. Today at least one of the two vehicles is in the Roy Rogers-Dale Evans Museum in Victorville, California.

46. *17th Annual Rodeo Magazine* (Madison Square Garden, 1942). An article that was probably written by Roy Rogers's publicity agent states that he went west to "take up cattle punching." This article has him driving a truck in Cincinnati.

47. It is now thought that the family used the 1923 Dodge truck to make this return trip to Ohio. In his Miller interview, Roy stated that they arrived back in Ohio in October.

48. Most sources state that he was able to go along by offering to "help out with the driving." It is assumed this trip was made in the car belonging to his sister's father-in-law. The *DISCoveries* interview states that he "hitched a ride," evidently a figure of speech.

49. McDowell interview.

50. Roy, in "Roy Rogers King of the Cowboys" (AMC-TV). I have never seen this in print. They were doing migrant farm work, and money apparently was very scarce. The first mention I have seen of a motorcycle is a source that states that he and his cousin tied their instruments onto the handlebars of a motorcycle. Roy had a lifelong love affair with motorcycles.

51. Johns was possibly 24 or 25. Divorce documents show that he was seven years older than Frances. Divorce documents filed May 13, 1936. Johns vs. Johns, No. 246-832, Jefferson Co., Kentucky. Also copy of letter from John T. Pigott, Jr., with Gibson, Dunn & Crutcher, law firm, to Clerk, Jefferson County, Kentucky, dated June 8, 1953, on file. Also copy of letter from Father F. X. Simcox, with Sacred Heart Mission, Waus, Mississippi, to Clerk, Jefferson County, Kentucky, dated November 19, 1954. Additional Simcox letter, dated December 3, 1954, both on file. All letters are part of public documents.

52. Marriage license No. 695362, Shelby County, Tennessee.

53. The exact time of this move is impossible to pin down despite the numerous accounts. It is calculated to be late 1930, but at this time the move itself remains undocumented. No published account seen by this researcher mentions her marriage to Johns. In *Happy Trails* the move to Chicago is placed immediately after seeing husband Tom for the last time, before her divorce is final, and after all her Memphis radio work. No mention is made here either, of August W. Johns. See also, *Motion Picture*, September 1944. According to studio publicity, Dale Evans Rogers was born on a cotton farm outside Dallas, was christened Fanny Octavia Smith, moved to Uvalde, got discovered, knocked about as a band canary, went to Chicago, toured, married Dale Butts in 1938, moved to an eight-room Spanish home in Westwood, California, made films, and made music with her husband, and yearned to be an advertising executive.

54. Stowell article. See also, Rogers and Rogers, *Happy Trails*. In 1979 the place still belonged to the Hiles family.

55. Marriage license, Leonard Slye, 1933. The DePew address is the one listed.

56. According to the liner notes for *The Man from Duck Run*, Capitol LP, this took place in 1930, but that doesn't agree with *Happy Trails* or *The Answer Is God*. It is stated in at least one source that this type of work lasted about two months.

57. Some sources state that Len and Andy and his cousin Stanley worked in the peach orchards. In their book *Sixgun Heroes*, Theodore L. Hake and Robert D. Cauler add grapes to the farm labor jobs of the trio, but this is the only mention of grapes discovered. An article in *20th Annual Rodeo Magazine* (Madison Square Garden, 1943), vol. 19, states that Len also worked as a tourist guide.

58. *Modern Screen*, November 1955.

59. Photo with captions published in numerous magazines.

60. Some sources date this as early as 1929, *Movie Life Yearbook*, 1946. Some accounts place it in 1931, others in 1932. The *DISCoveries* interview differs with all others, stating he was 18 at this time. The station was KMCS or KMIC Radio according to the *DISCoveries* interview, October 1991. Roy in an interview in late 1991 on WOAI Radio, Portsmouth, Ohio, gave the hours.

61. *Modern Screen* article, November 1955, *Happy Trails*, and *DISCoveries*, October 1991, vary from "several days later" to "next day" to "two days later." "King of the Cowboys" (AMC-TV, 1992): Roy identifies the man as Ed Bohlin (the spelling of his name is unclear). Bohlin became a major producer of silver-laden show saddles during the heyday of the silver screen cowboys. In a *Pulse* magazine, November 1991,

Griffith interview, Roy states: "To this day, I still don't remember what songs I sang, I was so scared. But I had a yodel in it, and they took my name and address." In the Miller interview, the manager's name was spelled "Ed Bowen." (This could be correct, but this interview contains many inaccuracies, such as "Saul Siegel" for Republic producer.)

62. This is the order of events related in most works that treat the subject in depth. It is often condensed and rearranged, however, as can be seen in the *Modern Screen* version of 1932:
    1. *Midnight Frolic* radio program.
    2. Several days later, agent called.
    3. Same agent needed singer for the Rocky Mountaineers.
    4. Performed in this group over KGER.
The Capitol Records LP *Man from Duck Run* liner notes, "Len and some other guys formed a group, The Rocky Mountaineers."

63. *Modern Screen*, November 1955, "The Truth About My First Wife." *Happy Trails* leaves out any reference to Len's first wife, as does Davis' *The Answer Is God*, published the same year as the magazine article that addresses the subject head on. The article, however, appears to be the only source revealing a "first wife" to any extent. The subject is given two sentences in Rothel's *The Roy Rogers Book*. For Lucile's address, see Marriage license No. 8928, Document No. 1744 (33-026092), Orange County, California. All other published matter author has seen shows Lucile being from Wilmington in Orange County. It is not known precisely when Len added the "e" to his surname, but it appears as early as this document.

64. Leonard Slye's "Affidavit of Husband No. D-124587," Los Angeles Superior Court, September 11, 1934.

65. According to Rogers and Rogers, *Happy Trails*, Nolan joined shortly after Len did but left because paydays were few and far between.

66. *Western Stars*, November 1948, gives Nolan the credit for placing this ad, but this seems to be the only instance of this statement and the article was full of misinformation.

67. In *Happy Trails*, Roy states that several of the others lived with him and his wife in a small house. Davis, *The Answer Is God*: "The rest of the gang bunked and boarded in his small cottage." In *Modern Screen*, November 1955, Roy is quoted as saying, "I moved in with the banjo player and two other musicians in South Los Angeles, and we slept crowded together on a cot and a couch we shoved together."

68. A photograph of the group in *Movie Life Yearbook*, 1947, shows Len, "Professor," Bob Nolan, "Slumber," "Hi," and "Lefty." It was very common in these times for all hillbilly or Western music entertainers to use nicknames, a tradition that has been witnessed heavily in Western Swing music groups from the 1930s to present day.

69. William Witney, *Trigger Remembered* (Toney, AL.: Earl Blair Enterprises, 1989). Also, letter to the author from Roy A. and Lexy Cloud, January 20, 1995.

70. In *The Woman at the Well*, Dale states that she spent "a few short years" in Chicago. She places her return in the same year as when she went to Louisville. No mention is made of Johns in any account. *Happy Trails* has her still in Chicago 1931-1932, working at Goodyear Co. as a file clerk. She states she and son Tommy returned to Texas on a train, paid for by her mother. After two weeks in the hospital and three months' rest, she and Tommy went to Louisville.

71. Johns vs. Johns divorce documents. In Frances Johns' "Deposition for Plaintiff No. 246 832," taken May 22, 1936, she refers to a "nervous breakdown" due to abuse of her and the child by her husband.

72. *Modern Screen*, November 1955.

73. Ibid.

74. No mention of this marriage has been found in any of the stories created by the Republic Studios publicity department, the information put together by Roy Rogers publicity people, press stories, magazine articles and biographers, until 1955, when apparently someone got wind of it and the *Modern Screen* article was written. The *Modern Screen* article is supposedly in Roy's own words, but it is a curious piece for what it leaves out more than for what it says. I found no other mention of this marriage until David Rothel's, *The Roy Rogers Book* (Madison, NC: Empire, 1987). Roy still documents Arline as his first wife, and spells her name "Arlene." Lucile Ascolese is not mentioned in either of two recently published biographies. He still refers to Arline as his first wife in interviews.

75. Documents and *Modern Screen*, November 1955, indicate that it was almost immediately after the wedding.

76. "Barnstorming" has always been a part of life for such entertainers. It involved playing one-night stands (or several nights) in town after town. Information from the Cincinnati Radio Interview provides the fall of 1931 or 1932 as the date of the tour. All documents support 1932.

77. Almost all the printed source material in the author's personal collection give this duration for the tour. In *Modern Screen*, November 1955, Roy states that it was six weeks before he saw his wife again. A document pertaining to case "No. D 124587, Superior Court, Los Angeles County, Lucille Slye vs. Leonard Slye, Complaint for Separate Maintenance/Leonard Slye vs. Lucille Slye, Cross-Complaint," filed August 29/September 5, 1934, indicates that the length of time was two months. The Zwisohn article relates that Len returned in September.

78. *Modern Screen*, November 1955. Davis, *The Answer Is God*, states that this latest band name wasn't even decided upon until their trip was well under way, so it is not known under what

name the agent was supposed to be advertising their performance tour. It was probably the "International Cowboys" name, however, which had been the band's name prior to the tour.

79. The *Modern Screen*, November 1955, article, written eight years after Roy's marriage to Dale Evans, is unique in that it addresses his first marriage, but completely leaves out any reference to the second one, which almost every fan in 1955 was aware of, the one to Arline Wilkins that lasted over ten years, from 1936 to 1946, when Roy Rogers was widowed. He and Arline filled the pages of many film magazines during those years. This magazine article leaves out Roswell, New Mexico, entirely and ends the tour in Lubbock, Texas, where the band heads back to California. All other articles leave out Lucile Ascolese.

80. Robert Joseph, *Movies Magazine,* June 1942, states that they borrowed a gun from the owner of a gasoline station and hunted jackrabbits with it. It also quotes Roy as saying they borrowed bread from the same fellow to go with their rabbit and carrots.

81. One source states that Arline lived across the street from the radio station. Another states that she drove to the station. Yet another published article quotes Roy saying it was a cake rather than a pie. The Smith article is in *Life* magazine, July 12, 1943, states that the pies were taken to the auto-camp. A photo, apparently taken that day, was used in "Roy Rogers King of the Cowboys" (AMC-TV) and shows Roy with Arline, her mother, and what looks like her entire family by their automobile. Roy, in the AMC-TV film, sums up this Roswell, New Mexico, story by saying, "and that's how I got my *first* wife, Arline" (author's italics). The author had, however, provided the information about Roy Rogers preceding wife to producer Len Morris of Galen Films, the producer of the documentary, while the author was serving as a research consultant.

82. According to Roy in *Modern Screen*, November, 1955, they went on to Lubbock, Texas, where they finally called it quits. In the AMC-TV film, Roy stated that they played Texas.

83. Republic Studio's publicity that was generated almost immediately after they released his first feature film includes the Cody, Wyoming, story and probably the real cowboy on a ranch story. According to Robert Joseph, *Movies Magazine,* June 1942, Roy went to work on the Sutherland Ranch right after he met Arline in Roswell (June 1933), stayed there for one year, and then headed to California. *Western Stars*, November 1948, states that the ranch work took place in Arizona. *Movie Life*, January 1945, suggests "a resort near Grand Canyon." *The Mountain Broadcast and Prairie Recorder*, March 1946, states that the ranch job occurred after the Rocky Mountaineers broke up. Then after a year on the ranch, Len became a tour guide for the Grand Canyon Tours. It is possible that some time was

spent on the ranch, but it is hard to see how the time spent could have possibly been anything close to a year, especially if the ranch was in New Mexico. If the ranch was in California, then Len could have worked there many hours in his spare time. The *17th Annual Rodeo Magazine* of Madison Square Garden even hints that Roy competed in rodeo events such as bull riding, bronc riding, steer wrestling, etc., prior to 1942, but states he was "through with that" (competing). According to *The Western Horseman*, April 1961, the ranch work took place while he was in his teens. By the end of 1931, one year after he arrived in California, Len was 20 years of age. That year and the previous ones are accounted for in all published materials and allow no time for ranch work. This article places the ranch experience right before his job picking fruit. It also mentions that Len sold shoes, but it is the first instance I have seen of this work.

In his book *Riders of the Range*, Kalton C. Lahue states that Len played neighborhood square dances while "he learned the western skills of roping and riding." *Movie Teen*, April-June 1947, places the ranch at which Roy worked in New Mexico. *Movie Fan Album* 1 (Winter 1946) places it in Montana. *17th Annual Rodeo Magazine* (Madison Square Garden, 1942) places the ranch in New Mexico. They quote Roy as saying, "we would go back punching cows and start out again as soon as we got fed up and a few dollars in our pockets."

84. *Modern Screen*, November 1955, "The Truth About My First Wife" by Roy Rogers.

85. The pay for this work? The *DISCoveries* interview, October, 1992, states that it was $14 a week. Rogers and Rogers, *Happy Trails*, say "no pay," and Davis, *The Answer Is God*, says, "little more than his supper."

86. An article by Rich Kienzle, "The Sons of the Pioneers," in *Country Music*, September-October 1987, states: "Nolan returned to a full-time job, but Slye and Spencer lured him away from his work to try performing again."

87. Kienzle places this in the fall of 1933.

88. The house has been described in all previously published material as having been on Bronson Avenue, which is close to Tamarind.

89. *Modern Screen*, November 1955. Court documents show that KFWB was located at the intersection of Bronson Avenue and Sunset Boulevard at the time.

90. Court records, statement by Leonard.

91. Ibid.

92. Ibid.

93. Rogers, *The Woman at the Well*.

94. Only Mrs. W. H. Smith is mentioned in Johns vs. Johns documents. Frances stated in 1936 that her son was with her mother in Irene, Texas. In *Happy Trails*, Dale states that she and her son returned to Texas from Louisville contradicting court documents.

95. Divorce documents. Also correspondence with the Louisville Free Public Library, April 1993. There was no residential listing in 1933-1935, for Mr. and or Mrs. August, A. W. or A. Johns. According to *Happy Trails*, she worked with a group "Romeos of Song" and with "Honey and the Flapjacks."

96. *Movie Life Yearbook*, 1946. Photograph of early group shows them in hillbilly attire, clowning for camera.

97. This was a common practice at the time, as it permitted the station to sound as if they had more acts than they actually had, thus creating more shows and more sponsors.

98. Court documents.

99. Court documents; statement by Lucile.

100. Court documents, Complaint for Separate Maintenance No. D-124587, Lucile Slye, plaintiff.

101. Possibly August 8; sources disagree.

102. Court documents, Case No. D-124587.

103. Ibid.

104. Ibid.

105. Ibid.

106. Court documents indicate that Bob Nolan was the only person living with him. Fifteen other boarders were living in the dwelling. Vernon Spencer and Hugh Farr had different phone numbers, another indication they were not residing here (*1993 Edition, The Thomas Guide, Los Angeles County Street Guide and Directory*).

107. Court documents. In Kelly interview, Roy is quoted as saying, "$9.00 a week for room and board."

108. Helen Weller, *Motion Picture*, November 1944. According to this article profiling Arline, she invented the excuse of attending school in order to see Roy after corresponding with him for a year. The article states that two years later they were married. (The wedding took place in June 1936.) Weller's article states that Arline appeared in L.A. in 1936 on "vacation." Weller states that when Len left Roswell, an understanding had sprung up, and the first year of their courtship was conducted by letter.

109. According to the Griffith interview, Roy stated that they remained in this capacity during 1934, 1935, and 1936.

110. *Movie Life Yearbook*, 1946. It is not known if this is the Ford Tudor Sedan. Roy was still wearing non-Western clothes at the time when he was not performing.

111. Will Rogers died in 1935 in an air crash in Alaska, with aviator Wiley Post.

112. WAOI interview. This has been often told, but a sworn affidavit made September 11, 1934, shows that he was spending $3 per month replying to fan mail.

113. Rich Kienzle. This film probably starred El Brendel. See Monroe article, *Movies* magazine, November 1940. This is the first mention of the film that the author has encountered. Siegel and

Siegel discounted everything prior to *Tumbling Tumbleweeds*.

114. Court documents. The real estate was a 40-acre tract in the county of Riverside, in the state of California.

115. Marriage License No. 6224, book L, page 509, Chaves County, New Mexico. According to sources having visited the Roy Rogers–Dale Evans Museum lately, the date of this marriage is shown there in large print as June 14, 1937, but every published source shows the date as June 14, 1936. Roy has always referred to Arline as his first wife. Len wore non-Western formal attire for the wedding vows.

116. Rogers, *The Woman at the Well*.

117. In a 1991 interview with Jackson Griffith, Roy said they went to work at KNX, a 50,000 watt station, in 1937. There have been a number of sources showing 1936.

118. Affidavit, interrogatory, and deposition, Frances O. Johns. Interrogatory, Mrs. John Brand stetter, friend for 1½ years, 502 Wendover Avenue, Louisville.

119. Divorce documents, Case No. 246832. Jefferson County, Kentucky, Circuit Court. In *Happy Trails*, Dale not only omits August Johns, but offers new account of next husband, R. Dale Butts, and her marrying in Dallas. In fact, he is not even mentioned by name.

120. *The Western Horseman*, April 1961, places the event in a "music store." The cowboy's name was Carter, according to Wm. Witney, *Trigger Remembered*, and according to Roy's account related by Bob Pontes in *Westerns and Serials* magazine 40 (Spring 1993). A totally different version of how Len got his break with Republic comes from cowboy star Ray "Crash" Corrigan, who took credit for introducing Roy to Siegel while the cowboy was working on his ranch. After much insistence on Corrigan's part, Siegel watched Len do some trick mounts and hired him. This story is told in the *Westerns and Serials* article by Pontes.

121. *Movies*, November 1940. An article by Don Monroe states that Siegel came upon Len sitting out in front of the casting department on the curb.

122. In *The Encyclopedia of Hollywood*, Scott and Barbara Siegel state that Len was a singer using the name of Dick Weston "long before he became an actor."

123. According to Witney, *Trigger Remembered*, Roy's contract was a "stock" contract, not known for its high pay or long term; it was a form of conditional contract.

124. Rogers and Rogers, *Happy Trails*. In an article in *The Western Horseman*, April 1961, Valentry gives the salary as $100 per week.

125. ARC would later become Columbia Records, but at this time the company issued records on numerous labels such as Oriole and Perfect.

126. "I Lived a Lie" (*Photoplay*, April 1948), by Dale Evans, as told to Erskine Johnson. Similar to Roy's "The Truth About My First Wife," muddies the waters even more by offering autobiographical detail totally out of accord with that related in numerous later books by Dale, and all other articles. Not only is the previous marriage to Johns still omitted as always, but the article skips the trip to Chicago from Memphis, has her returning home to Texas, then going to Louisville, Kentucky, to work, then back to Dallas, Texas, where she states that she met Robert Dale Butts. Other incredible information includes instead of divorcing her son's father, Thomas Fox (here the marriage is given as January 1927), she is *left a widow* at age seventeen (1929-1930). Supposedly in her own words, this article reveals "the whole story," but is an obvious attempt by Dale and or the studio to deal with Hollywood's discovery of her grown son, and in doing so, offers another of the many contrasting versions of her past.

Chapter 2

1. See Chapter 10. There are conflicting published and filmed accounts pertaining to the horse and to his age.

2. By 1942 articles with correct information on Roy's heritage appeared: *Movies*, June 1942, and *17th Annual Rodeo Magazine* (Madison Square Garden, 1942). Wyoming was stuck in Roy's publicity story as part of the 1933 Southwest tour, however.

3. *Film Illustrated Monthly*, May 1949.

4. Los Angeles Superior Court, County Records Center, Case #C-431373. Certified copies. Telephone conversation February 17, 1993.

5. *Variety* magazine. Evidence prepared by vaudeville Rogers for use in court included photos of his name on marquees in major cities; newspaper theater ads for his show by RKO, Paramount, and other circuits in New York, San Francisco, Vancouver, Buffalo, London, etc.; and a multitude of press clippings and ads from 1932 to 1937. Republic should have been aware of this actor.

6. Elise Miller Davis, *The Answer Is God* (New York: McGraw-Hill, 1955).

7. Roy and Dale Rogers, with Carlton Stowers, *Happy Trails* (Waco, TX: Word Books, 1979).

8. George E. Pitman, of Western Bit, Spur, and Cowboy Collectibles, San Gabriel, California, discussed Roy's saddles with me in correspondence dated December 18, 1992. I first heard of the "Dick Dixon model" in this letter. Mervin Bendewald, cowboy collector/dealer, New York City, also provided information.

9. William Witney, *Trigger Remembered* (Toney, AL: Earl Blair Enterprises, 1989).

10. Author's personal collection. This is probably the first example of early "pure" publicity; it states that Roy got his start "when a customer heard him singing in a shoemaker's shop, where he was carving out soles."

11. *Movie Life*, March 1948, stated that Dale was 5'2" tall, weighed 110 pounds, and had brown hair and green eyes. Most sources mentioning her early years refer to auburn hair and green eyes. Color photos show her with red, orange-red, and blonde hair.

12. George Shute, "Feud for Thought," *Real Screen Fun* (June 1939). Phillips Archives.

13. Elmer Sword, *Roy Rogers Hometown Photo Album* (Portsmouth, OH: Portsmouth Area Recognition Society, 1982). The theater was located at 718 Chillicothe Street; it was closed in 1958.

14. Sword, *Hometown Photo Album*. Numerous published photos document this visit.

15. According to Glenn Randall, he was hired as Roy's horse trainer in 1941. Nearly all accounts mention only Randall and position him as the first trainer.

16. Dale Evans Rogers, *The Woman at the Well* (Old Tappan, NJ: Revell, 1970).

17. Davis, *The Answer Is God*.

18. The clause allowed Len to exploit whatever rights that Republic might control while he was under contract to them to the name, likeness, etc., of the character "Roy Rogers."

19. The timing was right for such a move. Although Tom Mix had died on October 12, 1940, he would remain popular in name and image, and Tom Mix products would even be issued in the future. The Lone Ranger would have been big competition in this market, but there was a long period when he wasn't seen, from his 1939 film serial to 1949, when his television series began. Hopalong Cassidy, who was going strong and had become an American institution, was the major competition for Roy Rogers in market sales.

20. This amounts to $7,800 annually. When Autry settled his dispute with the studio after his strike, they agreed to $12,500 per film at six to eight films per year, or $75,000–$100,000 per year. David Rothel, *The Gene Autry Book* (Madison, NC: Empire Publishing, 1988).

21. William K. Everson, author of several books on the Hollywood Western film, referred to Roy Rogers as "Gene Autry's only serious rival in his article "Movie Cowboys," *Liberty* 1, no. 12 (Spring 1974).

22. Evans, *Woman at the Well*.

23. "A.M. Philadelphia" television show interview, August 1981.

24. According to Roy in *Happy Trails*, the little girl was already named. Several movie magazines report that Roy chose one of the two names and Arline the other. *Movie Life Yearbook*, 1946, says Arline chose "Cheryl" and Roy chose "Darlene."

25. Davis, *The Answer Is God*.

26. *Movies*, November 1940: "Today there is no one more happy than Gene Autry himself over Rogers' success. The two are fast friends, are constant visitors at each other's ranch, and best boosters for the other fellow." See accounts also in *Movie Stars Parade*, March 1942; *Screen Stars*, January 1947; and *Modern Screen*, October 1947. As incredible as it may sound, in January 1951, Gene Autry comic books were being offered on the Roy Rogers radio show over the Mutual network. See Chapter 4.

27. Court petition, Los Angeles Superior Court Case No. 479706, filed August 24, 1942, and October 6, 1942. It is still unknown when, or even if, Leonard Frank Sly legally became Leonard Franklin Slye, but he signed legal documents using "Slye" as early as 1932 and signed documents using "Franklin" as early as 1936.

28. It was a West not unlike the one this writer grew up in, where horses, cowboys, rodeos, and cattle-grazing blended in perfect harmony with small-town cafes, automobiles, trucks, and even airplanes.

29. "Roy Rogers," *Movie Fan Album* 1 (Winter 1946) states that they (Roy and company) had been traveling with the rodeos for the past four years.

30. Davis, *The Answer Is God*.

31. *Madison Square Garden Annual Rodeo Magazines. Madison Square Garden: 100 Years of History*, Joseph Durso, 1979. These rodeos were started in 1926; the performance lasted for several weeks each fall and pulled in crowds from all over the world. They offered the biggest purse of any rodeo. The rodeos were produced by Texan Everett Colborn, who also produced rodeos for Houston, Boston, and Cheyenne. Autry made his debut here in 1939.

32. *Movie Life Yearbook*, 1948. Davis, *The Answer Is God*.

33. Property Settlement Agreement: Butts vs. Butts. Dale, in *Happy Trails*, leaves out divorce from Butts. This book offers the most vague accounting of her life to date.

34. *20th Annual Rodeo Magazine* (Madison Square Garden, 1945).

35. *Motion Picture*, September 1944.

36. *Life*, July 12, 1943.

37. *The Mountain Broadcast and Prairie Recorder*, March 1946.

38. Ibid.

39. Ibid.

40. Some sources cite the figure $100,000. These billboards can be seen on the backs of *Annual Rodeo Magazines* and also appear in "Roy Rogers, King of the Cowboys" (AMC-TV).

41. *Motion Picture Herald* and other polls. Roy was voted this award every year from 1943 to 1954, and the last two of these years he wasn't even making films.

42. *Modern Screen*, November 1944.

43. *Annual Rodeo Magazine* (Madison Square Garden, 1943).

44. Ibid.

45. *Modern Screen*, November 1944.

46. Ibid.

47. The only other horse that would get even a fraction as much attention as Trigger would be Gene Autry's "Champion" or "Champ," but even that horse would not really come close to capturing the media's and public's attention to the extent Trigger did.

48. *Annual Rodeo Magazine* (Madison Square Garden, 1945): "He decided that Encino made him too lonely, and that he wanted a place with neighbors. One of his neighbors is 'Dick Haymes, the singing star.'"

49. *Movieland* 3, no. 9 (October 1945) refers to a "second annual Roy Rogers Rodeo." See also, *Screen Guide* 10, no. 10 (October 1945). Davis states in *The Answer Is God* that the rodeo was organized and went on tour in 1946.

50. *Liberty*, December 14, 1946; *Movie Life*, March 1948.

51. *Screen Guide*, 1945.

52. *Western Horseman*, April 1961. This article, one of several reporting the figure, places it at 1.11 million.

53. Witney, *Trigger Remembered*.

54. Dale Evans Rogers, *Dale—My Personal Picture Album* (Old Tappan, NJ: Revell, 1971). See also, *Motion Picture*, September 1944, and *Movie Life*, March 1948.

55. Los Angeles Superior Court, County Records Center, Case No. D-293361, Butts vs. Butts.

56. Ibid.

57. Bobby J. Copeland, "Masonic Cowboys," *Westerns and Serials* 40 (Spring 1993).

58. *Movie Life Yearbook* states 1,000 a day.

59. It was more likely that patterns were duplicated, rather than outfits. The term "double-eagle" is correct, according to bootmakers, but Roy used the term "thunderbird" in interviews.

60. *Liberty* 23, no. 50 (December 14, 1946).

61. *Screen Guide*, October 1946.

62. Roy Rogers, Jr., birth certificate.

63. Mrs. Prentice Wilkens, Arline's mother. There are several published accounts of this version. *Happy Trails* offers a different version: Roy was at home, Mrs. Wilkins was there, and he was preparing for a Sunday morning golf date with Art Rush when the call came.

64. Grace Arline Rogers' death certificate. Numerous published accounts have shown erroneous date, time, etc. Rovin's book places it on November 4th, 10 A.M., and states Roy talked to her at 9 A.M. from Chicago.

65. Ibid.

66. One wonders why Tom listed his mother as Dale Evans, when her name was Frances Octavia Butts.

67. *Photoplay*, April 1947.

68. *Roy Rogers World's Championship Rodeo Souvenir Program*, September 1947.

69. *The Western Horseman*, May-June 1948. The "thunderbird" was used in an ad of the company manufacturing this saddle. *Modern Screen*, April 1948, states that Roy was the first cowboy to use a plastic saddle. This one would be used frequently for photos that would appear in comics and was used in the film *Under California Stars*. Roy would own several. It was manufactured by the All-Western Plastics Co., Alliance, Nebraska, "Originators of Plastic Saddlery," according to *The Western Horseman*, November-December 1946, company ad. See also Chapter 12.

70. *Photoplay*, April 1947.

71. *Movie Life Yearbook*, 1948. Photos.

72. Correspondence dated April 25, 1993, and photos from former Lake Hughes school teacher Ms. J. Williams, of Lake Hughes, California.

73. The structure is now the Community Presbyterian Church of the Lakes. The architecture is the same, except that a steeple was added.

74. Murray County, Sulphur, Oklahoma, recorded in book 13, at page 254, January 9, 1948. No evidence has been found showing that Dale ever legally changed her name from Miss Smith, Mrs. Fox, Mrs. Butts, or Mrs. Rogers to Dale Evans in any state in which she resided from the 1930s to the present.

75. Roy stated this on the "This Is Your Life" television show, 1953. Books make no mention of this, but state that the minister was dressed in old period Western attire.

76. *Movie Stars Parade*, June 1948.

77. Ibid.

78. *Modern Screen*, April 1948.

79. Roy would often state that Gabby was like his father, his brother, and his buddy, all wrapped into one. Cincinnati radio interview, 1991; "A.M. Philadelphia" television show interview, August 1981.

80. *Life*, October 16, 1950.

81. Roy stated in published interviews and for David Rothel, in his 1987 work *The Roy Rogers Book*, that Trigger never sired a colt. He was probably referring to the original Trigger.

82. The trial was held in United States District Court, Central District of California, Los Angeles. Records of this trial are now in the possession of the National Archives, Laguna Niguel, California.

83. Roy was finally able to persuade General Foods to take a chance on a court victory. Their agreement included a "kick-out" in case he lost.

84. Case No. 13320, Civil, Accession No. 021-69H1117, Location 346609, Box 71.

85. Rogers and Rogers, *Happy Trails*.

86. Captioned photo appeared in *Open Road*, June 1952.

87. Court documents, Los Angeles Superior Court, Case No. 60C2740.

88. Certificate of Death, Los Angeles county, No. 14322.

89. *Double R Bar Ranch News*, January 1951.

90. Dale Evans, "Why I Am Fighting to End Child Abuse," *National Enquirer*, 1990s. Dale states that Sandy had been beaten by alcoholic parents, starved, and left to die in a motel room. He suffered from brain damage, poor coordination, eye problems, lack of bladder control, rickets, and curvature of the spine.

91. Sword, *Hometown Photo Album*.

92. Roy and Dale apparently had a passion for nicknames. According to Dale, "There was talk of nicknaming Robin 'Stormy,' but she was so placid and gentle, the name didn't fit."

93. An article in *American Collector* 10, no. 6 (June 1979) describes the gun as a "Model 12 Pigeon Grade Winchester" shotgun.

94. Complaint for Personal Injuries, No. 602740. Mabel Smeyne, aka Mabel Smaney, vs. Roy Rogers, et al.

95. Now that we know that there were a number of "Triggers," it is natural to wonder which one was being referred to in court by the defendant or if the plaintiff knew of all the horses that were used for "Trigger" in the film and which one she was alleging kicked her.

96. Dale's books and tabloid *Inside Story*.

97. The article both enlightens and disappoints. The first wife is covered in detail, as is Dale (wife number three), to whom he was married at this time. However, for reasons that may never be known, he did not discuss his second wife, Arline.

98. Rothel, *Roy Rogers*.

99. March-April 1993 correspondence from Mary Enroth, who was Cheryl's teacher at Kemper Hall. This is an Episcopal Sisters of St. Mary school, with a campus that is approximately 16 acres on Lake Michigan's shores. Mrs. Enroth recalls that Cheryl loved to ride horses. It is possible that Dale heard of this school by way of its retreat at Evergreen, Colorado.

100. Roy discussed his heart problems in an interview with Bob Thomas for AP in 1975. See also, Rogers and Rogers, *Happy Trails*. An "A.M. Philadelphia" television show interview places his first angina problems probably at this occurrence, about 1954-1955.

101. "Rodeo Ben," *The Western Horseman* (May 1958).

102. The author has been advised by Nancy Horsley in a telephone conversation May 29, 1993, that the esplanade has been removed by the city of Portsmouth, which is utilizing the space for downtown parking. The slabs with the prints are being preserved until a new site can be found. Money is being raised for a bronze statue of Roy rearing on Trigger.

103. Elmer B. Sword, Scioto County Photo History.

104. *TV Guide*, August 8-14, 1959.

105. Liner notes for *Sweet Hour of Prayer*, RCA Victor LPM 1439.

106. *Roy Rogers Comics*, January-February 1960.

107. McDowell interview, 1972.

108. *Movie Life*, February 1952, story and photos. See also, Certificate of Death, No. 1500, File No. 61-035809, Kern County, California, records; Kern County Sheriff's Office, Offense Report, Case No. RO 2392, April 4, 1961; Coroner's Report, No. 793.

109. Toches, Nick. *Country—Living Legends and Dying Metaphors in America's Biggest Music* (New York: Charles Scribner's Sons, 1977). Also: Reise, Randall. *Nashville Babylon* (Chicago: Congdon and Weed/Dist. by Contempory Books, 1988).

110. Muriel Davidson, *TV Guide*, December 8-14, 1962.

111. Witney, *Trigger Remembered*.

112. Roy Rogers, Jr. *Growing up with Roy and Dale* (Ventura, CA: Regal, 1986).

113. Rothel, *The Roy Rogers Book*. Interview with Roy, by Rothel.

114. David Rothel, *Those Great Cowboy Sidekicks* (Metuchen, NJ: Scarecrow, 1984). According to Dusty in *Growing Up with Roy and Dale*, Pat died in an auto accident. Roy states he was killed in an accident in Colorado Springs, Colorado, as well, in an interview on a Cincinnati radio station.

115. Original copyright: Roy Rogers, No. AA 450120, February 15, 1944.

116. "A.M. Philadelphia" television show interview.

117. Article by Suzanne Munshower in *Rona Barrett's Hollywood* 7, no. 3 (November 1975).

118. Magazine article in *Police Gazette*, 1973.

119. Fred Bodmer. Bodmer, a Portsmouth, Ohio, resident described his visit to the museum in an article with photos that appeared in the *Roy Rogers–Dale Evans Collector's Association Newsletter*, vol. 4, no. 26.

120. Rothel, *The Roy Rogers Book*, and numerous other sources previously listed.

121. Rogers and Rogers, *Happy Trails*.

122. *Rona Barrett's Hollywood* 7, no. 3 (November 1975).

123. "A.M. Philadelphia" television show interview, August 1981.

124. Ibid.

125. If this is the same colt discussed in David Rothel's *The Roy Rogers Reference and Trivia Book*, the correct spelling is "Triggaro."

126. The wrap-arounds, in which Roy and Dale talked to the audience and reminisced about the films with guests, were filmed in Tennessee and shown before, during, and after the Republic features. It has been reported that the copyrights by Republic had lapsed on the films used for this venture. Otherwise, considering the Rogers/Republic relationship and the fact that they would have had to be paid for the use of these films, it is doubtful this series would have been produced.

127. At least a dozen letters of inquiry were made to this company, without a single response.

128. *The Columbus Dispatch*, May 6, 1986.

129. U.S. Historical Society brochure, package, with letter from Roy.

130. Ibid.

131. Cincinnati radio interview, late 1991.

132. AP story dated April 19, 1992, Baltimore.

Chapter 7

1. *Gaylord DuBois Account Books*, on file at Michigan State University. Copy on file with author, courtesy Randall W. Scott and Roy White.

2. History of Dell Comics documents, on file. Courtesy Elizabeth McCreary. Used with permission.

3. "Terry and the Pirates," drawn by artist Milton Caniff, first appeared in October 1934. Source: *The Encyclopedia of American Comics* by Goulart.

4. *Official Overstreet Comic Book Price Guide* (New York: The House of Collectibles, annually).

5. *Official Overstreet Comic Books Price Guide*. See also, *The Photo-Journal Guide to Comic Books* by Gerber.

6. *Official Overstreet Comic Book Price Guide*.

7. In 1938, King Features Syndicate editors decided that they would adapt the radio show "The Lone Ranger," written by Fran Striker, (officially), into a comic strip. Ed Kressy wrote the stories, his wife adapted them for the comic strips, and Kressy drew them. The debut of the "Lone Ranger" in the newspapers was September 10, 1938. Dave Holland, *From Out of the Past—A Pictorial History of the Lone Ranger* (Granada Hills, CA: The Holland House, 1989).

8. *Large Feature #3* was also printed as Whitman #710. Issue #7 was also printed as Whitman #715. *Official Overstreet Comic Book Price Guide*; Gerber, *The Photo-Journal Guide to Comic Books*.

9. First appearance: *Saturday Evening Post*, single panel cartoon by Marge Henderson Buell, June 1935. *Official Overstreet Comic Book Price Guide*; Gerber, *The Photo-Journal Guide to Comic Books*.

10. History of Dell Comics speech to sales force in 1987, courtesy Elizabeth McCreary, Dell Publishing. Used with permission.

11. *Official Overstreet Comic Book Price Guide*.

12. Ibid.

13. *Modern Screen*, November 1944.

14. Examples: Donald Duck, #199, #328; Little Hiawatha, all issues; Little Joe, #1; Mickey Mouse, #268, #352; Porky Pig, #112, #156, #260,

#271; Goofy #468; Gerber, *The Photo-Journal Guide to Comic Books*.

15. *Official Overstreet Comic Book Price Guide*.

16. Holland, *From Out of the Past—The Pictorial History of the Lone Ranger*.

17. *The Western Horseman*. April 1961.

18. Ibid.

19. Arline never appeared in these photos with Roy and the girls, but in the movie magazines, pictures of all four of them were quite common. Dale appeared occasionally on the inside b&w shots, but never with Roy and the girls. (That really would not be appropriate, considering the time period in which these were shot, when Roy and Dale were not yet married.) Most of the Roy and Dale shots were taken on the film locations, and the shots of Roy and the girls were taken at his ranch home.

20. Scott, Randall W., *Gaylord DuBois Account Books*. Courtesy Ray White, 1992.

21. One of the most interesting aspects of these comics and the hundreds of photos they use is that this was the only medium that offered up many of these particular shots. Just as the films produced thousands of "stills" and associated publicity pictures from Republic, these comics were responsible for their own "stills."

22. Dell dipped far back into their files for the cover photo here.

Chapter 9

1. Bails, Jerry, and Hames Ware, eds. *The Who's Who of American Comic Books* (Detroit: Privately published, 1974).

2. Information and artwork courtesy Colin Jellicoe and Alan Smith.

3. Ibid.

4. Conversation with Till Goodan art collector Gary Parsons of Cowboy Classics, Fairview, Oklahoma, April 1993.

5. Bails and Ware, *Who's Who of American Comic Books*.

6. Ibid.

7. Visit to museum in 1992. Conversation, 1992, and correspondence, 1993, with Elvin Sweeten of the museum.

8. Smoky Mountain Knife Works sells sheets. Camillus Co. adv.

Chapter 10

1. Robert W. D. Ball and Ed Vebell, *Cowboy Collectibles and Western Memorabilia*, Schiffer Publishing, 1991. Information, photos.

2. *The Western Horseman*, various 1940s–1950s issues. The Tem-Tex Co. was a large producer of Western shirts for the L.A. area, and they sold mail-order.

3. A Tom Mix shirt of this description is seen in Ball and Vebell, *Cowboy Collectibles*.

4. *The Western Horseman*, March 1951. *25th Annual Rodeo Magazine* (Madison Square Garden, 1950). Eighth Avenue and adjacent streets near the Garden were the location of many Western attire and saddlery stores such as Dan's Trading Post, 307 W. 48th St., and there were other large stores in the city where Roy no doubt shopped, such as Kauffman's at 141 E. 24th St. and Miller's at 123 E. 24th St.

5. Letter from George E. Pitman (California cowboy collectibles authority), dated December 18, 1992, providing information on outfits by Turk, of Sherman Oaks, California, and photos of attire in his collection that was worn by one of Roy's doubles.

6. *The Western Horseman*, May 1958. Also known as Rodeo Ben; the store was located at 6240 N. Broad St.

7. Nudie's Rodeo Tailors, 5015 Lankershim Blvd. and then 11000 Victory. Another popular Western attire outfitter in L.A. was Weslows. Roy may have also used a cowboy tailor named Buck Bernie.

8. *Movie Stars Parade* 4, no. 8 (July 1944).

9. Ibid.

10. Smith. Article in *Life*, July 12, 1943.

11. *Movie Stars Parade* 4, no. 8 (July 1944). *The Mountain Broadcast and Prairie Recorder*, March 1946. Roy himself uses the "thunderbird" term for his boots ("A.M. Philadelphia" television show interview, August 1981). December 1992 telephone conversation with Joe Patrickus of J. P.'s Custom Hand-made Boots, Roy's licensed representative bootmaker in 1992. *Yippy Yi Yea* magazine, Winter 1992.

12. *Movie Stars Parade* 4, no. 8 (July 1944).

13. Roy is quoted by writer Beth Bright in "Ranch Flicker Talk," in *Ranch Romances*, January 1950: "Some people say my clothes are too flashy, but all real cowboys love to dress up in colorful shirts and scarfs."

14. *The Western Horseman*. April 1961. A "gold gun belt" is also mentioned.

15. Publicity photograph #704-8.

16. Ball and Vebell, *Cowboy Collectibles*.

17. Still photograph #R-1-47.

18. *Hollywood Studio* 14, no. 10 (May 1981).

19. *Radio-TV Mirror*, June 1952. Photos part of article "That Old Family Feeling."

20. Photograph of 1890s hat, Ball and Vebell, *Cowboy Collectibles*.

21. *The Western Horseman*, April 1961.

22. Photograph #RR-M-4, unknown event. Buckle shows steer head. See also, Lobby Cards, "Sunset in the West," 1950.

23. Publicity photograph #1623-16, *Eyes of Texas*.

24. Ibid.

25. Photograph #R-1-47, from film *Billy the Kid Returns*. *The Western Horseman*, March

1951. The Olsen-Stelzer Co., Henryetta, Texas, was very well-known. *Olsen-Stelzer Boot Catalog*, 1940s. Some of the common professional-quality bootmakers of the day were M. L. Leddy Co., Justin Boots, and Tony Lama Co., all in Texas. Many companies, Leddy for one, custom made boots. David Posada, 1647 Canuenga Blvd., in Los Angeles, advertised "World's Finest Boots," custom made for "cowboys, horsemen, movie stars, etc." in 1951.

26. Photograph with "Horse Sense" article, taken across from nation's Capitol. *Screen Stars*, December 1945.

27. One such pair, manufactured by L. White Boots and Saddle Shop, Fort Worth, Texas, is shown in ad of *25th Annual Rodeo Magazine* (Madison Square Garden, 1950).

28. Cover, *Roy Rogers Comics*, #60, December 1952. Boots are also shown on back of *The Western Horseman*, October 1953. The company was able to boast of "pure silk thread used in all stitching" and "skilled hand workmanship on all stitching and inlaying."

29. *The Western Horseman*, September-October 1946. Bohlin's address was 931 N. Highland Avenue.

30. *The Western Horseman*, September 1953. Roy Rogers licensee list, late 1940s–early 1950s. *Sears and Roebuck Catalogue*, 1953.

31. One of these silver-ornamented saddles, as well as other items, could possibly have come from Herman Friedrick Ranch Supplies, Inc., 797 Eighth Avenue, New York. Friedrick was a cowboy silversmith, and all silver work was done on premises, which were close to the Garden.

32. *The Western Horseman*, April 1961.

Chapter 11

1. William Witney, *Trigger Remembered* (Toney, AL: Earl Blair Enterprises, 1989).

2. Rothel, David, *The Great Show Business Animals*. (New York: A. S. Barnes & Co., Inc., 1980). There is another renowned rental stable in the area, named Fat Jones.

3. Elise Miller Davis, *The Answer Is God* (New York: McGraw-Hill, 1955). Roy stated in published and filmed interviews in later years that Trigger never once fell with him during his career. I suppose it is a question of which "Trigger" is being referred to at any given time.

4. See *The Western Horseman*, May-June 1946. This horse was being advertised at stud.

APPENDIX

The Roy Rogers Riders Club Rules and Creed

Source: Back of *Roy Rogers Riders Club Comic:* 1952.

One reading of the "Rules and Creed" can give the student of popular culture and the person researching the Western film cowboys of the 1940s–50s a good idea of how much positive influence these characters had on the youth of America during the time that they were riding the hardest, chasing all the bad guys out of town and selling cereal. In retrospect, an adult can recall the role models that helped to shape his or her character; parents, teachers, the Boy Scouts, and, you can bet, Roy Rogers, Gene Autry, and Hopalong Cassidy will top the list. The basic rules that were spelled out in codes such as this one came across in the films and on television in the way the hero treated his friends, the ladies, his horse, and even his guitar.

1. *Be neat and clean.* At our house, Dale and I are pretty strict about Cheryl, Linda, and Dusty keeping their rooms in neat order, putting away their toys when they're finished playing and hanging up their clothes. Remember, your mother is a busy person and just think of how much you can help if you keep your own things neat.

2. *Be courteous and polite.* Saying "please" and "thank you" may not seem too important, but the boys and girls who always remember to be polite to their parents, teachers and friends are the ones I always feel make the best Riders Club members.

3. *Always obey your parents.* Sometimes you might think your parents are asking you to do something you feel isn't necessary, or they may refuse to let you have your own way. Believe me, pardners, your parents are just doing what they feel will be best for you—remember, they were young once too, maybe felt the same way you do.

4. *Protect the weak and help them.* A true Riders Club member never tries to "bully" anyone, especially someone smaller or weaker than himself. Instead he tries to do whatever he can to help them grow stronger.

5. *Be brave, but never take chances.* Just remember the fellow who takes a "dare" isn't always the "hero." Bravery means doing whatever you can to help someone in trouble, but not taking reckless chances where you yourself might get hurt.

6. *Study hard and learn all you can.* Everyone has a job to do all his life, and when you're young, school is your "office," and your lessons are your "work." The work you do in school pays off with the best jobs when you grow older.

7. *Be kind to animals and care for them.* No matter what kind of a pet you have, always be sure to take good care of it, because that animal looks to you for protection and love. Animals are man's best friends, and to keep our friends we have to show them how much we care for them.

8. *Eat all your food and never waste any.* Boys and girls in this country are the luckiest in the world. We have so many hundreds of foods to choose from that we can have anything we want to eat. Thousands of youngsters in Asia and Europe hardly have anything to eat, and often have to go hungry. So, never waste any of your food, and then America will have food to share with the less fortunate in other countries.

9. *Love God and go to Sunday school regularly.* I hope all my Riders Club members go to Sunday school regularly, just like our own children do. Cheryl, Linda, and Dusty know that going to church in the morning is the most important part of every Sunday.

10. *Always respect our flag and our country.* We live in the greatest country in the world and it's up to all of us to do everything we can to show our love for America. Doing all we can to protect our freedom by following the laws of our country is one of the best ways in which we can show our love and respect.

Names and Name Changes of Roy and Dale

1911 Leonard Frank Sly (birth certificate).
1933 Leonard F. Slye (signed on marriage license).

1936 Leonard Franklin Slye (signed on marriage license). No documentation has been found showing a legal name change to Leonard Franklin Slye. Research continuing.

1938 Leonard Slye (shown on law suit).

1942 Roy Rogers. (Leonard Slye changed his name to "Roy Rogers." Sworn statement to court stated he was born Leonard Franklin Slye.)

1912 Lucille Wood Smith born October 30, 1912 (birth record). Frances Octavia Smith, born October 31, 1912. (In *Happy Trails*, Dale makes reference to a sworn affidavit given her by her parents. A diligent search has taken place, with no copy of this having been found in any public record thus far.)

1929 Frances S. Fox (divorce record).

1930–1938 Frances Johns (appears on marriage license to R. Dale Butts; also divorce documents, Johns vs. Johns, 1936).

Mid–1930s Marion Lee, Dale Evans (published accounting; first used in Louisville, Kentucky).

1938 Frances Johns/Frances Butts (marriage license). Dale Evans (published accounting).

1940–1944 "Dale Evans" (published accounting).

1945 Frances Butts (Butts/Butts divorce record).

1947 Dale Evans (marriage license). So far, I have been unable to document the names "Lucille Wood Smith"/"Frances Octavia Smith" being legally changed to "Dale Evans." According to a fellow researcher, Dale makes reference to such a change in a televised statement.

1953 Dale Evans Rogers. (Pen name, books, and possible legal name.)

1954 Lucille Wood Smith. (Published account of passport application. Legal name probably still not Dale Evans at that time.)

Birthdate Issue

Birth certificate shows "Leonard Frank Sly," Nov. 5, 1911. Of 21 published sources examined, ten give 1911 as Roy's birthdate and eleven give 1912.

1911 birthdate: *Country Music U.S.A.*, Bill Malone, 1968; *Sixgun Heroes*, Theodore Hake, Robert D. Cauler, 1976; *Box Office Buckaroos*, Robert Heide, John Gilman, 1982; *The Country Music Book*, Michael Mason (ed.), 1985; *The Harmony III. Enc. of Country Music*, Dellar, Cackett, Tompson, 1986; *The Roy Rogers Book*, David Rothel, 1987; *The New York Post* (March 1990); *The New York Daily News* (10-23-90); *The New York Post* (11-6-90); *The Country Music Hall of Fame and Museum* (plaque); *Double RR Bar News* 7 (December 1991); letter to readers from Dusty about Roy's 80th birthday, November 1991.

1912 birthdate: *TV-Radio Annual*, 1958; *The Encyclopedia of Folk, Country and Western Music*, Stampler, Landon, 1969; *The Country Music Encyclopedia*, Melvin Shestack, 1974; *Roy Rogers, King of the Cowboys*, Bob Carman, Dan Scapperotti, 1979; *The Film Encyclopedia*, Ephraim Katzl, 1979; *The Book of Movie Lists*, Gabe Essoe, 1981; *Heroes of the Range*, Buck Raney, 1987; *The Hollywood Walk of Fame*, 1987; *The BFI Companion to the Western*, Edward Buscombe, 1988; *The Encyclopedia of Hollywood*, Scott and Barbara Siegel, 1990.

Residences and Business Addresses of Roy Rogers

1911 412 E. 2d St., Cincinnati, Ohio

1912 Houseboat, Ohio River, Portsmouth, Ohio

1915–1916 1223 Mill St., Portsmouth, Ohio

1919 Unknown road, also Reed's Run, both near Duck Run community, rural Scioto County, Ohio

1920s 1910 Ohio Avenue, Cincinnati, Ohio

1933 4044 DePew St., Lawndale, Calif. (Now 165th St.)

1933 W. 88th St., Los Angeles

1934 Bronson St., Hollywood, Calif. (between Hollywood Blvd. and W. Sunset Blvd.)

1934 1453 Tamarind Avenue (1 block from Bronson St.)

1934 5841 Carlton Way, Hollywood, Calif.

1936–1941 "Five-room wooden house" (several published accounts without specific address)

1941 4704 Whiteoak Avenue, Encino, Calif. (former Spanish-style home of Don Ameche, six-room house)

1944 3734 Longridge Avenue, Van Nuys, Calif.

1945 Magazine article notes "three houses owned"

1945–1946 Lake Hughes Ranch (retreat) near Lancaster, Calif., "Sky Haven"; 3734 Longridge Avenue

1947 6147 Longridge Avenue, Van Nuys, Calif.

1948 6423 Ivarene Avenue, Hollywood Hills (former home of Noah Beery), 2 acres

1951 Encino. "Double R Bar Ranch," 5330 Amestoy Ave, 5 acres/9 acres

1953–1963 9839 Andora Ave., Chatsworth, "Double R Bar Ranch," 138 acres

1963 Hidden Valley, Calif.

1965 Apple Valley, Calif.

Other Properties:

- Dude Ranch, Las Vegas, Nevada, area
- Possibly the "chicken ranch" on which his folks lived in Encino
- Another such property in Van Nuys (neither documented)
- Possibly commercial property on which his car dealership sat (Ventura Blvd.) and the Western stores

- Possibly 24,000 acres of Arizona land (co-owner)
- Cottage at Big Bear Lake in California
- The most famous and photographed of all these, naturally, is the "Double R Bar Ranch," Chatsworth, where Roy lived for nearly ten years

Roy Rogers Enterprises
1418 No. Highland Avenue
Hollywood 28, Calif.

1948 The Roy Rogers Fan Service
Studio City, California

1959 Roy Rogers Building
Devonshire Avenue
Los Angeles, Calif.

1959 Roy Rogers Syndication, Inc./
Roy Rogers Frontiers, Inc.
357 No. Canon Drive
Beverly Hills, Calif.

1959 Arthur Rush/Rush, Inc.
357 No. Canon Drive

1959 Jim Osborne
13611 South Charlemagne
Bellflower, Calif.

1960s Roy Rogers' Apple Valley Inn
Post Office Box 5
Apple Valley, Calif.

Copyright Holding Companies

Sources: Comics, Whitman books, merchandise

1944–1947 Copyrights apparently held by Dell and Whitman
1948 The Rohr Co.
1949 Roy Rogers/Roy Rogers
1950 The Rohr Co.
1951 Roy Rogers Enterprises
1952 Roy Rogers Enterprises
1953 Roy Rogers Enterprises (year of the big merchandise push, large ads in national magazines, large amount of merchandise in Sears catalogue); Pledge to Parents
1954 Roy Rogers Enterprises (initiated the "Plus Brand")
1955 Frontiers, Inc.
1955 Roy Rogers Ent., a div. of Frontiers, Inc.
1956 Frontiers, Inc. Beverly Hills, Calif.; Empire State Bldg., N.Y.
1957 Frontiers, Inc.
1958 Roy Rogers-Frontiers, Inc.
1959 The Slys, Andrew and Mattie
6538 Hayvenhurst Avenue, Los Angeles, Calif.
1966 Don Gardner and Associates
1980s Golden Stallion, Inc.
1990s Dawn Licensing Agency, Inc., Verona, N.J.
Note: The letters ROHR are believed to represent Rogers, Osborne, Harvey, Rush; the Rogers and Rush could be switched.

1994 Guise Wite Studio. Information courtesy Merv Bendewald, N.Y.

Roy's Dogs

A Greenland husky
1940s "Queen," bird dog
1940s Lana and Joaquin, weimeraners; drum, hunting dog
1952 Ghost, hound
1940s–1950s Spur, German shepherd
1949 Bullet, German shepherd
1965 Bowser, coyote-chow mix
1965 Bambi, chihuahua
1965 Heidi, beagle

Marriages

Roy:

1933–1936 Lucile Ascolese
1936–1946 Grace Arline Wilkins
1947–Present Dale Evans

Dale:

1927–1929 Thomas F. Fox
1930–1936 August Wayne Johns
1937–1946 Robert Dale Butts
1947–Present Roy Rogers

Children

Thomas Frederick Fox, Jr. (Frances, Thomas)
Memphis, Tenn., born 1927

Cheryl Darlene Sly Rogers (Leonard, Arline adopted)
Dallas, Texas, born circa 1940, adopted 1941

Linda Lou Rogers (Leonard, Arline)
Los Angeles, born 1943

Roy Rogers, Jr. (Roy, Arline)
Los Angeles, born 1946

Robin Elizabeth Rogers (Roy, Dale)
Los Angeles, born 1950

Harry John David Hardy Rogers (Roy, Dale adopted)
Covington, Ky., born 1947, adopted 1953

Mary Little Doe Rogers (Roy, Dale; adopted)
Dallas, Texas, born 1952, adopted 1953

Marion Fleming (Roy, Dale; fostered)
Scotland, born circa 1941, fostered circa 1955
In Ai Lee (Deborah Lee) Rogers (Roy, Dale; adopted)
Korea, born 1952, adopted 1956

BIBLIOGRAPHY

This is a magazine and newspaper article bibliography only, and this is the first time such a bibliography has ever been published. Reference material is from my personal collection containing over 700 articles. I would also like to acknowledge the assistance of Professor Ray White of Ball State University and others for sharing with me information on articles from their collections. Books specifically on Roy and Dale are listed in Chapter 12.

Magazine Covers

The following publications show Roy Rogers on the cover:

Alan G. Barbour's Screen Nostalgia Illustrated 4 (1983).
American Collector 10, no. 6 (June 1979).
American Movie Classics 4, no. 3 (March 1991); 5, no. 11 (November 1992), backcover; 5, no. 12 (December 1992).
American Photographer 21, no. 2 (August 1988).
Annual Rodeo Magazine. Madison Square Garden. 27th, 1952; 29th, 1954; 30th, 1955; 33d, 1958.
Autograph Collector (November 1992).
Baltimore Sunday American. "T-Vue Time." December 2–8, 1956.
Barn Dance Magazine (Dale) 5 (1948).
Bell Theatre Program. Marietta, Georgia. July 21, 1945.
Canal TV (Argentina TV Guide) 3, no. 185 (1962).
The Card Collector's Bulletin 5 (1992).
Ciné Revue 32 (August 9, 1946).
The Christian Reader (September-October 1982).
Cinlandia. Mexico film publication published in California. (August 1943).
Classic Images 203, no. 4 (May 1992).
Col. Jim Eskew's Texas Rodeo Souvenir Pogram (1945).
Collecting Hollywood 1, no. 6 (June-July 1994).
Country America 3, no. 4 (February 1992).
Country Gentlemen, unknown date.
Country Post 4, no. 5 (September-October 1993).
Country Music 3, no. 7 (July 1975).
Cowboy Music World 1, no. 6 (March-April 1945).
Disc Collector 152 (Summer 1988).
DISCoveries 4, no. 10 (October 1991).
Dixie Gun Works, Inc. Catalogue. 1991.

Dodge News 19, no. 2 (circa 1954).
Double R Bar Ranch News (May-June 1953); (January-February 1954); (March-April 1954); (July-August 1955); (November-December 1955); (January-February 1956); (September-October 1957).
Double RR Bar News 1 (October 1990); 4 (April 1991); 5 (May 1991); 7 (October 1991); also numbers 7, 9, 13, 14, 15, 16, 17, 18 (no dates appear).
Favorite Westerns 1 (Winter 1981); 6 (1982); 9 (March 1983); 10 (April 1983); 18 (Summer 1984); 21 (Spring 1985); 27 (1988).
Florida State Fair Event Program. Unknown date.
Full Cry 53, no. 10 (November 1991).
Gems and Minerals (April 1968).
Good Ol' Days 25, no. 3 (September 1988); special issue—Western Stars of the Silver Screen, (Summer 1990).
Guideposts Magazine 13, no. 9 (November 1958); (February 1980); (March 1953).
Guns 4 (August 1958).
Hit Parader (April 1946).
Hollywood Studio Magazine 14, no. 10 (July 1982).
Hollywood Western (September 1950).
Inside Story 2, no. 3 (March 1956).
Intimate Lives of Movie Stars (September 25, 1953).
Jack and Jill 23, no. 7 (May 1961).
JET (February 19, 1953).
The Journal of the American Academy for the Preservation of Old Time Country Music 2, no. 6 (December 1992).
Ladie's Circle 6, no. 8 (March 1970).
Liberty Magazine. Unknown date; December 14, 1946.
Life 15, no. 2 (July 12, 1943).
Listen. First Quarter, 1951.

The Motorcycle Enthusiast (October 1958).
The Mountain Broadcast and Prairie Recorder (March 1946).
Movie Fan 3, no. 2 (August 1948); 5, no. 2 (November-December 1950).
Movie Life (January 1945); 10, no. 5 (March 1947); 11, no. 5 (March 1948); 12, no. 1 (November 1948); 12, no. 10 (August 1949); (April 1950).
Movie Life Yearbook 1, no. 3 (1946); 1948.
Movie Pix (1949).
Movie Play. Western Edition 3, no. 5 (January 1949).
Movie Spotlight. Western Edition 1, no. 2 (October 1949).
Movie Stars Parade (June 1945); 8, no. 7 (June 1948).
Movie Thrills (May 1950).
Movie Western 1, no. 2 (September 1950).
Music City News 29, no. 5 (December 1991).
National Western Jamboree (June 1949).
New York Mirror (October 5, 1958).
New York Sunday Mirror. November 19, 1950.
New York Sunday News. December 6, 1942.
New York Times Coloroto Magazine (September 21, 1958).
Our Dogs 1, no. 3 (Winter 1942).
Parade. December 20, 1959.
Philadelphia Inquirer. Colorama Section. February 7, 1954.
Portsmouth Convention and Visitors Bureau, 1992.
Possibilities (March-April 1986).
Private Clubs (September-October 1992).
Pulse 29, no. 5 (November 1991).
Que Magazine (c. 1952).
Quick 2, no. 8 (February 20, 1950).
Radio Hit Songs (1944).
Radio Life (c. 1946).
Rob Tucker's Memory Lane (August 1980).
Rodeo History and Records. Backcover Fall 1945).
Rodeo Magazine (Madison Square Garden). 27th Annual (1952); 29th Annual (1954); 30th Annual (1955).
Rodeo (Official Souvenir Program—Houston Fat Stock Show and Rodeo) 1950s.
Roy Rogers Collectors Monthly (1980s).
Roy Rogers-Dale Evans Collector's Assn. Newsletter 40 (Fall 1990); 43 (Spring 1992); 3, no. 21 (March-April 1986); 3, no. 23 (July-August 1986); 3, no. 24 (September-October 1986); 4, no. 25 (Spring 1987); 4, no. 26 (Spring-Summer 1987); 4, no. 28 (Fall 1987); 5, no. 30 (Spring 1988); 5, no. 31 (Spring-Summer 1988); 5, no. 33 (September-October 1988); 5, no. 34 (Winter 1988-89); 5, no. 35 (Spring 1989); 5, no. 36 (Spring 1989); 5, no. 37/38 (Spring 1989); 5, no. 42 (Summer-Fall 1991); 45 (Fall 1992); 5, no. 46 (Winter-Spring 1992); 5, no. 48 (Summer 1993).
Roy Rogers Homecoming Day. September 6, 1982.

Roy Rogers Hometown Photo Album. 1982.
Roy Rogers Official Souvenir Program (1951).
RRDECA Membership Directory 4, no. 49 (1987).
Saturday Evening Post 252, no. 3 (April, 1980).
The Scottish Rite Journal 98, no. 8 (August 1990).
Screen and Television Guide (May 1949).
Screen Guide 14, no. 5 (May 1949).
Screen Stars (July 1950).
Screen Stories (November 1948); 44, no. 1 (July 1950).
Smoky Mountain Knife Works Catalogue (Christmas-Winter, 1991).
Sunday News (New York). September 26, 1954.
This Month in San Antonio (June 1955).
TV Guide 5, no. 39 (September 26–October 2, 1952); 5, no. 45 (November 7, 1952); 5, no. 51 (December 19–25, 1952); 2, no. 29 (July 17–23, 1954); 4, no. 52 (December 28–January 3, 1952); (December 8–14, 1962).
TV Western and Movie 1, no. 3 (December 1958).
Under Western Skies 2 (April 1978).
1991-1992 Video Guide. October 25, 1992.
The Washington Post. November 29, 1992.
Western Comics Journal 1, no. 4 (October 1992); 1, no. 5 (November 1992).
Western Hollywood Pictorial (September 1950).
The Western Horseman (December 1949).
Western Stars. Unknown date, late 1940s; 1, no. 1 (November 1948-February 1949); 1, no. 3 (October-December 1949); 2 (1950).
Western Stories (November 1948–Feburary 1949).
Westerns and Serials 33 (1990); 38 (1992).
Who's Who in Western Stars, 1, no. 1 (1952); 1, no. 3 (1953).
World Championship Rodeo Program. Boston Garden Rodeo. October 19–30, 1955.

Magazine Articles

Advertising Age
Garfield, Bob. "Hot Weenies Cook Roy Rogers' Goose" 59, no. 36 (August 29, 1988): 65.
Meyers, Janet. "Roy Rogers Corral's 3 Approaches" 57, no. 34 (June 9, 1986): 52.
Meyer, Janey and Hume Scott. "Roy Rogers Sale Hits EPB" (Earl Palmer Brown Co. loses Roy Rogers' ad account) (February 5, 1990).
Scott, Hume. "Lassoing Roy Rogers" (June 4, 1990): 50.

Adweek
"Roy Rogers' Bricks Were More Important Than the Brand" (restaurant chain), Eastern Edition 31, no. 6 (February 5, 1990).

The Alkalizer, Miles Laboratories publication.
"Roy Rogers Is New Miles Star" 31, no. 6 (July-August 1946): 7.
"King of the Cowboys Rides for Miles" 11, no. 4 (September 1946): 1ff.

American Classic Screen
Rogers, Roy. "Roy Rogers: First Days at Republic" (Winter 1980): 34–36.
Singer, Stan. "Roy Rogers–Dale Evans Museum, in Touch with the Past" (Winter 1980): 37–39.

American Collector
Maloney, John. "Roy Rogers, Cowboy Turned Collector" 10, no. 6 (June 1979): 8–10.

American Magazine
"Horse Laugh" 139 (May 1945): 64.
Rogers, Roy. "Don't Shoot Ma!" 148 (August 1948).
Stump, Al. "Meet the Roy Rogers Family" (August 1953): 38.

American Mercury
Valentry, Duane. "A Man, a Horse, and a Guitar," pp. 131–33. Unknown date.

American Movie Classics
"Roy Rogers" (March 1992).

American Photographer
Schiffman, Bonnie (photographer). Cover photo of Roy Rogers, no story (July 1988).

American Rifleman
Evans, Dale. "At the Fork in the Road" (c. 1955).
Rogers, Roy. "My Light of Faith" (c. 1955).

Antique and Collecting Hobbies
Phillips, Robert W. "A Guide to 'King of the Cowboys' Collectibles" (7 b&w photos) 97, no. 6 (August 1992): 26–29.

Antique Trader
Phillips, Robert W. "Collecting Western Comics" (August 3, 1994): 10B–12B.
_____. "Roy Rogers King of the Cowboys" 1, no. 10 (July 1994): 42–45.

Antiques and Collecting
Phillips, Robert W. "Make-Believe Cowboys" 99, No. 4 (June 1994): 44–47.

Antique Week/Tri State Trader
Pelchner, William J. "Roy Rogers: King of 'Collectibles' Cowboys," November 26, 1984.

Baby Boomer Collectibles
Phillips, Robert W. "Being the Hero Meant Dressing the Part" (April 1994): 26–27, 66–68.

Back Stage
Levy-Malis, Elizabeth. "Roy Rogers Bites Back" (Restaurant's TV advertising) 31, no. 2, unknown date.

Barn Dance Magazine
"Roy Rogers" 5 (1948).

Big Reel
Phillips, Robert W. "Riding Herd on Silver Screen Cowboy Memorabilia" (September 1994): 144–145.

Billboard/The Billboard
Editorial Staff. "15 New Markets Order Autry-Rogers Westerns" [1 large b&w of Roy and Trigger] (May 7, 1955).
"Now, These Featured Pix Never Before on Television" (May 7, 1955).
Wood, Gerry. "Roy Rogers Deserves a Spot in the Hall" [Country Music Hall of Fame] (August 13, 1988): 35ff.
_____. "Predicting the Roy Rogers of the 90's" ["Who's Next in the 90's—Country Music"] (June 30, 1990): 33.
Morris, Edward. "Rogers & Co. Back on Happy Trails: RCA Album 'Tributes' King of the Cobwoys" 103, no. 38 (September 21, 1991).

Biography News
Stoops, B. H. "Dale Evans to Appear on Hartsville Program" 1 (March 1974): 227.
Reed, B. "Good Guy: Roy Rogers, Dale Evans Revive Memories" 1 (October 1974): 1196.

Box-office
"Roy Rogers Film Finishes Third Week of Shooting" 107 (August 18, 1975): 14.
"Roy Rogers, Cowboy King. Back in the Saddle Again" 111 (September 5, 1977).

Capitol News
Gillette, Lee. "Western Folk Music Goes Overseas" (Dale Evans) 6, no. 6 (June 1948): 10.

Ciné Revue
"Roy Rogers—le Roi des Cow-Boys." French Publication, 7 b&w photos included, 2 taken at Madison Square Garden (August 8, 1946).

Christian Advocate
Valentry, Duane. "At Home with Roy Rogers Clan" (April 30, 1953).

Christian Century
Gill, T. A. "Evangelist Three" (March 23, 1955): 370.

Christian Life
Wagner, W. "The Dale and Roy Trio" (August 1969): 20ff.
Houston, J. "What Do Women Really Want?" (October 1980): 22.

Christian Reader
Beane, B. B. "Living Legend" [Roy Rogers] (November 1980): 37.
Rogers, R., and Dale Evans, with Jane Curtis. "Dale and Roy: Riding Happy Trails" (September-October 1982): 5ff.
Roessing, W. "Roy Rogers on Sunset Trail" (January 1984): 9.
"An Undone Marriage" 18, no. 5 (September-October 1984): 99–104.

Christianity Today
"Roy and Dale on Country Crossroads" 16, no. 34 (February 4, 1972): 14.

Classic Film Collector
Polunsky, B. "Flicker Footnotes" [Dale Evans] (Summer 1976): 11ff.

Classic Images
Franklin, Grady. "Roy Rogers Goes Home to Big Ohio Welcome" 88 (October 1982): 14ff.
Phillips, Robert W. "From Rags to Western Riches" (4 b&w photos, 1 drawn likeness by Chero) 203 (May 1992): 10–11, 43.
_____. "New Book Documenting Roy Rogers' Comics" 203 (May 1992): 4.
_____. "Roy Rogers 'Firsts'" 205 (July 1992).
_____. "Rogers According to Yates" 216 (June 1993) 52.

Col. Jim Eskew's Texas Rodeo
Souvenir Program
"Roy Rogers . . . and Trigger," 1 b&w photo, p. 1.

Collectibles Illustrated
Caufield, Deborah. "When the Hollywood Cowboy Was King" 1, no. 1 (May-June 1982).
"Lunch Paileontologists Form Newsletter" (1 photo) 2, no. 1 (January-February 1983).
"Book Bin" (Photo, information on Sons of the Pioneers LP, Roy photo) 2, no. 1 (January-February 1983).

Collecting Hollywood
"The Roy Rogers Story" 1, no. 6 (June-July 1994): 42–46.

Collector's Showcase
Ingram, J. D. "Western Cowboy Comics" (photos of Roy Rogers Comics) 2, no. 10 (October 1991): 30ff.
Heide, Robert and John Gilman. "Movie Posters and Lobby Cards" 2, no. 10 (October 1991): 36ff.
"Showtime—Big D Super Collectibles Show" (photos of Roy Rogers collectibles) 2, no. 10 (October 1991): 72–73.

Colliers
"Roy Rogers" (1946).
Reid Ashton. "Hero on Horseback" (July 24, 1948): 27ff.

Consumer Reports
"Fast Food: A Survival Guide to the Greasy Kid Stuff" 53, no. 6 (June 1988): 355–361.

Comic Buyer's Guide
Horak, Carl J. "Tracking Down Tufts" (April 5, 1991).

The Comic's Journal
Jackson, Jack. "The Good, the Bad, and the Foreign Western Comics" (1 b&w photo, Roy Rogers related) 144 (September 1991).

Comics Source
Phillips, Robert W. "The Phillips Study of Western Comics" no. 9 (May 1994): 18–21.

Coronet
Shipp, Cameron. "Hollywood Saints in Ten Gallon Hats' ' 20, no. 3 (July 1946): 130–33.
"The Big Roundup" (1949).
Article on Roy Rogers/Dale Evans on NBC Radio and Television [b&w photos] (November 1953).

Country America
"Happy Trails" (3 color photos of Roy Rogers) 3, no. 2 (November 1990): 26–28.
Pond, Neil. "Roy Rogers, King of the Cowboys" (numerous color photos) 3, no. 4 (February 1992): 34–38.
Editorial Staff. "Country Almanac, Holly's Hero" 3, no. 8 (June 1992).

Country and Western Jamboree
"Frontiersman Blaze a New Trail" 3, no. 5 (August 1957): 21.

Country and Western Music
Elwood, Roger. "The Simple Faith of Roy Rogers and Dale Evans" (2 b&w photos) 1, no. 3 (August 1970): 31, 38–40.

Country Collectibles
Phillips, Robert W. "Cowboy Heroes" 6, no. 2 (Summer 1994): 68–69.

Country Fever
Fruin, Deborah. "The Last (Really) Good Guy" (4 color, 5 b&w photos) 1, no. 1 (August 1992): 448–52.
_____. "A Yippy-Ki-Yi-Ay Tribute to the King of the Cowboys" (1 color, 2 b&w photos) 1, no. 1 (August 1992).

Country Gentleman
Article about Roy and Dale's faith (March 1951).

Country Music
Russell, Peggy. "It Isn't Easy for Roy Rogers, Jr." 1, no. 6 (February 1973): 20.
Parks, Jack. "Hollywood's Singing Cowboys: They Packed Guitars, As Well As Six-Guns" 1, no. 11 (July 1973): 34–38.
Young, J. R. "Roy Rogers" 3, no. 10 (July 1975): 22ff.
Kienzle, Rich. "The Sons of the Pioneers" [several b&w photos] (September-October 1987): 40F-40G.
"Roy Rogers Album Specials" 133 (September-October 1988): 68.
Green, Douglas B. "Legends of Country Music: Roy Rogers" (5 b&w photos) 133 (September-October 1988): 38F-38G.
"Roy Rogers/Various Artists" (1 color photo) new LP "Tribute" review) 153 (January-February 1992).
Bane, Michael. "Roy Rogers Answers the Call/20 Questions with Roy Rogers" (3 color photos) 154 (March-April 1992): 32–33.

Country Music Journal from Nevada
Morris, Jesse. (Robert W. Phillips book review: *Singing Cowboy Stars*) 5 (Fall 1994).

Country Music Star Life
"Dale Evans and June Carter—Two Superstar Wives on Their Second Marriage" 1, no. 2 (circa 1970s): 45–47, 71.

Country Song Roundup
"Singing Rawhide" 1, no. 1 (July-August 1949): 10–11.
"A Day with Roy Rogers" 1, no. 3 (November-December 1949).
"Spotlight on the Stars" (1 b&w photo with dog) 1, no. 6 (June 1950): 12.
Sanders, George. "Hollywood Hoedown Lowdown" (1 b&w photo of Roy, Howard Duff, others) 13, no. 12 (August 1951): 10.
Delaney, Donna. "Roy Rogers Still King of the Cowboys" 34, no. 38 (August 1982): 27–30.
"Roy Rogers" (February 1991).
"Clint Black and Roy Rogers: Partners and Friends" 44, no. 392 (March 1992): 12–13.

Country Sounds
"The Sons of the Pioneers: Half a Century of the Tumbleweed Trail" [b&w photos] (November 1986): 6ff.

Cowboy Songs
"Roy Rogers" 3 (1948).
"Republic Pictures Presents 'Heart of the Rockies'" 15 (1950).

Cowboy Song Roundup
"A Day with Roy Rogers" 3 (1948).

Cue
"Wildwest Hero" 12, no. 42 (October 16, 1943): 13.
Sabol, Blair. "Cowboy Chic Bottoms Out" 48, no. 22 (November 9, 1979): 26–27.

Current Biography
"World's Top Boots and Saddles Star" (March 1948).
"Roy Rogers" (1983): 328–31. Month unknown.

Desert Magazines
Vol. 3, no. 2 (1987).

DISCoveries
Caroll, Tom and Jerry Osborne. "The Roy Rogers Interview" [1 b&w photo] (October 1991).

Dodge News
"The Roy Rogers Show with Roy and Dale" 19, no. 2 (circa 1954).

Double-R-Bar News
"Dusty's Corner" (reprint of portion of article appearing in *Coronet* magazine, November 1953) 1 (October 1990): 5.
"Trivia Treat" (reprint from *Lowell Sun* newspaper [Massachusetts], October 23, 1985, cartoon of Dale; artwork by Elvira and Tony Tallarko; 5 b&w photos of Roy, Dale, family;

Roy in comic art form by Bill Maunder) 1 (October 1990).
"Cover Art by Bob Brown" 2 (late 1990): 1.
"Date with Dale Show Dates" (on TBN Network, 4 b&w photos of Roy and Dale, Roy in comic art form) (late 1990).
Reprint of *People* magazine, October 22, 1990 (photo of Roy and Barbara Mandrell 3 (February 11, 1991).
Reprint of Roy, Dale, family in *Dell Comics 1950* 3 (February 1991).
Reprint, Dale Evans, "The Role I Liked Best" 3 (February 1991).
Reprint, Sydney Young, "Roy Rogers Rides Again," *Police Gazette*, 1976 (11 b&w photos, Roy Rogers related) 3 (February 1991). Reprint, "Roy Rogers—King of the Cowboys" (18 b&w photos from numerous sources, including 1940s publicity; *AC Comics*: Roy Rogers Festival, 1989, candid; Golden Boot Awards; *Rock Island Trail*; film publicity; and *Son of Paleface* 1952), brochure from U.S. Historical Society 4 (April 1991).
"Walt's Record Roundup." "The Recordings of Roy Rogers, Pt. 1" 5 (May 1991).
Rogers, Dusty. Letter to readers dated May 1, 1991 (2 b&w photos of Roy and Dale) 5 (May 1991).
———. Letter to readers 5 (July 1991).
"Walt's Record Roundup." "The Recordings of Roy Rogers, Pt. 2" (6 b&w photos of Roy and Dale) (July 1991).
Terry, Ruth. Letter about Roy from a former leading lady 7 (September 1991).
"Walt's Record Roundup." "The Recordings of Roy Rogers, Pt. 3" 7 (September 1991).
Rogers, Dusty. Letter to readers 7 (September 1991).
"Roy Rogers Highlights" 7 (September 1991).
"Roy Rogers-Dale Evans Fan Poll" (10 b&w photos of Roy and Dale) 7 (September 1991).
Rogers, Dusty. Letter to readers 8 (January 1992).
"Roy Rogers-Dale Evans Licensed Merchandise Program" (dated September 17, 1991) 8 (January 1992).
"Poll Results" (6 b&w photos of Roy and Dale) 8 (January 1992).
"Dale's Wisdom" 9 (February, 1992).
"Roy Rogers Interview, WIOI, Western Roundup with Jim Wilson and Zeke Mullins" (radio transcription) 9 (February 1992).
Rogers, Dusty. Letter to readers dated January 17, 1992 9 (February 1992).
"Walt's Record Roundup." "Roy Rogers Tribute," record reviews 9 (February 1992).
"Walt's Record Roundup." "The Recordings of Roy Rogers, Pt. 4" 9 (February 1992).
Reprint from *National Star,* October 21, 1975, "Roy Rogers, Back in the Saddle at 53" (6 b&w photos of Roy and Dale) 9 (February 1992).

Rogers, Dusty. Letter to readers 10 (March 1992).
"Collectibles." "The Roy Rogers Camera" 10 (March, 1992).
"Walt's Record Roundup." "The Roy Rogers Recordings, Pt. 5" (7 b&w photos of Roy and Dale) 10 (March 1992).
Photo reprint from *Screen Stars,* February 1949 11 (April 1992).
"Sons of the Pioneers, Pt. 1—Early Decca Years, 1934–1937" 11 (April 1992).
"Walt's Record Roundup," Special Bulletin 11 (April 1992).
"Collectibles." "American Tract Society Tracards" 11 (April 1992).
"Roy Rogers Quiz," "Movie Time" (1 b&w photo of Roy and Dale) 11 (April 1992).
"Walt's Record Roundup." "Sons of the Pioneers, Pt. 2—Standard Radio Transcriptions, 1934–1935" 12 (August 1992).
Rogers, Dusty. Letter to readers dated July 22, 1992, 12 (August 1992).
"Collectibles." "Roy Rogers; English Birthday Cards" (3 b&w photos of Roy, Dale) 12 (August 1992).

Double R Bar Ranch News
Newsletter of Roy Rogers Fan Club, 1940s–1950s.
McHale, Jewell D. P. (December 1948).
Coleman, Evelyn. "Vacationing with Roy Rogers" (May 1951): 4ff; "A Message from the King of the Cowboys" (January 1951): 1; "Personal Appearance Tour Great Success" (January 1951): 3; "Television Report" (January 1951): 4; "Our Roy Rogers Wins Many Honors" (January 1951): 5.
"Roy's Spring Tour in Central States Makes Smash Hit," p. 1; "New Hampshire Club Sets Good Example," p. 1; "RR-DEFC Member Wins Philadelphia Safety Contest," p. 2; "Dale Stages Happy Reunion with Jack Owens," p. 2; "Five Lucky Children to Win Bullet's First Puppies," p. 3; "Big Day in Tampa," p. 3; "A Travelling We Will Go," p. 3; "He's Got Their Number," p. 3; "W. H. Smith, Dale's Father, Dies April 10," p. 4; "Hollywood's Most Elegant Cowboy Car," p. 4; "*Angel Unaware* Reaches National Best Seller Status Within One Month," p. 6; "I'm Roy," p. 7; "Roy Builds Workshop for His Hobby Equipment," p. 7; "Roy Outwits the Villains Again," p. 8, May-June 1953.
"Texas School First in Safety Programs," p. 2; "Letter from Dale," p. 2; "Seattle Youngsters to be Roy's Guests in Hollywood," p. 2; "New Rogers Ranch Home, Western Dream Come True," pp. 3–5, 7; "Roy Rogers Show Now on 125 NBC-TV Stations," p. 6; "New Biography of Roy Seems Sure to Charm Fans Young and Old," p. 7, November-December 1955.

Dusty Trails
Phillips, Robert W. "Roy Rogers" (January-February 1990).

Esquire
Goodman, Mark. "The Singing Cowboy" [This is a highly offensive article to Rogers family and fans] (December 1975): 154ff.

The Evanstar
Johnson, Lois Blair. Continuing articles, newsletter of the Dale Evans Fan Club. C. 1950s.

Everweek
Lawrence, D. "Trigger Takes a Bow." July 4, 1943.

Family Magazine
"Roy Rogers" (January 1953).

Favorite Westerns
McCleary, Charles. "Don't Fence Me In" 1 (1981): 2–7.
_____. "Roy Rogers and Trigger in South of Caliente" 6 (1982): 21–23.
Roy and Gene cover 9 (1983).
Roy and Wonder Woman cover 10 (1983).
"Bells of Coronado" 18 (Summer 1984).
"Pals of the Golden West" 21 (1985).
Pontes, Bob. "Roy Rogers and I Have Something in Common" 27 (1988): 24.
Reinhart, Ted. "Roy Rogers . . . His Trails Are as Happy as Ever" 28 (1988): 11–13.

Film Album
Votsis, Gloria. "Dale Evans—Roy Rogers" [2 b&w photos] (Summer 1948).

Film Illustrated Monthly (English Publication)
Maxwell, Earl. "The Man from Cincinnati" (4 b&w photos) 2, no. 8 (September 1947).
"Roy Rogers" (full-page photo) 3, no. 6 (June 1948).
"Western News—Dale Back with Roy" (full-page photo of Roy, full-page photo of Dale) 4, no. 5 (May 1949): 14–15.

Film Stars
"Cause for Celebrating" [4 b&w photos] (September 1954): 8.

Filmland
Hayes, Gabby. "My Boy Roy" [6 b&w photos] (October 1950): 42–43.
"Hollywood Birthday Party" (May 1951).
Photo of Dale (October 1951).
"My Hero" (March 1953).

Flair
"Trigger's Trailer" (June 1950): 56–57.

Forbes
Gubernick, Lisa. "The Wal-Mart School of Music" 149, no. 5 (March 2, 1992): 72–76.

Gems and Minerals
Cox, Jack R. "Happy Rock Trails" (April 1968): 18ff.

Golden State
Gurlacz, Betsy. "Happy Trails Are Here Again" 8, no. 3 (Winter 1992).

Good Housekeeping
Baskette, Kirtley. "The Gift of Debbie" 160 (March 1965): 92–93.

Good Old Days
Wilkinson, Harry. "Looking Hollywood Way" 9, no. 7 (January 1973): 22–26, 50.
McClain, Jim. "The Queen of the West" (November 1985): 31–33.

Grit
Douglas, Ester. "Way of the Strong" (June 10, 1945).

Guideposts
Rogers, Roy. "I Didn't Get Away with It" (reprinted in *Faith Made Them Champions*, by Norman Vincent Peal, Guideposts Associates, Carmel, New York, 1954, pp. 53–56) 8 no. 1 (March 1953): 1–4.
Rogers, Roy and Dale Evans. "Bedlam Can Be Beautiful" 13, no. 9 (November 1958): 1–5.
_____. "When Healing Begins" 27, no. 1 (March 1972): 28–30.
_____. "A House Built on a Rock" (February 1980): 17ff.

Guns
August 1958.

The Hillbilly and Western Scrapbook
Roy Rogers 1 (c. 1948).

Hit Parade
September 1944.
April 1946.

Hollywood
Smithson, E. J. "Roy Rogers: Gentleman from Wyoming" 30, no. 12 (December 1941): 54–55.
Crocker, Betty. "Roy Rogers' He-Man Breakfast" 3, no. 3 (March 1942): 68–70.

Hollywood Album (British publication)
"The Changing Pattern" [8 b&w photos, 1 full-page color photo of Roy, Dale, and family] (c. 1950).

Hollywood Cowboy Heroes
"Roy Rogers, King of the Cowboys" (1 b&w photo), p. 69. Unknown date.

Hollywood Family
Story of Rogers family (November 1950).

Hollywood Family Album
"Roy's Robin: Her Heart Belongs to Dusty" (April 1952): 19–20.

Hollywood Family Life
Robin's first birthday covered (January 1951).

Hollywood Pictorial
Editorial Staff. "Roy Rogers" [special Western issue] (September 1950).

The Hollywood Reporter
"Roy Rogers Wins TV Decision" 116, no. 20 (October 19, 1951): 1ff.

Hollywood Studio/Great Western
"Roy Rogers" [Great Western Heroes Edition] (December 1977).

Hollywood Studios
Editorial Staff. "Roy Rogers" (March 1980).
Editorial Staff. "Roy Rogers" (August 1980).
"Roy Rogers—King of the Cowboys" (May 1981): 12–17.

Hollywood—Then and Now
Wiggins, Jim. "How to Write the Stars/Roy Rogers" (1 photo each of Roy and Dale) 24, no. 6 (June 1991): 25.
"Roy Rogers Expert" (Collector's corner: Robert W. Phillips collection, 1 b&w photo) 25, no. 6 (October 1992).

Hollywood Western
"Roy Rogers" (September 1950).

Hollywood Who's Who
"Roy Rogers" (contains Roy's Wyoming story) 1 (1941): 15.

Homesick Texan
Durham, Bill. "The Wild, Wild West Village" (Mid-summer 1990).

The Inside Collector
Kwasneiwski, William. "The Lunch Box" (June 1990): 86–91.
Phillips, Robert W. "Hot! Hot! Hot! It's *Happy Trails* While Collecting Roy Rogers" 5, no. 2 (December 1994).

Inside Edition
"After Hours: Happy Trails to You" (1 photo of Roy with fans) 4, no. 2 (December 1992).

Inside TV
Archerd, Armand. "The More the Merrier" (July 1953).
Branden, Elsie. "Hobby Lobby" (July 1953).
Editorial Staff. "So You Want to Marry a Star" [1 photo of Roy and Dale, Roy is wearing a badge] (October 1953): 23.
"It's Always Christmas" (1 b&w photo of Roy visiting children's hospital) 1, no. 6 (December 1953): 36–41.

Intimate Lives of Movie Stars
"Intimate Life of Roy Rogers," September 25, 1953.

Jack and Jill
Rogers, Roy. "My Television Adventures" [10 photos] (May 1961): 22–27.

Joe Franklin's Memory Lane News
"The Old Corral—Remembering Yesterday's Great Western Stars" and "Roy Rogers" (9 small b&w photos, 1 large full-page b&w photo) 1, no. 3 (February-March 1981): 18–20.
Crisp, Quentin. "Ties That Bind" (1 b&w photo of Roy) 1, no. 6 (January 1991): 76–81.

The Journal of Country Music

Green, Douglas B. "Foy Willing and the Riders of the Purple Sage — Teleways Transcriptions, 1946-1948" 6, no. 1 (Spring 1975).

"The Singing Cowboy" 7, no. 2 (May 1978).

Journal of the American Academy for the Preservation of Old Time Country Music

"Sons of the Pioneers" (October 1992).

Short biography and profile of Roy Rogers (cover photo, inside photos) 2, no. 6 (December 1992).

Ladie's Circle

"Roy Rogers, Dale Evans." Unknown date.

"Roy and Dale: Their 23 Years of Heartbreak and Joy" 6, no. 8 (March 1970): 20-21.

Latest Song Hits

"Song King of the Cowboys" 1, no. 2, April-May 1943.

Liberty

"Cowboy from Cincinnati" (December 14, 1946): 32-33.

Emerson, William K. "The Movie Cowboys" 1, no. 12 (Spring 1974): 44.

Liberty: Canada's Favorite Magazine

Rasky, Frank. "My Amazing Friend Roy Rogers" (September 1954).

Library Journal

Raferty, Bob. "Life with a Bestseller: Angel Unaware" (January 15, 1959): 232.

Life

Smith, H. Allen. "King of the Cowboys" (6 photos of Roy and Arline) 15 (July 12, 1943): 47ff.

"To the editor" [letter from an Autry fan and a letter from Gene Autry about Roy Rogers article] (August 2, 1943).

Editorial Staff. "Trigger Shows Off His Affectionate Nature with Roy Rogers" in "Life on the Newsfronts of the World" (November 5, 1954).

Look

"Roy Rogers Rides Again — and Again" (May 1, 1940): 40.

Houseman, William. "The U.S. Is Going Cowboy Nutty" (July 18, 1950).

"Meet the People — Which Hollywood Star Would You Like to Meet?" (1 b&w photo of Roy, Trigger, child). c. 1950s.

Lardner, John. "A Hoss Who Can Play Alone" (November 4, 1952).

Watters, Jim. "Classic Hollywood" 9, no. 5 (May 1986): 171-94.

Lunch Box Newsletter

Various issues, apparently. Information/photos, Roy Rogers, lunch boxes.

Madison Square Garden Official Annual Rodeo Magazine

"Rodeo Guest, Roy Rogers" (5 b&w photos). *17th Annual Rodeo Magazine* 16, no. 4 (1942).

"Roy Rogers and Trigger" [possibly written by Publications Director, Al Rackin] (1943).

"Roy Rogers and Trigger ... Favorites of Millions." *20th Annual Rodeo Magazine* 19 (1945).

"1945 World Championship Title Winners." *21st Annual Rodeo Magazine* 20, no. 3 (1946).

Whalen, Kathleen L. "Royalty of the Range." *27th Annual Rodeo Magazine* 26, no. 3 (1952).

Rackin, Al. "Roy Rogers, King of the Cowboys." *30th Annual Rodeo Magazine* 29, no. 2 (1955).

"Roy Rogers." *33rd Annual Rodeo Magazine* (1958).

Mature Living

Fair, Charlie. "Roy Rogers Festival Always Draws a Crowd" (August 1990).

Memory Lane, Rob Tucker's

"Roy Rogers." "Dale Evans" (August 1980).

Men's Health

Rogers, Roy. "How to Make a Quick Getaway" (May 1994).

Midnight

"How Roy Rogers Overcame His Cardiac Problems" (January 6, 1977): 29.

Model and Toy Collector

Phillips, Bob. "Bob Phillips' Cowboy Collectibles" no. 28, 30 (1994).

Modern Screen

"They Ride the Picture Plains" 20, no. 2 (January 1940): 66-67.

"Appearing in Republic's *Idaho*" 26, no. 5 (April 1943): 52.

Benjamin, George. "We Want Roy Rogers" (3 b&w photos) 29, no. 6 (November 1944).

"Pistol Packin' Papa" 31, no. 3 (August 1945): 56-57.

"Roy Rogers" (December 1946).

"State Fair" (10 b&w photos) 34, no. 1 (December 1946): 46-49.

Koleman, Evelyn. "Something for Dusty" 7, no. 8 (July 1947): 24-25.

Kinkead, Jean. "Family Man — Western Style" 35, no. 4 (September 1947): 56-92.

Schroeder, Carl. "The Case of Autry vs. Rogers" 35, no. 5 (October 1947): 42ff.

"Philadelphia Idyll" 36, no. 2 (January 1948): 52-55.

Miller, Cynthia. "They Knew What They Wanted" 36, no. 3 (February 1948): 14ff.

Morris, Mary. "They Wake up Dreaming" (April 1948): 28-29, 100-101.

"They Call Me Mother" 37, no. 3 (July 1948): 32ff.

"You Can't Come Between Roy and Dale" 37, no. 3 (August 1948): 27.

"By Invitation Only" (color, b&w photos) 37, no. 6 (November 1948): 48–51.

Rogers, Roy. "We're Together Again" 38, no. 6 (May 1949): 50ff.

Churchill, Reba, and Bonnie Churchill. "Westward Whoa" 39, no. 4 (September 1949): 42ff.

Evans, Dale. "Two Loves Have We" (December 1949): 32–33, 87.

Waite, Margaret. "All in the Family" 41, no. 2 (July 1950): 53ff.

"Cheryl's Debut" 14, no. 1 (November 1950): 80–81.

"By Popular Demand" 14, no. 9 (July 1951): 36–39.

Peterson, Marva. "Roy's Ranch" 43, no. 4 (September 1951): 64.

"Cheryl Steps Out" 14, no. 12 (October 1951): 42–45.

Trent, Susan. "Full House—Full Hearts" (4 color photos) 46, no. 3 (February 1953): 36ff.

Rogers, Roy. "The Truth About My First Wife" 49, no. 12 (November 1955): 29ff.

"Roy Rogers" [1 b&w photo] (February 1974).

"Editor's Page." Country Music Special Issue [photo of Roy] (Fall 1991).

"Clint Black's Newest Project: Roy Rogers and Lisa Hartman." Country Music Special—Garth Brooks and the Men of Country (February 1992).

Country Music Special Issue [full-page color picture of Roy] (February 1993).

Modern Television and Radio
Koleman, Evelyn. "A Reunion with Roy and Dale" (December 1948).

Motion Picture
Raymond, Louis. "King of the Cowboys" (Combined with *Hollywood Magazine*, 2 b&w photos) 65, no. 2 (April 1943).

Rogers, Roy, as told to Adrienne Ames. "How I Trained Trigger" 67, no. 1 (February 1944).

Bard, Richard. "Singing Steno" [Dale Evans] (September 1944): 72.

Weller, Helen. "Let's Pretend You're Mrs. Roy Rogers" (November 1944): 38ff.

Woolf, S. J. "An Artist Looks at Roy Rogers" 80, no. 3 (October 1945).

Photo of Roy with Arline [caption] (c. late 1945).

Samuels, Charles. "Hero on Horseback" 63, no. 2 (September 1946): 28ff.

Hoover, Helen. "Popping Questions at Roy Rogers" 72, no. 4 (May 1947): 300–314.

Hastings, Charles. "The War of the Cowboys" 74, no. 4 (November 1947): 44ff.

Editorial Staff. "The Money Makers—Roy Rogers" 75, no. 5 (June 1948): 48.

Weller, Helen. "Let's Pretend You're Mrs. Roy Rogers" (November 1948): 30ff.

Hastings, Robert. "Everybody's Top-Hand" [color photos by Mickey Marigold, Don Keyes] (1949): 36–37, 76–77.

Story by Dale (July 1950).

Motion Picture and Television
"Time for Living" (June 1954).

Motion Picture Herald
"The Biggest Money Making Stars of 1939" 137, no. 12 (December 23, 1939): 13–16.

Weaver, William R. "The Top Money Making Stars of 1940" 141, no. 13 (December 28, 1940): 13–16.

———. "The Biggest Money Making Stars of 1941" 145, no. 13 (December 27, 1941): 13–16.

———. "The Biggest Money Making Stars of 1942" 149, no. 13 (December 26, 1942): 13–16.

———. "The Biggest Money Making Stars of 1943" 153, no. 13 (December 25, 1943): 14–16.

———. "The Biggest Money Making Stars of 1944" 157, no. 13 (December 30, 1944): 12–15.

———. "The Biggest Money Making Stars of 1945" 161, no. 13 (December 29, 1945): 13–16.

"Dale Evans Has Fun in Western" (November 30, 1946).

Weaver, William R. "The Biggest Money Making Stars of 1946" 165, no. 13 (December 28, 1946): 13–16.

———. "The Biggest Money Making Stars of 1947" 170, no. 1 (January 3, 1948): 13–15.

———. "The Biggest Money Making Stars of 1948" 174, no. 1 (January 1, 1949): 13–15.

Rodeo Coverage. Photo of Roy in arena on horseback, visiting with singer Pat Boone and family, 177 (December 31, 1949).

Weaver, William R. "The Biggest Money Making Stars of 1949" 177, no. 14 (December 31, 1949): 13–15.

———. "The Biggest Money Making Stars of 1950" 181, no. 13 (December 30, 1950): 13–15.

———. "Rogers Verdict Sends TV into Vertical Spin" (October 27, 1951): 13ff.

Motion Picture Star Album
"Roy Rogers" (3 photos) 3 (1948).

The Motorcycle Enthusiast
Kraft, Ken. "Roy Rogers Rides Again" (October 1958)

The Mountain Broadcast and Prairie Recorder
Case, Floy. "Roy Rogers" (December 1946): 21, 23.

Henderson, Frame. "King of the Cowboys" [11 photos] (March 1946): 3–7.

Movie
"Roy Rogers" 6, no. 1 (September-October 1951): 28–29.

Movie Collector's World
Ward, Jim. "Cowboy King: A Prince of a Guy" 237 (May 2, 1986).

Movie Fan
"Roy Rogers" 1, no. 3 (Autumn 1946).

"Roy Rogers and Dale Evans" 3, no. 2 (August 1948): 56–57.

"Roy Rogers" 3, no. 4 (March-April 1949).

"Roy Rogers" 3, no. 3 (May-June 1949): 26–27.

"Roy Rogers" 4, no. 1 (September-October 1949): 56–57.

"Roy Rogers" 4, no. 2 (November-December 1949): 56–57.

"Roy Rogers" 4, no. 3 (January-February 1950): 50–51.

"Roy Rogers" 4, no. 5 (May-June 1950): 26–27.

Two pages on Roy 4, no. 10 (July 1950)

Two pages on Roy 4, no. 12 (September 1950)

"Roy Rogers" 5, no. 1 (September-October 1950): 54–55.

"Roy Rogers" (additional photo, p. 4) 5, no. 2 (November-December 1950): 16–17.

"Movie Fan Requests" (photo) 5, no. 2 (November-December 1950).

"Roy Rogers" 5, no. 3 (January-February 1981): 12–13.

"Roy Rogers" 5, no. 4 (March-April 1951): 28–29.

"Roy Rogers" 5, no. 4 (March-April 1951).

Two pages on Roy 5, no. 6 (March 1951).

Two pages on Roy 5, no. 8 (May 1951).

"Roy Rogers" 5, no. 5 (May-June 1951).

"Roy Rogers" 5, no. 5 (May 1951): 30–31.

Two pages on Roy 5, no. 10 (July 1951).

Two pages on Roy 5, no. 12 (November 1951).

"Roy Rogers" 6, no. 2 (November-December 1951): 36–37.

"Roy Rogers" 6, no. 3 (January-February 1952): 32–33.

"Roy Rogers" 6, no. 4 (March-April 1952): 36–37.

"Roy Rogers" 6, no. 5 (May-June 1952): 38–39.

"Roy Rogers" 6, no. 6 (July-August 1952): 38–39.

Sifikis, Carl. "Trigger, Roy Rogers Boss" 7, no. 6 (March 1953): 48–49.

Movie Fan Album
"Roy Rogers" 1 (Winter 1946): 22–23.

Movie Glamour
Three part story with photos (December 1950).

The Movie Greats
"The Cowboys" (Lynne Roberts [Mary Hart] is identified as Dale Evans). 3 (1971): 16–19.

Movieland
Albert, Dora. "Roy Rogers' Little Buckorina" (September 1943): 39.

"Roy Rogers Rodeo" 3, no. 9 (October 1945): 48.

Editorial Staff. "Horse Laughs" (April 1946): 44–45.

Simpson, Len. "Trigger Man" (October 1946): 35ff.

"A God Mother for Dusty" (July 1947): 24–25.

Editorial Staff. "Devoted Daddy" (January 1948): 60–61.

Evans, Dale. "Confessions of a Stepmother" (May 1948).

Covering Roy and Dusty at Ladd Party 8, no. 3 (August 1950).

Roy and Dale in Gallery of Fame 8, no. 9 (October 1950).

Robin and Dale, 9 no. 5 (June 1951).

"Roy Rogers' New Family" 9, no. 6 (July 1951).

"Roy Rogers" 9, no. 9 (October 1951).

Photo from *Place in the Sun* premiere, Roy and Dale in white suits, 9, no. 10 (November 1951).

Rogers, Roy. "My Ten Rules for a Happy Marriage" (October 1952): 46–56.

Balling, Freda D. "Life Is Now Complete" (April 1953): 60–64.

"Sheila Graham's Hollywood Family Album" (April 1953).

Movie Life
"A Day at Jane's House" 6, no. 2 (December 1942): 32–34.

"Roy Rogers and Trigger," "Trigger's Birthday Party" (2 b&w photos) 7, no. 1 (1943).

"18 Year Plan" 7, no. 4 (February 1944): 10.

Miller, Llewellyn. "Yellow Rose of Texas" [ad] (June 1944): 10.

_____. "Radio Roundup" (June 1944): 74.

Editorial Staff. "Family Man" (June 1944): 77.

"Ride'em Cowboy" 7, no. 12 (October 1944): 20.

"Movie Life of Roy Rogers" 8, no. 3 (January 1945): 20–25.

"Hep to Hitch" 8, no. 6 (April 1945): 64–65.

"Socko" 8, no. 10 (August 1945): 82–83.

"Trigger Goes Along on a Hospital Tour with Roy Rogers" 8, no. 10 (September 1945).

"Hay Trigger" 10, no. 3 (February 1946): 74–75.

"Along Radio Roy" (photo of Roy and Janet Blair) 10, no. 6 (May 1946): 53.

"Everything the Popsy Goes" 10, no. 7 (June 1946): 32–33.

"Home on the Range" 10, no. 7 (June 1946): 18ff.

"Feet First" 10, no. 9 (August 1946): 70.

"Setting the Style" (photo of Roy with Jane Wyman with caption, c. mid–1940s) 10, no. 10 (September 1946): 48.

"Heffer Heafting" 10, no. 4 (February 1947): 97.

"Bear Bear" 10, no. 5 (March 1947): 98–99.

"Lullabye for Dusty (with Roy on the Vocal)" 10, no. 7 (May 1947): 75.

"Movie Life's Corral of Horse Opera Heroes" 10, no. 5 (May 1947): 58–60.

"That a Way" 11, no. 1 (November 1947): 34.

"Movie Life's Corral" 11, no. 2 (December 1947): 63.

"For Dusty" [a new suit from a fan] (January 1948): 55.

"It Won't Be Long Now" 11, no. 3 (February 1948): 48–50.

Vallee, William Lynch. "Life Story in Pix of Roy's New Bride – Dale Evans" (March 1948): 58–64.

"All Join in (for a Big Celebration)" 11, no. 9 (July 1948): 66–69.

"The Buckaroo Bob" 12, no. 9 (July 1948): 25–27.

Editorial Staff. "Movie Life of Dale Evans and Roy Rogers." *Yearbook* (1948): 22–33.

"Dusty's King at the Rogers'-Evans Diggings" 11, no. 12 (October 1948): 44–48.

"Rogers Style" (also seen listed as "The Rogers Look") 12, no. 1 (November 1948): 35.

"Dale Votes" (November 1948).

"On Tour" 12, no. 2 (December 1948): 101.

Editorial Staff. "Dusty's Birthday Party" (c. January-May 1949).

"Men at the Mike" 12, no. 6 (April 1949): 82.

Editorial Staff. "Everybody's Happy (As Dale Evans Goes Back to Work with Roy Rogers)" (May 1949): 46–48.

"King and Handyman" (has dog "Spur" in article) 12, no. 10 (August 1949): 62–65.

"Home Sweet Hollywood—At Home with Roy Rogers" [may also be listed as "Hollywood Goes to Church"] (October 1949): 48–50.

"One Last Fling" 13, no. 1 (November 1949): 50–51.

"Roy and Gene Play Golf" 13, no. 6 (April 1950): 34–41.

"Trigger's New Trailer" 13, no. 8 (June 1950).

Editorial Staff. "Roy Rogers," 1950 *Yearbook*.

"Sombreros at Seven" (2 pages on Roy and Dusty at Alana Ladd's birthday party) 13, no. 10 (August 1950).

"Sitting Pretty, Roy Poses for Son Dusty" 13, no. 11 (September 1950): 87.

"The Stork's in Style" 13, no. 13 (October 1950)

"Cheryl's Debut" 14, no. 1 (November 1950).

"Roy and Dale on a Coon Hunt" (10 b&w photos) 4, no. 2. c. 1950.

"Love Him, Love His Dogs" (Roy and Bullet in Central Park, New York City) 14, no. 3 (January 1951): 48–51.

"How Busy Can You Get" (6 pages photos) 14, no. 5 (March 1951); 40–45.

"First Robin" 14, no. 8 (June 1951): 57.

"It's a Close Race" (Fan Club contest, 2 b&w photos of Roy and Fan Club president, Lillian Byrum of Greenville, Texas) 14, no. 9 (July 1951): 880.

"Roy Rogers and Dale Evans at Home" 14, no. 11 (August 1951): 6.

"Those Gay Rancheros" 14, no. 10 (August 1951): 42–47.

Photo of Roy recording 14, no. 11 (September 1951).

"Roy and Dale—From Saddles to Sails" (February 1952).

"Western Style—Roy Rogers and Rex Allen" (1 large b&w photo) 16, no. 5 (April 1953): 6.

"The Younger Set" (March 1955).

Movie Mirror

"Daddy" 2, no. 3 (1949).

Tully, Jim. "Roy Rogers" (September 1942).

"Western Hall of Fame" (June 1950).

"Trigger Travels in Style" (August 1950).

"Roy, Boy, Joy" (June 1951).

"They Went That-a-Way" (August 1951).

"Daddy" [1 page photo] (February 1952).

"Ranch Hand at Work" 3, no. 4 (April-May 1952): 38–39.

Rogers, Roy. "I Found God" (December 1953).

Movie Play

"Roy Rogers" 1, no. 2 (January 1946).

"Roy Rogers" (Winter 1946).

Unknown title article (January 1949).

Two pages on Roy, Dale, at Houston Rodeo (June 1950).

Two pages of Roy, photo with Gabby (September-October 1950).

"Dusty Visits the Set" (November 1950).

"Then and Now" (January 1951).

Roy Rogers family photos (February 1951).

"King Roy" [2 pages of photos] (March 1951).

Photos at play (April 1951).

Two pages on Roy (May 1951).

"Dale Evans Returns" (October 1951).

"Friends of the Fans" (October 1951).

"Roy Goes Back to the Farm" (December 1951).

Movie Play Western

"Ten Years with Roy Rogers" 5, no. 5 (c. 1948): 8–13.

Movie-Radio Guide

"Roy Rogers and Trigger Take Over NBC" (January 16-22, 1943): 8.

Movie Show

"Trigger Tricks" [8 b&w photos] (c. 1944).

"Bowling Date" (February 1944).

Albin, Jack. "Private Life of the 'King'" (4 color photos of Roy, family, 1 full-size photo using reverse negative). Unknown date.

"Cowboy Picnic" [5 b&w photos] (c. 1950s).

Movie Spotlight

"Roy Rogers" (October 1949).

"You Asked for It" (August 1950).

"Roy Rogers" (October 1950).

"Handyman Roy" (January 1951).

Photos, full page, Roy and Trigger (February 1950).

Rogers family at home (March 1951).

"Royal Doings" (June 1951).

Movie Star Parade

"Civil War in the Sagebrush" 2, no. 4 (March 1942): 13–15.

"Linda Lou" 3, no. 9 (August 1943): 72.

"Cowboy in Gotham" 4, no. 2 (January 1944): 44–45.

"Clothes Make the Cowboy" 4, no. 8 (July 1944): 34–35.

"Cowboy on Ice" 4, no. 10, (September 1944): 14–15.

Photo of Roy and Gene together (October 1944): 200.

Taylor, Lilli. "Shucks, It's Glamour" 4, no. 12 (December 1944): 38–39.

"Ridin' on Air" 5, no. 4 (March 1945): 25.

"Super Sagebrusher" 5, no. 7 (June 1945): 40–41.

"Heading Up" (September 1945).

"Roy Rodeo" 5, no. 1 (October 1945): 31.

"The King Goes to Town" 6, no. 3 (February 1946): 32–33.

"The King Plays Talent Scout" 6, no. 6 (May 1946): 26–27.

"Meet the Queen" 6, no. 12 (November 1946): 42.

"Heldorado Hi Jinx" 6, no. 12 (November 1946): 42–43.

"Win a Wee Trigger" 7, no. 12 (November 1947): 54–55.

"Roy and Dale in Honeymoon Hideaway" [15 photos of Roy, Dale, kids at new home] (June 1948).

Rogers, Roy. "You" (March 1949): 30–33.

"How Roy Changed My Life" 10, no. 3 (February 1950): 32ff.

"Sagebrush Sweethearts" 10, no. 5 (June 1950).

"Stormy" 11, no. 5 (June 1950).

"A Playmate for Dusty" (August 1950).

"Dog Days" (October 1950).

Photo of Roy and Dale with Trigger trophy (December 1950).

Full-page photo of Roy and Dale (January 1951).

"Stormy Takes a Bow" (photo of Roy, Dale, and Robin) 10, no. 6 (June 1951): 64.

Photo of Roy with golden hamsters, 11, no. 6 (July 1951).

"Read Your Bible with Roy Rogers" 12, no. 1 (November 1951).

Photo of Roy and Dale with Trigger trophy, 12, no. 2 (December 1951).

"He's a Young Cowhand" (11 b&w photos of Roy, Dale, Dusty, and Robin) 12, no. 2 (December 1951): 60–63.

"Roy Plays the Garden" [3 b&w photos] (September 1952): 18.

"Roy Rogers/Dale Evans" (January 1991).

Movie Star Parade Album

"Meet the Queen" 1, no. 2 (1947): 40–41.

"Lonely Buckaroo" no. 2 (1947): 36–37.

"Family Album" (1947).

"First Family" 1, no. 4 (1948): 44–45.

Movie Story

"Don't Fence Me In" 20, no. 140 (November 1945): 46–47.

Reed, Vivian. "A Merry Christmas Brunch" 20, no. 2 (December 1945): 12.

Movie Teen

Full-page portrait, Roy and Trigger (August 1950).

Full-page photo of Roy and Miss Movie Teen (March 1951).

Photo of Roy, Trigger, Donald O'Connor (November 1951).

Movie Thrills

"Coon Huntin'" 1, no. 4 (November 1943): 52–53.

"Not in the Script" (May 1950): 40–43.

"That Young Cowhand" (May 1950): 25–27.

"The Cowboy and His Mrs" [Portraits of Roy and Dale] (July 1950): 50–51.

"My Life with Roy" 1, no. 2 (July 1950): 22–25.

"For the Sportsmen" 1, no. 4 (September 1950): 16–17.

"Sunset in the West" 1, no. 4 (September 1950): 86.

"Rock Island Special" (September 1950): 50–51.

"For the Sportsman" [Roy Rogers at California sports show] (September 1950): 16–17.

"Previews: North of the Great Divide" 1, no. 4 (November 1950): 90–91.

Movie Western

"How I Teach My Children to Cook" 1, no. 1 (July 1950).

"Trigger, Jr." 1, no. 1 (July 1950).

"Lucky Penny" (1 photo) 1, no. 2 (September 1950): 8.

"Horses, Horses, Horses" (2 photos) 1, no. 2 (September 1950): 9–10.

"Dusty Grows Up"; (8 photos) 1, no. 2 (September 1950): 11–14, 78.

"The Rogers Family" 1, no. 3 (November 1950).

"Western Records" 1, no. 3 (November 1950).

"Down on the Farm" (July 1960).

Movie World

"In the Swim" (January 1951).

Movies

Monroe, Don. "Roy Rogers" (November 1940)

Joseph, Robert. "Hero of the Badlands — Roy Rogers" (June 1942): 24–27.

"Roy Rogers and Trigger — They're Co-Stars Now" (July 1943): 71.

"Roy Rogers in Pecos Bill" [in full color] (August-September 1947): 70.

"Pop Takes Over" (October 1947).

"Weddings" (May 1948).

"First Role" (December 1950).

Photos, Roy, Trigger, and Bullet (February 1951).

"I Doff My Stetson to Roy Rogers" (June 1951).

"I Doff My Stetson to Rev. Bill Alexander" (August 1951).

Music City News

Editorial Staff. "Fixtures to Happy Trails — Roy and Dale" (October 1979).

"Country Meets Western," "Star Gazin'" (January 1988): 6–7.

"Trade News," "The Stars Come Out in Music City" (December 1990): 3, 14, 60.

Harden, Lydia Dixon. "The King of the Cowboys Rides Again" 29, no. 5 (December 1991): 32–33.

"Roy Rogers Receives 'Living Legend Award'" (July 8, 1992).

Muzzle Loaders

Hacker, Rick. "Roy Rogers, King of the Muzzle-loading Families" (October 1990): 15.

The National Broadcast and Prairie Recorder

Henderson, Frame. "Star of Western Pictures" (Dale Evans) 3 (March 1945).

National Jamboree
"Roy Rogers Visits New York" (June 1949).
"Intimate Facts About the Queen: Meet the Real Dale" (November-December 1949): 19–21.

New York Times Magazine
Greenbaum, Lucy. "A Sinatra in a Sombrero" (November 4, 1945): 42.

Nation's Restaurant News
Carlino, Bill. "Roy Rogers 'Lunch Ladies' Resign Spatulas – Again: Fast-Food Chain Pulls TV Spot for Second Time Amid Complaints" (September 3, 1988): 12.
_____. "Roy Rogers Cans Ads: School Feeders' Complaints Bring End to Campaign" (September 5, 1988): 4.
Seligman, Bob. "Hardee's Ropes Roy Rogers" 24, no. 7 (February 12, 1990): 1ff.
Van Warner, Rick and Prewitt Milford. "Hardee's Pushes North with Roy's Conversions" 25, no. 9 (March 4, 1991): 48.
"Hardee's Creates Task Force to Finish Roy's Conversion" 25, no. 26 (June 10, 1991): 2.
Prewitt, Milford. "New Ads, Task Force Bouy NY Roy's Licensees: Hardee's Moves to Address Conversion Concerns of Roy Rogers Franchises in Metro Area" 25, no. 26 (July 8, 1991).

The New Captain George's Whizzbang
Miller, Don. "Let's Hear It Out There for Roy Rogers and to a Lesser Extent, Autry" 3, no. 2 (c. 1968-69): 18–21.

New York Herald Magazine
Rogers, Roy. "Bob Hope a Cowboy? Trigger Had a Horse Laugh" (June 1, 1952).

Newsweek
"King of the Cowboys" (March 8, 1943): 75–76.
"Back in the Saddle" 18 (January 14, 1974): 15.
"Out of the Saddle" (March 3, 1975): 9.
"Roy Rogers Eats Crow" 112, no. 9 (August 29, 1988): 42.

Nostalgia Illustrated
Martin, Bette. "The Cowboys" (April 1975): 44–50.

Oak Tree Express
"Dale Berry's Ranch House News" 1, no. 1 (November 1992).
"Roy Rogers, King of the Comic Book Cowboys," "Enjoying the Work of Stuntmen in Western Films" 1, no. 4 (May 1993): 4–5.

Omni
Long, Marion. "Paradise Tossed" (April 1988): 36ff.

Open Road
"Roy Rogers Plans a Boy's Ranch" 34, no. 6 (June 1952).

Outdoor Life
Anderson, W. E. A. "Roy Rogers Goes North" 137 (April 1966): 52–55.

People Weekly
Novak, Ralph. "After 23 Years Out of Films, Roy Rogers Is (Apologies, Gene) Back in the Saddle" (June 23, 1975): 56ff.
"Good Ol' Timers and Nashville Newcomers Mix It Up – With Smiles – on Country Music's Biggest Night" (October 22, 1980): 38–39.
Photo with caption: Roy and Dale attend the 20th Century-Fox party for Queen Elizabeth at Stage 9 in Hollywood (March 14, 1983).
Gross, Ken, and Suzanne Adelson. "Once Estranged, Roy Rogers and Roy Rogers, Jr. See Only Happy Trails" (August 17, 1987): 67–68.
Novak, Ralph. "Heroes and Friends" (October 29, 1990): 15.
_____. "Pix & Pans: Tribute by Roy Rogers and Various Artists" 37, no. 20 (May 25, 1992): 21.

Photo Story
Natterford, Jack. "Cowboy King" (January 1943).

Photoplay
"Cowboy with Sex Appeal" 19, no. 6 (November 1941): 64.
Tully, T. "Keep Punchin'" 21, no. 4 (September 1942): 51.
Delehanty, Thornton. "Cowboy in the Velvet" 25, no. 6 (November 1944): 47ff.
Waterbury, Ruth. "Life with Fathers" 272, no. 1 (June 1945): 40–41.
Photo of Roy, Gabby, Shug Fisher, script girl, and Peggy Stewart (c. 1945).
"Carnival Time" 29, no. 1 (June 1946): 44–45.
Arnold, Maxine. "Buckeye Buckaroo" (November 1946): 44ff.
Parsons, Louella. "Roy Rides Alone" (April 1947): 32–33.
Dusek, J. "I Was There" 32, no. 2 (January 1948): 54.
Evans, Dale. "I Lived a Lie" (April 1948): 62–63.
Mulvey, Kay. "Swing Your Partner" (December 1948).
Howe, Herb. "Photoplay Roundup" 36, no. 6 (November 1949): 54ff.
"Roy Rogers" (December 1951).
Endersley, Douglas A. "King of Them All" (June 1952).
Kingsley, K. "With Open Hearts" 43, no. 2 (February 1953): 82–83.
La Badie, D. W. "How I Faced My Drinking Problem" 78, no. 4 (October 1970): 60ff.

Photoplay Annual
Portrait of Roy, full page (January 1951).

Pic
Photos of Rogers' new home (October 1951).

"Spurs That Jangle Like a Cash Register" (November 1952).

Piccolo (Swedish Film Publication)
"Filmland in Kleur" (c. February 1950).

Picturegoer
"Roy Rogers" (September 11, 1948).

The Plain Dealer
Evans, Christopher. "Whoopie-Ti-Yi-Yo, It's the Roy Rogers Show" (May 28, 1989): 10–11.

Playboy
Friedenn, Neva. "Museums" 24, no. 5 (May 1977): 72.

Plus
Rogers, Dale Evans. "The Art of Being Alive — Part 3" 7, no. 10 (December 1986): 26–35.

Police Gazette
Young, Sydney. "Still Going Strong at 62 — Roy Rogers Rides Again" (1973).

Possibilities
Dunn, Jeanne A. "The Happy Trails of Roy Rogers and Dale Evans" (March-April 1986).

Praise The Lord
"Roy Rogers and Dale Evans" 21, no. 7 (July 1994): 3.

Pulse
Griffith, Jackson. "Country and Western's Trigger Happy Elder Spokesman Teams Up with a Few Young Guns" 99 (November 1991).

Que
"Those Adult Westerns on TV" [drawing of Roy and Trigger] (January 26, 1957): 10.

Quick
"King of the Cowboys" (8 photos) 2, no. 8 (February 20, 1950): 48–51.
"For Sale" (February 4, 1952).

Radio Album
"The More the Merrier," exclusive edition (1957).

Radio and Television Mirror
Blair, Dorothy. "Come and Visit Roy Rogers" 32, no. 3 (August 1949): 60ff.

Radio Mirror
"Cover Girl" 21, no. 1 (November 1943): 12–13.

Radio TV Mirror
"What's New from Coast to Coast" (photo of Roy and Gale Storm) 43, no. 1 (December 1943): 10.
Valentry, Duane. "That Old Family Feeling" (June 1952): 46–47.
"Tomorrow the Sun Will Shine Again" (February 1953).

Ranch Romances
Bright, Beth. "Ranch Flicker Talk" (January 1950): 3.

"Roy Rogers, Dale Evans and Little Robin Elizabeth" [1 b&w photo] (February 1951): 12–13.

Read
Lee, Rosalind. "King of the Cowboys" (August 1944).

Real Screen Fun
Shute, George. "Feud for Thought" (June 1939).

Reporter (Frisch's Restaurant Publication)
"King of the Cowboy's Headin' Home" 35, no. 3 (June 1988): 1ff.

Republic Reporter
"Rogers Bully in Wall Street Cowboy" (September 6, 1949): 1–2.

Restaurant Business Magazine
"Happy Trails for Hardee's: Buys Roy Rogers for $365M" 89, no. 4 (March 1, 1990): 200.

Restaurants and Institutions
Bertagnoli, Lisa. "Sweet Stuff, Seniors, and Southern Style: Roy Rogers Adds Breakfast Cinnamon Rolls to Satisfy Sweet-Toothed On-the-Go Customers" 98, no. 1 (January 8, 1988): 142ff.

Rodeo History
Clancy, Foghorn. "Roy Rogers, King of the Cowboys" [back cover] (Fall 1945): 28.

Rona Barrett's Hollywood
Munshower, Suzanne. "Roy Rogers — Back in the Saddle" 7, no. 3 (November 1975): 19, 52–53.

Roy Rogers and His World's Championship Rodeo Programs
[Insert for appearance at Indianapolis, Indiana] (September 29–October 5, 1948).

Roy Rogers–Dale Evans Collectors Assn. News
All volumes through #43, Portsmouth, Ohio (1984–1992).
White, Ray. "The Roy Rogers Show: A Decade of Radio Adventure, 1944–1945," Pt. 1: 1944–1951; continued, 5, no. 33 (September-October 1988).
———. "The Roy Rogers Show: A Decade of Radio Adventure, 1944–1945" Pt. 1: 1944–1951; continued (Winter 1988-89).
Phillips, Robert W. "Bob Phillips on Roy Rogers" 43 (Spring 1992).
Phillips, Bob. "The Dell Westerns" 45 (Fall 1992).
———. "The Roy Rogers Books" 45 (Fall, 1992).
Johnson, Carol. "The Sons of the Pioneers — A Roundup" 45 (Fall 1992).

Roy Rogers Official Souvenir Program
c. 1958

Rural Radio
Dale Evans cover 1, no. 7 (August 1938).

Rustic Rhythm
"Junior Photo Gallery" (June 1957): 46.

Saturday Evening Post
Martin, Pete. "Cincinnati Cowboy" 217 (January 1945): 26ff.
Rogers, Roy. "The Role I Liked Best" (April 27, 1948).
Brown, Joan Winmill. "Roy Rogers and Dale Evans—A Marriage Made in Heaven" 252 (April 1980): 50–53.

Saturday Review
Haverstick, John. "Two Souls in the Saddle" (December 10, 1955): 19–20.

The Scottish Rites Journal
Kemmerer, Walter L. "Roy Rogers, 33 Degree Recollections" 98, no. 8, (August 1990).

Screen Album
"Roy Rogers" 24 (Fall 1943): 44.
"Roy Rogers" 25 (Winter 1944).
Story, photos (May 1950).
"Roy Rogers" (July 1950).
Story on Dale (November 1950).
Two pages photos (Spring 1951).
Roy and Dale 5, no. 10 (July 1951).
Two pages on Roy, 5, no. 12 (September 1951).
Photo of Dale and kids (November 1951).
"Just Like Her Maw" (Fall 1951).

Screen and Television Guide
"Blue Jean Jamboree" (May 1949).

Screen and TV Album
"Gallopin' Greats" (1950s): 59–61.

Screen Annual
Four pages on Roy, Cheryl, Rocky Lane (April 1951).

Screen Facts
Cocci, John. "Films of Roy Rogers" 2, no. 5 (1963): 68ff.
———. "Additional Roy Rogers Films" (1968).

Screen Greats
"The Great Love Teams" Roy and Dale 3 (1990): 161.
"Rogers and Evans; 35 Films" 3 (1990).

Screen Guide
"Screen Guide's 1944 Poll Results" (February 1945).
Photo of Roy and Dale dancing, Dale not wearing Western attire (c. mid-1940s).
"He Can't Take It with Him" [14 b&w photos taken at Madison Square Garden Rodeo] (c. 1945).
Interview with Roy (January 1946).
"Roy Rogers Adopts a Home Town" 11, no. 10 (October 1946): 27–29.
Photo, oversize, color, of Roy and Trigger (c. 1946).
"Dale Turns Dude" (July 1947): 84–86.
"Stars Behind the Camera" [2 b&w photos] (c. 1947).
Rogers, Roy. "Self Portrait" (August 1948): 43.

"Screen Guide Visits Roy Rogers" (April 1950): 32–35.
"Mr. and Mrs. Roy Rogers Rough It" (July 1950): 46–49.
"Roy Rogers" (August 1950).
"How the Roy Rogers Live" [8 pages b&w photos] (March 1951): 34–41.
Photo of Roy and Robin (June 1951).
"Roy Rogers Ranch" (August 1951).
Four pages on Roy with notes by Dale (October 1951).
Photo of Roy (November 1951).

Screen Romances
"Heart of the Golden West" (December 1942).
"San Fernando Valley" 28, no. 186 (November 1944).

Screen Stars
"Prairie Canary" (October 1944): 24–25.
Photo of Roy Rogers, Gene Autry in New York, 2, no. 3 (December 1944).
"Those Real Nice Rogers" 2, no. 3 (December 1944): 14–16.
"Those Real Nice Rogers" [photo of Arline, Roy, girls] (c. 1945).
Rogers, Linda Lou. "Babes in Hollywood" 3, no. 6 (September 1945): 26–27.
"Horse Sense" (December 1945): 32–33.
Webster, Robert. "Debunking the Autry-Rogers Feud" 6, no. 4 (January 1947): 48ff.
Mann, May. "Magnificent Mothers" 6, no. 6 (March 1947).
"Rex Allen" [talks about Roy Rogers] (October 1949).
Canfield, Alyce. "Dinner with Roy Rogers" 8, no. 11 (February 1951).
"Ranching the Rogers Way" (18 b&w photos) 8, no. 11 (February 1951).
"Roy Rogers" (2 photos) 9 no. 1 (April 1951).
Rogers, Roy. "Westerns Are Good for Children" 9, no. 3 (June 1951): 62–64.
Rogers, Roy. "Why I Go to Church" 9, no. 7 (October 1951): 16–17.
"Western Birthday Party" 10, no. 3 (June 1952).
"Roy Gets a Break" 12, no. 5 (November 1954): 32–33.

Screen Stories
"Grand Canyon Trail" (November 1948): 43–45, 93–98.
"Susanna Pass" (June 1949): 34–36, 98–100.
"Down Dakota Way" (September 1949): 57–58, 90–92.
"Trigger, Jr." (July 1950): 39–41, 68–70.
"Sunset in the West" (September 1950).
"North of the Great Divide" (November 1950).
"Bells of Coronado" (December 1950).
Fidler, Jimmie. "Jimmie Fidler in Hollywood" 44, no. 6 (December 1950).
"Trail of Robin Hood" (February 1951).
"Heart of the Rockies" 45, no. 5 (May 1951).
"South of Caliente" (July 1951).

Screen Thrills
"The Ace of Stuntmen" [photo of Roy with stunt-
man David Sharpe] (October 1963): 26.
Rinehart, Ted. "Dale Evans: A Very Fine Lady"
6 (1976): 28–29.

Screen World
Story: Roy (June 1951).

Screenland
Evan, Delight. "Roy Rogers" (September 1941).
Zeitlin, Ida. "Roy Rogers' Wife Talks" (June
1942).
"Roy Rogers' Wife Talks" 46, no. 2 (December
1942): 30–31.
Bowers, Lynn. "Through Hell-Dorado with Roy
Rogers" (September 1946): 50–51, 79–86.
"Just Call Him Dusty" 51, no. 9 (July 1947): 51.
"The Roy Rogers Safety Trophy" (December
1949): 20.
"Roy's Way of Life Is Mine" (January 1951).
"People" 1, no. 1 (May 12, 1975).

Senior Times
Wilder, A. J. "King of the Cowboys—Queen of
the West" 2, no. 14 (November 21, 1989).

Shotgun News
"Jim Carpenter Presents SGNIX West Bally's
Grand, Reno, Nevada" (November 1990).

Show
La Badie, D. W. "The Last Roundup" 2, no. 9
(September 1962): 74.
"Career Notes" 2, no. 9 (September 1966): 77.

Silver Screen
Marsh, P. "Kissless Heroine" 17, no. 8 (June
1947): 61.
"Love Thy Neighbor" [full page color photo of
Roy] (January 1951).
"Cowboy Picnic" [2 photos] (April 1951).
"Never Stop Dreaming" (July 1951): 54–55.

Song Hits
Rogers, Roy. Monthly column, "Songs of the
West" 6, no. 11 (April 1943).
———. Monthly column, "Songs of the West" 10,
no. 1 (June 1946).
"The Man from Oklahoma" 9, no. 6 (November
1945): 10.

Song of the West
"Winter Trip to Roy Rogers Museum" (Spring
1989): 18.

Sports Afield
Rogers, Roy. "My Best Shot" (September 1951).

Star
Langley, Norma. "Living Legends" (January 20,
1987).

The Star Weekly (Toronto, Canada)
Color photo of Roy and Dale (December 30,
1950).

TDC, The Discovery Channel
"Wild, Wild Westerns" 5, no. 11 (March 1989): 61.

Television and Screen Guide
"Sunday Best" (October 1948): 24–27.
Rogers, Roy. "What'll I Do for My Oldest
Daughter?" (July 1951): 54.
"The Roy Rogers' New Ranch" (August 1951):
46–49.
"Roy Rogers" (October 1951): 40.

This Week
Trigger's television debut (December 1950).

Time
"Man and Wife" (Religion) 65 (March 7, 1955):
55–56, 58.
"People" (May 12, 1975): 40.
"Only Kidding, Lunch Ladies" (food chain runs
ads mocking school cafeteria lunches) 136,
no. 10 (September 3, 1990): 59.

Total
Morrison, Mark. "Tall in the Saddle" (November
28–December 4, 1992): 14.

Tournament of Roses Parade
Various editions with possibly Roy and Dale on
cover, 1950s.

Town and Country
"Roy Rogers and Dale Evans Museum" (March
1982): 116–17.

Toy Box
Phillips, Robert W. "Cowboy Comic Book Col-
lectibles" 1, no. 4 (March 1993): 31–33.
"Once Upon a Time" 2, no. 2 (Fall 1993): 48–51.

Tradition
"News," Roy Rogers honored in Los Angeles
(May–June 1992): 13.

Trailblazers
"Happy Trails" 5, no. 12 (December 1983): 23–25.

True Movie and Western
"Roy Rogers" (January–March 1951).
"Roy Rogers" (April 1951).

TV and Movie Screen
"King at Work" 1, no. 4 (May 1954): 54–55.

TV and Movies Western
"Roy Rogers" 1, no. 3 (December 1958).
Rasky, Frank. "Roy Rogers and Trigger" 1, no. 5
(April 1959): 14–17.

TV Fan
"And a Little Child Shall Lead Them" (February
1951).
"All Trails Lead to Home" (February 1954): 22–
27.

TV Guide
"Kids: You Can Meet Roy Rogers" (September
26, October 2, 1950).
"The Roy Rogers Show" [pre-national] (Early
1950s).

"Here Comes Roy Rogers" (December 28, 1951–January 3, 1952): 8.

"Who Are the BEST in Television?" (December 19–25, 1952).

"Roy Rogers, Businessman" (also listed as "Roy Rogers Is Big Business") 1, no. 6 (December 19–25, 1952): 8–9.

Reviews: Program of the Week, "The Roy Rogers Show" 2, no. 24 (June 11, 1954): 20.

Jenkins, Dan. "Children Made Roy King of the Cowboys" (July 17, 1954): 8–9.

"And He's Not Even Dreaming" (June 4, 1955): 20–21.

"What Makes Fan Clubs Tick" 3, no. 24 (June 11, 1955): 4–5.

"Who's Got the Last Laugh" (June 23, 1957): 28–29.

Whitney, Dwight. "Meanwhile, Back at Their Ranches" 7, no. 32 (August 8, 1959): 17–19.

Davidson, M. "Are They Going to Be Headed Off at the Pass?" 10, no. 49 (December 8, 1962): 10–12.

"They've Been Branded," 2000th Issue, Commemorative Edition, 7 (December 12–18, 1988).

"Cartoon Cowpoke" (1992): 50.

Stebbin, Gregg. "What I Watch" (1 photo) 41, no. 18 (May 1–7, 1993): 5.

TV People

Rogers, Roy. "This Is My Life Story" 4, no. 2 (April 1956): 45ff.

TV Pictorial

"Hook, Line and Showman," pp. 12–14. (1950s).

TV Picture Life

Lucas, Bob. "Giant All-Star Western Roundup" (April 1961): 42–47.

TV Movie Fan

"Good Partners—Gene Autry/Roy Rogers" 1, no. 3 (June 1957): 20–21.

TV Personalities Biographical Sketch Book

Wood, C. "Roy Rogers" (1954): 137.
_____. "Dale Evans" (1954): 138.

TV Picture Life

"Back at the Ranch" (June 1957).

TV-Radio Album

"Roy's Lucky Seven" (1957): 30–31.

TV Radio Annual

"Who's Who in Adventure—Roy Rogers" (1958).

TV Radio Mirror

Arnold, Maxine. "Tomorrow the Sun Will Shine Again" (February 1953).

"Answer to Prayer" (May 1953).

TV Screen

"Roy and Dale Rogers Have Built Their World Around Home and Children" (April 1951).

TV Stage

O'Leary, Dorothy. "Trigger's Folks" (3 b&w photos) 2, no. 5 (August 1955): 36ff.

Rogers, Cheryl D. "My Dad, Roy Rogers" 4, no. 3 (May 1957): 40ff.

TV Star Annual

"Range Riders—Roy Rogers" (1956).

"The Roy Rogers Show" (1957).

"Outdoor Man" (May 1957): 67.

TV Star Parade

"Cowboy Close-Up! Gene Autry, Roy Rogers..." 1, no. 8 (Fall 1951): 50–56.

Photo of Roy, Dale, Trigger (September 1951).

"They Came This a Way" 1, no. 8 (Fall 1951): 76–79.

"Roy Rogers Safety Award" 1 (December 1953): 56–57.

TV Western

"Roy Rogers" (March 1958).

"Our Two Angels Will Never Be Lonely Now" (1964).

TV Western Roundup

"King of the Cowboys" (1957): 23–24.

"Second-Bananas, Cactus Style" (1957).

TV World

"Roy Rogers and Dale Evans at Home" (June 1954).

TWA Ambassador

Morgan, James. "Conversations with the Cowboy King" (October 1976): 16ff.

Under Western Skies

Dover, Bill. "Roy Rogers and Dale Evans" 2 (April 1978): 5–45.

Unknown

Spanish/Mexican film publication (large photo, caption, Roy and Trigger), taken from series used for exhibit cards (c. 1941-42): 14.

"Roy and Trigger Thrill New York" [7 b&w photos] (c. 1942): 54–55.

Watkins, Willard. "Roy Rogers Is One Cowboy Star Who Thrills the Big Sisters as Well as the Kid Brothers" (c. 1943).

Full page color photo of Roy, standing behind fence, facsimile signature (April 1943).

Photo, caption, of infant, Linda Lou, Roy, Arline (c. Summer 1943).

Photo, caption, Roy holding foal (Summer 1944).

"Horse Opera-tor," "The Movies" [7 b&w photos, Roy and Trigger, at what appears to be a rodeo performance] (c. 1944).

"Texas Rose" [1 b&w photo, Roy and Dale] (c. 1944).

Photo, b&w, Roy boarding train with girls (c. 1944).

Photo, b&w, Roy in front of pigeon pen, with pigeons flying (c. mid-1940s).

Four photos, b&w, from "Lake Placid Serenade" location (c. 1944).

Full-size color photo of Roy with guitar, caption mentions film *San Fernando Valley* (c. Fall 1944).

"Shucks, It's a Cinch" [6 b&w photos] (c. 1945).

Photos, b&w, Roy, Arline, Linda Lou; Roy and Arline at piano (c. 1945).

"Roy Rogers" [6 b&w photos] (c. 1945).

"One Man Horse" [3 photos, Roy and Dale on Trigger] (c. Summer 1945).

Photo, b&w, of Roy, Dale, entertaining servicemen at Hollywood Canteen (c. 1945).

Photo, b&w, Roy, Arline, during night out (c. 1945).

Photo, b&w, Roy doing radio interview with Paula Stone (c. 1945).

Photo, color, full-page, Cheryl on pony beside Roy, facsimile signature (c. 1945): 46.

Photo, Roy with Mervyn LeRoy at Warner Brothers–Joan Crawford Party (c. December 1945).

Photo, Roy and Edith Fellows at Warner Brothers–Joan Crawford party (c. December 1945).

Photo, Roy with Boy Scout troop at ceremony in Beverly Hills (c. mid-1940s).

Photo, color, full-page, Roy (c. mid-1940s).

Photo, caption detailing dazzling cowboy outfits (c. 1946).

Photo, color, Roy, Trigger; caption mentioning film *My Pal Trigger*, reverse negative used (c. Spring 1946).

"Their Little Buckaroo" [photo Roy, Dale, Dusty] (c. 1949).

Photo, Roy, Dale, in New York City's Stork Club (c. 1949).

Photo, large color, Roy leaning on wagon wheel, wagon [back of photo is picture of Pat Crowley] (c. 1948).

"I Don't Drink" [photo, Roy, Dusty on set] (c. 1948).

"Weddings and More Weddings" [6 b&w photos, Roy, Dale, wedding] (c. 1948)

Photo, b&w, Roy, Dale, Judy Canova, Harry Von Zell, others at National Safety Council Meeting at Ambassador Hotel (c. late 1940s).

Photo, color, full-page, Roy, Dale, Dusty, Linda Lou, and Cheryl (c. 1949).

Photo, b&w, Roy, Dale, Pal, and Trigger (c. 1949).

Photo, color, full-page, caption mentioning film *The Far Frontier* (c. 1949).

Photo, b&w, Roy and child at personal appearance in Los Angeles (c. 1950s).

Photo of Dale giving Roy a drink of water (c. 1950s).

Photo, b&w, Roy with Eilene Jannsen and Michael Chapin (c. 1950s).

"Papa, Won't You Play" (c. 1950).

"On TV" [3 photos, b&w, Roy, Trigger, Bullet, on "Gabby Hayes Show"] (c. 1950).

Photo of Roy, Dale, during night out; caption mentions *Son of Paleface* (c. 1951).

"Four Little 'Squares'" (1953).

"What Hollywood Wears – Roy and Dale" [3 photos, color, Roy and Dale in matching outfits by Traxel] (c. 1950s).

Crowley, Mark. "Why the Stars Fear Adoption Blackmail" [1 b&w photo] (c. 1950s): 17–19.

Photo of Roy and Dale, over AFNS radio (c. 1950s).

Photo of Roy, Rex Allen, Monte Hale (c. mid-1950s).

Photo of Roy, Dale, Cheryl, Linda Lou, Dusty, all on Trigger (c. mid-1950s).

Whitney, D. "Autry, Rogers, Vintage Cowpokes" (Aug. 8, 1959): 17–19.

Spencer, Harry C. "Movies for the Family: Trail of Robin Hood," "For Some Reason, Roy Rogers, Perhaps the Best Western Star on the Screen Today, Has Not Been Released for Television" (c. 1951).

"The Children Nobody Wanted" (early 1960s).

"Hero to Kids – And Grown-Ups" (c. 1968): 39.

"Cowboy Roundup" [Tribute at Gene Autry Western Heritage Museum] (April 27, 1992).

Gregory, Jack. "Our Two Angels Will Never Be Lonely Now" (probably *Motion Picture* or *Movie Play*), c. 1964.

Photo, full-page, Roy in swimming trunks, eating hot dog.

Variety

"Rep Pay Off Rogers, Keeps Tag for Oats Star" (c. 1938–39).

"Republic Offers R.R. TV Rights in New Pact, But Star Still Balks" (May 28, 1951).

"Roy Rogers Sues Rep., TV Subsid to Nip Their Sales of His Pix" (June 27, 1951).

"Adman, Wayne Tiss Aids RR in TV Test Suit" (September 20, 1951).

"Roy Rogers, in Court Admits Talking Deal with REP, Quaker Oats to Show Pix on TV" (September 24, 1951).

"REP's Legal-Eagle Claws Art Rush as RR TV Test Suit Grinds On" (September 26, 1951).

"REP Attorney Puts Roy Rogers' Mgr. in Suit Hot Spot" (September 27, 1951).

"REP Coming to Bat as RR Suit Starts Last Lap" (October 1, 1951).

"Jurist's Comments Baffle Both Sides in Roy Rogers Suit" (October 5, 1951).

"Rogers' Suit Down to Near Bare Facts: Yates Up Next" (October 8, 1951).

"Roy Rogers' Attorney Claims REP Backed Out of TV Deal." October 11, 1951.

"Details of RR–General Foods Deal Come to Light in REP Suit" (Rogers, Autry vs. Republic suit) (October 12, 1951).

"REP Attorney Pulls Courtroom Coup in Rogers' Test Suit" (October 21, 1951).

"See Oldies in Continued Sale to TV Despite Rogers' Win Over Republic" (October 24, 1951): 2ff.

"Roy Rogers to Top Houston Stock Show" (October 31, 1951): 4.

"Roy Rides Again for Gen. Foods" (May 5, 1954): 37.

"Rogers Likely to Pull out of CNE in Union Tug of War" (Canadian National Exhibition) (June 2, 1954): 53.

"See Rogers' Visit as 'Better Than School'" (July 14, 1954).

"Rogers and Autry Video Rights Case to U.S. Top Court" (August 4, 1954): 11.

"Lots of Offers for Autry-Rogers Pix, but REP Waits" (September 1, 1954): 49.

"Dale Evans Will Be Filming Religious Talk Show" (April 25, 1973).

"Roy Rogers Promotion: Dixie Remembers Him" (November 29, 1975): 23.

Video Guide

Curtright, Bob. "Roy Rogers" (October 25, 1992).

Video Review

Everson, William K. "Critic's Choice: Tape 'Em Cowboys" (September 1980).

Washingtonian

Weiss, Michael J. "The Selling of a Burger" (Roy Rogers chain food advertisement) 24, no. 9 (June 1989): 103ff.

Western Film and Memorabilia Program

Hagan, Bill. "Film Program." "Shokus Video." "AC Comics" [3rd Annual Western Film and Memorabilia Festival Souvenir Program] (November 1-12, 1988): 4-5, 27, 35, 39.

Western Hollywood Pictorial

"Trigger, Jr." (September 1950).

"Roy Rogers" (September 1950).

The Western Horseman

Rogers, Roy, and Aaron Dudley. "Trigger: First Get a Good Horse" (December 1949).

Valentry, Duane. "A Horse Named Babe" [6 photos] (April 1961): 56ff.

"They Went That-A-Way" (January 1989): 22.

Brown, Mary Remington. "Four-Legged Stars of the Silver Screen" (March 1991): 58ff.

Western Movie Hits

"Roy Rogers TV Album: 'Mayor of Ghost Town,' 'The Feud,' 'Knockout'" 1, no. 2 (November 2, 1953): 25-33.

Western Screen Hits

"My Pal Trigger." Roy Rogers novelette 1, no. 1 (1952): 25-33.

Western Stars

"Roy Rogers" 1, no. 1 (November 1948–February 1949): 10-15.

Editorial Staff. "Roy Rogers" 1, no. 1 (November 1948–February 1949).

"The Far Frontier" 1, no. 2 (March-June 1949): 26-27.

"Just Plain Folks" 1, no. 2 (March-June 1949): 22-25.

"The Golden Stallion" 1, no. 3 (October-December 1949): 26-29.

Evans, Dale. "Now They Call Me Ma" 1, no. 3 (October-December 1949): 14-19.

"The Trail to Fame" 1, no. 3 (October-December 1949): 12-13.

Randall, Glenn "I'll Match Roy Against Any Texas Line Rider" 1, no. 3 (October-December 1949): 20-25.

Slye, Andrew E. "A Son to Be Proud of" 1, no. 3 (October-December 1949): 4-7.

Spencer, Tim. "We Sang for Our Supper" 1, no. 3 (October-December 1949): 8-11.

"Roy Rogers" 1, no. 2 (1950).

"Bells of Coronado" 1, no. 4 (January-March 1950): 52-55.

"Twilight in the Sierras" 1, no. 5 (April-June 1950): 42-45.

Rogers, Roy. "How to Keep Fit" 1, no. 6 (July-September 1950).

"Ride with the Best of 'Em" 1, no. 6 (July-September 1950).

"Day by Day with Roy Rogers" (a week's diary entries) 1, no. 6 (July-September 1950): 87.

"Western Album: Dale Evans" 1, no. 6 (July-September 1950): 41.

Westerns and Serials

Copeland, Bobby J. "1989 Roy Rogers Festival" (all editions have Roy Rogers related art, ads) 33 (1990).

"The Roy Rogers Festival" 36 (1991).

Phillips, Robert W. "The Roy Rogers Comic Books" 39 (1992): 14-18.

Westways

Cuppett, Annis. "Special People" (February 1981): 62-65.

Who's Who in Hollywood

Cover photo; photo inside (April 1951).

Five pages on family (October 1951).

Photo, Roy, Dale, Robin (December 1951).

"Roy Rogers" (1953).

"Way Out West in Hollywood" (1956).

Who's Who in Western Stars

"Roy on the Air: Ridin' the Range for Sugar Crisp" 1, no. 1 (1952): 16-17.

"Roy's Career: 15 Years Ago—He'd Swap a Song for a Sandwich" 1, no. 1 (1952): 4-5.

"Roy's Career: Today—Even His Horse Has Cream in His Oats" 1, no. 1 (1952): 6-7.

"Roy's Kids: Local #1 of the Roy Rogers Fan Club" 1, no. 1 (1952): 8-9.

"Roys Pictures: *Pals of the Golden West*" 1, no. 1 (1952): 10-13.

"Lots of Laughs—And Music Too" 1, no. 1 (1952): 18-20.

Rogers, Roy. "A Slice of My life" 1, no. 2 (1952): 4-11.

"Roy Rogers Enterprises" 1, no. 1 (1952): 14-15.

_____. "Our House Is Full Once More" 1, no. 3 (November 1953).

"Outlaws of Paradise Valley" 1, no. 3 (November 1953): 10–13.

"Pat's Inheritance" 1, no. 3 (November 1953): 14–18.

WIBW Roundup
Photo, caption, Roy Rogers and Ambrose Haley, 30 (September 1947): 11.

Wrangler's Roost
Hickey, Bruce. "Bruce Hickey Meets Roy Rogers" 77 (1987).

Yippy-Yi-Yea
Phillips, Bob. "This Time I Want to Be Roy Rogers" (Winter 1992): 72–75.
Phillips, Robert. "The Roy Rogers Story" 3, no. 1 (Summer 1994): 66–69.

You
Reed, Dana. "Roy Rogers Says: 'God Set Your Trail'" (November 1950).

Newspaper Articles

Christian Science Monitor
Loercher, Diana. "'Cowboy King' Stars in a New Western." September 7, 1977.

The Columbus Dispatch (Ohio)
Bloom, Bob. "Cowboy Stars at Roy Rogers Festival." May 6, 1986.
"Cowboy Backing Robertson." August 20, 1986.

The Community Common (Portsmouth, Ohio)
Rickey, E. E. "A King for President." March 4, 1984.
"Roy Rogers Visits Scioto County." 1986.

Connersville News-Examiner (Indiana)
"Happy Birthday Roy" (photo of Roy and Dale with caption). November 5, 1992.

The Courier-Journal (city unknown)
"A Road of Fame and Fortune." July 6, 1992. People section.
"Rogers Signs Deal with Old Film Studio." July 6, 1992. People section.

Dallas Times Herald
"Golden Boot." August 21, 1988. (Associated Press.)
Henderson, Jim. "Hold Your Horses—Or Trigger May Be Dinner in France." July 21, 1991.

Family Weekly
Rogers, Dale Evans. "Hear the Children Cry." July 23, 1978.

Fort Worth Star Telegram
"Star Roy Rogers Arranges Gift of Cowboy Boots for Boy's Ranch." C. 1940s–50s.
"Back in the Saddle Again." October 20, 1978.
"Pat Robertson Supporters Hope to Trigger Votes with Roy Rogers." C. 1980s.

"Back in the Saddle Again." September 30, 1991. Interview with Roy. August 2, 1992.

The Greenpoint Gazette (New York)
Phillips, Bob. "To Roy Rogers Restaurant." March 1992.

Hutchinson News (Kansas)
Edwards, Joe. "Roy Rogers Reviews His Life with 'Tribute.'" September 8, 1991. (Associated Press.)

Indianapolis News
"Western at Alamo." March 28, 1941.

Inside Story
Shaw, Manuel. "What They Don't Tell the Kiddies About Roy Rogers." C. 1950s.

Kansas City Star (Missouri)
"Cartoon Cowpoke" (photo of Roy rearing on Trigger). May 23–29, 1992. TV section.
"Cowboys, Dictators, and Baseball." October 1992.
Hetterick, Scott. "Film Tells Tale of Cowboy King—Roy Rogers." November 30, 1992.
Garron, Barry. "Happy Trails." December 3, 1992.
"For Roy and Dale." April 26, 1993.

Los Angeles Examiner (L.A. Herald Examiner)
"Happy Trails to Hollywood from Roy and Dale." November 30, 1981.
"Roy Rogers." August 4, 1992.

The Muncie Star (Indiana)
Prescott, Jean. "Roy Rogers Is Back to Remember Those Happy Trails." December 2, 1992.

National Enquirer
Evans, Dale. "Why I Am Fighting to End Child Abuse." 1978.
"Roy Rogers Fans: He Needs You Now." Late 1990.
Coates, Julia, "Thanks Pardners!" Late 1990.

National Star
Thompson, Douglas. "Back in the Saddle at 63." October 21, 1975.

New York Daily News
"Roy Rogers." December 6, 1942.
"Roy Rogers in Person with Trigger." October 1, 1944.
"Trigger Tricks for Kiddies." October 18, 1944.
"Cowboy." November 6, 1990.
Greene, Bob. Unknown title. July 21, 1992.
Nye, Doug. "How the West Is Rerun." April 25, 1993.

New York Mirror
"Roy Rogers" (photo, caption, Roy and singer, Pat Boone and family at Madison Square Garden Rodeo). October 12, 1958. Sports Final edition.

New York Mirror Magazine
"The Roy Rogers Nine on a Horse." October 5, 1958. 14 ff

New York News Coloroto Magazine
"Dale Evans, Roy Rogers and Trigger." September 21, 1958.

New York Post
Bragsiotti, Mary. "Just Plain Folks." September 19, 1948.
Burden, Martin. "Saddle Hymn of the Republic—By Roy." March 1990.
"Roy Rogers Undergoes Heart Surgery—Doin' Fine." October 23, 1990.

New York Sun and Mirror Magazine
"Roy Rogers and Dale Evans." January 30, 1949.

New York Sunday Mirror
November 19, 1950.

New York Times
Strauss, Theodore. "Little Dogies, Git Along." October 4, 1940.
Brady, Thomas. "Some Hollywood Highlights." February 8, 1942.
_____. "On the Firing Line." February 15, 1942.
_____. "Charity, Hope and Faith in Filmland." September 20, 1942.
Strauss, Theodore. "King of the Cowboys." October 25, 1942.
Stanley, Fred. "Hollywood Shivers." May 28, 1944.
_____. "Hollywood Bulletins." November 18, 1945.
Pallette, Elizabeth. "Built by Horses." February 2, 1947.
Weiler, A. H. "By Way of Report." November 16, 1947.
Spiro, J. D. "Hollywood and TV." July 1, 1951.
"Roy Rogers Ruling Bars Film Sale to TV." October 19, 1951.
Pryor, Thomas M. "TV-Movie Tie-Ins Remain Confused." May 15, 1952.
"Hollywood Edict: Ruling on Use of Autry, Rogers Films May Set Pattern of Best Sellers." July 13, 1954.
"Karl Farr Dies at 52—Member of the Sons of the Pioneers Collapses on Stage." September 21, 1966.
Zavatsky, Bill. "Some Japanese Poems About Roy Rogers" (excerpt from author's book on theories of rain and other poems). 1975.
Schneider, S. "Cable TV Notes: After 200 Years, a Handel Tribute Gets It Straight." December 29, 1985.
Fabrikant, Geraldine. "Roy Rogers to Cancel Ad." August 19, 1988.
"Marriott Plans Retreat from Fast Food Wars." December 19, 1989.
"Roy Rogers Chain Is Sold to Hardee's." January 31, 1990.
Brown, Patricia Leigh. "Western Wind Across Urban Plains." 1990.

"People." May 12, 1977.
Patten, Phil. "The Dude Is Back in Town." April 18, 1993.

New York Times Magazine
"Roy Rogers Portrait." April 28, 1957.

The News (Frederick, Maryland)
Luce, Nancy. "It Was Happy Trails." May 29, 1987.

The Ohio Conservation Bulletin
Greer, Ernest. "Learning to Be Safe Hunters." January 1960.

The Packet (Toronto, Canada)
Story and photos. January 7, 1993.

Parade Magazine (newspaper supplement)
"Christmas at Our House." December 20, 1959.

The Portsmouth Times (Portsmouth, Ohio)
Stowell, George. "It Was Uncle Bill Slye, now 69, Who Started Roy Rogers on Music Career." 1948.

Providence Journal (Rhode Island)
"Well at Least Some Rumors Are Correct." c. 1980s.

Record-Searchlight (Redding, California)
Lease, Betty. "Dale Evans Off Her Horse but Not Ready for Rocker." January 16, 1986.

St. Petersburg Independent (all Florida weekly magazine)
"Roy Rogers and Trigger Come to Florida State Fair." February 1, 1959.

Star Tribune (Caspar, Wyoming)
Nye, Doug. "Roy Rogers, at 81, Is Still King of the Cowboys." January 17, 1993.

Sunday News (New York)
"Roy Rogers." December 6, 1942.
Muir, Florabel. "The West's ROY-al Family" (2 color photos). September 26, 1954.
"At Home with Dale Evans" (5 b&w photos). September 25, 1966.

The Tennessean (Nashville)
Hill, Leonard. "Dale Evans 70 Years Young Today." October 31, 1982.
Rothberg, Donald M. "Cowboy Urges U.S. to Draft Pat Robertson for President." August 20, 1986.

Toronto Star Weekly
Roy and Dale with story about Westerns. December 1951.
Hall, Gladys. "Galahad on the Gallop." November 1979.

Toronto Sun (Canada)
"Showbiz Reaction." January 7, 1993.

Tulsa World

Watkins, Brandon (Robert W. Phillips book review: *Singing Cowboy Stars*). November 2, 1994.

Unknown Publications

"Cowboy King Endorses Panhandle Yo-Yo." RR merchandise, Western Plastics, Inc. (b&w photo of Roy with owner of plastics company). Scottsbluff, Arizona. 1950s.

Mink, Ken. "Installment Purchase of Horse Led Roy to Film Career" (Scripps-Howard News Service). C. 1986.

"Buckles Holding Up Cowboy Legend." Norman, Oklahoma. C. 1986.

"Happy Cowboy Couple." Hollywood, California. 1987.

"Golden Boot." Baltimore, Maryland. August 21, 1988.

"Paying Homage to Roy and Dale." c. 1992.

"Singing Cowboy Working on Series." Victorville, California (Associated Press). c. 1992.

"Cowboy Dreams Come True for Boy." Hollywood, California (Associated Press). c. 1992.

"Roy Rogers Rides Again." Beverly Hills, California (Associated Press). April 19, 1992.

Syndicated interview with Roy (Knight-Ridder). July 13, 1992.

USA (Weekend)

Martin, Joe. "Are Roy and Dale Taking Separate Happy Trails?" August 14–16, 1987.

USA Today

"Roy Still Quick on Trigger." July 2, 1985.

Zimmerman, David. "Roy and Dale Are Back in the Saddle." March 19, 1986.

"Country Singer Pair Up for Two-Part Harmony." September 14, 1990.

"Rogers and Black, A Couple of Singing Cowboys." October 2, 1991.

Wall Street Journal

Goad, Pierre. "Trying to Assimilate Roy Rogers Outlets, Hardee's Is Ambushed by Irate Clientele." c. 1992.

Washington Post

Farhi, Paul. "Marriott to Sell 800 Restaurants; Bob's Big Boy, Roy Rogers Chains Going on the Block." January 30, 1990.

_____. "Marriott to Sell Its Roy Rogers Chain to Hardee's." January 30, 1990.

Hsu, Spencer S. "Roy Rogers Pulls Plugs on TV Ads." August 21, 1990.

Frank, Jeffrey A. "Roy's Last Roundup; Can a Wing Taste As Sweet by Any Name?" December 21, 1990.

Walsh, Sharon Warran, and Mark Potts. "Giddap: Roy Rogers Restaurants Introduce New Burgers." April 28, 1991.

"TV Week" (supplement, cover photo, biography, two-page feature). November 29, 1992.

Wichita Eagle-Beacon (Kansas)

Rush, Duke. "Reel Cowboy Hollywood Buckaroo Era Sires Line for Collector." 1982.

"Roy Rogers." May 17, 1983.

Duffy, Mike. "'Happy Trails' Show, Brings Back Roy, Dale." June 29, 1986.

Levenbrown, Cheryl. "Autry's Back in the Saddle Again." November 1988.

Edwards, Joe. "Still King of the Cowboys." September 19, 1991 (Associated Press).

INDEX